Volume I: To 1650

DISCOVERING THE GLOBAL PAST

A LOOK AT THE EVIDENCE

FOURTH EDITION

Merry E. Wiesner
University of Wisconsin—Milwaukee

William Bruce Wheeler
University of Tennessee

Franklin M. Doeringer
Lawrence University

Kenneth R. Curtis
California State University Long Beach

WADSWORTH
CENGAGE Learning™

Australia • Brazil • Japan • Korea • Mexico • Singapore • Spain • United Kingdom • United States

WADSWORTH
CENGAGE Learning™

Discovering the Global Past; A Look at the Evidence, Fourth Edition, Vol. I: To 1650
Wiesner, Wheeler, Doeringer, Curtis

Senior Publisher: Suzanne Jeans

Senior Sponsoring Editor: Nancy Blaine

Associate Editor: Adrienne Zicht

Editorial Assistant: Emma Goehring

Senior Marketing Manager: Katherine Bates

Marketing Coordinator: Lorreen Pelletier

Marketing Communications Manager: Caitlin Green

Senior Content Project Manager: Carol Newman

Senior Art Director: Cate Rickard Barr

Senior Print Buyer: Betsy Donaghey

Senior Text Rights Acquisition Specialist: Katie Huha

Senior Image Rights Acquisition Specialist: Jennifer Meyer Dare

Production Service: MPS Limited, a Macmillan Company

Cover Designer: Harold Burch, New York City

Cover Image: Men making wine, plucking poultry, and bringing offerings to the dead. Detail of a wall painting in the tomb of Nakht, scribe and priest under Pharaoh Tuthmosis IV (18th Dynasty, 16th–14th BCE). © François Guenet / Art Resource, NY.

Compositor: MPS Limited, a Macmillan Company

Library of Congress Control Number: 2010937461

ISBN-13: 978-1-111-34142-8

ISBN-10: 1-111-34142-7

Wadsworth
20 Channel Center Street
Boston, MA 02210
USA

Cengage Learning is a leading provider of customized learning solutions with office locations around the globe, including Singapore, the United Kingdom, Australia, Mexico, Brazil and Japan. Locate your local office at **international.cengage.com/region**

Cengage Learning products are represented in Canada by Nelson Education, Ltd.

For your course and learning solutions, visit **www.cengage.com**

Purchase any of our products at your local college store or at our preferred online store **www.cengagebrain.com.**

Printed in the United States of America
1 2 3 4 5 6 7 14 13 12 11

CONTENTS

CHAPTER FIVE
International Religious Communities
(300 B.C.E.–800 C.E.)   106

CHAPTER SIX
Vikings and Polynesians: Exploring New Worlds
(300–1100)   138

CHAPTER SEVEN
Two Faces of "Holy War": Christians and Muslims (1095–1270s)   179

CHAPTER EIGHT
Fiction and the Emotions in Japanese, Arabian, and Irish Culture (1000–1400 C.E.)   202

[VIII]

CHAPTER ELEVEN
Sacred Journeys: Pilgrimages in Buddhism and Islam (629–1324) 293

CHAPTER TWELVE
The Well-Educated Man: Students and Scholars in China, Paris, and Timbuktu (1180–1600) 344

CHAPTER THIRTEEN
Facing the Black Death (1300–1400) 375

CHAPTER FOURTEEN
Cross-Cultural Encounters: Travel, Religion, Conquests, and Trade (1400–1700)   410

PREFACE

Almost from the founding of the United States itself, those who chose to call themselves "Americans" maintained a deep and abiding curiosity about and interest in other lands and their peoples. Indeed, although they often were characterized as provincial, narrow, and even rustic, Americans read all they could find about faraway peoples, flocked to lectures and lyceums offered by world travelers in the early nineteenth century, packed into nineteenth- and twentieth-century expositions and world's fairs to see "exotic" peoples, and even more recently became a "nation of tourists."

To convert this widespread curiosity into a deeper knowledge, schools began to offer classes in World History. In 1821, the first high school–level World History course was offered, at the Boston English High School, and a World History textbook (by Samuel G. Goodrich) appeared in 1828 to serve the growing teacher and student interest. Colleges and universities followed suit quickly thereafter, and in 1885, historian Mary D. Sheldon of Wellesley College first introduced the examination and analysis of primary sources into her World History (it was called "General History") course.[1]

The advent of professionally trained historians in the late nineteenth and early twentieth centuries, however, nearly spelled the end of the World History course. Essentially, these new professors charged that by trying to teach everything, the result was to teach nothing—or at least nothing in depth. By 1915, fewer than 5 percent of the high schools surveyed by the U.S. commissioner of education still taught a World History course. And after the introduction of the Western Civilization course (at Columbia University in 1919), colleges and universities too abandoned the single course in World History.[2]

And yet the curiosity that prompted the first World History courses in the early nineteenth century never abated. Indeed, with the recent emergence of the "global village," interest grew significantly. In 1982, the World History Association was founded, in part to encourage the reintroduction of World History courses and in part to assist people eager to teach such a course. As William H. McNeill, one of the founders of the modern movement to reintroduce World History courses, put it, "Surely it takes only a little common sense to see that some sort of world history is the *only* way a college can do justice to

---

1. Gilbert Allardyce, "Toward World History: American Historians and the Coming of the World History Course," in *Journal of World History*, vol. I (Spring 1990), pp. 23–76, esp. 45 and 47.
2. Ibid., pp. 30, 47.

students who live in a world where events in Asia, Africa, and Latin America are as likely to involve the United States in critical action as anything happening in Europe or North America."[3]

Discovering the Global Past emerged from this newer movement of World History, and the response to the First Edition was a gratifying one. It means that Mary D. Sheldon at Wellesley College over a century ago understood how to tap the already high level of student curiosity about faraway people. In our opinion, it also means that William H. McNeill had it right: that students understand not only the satisfaction of studying world history, but, in today's world, its *necessity*. This book honors both of these historians, as well as the countless numbers of curious and challenging students and their equally challenging teachers.

The primary goal of *Discovering the Global Past: A Look at the Evidence* is to allow students enrolled in world history courses to *do* history in the same way that we as historians do—to examine a group of original sources to answer questions about the past. The unique structure of this book clusters primary sources around a set of historical questions that students are asked to "solve." Unlike a source reader, this book prompts students to actually *analyze* a wide variety of authentic primary source material, to make inferences, and to draw conclusions in much the same way that historians do.

The evidence in this book is more varied than that in most source collections. We have included such visual evidence as coins, paintings, statues, literary illustrations, historical photographs, maps, cartoons, advertisements, and political posters. In choosing written evidence we again have tried to offer a broad sample—eulogies, wills, court records, oral testimonies, and statistical data all supplement letters, newspaper articles, speeches, memoirs, and other more traditional sources.

For students to learn history the way we as historians do, they not only must be confronted with the evidence but must also learn how to use that evidence to arrive at a conclusion. In other words, they must learn historical methodology. Too often methodology (or even the notion that historians *have* a methodology) is reserved for upper-level majors or graduate students; beginning students are simply presented with historical facts and interpretations without being shown how these were unearthed or formulated. Students may learn that historians hold different interpretations of the significance of an event or individual or different ideas about causation, but they are not informed of how historians come to such conclusions.

Thus, along with evidence, we have provided explicit suggestions about how one might analyze that evidence, guiding students as they reach their own conclusions. As they work through the various chapters, students will discover both that the sources of historical information are wide-ranging and that the methodologies appropriate to understanding and using them are equally diverse. By doing history themselves, students will learn how intellectual

3. Ibid., p. 72. Italics added.

historians handle philosophical treatises, economic historians quantitative data, social historians court records, and political and diplomatic historians theoretical treatises and memoirs. They will also be asked to consider the limitations of their evidence, to explore what historical questions it cannot answer as well as those it can. Instead of remaining passive observers, students become active participants.

Each chapter is divided into six parts: The Problem, Background, The Method, The Evidence, Questions to Consider, and Epilogue. Each of the parts relates to or builds upon the others, creating a uniquely integrated chapter structure that helps guide the reader through the analytical process. "The Problem" section begins with a brief discussion of the central issues of the chapter and then states the questions students will explore. A "Background" section follows, designed to help students understand the historical context of the problem. The section called "The Method" gives students suggestions for studying and analyzing the evidence. "The Evidence" section is the heart of the chapter, providing a variety of primary source material on the particular historical event or issue described in the chapter's "Problem" section. The section called "Questions to Consider" focuses students' attention on specific evidence and on linkages among different evidence material. The "Epilogue" section gives the aftermath or the historical outcome of the evidence—what happened to the people involved, the results of a debate, and so on.

Within this framework, we have tried to present a series of historical issues and events of significance to the instructor as well as of interest to the student. We have also aimed to provide a balance among political, social, diplomatic, intellectual, and cultural history. In other words, we have attempted to create a kind of historical sampler that we believe will help students learn the methods and skills used by historians. Not only will these skills—analyzing arguments, developing hypotheses, comparing evidence, testing conclusions, and re-evaluating material—enable students to master historical content; they will also provide the necessary foundation for critical thinking in other college courses and after college as well.

Because the amount of material in global history is so vast, we had to pick certain topics and geographic areas to highlight, though here too we have aimed at a balance. Some chapters are narrow in focus, providing students with an opportunity to delve deeply into a single case study, while others ask students to make comparisons among individuals, events, or developments in different cultures. We have included cultural comparisons that are frequently discussed in World History courses, such as classical Rome and Han China, as well as more unusual ones, such as peasant family life in early modern central Europe and Southeast Asia.

Discovering the Global Past is designed to accommodate any format of the World History course, from the small lecture/discussion class at a liberal arts or community college to the large lecture with discussions led by teaching assistants at a sizable university. The chapters may be used for individual assignments, team projects, class discussions, papers, and exams. Each is self-contained, so that any combination may be assigned. The book is not intended to replace a standard textbook, and it was written to accompany any World History text the instructor chooses. The Instructor's Resource Manual, written by the authors of the text, offers further suggestions for class discussion, as well as a variety of ways in which students' learning may be evaluated and annotated lists of recommendations for further reading.

A note on spellings: Many of the sources presented in this book were originally written in a language other than English, and often in an alphabet other than the Western (Roman) one. Over the centuries, translators have devised various means of representing the sounds of other languages, and these conventions of translation have also changed over time. In general, we have used the most current spelling and orthographic conventions in our discussions and have left spellings as they appeared in the original translation in the sources. This means, for example, that Indian, Arabic, and Japanese words often have diacritical marks in the sources but not in our own material. For Chinese, in our own text we have used the pinyin system developed by the Chinese in the 1950s, with pinyin spellings indicated in brackets in the sources, most of which use the older Wade-Giles system.

New to the Fourth Edition

Volume I includes two entirely new chapters: Fiction and the Emotions in Japanese, Arabian, and Irish Culture (Chapter 8) and Cross-Cultural Encounters: Travel, Religion, Conquests, and Trade (Chapter 14; this chapter is also Chapter 1 in Volume II). Volume II includes two new chapters: The Age of Revolutions in the Atlantic World (Chapter 6); and Reform and Reaction in the Soviet Union and China at the End of the Cold War (Chapter 14).

In addition to the four new chapters, each volume has been carefully revised throughout. Several chapters have been heavily modified to offer a clearer emphasis on key topics in global history.

In Volume I, Chapter 2 now includes an excerpt from the creation account, *Kojiki*, Japan's oldest written chronicle. In addition, some of the sources have been shortened. In Chapter 3, the material on Egypt has been cut, which allows this chapter to focus more closely on Archaic and Classical Greece, Buddhist India, classic Maya, and western Africa. As a result, the following sources have been cut: Tut-ankh-amon and his wife Ankhesenam, Nebamum Hunting Birds, Statues of King Ramesses II and his Wife, and Wall Painting from Nefertari's Tomb near Thebes. In Chapters 4 and 5, some of the sources have been shortened. In Chapter 6, the Problem section has been expanded to include a brief discussion of material culture. In Chapter 7, the three European Christian accounts have been shortened and three additional accounts have been added, including two new accounts of the Third Crusade from Geoffrey de Vinsauf and Ambrose and one new account of the Seventh Crusade from Jean de

Joinville. Chapter 9 has been recast as a chapter on Mongol conquests, focusing on the clash between the beneficial and negative effects of this conquest. As a result, new sources have been added, including a Persian miniature illustrating a Mongol attack on a city, an excerpt on the destruction of Riazan, and an excerpt of the account of John de Plano Carpini. To accommodate these new sources, we have cut the Chinese-style portrait of Chingis Khan, Güyük Khan's letter to Pope Innocent IV, and Isfandiyar Fights with the Dragon. In Chapter 10, the source From Bernardino de Sahagún, The Florentine Codex has been cut. In Chapter 11, the material on Christianity has been cut, which allows this chapter to focus more closely on Buddhism and Islam. As a result, the following sources have been cut: Annalist of Nieder-Altaich: "The Great German Pilgrimage of 1064–65;" Icelandic Pilgrim's Guide; and From Guillaume de Deguileville, The Pilgrimage of Human Life. A new excerpt has been added on the Travels of Ibn Jubayr.

In Volume II, Chapters 3, 4, and 5 have been reorganized: Chapter 3 is now on the Confucian Family: Social Tyranny or Group Harmony; Chapter 4 is now on Gender, Labor, and Property in Rural Societies; and Chapter 5 is now on the Sweet Nexus: Sugar and the Origins of the Modern World. Chapter 3 has been recast to focus on the contrast between the modern and traditional views of the individual and the family. The Sample Contracts for Purchasing a Concubine and Selling a Son has been cut, and the excerpt from Classic of Filiality, or Xiao Jing has been replaced with a new excerpt from this source. Additionally, the following sources have been added: Zhong Yong (Chung Yung)—Doctrine of the Mean and The Sacred Edict of the Kangxi Emperor. Chapter 4 has been expanded to include coverage of gender. As a result, the following sources have been expanded: the Lê Code, Vietnam; the Agama Law Code, Java; William Marsden, The History of Sumatra; and the Law Code of the Territory of Salzburg, Austria. Also, A Female Dairy Farmer in Nuremberg, Germany has been cut. In Chapter 8, Oral Records of "Crossing Nomugi Pass" to Work in the Suma Mills has been replaced with "Song of the Living Corpses," Japanese Workers Song. We have cut the previous edition Chapter 12: The Industrial Crisis and the Centralization of Government, so now Chapter 12 is on Total War and Chapter 13 is on the Suez Crisis. In Chapter 12, we replaced Iwao Nakamura, Recollections of August 6, 1945, with the End of a Bake Shop: Reminiscence of Arakawa Hiroyo. In Chapter 15, we added the following new sources: Wayne Grudem, Bible Doctrine; James Dobson Mourns Obama Victory, Forecasts Significant Abortion Promotion; Ayatollah Khomeini, New Year's Message, March 21, 1980; Osama bin Laden Address "The Towers of Lebanon," October 29, 2004; Mahmoud Ahmadinejad Speech, October 26, 2005; Menachem Mendel Schneerson, "What Makes a Jew 'Jewish'?"; David Gardner (journalist) on K.S. Sudarshan; and "Hindu Party Seeks to Ban Foreign Churches in India." We have cut the following sources: After the Attacks: Finding Fault; Interview with Randall Terry; Sayyid Qutb, "Religion and Society in… Islam"; and Frontline Interview with Osama bin Laden.

Acknowledgments

We would like to thank the many students and instructors who have helped us in our efforts. We extend our gratitude to the following professors who have helped us and criticized the manuscript through its development:

Martin J. Blackwell, *Gainesville State College*

Andrew F. Clark, *University of North Carolina, Wilmington*

Terry D. Goddard, *Northwest Vista College*

Mark Hampton, *Lingnan University*

Kenneth J. Orosz, *University of Maine, Farmington*

Alice K. Pate, *Columbus State University*

Beatrice Spade, *Colorado State University, Pueblo*

In addition to our colleagues across the United States, we would like to thank especially our colleagues at the University of Wisconsin—Milwaukee; the University of Tennessee, Knoxville; Lawrence University; and California State University Long Beach. Merry E. Wiesner wishes especially to thank Darlene Abreu-Ferreira, Barbara Andaya, Judith Bennett, Susan Besse, Philip C. Brown, Martha Carlin, Jean Fleet, Charlotte Furth, Faye Getz, Anne Good, Michael Gordon, Abbas Hamdani, Anne Hansen, Jean Johnson, Teresa Meade, Jeffrey Merrick, Barbara Molony, Sheilagh Ogilvie, Jean Quataert, Irene Silverblatt, Andrea Stone, Hitomi Tonomura, Jane Waldbaum, and Charlotte Weber. Bruce Wheeler would like to thank Jay Rubenstein, Robert Bast, Palmira Brummett, Thomas Burman, Todd Diacon, and Catherine Higgs. Franklin M. Doeringer wishes to thank all of his colleagues in the Lawrence University Department of History for their support and interest in this project. J. Michael Hittle and Edmund M. Kern deserve particular mention for reading over portions of manuscript and offering helpful comments. He also expresses his gratitude to Jane Parish Yang and Kuo-ming Sung in the Department of Chinese and Japanese for their suggestions on material pertaining to China and East Asia. Finally, he extends special thanks to Peter J. Gilbert of the Lawrence Library for his unflagging help in tracking down elusive sources and obscure references. Kenneth R. Curtis would especially like to thank Christos Bartsocas, Francine Curtis, Steve Curtis, Ross Dunn, Tim Keirn, Lezlie Knox, Emilie Savage-Smith, Donald Schwartz, Andrew Jenks, and his coauthors.

Finally, we would like to thank Nancy Blaine, Adrienne Zicht, and the rest of the staff at Cengage Learning for their support.

M.E.W.
W.B.W.
F.M.D.
K.R.C.

DISCOVERING THE GLOBAL PAST

CHAPTER ONE

THE NEED FOR WATER

IN ANCIENT SOCIETIES

(3100 B.C.E.–100 C.E.)

The title of the course for which you are using this book is most likely some variation on "World Civilization." The meaning of *world* is self-evident, but why *civilization?* What distinguishes human cultures that are termed civilizations from those that are not? Though there are great differences among civilizations, all civilizations have a few features in common. The most important of these is the presence of cities; indeed, the word *civilization* comes from the Latin word *civis*, meaning "resident of a city, or citizen." Historians and archaeologists generally define a city as a place where more than five thousand people live. Remains of the earliest communities of this size have been discovered in ancient Mesopotamia, or present-day Iraq.

Why should the presence of cities be the distinguishing mark of cultural development? It is not the cities themselves but what they imply about a culture that makes them so important. Any society in which thousands of people live in proximity to one another must agree in general to certain laws or rules governing human behavior. These may be either part of an oral tradition or, as they were in ancient Mesopotamia, written down. A city must also make provision to assure its residents of a constant supply of food, which involves not only transporting food into the city from the surrounding farmland but also storing food throughout the year and preserving stockpiles for years when harvests are poor. In addition to demonstrating that people could transport and store food effectively, the presence of cities also indicates that people were producing enough surplus food to allow for a specialization of labor. If the whole work force had been devoted to farming, no one would have been available to build

Chapter 1

The Need for

Water in

Ancient Societies

(3100 B.C.E.–

100 C.E.)

roads, produce storage bins, or enforce the laws on which the city depended. This specialization of labor eventually allowed some members of society the opportunity and time to build structures and produce goods that were not directly essential to daily survival. Urban residents in Mesopotamia began to erect large buildings and to decorate them with sculptures, paintings, and mosaics, to write poetry and history, and to develop religious and philosophical ideas, all of which we consider essential to a civilization. As the cities themselves grew, they needed greater and greater amounts of food, which led to further technological development.

The civilization of ancient Mesopotamia flourished in the valley of two rivers, the Tigris and the Euphrates, and other early civilizations were located in river valleys as well—the Nile in Egypt, the Indus in India, and the Yellow in China. In all of these areas, except perhaps the Indus Valley, the amount of natural rainfall is not enough to sustain the level of agricultural production required for urban populations; irrigation using river water is necessary. Rather than proving a block to further development, however, the need for irrigation in these river valleys may have been the very catalyst that prompted the growth of cities. We may never be able to know this for sure, because irrigation systems were already in place before written records appeared, and because cities and irrigation expanded together. We do know that neither could have existed without the other in Mesopotamia; cities could survive only where there was a food surplus created by irrigation, and irrigation could be implemented only where there were enough people to construct and maintain ditches and other components of the system.

Supplying cities with water was not simply a technological problem, but one with economic, legal, social, and political implications as well. We can see this significance even in words themselves: The word *rival* originally meant those who shared, and quarreled over, the water in a *rivus,* or "irrigation channel." Your task in this chapter will be to use both visual and written evidence of ancient water systems to answer the following question: How did the need for a steady supply of water affect the technological, economic, political, and legal development of ancient societies?

BACKGROUND

Though the earliest of the world's civilizations all grew up in river valleys, the technical and organizational problems they confronted were very different because the character of the rivers differed tremendously. The Tigris and Euphrates flowed very fast, carrying soil as well as water down from the highlands. This soil was extremely rich and created new farmland where the rivers emptied into the Persian Gulf. (The ancient Persian Gulf ended more than 100 miles north of its modern-day shoreline; all of that land was created as the rivers filled in the delta.) The soil also filled in the irrigation ditches, which meant that they had to be cleaned out constantly. Every year this deposit was piled on the banks until they grew so high that the cleaning could no longer be accomplished easily. At this point a new ditch was cut and the old one abandoned, a process that entailed a great deal of work and required the cooperation of everyone whose land was watered by that particular ditch.

Mesopotamian farmers used several types of irrigation. They leveled large plots of land adjacent to the rivers and main canals, building up dikes around them in what is termed basin irrigation. During the spring and other high-water times of the year, farmers knocked holes in the dikes to allow water and fresh soil in. Once the sediment had settled, they let the water flow back into the channel. Workers also built small waterways between their fields to provide water throughout the year, developing a system of perennial irrigation. In the hillier country of northern Mesopotamia, farmers built terraces with water channels running alongside them. The terraces provided narrow strips of flat land to farm, and the waterways connected to brooks and streams.

Farmers could depend on gravity to bring water to their fields during spring and flood times, but at other times water-raising machines did the work. Technicians built many different types of machines, some of which are still in use in many parts of the world today. These solved some problems, but created others; for example, farmers with machines could drain an irrigation ditch during times of low water, leaving their neighbors with nothing. How were rights to water to be decided? Solving this problem was extremely important, and the first recorded laws regarding property rights in fact involve rights to water, not rights to land. In Mesopotamia, land was useless unless it was irrigated.

Many of the irrigation techniques developed in Mesopotamia spread to Egypt or were developed independently there. Egypt, because it received even less rainfall than Mesopotamia, was totally dependent on the Nile for watering crops. Fortunately, the Nile was much easier to use than the Tigris and Euphrates because it flooded regularly, allowing easy basin irrigation. The Nile was so predictable, in fact, that the Egyptians based their 365-day calendar on its annual flooding. The Egyptians also constructed waterways and water-lifting machines for perennial irrigation. Here as well, irrigation both caused and resulted from the growth of cities. Moreover, it contributed to the power of the kings, whom the Egyptian people regarded as somehow responsible for the flood of the Nile.

The harnessing of the Yellow River in China was also closely related to the growth of centralized state power there. The Yellow is a very violent river and carries a great amount of silt— twelve times as much as the Tigris and Euphrates, and seventy times as much as the Nile. The silt, caused by deforestation and erosion in the highlands, raises the bed of the Yellow River by

Chapter 1

The Need for
Water in
Ancient Societies
(3100 B.C.E.–
100 C.E.)

three feet every century, necessitating either constant dredging of irrigation canals or the continual building of higher dikes to hold back the river. The violence of the Yellow River floods—which have continued into the twentieth century—has changed the river's lower course dramatically throughout recorded history and has always led to devastation and social upheaval. Engineers in the Yellow River valley thus needed waterworks that would both protect cities and villages from flooding and at the same time irrigate fields; the earliest attempts to do both began in the seventh century B.C.E. In addition, the states that developed in the Yellow River valley received most of their taxes in the form of grain, which needed to be transported to the capital or to armies under state command. Along much of its course, the Yellow was too turbulent for transport, so canals were dug for grain barges. These three goals—flood control, irrigation, and grain transport—were not always compatible. In addition, competing armies often used waterworks as weapons, flooding the land of their rivals by building or destroying dikes. (Such tactics have also continued into the twentieth century; the dikes of the Yellow River were broken as a strategic move in 1938 during the Sino-Japanese War.)

Some of the earliest large-scale waterworks in China were the Hong Guo system of canals connecting the Yellow River with the Bian and Si Rivers, dating from the fifth or fourth century B.C.E., and the Zhengguo irrigation canal, first completed in 246 B.C.E. and still in use today. Branch canals dug from the major arteries created large irrigated areas, and farmers built water-lifting machines for

the perennial irrigation of their plots. As in Mesopotamia, water rights were a contentious issue, and special officials charged with the regulation of water were appointed as early as the second century B.C.E.

Though sewers were rare in the ancient world, pipes and conduits bringing water into cities and buildings were quite common in some areas. In China, earthenware pipes fitted together in sections have been excavated from as early as the second century B.C.E., and bamboo piping appears in illustrations from slightly later. The most extensive system for bringing water into cities in the ancient world was the one built for Rome. Like the three civilizations we have already discussed, Rome also grew up on the banks of a river, the Tiber, but substantial natural rainfall in the area made extensive irrigation for agricultural purposes unnecessary. Farmers did build drainage ditches, for much of the land around Rome was marshy and was usable for agriculture only when drained. Rome's primary water problem was the lack of good drinking water; the Tiber was often brackish and unpleasant, or even unhealthy, to drink. The Chinese solved the problem of unhealthy drinking water very early by boiling theirs, but the Romans instead learned from their Near Eastern neighbors and built aqueducts, covered or uncovered channels that brought water into the cities from pristine lakes and springs. The first of Rome's aqueducts was built in 312 B.C.E., and the system was expanded continuously up to about 150 C.E. Over 300 miles of aqueducts served the city of Rome alone, with extensive networks in the outlying provinces as well. Roman engineers went to great lengths to avoid valleys but were occasionally forced to construct enormous bridges to carry the aqueduct across a gorge. Some of these bridges were over 150 feet high, and a few, such as that in Segovia, Spain, still serve to bring water to city residents. Roman construction techniques, such as the use of the arch and water-resistant cement, allowed them to build water systems undreamed of in Mesopotamia and Egypt. Legal problems were not as easily solved, however, and disputes about water rights occurred throughout Rome's long history.

THE METHOD

Historians use a wide variety of sources when exploring ancient irrigation and water-supply systems. Many of these systems were created before the development of writing, so archaeological evidence—the actual remains of ancient ditches, machines, or aqueducts—is extremely important, particularly when tracing technological development. Even when such evidence itself has completely disappeared, valuable traces remain. As you will discover in this chapter, modern landscapes often reveal the ancient uses of the land through patterns of depressions and discoloration.

The easiest way to see these patterns is through aerial photography. Analyzing aerial photographs can be difficult, for it takes a great deal of training to learn how to read ancient land-use patterns through the overlay of modern development. Occasionally the older patterns can be quite clear, however, and with only a bit of additional information, you can begin to decode them. Source 1 is an aerial photograph of the site of a pre-Roman city in Italy. Examine the picture carefully. Can you see the old grid pattern of drainage ditches, which shows up as light and dark marsh grass? The dark lines are ancient drainage ditches, the lighter areas are ancient fields, and the white parallel lines superimposed on top are part of a modern drainage system. To examine the ancient system, you will mentally have to strip away the modern system. What do you think the broader black strip at the top left is? Look at the flatness of the landscape. Would silting in be a problem?

A more sophisticated type of aerial photography involves the use of satellites, rather than airplanes. Satellites can take extremely detailed pictures of the earth's surface that reveal natural and artificially constructed features, both ancient and contemporary. The sharpest images are produced by high-resolution military satellites whose pictures are not available to the public, but low-power images produced by LANDSAT, the only U.S. commercial imaging satellite system, are adequate for most archaeological and historical purposes. Source 2 is a map of the major ancient irrigation ditches between the Tigris and Euphrates Rivers identifiable in a recent LANDSAT image. What does the extent of the system reveal about Mesopotamian technology? What does the size of this network imply about the political

Chapter 1

The Need for

Water in

Ancient Societies

(3100 B.C.E.–

100 C.E.)

systems in this area—that is, would you expect the cities in Mesopotamia to be politically unified? hostile to each other? New technologies such as LANDSAT imagery not only answer elusive questions, but also guide future research. How could you use this map to plan further investigations of irrigation systems?

Aerial photography provides visual evidence of entire irrigation systems, but not of the specific tools and machines used to build them or to lift water to the fields. For these we must look to the remains of the tools themselves, or to depictions of them in tomb paintings, scrolls, mosaics, and pottery. Source 3 is the earliest depiction of irrigation ditches that has survived from ancient Egypt, carved on the head of a ceremonial mace dating from around 3100 B.C.E. The large figure in the middle is one of the early kings of Egypt, holding a hoe, flanked by two palm-fan bearers and a man holding a basket for the dirt dug up by the hoe. At the bottom are two other workmen, also with hoes, excavating or deepening the ditches. Based on what you already know about Egyptian society, would you expect the king himself to be digging ditches? Why might this mace, which signified royal authority, show the king involved in building irrigation ditches?

Some of the machines depicted in ancient paintings are still in use today, showing that many techniques for lifting water have not changed at all for thousands of years. Sources 4 to 7 show four different machines for raising water that we know were in use in ancient times: the shaduf, the saqiya, the square-pallet chain pump,

and the noria. To assess their role and importance, you have to think about a number of different factors while you examine the four diagrams. Some of these factors are technical: How complicated is this machine to build? Does it have many moving parts to keep in good repair? How much water can it lift? How high can it lift it? Can it work with both flowing and stationary water? Some of the factors are economic: Does the machine require a person to operate it (thus taking a worker away from other types of labor)? Does it require a strong adult, or can it be operated by a child? Does it require the power of an animal, which must be fed and cared for? Some of the factors are both economic and political: Does the machine require more raw materials to build than one family would be likely to possess? Does it require any raw materials, such as metal, that would have to be imported? (Such questions are political because someone has to decide which families get the raw materials necessary for their fields.) Some of the factors are legal: Does the machine raise so much water that distribution would have to be regulated? At this point, you may want to make a chart summarizing your assessment of the advantages and disadvantages of each machine; such a study aid will help you make your final conclusions.

We now turn from visual to written sources. Because water was so important, mention of water systems appears very early in recorded human history. Sources 8 to 12 are written accounts of the construction or operation of water systems. Source 8 presents the sections from the Code of Hammurabi, a

Babylonian legal code dating from 1750 B.C.E., that refer to irrigation. Source 9 is a description of the building of the Zhengguo [Chêng Kuo] Canal in the third century B.C.E., written by the historian Sima Qian about 150 years later. In Source 10, the Roman historian Suetonius records the water-system projects undertaken by the Emperor Claudius during his reign (41–54 C.E.). Source 11 is a report of the activities of Shao Xinchen [Hsin-Ch'en], an administrator during the Han dynasty in China, dating from sometime before 33 B.C.E. Source 12 is a discussion of some of the problems associated with Rome's water system, written about 100 C.E. by Frontinus, who was commissioner of the water supply. Finally, Source 13 is a memorial dating from the first century B.C.E. by Jia Rang [Chia Jang], a specialist in flood control, answering an imperial decree that asked for opinions on river conservancy.

As you read these sources, notice first of all the technical problems that each author addresses. What particular problems in controlling, tapping, transporting, and storing water are discussed? What solutions are suggested? Then look at legal problems, most clearly presented in the selection by Frontinus and the Code of Hammurabi. How were people misusing or harming the water systems? What penalties did they incur? Who controlled the legal use of water and decided how water was to be distributed?

The written sources also include information about political and economic factors in ancient water-supply systems that is nearly impossible to gain from archaeological evidence. Careful reading can give you an insight into who paid for the construction of such systems and who stood to profit—financially or politically—from their use. What reasons other than the simple need for water led rulers to build water systems? What political and economic factors entered into decisions about how water was to be distributed?

Chapter 1
The Need for
Water in
Ancient Societies
(3100 B.C.E.–
100 C.E.)

THE EVIDENCE

Source 1 from Leo Deuel, Flights Into Yesterday: The Story of Aerial Archaeology *(New York: St. Martin's Press, 1969), p. 236. Photograph: Fotoaerea Valvassori, Ravenna.*

1. Aerial Photograph of Pre-Roman City in Italy

Source 2 *from Robert MaC. Adams,* Heartland of Cities; Surveys of Ancient Settlements and Land Use on the Central Floodplains of the Euphrates *(Chicago: University of Chicago Press, 1981), p. 34.*

2. Major Ancient Levees Identifiable in LANDSAT Imagery

Chapter 1

The Need for

Water in

Ancient Societies

(3100 B.C.E.–

100 C.E.)

Source 3 from Walter B. Emery, Archaic Egypt *(Baltimore: Penguin, 1961), p. 43.*

3. Early Egyptian King Cutting an Irrigation Ditch, Drawn from Mace-head Carving, 3100 B.C.E.

Sources 4 through 7 adapted from sketches by Merry E. Wiesner.

4. Shaduf

5. Saqiya

6. Square-Pallet Chain Pump

7. Noria

Chapter 1

The Need for

Water in

Ancient Societies

(3100 B.C.E.–

100 C.E.)

Source 8 from Robert F. Harper, The Code of Hammurabi *(Chicago: University of Chicago Press, 1904).*

8. Sections from the Code of Hammurabi Referring to Irrigation, 1750 B.C.E.

53. If a man neglects to maintain his dike and does not strengthen it, and a break is made in his dike and the water carries away the farmland, the man in whose dike the break has been made shall replace the grain which has been damaged.

54. If he is not able to replace the grain, they shall sell him and his goods and the farmers whose grain the water has carried away shall divide [the results of the sale].

55. If a man opens his canal for irrigation, and neglects it and the water carries away an adjacent field, he shall pay out grain on the basis of the adjacent field.

56. If a man opens up the water and the water carries away the improvements of an adjacent field, he shall pay out ten *gur* of grain per *bur* [of damaged land]. . . .

66. If a man has stolen a watering-machine from the meadow, he shall pay five shekels of silver to the owner of the watering-machine.

Source 9 from Joseph Needham, Science and Civilization in China, *Vol. 4, Pt. 3 (Cambridge: Cambridge University Press, 1974), p. 285.*

9. Sima Qian's Description of the Building of the Zhengguo Canal, ca. 100 B.C.E.

(The prince of) Han,[1] hearing that the State of Chhin[1] [Qin] was eager to adventure profitable enterprises, desired to exhaust it (with heavy activities), so that it should not start expanding to the east (and making attacks on Han). He therefore sent the hydraulic engineer Chêng Kuo [Zhengguo] (to Chhin) to persuade deceitfully (the king of) Chhin to open a canal from the Ching [Qing] River, from Chung-shan [Zhongshan] and Hu-khou [Hukou] in the west, all along the foot of the northern mountains, carrying water to fall into the river Lo in the east. The proposed canal was to be more than 300 *li*[2] long, and was to be used for irrigating agricultural land.

1. Han and Chhin were two states that bordered the Yellow River.
2. 300 *li* = 100 miles.

Before the construction work was more than half finished, however, the Chhin authorities became aware of the trick. (The king of Chhin) wanted to kill Chêng Kuo, but he [the engineer] addressed him as follows: "It is true that at the beginning I deceived you, but nevertheless this canal, when it is completed, will be of great benefit to Chhin. I have, by this ruse, prolonged the life of the State of Han for a few years, but I am accomplishing a work which will sustain the State of Chhin for ten thousand generations." The (king of) Chhin agreed with him, approved his words, and gave firm orders that the canal was to be completed. When it was finished, rich silt-bearing water was led through it to irrigate more than [667,000 acres] of alkali land. The harvests from these fields attained the level of [16 bushels] per *mou* [i.e. they became very abundant]. Thus Kuanchung (the land within the passes) became a fertile country without bad years. (It was for this reason that) Chhin became so rich and powerful, and in the end was able to conquer all the other feudal States. And ever afterwards the canal (bore the name of the engineer and) was called the Chêngkuo Canal.

Source 10 from Naphtali Lewis and Meyer Reinhold, Roman Civilization *(New York: Columbia University Press, 1955), pp. 151–152.*

10. Suetonius's Description of the Water Projects Undertaken by Emperor Claudius (r. 41–54 C.E.)

The public works which Claudius completed were great and essential rather than numerous; they were in particular the following: an aqueduct begun by Caligula; also the drainage channel of Lake Fucine and the harbor at Ostia, although in the case of the last two he knew that Augustus had refused the former to the Marsians in spite of their frequent requests, and that the latter had often been considered by the deified Julius but given up because of its difficulty. He brought to the city on stone arches the cool and abundant springs of the Claudian aqueduct . . . and at the same time the channel of the New Anio, distributing them into many beautifully ornamented fountains. He made the attempt on the Fucine Lake as much in the hope of gain as of glory, inasmuch as there were some who offered to drain it at their own cost provided the land that was drained be given them. He finished the drainage canal, which was three miles in length, partly by leveling and partly by tunneling a mountain, a work of great difficulty requiring eleven years, although he had 30,000 men at work all the time without interruption.

Chapter 1

The Need for

Water in

Ancient Societies

(3100 B.C.E.–

100 C.E.)

Source 11 from Cho-yun Hsu, Han Agriculture: The Formation of Early Chinese Agrarian Economy *(Seattle: University of Washington Press, 1980), pp. 268–269. Copyright © 1980. Reprinted by permission of the University of Washington Press.*

11. Activities of Shao Xinchen, Han Dynasty, before 33 B.C.E.

[Shao] Hsin-ch'en [Xinchen] was promoted to be grand administrator of Nanyang. . . . Hsin-ch'en was a person of energy and plans; he took an interest in creating benefits for the people and regarded it as his urgent task to enrich them. Crossing in and out of the fields, stopping and resting even at remote villages and cantons, and having very little time for quiet living, he personally encouraged farming.

As he traveled about, he inspected the waters and springs in the commandery. He dug canals and ditches and built water gates and dikes in several tens of places in all to expand the irrigated land, which increased year by year to as much as [500,000 acres]. The people obtained benefits from this and had a surplus of stores.

Hsin-ch'en formulated regulations for the people concerning the equitable distribution of water. They were inscribed on stones and set up at the boundaries of the fields to prevent disputes over the distribution [of water].

Source 12 from B. K. Workman, editor and translator, They Saw It Happen in Classical Times *(New York: Barnes & Noble, 1964), pp. 179–181.*

12. Frontinus's Discussion of Rome's Water System, ca. 100 C.E.

The New Anio[3] is drawn from the river in the district of Sinbrinum, at about the forty-second milestone along the Via Sublacensis. On either side of the river at this point are fields of rich soil which make the banks less firm, so that the water in the aqueduct is discoloured and muddy even without the damage done by storms. So a little way along from the inlet a cleansing basin was built where the water could settle and be purified between the river and the conduit. Even so, in the event of rain, the water reaches the city in a muddy state. The length of the New Anio is about 47 miles, of which over 39 are underground and more than 7 carried on structures above the ground. In the upper reaches a distance of about two miles in various sections is carried on low structures or arches. Nearer the

3. An aqueduct completed under the emperor Claudius in 52 C.E.

city, from the seventh Roman mile-stone, is half a mile on substructures and five miles on arches. These arches are very high, rising in certain places to a height of 109 feet.

. . . All the aqueducts reach the city at different levels. So some serve the higher districts and some cannot reach loftier ground. For the hills of Rome have gradually increased in height because of the rubble from frequent fires. There are five aqueducts high enough at entrance to reach all the city, but they supply water at different pressures. . . .

Anyone who wants to tap water for private consumption must send in an application and take it, duly signed by the Emperor, to the Commissioner. The latter must take immediate action on Caesar's grant, and enroll one of the Imperial freedmen to help him in the business. . . . The right to water once granted cannot be inherited or bought, and does not go with the property, though long ago a privilege was extended to the public baths that their right should last in perpetuity. . . . When grants lapse, notice is given and record made in the ledgers, which are consulted so that future applicants can be given vacant supplies. The previous custom was to cut off these lapsed supplies at once, to make some profit by a temporary sale to the landowners or even to outsiders. Our Emperor felt that property should not suddenly be left without water, and that it would be fairer to give thirty days' notice for other arrangements to be made by the interested party. . . .

Now that I have explained the situation with regard to private supply, it will be pertinent to give some examples of the ways in which men have broken these very sound arrangements and have been caught red-handed. In some reservoirs I have found larger valves in position than had been granted, and some have not even had the official stamp on them. . . .

Another of the watermen's intolerable practices to make a new outlet from the cistern when a water-grant is transferred to a new owner, leaving the old one for themselves. I would say that it was one of the Commissioner's chief duties to put a stop to this. For it affects not only the proper protection of the supply, but also the upkeep of the reservoir which would be ruined if needlessly filled with outlets.

Another financial scheme of the watermen, which they call "puncturing," must also be abolished. There are long separate stretches all over the city through which the pipes pass hidden under the pavement. I found out that these pipes were being tapped everywhere by the "puncturers," from which water was supplied by private pipe to all the business premises in the area, with the result that only a meagre amount reached the public utilities. I can estimate the volume of water stolen in this way from the amount of lead piping which was removed when these branch pipes were dug up.

Chapter 1

The Need for

Water in

Ancient Societies

(3100 B.C.E.–

100 C.E.)

Source 13 from Cho-Yun Hsu, Han Agriculture: The Formation of Early Chinese Agrarian Economy (Seattle: University of Washington Press, 1980), pp. 266–267. Copyright © 1980. Reprinted by permission of the University of Washington Press.

13. Memorial from Jia Rang, 1st century B.C.E.

[Jia Rang memorialized:] ". . . Digging canals has three benefits; not digging them has three detriments. When the people are constantly exhausted by preventing floods, half of them lose their livelihood. When the water overflows the land and when the accumulated moisture evaporates, the people are made ill by the humid atmosphere. All the trees rapidly rot away, and the soil, turning alkaline, does not produce grain. When the river breaks the dikes and overflows, destruction ensues, and [the victims] become food for fish and turtles. These are the three detriments.

"If there are canals for irrigation, then the salt is washed down to the marshy ground and the spreading of the silt increases fertility. Where formerly millet and wheat were raised, even nonglutinous and glutinous rice can be produced; the productivity is increased fivefold in the high-lying land and tenfold in low-lying land. Furthermore, there is the advantage of transportation by water. These are the three benefits."

[Jia Rang next considers the possible types of irrigation projects, and proposes the building of large-scale dikes as the best policy. He describes two other alternatives to pursue if new dikes are not possible: digging new irrigation canals and repairing the old dikes. He assesses these two choices as follows.]

"At present, the number of functionaries and conscript laborers for embankments along the Yellow River in each commandery is several thousand, and the costs of cutting and buying wood and stone are several tens of millions yearly [an amount] that is sufficient to dig canals and construct water gates. Furthermore, when the people benefit from irrigation, they will urge one another to make canals, and they will not be weary even if the work is strenuous. At the same time the people's fields will be cared for and the dikes on the Yellow River will be completed. This will indeed enrich the state, make the people secure, create profit, and do away with calamities, and it will endure for several hundred years. Therefore, I consider this a medium policy. Repairing the old dikes by means of increasing the height and thickness would cost limitlessly, and we would frequently encounter calamities. This would be the worst policy."

QUESTIONS TO CONSIDER

Now that you have looked at both visual and written evidence, you will need to compile and organize the information gained from each type of source to achieve a more complete picture. Because sources for the earliest periods of human development are so scant, we need to use every shred of evidence available and use it somewhat creatively, making reasonable speculations where there is no specific evidence.

Take all the evidence about technical problems first. Keeping in mind that the ancient world had no power equipment, and no tools more elaborate than axes, hammers, saws, and drills (the Chinese and Romans also had planes and chisels), what would you gauge to be the most difficult, purely technical problem involved in constructing water systems? in keeping them operating? The four diagrams of the water-raising machines are arranged in the chronological order of their development, with the shaduf as old as 2500 B.C.E. and the other three introduced hundreds of years later. Looking at your chart of the advantages and disadvantages of each machine, how do the later machines improve on the shaduf? What additional problems do these improvements create? What types of technological experimentation did the need for water encourage?

Technological advance is not always an unmitigated blessing. For example, water standing in irrigation ditches can become a fertile breeding ground for mosquitoes and other carriers of disease. Cities that depend on irrigation suffer food shortages and famine when ditches cannot be kept clear or when river levels drop. Furthermore, the diversion of so much of their water makes rivers much smaller when they finally reach their deltas, which means that the deltas become increasingly salty from sea water and eventually become unable to support the kinds of plant and animal life they originally sustained. Judging by the aerial photograph and the LANDSAT map, would you expect any of these problems in ancient Italy or Mesopotamia? In the written sources, do you find evidence of problems in the Chinese and Roman water systems that were caused by technological advance? Are any suggestions made for solving these?

Now think about what you have learned about the economic issues associated with water systems. You have no doubt noticed that tremendous numbers of people were needed to construct irrigation ditches and aqueducts. Some of the written sources, such as Suetonius and Jia Rang, give exact figures as to the number of workers. The size and complexity of the systems depicted in all the sources also imply huge work forces, given the lack of elaborate equipment. The rulers of Mesopotamia, Egypt, China, and Rome did not view the need for mass labor as an obstacle, but rather saw it as a solution to the problem of unemployment. Legend has it that the Roman emperor Vespasian, when offered a labor-saving machine, refused to use it on the grounds that it would put people out of work and lead to social unrest in Rome. You may approve of this concern for full employment, but it should also tell you something about the value of labor in ancient societies.

[17]

Chapter 1

The Need for

Water in

Ancient Societies

(3100 B.C.E.–

100 C.E.)

What would you expect wages to be for construction workers? What class of people would you expect to find working on these water systems?

Large numbers of workers were needed not only in construction, but also in the maintenance of irrigation systems and the operation of water-lifting machines. What does this tell you about the value of labor? What would happen with the sudden drop in the population, such as that caused by a famine or epidemic? How would a loss of workers affect the available food supply?

The sources also reveal information about political factors associated with water systems. What does their construction indicate about the power of rulers to coerce or hire labor? How do rulers control the building and maintenance of machines and ditches? How might this affect the power and independence of local communities or of individual families? What can you surmise about the role water played in expanding centralized political power or in disputes between rival dynasties?

Finally, the sources provide evidence of legal changes necessitated by the search for, and limits of, water. Actions that had previously been unrestricted and unregulated now came under the control of public authorities, which meant that the number of enforcement agents and courts had to increase. What would this expansion of bureaucracy do to taxation levels? How did political concerns shape the regulations?

You are now ready to answer the question posed at the beginning of the chapter: How did the need for a steady supply of water affect the technological, economic, political, and legal development of ancient societies?

EPILOGUE

The irrigation and water supply systems of the ancient world required not only huge amounts of labor, but also strong central states to coerce or hire that labor and to enforce laws that kept the channels flowing. For example, each Mesopotamian city managed its own irrigation system, but the wealthy and advanced cities were attractive targets for foreign conquerers. The political history of ancient Mesopotamia was one of wave after wave of conquerers invading from the north—the Akkadians, Babylonians, Assyrians, Persians, Greeks, and finally Romans. Most of these conquerers realized the importance of irrigation and ordered the vanquished residents to maintain or expand their systems. When the Muslims conquered the area in the seventh century, they studied Mesopotamian techniques and spread these westward across northern Africa and into Spain, where centuries-old Roman irrigation systems were disintegrating.

In between these powerful conquerers, however, and after the thirteenth century, when the area was overrun by the Mongols, the irrigation ditches were often not maintained, and they silted in irreparably. The fertile farmland that had been built up in the delta became salinized from the salty waters of the Persian Gulf, making it useless for cultivation. Once the irrigation ditches were no longer functional, the cities could not survive. Centuries of irrigation combined with too little fertilization made even irrigated land less and less productive.

The benefits and problems brought by irrigation are not limited to the ancient world, however, but can be seen in many modern societies. A striking contemporary example comes from one of the parts of the world we have been studying in this chapter. Throughout the twentieth century, Egypt expanded its irrigation system fed by the Nile with a series of dams, culminating in the Aswan High Dam, begun in 1960 to provide hydroelectric power and limit the free flow of water at the height of the flood season. The enormous reservoir created by the dam can also be tapped at low water times to allow for perennial irrigation. The dam does all of the things it was intended to do very well, but has also introduced some unexpected problems. The river's regular flooding had brought new fertile soil to the Nile Valley and carried away the salts that result from evaporation. Once the dam stopped the flooding, Egyptian fields began to need artificial fertilizer to remain productive, a supplement few farmers could afford. Because the soil of the Nile Valley contains much clay and so drains very slowly, the dam's steady supply of water makes many fields waterlogged and unusable. The large reservoir created by the dam sits in the middle of the Sahara Desert, losing tremendous amounts to evaporation and decreasing the total flow of water in the Nile significantly. The artificial lake also put many acres of farmland under water and forced the relocation of tens of thousands of people. The current drought in northern Africa has further lowered the level of the Nile, shrinking the amount of hydroelectric power the river can generate. Ending the flooding also allowed snails that carry bilharzia (schistosomiasis) to proliferate in the fields and irrigation ditches; bilharzia is an intestinal parasite that severely weakens its victims. Thus, like the dikes in ancient China that could be broken by flood or foreign conquest, or the levees of the Mississippi that gave way in the floods of 1993, or the irrigation of the southwestern United States that is draining underground aquifers, the Aswan High Dam has proved a mixed blessing to modern Egypt.

As you reflect on what you have discovered in this chapter, you may want to think about problems associated with the distribution of water in your own area. How does the need for water affect the political and economic structures of your city or state? What technological solutions has your area devised, and how have these worked?

CHAPTER TWO

WRITING AND POWER:

DEFINING WORLD-VIEWS

(1750 B.C.E.–250 C.E.)

According to Islamic tradition, when the angel Gabriel first revealed himself to Muhammad around the year 610, among the first words he spoke to Muhammad were these:

> In the name of the Lord who created all things. He has taught us the use of the pen. He taught us that which we know not.[1]

Although there is no record that Muhammad himself could either read or write, there is little doubt that the man who ultimately would be revered by Muslims as the Prophet understood the power that literacy gave to those who could read and write, a power that literate people held over those who were not literate. Thoughts could be shaped, codified, and transmitted over both distance and time. Laws (whether political, economic, or religious) could be written down and interpreted or enforced by those who could record or read them. Perhaps more important, writing gave to some the power to bind a people together by giving them a shared history, a common literature, a united world-view, and even a shared *cosmology* (a branch of philosophy that deals with the origin, process, and structure of the universe). And while the oral traditions of nonliterate peoples could be powerful, effective, and in some ways even more "democratic" (in that all who heard could thereby participate in the carrying on of laws, religion, and history), writing possessed certain advantages over an oral tradition. Indeed, later historians have asserted that, along with the discovery of fire, the domestication of animals, and the division of labor, the evolution of writing was an indispensable factor in human

---

1. Qur'an (Koran) XCVI, 1–5.

development and the growth of civilizations.[2]

Throughout history, virtually every culture has had its own explanation of how the world was created (cosmology) and what place humans were meant to occupy in that world. In addition to commercial information and law codes, a people's explanations of creation were one of the first things they wrote down, thus demonstrating the people's own belief in the superiority of written over oral transmission. By studying these written explanations of creation, historians can come to understand a particular people's value system, its view of itself, and the relationship of the people to the world, to the universe, and to a god or gods. In addition, historians can gain an understanding of a people's own view of history. To a particular people, is history linear (resembling a straight line, from event to event), cyclical (circular, with patterns recurring), of another form, or formless (with events occurring purely at random, by chance)? In sum, by studying a people's accounts of creation, historians can learn a remarkable amount about how the people thought and even why they behaved as they did.

Your tasks in this chapter will require you to use all your analytical reading skills plus a good deal of historical imagination. In the Evidence section of this chapter you will find six written creation accounts—one from Atra-hasis of ancient Babylonia, one from the Rig Veda of ancient India, one from the Torah (the first five books of both the Jewish and Christian Bibles) of the Israelites, one from the Yijing (or I Ching, the Book of Changes) of ancient China, one from the Popol Vuh of the Mayan civilization of Central America, and one from the *Kojiki*, Japan's oldest written chronicle. First, you must read each account to learn how each of these peoples sought to explain the creation of the world. Then, using your historical imagination, show what each creation account tells us about the people who thought it critical enough to write it down—their value system, their view of history, their relationship to the universe as well as to a god or gods. In essence, then, you will be studying the cosmologies of six ancient peoples, an extremely important exercise for historians.

2. See Colin Cherry, *On Human Communication* (New York: John Wiley & Sons, 1957), p. 31. See also Jared Diamond, *Guns, Germs, and Steel: The Fates of Human Societies* (New York: W.W. Norton, 1997), ch. 12.

BACKGROUND

Forms of "written" communication are nearly as old as humanity itself. Cave paintings and etchings[3] surely were intended to transmit simple messages as well as to provide means of self-expression. Message sticks (Australia), wampum belts (Native Americans), shell designs (Nigeria), knotted cords (Tibet, Polynesia, parts of Africa),

3. Carvings or etchings on cave walls are referred to by archaeologists as petroglyphs; cave paintings are called petrograms.

Chapter 2

Writing and

Power: Defining

World-Views

(1750 B.C.E.–

250 C.E.)

bean patterns (pre-Inca Peru), and the like—all were used to communicate uncomplicated messages.

Beginning about six thousand years ago, however, people began to develop more complex and codified (systematic, with rules) forms of written communication. Evolving first among the Sumerians of the Fertile Crescent—the land between the Tigris and Euphrates Rivers—in approximately 3500 B.C.E., various types of writing on stone, clay tablets, and papyrus[4] emerged independently in Egypt, China, the Near East, Crete, Cyprus, and (by about 1000 B.C.E.) Central America. Ultimately, various cultures developed over two hundred written scripts, approximately eighty of which are still in use today.[5]

Wherever writing developed and whatever particular form it took, all types of writing can be divided into two general systems: *ideographic* and *phonetic*. Ideographic writing, known also as thought writing, evolved from using pictures to represent things or thoughts (Sumerian pictorials, Egyptian hieroglyphics, and Chinese pictographs, among others). The advantage of ideographic writing is that it is not tied to any particular spoken language and thus can be understood by people speaking a variety of tongues and dialects. The principal disadvantage of ideographic writing is that it requires the memorization of an immense number of different signs, or ideograms—four to six thousand, for example, for literate Chinese. On the other hand, in phonetic writing, each sign (or letter, in our writing) represents a particular sound, and signs are combined to make the sounds for particular words. For example, most Western Europeans employ a form of phonetic writing that uses the signs of the Roman alphabet. Regularized in the sixth century B.C.E., the Roman alphabet originally contained twenty-one signs (letters); the number was later expanded to twenty-six.[6] The chief advantages of phonetic writing are that only a few signs need to be memorized and that these signs can be grouped in an almost endless number of sound combinations to make words and to create new words.[7]

Wherever writing developed, those who mastered this skill often wielded great power and commanded enormous respect. In Egypt, scribes were exempt from physical labor, taxation, and military service. As one scribe wrote, "Put writing in your heart that you protect yourself from hard labor of any kind." Scribes were likewise respected in Mesopotamia, among the

4. **papyrus:** a type of paper, developed by the Egyptians around 3100 B.C.E., that was made from the inner stems of the papyrus plant, which were pressed together with some form of adhesive; after being written on, the papyrus then was rolled into scrolls.

5. Of all the written scripts known to have existed, over twenty still are undecipherable. People who decipher ancient inscriptions or writings are known as epigraphers. For more on this exciting profession, see John Chadwick, *The Decipherment of Linear B* (Cambridge, England, 1958); Carol Andrews, *The Rosetta Stone* (London, 1981); Michael D. Coe, *Breaking the Maya Code* (New York: Thames and Hudson, 1992).

6. The letters *W, J, Y, Z,* and *U* were added later. Note, however, that the English language contains around 40 sounds (phonemes) that are expressed using the 26 letters—for example, the multiple sounds expressed by the letter "a," "e," etc.

7. An unabridged English dictionary contains approximately 500,000 words, and hundreds of new words are added to the language each decade.

Aztecs of Central America, and later in the nations of Islam. In ancient Japan the position of scribe was hereditary, and scribes were referred to as *Fumi no Obito* (Chiefs of Writing). Most societies founded schools to teach royalty, nobility, and scribes the craft of writing, but in no early culture was universal literacy considered either necessary or desirable. This was because those in power quickly realized that those who could write possessed the capacity to shape the thoughts of those who could not. The illiterate would gather (or would be forcibly gathered) to listen to the readings of edicts, proclamations, laws, or religious texts and liturgies.[8]

As noted above, along with commercial agreements and legal codes, one of the first things a people committed to writing was their own explanation of the creation of the universe, the world, and human beings. Such creation accounts often bound a people together and formed a philosophical foundation for their thoughts and actions. In this chapter, you will be analyzing the creation accounts of the Babylonians of the Fertile Crescent (written down sometime between 1750 and 1400 B.C.E.), the Indo-Aryans of ancient India (Rig Veda, written down ca. 600 B.C.E.), the Israelites of ancient Israel (the Torah, traditionally first read publicly by the scribe Ezra in Jerusalem in 444 B.C.E.),[9] the Zhou dynasty of ancient China (Yijing, parts of which can be dated roughly at 1000 B.C.E., although the section you will be reading dates from around the third century B.C.E.), the

Mayas of Central America (Popol Vuh, almost surely transcribed from ancient oral accounts and written down before the Classical Period of Mayan civilization, which began in approximately 250 C.E.), and the Japanese (*Kojiki*, or *Record of Ancient Matters*, compiled by O No Yasumaro in 712 C.E.).

Historians generally agree that Mesopotamia,[10] the area between the Tigris and Euphrates Rivers (in modern-day Iraq), was the scene of the earliest civilization. It was here that a people known as Sumerians domesticated plants and animals; devised an irrigation system; constructed cities such as Ur, Uruk, and Lagash; established trade routes to lands as far away as Egypt; and developed what was probably the world's first writing system, at first pictographic but ultimately evolving into a phonetic system. Later conquerors of the Sumerians, such as the Babylonians,[11] adopted much of Sumerian culture, including its writing and its cosmology. Atra-hasis (Source 1), the Babylonian creation account, borrowed heavily from the Sumerians.

The Indo-Aryans migrated to present-day India from the northwest around 1500 B.C.E., either conquering the earlier Indus civilization or moving in after its fall. Originally a warlike and pastoral people, the Aryans quickly adapted themselves to a sedentary, food-producing life. Politically, their Vedic society was divided into a strict caste system of priests

10. **Mesopotamia:** a Greek word meaning "land between the rivers."

11. The Babylonians were known as Amorites, a Semitic people who invaded Sumer from the west and built the city of Babylon. Their most famous ruler was Hammurabi, the author of a comprehensive law code for Babylon.

8. **liturgy:** a prescribed form for a public religious service; many religions have written down their liturgies in prayer books or missals.

9. See Nehemiah 8:1–8.

Chapter 2

Writing and

Power: Defining

World-Views

(1750 B.C.E.–

250 C.E.)

(Brahman), warriors (Kshatriya), peasants (Vaishya), and serfs (Shudra). Although the original Aryan conquerors were illiterate, the preceding Indus Valley civilization had developed a writing system that was a mixture of ideographic and phonetic forms.[12] By roughly 700 B.C.E., however, Vedic society had developed its own form of writing known as Brahmi, apparently derived from a North Semitic script.

In Vedic society, writing apparently was first used in political contexts, but soon was adopted by the Brahman to systematically collect songs, hymns, histories, and other materials that had been passed orally from generation to generation. The oldest of those collections was the Rig Veda (Source 2),[13] a collection of 1,017 hymns or songs divided into ten chapters or books. Some of these songs had been present in Vedic society at least since the Indo-Aryan migration to northern India in roughly 1500 B.C.E. It is here that the society's creation accounts can be found. The Rig Veda was a sacred book of Brahmanism, an early form of Hinduism.

In China, the Shang dynasty (ca. 1523–1027 B.C.E.) was overthrown by the Zhou (Chou), once-loyal dependents of the Shang whose military technology (including horse-drawn chariots) gave them the upper hand over their former masters. But the Zhou were wise enough to retain much of Shang culture, including its system of writing and its religious beliefs. A major part of those beliefs had to

do with divination, the art of foretelling the future. Priests would take the bottom shell of a tortoise, pierce the shell with a small hole, ask a question, and then apply heat to the hole in the shell. The resulting cracks in the shell formed various patterns that the priests could then interpret in order to predict future events. By around 200 B.C.E., the Yijing (or Book of Changes) had been completed and served as an interpretive guide that substituted eight trigrams (sets of three parallel lines) and sixty-four hexagrams (six parallel lines) for the cracks in the tortoise shell. The Yijing is less a religious book than it is a volume of philosophy and ethics, and it was considered important enough to escape the great book burning of 213 B.C.E. It is in the Yijing (Source 4) that the Chinese creation account can be found.

About the time that the Indo-Aryans were moving into India and the Shang dynasty was in the process of controlling the eastern half of the Yellow River Valley, in Mesopotamia and the Arabian peninsula groups of homeless nomads (referred to in Mesopotamian and Egyptian sources as "Habiru") wandered across the semiarid landscape grazing their herds. One of these groups came to be known as "Hebrews," or "Israelites" or "Jews."[14] Sometime after 1550 B.C.E., the Jews voluntarily migrated to Egypt to escape a drought, but soon were enslaved by the Egyptians. Around

---

12. The Indus script is one of those that is still a mystery.

13. **Veda:** "wisdom, or the path to wisdom."

14. At the time, "Hebrew" referred to a social category, whereas "Israelite" was used to describe all the people of the group; "Jews" derived from the southern kingdom's surviving tribe of Judah.

1200 B.C.E., the Jews either abandoned or escaped from Egypt. The decline of both the Egyptian and Hittite empires had left a power vacuum along the eastern coast of the Mediterranean Sea, and it was here that the Israelites ultimately settled, fighting off Philistines and other peoples in order to seize and hold the land. Sometime after 925 B.C.E. (the traditional death of King Solomon), the Israelites broke into two kingdoms. The northern kingdom was destroyed by Assyrian invaders, while the southern kingdom (Judah) survived for another century and a half, until the Babylonian captivity.

Written Hebrew was one of the several offshoots of North Semitic script (another, as we have seen, was Brahmi) and was in use as early as ca. 800 B.C.E. The form of Hebrew writing known as Square Hebrew (for the rectangular shaping of the letters) traditionally owed its adoption to the scribe Ezra in the fifth century B.C.E. Like all Semitic scripts, Hebrew is consonantal—that is, phonetic with consonant letters or sounds (in the case of Hebrew, twenty-two), but no vowels.

Similar to the early writings of other peoples, the Torah contains the Jews' creation account, history, and laws. Traditionally, authorship is credited to Moses, although a majority of biblical scholars assert that the Torah comes from more than a single source. According to ancient tradition, Joshua had the Torah "engraved upon the stones of the altar" of the tabernacle sometime before 1100 B.C.E., a claim that most scholars dispute as much too early (the fifth century B.C.E. is more likely). Like those of other peoples, the Israelites' explanation of creation (Source 3, from the book of Genesis, which began to be stabilized around 720 B.C.E.) tells historians a great deal about the Jewish people themselves.

About the time the Jews left Egypt, a group of people in what is now known as Central America were establishing sedentary villages and even towns. No longer an exclusively hunter-gatherer society, the Mayas were raising corn (which constituted roughly 70 percent of their diet), beans, squash, pumpkins, and tomatoes and were supplementing that diet with hunted deer, turkey, and wild birds as well as with fish. They terraced the hillsides to grow more food and developed a remarkable irrigation system and network of canals for their crops.

By approximately 250 C.E., the Mayas had founded over fifty independent city-states that encompassed around 100,000 square miles (about the size of present-day Ecuador); had constructed magnificent stone temples, palaces, tombs, and monuments; had established a flourishing economy and extensive trade networks; had developed an accurate calendar (known as the Long Count); had created a system of writing; and, according to Mayan expert Michael Coe, had "reached intellectual and artistic heights which no others in the New World, and few in the Old, could match at that time."[15]

The Mayan system of writing used logographs (hieroglyphs or symbols that represent sounds or whole

15. Michael D. Coe, *The Maya*, 6th ed. (London: Thames and Hudson, 1999), p. 81.

[25]

Chapter 2

Writing and

Power: Defining

World-Views

(1750 B.C.E.–

250 C.E.)

words, such as $ for dollar). Like the Long Count calendar, the system was comparatively complex, and scribes were held in high esteem. By the time Europeans arrived, the Mayas had many books, most of them written on deerskins or bark paper. Peter Martyr, who accompanied the conquistador Hernando Cortés on his conquest of Cozumel Island, reported, "They also have, O Holy Father, innumerable books." In an effort to wipe out Native American "paganism," however, Bishop Diego de Landa burned every Mayan book or manuscript he could find, so that today only four such books still exist.[16]

No original Mayan text of the Popol Vuh (Source 5) exists. But in the late 1600s Francisco Ximenez (1666–1729?), a Dominican parish priest, completed a translation of the Popol Vuh (which he called "The Book of the People"). Whether Ximenez altered the original in any way is unknown. An English translation of the Popol Vuh was not published until 1950.[17]

At the beginning of the Classical Period of Mayan civilization (approx. 250–300 C.E.), the people of Japan had not emerged very far from the Stone Age. Agriculture was largely undeveloped, as people engaged principally in hunting, fishing, and gathering. No tools beyond polished stone implements have been found, evidence that metallurgy still was unknown. Political units did not extend farther than individual villages.

Beginning around 300 B.C.E., however, waves of migrants began arriving in the Japanese islands, coming mostly by way of the Korean peninsula. These immigrants brought with them, among other things, wet-rice agriculture, iron-working, stoneware, the use of the horse, centralized government, Buddhism, and Chinese writing and writing techniques (the brush, ink, and later the use of paper). Because of the different structures of the Chinese and Japanese languages, Chinese written characters had to be altered for Japanese use.[18]

What does the creation account of each of the peoples excerpted in the Evidence section tell us about the people themselves? What can we discover about how they viewed the universe, themselves, the role of a god or gods, and the unfolding of history itself?

16. For Peter Martyr's statement, see Bruce Love, *The Paris Codex: Handbook for a Maya Priest* (Austin: University of Texas Press, 1994), p. xv. On Diego de Landa, see Jared Diamond, *Collapse: How Societies Choose to Fail or Succeed* (New York: Viking, 2005), p. 159. For the fascinating story of deciphering Mayan writing, see Michael D. Coe, *Breaking the Maya Code* (New York: Thames and Hudson, 1992). Actually, as of 1999 only about one-half of the logographs had been deciphered. See *The New York Times*, May 16, 2006.

17. A good history of the Popol Vuh may be found in the introduction to the first English translation. See Delia Goetz and Sylvanus G. Morley, *Popol Vuh: The Sacred Book of the Ancient Quiche Maya* (Norman: University of Oklahoma Press, 1950), pp. 3–75.

18. Japanese tradition tells of pre-Chinese writing dating from "the age of the gods," but the evidence is not totally convincing. See William Wayne Farris, *Sacred. Texts and Buried Treasures: Issues in the Historical Archaeology of Ancient Japan* (Honolulu: University of Hawaii Press, 1998), pp. 70–98.

THE METHOD

When people today consult the Rig Veda, the Torah, or the Yijing, most do so either as part of their religious worship or as an inspirational guide. Each of these writings, however, also is a historical document that can be examined and analyzed for what that document tells us about those who created it and those who preserved and venerated it.

As you might expect, historians approach such a document in quite different ways from members of a group for which the document is an important part of their creed or philosophy. To begin with, whenever it is possible, historians prefer to read the document in its oldest version and in its original language. In that way, mistakes made in copying or translating, as well as purposeful additions to or deletions from the original text, will not lead the historians into errors of judgment. Second, it is important to historians to know as closely as possible the date (or dates) of the document's creation. This information is valuable to historians because it enables them to study the context and understand more about the people who were living during that period, the events taking place, and the ideas in circulation. Historians call this process learning about the "climate of opinion" of a particular time period. Unfortunately, very early documents (such as the ones you will be working with in this chapter) cannot be dated very precisely because they were written down only after a long period of oral transmission.

After completing these early steps, historians then are prepared to examine the document itself. When dealing with creation accounts, historians ask of each written account a series of questions: How does the account explain the creation of the universe, the world, and human beings? Is the creation divinely inspired—in other words, did a god or gods play an active role in the creation process, and for what purpose? Are human beings merely one among many objects of creation, *or* are human beings the pinnacle of the creation process? In return for creation and care, do human beings have any obligation to their creator? Finally, is the creation process in the account lineal (proceeding sequentially along a line from one event to another), cyclical (circular), of another pattern, or without pattern (formless)?

Having subjected each creation account to this series of questions, historians then are ready to ask what each document reveals about the people who created it. This will take some reading in your text about the people under scrutiny, as well as a considerable amount of historical imagination. For example, if each creation account can be seen as a life guide for those who venerate it, what does the account encourage or compel (or forbid) the true believers to do? Is the creation process *reproduced* in the lives of true believers (from birth to death)? What does that process tell you about the people who created the account?

Finally, you are ready to compare the six creation accounts and the people who committed them to memory and later to writing. Historians call

Chapter 2

Writing and

Power: Defining

World-Views

(1750 B.C.E.–

250 C.E.)

this process *comparative textual analysis*, and it is one of the most basic methods of investigation used throughout all the humanities (literature, philosophy, linguistics, history, and the like). As you compare these accounts and their creators, using the questions above as initial guides, be careful *not* to fall into the habit of thinking of certain cultures or peoples as "inferior" or "superior" on the basis of how far or near a particular group's beliefs are to your own beliefs or philosophy. This is a common trap, and you must make every effort to avoid it. After all, each of the creation accounts you will be examining and analyzing was preserved by a people or peoples for thousands of years. All except Atra-hasis have become the foundation for one or more current religions or philosophies, and as such have been deemed satisfying by a group or groups for many, many generations. Historians, therefore, approach these sources with great sensitivity and respect.

Atra-hasis (Source 1), as noted above, was lost for two millennia, surviving only in some Hebrew traditions that became part of the Book of Genesis (Atra-hasis was a man who was warned of a flood by the god Enki and was urged to build a boat and escape with his family and a selection of animals). The Rig Veda (Source 2) is the oldest of the sacred texts of modern Hinduism (733 million followers in 1992). The Torah (Source 3) is considered sacred to Jews (18 million), Christians (1.8 billion), and Muslims (971 million), all of whom are referred to by Muslims as People of the Book. The Yijing (Source 4) is one of the bases of Confucianism (195 million adherents is only a guess), a westernization of the name of the great teacher K'ung Fu-tze (551–479 B.C.E.). The Popol Vuh (Source 5) was the sacred text of the ancient Mayas and contained Mayan cosmology, history, popular traditions, and religious beliefs. It was revered by millions of people for at least 1,400 years prior to European conquest.

Finally the *Kojiki* (compiled and written down in 712 C.E.) of Japan offers the people not only a *cosmology* but some other ideas that later would become important to the Japanese.

As you read the Evidence, be sure to take notes. One effective way of organizing your thoughts is to divide your note pages into two parts. On the left side of the page, summarize the creation account you are reading. Then, on the right side, summarize your thoughts (and questions) about the value system, the view of history, and the relationship between beings that you are able to infer from the creation account.

THE EVIDENCE

Source 1 from W. G. Lambert and A. R. Millard, Atra-hasis: The Babylonian Story of the Flood *(Oxford: Oxford University Press, 1969), pp. 57, 59, 61.*

1. Excerpts from Atra-hasis

[The account begins with a universe that contained only the gods. The three senior gods (Anu, Enlil, and Enki) agree to divide the universe into three spheres of influence, with Anu in charge of heaven, Enlil of earth, and Enki of the water beneath the earth. The junior gods, required by Enlil to work, revolt against the senior gods. Thus the three senior gods call on Belet-ili,[19] the birth goddess, to create workers to serve the gods.]

While [Belet-ili, the birth-goddess], is present,
Let the birth-goddess create offspring
And let man bear the toil of the gods.
They summoned and asked the goddess,
The midwife of the gods, wise Mami,
'You are the birth-goddess, creatress of mankind,
Create *Lullu*[20] that he may bear the yoke,
Let him bear the yoke assigned by Enlil,
Let man carry the toil of the gods.'
Nintu opened her mouth
And addressed the great gods,
'It is not possible for me to make things,
Skill lies with Enki.
Since he can cleanse everything
Let him give me the clay so that I can make it.'
Enki opened his mouth
And addressed the great gods,
'On the first, seventh, and fifteenth day of the month
I will make a purifying bath.
Let one god be slaughtered
So that all the gods may be cleansed in a dipping . . .
So that we may hear the drum for the rest of time
Let there be a spirit from the god's flesh.
Let it proclaim living (man) as its sign. . . .
From the flesh of the god [there was] a spirit.
It proclaimed living (man) as its sign,
And so that this was not forgotten [there was] a spirit.
After she had mixed that clay
She summoned the Anunnaki, the great gods.
The Igigi, the great gods,
Spat upon the clay.
Mami opened her mouth
And addressed the great gods,

19. Interestingly, Belet-ili, the birth goddess, is also referred to as Mami or Mama.
20. **Lullu:** man.

Chapter 2

Writing and

Power: Defining

World-Views

(1750 B.C.E.–

250 C.E.)

'You commanded me a task, I have completed it;
You have slaughtered a god together with his personality.
I have removed your heavy work,
I have imposed your toil on man.
You raised a cry for mankind,
I have loosed the yoke, I have established freedom.'
They heard this speech of hers,
They ran together and kissed her feet (saying),
'Formerly we used to call you Mami,
Now let your name be Mistress-of-All-the-Gods (Belet-kala-ili) . . .

[*As the number of humans increased, their noise bothered the gods. Therefore Enlil tried to reduce the human population through plagues and other devices. It was in this context that he summoned up the flood, from which Atra-hasis and his family escaped. It is likely that, while in captivity in Babylon, the Hebrew people heard this account.*]

Source 2 from Franklin Edgerton, trans., The Beginnings of Indian Philosophy *(Cambridge, Mass.: Harvard University Press, 1965), pp. 60–61, 67–68, 73, 74.*

2. Excerpts from Book 10 of the Rig Veda

10.72[21]

1. We will now proclaim the origins of the gods to win applause (from any) who shall behold them in a later age, as the hymns are chanted.

2. Brahmanaspati (the Lord of the Holy Word) smelted them together, as a smith. In the primal age of the gods the Existent was born from the Non-existent.

3. In the first age of the gods the Existent was born from the Non-existent. After it (the Existent) the regions were born—(after) it, from the (World-mother) in labour.

4. The world was born from the (World-mother) in labour; from the world the regions were born. From Aditi Daksa was born, from Daksa likewise Aditi (was born).[22]

---

21. The Rig Veda is organized into ten books totaling 1,017 hymns. The number 10.72 means hymn #72 of book #10.

22. Aditi "is Mother, is Father, is Son . . . is all that is born, that will be born" (Rig Veda, 1.89). Normally, however, Aditi is taken to mean the Great Mother from whom the world was born, as well as the mother of the gods themselves. Daksa is masculine and often referred to as the "primordial cause," the original power of wisdom. Daksa's personification fluctuates throughout the Vedas.

5. Aditi, verily, was born, who is thy daughter, O Daksa. After her the gods were born, the blessed ones, companions of immortality.

6. When, O gods, there in the flood you stood, holding fast to one another, then from you, as from dancers, thick dust arose.

7. When, O gods, like wizard-priests, you made the worlds to swell, then you brought forth the sun that had been hidden in the sea.

8. There were eight sons of Aditi, which were born of her body. She went to the gods with seven; the (Sun-)bird she cast away.

9. With seven sons Aditi went to the primal generation (of gods). She brought back the (Sun-)bird for alternate procreation and death.

10.129

1. Non-existent there was not, existent there was not then. There was not the atmospheric space, nor the vault beyond. What stirred, where, and in whose control? Was there water, a deep abyss?

2. Nor death nor immortality (mortals nor immortals) was there then; there was no distinction of night or day. That One breathed without breath by inner power; than it verily there was nothing else further.

3. Darkness there was, hidden by darkness, in the beginning; an undistinguished ocean was This All. What generative principle was enveloped by emptiness—by the might of (its own) fervour That One was born.

4. Desire (creative, or perhaps sacrificial, impulse) arose then in the beginning, which was the first seed of thought. The (causal) connection (bandhu) of the existent the sages found in the non-existent, searching with devotion in their hearts.

5. Straight across was stretched the (dividing-)cord of them (i.e., of the following); below (what) was there? above (what) was there? Seed-bearers (male forces) there were, strengths (female forces) there were; (female) innate power below, (male) impellent force above.[23]

6. Who truly knows? Who shall here proclaim it—whence they were produced, whence this creation? The gods (arose) on this side (later), by the creation of this (empiric world, to which the gods belong); then who knows whence it came into being?

---

23. A suggestion that the world was created by some sort of cosmic intercourse between male powers and female powers. But, as Edgerton suggests, verses 6 and 7 strongly imply that the poet feels that he has gone too far. See *Beginnings of Indian Philosophy,* p. 73. See also Abinash Chandra Bose, *Hymns from the Vedas* (New York: Asia Publishing House, 1966), pp. 303–305.

Chapter 2

Writing and

Power: Defining

World-Views

(1750 B.C.E.–

250 C.E.)

7. This creation, whence it came into being, whether it was established, or whether not—he who is its overseer in the highest heaven, he verily knows, or perchance he knows not.

Source 3 from The Torah: A Modern Commentary *(New York: Union of American Hebrew Congregations, 1981), pp. 18–20, 29–30, 116–117. Copyright © 1981. Reprinted by permission of Union for Reform Judaism.*

3. From the First Book of Moses, called Genesis

CHAPTER 1

1] When God began to create the heaven and the earth—**2]** the earth being unformed and void, with darkness over the surface of the deep[24] and a wind[25] from God sweeping over the water—**3]** God said, "Let there be light"; and there was light. **4]** God saw that the light was good, and God separated the light from the darkness. **5]** God called the light Day, and the darkness He called Night. And there was evening and there was morning, a first day.

6] God said, "Let there be an expanse in the midst of the water, that it may separate water from water." **7]** God made the expanse, and it separated the water which was below the expanse from the water which was above the expanse. And it was so. **8]** God called the expanse Sky. And there was evening, and there was morning, a second day.

9] God said, "Let the water below the sky be gathered into one area, that the dry land may appear." And it was so. **10]** God called the dry land Earth, and the gathering of waters He called Seas. And God saw that this was good. **11]** And God said, "Let the earth sprout vegetation: seed-bearing plants, fruit trees of every kind on earth that bear fruit with the seed in it." And it was so. **12]** The earth brought forth vegetation: seed-bearing plants of every kind, and trees of every kind bearing fruit with the seed in it. And God saw that this was good. **13]** And there was evening and there was morning, a third day.

14] God said, "Let there be lights in the expanse of the sky to separate day from night; they shall serve as signs for the set times—the days and the years; **15]** and they shall serve as lights in the expanse of the sky to shine upon the earth." And it was so. **16]** God made the two great lights, the greater light to dominate the day and the lesser light to dominate the night, and the stars.

24. Some Hebraic scholars point out that this phrase ("surface of the deep") echoes a "Mesopotamian creation story where it is told that heaven and earth were formed from the carcass of the sea dragon, Tiamat." *The Torah: A Modern Commentary*, p. 18.

25. **wind:** also translated as "spirit."

17] And God set them in the expanse of the sky to shine upon the earth, 18] to dominate the day and the night, and to separate light from darkness. And God saw that this was good. 19] And there was evening and there was morning, a fourth day.

20] God said, "Let the waters bring forth swarms of living creatures, and birds that fly above the earth across the expanse of the sky." 21] God created the great sea monsters, and all the living creatures of every kind that creep, which the waters brought forth in swarms; and all the winged birds of every kind. And God saw that this was good. 22] God blessed them, saying, "Be fertile and increase, fill the waters in the seas, and let the birds increase on the earth." 23] And there was evening and there was morning, a fifth day.

24] God said, "Let the earth bring forth every kind of living creature: cattle, creeping things, and wild beasts of every kind." And it was so. 25] God made wild beasts of every kind and cattle of every kind, and all kinds of creeping things of the earth. And God saw that this was good. 26] And God said, "Let us make man in our image, after our likeness. They shall rule the fish of the sea, the birds of the sky, the cattle, the whole earth, and all the creeping things that creep on earth." 27] And God created man in His image, in the image of God He created him; male and female He created them. 28] God blessed them and God said to them, "Be fertile and increase, fill the earth and master it; and rule the fish of the sea, the birds of the sky, and all the living things that creep on earth."

29] God said, "See, I give you every seed-bearing plant that is upon all the earth, and every tree that has seed-bearing fruit; they shall be yours for food. 30] And to all the animals on land, to all the birds of the sky, and to everything that creeps on earth, in which there is the breath of life, [I give] all the green plants for food." And it was so.[26] 31] And God saw all that He had made, and found it very good. And there was evening and there was morning, the sixth day.

CHAPTER 2

1] The heaven and the earth were finished, and all their array. 2] On the seventh day God finished the work which He had been doing, and He ceased on the seventh day from all the work which He had done. 3] And God blessed the seventh day and declared it holy, because on it God ceased from all the work of creation which He had done.

4] Such is the story of heaven and earth when they were created.

When the LORD God made earth and heaven—5] when no shrub of the field was yet on earth and no grasses of the field had yet sprouted, because the LORD God had not sent rain upon the earth and there was no man to till the soil, 6] but a flow would well up from the ground and water the whole surface of the

---

26. Many biblical scholars assert that humans and other animals were herbivores (exclusively vegetarian) until after the Flood, when they became omnivores (eating all kinds of food, including the flesh of other animals). See Genesis 9:3 and Isaiah 11:7.

Chapter 2

Writing and

Power: Defining

World-Views

(1750 B.C.E.–

250 C.E.)

earth—**7]** the LORD God formed man from the dust of the earth. He blew into his nostrils the breath of life, and man became a living being.

8] The LORD God planted a garden in Eden, in the east, and placed there the man whom He had formed. **9]** And from the ground the LORD God caused to grow every tree that was pleasing to the sight and good for food, with the tree of life in the middle of the garden, and the tree of knowledge of good and bad. . . .

15] The LORD God took the man and placed him in the garden of Eden, to till it and tend it. **16]** And the LORD God commanded the man, saying, "Of every tree of the garden you are free to eat; **17]** but as for the tree of knowledge of good and bad, you must not eat of it; for as soon as you eat of it, you shall die."[27]

18] The LORD God said, "It is not good for man to be alone; I will make a fitting helper for him." **19]** And the LORD God formed out of the earth all the wild beasts and all the birds of the sky, and brought them to the man to see what he would call them; and whatever the man called each living creature, that would be its name. **20]** And the man gave names to all the cattle and to the birds of the sky and to all the wild beasts; but for Adam no fitting helper was found. **21]** So the LORD God cast a deep sleep upon the man; and, while he slept, He took one of his ribs and closed up the flesh at that spot. **22]** And the LORD God fashioned the rib that He had taken from the man into a woman; and He brought her to the man. **23]** Then the man said, "This one at last / Is bone of my bones / And flesh of my flesh. / This one shall be called Woman, / For from man was she taken." **24]** Hence a man leaves his father and mother and clings to his wife, so that they become one flesh.

[*Disobeying God's command, Adam and Eve ate the forbidden fruit, were cursed by God, and were banished from the Garden. Their first two children were Cain and Abel. Out of jealousy, Cain murdered Abel and was even further banished. Adam and Eve had many more children. After several generations, humans had become corrupt, and God determined to punish them by flooding the land. He warned righteous Noah, who gathered his family and all species in an ark, which survived the flood. Many generations later, people attempted to build a tower to reach heaven, but were confounded by God, who caused them to begin speaking different languages. Many generations later, God appeared to Abram, offering to make a covenant (contract) with him.*]

CHAPTER 17

1] When Abram was ninety-nine years old, the LORD appeared to Abram and said to him, "I am El Shaddai.[28] Walk in My ways and be blameless. **2]** I will establish My covenant between Me and you, and I will make you exceedingly numerous."

27. Given the fact that Adam did not die immediately upon eating the forbidden fruit, perhaps a better translation might be "you shall lose your immortality."

28. **El Shaddai:** God Almighty.

4. From Yijing, Commentary on the Appended Judgments

Heaven is high, the earth is low; thus the Creative and the Receptive are determined. In correspondence with this difference between low and high, inferior and superior places are established.

Movement and rest have their definite laws;[29] according to these, firm and yielding lines are differentiated.

Events follow definite trends, each according to its nature. Things are distinguished from one another in definite classes. In this way good fortune and misfortune come about. In the heavens phenomena take form; on earth shapes take form. In this way change and transformation become manifest.

Therefore the eight trigrams succeed one another by turns, as the firm and the yielding displace each other.[30]

Things are aroused by thunder and lightning; they are fertilized by wind and rain. Sun and moon follow their courses and it is now hot, now cold.

The way of the Creative brings about the male.

The way of the Receptive brings about the female.

The Creative knows the great beginnings.

The Receptive completes the finished things.

The Creative knows through the easy.

The Receptive can do things through the simple.

What is easy, is easy to know; what is simple, is easy to follow. He who is easy to know attains fealty. He who is easy to follow attains works. He who possesses attachment can endure for long; he who possesses works can become great. To endure is the disposition of the sage; greatness is the field of action of the sage.

By means of the easy and the simple we grasp the laws of the whole world. When the laws of the whole world are grasped, therein lies perfection. . . .

The Book of Changes contains the measure of heaven and earth; therefore it enables us to comprehend the tao[31] of heaven and earth and its order.

29. The *Book of Changes* is concerned primarily with understanding and predicting what appears to be constant and random change. ("Everything flows on and on like this river, without pause, day and night."—K'ung Fu-tze)

30. **displace each other:** an example of cyclical change.

31. **tao:** the way.

Chapter 2

Writing and

Power: Defining

World-Views

(1750 B.C.E.–

250 C.E.)

Looking upward, we contemplate with its help the signs in the heavens; looking down, we examine the lines of the earth. Thus we come to know the circumstances of the dark and the light. Going back to the beginnings of things and pursuing them to the end, we come to know the lessons of birth and of death. The union of seed and power produces all things; the escape of the soul brings about change. Through this we come to know the conditions of outgoing and returning spirits.

Since in this way man comes to resemble heaven and earth, he is not in conflict with them. His wisdom embraces all things, and his tao brings order into the whole world; therefore he does not err. He is active everywhere but does not let himself be carried away. He rejoices in heaven and has knowledge of fate, therefore he is free of care. He is content with his circumstances and genuine in his kindness, therefore he can practice love.

In it are included the forms and the scope of everything in the heavens and on earth, so that nothing escapes it. In it all things everywhere are completed, so that none is missing. Therefore by means of it we can penetrate the tao of day and night, and so understand it. Therefore the spirit is bound to no one place, nor the Book of Changes to any one form. . . .

[Here Pao Hsi (also known as Baoxi or Fuxi) studied the patterns in the heavens and on the earth and from this constructed the eight trigrams based on the cracks in a tortoise shell, which was developed into the system of Yijing, *or* The Book of Changes. *Then arose Shennong, the teacher of agriculture to humans.]*

The Yellow Emperor, Yao, and Shun allowed the upper and lower garments to hang down, and the world was in order. They probably took this from the hexagrams of THE CREATIVE and THE RECEPTIVE.

They scooped out tree trunks for boats and they hardened wood in the fire to make oars. The advantage of boats and oars lay in providing means of communication. (They reached distant parts, in order to benefit the whole world.) They probably took this from the hexagram of DISPERSION.

They tamed the ox and yoked the horse. Thus heavy loads could be transported and distant regions reached, for the benefit of the world. They probably took this from the hexagram of FOLLOWING.

They introduced double gates and night watchmen with clappers, in order to deal with robbers. They probably took this from the hexagram of ENTHUSIASM.

They split wood and made a pestle of it. They made a hollow in the ground for a mortar. The use of the mortar and pestle was of benefit to all mankind. They probably took this from the hexagram of PREPONDERANCE OF THE SMALL.

They strung a piece of wood for a bow and hardened pieces of wood in the fire for arrows. The use of bow and arrow is to keep the world in fear. They probably took this from the hexagram of OPPOSITION.

In primitive times people dwelt in caves and lived in forests. The holy men of a later time made the change to buildings. At the top was a ridgepole, and sloping down from it there was a roof, to keep off wind and rain. They probably took this from the hexagram of THE POWER OF THE GREAT.

In primitive times the dead were buried by covering them thickly with brushwood and placing them in the open country, without burial mound or grove of trees. The period of mourning had no definite duration. The holy men of a later time introduced inner and outer coffins instead. They probably took this from the hexagram of PREPONDERANCE OF THE GREAT.

In primitive times people knotted cords in order to govern. The holy men of a later age introduced written documents instead, as a means of governing the various officials and supervising the people. They probably took this from the hexagram of BREAKTHROUGH.

Source 5 from Delia Goetz and Sylvanus G. Morley, trans., Popol Vuh: The Sacred Book of the Ancient Quiche Maya *(Norman: University of Oklahoma Press, 1950), pp. 81, 83–86, 89.*

5. From Popol Vuh, "The Book of the People"

This is the first account, the first narrative. There was neither man, nor animal, birds, fishes, crabs, trees, stones, caves, ravines, grasses, nor forests; there was only the sky.

The surface of the earth had not appeared. There was only the calm sea and the great expanse of the sky.

There was nothing brought together, nothing which could make a noise, nor anything which might move, or tremble, or could make noise in the sky.

There was nothing standing; only the calm water, the placid sea, alone and tranquil. Nothing existed.

There was only immobility and silence in the darkness, in the night. Only the Creator, the Maker, Tepeu,[32] Gucumatz,[33] the Forefathers,[34] were in the water surrounded with light. . . .

The Tepeu and Gucumatz came together; then they conferred about life and light, what they would do so that there would be light and dawn, who it would be who would provide food and sustenance.

Thus let it be done! Let the emptiness be filled! Let the water recede and make a void, let the earth appear and become solid; let it be done. Thus they spoke. Let there be light, let there be dawn in the sky and on the earth! There shall be neither glory nor grandeur in our creation and formation until the human being is made, man is formed. So they spoke.

32. **Tepeu:** king, or conqueror.
33. **Gucumatz:** the Feathered Serpent.
34. **Forefathers:** literally, "those who beget children."

Chapter 2

Writing and

Power: Defining

World-Views

(1750 B.C.E.–

250 C.E.)

Then the earth was created by them. So it was, in truth, that they created the earth. Earth! they said, and instantly it was made.

Like the mist, like a cloud, and like a cloud of dust was the creation, when the mountains appeared from the water; and instantly the mountains grew.

Only by a miracle, only by magic art were the mountains and valleys formed; and instantly the groves of cypresses and pines put forth shoots together on the surface of the earth. . . .

[*Then animals, birds, and serpents were created. But since they could not speak like humans and thus were unable to praise and worship their creators, the Creator, the Maker, and the Forefathers condemned them to be eaten.*]

"Let us try again! Already dawn draws near: Let us make him who shall nourish and sustain us! What shall we do to be invoked, in order to be remembered on earth? We have already tried with our first creations, our first creatures; but we could not make them praise and venerate us. So, then, let us try to make obedient, respectful beings who will nourish and sustain us." Thus they spoke.

Then was the creation and the formation. Of earth, of mud, they made [man's] flesh. But they saw that it was not good. It melted away, it was soft, did not move, had no strength, it fell down, it was limp, it could not move its head, its face fell to one side, its sight was blurred, it could not look behind. At first it spoke, but had no mind. Quickly it soaked in the water and could not stand.

And the Creator and the Maker said: "Let us try again because our creatures will not be able to walk nor multiply. Let us consider this," they said.

Then they broke up and destroyed their work. . . .

[*The second attempt was to carve a man out of wood.*]

And instantly the figures were made of wood. They looked like men, talked like men, and populated the surface of the earth.

They existed and multiplied; they had daughters, they had sons, these wooden figures; but they did not have souls, nor minds, they did not remember their Creator, their Maker; they walked on all fours, aimlessly.

They no longer remembered the Heart of Heaven and therefore they fell out of favor. It was merely a trial, an attempt at man. At first they spoke, but their face was without expression; their feet and hands had no strength; they had no blood, nor substance, nor moisture, nor flesh; their cheeks were dry, their feet and hands were dry, and their flesh was yellow.

Therefore, they no longer thought of their Creator nor their Maker, nor of those who made them and cared for them.

These were the first men who existed in great numbers on the face of the earth. . . .

[*Because these wooden men and women did not honor or worship their creator, they were destroyed in a flood. Their descendants, monkeys, lived in the forest and resembled humans. The few people who escaped the deluge did praise the gods and thus became true human beings.*]

Source 6 from Tales from the Kojiki, *trans Yaichiro Isobe, 1928.*

6. From "The Beginning of the World," in Kojiki (a modern translation of the 712 C.E. compilation by O No Yasumaro)

[The account begins with the births of the deities, of the August Center of Heaven.]

Many gods were thus born in succession, and so they increased in number, but as long as the world remained in a chaotic state, there was nothing for them to do. Whereupon, all the Heavenly deities summoned the two divine beings, Izanagi and Izanami, and bade them descend to the nebulous place, and by helping each other, to consolidate it into terra firma. "We bestow on you," they said, "this precious treasure, with which to rule the land, the creation of which we command you to perform." So saying they handed them a spear called Ama-no-Nuboko, embellished with costly gems. The divine couple received respectfully and ceremoniously the sacred weapon and then withdrew from the presence of the Deities, ready to perform their august commission. Proceeding forthwith to the Floating Bridge of Heaven, which lay between the heaven and the earth, they stood awhile to gaze on that which lay below. What they beheld was a world not yet condensed, but looking like a sea of filmy fog floating to and fro in the air, exhaling the while an inexpressibly fragrant odor. They were, at first, perplexed just how and where to start, but at length Izanagi suggested to his companion that they should try the effect of stirring up the brine with their spear. So saying he pushed down the jeweled shaft and found that it touched something. Then drawing it up, he examined it and observed that the great drops which fell from it almost immediately coagulated into an island, which is, to this day, the Island of Onokoro. Delighted at the result, the two deities descended forthwith from the Floating Bridge to reach the miraculously created island. In this island they thenceforth dwelt and made it the basis of their subsequent task of creating a country. Then wishing to become espoused, they erected in the center of the island a pillar, the Heavenly August Pillar, and built around it a great palace called the Hall of Eight Fathoms. Thereupon the male Deity turning to the left and the female Deity to the right, each went round the pillar in opposite directions. When they again met each other on the further side of the pillar, Izanami; the female-Deity speaking first, exclaimed: "How delightful it is to meet so handsome a youth!" To which Izanagi, the male Deity, replied: "How delightful I am to have fallen in with such a lovely maiden!" After having spoken thus, the male Deity said that it was not in order that woman should anticipate man in a greeting. Nevertheless, they fell into connubial relationship, having been instructed by two wagtails which flew to the spot. Presently the Goddess bore her divine consort a son, but the baby was weak and boneless as a leech. Disgusted with it,

[39]

Chapter 2

Writing and

Power: Defining

World-Views

(1750 B.C.E.–

250 C.E.)

they abandoned it on the waters, putting it in a boat made of reeds. Their second offspring was as disappointing as the first. The two Deities, now sorely disappointed at their failure and full of misgivings, ascended to Heaven to inquire of the Heavenly Deities the causes of their misfortunes. The latter performed the ceremony of divining and said to them: "It is the woman's fault. In turning round the Pillar, it was not right and proper that the female Deity should in speaking have taken precedence of the male. That is the reason." The two Deities saw the truth of this divine suggestion, and made up their minds to rectify the error. So, returning to the earth again, they went once more around the Heavenly Pillar. This time Izanagi spoke: first saying: "How delightful to meet so beautiful a maiden!" "How happy I am," responded Izanami, "that I should meet such a handsome youth!" This process was more appropriate and in accordance with the law of nature. After this, all the children born to them left nothing to be desired. First, the island of Awaji was born, next, Shikoku, then, the island of Oki, followed by Kyushu; after that, the island Tsushima came into being, and lastly, Honshu, the main island of Japan. The name of Oyashi-ma-kuni (the Country of the Eight Great Islands) was given to these eight islands. After this, the two Deities became the parents of numerous smaller islands destined to surround the larger ones. . . .

[Later in the Kojiki the first emperor of Japan was created by the Sun Goddess Amaterasu and the Storm God Susa-no-o on the Plain of High Heaven, after which he descends wrapped in a sacred robe to take his place as the earthly ruler. See Matsumura Kazuo, "Ancient Japan and Religion," in Paul L. Swanson and Clark Chilson, eds., Nanzan Guide to Japanese Religions *(Honolulu: University of Hawaii Press, 2006), p. 131.]*

QUESTIONS TO CONSIDER

One of the first truths that historians come to appreciate is that people from different cultures not only think differently about various subjects (such as life, death, and cosmology) but also use different thought patterns when attempting to solve a problem. Thus we must determine not only what people of the past think, but also how they think.[35]

Accounts or interpretations of creation are excellent sources from which to deduce not only how a particular culture thinks about creation, but how it thinks in general.

Sumero-Babylonian traditions had more than one account of the creation and of the early history of human beings, of which Atra-hasis is probably the oldest. Written in cuneiform script using a stylus on soft clay that later was baked to harden it, the Atra-hasis creation epic is still fragmentary,

35. The same can be said about the study of writing itself. For example, fewer than half of the systems of writing that exist (or are known to have existed) begin at the top left of a page and move from left to right, then drop down one line and repeat the process. Some peoples' systems require writing right to left, some vertically (either top to bottom or bottom to top), and some circularly, and a few (like the Aztec script of Central America) have no particular form at all.

and parts of the broken tablets are still being discovered in excavations.

Why did the gods decide to create human beings? What, therefore, is the purpose of humans? How were the first humans constructed by Belet-ili? What materials were used? Why was it necessary to kill the junior god We-ila? What was We-ila's "contribution" to humans? In your opinion, what does this tell about the Babylonians' concept of human beings? Of their gods?

The first thing that we discover about Vedic culture is that it has not one creation account but several. In Rig Veda 10.72, the creation of the universe is compared to the birth of a human child. Who is Aditi, and what function does she perform? But how was Aditi created (see verses 2–5)? Note that these verses have a cyclical pattern: Aditi is born and gives birth and in turn is born. This cyclical thought pattern would become a key component of Hindu philosophy (Westerners are most familiar with it in the Hindu doctrines of *karma* and reincarnation).

In R.V. 10.129, the author begins by emphasizing the nothingness that preceded creation. And then, mysteriously, That One was born. But what role (if any) did That One play in creation? What about the male forces and female forces? Where did those forces come from? What feelings does the author convey in verses 6 and 7?

The narrative of creation in the Torah is a familiar one to Jews, Christians, and Muslims, and is quite different from the accounts in the Rig Veda. Almost immediately, however, we see that we are confronted not with *one* creation account in the Torah, but with *two*. Notice that Genesis 1:1 through 2:4 contains

one account and, immediately following, Genesis 2:5–24 is *another* account, in some ways markedly different. In your view, what are the principal differences between the two creation accounts in Genesis? Can you explain why there are two accounts? Why do you think that both accounts were included and have remained stable fixtures in Genesis for over 2,700 years?

In the Torah, it is extremely clear that the Israelites (and the later Christians and Muslims) were strict monotheists. Moreover, the one god of the Torah exhibits human traits—intent, desire, love, satisfaction, anger, and other emotions—and is given a voice that speaks to many people. And even more important, God has made some specific promises to and demands on the humans He created, most especially the ancient Israelites (the "Chosen People," as explicitly stated in Genesis 17:2). What were those demands? What was the covenant?

In contrast to the Torah, the Yijing not only lacks an account of a divinely inspired or god-caused creation, but also seems almost unconcerned about these questions at all. Gods do appear (Heaven, the high god, is most prominent), but more as abstract models for humans to emulate than as powers to worship or obey. Instead, the Yijing is a search for order, for patterns that can be discovered in the heavens and then later on earth—the patterns of birth and of life and of death.

How can the Creative and the Receptive be seen in the universe? Can any patterns be discerned and applied to the world? In this way, "man comes to resemble heavens and earth, he is not in conflict with them." One can

Chapter 2

Writing and

Power: Defining

World-Views

(1750 B.C.E.–

250 C.E.)

see day and night (and day again) in the heavens. To what could you compare that cycle on earth?

How is Pao Hsi (Baoxi) treated in the Yijing? Obviously, he was not a god, but he was nicknamed "the inventor" by millions in later years. What did Pao Hsi "invent"? The remainder of the excerpt traces a line of creative leaders or sages. What were their contributions? How did they "discover" these things? What was the final (the highest) gift of the holy men? Finally, how did those who venerated the Yijing think about creation?

The creation account in the Popol Vuh is a fascinating one, similar in some ways to other explanations of creation. Why were the gods dissatisfied with the animals and birds they created? Therefore, what role did the gods assign to the animals and birds? How is that similar to other accounts

(see Genesis 1:28–30)? Why did the gods view their early efforts at creating human beings unsuccessful? What "lessons" were humans supposed to learn from the Popol Vuh creation account? In what ways are those "lessons" similar to those in other accounts?

Like the Babylonian, Indian, and Chinese creation accounts, the *Kojiki* likens the creation of the world by the gods to human intercourse and childbirth. Why do you think this is so? On the other hand, the Japanese account is unique, especially in the children of Izanagi and Izanami. Who (what) are they? What effect do you think this creation account had on the collective mentality of the Japanese people? Finally, why were Izanagi's and Izanami's earlier efforts at having children unsuccessful? What is the point of that part of the creation account?

EPILOGUE

The development of writing held out many advantages for a culture. Important commercial agreements (water rights, real estate titles, merchant contracts, bills of sale) could be recorded and handed down with considerably more precision, often giving the ownership of property and goods more security and status. Laws and proclamations also could be codified, read in public, and enforced with more regularity. Finally, works of religion, philosophy, and literature could bind a people together, give them a sense of their past and of mission,

and shape and mold their collective thought.

For these reasons, a people's written accounts of creation were never merely interpretations of the origins of the universe, the world, and human beings. The Torah revealed the Jews' (and later Christians' and Muslims') belief in a purposeful deity who created humans for a specific purpose and made a covenantal agreement with Abraham and his descendants that required worship and obedience to God's laws in return for God's blessing and protection. Not only did the Rig Veda strengthen Indian thinking about the cyclical laws that governed birth, life, and death, but it also legitimized the Aryan caste system of priests, warriors, peasants, and serfs. The Yijing called the Chinese to meditation about the interrelationships of all things—past, present, and future. Indeed, these creation accounts as well as all others (and there are literally dozens) contain much more than a simple relating of origins.

Developing a system of writing, however, was no guarantee of a people's dominance or even survival. In the case of the Mayas, rapid population growth in the Classical Period (roughly 250–900 C.E.) caused significant damage to the environment, as deforestation to grow more food resulted in soil erosion and extended periods of drought. In addition, research on Mayan skeletal remains shows that their health was declining, in large part because the diet lacked sufficient protein. Finally, internal warfare severely sapped their resources. In the end, the Mayas abandoned their impressive towns and cities, which were not rediscovered until the late eighteenth and early nineteenth centuries.[36]

Just as writing offered cultures that possessed it certain advantages, so also the ability to read and write elevated certain individuals, elite groups, and classes *within* a culture. To begin with, it was these people who had the power to make and enforce laws, to mold and sanction beliefs, and to exercise authority over the illiterate. As soon as a particular group had established a political or religious canon,[37] its next step often was to punish those who violated or opposed the established orthodoxy.

There is little doubt that literate elites tried to limit the spread of writing. But ultimately such restraint was almost impossible. The invention of the printing press in the mid-fifteenth century in Mainz (Germany) made it possible for writing to reach an almost limitless audience.[38] As a result, literacy in Western Europe increased dramatically. Once political and religious canons could be read by many, however, disputes erupted, often over the "proper" interpretation of these canons. Yet once Pandora's box had been opened, it was nearly impossible to close it again.

Ultimately, widespread literacy strengthened the cultures in which it occurred and gave them great advantages over those in which literacy was more limited or confined. In the long run, near-universal literacy tended to support political stability and continuity, in part because of earlier political revolts and changes that, ironically, literacy often had instigated, and in part because literate cultures could develop and disseminate technology and economic systems that more often led toward economic abundance. It may be no accident that in the world's most prosperous economies (Germany, Japan, the United States, the Scandinavian nations, the United Kingdom, France, and the like), illiteracy is negligible and political stability is prevalent, whereas in the world's poorest nations

36. See Diamond, *Collapse*, pp. 157–176.

37. **canon:** code of law.

38. In fact, printing, movable type, and paper all had been invented in China over five hundred years earlier.

Chapter 2

Writing and

Power: Defining

World-Views

(1750 B.C.E.–

250 C.E.)

(such as Chad, Niger, Afghanistan, and Bangladesh), illiteracy is rampant and political systems are extremely unstable.[39]

39. Estimates from 1995 show Niger with an astounding 86 percent illiteracy, Afghanistan with 68.5 percent, Bangladesh with 62 percent, and Chad with 52 percent (*The World Almanac and Book of Facts,* 1999).

It would take centuries before the relationship between widespread literacy, economic abundance, and political stability would be fully understood. And yet as early as the prophet Muhammad, people appreciated the fact that writing meant power, and that the pen (or carving tool or stylus or quill or brush or whatever writing instrument) could be mightier than the sword.

CHAPTER THREE

REPRESENTING THE HUMAN FORM

(600 B.C.E.–1500 C.E.)

THE PROBLEM

In the last chapter, you explored the role that writing and written texts played in shaping the world-views of several early civilizations. As important as they are, however, written texts are only one of the types of sources available for learning about early cultures.

In many of the world's cultures, the transmission of information continued to be entirely oral, and in those that developed writing, the number of people who could read and write was very small, so that written texts were not a part of most people's lives. However, almost all of the world's cultures produced decorated items or adorned the walls of some buildings. These objects and decorations are what we would now call "art," and they can provide important evidence about both literate and nonliterate cultures.

Artistic evidence has been used to answer a wide range of historical questions about early cultures. Some of these are technical: What level of engineering skill in a culture would enable it to construct certain types of buildings? What technological processes did a culture use in the production of pottery, metalwork, or other items? Some are economic: What proportion of a culture's wealth went into the production of what types of artistic products? Who paid for and benefited from artistic production? Some questions are aesthetic: How skillful were certain artists? How would one describe an individual artist's or a civilization's style, particularly in comparison to those of others? Some are cultural: Why were certain subjects depicted, and depicted the way they were? What did a civilization view as important enough to include in its permanent visual record?

The questions that we might term aesthetic or cultural are perhaps the most tricky for historians or art historians, particularly if they involve comparisons between civilizations.

Assessing the skill of an artist requires not only appreciating the technical aspects of production, but also understanding ideas about the purpose of artistic products as well as the cultural context in which the artist worked. We may be able to say immediately that we "like" or "don't like" an artistic product, but we certainly need information on the culture in which it was created to assess its meaning and use it as historical evidence. It is often difficult to gain much understanding of a culture from a few pieces of artistic evidence, particularly when we view them, not where they were intended to be displayed, but on a gallery wall or in a museum case. Thus, using artistic evidence is in some ways a circular process: We learn about a culture from the available written and artistic sources, then use that background to analyze a single piece of art, which may in turn make us change or refine our ideas about the written record or other artistic creations, and eventually may lead to new conclusions about the culture as a whole.

Analysis of individual pieces of artistic evidence is thus an important tool for historians. It is often difficult to view pieces in their original setting—they may have been removed, or we may not be able to travel to distant lands—so our only access to such evidence is via museums or in books of reproductions. In this chapter we use such reproductions of sculpture and painting to investigate four different cultures: Archaic and Classical Greece (600–350 B.C.E.), Buddhist India (200 B.C.E.–600 C.E.), classic Maya (600–900 C.E.), and western Africa during the ascendancy of Ile-Ife and Benin (1100–1500 C.E.). In all four of these cultures, one of the most common subjects for artistic presentation was the human form. Our questions for this chapter, questions that are aesthetic and cultural, focus on this one subject: How do these cultures depict the human form? What do these depictions tell us about the values of these cultures?

BACKGROUND

Though most historians and art historians regard some knowledge of a culture as important for an understanding of its artistic products, there are those who discount such a prerequisite. Some people, though usually not art historians, assert that aesthetic judgments are not culturally or historically based, but rather derive from universal standards, so that "good" art, or at least a masterpiece, is recognizable to all.

Others contend that knowing about a culture shapes one's impressions too strongly, making it impossible to view an artistic product objectively. To them what is most important is seeing with a fresh eye, and they stress that to use visual evidence correctly, we must both sharpen our powers of observation and also *unlearn* previous ideas about art.

You may agree with either or both of these arguments and wish to test them with this chapter. To do this, turn immediately to the Evidence and look carefully at each sculpture or painting.

Record your general impressions, and also write down your initial responses to the central questions for the chapter. (This will enable you later to assess how much even a slight understanding of a culture may alter your viewing.) Do any of these impressions or answers come from what you already know about any one of these cultures, or do they come solely from looking at the art?

As we turn now to background information, we begin with characteristics common to all of the sources. For each of the four cultures, the sculptures and paintings are arranged roughly in chronological order, though they span different amounts of time. All the pieces served some sort of religious or political function and come from tombs, religious buildings such as temples, or royal residences. In all of these cultures except Classical Greece, rulers were regarded as links between human society and the gods, so that the distinction between the religious and political realms is somewhat artificial; even in Greece, religion was viewed as having a political function, binding the residents of one area together. All the pieces were created in cultures that believed in *anthropomorphic* gods; in other words, at least some of their gods were conceptualized in human form so that human form and divine power were linked. In all four cultures, making an image of a god or a godlike hero or leader and honoring that image were seen as meritorious, and thus the creative process was linked to spiritual and religious values.

Many of the earliest Greek depictions of the human form were from tombs or temples, the male *kouros* and female *kore* figures, erected in memory of an individual or by a living person to fulfill a vow to the gods. These large stone sculptures began to be made in Greece beginning in the mid-seventh century B.C.E. The portrayal of the human body in Greece changed rapidly over the next two hundred years, with sculptors basing their work more and more on actual human anatomy. This concern with the way that the body actually looked can also be observed in Greek painting. Unfortunately, most large-scale Greek paintings have been lost, but Greek pottery was frequently decorated with painted figures and scenes that allow us to see human forms in a setting.

Along with the kore and kouros figures, Greek statuary from the Archaic period (about 630–480 B.C.E.) also portrayed gods and mythological heroes, who are sometimes part divine and sometimes fully human. Because the gods bore no physical sign of their divinity, it is often difficult to tell exactly who is being depicted unless the subject is accompanied by a standard symbol such as the sea god Poseidon's trident or the hero Herakles' lion skin. Gods and heroes continued to be the most common subject matter for Greek sculpture in the Classical period (about 480–330 B.C.E.), with actual historical events shown only rarely, although mythological events appear frequently, especially in reliefs.

Greek pottery often shows mythological scenes, but it also depicts everyday life—women weaving, men banqueting, people going in and out of doors. Some of its subjects are pornographic, showing men with prostitutes or gods and satyrs chasing nymphs. Because of such subject matter, pottery has traditionally been viewed as having no religious or ceremonial significance. This view has recently changed somewhat, as scholars have recognized that, for example, the banqueting scenes not only depict the setting in which the pottery was actually used, but also envision a certain type of afterlife for those using it. The doors may not be simply entrances of houses, but also the gateway between this life and the next. The mythological scenes are not simply decorative, but are meant to reinforce cultural norms.

The Greek view of the human body was determined by philosophy as well as religion, particularly after the time of Plato (427–347 B.C.E.). Plato saw the human body as in some ways a microcosm of the universe (an idea that influenced Western thought until the time of the Renaissance), a universe that was itself a living creature. Both the body and the universe are material and perishable, but the soul is immortal, as is the perfect form of the universe and all that exists within it. For Plato, these perfect forms, which are sometimes called "ideal types," were not simply mental constructs but had an existence somewhere and were actually more "real" than the transitory, material world around us. (The notion of ideal types, or idealism, has also been a long-lasting one in Western thought. It operates, for instance, in many people's understanding of such concepts as justice. Their concept of a just society comes not so much from observing societies that actually exist in the world as from abstract principles

regarding what might be termed "ideal justice.") As a proponent of idealism, Plato scorned the attempts of the artists and sculptors who were his contemporaries to depict the human body based on visual observation. Plato thought the chief purpose of art was to represent eternal forms as understood by the soul, not to imitate fleeting external appearances. He praised Egyptian art for its elevated portrayals, and he regarded mathematical forms as the most beautiful because their beauty was absolute and not based on—or biased by—either intellectual or physical points of view.

In many ways, sculptors in India working within both Buddhist and Hindu traditions fit Plato's ideal better than did his Athenian contemporaries. In Indian religion and philosophy, the purpose of sculpture is not to depict the physical body but to give concrete shape to an invisible spirit within the body. Indian artists sought to give visible form to the living principles within the body, conceptualized as breath (*prana*) and sap (*rasa*). *Prana* pushes against the walls of the body, making the skin appear taut and keeping the body erect, so that the muscles are less important. Indian sculpture does not aim to record the appearance or structure of the body, but instead to express the awareness of life within the body, of the breath that sustains and moves the body. Sculptors achieve this, not by looking at other bodies as models, but by feeling the breath and pulse of life within their own bodies and by meditating or contemplating. There is a link between the body and the natural world, which also has breath and sap. When a sculpture was completed, it was consecrated by a priest, given the breath of life. Then it was placed in a position within a temple where it could be seen, worshiped, and perhaps eventually copied, for the replication of images was considered auspicious.

Buddhist teachings did not reject earlier Indian ideas about art or the body, but built on them. The religious teachings generally termed Buddhism were first taught in India by Siddhartha Gautama, a nobleman living in the sixth century B.C.E. who came to be known as the Buddha, or the Awakened One. Buddhist teachings are extremely complex, although at their heart is an emphasis on morality, meditation, and achieving wisdom. Part of the wisdom one strives to achieve is the understanding that there is nothing permanent, including the individual soul, and that the ideal state of being (*nirvana*) is a life that transcends individual desires. On achieving nirvana, an individual would become awakened to a transcendental eternal realm of being, that is, a buddha.

Over the centuries, many divisions developed within Buddhism, one of the most significant being a split beginning in the first century B.C.E. over how strictly one needed to follow the Buddhist path in order to achieve nirvana. Mahayana Buddhism taught that many people, not simply a small spiritual elite of monks, could become fully buddha, an idea that gave this branch of Buddhism a wide popular base. As it spread, Mahayana Buddhism absorbed a number of local deities, transforming them to fit with Buddhist ideas by turning them into guardians of the Buddha, or *bodhisattvas*. A bodhisattva is a being who has almost achieved nirvana but decides instead to turn away from this final, blissful, transcendental state to help others on their way to becoming buddha. Although bodhisattvas had human bodies, they were no longer subject to the physical limitations of human life and were often worshiped in their own right. Their merits could be shared by their worshipers, and their intervention, combined with devotion, could allow the worshiper to achieve nirvana. The Buddha himself had been a bodhisattva in his earlier lives, and stories of his actions and exploits during these previous lives became an important part of Buddhist literature.

Though there was no explicit prohibition on portraying the Buddha as Buddha, there are no images of him until several centuries after his death; he was symbolized by an empty throne or a hemispheric mound containing a relic, termed a *stupa*. With the spread of Mahayana Buddhism, people became more devoted to Buddha's person and not simply his teachings, so they wanted physical likenesses. Images of the Buddha showed up first on coins and temple railings and, by the first century C.E., as free-standing sculpture. Sculptors adopted existing ideas about portraying the body to the portrayal of the Buddha's body, striving to produce a sacred image that both transcended and represented perfect human beauty. The links between the body and the natural world were stressed in the shapes of the Buddha's body parts, and a system of proportions was developed based on the height of the head or the breadth of the finger. These calculations for the correct proportions of the Buddha were based not on actual human anatomy, but on the magical properties of certain numbers, and they became the standard for images of the Buddha for centuries.

Among the Mayas, most large-scale art was produced to record the deeds and actions of rulers; Maya buildings are almost like billboards, with huge reliefs depicting religious and political messages. It was thus important that the individuals depicted be recognized, which Maya artists accomplished sometimes by showing them with specific distinctive physical features, but more often by identifying them by name in the writing that almost always accompanies pictures of people. The Mayas built pyramids, which served both as temples and as graves for kings, who were viewed as interceding between the gods and people both in this life and after death; concerns about the afterlife show up in much Maya art.

The Mayas were not unified under a single ruler, but lived in cities ruled by separate royal lineages. Scholars used to think that the Mayas were a peaceful people concerned primarily with astronomical and religious issues; this view was altered dramatically after 1960, when scholars began to learn to read Maya writing, which told of great battles and extolled rulers who were victorious over other kings. Writing and art also portray gruesome bloodletting rituals involving kings and their families as well as captives; blood was a potent substance for the Mayas, and the blood of their rulers was particularly powerful. (All hereditary aristocracies conceptualize what

distinguishes rulers from everyone else in terms of blood, of course; even the weak monarchs of today have "royal blood.") Maya writing is a combination of signs that stand for certain whole words and phonetic symbols; it was painted with a brush on pottery and in books made from the bark of fig trees, and inscribed on stone, wood, jade, and shell objects. The earliest writing dates from the first century B.C.E.; because Maya artists included the dates on the events they depicted (and because scholars have learned how to interpret these dates), we are able to trace some aspects of their history very specifically. Artists and scribes belonged to certain families and sometimes included their own names as well as those of their subjects on their work, so that, unlike the case with many ancient peoples, we can know the identity of certain artists. Writing and artistic production were viewed as in some ways beyond human capacity, and a number of gods were associated with writing; these god-scribes are sometimes portrayed as animals—as rabbit-scribes, as in Source 13, or, more commonly, as monkey-scribes.

The sculptures and paintings reproduced here all date from the period 600–900 C.E., which scholars label the late classic period. (Like that of ancient Greece, Maya cultural history is generally divided into preclassic, classic, and postclassic periods.) During that period, the Mayas living in hundreds of large and small cities, ruled by lineages that both intermarried and engaged in warfare with one another, built large buildings, and recorded their own histories. These reproductions come from three of those cities, Palenque, Bonampak, and Yaxchilan, all located in the southwestern part of the area inhabited by Maya people, now in southern Mexico.

Given the warm and damp climate of central America, most painted Maya artwork has disappeared; most of what survives is thus carved or formed out of more permanent materials such as stone, stucco, or jade. (Many books were also destroyed by Spanish Christian authorities in the sixteenth and seventeenth centuries because these authorities considered Maya writing, which often concerned religious and mythological subjects, to be demonic; only four preconquest Maya books survive today.) Much of this is in the form of reliefs carved on vertically set slabs of stone (called *stelae*) or panels, and some of it is very difficult to see because it has weathered over the centuries, so that art historians and archaeologists make drawings of the pictures and writing in order to study them more closely. Source 12 is, in fact, a copy based on the original painting, as the painting itself is very faint and difficult to see. Many of these reliefs are also extremely complex, with writing, people, gods, and natural objects entwined and interwoven over the entire surface; all of these have symbolic meanings, and deciphering them is thus very complicated. The objects shown here are therefore somewhat unusual in that they are relatively simple and the carvings are still sharp enough to be seen without the aid of a drawing.

In other ways, the pieces reproduced here are quite typical of Maya art. In contrast to the Greeks, who showed the human form primarily through the depictions of gods and heroes, the Mayas showed actual people and actual historical events, although rulers were often dressed as gods. Source 10 is a stucco portrait head of King Pacal of Palenque (ruled 615–683) from his burial tomb; Source 11 shows a king of Yaxchilan, Shield Jaguar, and his wife, Lady Xoc, in a bloodletting ritual that took place on October 28, 709; Source 12 is one of the wall murals from Bonampak, which portray various events in the life of the ruler Chaan-muan from the 790s. In all of these, and in the portrayal of a mythological scene in Source 13, bodies are shown in realistic proportions, with clothing and accessories depicted in great detail. In the reliefs and the painting, people are shown primarily in a side view, with the heads always shown from the side. This allows the artist to highlight one of the most distinctive aspects of the ideal human form for classic-period Mayas: the flat, elongated forehead, achieved by molding infants' skulls in this shape while they were still pliable. Nobles and deities are also generally portrayed with large, curved noses, another sign of status (this is sometimes enhanced, as it is in Source 10, with a decorative nosepiece, probably made of latex rubber). Captives and conquered peoples, by contrast, are often shown with blunt noses and domed foreheads.

Like that of the Mayas, much of the art from Nigeria in the eleventh through the sixteenth centuries that has survived comes primarily from royal courts, where professional artists—smiths, sculptors, jewelers, and

[51]

so on—produced items for royal families and other powerful individuals. Not surprisingly, much of this art depicts kings and queens, either alone or surrounded by their supporters, servants, and assistants. There were a number of small kingdoms in this area during this period, linked both politically and artistically. According to tradition, in the thirteenth century the people of Benin (called the Edo people) asked the ruler or *oni* of the Yoruba kingdom of Ile-Ife to send them a king. This *oni*, Oranyan, sent one of his sons, who became the first king or *oba* of Benin. The first *oni* of Ile-Ife is regarded as the son of the Yoruba god of creation, Olorun, and Ile-Ife continued to be viewed as the spiritual and mythical center of the world by the rulers of Benin; subsequent rulers in Benin continued to receive their symbols of office from the *oni* of Ile-Ife. Those rulers also admired the art of Ile-Ife, for tradition holds that a later *oba* of Benin requested that the *oni* of Ile-Ife send him a bronzesmith to teach the smiths in his kingdom.

Given these connections, it is not surprising that the earliest art from Benin looks much like that of Ile-Ife, but within a relatively short period of time, artists from Benin had developed a completely different style. The portraits from Ile-Ife, especially those in terra cotta, depict men and women with extremely individualized features; careful attention is given to the contours and musculature of the face. Many of them are wearing elaborate headdresses that indicate their high status, or have holes on the face, indicating that originally crowns or other

royal regalia were attached. Some have holes around the mouth and chin for the attachment of a beaded veil, common for Yoruba kings. (The striping pattern on some faces is thought to represent a veil.) The terra-cotta heads come from full figures, whereas those made from metal were crafted simply as heads and may have been used to show off royal garments and symbols of office. The exact identity of most of these portraits is unknown, although Source 15 is regarded by many scholars as representing the *oni* Obalufon. Though the portraits are individualized, they are also somewhat idealized: Like portraits of the Buddha, they show only people with calm and peaceful expressions, which was viewed as reflecting inner dignity and self-control; like Greek sculpture, they show only women and men in the prime of life.

In contrast to the portraits from Ile-Ife, which generally show single individuals without much decoration, those from Benin often show multiple figures and, like Maya reliefs, are loaded with symbolic and ceremonial objects. Though they continued to have contacts with artists in Ile-Ife, artists in Benin appear to have become less interested in capturing the individuality of their subjects than in providing information about court life and events; individuals are identified by clothing and symbols representing their office, not by distinctive facial features. The *oba*, his relatives, and other chiefs are generally shown with symbols of power, such as fish, leopards, or elephant trunks, and wearing huge necklaces and headdresses of red coral beads. These beads were restricted to the royal family and high court officials, as they were believed to have been stolen from Olokun, the god of the seas and waters and the source of all worldly riches; when the king was wearing beaded garments, he was regarded as having powers similar to those of a god.

Many of the artistic items that have survived from Benin in this period are ceremonial plaques showing the *oba* and other individuals, an artistic form that may have been modeled on-pictures in books brought to Africa by Portuguese missionaries and merchants. In contrast to the depiction of the human form in Maya art, in Benin figures are shown frontally, usually standing, although the *oba* himself is occasionally seated. The plaques are symmetrical, with the *oba* or symbols that represented him in the middle; this fit with Edo ideas of the perfect hierarchical society, in which everything revolved around the *oba*, the axis of the world. The figures are not only positioned but also proportioned according to their status; the *oba* is the largest, with various other figures of different sizes around him. All of the figures are usually placed against a flat background carved with "river-leaves," the leaves of the water-god Olokun, whose domain was thought to surround that of the earthly *oba*. The figures themselves do not stand on anything, but float on this background. The heads are often slightly enlarged in relation to the body, for the Yoruba people of Ile-Ife and the Edo people of Benin regarded the head as the site of a person's nature (*iwa*) and life force (*ase*); as in India, the purpose of representations of the body was to make these living principles within the body visible.

THE METHOD

The single most important method for using visual sources was stated at the beginning of the Background section—**look at them.** This may seem self-evident, and we may feel that our "looking" skills are well honed because of the visual culture of advertising and television in which we live. Too often, however, we view visual material as merely illustrations of a text (this is often how graphics are integrated into textbooks) and don't really look at the images themselves. To answer the first question in this chapter, turn to the Evidence (which you may already have done if you decided to do the pretest suggested in the Background section).

Look at the artistic evidence from Greece, Sources 1 through 5. What do you notice most about these figures; in other words, what details stand out? What words would you use to describe the individuals as they are portrayed? How do their expression and stance sway your description? Comparing the kore and kouros figures from the early sixth century B.C.E., Sources 1 and 2 with the vase painting in Source 3 and the sculpture in Source 4, what changes do you see in the representation of the human form? What differences do you see between the depiction of female and male forms

[53]

in Source 3? Now look at Source 5, which is about one hundred years more recent than Source 4 and is one of the first depictions of the nude female form in Greek art. (Until this period, the only women depicted nude were prostitutes; even Aphrodite, the goddess of love and-beauty, was shown clothed.) What words would you use to describe Aphrodite as she is shown here? Looking at Sources 4 and 5, what differences do you see in the way male and female bodies are depicted?

Now look at the examples from India, Sources 6 through 9. What details stand out in these portrayals? How would you describe the body of the female deity (*yakshi*) in Source 6? How would you compare this with the female bodies portrayed in Greek art? Sources 7 and 8 show the Buddha. How does his body differ from the bodies in the other sources? How would you describe his expression and demeanor? How would you compare the treatment of clothing in these two sculptures with the treatment of clothing in Greek sculpture? Source 9 is a bodhisattva, usually identified as Vajrapani because he is holding a thunderbolt. (Bodhisattvas can often be identified only by items they wear or carry, for no names are inscribed on these sculptures. Greek statues were mostly inscribed, but the inscriptions have often been destroyed or are missing, so that we identify them as well by their dress or other details.) How would you describe the bodhisattva's body? his stance? his clothing? How would you compare these with those of the Buddha? with those of a Greek male body such as the one in Source 4?

Now look at the Maya examples, Sources 10 through 13. How would you describe the portrayal of the ruler's body in Sources 11 and 12? How would you compare that to the portrayal of the captives' bodies in Source 12? How would you compare the portrayal of male and female bodies, both those of Shield Jaguar and Lady Xoc in Source 11 and those of the goddesses who serve God L in Source 13? What do you notice about the clothing and head-dresses of the kings and nobles? How do these compare with the clothing of the gods and goddesses? Source 12 shows King Chaan-muan's judgment of prisoners after their defeat in a great battle (shown on other wall paintings in this room). How does the artist use the placement of figures and their body positions to enhance the effect of the action and communicate the status of the people portrayed? How would you compare this with the other paintings of humans in action, such as that of Theseus and the Amazons in Source 3? How would you describe God L and his attendants in the scene of the underworld in Source 13?

Now look at the examples from Ile-Ife and Benin, Sources 14 through 17. How would you describe and compare the expressions of the individuals in Sources 14 and 15? How does the artist who made Source 16 communicate the status of the individual portrayed? How does the artist who made Source 17 communicate the status of the various individuals portrayed? What do you notice about the dress and headdresses of the individuals in Source 17? Sources 14 and 15 come from one culture, the Ile-Ife, and Sources 16 and 17 from another culture, Benin, that was nearby but developed slightly later. How would you compare the portrayal of the human form in the two cultures? Most of the individuals portrayed represent rulers, just as do most of the individuals in the Maya examples. How would you compare the portrayal of rulers in these cultures?

From looking at the Sources and considering questions like those suggested above, you can formulate your answer to the first question for this chapter: How do these four cultures depict the human form? Answering the second question—what do these depictions tell us about the values of these cultures?—involves extrapolating from the sources and combining your observations with your previous knowledge of the cultures. Here you (or any historian) must be more speculative, for we generally can't know exactly how individuals living at the time a statue or painting was made looked at it, or how their view of the artist's intent differed from ours. We must also be especially careful, when using visual sources, to choose ones that are representative or typical rather than unusual. (On this issue, you will have to either trust our choice of evidence or do some further research in books of reproductions or museums in your area.)

These reservations apply, of course, just as much to historical arguments based on written sources as to those based on visual evidence, and in both cases the best method of historical interpretation is the same: Stick as closely as possible to arguments that are based on the sources themselves. In this case, then, your exploration of the values of these cultures needs

to be based primarily on the careful observations you have already made.

Think about your observations of the depiction of the body in Greek art. Whose bodies are shown? What does their stance or expression indicate were admirable qualities in such individuals? Why might the depiction of the body become more anatomically accurate earlier than that of the head? Why might the Greeks have portrayed men nude, even in scenes (such as the battle scene in Source 3) in which men were not normally naked? What might account for the differences in the portrayal of male and female nudes you noted in Sources 4 and 5? Though we generally think of nakedness as revealing, are there certain facts that nakedness obscures?

Now turn to the Indian art. What does Source 6 indicate about cultural attitudes toward the female body? How does this portrayal of a goddess differ from those of Greek female deities, such as Aphrodite in Source 5? What does the Buddha's expression indicate about the qualities admired in a leader? How does this differ from the qualities suggested in the depictions of Greek heroes? What do the differences you have noted between the Buddha and the bodhisattva indicate about attitudes toward each of these revered individuals?

Now turn to the Maya art. What does the portrayal of Lady Xoc engaged in a bloodletting ritual along with her husband indicate about the status of noblewomen in Maya culture? What might the similarities in the portrayals of the gods and goddesses in Source 13 and the humans in the other sources indicate about Maya ideas of the relationship between the human and the divine? What might the judgment scene in Source 12 indicate about the handling of prisoners and about Maya attitudes toward nakedness? How would you compare this with Greek attitudes toward nakedness?

Next, think about the western African art. What might the two heads from Ile-Ife (and others like them) indicate about the relative status of men and women in the upper classes? How does this compare with the impression you have gained from the art of the other cultures in this chapter? In modern cultures, veiling is often perceived as negative, a restriction of the individual. Thus, why might rulers, of all people, wear veils that covered part of their faces? What might this indicate about west African ideas of rulership, as compared with those of classic-era Mayas?

THE EVIDENCE

Source 1: Archaeological Receipts Fund/National Archaeological Museum, Athens.

1. Anavyssos Kouros, Attica near Athens, ca. 525 B.C.E.

Source 2: Archaeological Receipts Fund/Acropolis Museum, Athens.

2. Peplos Kore, Athens, ca. 530 B.C.E.

Source 3: Courtesy of the Trustees of the British Museum.

3. **Theseus and the Amazons, from an Attic Red-figured Krater,[1] ca. 440 B.C.E.**

1. **Krater:** a wide, two-handled bowl common in ancient Greece.

Source 4: Alinari/Art Resource, NY.

4. Polykleitos, *Doryphoros* or *"The Canon,"* ca. 440 B.C.E. (Roman copy)

Source 5: Biblioteca Apostolica Vaticana.

5. Praxiteles, *Aphrodite of Knidos,* ca. 340 B.C.E. (Roman copy)

Source 6: Werner Forman/Topham/The Image Works.

6. Yakshi, from a Pillar at the Great Stupa of Bharhut, ca. 100 B.C.E.

Source 7: John C. Huntington.

7. **Standing Buddha, from Gandhara, ca. 200** C.E.

Source 8: Borromeo/Art Resource, NY.   *Source 9: © The Art Archive/Corbis.*

**8. Buddha with Halo, from
Sarnath, Gupta Period, 5th Dynasty**

**9. Tibetan Sculpture of the
Bodhisattva Vajrapani**

10. Head of Pacal the Great, from His Tomb at Palenque, 684 C.E.

11. Door Lintel Showing King Shield Jaguar and Lady Xoc in a Bloodletting Ritual, 709 C.E.

Source 12: From copies made by Antonio Tejeda Fonseca, in Mary Ellen Miller, The Murals of Bonampak *(Princeton: Princeton University Press, 1986). Photograph © Tozzer Library of Harvard College Library, Harvard University.*

12. Mural at Bonampak Showing King Chaan-muan Judging Defeated Enemies, 792 C.E.

Source 13: The Art Museum, Princeton University. Museum purchase, gift of the Hans A. Widenmann (Class of 1918) and Dorothy Widenmann Foundation. © 2001 Trustees of Princeton University. Roll-out photo © Justin Kerr.

13. Vase Painting Showing God L, Several Goddesses, and Rabbit-Scribe, ca. 600–900 C.E.

14. Terra-cotta Head of a King, Ife, ca. 1000–1200 C.E.

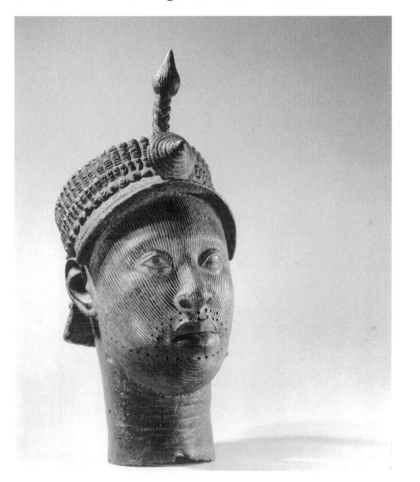

15. Copper Obalufon Mask, Ife, 1000–1200 C.E.

16. Brass Head of Queen Mother, Benin, ca. 1500

17. Brass Plaque Depicting the Oba Esigie, Benin, ca. 1500

QUESTIONS TO CONSIDER

As you examine the evidence for this chapter, you may be discovering that your viewing is shaped to a greater or lesser extent both by what you already know about one or more of the cultures and by your previous experience with sculpture and paintings of the human form. Some of the sources may thus seem very familiar, whereas others may appear strange and exotic. This has caused some people who work with visual evidence to deny that we can ever view things with the "fresh eye" that other scholars deem indispensable. Does your experience in working with the evidence in this chapter lead you to support either side of this dispute? If you did the pretest, did your observations and impressions change after reading the Background section?

Though all of the evidence in this chapter depicts the human form, some of the portrayed individuals were regarded as fully human, some as fully divine, and many as both human and divine or as moving between a human and a divine state. Do these differences affect the way these individuals are depicted? What does this tell you about the five cultures?

When making any sort of cultural comparison, it is often easiest to think in terms of similarities and differences. What similarities have you found in the depictions of the human body among the four cultures? Are there any words that you could use accurately to describe the bodies in all or most of the sources? Do any of these words suggest cultural values that may be similar? Do any two of the cultures handle representations of the human body in a similar fashion? What might this tell you about other ways in which these two cultures are similar? What do you see as the most important differences among the sculpture and painting from the five cultures? Are any of these the result of technological differences (such as differences in the material out of which the sculpture is made), or do they indicate cultural differences?

You are now ready to answer the central questions for this chapter: How do these four cultures depict the human form? What do these depictions tell us about the values of these cultures?

EPILOGUE

In all of the cultures we have investigated here, a certain way of depicting the human form came to be accepted as the norm and was then copied extensively. This copying took place both within a single culture, as artists learned the expected forms and styles, and between cultures, as artists traveled to new places or adopted the styles of works made elsewhere.

The way in which the human body was portrayed in fourth-century B.C.E. Greece (Sources 4 and 5) was influential. These depictions came to be regarded by later Greeks and Romans as the ultimate standard of perfection, and these pieces were copied and recopied hundreds of times. (This is very fortunate, for the Greek originals have in many cases been lost, and what remains are Roman copies; Sources 4 and 5 are actually Roman copies of the originals.) The Roman historian Pliny (ca. 23–79 C.E.), in fact, noted that Polykleitos' sculpture of the athlete (Source 4) was "called the Canon by artists, who drew from it the rudiments of art as from a code," and judged Praxiteles' Aphrodite (Source 5) the finest statue "not only by Praxiteles but in the whole world."[2] When Romans took or copied Greek images, they generally took them out of their religious setting as temple statuary and placed them in gardens, homes, or public squares. The statues thus lost their religious functions as objects of veneration and became secular objects prized primarily for their aesthetic appeal.

Greek style from this period, which has come to be called classical in the West, has been consciously emulated during many periods since, including the Italian Renaissance, the French Revolution, and the early decades of the United States. You need only to visit your state capitol or other local government buildings to assess the ways in which classical Greek standards still influence our portrayal of heroes and leaders.

Like Greek art, Buddhist art in India is generally regarded as having gone through a formative period and then achieved a level of perfection regarded as classical. Source 7 comes from the

2. Pliny, *Historia naturalis*, xxxiv, 55, and xxxvi, 20. Quoted in Gisela M. A. Richter, *A Handbook of Greek Art* (New York: Da Capo Press, 1987), pp. 120, 141.

formative period, from an area of western India called Gandhara (now a part of Afghanistan) in which artists may have been influenced by Greek statues or sculptors. Sources 8 and 9 come from northern India or Nepal in the Gupta period (ca. 300–600 C.E.), a time during which the Gandharan merged with styles from other parts of India. The Gupta period was one of Indian cultural expansion into central and southeastern Asia, and Gupta styles were copied over a very broad area. In areas of southeast Asia, such as Cambodia, where the ruler was viewed as a god-king, the statues often looked slightly like the ruling king, although they still were not portraits in the modern sense. Unlike Greek statuary, Buddhist images did not lose their religious function, for they were copied because of their sanctity, not solely because of their artistic merit. Images modeled on those of Gupta India are still produced today for use in worship, particularly in areas where Buddhism is strong, such as Sri Lanka and parts of southeast Asia.

As we have seen, Maya art also had a classical period, the time from roughly 200 to 900 C.E., during which most of the dynastic records were kept and the most elaborate images were carved and painted. The Mayas themselves drew on the artistic traditions of the Olmecs, who had preceded them as a major civilization in Mexico, and passed on many of their artistic and architectural achievements to various groups that later dominated central America, including the Toltecs and the Aztecs. Maya art after the classical period, such as that at Chichén Itzá in the Yucatan, blended classical Maya elements, such as reliefs of warriors with clothing and ornaments similar to those in the sources in this chapter; elements from other groups in Mexico, such as round temples and depictions of the atlatl (a type of spear-thrower); and new elements, such as long colonnades of pillars.

In western Africa, we have already noted one example of external influence, the ways in which the art (and perhaps artists) from Ile-Ife shaped that of Benin; art from Ife also influenced art in other centers of Yoruba culture, as well as in more distant parts of Africa to which Ile-Ife was connected by trading networks. West Africa provides examples of long-standing traditions and the influence of earlier styles within a single culture as well, for ideas about the ways in which the portrayal of the human form expresses the inner character and life force continue to be important for artists throughout Nigeria today. In fact, of all the items reproduced here, the only one that remains

in its original setting and maintains much of its original significance is the bronze Obalufon mask (Source 15), which is still in a shrine in the palace of the *oni* reigning at Ife in central Nigeria. Thus, like Greek statuary and Gupta images of the Buddha, images of the human form from western Africa are shaping portrayals of the body by contemporary artists.

Because of the international nature of today's artistic culture, artists are not restricted to their own tradition in terms of their portrayal of the human form. They may intentionally copy or pattern what they do on centuries-old images from many cultures, or they may unintentionally bring aspects of items or images they have seen into their work. As you may have discovered in this chapter, seeing (and creating) with completely fresh eyes may be very difficult, even in an artistic culture, like that in the contemporary West, that prizes the new more than the traditional.

CHAPTER FOUR

HAN AND ROME:

ASSERTING IMPERIAL AUTHORITY

(300 B.C.E.–400 C.E.)

Shi Huangdi, the Chinese monarch who in 221 B.C.E. created the first truly imperial realm in East Asia, awed his advisers by the scale of his success. "Now your Majesty has raised a righteous army to punish the oppressors and bring peace and order to all under heaven, so that everywhere within the seas has become our provinces and districts," they told him, observing that this was a feat "which has never once existed from remote antiquity onwards."[1] In their eyes, he had conquered not a kingdom but a world. And because no one to their knowledge had ever done so before, they had

trouble envisioning a state that was able to govern on such a vast scope. Half a world away, the leaders of Rome faced a nearly identical problem. Having wrested North Africa, present-day Spain, and southern France away from Carthage in 201 B.C.E. and then conquering Greece and Anatolia (contemporary Turkey) by 133 B.C.E., the city-state of Rome found itself in control of nearly all of the Mediterranean world.

Emerging almost simultaneously at opposite extremes of Eurasia, these two great empires welded their respective spheres together with such success that they initiated new stages of political development. No longer mere regional powers, they had become world states whose rule extended over many different peoples and cultures. As such, they had to be redefined and justified in new and broader terms. Although their immense size made this endeavor somewhat unique, the Roman and Han empires were by no means the first to face such a task.

1. These remarks appear in a biography of Shi Huangdi in the *Records of the Historian (Shiji)* by the historian Sima Qian. The version quoted here comes from Raymond Dawson's translation, *Historical Records* (New York: Oxford University Press, 1994), p. 84. By permission of Oxford University Press.

Chapter 4

Han and Rome:

Asserting Imperial

Authority

(300 B.C.E.–

400 C.E.)

Throughout history rulers have tried to secure the loyalty and obedience of their people by portraying their authority and the state through which they exercised it in the best possible light.

Such efforts to legitimize political power offer important insights into the way people in different times and cultures have viewed the state and political authority. Current states, for example, generally present themselves as embodiments of a single ethnic group or "nation," whose members share a common language and culture. According to modern beliefs, such national groups form a "people" with a "natural right" to self-rule. So governments today claim to derive their authority from their people and to reflect popular opinion in their policies. The idea of popular sovereignty seems reasonable today because it accords with current assumptions about human nature and politics. But people of other times and places with different assumptions might well consider the concept absurd.

To presume, then, that the people of the Han and Roman empires understood political authority much as modern people do courts problems. Conquerors of many peoples and cultures, these empires exemplified a very different kind of multinational state that had to be justified in terms of universality rather than exclusivity. Efforts to portray these empires as nation-states or even as ancestral forms of modern nations involve all sorts of anachronistic assumptions that project present ideas into the past. To overcome this danger, we need to discover how the builders of the Han and Roman states conceived of political authority within the constraints of their own political traditions. And that is the task facing you in this chapter. In the Evidence section, you will find two sets of primary materials dealing with imperial rule, one Roman and one Chinese. Investigate both to determine the answers to these questions: How did each of these peoples redefine political authority to suit a new level of world mastery? What do their views of imperial authority tell us about the ways in which they understood the state and its power?

BACKGROUND

Neither the Han nor the Roman empire emerged through a sudden, unexpected revolution. On the contrary, both evolved as final, logical outcomes of long processes of regional integration. Some general remarks about the origins of these empires, therefore, will provide a context for better understanding their transformation from regional to world powers. Tracing their rise will also provide insight into the political traditions to which they were heir. For though both innovated freely, they primarily shaped new identities by reinterpreting older, indigenous ideas and institutions. As a result, it would be difficult to understand how the builders of these empires conceived of them without reference to the historical circumstances out of which each evolved.

The Han state clearly owed a heavy debt to the past. For one thing, much of its institutional structure derived directly from the short-lived Qin dynasty, officially inaugurated by Shi Huangdi in 221 B.C.E.[2] Despite that conqueror's boast that his dynasty would rule the new empire for ten thousand years, his early death little more than a decade later created a power vacuum that brought its swift collapse. For a few years, civil war raged as rival provincial leaders restored local kingdoms and vied with one another for regional mastery. But finally one warlord, Liu Bang, overcame all other contenders and reimposed imperial unity. The Han dynasty, which he proclaimed in 202 B.C.E., proved a far more lasting regime than the one it replaced, surviving in its basic form for nearly four centuries before it was swept away by rebellion and mutiny in a series of upheavals that began in 184 C.E.

Despite the change of rulers, much of the basic structure of the Qin regime persisted under the Han, whose early rulers slowly modified its institutions to meet changing conditions. Throughout history, therefore, Qin and Han have often been linked together and deemed, as they will be here, but two phases of a single stage of imperial development. The fact that ancient records carefully distinguish between them, however, points up an important difference between the Chinese political

tradition and the European: In China, states were named in terms of dynasties, or ruling families, rather than in terms of territories, peoples, or institutional structures. Viewed from this perspective, Rome would appear to be not one but a series of different empires, named after successive ruling houses like the Julian and Flavian lines.

Though novel in scope, neither the Qin nor the Han ascension marked an abrupt departure from earlier political patterns. Indeed, much of their imperial system evolved out of the efforts of territorially more limited kingdoms, some ethnically Chinese and some not, to create centralized monarchies during the preceding third and fourth centuries B.C.E. Qin was itself initially just one of a half-dozen or so of these kingdoms, which fought so incessantly with one another during these centuries that later ages termed the era the Warring States Period. Because it succeeded in centralizing faster than its rivals, Qin proved better able to mobilize its resources and so conquered them. But many of these rivals, too, including Qin's chief contender for imperial mastery, a great southern kingdom called Chu, followed their own programs of centralization. Out of their collective experiments evolved many important, new institutions like autocratic kingship, centralized provincial administration, civil bureaucracy, mass military organization, and standardized legal codes, all of which the later Qin and Han empires adapted to their own purposes.

The Warring States era also supplied a diverse body of new ideas about the nature and purpose of the state. As in earlier times, Confucianism remained

---

2. Chinese terms appear in the modern *pinyin* system of romanization, with the often more familiar Wade-Giles spelling sometimes given in parentheses. The name Qin sounds approximately like the English word "chin," and the first emperor's title is pronounced something like *shur hwang dee*.

Chapter 4

Han and Rome:

Asserting Imperial

Authority

(300 B.C.E.–

400 C.E.)

a significant intellectual force. A practical political doctrine developed from the ideas taught by Confucius (in *pinyin* Kung Fu Zi, ca. 551–479 B.C.E.), early Confucianism advocated government based on ethical principles rather than on mere expediency or a ruler's whims. Confucius himself directed his followers to seek such principles in an old ruling house called the Zhou, claiming that its kings exemplified the highest ethical ideal, a rare quality called *ren*, translated variously as humanity, goodness, and benevolence. Later followers like the idealistic Mencius (Mengzi, ca. 371–288 B.C.E.) and the third-century B.C.E. rationalist Xunzi (Hsün Tzu) offered updated Confucian interpretations to suit the altered conditions of the Warring States Period. All, however, insisted that inherent human goodness made coercion unnecessary and argued that governments should rely on moral persuasion rather than force to win support. Only "sages," people endowed with extraordinary ethical virtue and intellectual ability, could in their view establish such regimes, and thus they claimed that rulers should turn government over to a well-trained, upright elite.

Other schools of thought, however, advocated different modes of sagely rule. Proponents of a political brand of Daoism (Taoism), a doctrine associated with a sixth-century B.C.E. figure named Laozi (Lao Tzu), proposed a doctrine of paternalistic, *laissez-faire* rule. In their view, secretive sage rulers trusted in the great Way (*Dao*) that orders the natural world to keep their people content and harmonious. And a group known as the Legalists propounded a theory of outright

autocracy. Likening most people to unruly animals, they claimed that the only means to achieve any social order was to allow those few individuals who overcame their base emotions to serve as enlightened despots. Using a strict system of rewards and punishments, these elevated autocrats were then to train their fellow humans to behave in orderly ways, much as dogs are trained.

Despite wide disagreement on how to achieve order and stability, all these schools of thought bequeathed a common legacy to later empires. First, all anticipated an end to the era of multiple kingdoms. Although they sharply differed as to how unification of their cultural world would be achieved, none doubted its likelihood—or desirability. They thus spoke of a state including all *Tianxia,* or "Underheaven," that is, a state stretching across the entire earth. Their idea of a world-wide state, however, was colored by assumptions of cultural difference.

For they expected this realm to develop around a core area located in the Central Plains of north China, the homeland of ethnic Chinese, then known as the *Xia*. Much earlier, at the start of the first millennium B.C.E., when united under the loose rule of the Zhou dynasty, this region had dominated regional politics. The collapse of Zhou power in the eighth century B.C.E. brought political fragmentation and the loss of regional mastery. But the people of this area continued to enjoy high cultural status in the centuries that followed, winning their petty principalities recognition as the *zhung guo* or "central states." When arguing for regional integration, Warring States thinkers reinterpreted the meaning of this term, understanding it to mean a single Central State that could serve as the core of a greater world polity.

Advocates of integration also fostered the belief that a world-state would be founded by the same kind of *sheng ren* or "sage" that was said to have founded the Zhou dynasty. Thus they encouraged a second assumption: that Underheaven would be united by a special kind of person. Unique to this tradition, the sage had no counterpart in Western thought. The figure may have evolved out of the semidivine forebears of ancient north Chinese clans, to whom old foundation myths ascribe all sorts of wondrous powers. But by Warring States times, sages seem to have been seen as purely human geniuses who personally created all of human culture, including its social and political order. Already, a number of thinkers were advancing historical schemes in which a line of sages seemingly guided humankind out of barbarism and onto the path of civilization. These schemes encouraged the idea that all great changes, including the founding of new states, depended on the leadership of such an event-making figure.

Warring States thinkers introduced a third assumption about any future world-state. Caught up in a wave of recent cosmological speculation, many argued that a strict correspondence existed between natural and human order. In their opinion, all political shifts occurred in concert with larger changes in the natural world. Confucian writers developed a special version of this idea, claiming that a conscious power whom they called *Tian* or "Heaven" willed this correspondence. Borrowing from old apologists who had justified the Zhou monarchy's power on the basis of Heavenly authority, Mencius claimed that Heaven gave true sages a special Heavenly Mandate or charge to found new regimes. He thus helped to revive an old Zhou belief that its kings were "Sons of Heaven," destined to serve as its agent among all humankind. From such concepts emerged a unique theory that universal states would rise and fall in dynastic cycles responsive to Heavenly bidding.

Rome, too, inherited a rich legacy from its Mediterranean forerunners. But it developed out of a very different milieu, one in which city-states rather than regional kingdoms dominated the political scene. The political tradition connected with such city-states celebrated the uniqueness and autonomy of small communities in which a select citizenry enjoyed special privileges. Even in imperial times, the Romans continued to identify with their own distinct origin as a small Latin "republic." Based on the idea of a *res publica*, or "public thing," held in common by a body of people, the ancient republic was a form of government in which authority was thought to reside in a group of citizens rather than in one family or one individual. Only those whom the citizens chose to represent them could thus legitimately rule the community. In early Rome, as in most Mediterranean city-states, only a small portion of the community actually possessed citizenship and could select rulers. Nonetheless, even this limited form of

Chapter 4

Han and Rome:

Asserting Imperial

Authority

(300 B.C.E.–

400 C.E.)

popular participation in government created a strong sense of communal identity that was lacking in East Asia. Compared to the highly standardized Qin–Han imperial system, in which provincial administrations tolerated no local deviation nor any form of communal power, the Roman Empire appeared more like a federation of semiautonomous cities and provinces than like a fully integrated domain.

In its earliest stages, of course, the Roman Empire arose out of just such a league. Beginning as a small Latin city-state on the Tiber River in central Italy in the eighth century B.C.E., it gradually expanded through the conquest of neighboring cities until by 272 B.C.E. it controlled the whole of the Italian peninsula. Thereafter, the decline of Greek power to the east and the rise of a rival Carthaginian hegemony in the west drew Rome into a wider involvement in the Mediterranean world. Within less than a century and a half more, the Roman republic extended its rule over most of the Mediterranean basin. This imperial success, however, placed an enormous burden on Rome's republican institutions, creating a period of political crisis during the mid–first century in which factional strife and civil war threatened to destroy the state.

This process intensified when the chief republican institution, a patrician council known as the Senate, accorded Julius Caesar dictatorial powers so that he could carry out a program of comprehensive reform. Although out of deference to republican tradition Caesar rejected the outright title *rex* ("king"), he became a monarch in all but name in 44 B.C.E. when the Senate voted him a lifetime dictatorship. His assassination that year briefly halted the transition toward monarchical rule, but it resumed little more than a decade later when Caesar's grandnephew Octavian convinced the Senate to name him dictator, too. By a further act of the Senate in 27 B.C.E., Octavian became *imperator* or "emperor," and under the new title Augustus completed the transition from republic to monarchy. From then until the empire's disintegration in the early fifth century, Caesarian-style emperors ruled over the Roman state.

Although an outgrowth of the Roman political situation, this monarchy increasingly reflected the influence of the Hellenistic[3] states of the eastern Mediterranean that Rome eventually absorbed. Most of these were monarchies still ruled by descendants of the followers of Alexander the Great, the Greek conqueror who in the fourth century B.C.E. briefly created the predecessor of a Mediterranean world-state by annexing the Persian Empire to his own much expanded kingdom of Macedonia. Fascinated by Near Eastern forms of kingship, Alexander had himself declared a god like the Egyptian pharaohs and ruled in the autocratic manner of the Persian warrior kings. Although Alexander's empire broke apart after his death, successors in Egypt and Asia Minor kept alive the tradition of posing as god kings, bequeathing it in turn to their Roman conquerors in the first century B.C.E.

3. **Hellenistic:** refers to the people of the eastern Mediterranean who after the time of Alexander the Great became Greek in their ways and outlook, though not necessarily Greek in ancestry; it derives from the word *Hellene,* the name the ancient Greeks gave themselves.

In other areas, too, Hellenistic culture and thought influenced Roman political life. Two Athenian philosophers of the fourth century B.C.E., Zeno and Epicurus, proved particularly influential on later Roman thought. Epicurus, a strict materialist, denied that there was any purpose or meaning to the world other than what humans made of it. He thus counseled followers to seek a quiet life of simple human pleasures. Zeno argued an almost opposite position, contending that a divine spirit worked mysteriously through all things to manifest cosmic harmony. Humans, he felt, provided a special medium through which this spirit operated. He accordingly urged people to recognize human fellowship and to dedicate themselves to a life of service to others and, through it, to the purpose of the divine will. In speaking of a broader human fellowship united by a common purpose, Zeno gave the Mediterranean area a concept of world community that could replace the localism of the city-state. His doctrine, known as Stoic philosophy, thus promoted a more cosmopolitan outlook on the eve of Rome's great expansion.

These Hellenistic ideas helped prepare the way for Rome's creation of an empire by providing terms with which to envision a universal state. Hellenistic writers, especially the Stoics, popularized the idea that the Mediterranean basin formed a single cultural domain, called the "ecumene,"[4] because its inhabitants, whatever their language and ethnicity, shared a common legacy of Greek ways and Greek thought. Out of this developed the later concept of a single Western civilization made up of diverse peoples united by a common classical tradition. Hellenistic thinkers, however, wanted political as well as cultural integration. They thus encouraged hopes that a divine, or at least a divinely inspired, figure would emerge to unite the whole Mediterranean world and help humankind realize its oneness in a new kind of universal state. Rome's eventual conquest of most of this area naturally seemed a fulfillment of their prophetic desires. And Roman emperors easily came to equate their *imperium* or "rule" with an assumed divine mission to order the entire globe, or *orbis terrarum* (literally "world sphere") as they called it.

4. **ecumene:** from the Greek word *oikoumene* ("the inhabited world"); the term, like the Chinese "underheaven," signifies a worldwide or universal sphere.

THE METHOD

The problem at issue here—how the builders of the Han and Roman empires understood their imperial authority—certainly involves aspects of political and institutional history. Yet, it pertains more to what people thought than to what they did. The study of what people of the past thought falls largely in the realm of intellectual history, a branch of history that seeks to trace the development of ideas and their

Chapter 4

Han and Rome:

Asserting Imperial

Authority

(300 B.C.E.–

400 C.E.)

impact on society. For all that they may appear to lack the concreteness of political events and institutions, ideas too can be recovered, providing we tap the right kind of evidence.

Written materials, of course, yield the most information on complex political ideas, for they typically reveal them in the fullest detail. Government documents like degrees, announcements, and commemorative statements give evidence of the official perspective, whereas individual histories, critiques, memoirs, and letters reveal something of the private viewpoints of the time. But written materials by no means exhaust all possibilities. As any visitor to a modern capital city quickly discovers, buildings, monuments, and artworks also express public ideals in powerful ways. Unlike written documents, which make sense only to literate elites, materials of this sort "speak" to a broader segment of the population through the language of visual symbols. In earlier times, when education and literacy were restricted, they probably played a greater role than written texts in conveying basic notions of the state and political authority to the populace. For that reason, we include visual materials as well as written documents in the Evidence section of this chapter.

Evidence presented here on the early Chinese empire includes both sorts of artifact. Source 1 is a selection from a famous biography of Qin Shi Huangdi contained in an early Chinese history of the world called the *Shiji*, or *Records of the Historian*. Compiled in the late second century

B.C.E. by the Han scholar Sima Qian, it incorporates a number of older documents along with the texts of certain stone inscriptions made at the first emperor's own order in 219 and 218 B.C.E. The photographs that serve as Sources 2 and 3 illustrate this emperor's tomb. Source 4 includes parts of essays written by Dong Zhongshu (Tung Chung-shu), a Confucian adviser to Han emperor Wudi (Wu-ti, r.-141–87 B.C.E.), and Source 5 is the text of a decree issued by Han emperor Wendi (Wen-ti) in 178 B.C.E. Sources 4 and 5 both reflect later views of the Qin-Han monarchy.

The Roman material, too, is visual as well as textual. Source 6, an excerpt from the *Res Gestae Divi Augusti*, or *The Achievements of the Divine Augustus*, sets forth the feats for which Rome's first emperor, Caesar Augustus (r. 27 B.C.E.–14 B.C.E.), wished to be remembered in his own words. Source 7, an excerpt from a work called *Roman History*, presents a different view of the accomplishments of Augustus by the third-century historian Cassius Dio. Source 8, a Roman coin, and Sources 9 and 10, a Roman monument called Trajan's Column, present visual images of the monarchy that were intended to influence the less literate. Additional official statements by later Roman emperors comprise Sources 11 and 12; both of these are inscriptions carved on the walls of public temples in the eastern part of the Roman Empire.

As Sources 1 and 5 demonstrate, political ideas tend to be discussed most intensely when governments first emerge or when they undergo crisis.

More apt to feel threatened and vulnerable at these times, leaders often take much greater pains than normal to explain their actions so as to consolidate their power. They issue special proclamations asserting their legitimacy and experiment with new guises through which to portray themselves and their power. Rivals, too, speak out more freely at such moments, whether to challenge authority or to voice alternative views. Material from such critical moments, therefore, provides an especially rich source of political ideas, and you will find a number of such items included here. But even the less intense level of political "talk" that continues in ordinary times may reflect important aspects of a political tradition. Governments, for example, often take advantage of routine statements to reaffirm basic ideals and conventional claims, as do private interests. The very repetitiousness of such messages may, in fact, prove more revealing of commonplace assumptions than more carefully authored statements.

In assessing the following materials, try to distance yourself from modern political assumptions and look for the unfamiliar. One way to do so is to pay special attention to the unusual terms and images that appear with any frequency. In written sources, "keywords," or special terms that appear again and again and seem critical to an understanding of the text, provide a useful starting point for analysis. Because their uniqueness makes modern translation difficult, many will appear in their original language, like the Latin *imperium* or the Chinese *huangdi*. But even when translated, most of these should catch your eye because of their oddity, if not their frequency. Where in modern political discourse, for example, would you find people talking about "sages" or "ovations"? Write these words down and note any passages that offer hints to their meaning. You may have to work back and forth among several of these passages, using clues from one to illuminate others. But if you do so carefully for both sets of evidence, you should end up with a basic vocabulary list of important political terms for each of the two traditions. In a similar way, look for significant factors in the visual materials to add to your list, and ask yourself if they correlate in any way to the keywords.

An approach of this sort, which requires you first to identify the basic words and images of the evidence, will force you to respect the integrity of the evidence and enable you to confront it on its own terms. But doing so will not automatically give you an answer to the central question of this chapter—how did the builders of the Han and Roman empires conceive of and justify their political authority? To get to that point, you will need to ask yourself what each set of key elements collectively indicates about the nature of imperial rule. Keeping a few fundamental considerations in mind at this point should help you piece the evidence together into a larger picture. First, ask yourself what in each case the state seems to embody. Is it a land, an ideal, a people, or something else? A second, closely related question to consider involves the purpose of imperial rule. Modern states, which usually claim to represent a nation,

Chapter 4

Han and Rome:

Asserting Imperial

Authority

(300 B.C.E.–

400 C.E.)

often cite securing the liberty and well-being of their people as their primary purpose. But throughout history other kinds of states have asserted different ends. Some, for example, have claimed to be embodiments of religious movements or churches with divine purposes to fulfill. Others have posed as bearers of cultural traditions, which they presume to defend or promote. Frequently they link this purpose to some higher order or power that thus bestows an ultimate sanction on their power. Logically, a third question to consider, then, is who or what authorizes imperial rule.

Once you have reached some general conclusions about the way in which Han and Roman rulers each understood their imperial authority, compare the differences and similarities between them. Juxtaposing one against the other should highlight what is unique to each. You will no doubt remark with what distinct "voices" early Chinese and Roman sources speak; patterns of rhetoric and style differ as much as, if not more than, basic political beliefs. Think what these differences imply about the gulfs between cultures and the difficulty of interpreting one in terms of the other. Yet, at the same time, note how similar some Roman and Chinese ideas of authority seem relative to the modern notion of popular sovereignty. How do you think people today would react to these ideas? Time, in this case centuries, creates gaps between people that are not easily bridged.

THE EVIDENCE

Source 1 from Raymond Dawson, Historical Records *(New York: Oxford University Press, 1994), pp. 63–70. Reprinted from* Sima Qian: Historical Records, *translated with an introduction and notes by Raymond Dawson. By permission of Oxford University Press.*

1. From Sima Qian,
The Annals of Qin,
ca. second century B.C.E.

Now Qin for the first time had unified all under Heaven and instructions were given to the Chief Minister and the Imperial Secretary saying: ". . . With my own insignificant person I have raised troops to punish violence and chaos and, with the support of the sacred power of the ancestral temples, the six kings have all admitted their crimes, and order is magnificently restored in all under Heaven. Now if the title is not changed there will be no means of praising these achievements and transmitting them to later generations. You are to discuss the imperial title."

Chief Minister Wang Wan, Imperial Secretary Feng Jie, Superintendent of Trials Li Si, and others all said: ". . . Now Your Majesty has raised a righteous army to punish the oppressors and bring peace and order to all under Heaven, so that everywhere within the seas has become our provinces and districts and the laws and ordinances have as a result become unified. This is something which has never once existed from remote antiquity onwards, and which the Five Emperors did not attain. Your servants have carefully discussed this with the scholars of broad learning and, as in antiquity there was the Heavenly August, the Earthly August, and the Supreme August, and the Supreme August was the most highly honoured, so your servants, risking death, submit a venerable title, and propose that the King should become 'the Supreme August.' His commands should be 'edicts,' his orders should be 'decrees,' and the Son of Heaven should refer to himself as 'the mysterious one.' " The King said: "Omit the word 'supreme' and write 'august' and pick out the title of 'emperor' used from remote antiquity, so that the title will be 'August Emperor.' The rest shall be as you suggest." And an edict was issued saying that it should be done. King Zhuangxiang was to be posthumously honoured as "the Supreme August on High."

The Chief Minister Wang Wan and others said: "The states are newly defeated and the territories of Yan, Qi, and Chu are distant, so if we do not establish kings for them there will be no means of bringing order to them. We beg to set up your sons in authority, but it is up to the Supreme One alone to favour us with his agreement." The First Emperor handed down their suggestion to the ministers, and they all thought this would be expedient. But the Superintendent of Trials Li Si advised: ". . . To establish feudal states would not be expedient." The First Emperor said: "It is because of the existence of marquises and kings that all under Heaven has shared in suffering from unceasing hostilities. When, thanks to the ancestral temples, all under Heaven has for the first time been brought to order, if states are reintroduced, this will mean the establishment of armies, and it would surely be difficult to seek peace in those places. The advice of the Superintendent of Trials is right."

So the Empire was divided into thirty-six provinces, and a governor and army commander and an inspector were established for each. The people were renamed "the black-headed people," and there were great celebrations. The weapons from all under Heaven were gathered in and collected together at Xianyang and were melted down to make bells and stands and twelve statues of men made of metal, each 1,000 piculs in weight, to be set up in the courts and palaces. All weights and measures were placed under a unified system, and the axle length of carriages was standardized. For writings they standardized the characters.

In the twenty-eighth year the First Emperor travelled eastwards through his provinces and districts and ascended Mount Zouyi. He set up a stone tablet,

Chapter 4

Han and Rome:

Asserting Imperial

Authority

(300 B.C.E.–

400 C.E.)

and after discussion with the various Confucian scholars of Lu an inscription was carved on the stone extolling the virtue of Qin. They also discussed the matter of the *feng* and *shan* sacrifices[5]. He made the *shan* sacrifice at Liangfu. The stone tablet that he had set up was inscribed with the following words:

When the August Emperor came to the throne, he created regulations and made the laws intelligent, and his subjects cherished his instructions.

In the twenty-sixth year of his rule, he for the first time unified all under Heaven, and there were none who did not submit.

In person he made tours of the black-headed people in distant places, climbed this Mount Tai, and gazed all around at the eastern limits.

His servants who were in attendance concentrated on following his footsteps, looked upon his deeds as the foundation and source of their own conduct, and reverently celebrated his achievements and virtue.

As the Way of good government circulates, all creation obtains its proper place, and everything has its laws and patterns.

His great righteousness shines forth with its blessings, to be handed down to later generations, and they are to receive it with compliance and not make changes in it.

The August Emperor is personally sage, and has brought peace to all under Heaven, and has been tireless in government.

Rising early and retiring late, he has instituted long-lasting benefits, and has brought especial glory to instructions and precepts.

His maxims and rules spread all around, and far and near everything has been properly organized, and everyone receives the benefits of his sagely ambitions.

Noble and base have been divided off and made clear, and men and women conform in accordance with propriety, and carefully fulfil their duties.

Private and public are made manifest and distinguished, and nothing is not pure and clean, for the benefit of our heirs and successors.

His influence will last to all eternity, and the decrees he bequeaths will be revered, and his grave admonitions will be inherited for ever.

. . . He then went south and ascended Langye and, since he greatly enjoyed it, he stayed for three months. Then he moved 30,000 households of the black-headed

5. *feng* and *shan* **sacrifices:** sacrifices to Heaven appropriate only to a supreme ruler.

[86]

people to the foot of Langye terrace, giving them tax and labour exemption for twelve years. When he built Langye terrace, he set up a stone inscription extolling the virtue of Qin, to make clear that he had achieved his ambition. It said:

In his twenty-eighth year, the August Emperor makes a beginning.

Laws and standards are corrected and adjusted, as a means of recording the myriad things.

Thus he clarifies human affairs, and brings concord to father and son.

With sagacity, wisdom, humaneness, and righteousness, he has made manifest all principles.

In the east he has pacified the eastern lands, and thus he has inspected officers and men.

When this task had been magnificently accomplished, he then turned towards the sea.

Through the achievements of the August Emperor, the basic tasks are diligently worked on.

Farming is put first and non-essentials are abolished, and it is the black-headed people who are made wealthy.

All people under Heaven, have heart and mind in unison.

Implements are given a uniform measure, and the characters used in writing are standardized.

Wherever the sun and moon shine, wherever boats and carts carry goods.

Everyone completes his destiny, and nobody does not get what he wants.

He makes things move in accord with the seasons, such is the August Emperor.

Source 2: Liu Liqun/ChinaStock.

2. Grave Mound of Qin Shi Huangdi at Mt. Li

3. Flanking Pit of Excavated Tomb of Qin Shi Huangdi

4. From Dong Zhongshu (Tung Chung-shu), Essays on Kingship

HOW THE WAY OF THE KING JOINS THE TRINITY

Those who in ancient times invented writing drew three lines and connected them through the middle, calling the character "king" [王]. The three lines are Heaven, earth, and man, and that which passes through   the middle joins the

Chapter 4

Han and Rome:

Asserting Imperial

Authority

(300 B.C.E.–

400 C.E.)

principles of all three. Occupying the center of Heaven, earth, and man, passing through and joining all three—if he is not a king, who can do this?

Thus the king is but the executor of Heaven. He regulates its seasons and brings them to completion. He patterns his actions on its commands and causes the people to follow them. When he would begin some enterprise, he observes its numerical laws. He follows its ways in creating his laws, observes its will, and brings all to rest in humanity. The highest humanity rests with Heaven, for Heaven is humaneness itself. It shelters and sustains all creatures. It transforms them and brings them to birth.

The ruler holds the position of life and death over men; together with Heaven he holds the power of change and transformation. There is no creature that does not respond to the changes of Heaven. The changes of Heaven and earth are like the four seasons. When the wind of their love blows, then the air will be mild and the world teem with life, but when the winds of their disfavor come forth, the air will be cold and all things die. When they are joyous the skies are warm and all things grow and flourish, but from their wrath comes the chill wind and all is frozen and shut up.

THE THREEFOLD OBLIGATIONS OF THE RULER

The ruler is the basis of the state. In administering the state, nothing is more effective for educating the people than reverence for the basis. If the basis is revered then the ruler may transform the people as though by supernatural power, but if the basis is not revered then the ruler will have nothing by which to lead his people. Then though he employ harsh penalties and severe punishments the people will not follow him. This is to drive the state to ruin, and there is no greater disaster. What do we mean by the basis? Heaven, earth, and man are the basis of all creatures. Heaven gives them birth, earth nourishes them, and man brings them to completion. Heaven provides them at birth with a sense of filial and brotherly love, earth nourishes them with clothing and food, and man completes them with rites and music. The three act together as hands and feet join to complete the body and none can be dispensed with. . . .

Source 5 from Dun J. Li, The Essence of Chinese Civilization *(New York: Van Nostrand, 1967), pp. 116–117.*

5. Han Wendi (Wen-ti), *On the Eclipse of the Sun*

I have heard that Heaven installs rulers to govern the people it creates and that it will warn a ruler with natural disasters if he has lost virtue or if his rule has become unjust.

On the eleventh month of this year there was an eclipse of the sun. No natural disaster can be more serious than this: Heaven has reproached me!

I have inherited the duty of protecting the temples of our imperial ancestors. A simple and insignificant person though I was, I was called to become the king of all people and scholars. I am solely responsible for all occurrences on earth, be they good or evil. In administering the vast empire, I am assisted by some of my closest minister-advisers.

I have lost my virtue indeed as my inability to take care of my people has aroused the wrath of the sun, the moon, and the stars. Let it be known that immediately after this decree is issued, all of you should think seriously about my shortcomings and inform me on happenings that I have not been able to hear and see myself. Report your findings to me directly! Moreover, you are urged to recommend to me the virtuous, the upright, the honest, and the outspoken so that I can benefit from their counsel and advice. Be it also decreed that all of you are to be diligent at your tasks and that you are to reduce taxes and corvée [enforced labor] duties among my subjects.

Source 6 from Res Gestae Divi Augusti *in Naphtali Lewis and Meyer Reinhold, eds.,* Roman Civilization: Selected Readings, *vol. 1 (New York: Columbia University Press, 1955), pp. 562–572. Copyright © 1955 Columbia University Press. Reprinted with permission of the publisher.*

6. From Caesar Augustus,
The Achievements of the
Divine Augustus

Below is a copy of the accomplishments of the deified Augustus by which he brought the whole world under the empire of the Roman people, and of the moneys expended by him on the state and the Roman people, as inscribed on two bronze pillars set up in Rome.

1. At the age of nineteen, on my own initiative and at my own expense, I raised an army by means of which I liberated the Republic, which was oppressed by the tyranny of a faction. For which reason the senate, with honorific decrees, made me a member of its order in the consulship of Gaius Pansa and Aulus Hirtius [43 B.C.E.], giving me at the same time consular rank in voting, and granted me the *imperium*. It ordered me as propraetor, together with the consuls, to see to it that the state suffered no harm. Moreover, in the same year, when both consuls had fallen in the war, the people elected me consul and a triumvir for the settlement of the commonwealth.

3. I waged many wars throughout the whole world by land and by sea, both civil and foreign, and when victorious I spared all citizens who sought pardon.

Chapter 4

Han and Rome:

Asserting Imperial

Authority

(300 B.C.E.–

400 C.E.)

Foreign peoples who could safely be pardoned I preferred to spare rather than to extirpate. About 500,000 Roman citizens were under military oath to me. Of these, when their terms of service were ended, I settled in colonies or sent back to their own municipalities a little more than 300,000, and to all of these I allotted lands or granted money as rewards for military service. I captured 600 ships, exclusive of those which were of smaller class than triremes.

4. Twice I celebrated ovations, three times curule triumphs, and I was acclaimed *imperator* twenty-one times. When the senate decreed additional triumphs to me, I declined them on four occasions. . . .

6. In the consulship of Marcus Vinicius and Quintus Lucretius, and again in that of Publius Lentulus and Gnaeus Lentulus, and a third time in that of Paullus Fabius Maximus and Quintus Tubero [in 19, 18, and 11 B.C.E.], though the Roman senate and people unitedly agreed that I should be elected sole guardian of the laws and morals with supreme authority. . . .

10. My name was inserted, by decree of the senate, in the hymn of the Salian priests. And it was enacted by law that I should be sacrosanct in perpetuity and that I should posseses the tribunician power as long as I live. I declined to become *pontifex maximus* in place of a colleague while he was still alive, when the people offered me that priesthood, which my father had held. A few years later, in the consulship of Publius Sulpicius and Gaius Valgius, I accepted this priesthood, when death removed the man who [had] taken possession of it at a time of civil disturbance; and from all Italy a multitude flocked to my election such as had never previously been recorded at Rome. . . .

20. I repaired the Capitol and the theater of Pompey with enormous expenditures on both works, without having my name inscribed on them. I repaired the conduits of the aqueducts which were falling into ruin in many places because of age, and I doubled the capacity of the aqueduct called Marcia by admitting a new spring into its conduit. I completed the Julian Forum and the basilica which was between the temple of Castor and the temple of Saturn, works begun and far advanced by my father, and when the same basilica was destroyed by fire, I enlarged its site and began rebuilding the structure, which is to be inscribed with the names of my sons; and in case it should not be completed while I am still alive, I left instructions that the work be completed by my heirs. In my sixth consulship [28 B.C.E.] I repaired eighty-two temples of the gods in the city, in accordance with a resolution of the senate, neglecting none which at that time required repair. In my seventh consulship [27 B.C.E.] I reconstructed the Flaminian Way from the city as far as Ariminum, and also all the bridges except the Mulvian and the Mínucian. . . .

26. I extended the frontiers of all the provinces of the Roman people on whose boundaries were peoples not subject to our empire. I restored peace to the Gallic and Spanish provinces and likewise to Germany, that is to the entire

region bounded by the Ocean from Gades to the mouth ⸱
caused peace to be restored in the Alps, from the region neare Elbe river. I
Sea as far as the Tuscan Sea, without undeservedly making w⸱e Adriatic
people. My fleet sailed the Ocean from the mouth of the Rhine eastwinst any
the territory of the Cimbrians, to which no Roman previously had ⸱s far as
either by land or by sea. . . .   ⸱ated

34. In my sixth and seventh consulships, after I had put an end to the ⸱
wars, having attained supreme power by universal consent, I transferred th⸱
state from my own power to the control of the Roman senate and the people. For
this service of mine I received the title of Augustus by decree of the senate, and
the doorposts of my house were publicly decked with laurels, the civic crown
was affixed over my doorway, and a golden shield was set up in the Julian senate house, which, as the inscription on this shield testifies, the Roman senate
and people gave me in recognition of my valor, clemency, justice, and devotion.
After that time I excelled all in authority, but I possessed no more power than
the others who were my colleagues in each magistracy.

35. When I held my thirteenth consulship, the senate, the equestrian order,
and the entire Roman people gave me the title of "father of the country" and
decreed that this title should be inscribed in the vestibule of my house, in the
Julian senate house, and in the Augustan Forum on the pedestal of the chariot
which was set up in my honor by decree of the senate. At the time I wrote this
document I was in my seventy-sixth year. . . .

Source 7 from Cassius Dio, Roman History *in Naphtali Lewis and Meyer Reinhold, eds.,*
Roman Civilization: Selected Readings, *vol. 1 (New York: Columbia University Press, 1955),*
pp. 557–559. Copyright © 1955 Columbia University Press. Reprinted with permission of the
publisher.

7. From Cassius Dio, *Roman History*

POWERS AND TITLES OF THE EMPEROR

In this way the power of both people and senate passed entirely into the hands
of Augustus, and from this time there was, strictly speaking, a monarchy; for
monarchy would be the truest name for it, even if two or three men later held the
power jointly. Now, the Romans so detested the title "monarch" that they called
their emperors neither dictators nor kings nor anything of this sort. Yet, since
the final authority for the government devolves upon them, they needs must be
kings. The offices established by the laws, it is true, are maintained even now,
except that of censor; but the entire direction and administration is absolutely
in accordance with the wishes of the one in power at the time. And yet, in order

Chapter 4

Han and Rome:
Asserting Imperial
Authority

(300 B.C.E.–
400 C.E.)

appearance of having this authority not through their power to preser of the laws, the emperors have taken to themselves all the offices but by me titles) which under the Republic possessed great power with the (inclur the people—with the exception of the dictatorship. Thus, they very conscome consuls, and they are always styled proconsuls whenever they ofitside the *pomerium*. The title *imperator* is held by them for life, not only by ße who have won victories in battle but also by all the rest, to indicate their psolute power, instead of the title "king" or "dictator." These latter titles they have never assumed since they fell out of use in the constitution, but the actuality of those offices is secured to them by the appellation *imperator*. By virtue of the titles named, they secure the right to make levies, collect funds, declare war, make peace, and rule foreigners and citizens alike everywhere and always—even to the extent of being able to put to death both *equites* and senators inside the *pomerium*—and all the other powers once granted to the consuls and other officials possessing independent authority; and by virtue of holding the censorship they investigate our lives and morals as well as take the census, enrolling some in the equestrian and senatorial orders and removing others from these orders according to their will. By virtue of being consecrated in all the priesthoods and, in addition, from their right to bestow most of them upon others, as well as from the fact that, even if two or three persons rule jointly, one of them is *pontifex maximus*, they hold in their own hands supreme authority over all matters both profane and sacred. The tribunician power, as it is called, which once the most influential men used to hold, gives them the right to nullify the effects of the measures taken by any other official, in case they do not approve, and makes their persons inviolable; and if they appear to be wronged in even the slightest degree, not merely by deed but even by word, they may destroy the guilty party as one accursed, without a trial. The emperors, it should be explained, do not think it lawful to be tribunes, inasmuch as they all belong to the patrician class, but they assume the power of the tribunes in its entirety, as it was at its height; and the number of the years of their rule is counted from the assumption of this power, the theory being that they receive it annually along with those who actually hold the office of tribune. These, then, are the institutions they have taken over from the Republic, each essentially in its traditional form and with the same title, so as to give the impression of possessing no power that has not been granted them. . . .

Thus by virtue of these Republican titles they have clothed themselves with all the powers of the government, so that they actually possess all the prerogatives of kings without the usual title. For the appellation "Caesar" or "Augustus" confers upon them no actual power but merely shows in the one case that they are the successors of their family line, and in the other the splendor of their rank. The name "Father" perhaps gives them a certain authority over us all— the authority which fathers once had over their children; yet it did not signify this at first, but betokened honor and served as an admonition both to them to love their subjects as they would their children, and to their subjects to revere them as they would their fathers. . . .

8. Roman Coin of the Reign of Emperor Nero (r. 54–68)

CAESAR

AVG(VSTVS)

GER(MANICVS)

P(ONTIFEX) M(AXIMVS)

TR(IBVNICIA) P(OTESTAT)

IMP(ERATOR)

P(ATER) P(ATRIAE)

NERO CLAVD(IVS)

9. Trajan's Column, Rome

Source 10 from Bildarchiv Foto Marburg/Art Resource, NY.

10. Detail from Trajan's Column

Chapter 4

Han and Rome:

Asserting Imperial

Authority

(300 B.C.E.–

400 C.E.)

Source 11 from V. Ehrenberg and A. H. M. Jones, trans., Documents Illustrating the Reigns of Augustus and Tiberius, 1976, p. 72.

11. Roman Temple Inscription in Myra, Lycia (Asia Minor)

Divine Augustus Caesar, son of a god, imperator of land and sea, the benefactor and saviour of the whole world, the people of the Myrians.

Marcus Agrippa, the benefactor and saviour of the province, the people of the Myrians.

Source 12 from E. M. Smallwood, trans., Documents Illustrating the Principates of Gaius, Claudius and Nero, 1967, p. 64.

12. Edict and Speech of Nero to the Greeks

Imperator Caesar proclaims:

Since I wish to reward most noble Greece for its good will and piety towards me, I order that as many as possible from this province attend at Corinth on November 29th.

When crowds had gathered in convention, he delivered the following address:

Men of Greece, I bestow upon you an unexpected gift—though anything may be anticipated from my generosity—a gift of such a size that you were incapable of asking for it. All you Greeks who inhabit Achaea and what until now was the Peloponnese, receive freedom and immunity from taxation, something you have not all had even in your most prosperous times, for you have been slaves either to foreigners or to each other. I wish that I might have bestowed this gift when Greece was at her peak, so that more might enjoy my beneficence. For this reason I hold the times to blame for having reduced the size of my beneficence. But, as it is, I bestow the beneficence upon you not out of pity but out of good will and I reward your gods, whose constant care for me on land and sea I have enjoyed, because they have made it possible for me to bestow such great benefactions. For other principes have conferred freedom on cities, but only Nero has done so even on a province.

> [*In response, the following decree*
> *of Acraephia was issued,*
> *proclaiming Nero a god.*]

The high-priest of the Augusti for life and of Nero Claudius Caesar Augustus, Epaminondas, son of Epaminondas, proclaimed (submitted by him for prior consideration to the council and people):

Since the lord of the entire world, Nero, pontifex maximus, in his 13th year of tribunician power, father of his country, New Sun that has shone on the Greeks, has decided to bestow beneficence upon Greece and has rewarded and shown piety towards our gods, who have stood by him everywhere for his care and safety; since he, Nero, Zeus the Liberator, the one and only greatest imperator of our times, friend of the Greeks, has bestowed the eternal indigenous, native freedom that had formerly been taken from the Greeks, he has shown his favour, he has brought back the autonomy and freedom of the past and to this great and unexpected gift has added immunity from taxation, quite complete, which none of the previous Augusti gave us. For all these reasons it has been decided by the magistrates and councillors and people to worship him at the existing altar dedicated to Zeus the Saviour, and to inscribe upon it "To Zeus the Liberator, Nero, forever" and to erect statues of Nero Zeus the Liberator and the goddess Augusta Messallina in the temple of Ptoian Apollo to share it with our ancestral gods, so that, when these things have been done, our city may be seen to have poured out every honour and piety upon the house of the lord Augustus Nero; it has also been decided to inscribe the decree on a column set beside Zeus the Saviour in the market-place and on the temple of Ptoian Apollo.

QUESTIONS TO CONSIDER

As you read and studied the individual pieces of evidence looking for clues about the ways the builders of the Han and Roman empires conceived of and justified imperial authority, you probably noted some shifts of emphasis. Later rulers and their advisers often embellished the ideas of the founding emperors. The founder of the Chinese empire, Qin Shi Huangdi, based much of his claim to an exalted imperial position on his success in conquering "all lands within the four seas." But subsequent rulers, who were not themselves conquerors, needed to develop other justifications for their power. Do you detect a similar shift in the Roman materials?

The stone inscriptions in Source 1 probably best reflect Qin Shi Huangdi's own view of his authority. Though they hail his military victories and worldwide conquest, note the claim that he inaugurated a new age by unifying the Six States and standardizing all laws and norms "wherever the sun and moon shine." Note, too, the references to his sageliness, a quality reflected in the title *Huangdi* (*Huang-ti*), which he adopted. Both words compounded into this title, though often translated "August Emperor" as here, came from terms applied to

Chapter 4

Han and Rome:

Asserting Imperial

Authority

(300 B.C.E.–

400 C.E.)

ancient sages whom tradition portrayed as the creators of human civilization. What does "sage" seem to imply in the emperor's biography? Why do you think the first emperor identified himself with this figure?

In addition to setting up stone markers and other monuments to celebrate his accomplishments while alive, Shi Huangdi constructed a huge tomb out on a plain some fifty kilometers away from his capital city to preserve his fame in death. This practice, which Han emperors continued on a more modest scale, gave him another way to shape his public image. Revisit Source 2, the photograph of his burial mound at Mt. Li. Originally an earthen pyramid 47 meters tall, this mound stood within a 2-square-kilometer enclosure that contained a virtual underground palace. As the detail of one of the excavations shows (Source 3), the area all around was honeycombed with pits filled with thousands of pottery figures. The overwhelming majority of these figures are soldiers like those shown here. What image of authority does this monument and its legions of clay figures imply? How does it compare with the images of conqueror, unifier, and sage presented in the biography?

Qin Shi Huangdi tried to link his rule with higher powers. These included his own deified ancestors and an impersonal cycle of cosmological forces believed to shape human events. But later Han emperors, who patronized Confucianism, elaborated this tendency further. In Source 4, Dong Zhongshu (Tung Chung-shu), a court Confucian adviser, explains how a ruler serves the higher moral power of Heaven, the deity with whom Confucians linked cosmic order. What does his statement that "the king is but the executor of Heaven" imply about the nature of imperial authority? What purpose does it ascribe to the state? And what does it mean to say "the ruler is the basis of the state"? Source 5, a decree issued by the Han Emperor Wendi, expresses the full development of the idea that Han emperors had a special mandate from Heaven to rule. But note that an emperor could lose this charge. Confucians argued that since Heaven gave ethical rulers mandates to rule, it could likewise withdraw authority from the unworthy. What according to Wendi's decree seems to bring Heaven's displeasure—and how does he expect Heaven to show it? Confucians used the doctrine of heavenly warnings to press for a professional bureaucracy schooled in their values as a check on arbitrary rule. Can you gather from this decree how the doctrine empowered imperial officials as well as emperors?

Source 6, *The Achievements of the Divine Augustus*, or *Res Gestae Divi Augustus*, issued by Augustus Caesar, provides a comparable Roman counterpart to Qin Shi Huangdi's stone inscriptions. It, too, came to be inscribed on stone, as copies were carved on the walls of temples throughout the Roman Empire. More autobiographical and personal than Shi Huangdi's inscriptions, it nonetheless served much the same purpose: to explain Augustus's new titles and power. Notice, however, that despite the name of the work, Augustus himself makes no claim to divinity here. Nor does he presume to be a new kind of ruler by right of any transcendent power, divine or natural. Although he points out how he has enlarged the Roman Empire, he does not claim to be a world conqueror, much less the creator of a new state. Saying only that he "liberated the Republic, which was oppressed by the tyranny of a faction," he presents himself as a restorer, not an innovator, and carefully professes not to transgress "the traditions of our ancestors."

Yet, as Augustus notes, not only did the Roman people elect him consul, the highest executive office in the Republic, the Senate voted him the extraordinary title of *imperator*, or emperor. Again and again he attributes his authority to these two sources. Their importance in the state was symbolized by the universal inscription S.P.Q.R., signifying *Senatus Populusque Romanus* ("The Senate and the Roman People"), on Roman standards and monuments. As the "sole guardian of the laws and morals with supreme authority" elected by the Roman Senate and people, what kind of imperial ruler did Augustus presume to be? In keeping with his elected offices, Augustus often preferred to use another title bestowed upon him by the Senate—*princeps*, meaning "first" among his fellow citizens. What kind of legitimization do these claims imply? In what sense did it qualify him to assume the title "father of the country," which he asserts so prominently at the end of this laudatory piece.

In his *Roman History*, the third-century historian Cassius Dio questions Augustus's pose as mere restorer of the Republic. In Source 7, an excerpt from this work, Cassius Dio argues that Augustus and subsequent Roman emperors actually wrested all power from the Senate and people and instituted an autocratic system of monarchy in which the *imperator* became an absolute ruler. Behind the façade of their republican titles, he charges, Augustus and his successors assumed "all the prerogatives of kings without the usual title." They absorbed not only all civil authority in this way, he says, but other authority, too. For they took the title *pontifex maximus*, or high priest of the official Roman pantheon of gods, along with their profane offices and honors. Indeed, one of the few surviving statues of Augustus portrays him in this priestly role. What support do you suppose he and his successors expected to add to their status through this title?

Later emperors continued to present themselves as high priest as well as civic father, chief executive, and, of course, heir to Augustus. Look at Source 8, a *sesterius* or bronze coin minted during the time of Emperor Nero (r. 54–68). Long accustomed to commemorating leading citizens on state coinage, the Romans found it natural to mint money bearing imperial portraits under the empire. These portraits and the legends accompanying them, of course, provided emperors with an excellent way to propagandize their public images. Notice all the names and titles appearing on the face of the coin reproduced here. Beginning at the lower left, the coin gives the emperor's personal name, Nero Claudius, then affirms his relationship to Caesar Augustus through his adopted father, Germanicus. Then

[101]

Chapter 4

Han and Rome:

Asserting Imperial

Authority

(300 B.C.E.–

400 C.E.)

around the rim follow abbreviated versions of his four most prized titles: PM for *Pontifex Maximus*, TRP for *Tribunicia Potestate* or tribuneship (an office supposedly representing the lower or plebeian class of the empire), IMP for *Imperator,* and PP for *Pater Patriae* or "father of the country." How do these titles compare with those assumed by Augustus?

Besides asserting civil and religious authority, a number of later emperors chose to portray themselves as military commanders and conquerors. Emperor Trajan (r. 98–117), who began his political career as a general, especially popularized this role. He not only commissioned statues of himself in full armor and minted coins bearing his image as a warrior, but raised a great column in Rome to depict his generalship. Source 9 shows this column. Although built primarily to hold aloft a huge statue of Trajan in military dress, the column also publicizes his most famous campaign, a war fought against the Dacians on the Balkan peninsula. Battle scenes like the one shown in Source 10 spiraled up its entire length, recalling a tradition of battlefield leadership going back to Alexander the Great and the Persian monarchs whom he imitated. Like similar monuments and victory arches raised in Rome by other emperors, Trajan's Column openly celebrates military conquest. What kind of imperial authority do these images evoke?

The image of a world conqueror closely parallels another theme that eventually affected the way Roman emperors characterized themselves and their authority: the tradition of world

savior. In the eastern lands of the empire, rulers had often claimed not only to represent gods but to *be* gods in their own right. Rome's newly conquered subjects in this quarter, therefore, readily accorded the emperors divine status. Source 11, a commemorative inscription from the time of Caesar Augustus carved on a temple in Myra, a city on the Mediterranean coast in present-day Turkey, shows this trend well underway. Note how it characterizes the first emperor as "divine Augustus Caesar" and calls him "son of a god," implying that his adoptive father, Julius Caesar, was divine, too. And observe how it lauds him as "benefactor and savior of the whole world," far more than just a restorer of Roman liberties.

By the time of Nero, the cult of imperial divinity encouraged even more exaggerated claims, like those in Source 12, an inscription from Acraephia. Issued by a priest in the service of the Augusti, or imperial cult, on the occasion of Nero's decision to grant many Greek cities special tax immunity, it equates Nero, "lord of the entire world," with the greatest of Greek gods, Zeus—here characterized as Liberator and Savior. By the end of the fourth century, Emperor Diocletian, who ruled from the eastern half of the realm, regularly equated himself with Zeus or his Roman equivalent, Jupiter. Contrast this form of divine monarchy with Augustus's own more modest view of sovereignty. How does it change the nature and justification of imperial authority?

As you compare this vision of a divinely led empire with the Han idea of a Heavenly ordained ruler, ask yourself why religious beliefs of this sort became so entwined with political institutions in both imperial traditions. How would people today react if their leaders claimed to have special divine or religious powers? Modern assumptions about the separation of state and religion make it difficult for us to understand why political supremacy might be equated with sacred power. But clearly this equation occurred in both ancient Rome and China. What other common features do you find in these two traditions that contrast with modern practice or belief? Think for a moment about the gender implied in all of these images of imperial rule. How different would it be if the Han rulers had claimed to be "children" of Heaven or the Roman emperors proclaimed themselves "parents" of the country. What does the masculine nature of the expressions imply about ancient Roman and Chinese notions of power?

EPILOGUE

Although extremely powerful for a few centuries, neither Han nor Rome proved immune to eventual decay. Internal conflicts and divisions strained their administrative structures to the breaking point, and as central authority ebbed, their empires fragmented in the face of rebellions and invasions. To their subjects, this collapse entailed far more than the end of political regimes. It meant the break-up of world order and the start of extended eras of change, turmoil, and insecurity at both ends of the Eurasian continent. Among other results, such change brought an end to regional unity and world-states.

The Han collapsed first, following a generation of court intrigues and coups in the second half of the second century that allowed imperial power to drift away from reigning emperors into the hands of palace eunuchs who lacked any claim to virtue or legitimacy. Uncertain of the bureaucracy's loyalty, they hesitated in the face of a wave of popular insurrections that exploded in the Yellow River plain in 184 following a devastating plague. United by millenarian bands known as Yellow Turbans, pledged to found a revolutionary "Heavenly State of Great Peace," the rebels nearly toppled the Han. For lack of central forces, provincial governors and local elites had to organize their own resistance against the rebels. After quelling the rebellions, therefore, they refused to disband their forces and relinquish local control. Nervously building up their power, they became de facto warlords and began to vie with each other for wider influence. Eventually one of their number, a general named Cao Cao, set himself up in the capital as protector of the impotent throne and used his armies to prolong nominal Han rule for a few decades more. But when his son deposed the last Han emperor in order to ascend the throne himself in 220, many provincial magnates refused to recognize his authority and partitioned the empire into warring fragments. Despite a brief reunification of the imperial territories

Chapter 4

Han and Rome:

Asserting Imperial

Authority

(300 B.C.E.–

400 C.E.)

at the end of the third century, further civil strife soon broke out again, and all hope of imperial restoration crumbled as waves of invaders swept across the frontiers to engulf north China.

Imperial Rome lasted longer, but eventually it, too, fragmented. Although for reasons different from those in China, rivalry around the throne weakened the monarchy. Left with inadequate resources, provincial leaders failed to deal with mounting domestic problems and frontier dangers. Emperor Diocletian (r. 284–305) and his immediate successors tried to overhaul the administrative structure of the empire and enhance imperial prestige. Constantine (r. 306–337), who shifted the capital away from Rome to his namesake city, Constantinople, enjoyed brief success. But the benefits of these belated reforms did not last long, and by the end of the fourth century, the decline had begun anew. Eventually the relentless pressure of German tribes along the Rhine and Danube frontier brought about the empire's final collapse. Following the Gothic invasion and sack of Rome in 410, outsiders overran and divided up the empire's western half. With the loss of Rome and most of the Latin-speaking lands, the eastern half, ruled from Constantinople, began to evolve into a very different kind of Greek empire known as Byzantium.

Despite their fall, both empires left enduring legacies of institutions and ideas, including ideals of universal empire and imperial authority. After a lapse of nearly three and a half centuries, East Asians succeeded in resurrecting a great imperial state under the Sui and Tang dynasties of the sixth through the ninth centuries. Though altered in subsequent centuries, this imperial state essentially survived intact until 1911, when the last *huangdi,* or sage lord, abdicated in the face of the revolution that instituted a westernized Chinese republic. And to this day, the Chinese still call themselves in their own language *Han ran*—the "people of Han." In the West, the imperial ideal proved more elusive, and though Europeans tried on occasion to revive the Roman Empire, none of their endeavors fully succeeded. Justinian's effort in the sixth century to rebuild it from a Byzantine base failed, as did Charlemagne's ninth-century attempt to restore it from his Frankish kingdom. Yet the mystique of the Caesars persisted into modern times, leading the Germans and Russians to appropriate the name for their rulers in *Kaiser* and *Czar.* Napoleon, who rode to power in France on the first tide of modern nationalism, showed how powerful that aura remained at the start of the nineteenth century when he gladly abandoned republican scruples to grasp the old title *imperator* for himself. And both Mussolini and Hitler evoked it again in the twentieth century in the symbols of their authoritarian power. As many have observed, the papacy preserves a more benign version of the Roman monarchy into the present.

The lasting power of these imperial ideals suggests that they embodied some of the most deeply rooted assumptions and beliefs from within

[104]

their respective cultural spheres. A final point worth considering, therefore, is the degree to which they may continue to influence contemporary political life. Some, for example, claim to see vestiges of assumed sagehood in the "great Helmsman" Mao Zedong (Mao Tse-tung), who, after all, proclaimed the advent of a new socialist age with global significance from a balcony overlooking Tiananmen Square in Beijing—a square whose very name, derived from the adjacent entrance to an old imperial palace, means the Gate of Heavenly Peace! And how many modern republics still revere a military figure who became "father of his country" by virtue of restoring the lost liberty of a people through some presumed divine grace?

CHAPTER FIVE

INTERNATIONAL RELIGIOUS

COMMUNITIES

(300 B.C.E.–800 C.E.)

In the last chapter, we examined the growth of large empires in the ancient world, noting the technical and bureaucratic structures that enabled them to grow and flourish. In this chapter, we explore another way in which large territories were brought or held together: through allegiance to a set of religious ideas or a religious figure. Of the thousands of religions practiced in the world today, three claim large numbers of adherents throughout the world: Buddhism, Christianity, and Islam. Each of these began as a small group of followers around a single leader and then was transformed, slowly or quickly, into an international religious community. In the case of Buddhism and Christianity, this occurred several centuries after the lives of the initial leaders, Siddhartha Gautama, called the Buddha (ca. 563–483 B.C.E.), and Jesus of Nazareth (ca.

5 B.C.E.–29 C.E.). In the case of Islam, this growth began during the lifetime of the initial leader, Muhammad (ca. 570–632 C.E.), and continued for many centuries after his death.

For each of these religions, the transformation from small sect to international community was accomplished by individuals who also had what we would term secular political power; in other words, they were political as well as religious leaders. In-the case of Buddhism, the person generally regarded as dramatically expanding Buddhism both within and beyond the Indian subcontinent was the Mauryan emperor Ashoka (ruled ca. 273–232 B.C.E.). In the case of Christianity, the Roman emperor Constantine (ruled 306–337 C.E.), the first emperor to become a Christian, is usually seen as the key figure. In the case of Islam, Muhammad himself and the-first four caliphs who succeeded him, termed the "patriarchal caliphs"—Abu Bakr (ruled 632–634),

Umar (ruled 634–644), Uthman (ruled 644–656), and Ali (ruled 656–661)—spread Islam across Arabia and into Persia and North Africa, setting the pattern for later, more extensive expansion into Europe, Africa, and Asia.

In each of these cases, the individuals involved, or those close to them, have left us a record of these transformations and what they were attempting to accomplish. Your task in this chapter will be to use a variety of sources to answer these questions: How did political leaders within Buddhism, Christianity, and Islam encourage the growth of their chosen religious community? What differences and similarities do you see in their actions and in what they viewed as most important in the lives of these communities?

BACKGROUND

Studying the history of any religious movement can pose special problems for historians. We may have more trouble achieving unbiased assessments of the history of religion than of other historical topics because of our intellectual, spiritual, or emotional commitments to certain religious ideas. This does not mean, however, that we should avoid religious topics—to do so would make it impossible for us to understand the past—but instead that we should be aware of our own prejudices and approach all religions with respect. Our job as historians is to understand people's religious ideas within their historical context and to see how religious faith has manifested itself in historically observable phenomena; it is not to judge whether certain religious ideas are right or wrong, true or false.

Difficulties in being objective when studying the history of religion can stem not only from our own personal religious commitments, but also from the nature of the sources available.

Very few religious sources were written simply to describe what happened; more often, they were written to express central doctrines or to win converts. Even those sources that do describe historical events, such as the actions of the political leaders we are examining in this chapter, were often written for the added purpose of spreading the faith. Many of these were composed long after the events occurred, and so later developments colored the ways in which they were recorded. In some cases, these written records were based on extensive oral traditions, but they are now our only source for the events they describe, and we have no way to check their accuracy. They may relate events that were viewed at the time as clearly miraculous—visions in the sky, voices from heaven—but also as having actually happened. Luckily, we as historians do not need to take a stand on the historicity of such events. What is important for us is that people believed that they had happened and acted accordingly.

In talking about any religious group, we often make distinctions between history, tradition, and myth, but the lines between these are never sharp and

Chapter 5
International
Religious
Communities
(300 B.C.E.–
800 C.E.)

are frequently contested. It is important to recognize, however, that tradition and myth are not the same; when historians use the phrase "according to tradition, . . . " they are not saying that an event is completely mythological but simply commenting on the limits of their sources. In many religions, deep divisions developed quite early not only about the religious meaning of certain events, but also about when certain things happened and whether they happened at all. Thus, not only can our sources be obscure, they can also be contradictory. Often there is no way to resolve the contradiction, and we simply have to say "according to this tradition . . . whereas according to that tradition. . . . " These divisions within religions were often more bitterly contested than differences between religions, and indeed, discords within religions continue to shape the contemporary world in profound and sometimes violent ways.

Keeping in mind these cautionary thoughts about the evaluation of all religious sources, we can now focus more specifically on the context for the sources we include here. Because we are examining the actions of certain leaders in regard to their religious communities, the evidence focuses on that aspect of their reigns. Your textbook can provide you with more general information about Ashoka and the Mauryan Empire, Constantine's reign in the Roman Empire, and the lives of Muhammad and the patriarchal caliphs.

The Mauryan emperor Ashoka was the grandson of the founder of the Mauryan Empire, Chandragupta, who had defeated one of the generals of Alexander the Great in 304 B.C.E. and expanded his holdings to include most of the Indian subcontinent. Ashoka grew up at the royal court at Pataliputra in the Ganges River valley, where many religious traditions mingled—Brahmanism, Jainism, Buddhism—and where ideas about the role of the ruler were openly debated and discussed. The most extensive consideration of these was a treatise on government traditionally attributed to one of Chandragupta's ministers, the Brahmanical teacher Kautilya, titled *Arthashastra*, in which power and benevolence were described as the two main objectives of kingship.

At some point in his life, Ashoka accepted Buddhism, although traditions vary about exactly who converted him. They also vary about the timing of some events within Buddhism that probably occurred during or shortly before or after Ashoka's reign, such as formal splits because of disagreements about various interpretations of the Buddha's teaching. Certain aspects of the practice and prevalence of Buddhism at that time are very clear, however: We know, for example, that people often went on pilgrimages to the holy places associated with the Buddha's life, built mounds called *stupas* to house Buddhist relics, and supported communities of monks and nuns called the *sangha*; Buddhism was well established in central India, and had begun to spread north to Kashmir and south to the Deccan plateau; and a canon of sacred texts, attributed to the Buddha, had begun to appear.

Like Ashoka, the Roman emperor Constantine underwent a religious conversion some time after he became an adult, though there are discrepancies in the sources and differences of opinion among historians about exactly when this was and how complete an acceptance and understanding of Christianity Constantine evidenced. Constantine was the son of Emperor Constantius, but his claim to the throne was challenged by a number of rivals. Though his troops elected him emperor in 306, the emperorship itself was divided at the time in a complex way, and Constantine did not become sole sovereign until 324, after he had defeated all other claimants. Much of Constantine's early reign was thus spent in warfare, and he became extremely concerned with establishing structures and institutions that would make the Roman Empire more united.

Christianity appeared to Constantine to be just such a unifying force. Christianity had originally been largely ignored by high-level Roman authorities, who regarded it as a sect within Judaism and therefore of little consequence. There were sporadic persecutions in the first century c.e., but there was no concerted campaign to annihilate Christianity. These persecutions may have actually helped Christianity spread, as the heroism of martyrs often impressed those who watched their public executions and who later became Christians themselves. As more non-Jews converted, Roman authorities became more concerned, particularly because Christians refused to participate in the sacrifices and ceremonies honoring the traditional Roman gods. These ceremonies were patriotic as well as religious to the Romans, for they were carried out for the good of the state and often specifically held to assure military victory. Persecution was thus stepped up in the second and

third centuries, and it became particularly vicious during the reigns of those emperors who were most concerned about the health of the empire. By this point it was too late to stop the spread of Christianity, which had a growing following among people of all classes throughout the Roman Empire and a strong bureaucratic structure based on regional officials termed bishops. There is great disagreement among historians about how much of the Roman population had become Christian by the time of Constantine, but it was certainly a sizable minority.

The history of Islam is very different from that of Buddhism and Christianity in that it was both a religious and a political community from the beginning; Muhammad was in some ways his own Constantine. Like both Ashoka and Constantine, Muhammad experienced a religious conversion when he was an adult, but, unlike them, he was a merchant rather than a ruler. He lived in Mecca, an important trading and religious center on the Arabian peninsula, which was divided into different tribal groups and lacked the leadership of a single ruler. Muhammad's conversion involved visions of angelic beings who ordered him to preach a message of a single God and to become God's Prophet, which he began to do in his hometown of Mecca. While he slowly gathered followers there, he also provoked a great deal of resistance and in 622 migrated with his followers to Medina—this event, termed the *hijra*, marks the beginning of the Muslim calendar. At Medina, Muhammad was much more successful, and by his death in 632 he had unified most of the Arabian peninsula into a religious/political

Chapter 5
International
Religious
Communities
(300 B.C.E.–
800 C.E.)

community (termed the *umma*) of *Muslims*, a word meaning "those who comply with or submit to God's will." (The first umma was formed by the Charter of Medina in 622 and included the local Jewish community, which established a precedent for the later protection of Jews under Islam.)

Muhammad's revelations were written down by his followers during his lifetime and shortly thereafter were organized into an authoritative text, the Qur'an, regarded by Muslims as the direct words of God (Allah) to his prophet Muhammad and therefore especially revered. (These revelations were in Arabic. If Muslims use translations into other languages, they do so alongside the original Arabic.) At the same time, other sayings and accounts of Muhammad, which gave advice on matters that went beyond the Qur'an, were collected into books termed *hadith;* Muslim tradition (*sunna*) consists of both the Qur'an and the hadith. Unfortunately for the Muslim community, neither the Qur'an nor the hadith gave clear guidance about how successors to Muhammad were to be chosen, but a group of Muhammad's closest followers elected Abu Bakr, who was a close friend of the Prophet's and a member of a small tribe affiliated with

the Prophet's tribe, as caliph, meaning "successor." This election set a precedent for the ratification of the subsequent patriarchal caliphs, though it was unsuccessfully opposed militarily by other Arab tribes. A more serious challenge developed later among supporters of the fourth caliph, Ali. Ali claimed the caliphate because of his blood ties with Muhammad—he was the Prophet's cousin and son-in-law—and because Muhammad had designated him as *imam,* or "leader." He was assassinated in 661, five years after becoming caliph, and his supporters began to assert that he should rightly have been the first caliph and that all subsequent caliphs were usurpers. These supporters of Ali—termed *shi'at Ali* or *Shi'ites*—saw Ali and subsequent imams as the divinely inspired leaders of the community, whereas the larger body of Muslims who accepted the first elections—termed *Sunnis*—regarded the caliphs as political leaders. Since Islam did not have an organized church and priesthood, the caliphs had an additional function of safeguarding and enforcing the religious law (*sharia*) with the advice of scholars (*ulama*), particularly the jurists, judges, and scholastics who were knowledgeable about the Qur'an and hadith.

THE METHOD

In reading the two central questions for this chapter, you no doubt noted that the first is largely informational and the second is comparative. This order is

not accidental, for historians must first uncover information about past societies before they can begin to make comparisons. Indeed, many historians choose to devote their entire lives to the intensive study of a single culture and time period and are not especially interested in comparative questions. World history courses, including probably the one you are enrolled in, tend to provoke comparative questions, however, and some historians would argue that to a certain degree *all* history is comparative. By this they mean that we approach all other cultures from the vantage point of our own, and thus we can understand them only by comparing them to what is familiar and known. They stress that these comparisons may be implicit, but they are inescapable. Other historians, though, dispute this point and argue that the best history writing seeks to be highly objective and, as much as possible, to constrain the historian's own cultural background from intruding.

Whatever they think about *implicit* comparisons, historians who make *explicit* comparisons in their work recognize that these must be derived and expressed very carefully. Not only must historians think about the ways in which the events, individuals, or developments that are the subjects of their study are comparable, but they must also think about the ways in which the sources available to them are comparable. Very often the types of records left by one culture are quite different from those left by another, even regarding matters as central as political leadership. Thus, as you begin to make comparisons between the actions and ideas of the leaders who are the focus of this chapter, you will need to think about how your ideas—and the connections and comparisons you are making—are shaped by the types of sources you are using.

Most of the sources for this chapter are written; they consist primarily of pronouncements of the political leaders themselves or the writings of historians or other commentators who were members of the leader's community. In no case does our evidence come from someone who was hostile to the individuals or their actions. (This is another aspect of the evidence you need to keep in mind.) Your primary method will be careful reading, and we advise you first to work on gathering information and then to go back and make your comparisons. You may find it useful to list all the actions and ideas of the leaders described in the sources, so as to summarize their roles in your own words before you begin to make comparisons.

Sources 1 through 3 all relate to King Ashoka. Source 1 is a selection of some of the so-called rock and pillar edicts, which are the best record we have of Ashoka's reign. These are inscriptions that King Ashoka ordered carved in stone on large rocks in prominent places or on tall pillars that he had erected for this purpose. The edicts are found in a number of different locations throughout Ashoka's large empire, particularly along the borders. They were written in Prakrit, the language spoken at Ashoka's time, and are the oldest surviving written documents of historical importance in India. Read these edicts carefully. What convinced Ashoka that he should change the way he was ruling and acting? What does he now see as the main aim of his reign? What actions has he done to promote this aim? How does he relate to the community of Buddhist monks and nuns (the sangha, sometimes spelled Samgha)? How does he say he treats those who follow religions other

Chapter 5
International
Religious
Communities
(*300 B.C.E.–*
800 C.E.)

than Buddhism, and how does he advise his subjects to treat people with different religious ideas?

Source 2 is a photograph of one of the Ashokan pillars, topped with a single lion. (Other pillars are topped with three lions, an emblem that is now on the state seal of India and Indian coins, or lions and the Buddhist wheel of law, an emblem reproduced on India's flag.) Each of these pillars—more than thirty have been discovered—was transported hundreds of miles from the same quarry and polished very smooth before it was inscribed. Why might Ashoka have regarded this effort as important? Why would pillars such as these be an effective way to relay the information you have just read? How would the pillars complement the visits by officials and by Ashoka himself?

The other major type of source we have for Ashoka's reign is legends, oral traditions about him that did not die out when the Mauryan Empire collapsed but spread throughout India and beyond its borders. Some of these were written down in the Pali language as part of the chronicles from the island of Sri Lanka, where Buddhist tradition holds that Ashoka's son Mahendra and daughter Samghamitra spread Buddhism. Others were written down in Sanskrit in northern India and gradually collected into a single text called the *Asokavadana*. Source 3 is from this text, relating an incident from Ashoka's life after he converted to Buddhism. When we use legends and oral traditions in historical investigations, the most important question to ask ourselves is not whether the events really happened, but why followers of

an individual tell and retell them—in other words, how these oral traditions worked to support the followers' ideas. Why would the Buddhist followers of Ashoka tell this story? How does it fit with Ashoka's statements about his own ideas and reign as inscribed in the rock and pillar edicts?

Sources 4 through 6 concern the Roman emperor Constantine. Like the evidence about Ashoka, many of the records that survive from Constantine's reign are official edicts and proclamations, though these were written on papyrus and parchment rather than being inscribed on pillars. Source 4 comprises a series of edicts issued by Constantine regarding Christianity, beginning with the original edict of toleration from 311 signed by three of the then four rulers of the Roman Empire: Lactantius, Licinius, and Constantine. The remaining edicts were issued by Constantine alone and are reprinted here in chronological order. They cover a range of actions that Constantine took either directly on behalf of the Christian church or because he was inspired by Christian ideas. Some indicate his opinion toward those following other systems of belief. Reading them will allow you to begin developing your ideas about Constantine's role.

The most important record we have of Constantine's life is a biography written shortly after his death by the historian and Christian bishop Eusebius of Caesarea (ca. 263–339?), a close adviser to Constantine. As Constantine's friend and an official in the Church, Eusebius expressed a particular point of view in his biography, but many of the events he discusses, such as Constantine's proclamations and military battles, are recorded in other sources as well. Other events are not verifiable, but, as with the legends surrounding King Ashoka, the stories about Constantine came to be considered true by later Christians. Source 5 is a series of selections from Eusebius's *Life of Constantine.* As you read these excerpts, note the actions Constantine takes in regard to the Christian church and the statements he makes about it. What convinces Constantine that he should become a Christian? How does he relate to the bishops, the Church's key officials? What does he see as most important for the Church? How do the events related here fit with the imperial edicts you read in Source 4? How might Eusebius's position as an official in the Church shape the way he reports history?

Like Ashoka, Constantine erected large monuments to his rule, most notably the Arch of Constantine in Rome. In Source 5, you discover smaller ways in which he portrayed his religious sentiments and celebrated his reign, through coins and portraits. Source 6 shows two of these coins, one portraying Constantine with a halo and another, two soldiers with the *labarum,* the special standard that was made for the army after Constantine's vision. Why might Constantine have thought it important to issue coins with symbols such as these? Why would coins be an effective means of communicating ideas?

When we turn to the transformation of Islam from small sect to international religious community, we can no longer look at the actions of just one individual, but we must explore those of a series of rulers. Here we have four basic types of sources: the Qur'an, the hadith, histories and biographies written after the fact, and legal or other commentaries on the actions of rulers and ideas about rulership. As you read Sources 7 through 10, you need to think about how the purpose for which each was written might have shaped the discourse.

Source 7 is several verses from the Qur'an regarding the duties of believers to authorities, the rewards for believers, the treatment for those who did not accept the Prophet's words, and the attitudes Muslims were to have toward Jews and Christians. Source 8 is a selection of sayings ascribed to the Prophet from three different collections of hadith, again addressing the duties of believers toward their leaders and leaders toward the community. Because the hadith record sayings and traditions that were handed down orally for several generations, they are generally prefaced by a listing of the names of those who related them back to the early years of Islam. According to both the Qur'an and the hadith, what are the most important duties of the leaders toward the community? of the community toward leaders? What developments are to be most guarded against? How are those who are not Muslims to be treated?

Source 9 is a selection from the earliest biographer of Muhammad whose work has survived, Ibn Ishaq, who was born in Medina in 707 and died in Baghdad in 773. (The Muslim calendar uses the hijra, Muhammad's migration from Mecca to Medina in 622, as its starting date, written as A.H.; in that dating system, Ibn

Chapter 5
International
Religious
Communities
(300 B.C.E.–
800 C.E.)

Ishaq's dates are A.H. 85–151.) As with Eusebius's biography of Constantine, many of the incidents recorded have been confirmed by archaeological findings and other sources, so that it is regarded as generally reliable, though, like Eusebius, the author writes from the point of view of a committed follower and admirer. As you read Source 9, note the kinds of actions by which Muhammad spread his message. How were those who opposed him to be handled? What were the most important aspects of the Muslim community? Source 10 is from the *Book of Land-tax* by Abu Yusuf (died A.H. 182/798 C.E.), a legal scholar who wrote a lengthy book of advice for his sovereign, the caliph Harun al-Rashid. Though this evidence comes from a later period, Abu Yusuf relates a number of incidents about the earliest caliphs as part of his instructions to the present one. What actions and advice of the patriarchal caliphs Abu Bakr and Umar does he describe and praise here? What do they advise their successors?

Unlike Christianity and Buddhism, Islam avoided portraying humans or animals in its sacred art; thus the Qur'an and the hadith are never illustrated with figures, though they are often decorated with lavish designs. This convention did not extend to histories, however, and Source 11 is an illustration from one of the most famous Muslim histories, the *Jami' al-tawarikh* (World History) of Rashid al-Din, an adviser to the Muslim ruler Uljaytu (ruled 1304–1316 C.E.). This work was produced, of course, long after the early development of Islam, but its text and illustrations depict what later Muslims saw as important from their early history. Source 11 is a picture of Muhammad (the figure on the far right), addressing Ali and other Muslim leaders before the battle of Badr in the year A.H. 2, which was the first victory of Muhammad's followers against the Meccans. What aspects of Muhammad's leadership does this painting highlight?

You should now have a list of actions and ideas for each of the three individuals—and their religious communities—that are the focus of this chapter, and you have probably begun to see ways in which to compare them. As you develop your comparisons further, you may wish to turn to the Questions to Consider section for additional suggestions.

Source 1 from The Edicts of Aśoka, *ed. and trans. N. A. Nikam and Richard McKeon (Chicago: University of Chicago Press, 1959), pp. 27–29, 30, 34–35. Copyright © 1959. Reprinted by permission of publisher, The University of Chicago Press.*

1. Selections from Ashoka (Aśoka), Rock and Pillar Edicts

The Kaliṅga country[1] was conquered by King Priyadarśī, Beloved of the Gods,[2] in the eighth year of his reign. One hundred and fifty thousand persons were carried away captive, one hundred thousand were slain, and many times that number died.

Immediately after the Kaliṅgas had been conquered, King Priyadarśī became intensely devoted to the study of Dharma,[3] to the love of Dharma, and to the inculcation of Dharma.

The Beloved of the Gods, conqueror of the Kaliṅgas, is moved to remorse now. For he has felt profound sorrow and regret because the conquest of a people previously unconquered involves slaughter, death, and deportation.

But there is a more important reason for the King's remorse. The Brāhmaṇas and Śramaṇas [the priestly and ascetic orders] as well as the followers of other religions and the householders—who all practiced obedience to superiors, parents, and teachers, and proper courtesy and firm devotion to friends, acquaintances, companions, relatives, slaves, and servants—all suffer from the injury, slaughter, and deportation inflicted on their loved ones. Even those who escaped calamity themselves are deeply afflicted by the misfortunes suffered by those friends, acquaintances, companions, and relatives for whom they feel an undiminished affection. Thus all men share in the misfortune, and this weighs on King Priyadarśī's mind.

[Moreover, there is no country except that of the Yōnas (that is, the Greeks) where Brahmin and Buddhist ascetics do not exist] and there is no place where men are not attached to one faith or another.

Therefore, even if the number of people who were killed or who died or who were carried away in the Kaliṅga war had been only one one-hundredth or one one-thousandth of what it actually was, this would still have weighed on the King's mind.

King Priyadarśī now thinks that even a person who wrongs him must be forgiven for wrongs that can be forgiven.

1. **Kaliṅga:** the modern state of Orissa on the east coast of India.
2. **King Priyadarśī:** Ashoka's name for himself, meaning "Beloved of the Gods."
3. **Dharma:** a complex term with many shades of meaning, involving piety, morality, ethics, order, duty, mutual understanding, justice, and peace.

Chapter 5

International

Religious

Communities

(300 B.C.E.–

800 C.E.)

King Priyadarśī seeks to induce even the forest peoples who have come under his dominion [that is, primitive peoples in the remote sections of the conquered territory] to adopt this way of life and this ideal. He reminds them, however, that he exercises the power to punish, despite his repentance, in order to induce them to desist from their crimes and escape execution.

For King Priyadarśī desires security, self-control, impartiality, and cheerfulness for all living creatures.

King Priyadarśī considers moral conquest [that is, conquest by Dharma, *Dharma-vijaya*] the most important conquest. He has achieved this moral conquest repeatedly both here and among the peoples living beyond the borders of his kingdom. . . .

Wherever conquest is achieved by Dharma, it produces satisfaction. Satisfaction is firmly established by conquest by Dharma [since it generates no opposition of conquered and conqueror]. Even satisfaction, however, is of little importance. King Priyadarśī attaches value ultimately only to consequences of action in the other world.

This edict on Dharma has been inscribed so that my sons and great-grandsons who may come after me should not think new conquests worth achieving. If they do conquer, let them take pleasure in moderation and mild punishments. Let them consider moral conquest the only true conquest.

This is good, here and hereafter. Let their pleasure be pleasure in morality [*Dharma-rati*]. For this alone is good, here and hereafter. . . .

My highest officials, who have authority over large numbers of people, will expound and spread the precepts of Dharma. I have instructed the provincial governors, too, who are in charge of many hundred thousand people, concerning how to guide people devoted to Dharma.

King Priyadarśī says:

Having come to this conclusion, therefore, I have erected pillars proclaiming Dharma. I have appointed officers charged with the spread of Dharma, called *Dharma-mahāmātras*. I have issued proclamations on Dharma. . . .

King Priyadarśī says:

My officers charged with the spread of Dharma are occupied with various kinds of services beneficial to ascetics and householders, and they are empowered to concern themselves with all sects. I have ordered some of them to look after the affairs of the Saṁgha [the Buddhist religious orders], some to take care of the Brahmin and Ājīvika ascetics, some to work among the Nirgranthas [the Jaina monks], and some among the various other religious sects.

King Priyadarśī honors men of all faiths, members of religious orders and laymen alike, with gifts and various marks of esteem. Yet he does not value either gifts or honors as much as growth in the qualities essential to religion in men of all faiths.

[116]

This growth may take many forms, but its root is in guarding one's speech to avoid extolling one's own faith and disparaging the faith of others improperly or, when the occasion is appropriate, immoderately.

The faiths of others all deserve to be honored for one reason or another. By honoring them, one exalts one's own faith and at the same time performs a service to the faith of others. By acting otherwise, one injures one's own faith and also does disservice to that of others. For if a man extols his own faith and disparages another because of devotion to his own and because he wants to glorify it, he seriously injures his own faith.

Therefore concord alone is commendable, for through concord men may learn and respect the conception of Dharma accepted by others.

King Priyadarśī desires men of all faiths to know each other's doctrines and to acquire sound doctrines. Those who are attached to their particular faiths should be told that King Priyadarśī does not value gifts or honors as much as growth in the qualities essential to religion in men of all faiths. . . .

Aśoka [Ashoka], Beloved of the Gods, issues the following proclamation:

For more than two and a half years, I have been a lay disciple [*upāsaka*] of the Buddha. More than a year ago, I visited the Saṁgha [the Buddhist religious orders], and since then I have been energetic in my efforts. . . .

The Saṁgha of the monks and the Saṁgha of the nuns have each been united to continue united as long as my sons and great-grandsons rule and as long as the sun and moon shine.

The monk or nun who disrupts the Saṁgha shall be required to put on white robes [instead of the customary yellow][4] and to live in non-residence (*anabasasi*). It is my desire that the Saṁgha be united and endure forever.

Everywhere in my dominions local, provincial, and state officials shall make a tour of their districts every five years to proclaim the following precepts of Dharma as well as to transact other business:

Obedience to mother and father; liberality to friends, acquaintances, relatives, priests, and ascetics; abstention from killing living creatures; and moderation in spending money and acquiring possessions are all meritorious.

---

4. **to put on white robes:** to leave the order of monks or nuns.

[117]

Chapter 5
International
Religious
Communities
(300 B.C.E.–
800 C.E.)

2. Ashokan Pillar with a Single-Lion Capital at Vaishali, India

Source 3 from John S. Strong, The Legend of King Aśoka: A Study and Translation of the Aśokāvadāna *(Princeton: Princeton University Press, 1983), pp. 234–236. © 1983 Princeton University Press. Reprinted by permission of Princeton University Press.*

3. From the *Asokavadana*

Not long after King Aśoka had come to have faith in the Teaching of the Buddha, he started honoring Buddhist monks, throwing himself at their feet wherever he saw them, in a crowd, or in a deserted place.

Now Aśoka had a minister named Yaśas, and although he had the utmost faith in the Blessed One,[5] he said, one day, to the king: "Your majesty, you ought not to prostrate yourself before wandering mendicants of every caste, and the Buddhist monks do come from all four castes."

To this Aśoka did not immediately respond. Sometime later, however, he told all his ministers that he needed to have the heads of various sorts of creatures, and he asked one of them to bring him the head of such and such an animal, and another to bring him the head of another animal, and so on. Finally, he ordered Yaśas to bring him the head of a human being.

Now when the ministers had gathered all these heads, Aśoka ordered them to go to the market place and sell them. Soon, all of the heads had been sold, except Yaśas's human head that no one would buy. Aśoka then told Yaśas to give his head away, but, even though it was gratis, still no one would take it.

Ashamed at his lack of success, Yaśas came back to Aśoka and said:

O king, the heads of cows, asses, sheep, deer, and birds—
  all were sold to people for a price;
but no one would take this worthless human head,
  even free of charge.

"Why is that?" Aśoka asked his minister, "why wouldn't anyone accept this human head?"

"Because it disgusted them," Yaśas replied.

"Oh?" said the king, "is it just this head that is disgusting or the heads of all human beings?"

"The heads of all humans," answered Yaśas.

"What?" said Aśoka, "is my head disgusting as well?"

Out of fear, Yaśas did not want to tell him the real fact of the matter, but the king ordered him to speak the truth, and finally he answered: "Yes."

After forcing this admission out of his minister, Aśoka then revealed to him his purpose in doing so: "You, sir, are obsessed with matters of form and superiority, and because of this attachment you seek to dissuade me from bowing down at the feet of the monks."

5. **the Blessed One:** the Buddha.

Chapter 5

International

Religious

Communities

(300 B.C.E.–

800 C.E.)

But if I acquire some merit
by bowing down a head so disgusting
that no one on earth would take it,
even free of charge,
what harm is there in that?
You, sir, look at the caste (jāti)
and not at the inherent qualities of the monks.
Haughty, deluded, and obsessed with caste,
you harm yourself and others.
When you invite someone,
or when it is time for a wedding,
then you should investigate the matter of caste,
but not at the time of Dharma.
For Dharma is a question of qualities,
and qualities do not reflect caste.
If a man of prominent family
happens to resort to vice,
the world censures him.
How then should one not honor virtue
when displayed by a man of low birth?
It is on account of men's minds
that their bodies are reviled or honored;
the minds of the Buddhist monks are pure,
therefore I honor them.

Source 4 from (a) Henry Bettenson, ed., Documents of the Christian Church *(Oxford: Oxford University Press, 1963), p. 15; (b–f) Theodosian Code, trans. and rpt. Maude Aline Huttman,* The Establishment of Christianity and the Proscription of Paganism, *Columbia University Studies in History, Economics and Public Law, no. 60 (New York: AMS Press, 1967), pp. 152, 154, 161–162, 163, 164.*

4. Constantinian Edicts

A. *EDICT OF TOLERATION,* 311

Among our other regulations to promote the lasting good of the community we have hitherto endeavoured to restore a universal conformity to the ancient institutions and public order of the Romans; and in particular it has been our aim to bring back to a right disposition the Christians who had abandoned the religion of their fathers. . . . 3. After the publication of our edict ordering the Christians to conform to the ancient institutions, many of them were brought to order through fear, while many were exposed to danger. 4. Nevertheless, since many still persist in their opinions, and since we have observed that they now neither show due reverence to the gods nor worship their own God, we therefore, with our wonted clemency in extending pardon to all, are pleased to grant indulgence to these men, allowing Christians the right to exist again and to set up their places of worship; provided always that they do not offend against public order. 5. We will in a further instruction explain to the magistrates how they should conduct themselves in this matter. In return for this indulgence of ours it will be the duty of Christians to pray to God for our recovery, for the public weal and for their own; that the state may be preserved from danger on every side, and that they themselves may dwell safely in their homes.

B. OCT. 31, 313 (?)

The Emperor Constantine Augustus. We have learned that the clergy of the Catholic Church are so harrassed by a faction of heretics as to be burdened with nominations to office and common public business, contrary to the exemptions granted to them. Wherefore, it is ordered that if your gravity[6] should find anyone thus annoyed, another man is to be substituted for him, and from henceforth, men of the religion above mentioned are to be protected from wrongs of this kind.

C. MARCH 21, 315 (316?)

The same [Constantine] Augustus to Eumelius.[7] If any one, on account of the crimes in which he is detected, should be condemned to the arena or the mines, by no means let him be branded in the face, although both on his hands and legs the penalty of his condemnation may be marked in a single brand; while the face which is formed in the likeness of heavenly beauty shall not be dishonored.

D. MAY 15, 319

The same [Constantine] Augustus to the People.

We prohibit all soothsayers, priests of prophecy, and those who are wont to administer such rites, from entering a private house, or, under the guise of friendship, from crossing another's threshold. And if they despise this law penalties shall be meted out to them. You, who think this applies to yourselves, go to the public altars and shrines, and celebrate your customary ceremonies, for we do not forbid the full services of ancient tradition from being conducted in the day time.

---

6. It is unclear to whom this edict was addressed.
7. **Eumelius:** the Vicar of Africa.

E. DEC. 17, 320 (321?)

The Emperor Constantine to Maximus.[8]

If a part of our palace, or any other public building, be struck by lightning, let the customs of the old religion be observed and the haruspices[9] be consulted for the meaning of the omen, and let their words be very carefully brought together and reported to us. Permission for the practice of the custom should also be granted to others, provided that no household sacrifices are made, for these are specifically forbidden.

F. JULY 3, 321

The same [Constantine] Augustus to the People.

Every man, when dying, shall have the right to bequeath as much of his property as he desires to the holy and venerable Catholic Church. And such wills are not to be broken.

Source 5 from Eusebius, Life of Constantine the Great, *trans. Ernest Cushing Richardson, Library of Nicene and Post-Nicene Fathers, second series, vol. 1. (Grand Rapids, Mich.: Eerdmans, 1979), pp. 489, 490–491, 494, 513–514, 523, 525–526, 534, 544, 545, 546.*

5. Selections from Eusebius, *Life of Constantine*

Thus then the God of all, the Supreme Governor of the whole universe, by his own will appointed Constantine, the descendant of so renowned a parent, to be prince and sovereign: so that, while others have been raised to this distinction by the election of their fellow-men, he is the only one to whose elevation no mortal may boast of having contributed. . . .

Being convinced, however, that he [Constantine] needed some more powerful aid than his military forces could afford him, on account of the wicked and magical enchantments which were so diligently practiced by the tyrant,[10] he sought Divine assistance, deeming the possession of arms and a numerous soldiery of secondary importance, but believing the co-operating power of Deity invincible and not to be shaken. He considered, therefore, on what God he might rely for protection and assistance. . . .

8. **Maximus:** the Prefect of the City of Rome.

9. **haruspices:** a traditional Roman religious authority who interpreted the meaning of lightning and other natural events.

10. **the tyrant:** referring to two of Constantine's rivals for authority in the empire, Severus and Galerius.

Accordingly he called on him with earnest prayer and supplications that he would reveal to him who he was, and stretch forth his right hand to help him in his present difficulties. And while he was thus praying with fervent entreaty, a most marvelous sign appeared to him from heaven, the account of which it might have been hard to believe had it been related by any other person. But since the victorious emperor himself long afterwards declared it to the writer of this history,[11] when he was honored with his acquaintance and society, and confirmed his statement by an oath, who could hesitate to accredit the relation, especially since the testimony of after-time has established its truth? He said that about noon, when the day was already beginning to decline, he saw with his own eyes the trophy of a cross of light in the heavens, above the sun, and bearing the inscription, CONQUER BY THIS. At this sight he himself was struck with amazement, and his whole army also, which followed him on this expedition, and witnessed the miracle.

He said, moreover, that he doubted within himself what the import of this apparition could be. And while he continued to ponder and reason on its meaning, night suddenly came on; then in his sleep the Christ of God appeared to him with the same sign which he had seen in the heavens, and commanded him to make a likeness of that sign which he had seen in the heavens, and to use it as a safeguard in all engagements with his enemies.

At dawn of day he arose, and communicated the marvel to his friends: and then, calling together the workers in gold and precious stones, he sat in the midst of them, and described to them the figure of the sign he had seen, bidding them represent it in gold and precious stones. And this representation I myself have had an opportunity of seeing.

Now it was made in the following manner. A long spear, overlaid with gold, formed the figure of the cross by means of a transverse bar laid over it. On the top of the whole was fixed a wreath of gold and precious stones; and within this, the symbol of the Saviour's name, two letters indicating the name of Christ by means of its initial characters, the letter P being intersected by X in its centre: and these letters the emperor was in the habit of wearing on his helmet at a later period. . . .[12]

Thus the pious emperor, glorying in the confession of the victorious cross, proclaimed the Son of God to the Romans with great boldness of testimony. And the inhabitants of the city, one and all, senate and people, reviving, as it were, from the pressure of a bitter and tyrannical domination, seemed to enjoy purer rays of light, and to be born again into a fresh and new life. All the nations, too, as far as the limit of the western ocean, being set free from the calamities which had heretofore beset them, and gladdened by joyous festivals, ceased not to praise him as the victorious, the pious, the common benefactor: all, indeed, with

11. that is, Eusebius.

12. This sign—a cross and the first two letters in Christ's name on the top of a long pole—was called the *labarum*.

Chapter 5
International
Religious
Communities
(300 B.C.E.–
800 C.E.)

one voice and one mouth, declared that Constantine had appeared by the grace of God as a general blessing to mankind. . . .

The emperor also personally inviting the society of God's ministers, distinguished them with the highest possible respect and honor, showing them favor in deed and word as persons consecrated to the service of his God. Accordingly, they were admitted to his table, though mean in their attire and outward appearance; yet not so in his estimation, since he thought he saw not the man as seen by the vulgar eye, but the God in him. He made them also his companions in travel, believing that He whose servants they were would thus help him. Besides this, he gave from his own private resources costly benefactions to the churches of God, both enlarging and heightening the sacred edifices, and embellishing the august sanctuaries of the church with abundant offerings.

He likewise distributed money largely to those who were in need, and besides these showing himself philanthropist and benefactor even to the heathen, who had no claim on him; and even for the beggars in the forum, miserable and shiftless, he provided, not with money only, or necessary food, but also decent clothing. . . . In short, as the sun, when he rises upon the earth, liberally imparts his rays of light to all, so did Constantine, proceeding at early dawn from the imperial palace, and rising as it were with the heavenly luminary, impart the rays of his own beneficence to all who came into his presence. It was scarcely possible to be near him without receiving some benefit, nor did it ever happen that any who had expected to obtain his assistance were disappointed in their hope. . . .

> [*In an edict to the provinces,*
> *Constantine stated:*]

"My own desire is, for the common good of the world and the advantage of all mankind, that thy people should enjoy a life of peace and undisturbed concord. Let those, therefore, who still delight in error, be made welcome to the same degree of peace and tranquillity which they have who believe. For it may be that this restoration of equal privileges to all will prevail to lead them into the straight path. Let no one molest another, but let every one do as his soul desires. Only let men of sound judgment be assured of this, that those only can live a life of holiness and purity, whom thou callest to a reliance on thy holy laws. With regard to those who will hold themselves aloof from us, let them have, if they please, their temples of lies: *we* have the glorious edifice of thy truth, which thou hast given us as our native home. We pray, however, that they too may receive the same blessing, and thus experience that heartfelt joy which unity of sentiment inspires. . . ."

[*In 325, Constantine called the Council
of Nicaea and addressed the bishops
assembled-there as follows.*]

"[I]n my judgment, intestine strife within the Church of God is far more evil and dangerous than any kind of war or conflict; and these our differences appear to me more grievous than any outward trouble. . . .

"Delay not, then, dear friends: delay not, ye ministers of God, and faithful servants of him who is our common Lord and Saviour: begin from this moment to discard the causes of that disunion which has existed among you, and remove the perplexities of controversy by embracing the principles of peace. For by such conduct you will at the same time be acting in a manner most pleasing to the supreme God, and you will confer an exceeding favor on me who am your fellow-servant. . . ."

All these things the emperor diligently performed to the praise of the saving power of Christ, and thus made it his constant aim to glorify his Saviour God. On the other hand he used every means to rebuke the superstitious errors of the heathen. Hence the entrances of their temples in the several cities were left exposed to the weather, being stripped of their doors at his command; the tiling of others was removed, and their roofs destroyed. . . .

How deeply his soul was impressed by the power of divine faith may be understood from the circumstance that he directed his likeness to be stamped on the golden coin of the empire with the eyes uplifted as in the posture of prayer to God: and this money became current throughout the Roman world. His portrait also at full length was placed over the entrance gates of the palaces in some cities, the eyes upraised to heaven, and the hands outspread as if in prayer. . . .

With regard to those who were as yet ignorant of divine truth, he provided by a second statute that they should appear on each Lord's day on an open plain near the city, and there, at a given signal, offer to God with one accord a prayer which they had previously learnt. He admonished them that their confidence should not rest in their spears, or armor, or bodily strength, but that they should acknowledge the supreme God as the giver of every good, and of victory itself. . . . The emperor himself prescribed the prayer to be used by all his troops. . . .

Hence it was not without reason that once, on the occasion of his entertaining a company of bishops, he let fall the expression, "that he himself too was a bishop," addressing them in my hearing in the following words: "You are bishops whose jurisdiction is within the Church: I also am a bishop, ordained by God to overlook whatever is external to the Church." And truly his measures corresponded with his words; for he watched over his subjects with an episcopal [as a bishop] care, and exhorted them as far as in him lay to follow a godly life.

Chapter 5
International
Religious
Communities
(300 B.C.E.–
800 C.E.)

Source 6: Top photograph from the Ashmolean Museum, Oxford. Bottom photograph is Courtesy of the Trustees of the British Museum.

6. Two Constantinian Coins

Source 7 from A. J. Arberry, The Koran Interpreted *(Oxford: Oxford University Press, 1964). Reprinted by permission of HarperCollins Publishers Limited.*

7. Selections from the Qur'an

O you who believe! Obey God and obey the Prophet and those of you who hold authority.   (Sura 4:59)

God has promised those of you who believe and do wholesome deeds that He will surely make you successors in the land, as he made successors of those before you, and He will surely establish for them as their service (*dīn*) what He approves for them, and exchange for them, after their fear, security: "They shall serve Me, not associating with Me anything."   (Sura 24:55)

There is no compulsion in matters of faith. Distinct now is the way of guidance from error. He who turns away from the forces of evil and believes in God, will surely hold fast to a handle that is strong and unbreakable, for God hears all and knows everything.   (Sura 2:256)

Say (O Muslims): We believe in God and that which is revealed unto us and that which was revealed unto Abraham and Ishmael and Isaac and Jacob, and the tribes, and that which Moses and Jesus received, and that which the Prophets received from their Lord. We make no distinction between any of them, and unto Him we have surrendered.   (Sura 2:136)

Source 8 from (a) Al-Muttaqi, Kanz-al-'Ummāl, *in Bernard Lewis, ed. and trans.,* Islam from the Prophet Muhammad to the Capture of Constantinople, *vol. 1 (New York: Oxford University Press, 1987), p. 150; (b) Al-Khaṭīb al-Tibrīzī,* Niches of Lamps, *in John Alden Williams, ed.,* Themes of Islamic Civilization *(Berkeley: University of California Press, 1971), pp. 65–67; (c) An-Nawawī,* The Forty Traditions, *in Arthur Jeffrey, ed.,* A Reader on Islam: Passages from Standard Arabic Writings Illustrative of the Beliefs and Practices of Muslims *(Gravenhage: Mouton and Company, 1962), p. 154.*

8. Selections from the Hadith

a. I charge the Caliph after me to fear God, and I commend the community of the Muslims to him, to respect the great among them and have pity on the small, to honor the learned among them, not to strike them and humiliate them, not to oppress them and drive them to unbelief, not to close his doors to them and allow the strong to devour the weak.

Chapter 5

International

Religious

Communities

(300 B.C.E.–

800 C.E.)

b. Bukhārī and Muslim, from Abū Hurayra: The Messenger of God, may God's blessing and peace be on him, said "Whoever obeys me obeys God, and whoever disobeys me disobeys God. Whoever obeys the Commander obeys me, and he who disobeys him disobeys me."

Muslim, from Umm al-Ḥuṣayn: The Messenger, may God bless him and give him peace, said "Even if a mutilated slave is made your commander, and he leads you in accord with the Book of God, hear him and obey."

Bukhārī, from Anas: The Messenger of God, the blessing of God and peace be upon him, said "Hear and obey, though an Abyssinian slave with a head like a raisin be placed over you."

Bukhārī and Muslim, from 'Umar's son: The Messenger of God—God's bene-diction and peace upon him—said "Hearing and obeying are incumbent on a Muslim man, so long as he is not ordered to disobey God. When he is ordered to do that, there is no hearing it and no obeying." 'Alī reported a simi-lar tradition.'

Bukhārī and Muslim, from 'Umar's son: The Messenger said—may God give him peace and blessing—"Is not each of you a shepherd, who must answer for his flock? The Imām of the people is a shepherd, and is answerable for his flock. A man is the shepherd of the people in his house, and he is answerable for his flock. A woman is shepherdess of her husband's house and children, and is answerable for them, and a slave is the shepherd of his master's wealth and is answerable for that. Thus each of you is a shepherd, and each of you is responsible for his flock."'

Muslim, from 'Arfaja: I heard the Messenger of God, peace and God's bless-ing be upon him, say "If anyone comes to you when you are united under one man, and tries to split you or divide your Umma, then kill him."'

Bayhaqī, from 'Umar's son: The Prophet, God bless him and give him peace, said "The Government (*al-Sultān*) is the shadow of God on the earth; all of His servants who are oppressed shall turn to it. When it is just, it shall be rewarded, and the flock must be grateful. When it is tyrannical, the burden is upon it, and the flock must be patient."'

c. From Abu Najih al-Irbad ibn Sariya, with whom may God be pleased, who said: The Messenger of God, may God's blessing and peace be upon him, preached a sermon whereby our hearts were made afraid and our eyes dropped tears, so we said: "O Messenger of God, it is as though this were a farewell sermon, so give us a testamentary exhortation." He said: "My testamentary exhortation to you is that you have a pious fear of God, magnified and exalted be He; that you hearken and obey, even though it should be a slave who is appointed over you. He among you who lives long enough will see great disagreement, so take care to observe my custom and the custom of the Rightly Guided Caliphs [that is, the first four: Abu Bakr, Umar, Uthman, and Ali], holding on to them with your molar teeth. Beware of matters newly introduced, for every innovation is an error." So Abu Dawud relates it, as does al-Tirmidhi, who says, "An excellent, sound Prophetic tradition."

Source 9 from Ibn Ishaq, The Life of Muhammad, Apostle of Allah, *ed. and trans. Michael Edwards (London: The Folio Society, 1964), pp. 35, 36–37, 41, 54, 65, 74, 104, 150, 156–157, 165. Copyright © 1964. Permission of the Royal Asiatic Society, Great Britain and Ireland.*

9. Selections from Ibn Ishaq, *The Life of Muhammad, Apostle of Allah*

When Muhammad was forty years old Allah sent him as a prophet of mercy to the people of the visible and of the invisible worlds, and to all mankind. . . .

Every year the apostle of Allah spent a month praying at Hira and fed the poor who came to him; and when he returned to Mecca he walked round the Kaba[13] seven or more times, as it pleased Allah, before entering his own house. In the month of Ramadan,[14] in the year when Allah designed to bestow grace upon him, the apostle of Allah went to [Mount] Hira as usual, and his family accompanied him. In the night the angel Gabriel came with the command of Allah. The apostle of Allah later said, "He came while I was asleep, with a cloth of brocade whereon there was writing, and he said, 'Read.' I replied, 'I cannot read it.' Then he pressed the cloth on me till I thought I was dying; he released his hold and said, 'Read.' I replied, 'I cannot read it.' And he pressed me again with it, till I thought I was dying. Then he loosed his hold of me and said, 'Read.' I replied, 'I cannot read it.' Once more he pressed me and said, 'Read.' Then I asked, 'What shall I read?' And I said this because I feared he would press me again. Then he said, 'Read in the name of the Lord thy creator; who created man from a drop of blood. Read, thy Lord is the most bountiful, who taught by means of the pen, taught man what he knew not.' Accordingly I read these words, and he finished his task and departed from me. I awoke from my sleep, and felt as if words had been graven on my heart.

"Afterwards I went out, and when I was on the centre of the mountain, I heard a voice from heaven, saying, 'O Muhammad! Thou art the prophet of Allah, and I am Gabriel.' I raised my head to look at the sky, and lo! I beheld Gabriel in the shape of a man with extended wings, standing in the firmament, with his feet touching the ground. And he said again, 'O Muhammad! Thou art the apostle of Allah, and I am Gabriel.' I continued to gaze at him, neither advancing nor retreating. Then I turned my face away from him to other parts of the sky, but in whatever direction I looked I saw him in the same form. I remained thus, neither advancing nor retreating, and Khadija [Muhammad's first wife] sent messengers to search for me. They went as

---

13. **Kaba:** a house containing a black stone venerated by Arabs before Muhammad, which was retained as the most holy place in Islam.

14. **Ramadan:** ninth month of the Muslim lunar year, which came to be viewed as holy because the first of Muhammad's revelations occurred during this month.

[129]

Chapter 5

International

Religious

Communities

(300 B.C.E.–

800 C.E.)

far as the highest part of Mecca and again returned to her, while I remained standing on the same spot, until the angel departed from me and I returned to my family. . . ."

Soon several men and women had made their profession of Islam and it was much discussed in Mecca. Then Allah commanded his apostle to make public the revelation and to invite the people to accept it; hitherto, for the three years since his first revelation, it had been kept secret by the apostle. Allah said to him, "Publish that which thou hast been commanded, and turn away from the idolaters. . . ."

The apostle of Allah never failed to attempt the conversion of any man of note or position who came to Mecca. . . .

> [*Muhammad and his followers left*
> *Mecca for Medina.*]

The apostle of Allah remained in Medina until the following year when his mosque and his dwellings were built. He worked on them with his own hands to encourage his followers. Islam in Medina soon became so complete that only a handful of houses remained whose tenants had not made profession of Islam.

> [*After a defeat of Meccan forces,*
> *Muhammad said:*]

"'. . . Whenever you win plunder, a fifth shall belong to Allah and His apostle, and his kindred, and orphans, and the poor, and the traveller.

"'. . . When you meet an army in battle, stand firm and remember Allah, that you may prosper; and do not quarrel, lest My cause should suffer. . . . But if they incline to peace, do you also incline to peace; and trust in Allah, for He heareth and knoweth all things. . . .'"

The apostle sent out expeditions to the surrounding territory to invite the people to Allah, but not to kill. . . . The apostle of Allah specially exhorted the rich to furnish money and beasts of burden and they did so, hoping for the eternal reward; Uthman was the most liberal of them, and the apostle said, "Allah! Be pleased with Uthman; for I am pleased with him!"

When the apostle of Allah had conquered Mecca and completed the campaign of Tabuk, and when al-Taif[15] had surrendered and made profession of Islam, deputations of Arabs arrived from all directions. This, the ninth year after the Hijra, was called the Year of Deputations. The Arabs had delayed professing Islam until they saw how the affair between the apostle and the Quraysh[16] would end, because the Quraysh were the leaders of men, the people of the Kaba and of the sacred territory, and they were acknowledged as the

15. **Tabuk** and **al-Taif:** cities in the northern part of Arabia.
16. **Quraysh:** Muhammad's tribe, the leading tribe in Mecca.

descendants of Ishmael, son of Abraham. Not one chief of the Arabs denied this. But when Mecca was conquered and the Quraysh submitted to Islam, the Arabs knew that they themselves were not strong enough to wage war or to show enmity to the apostle of Allah. So they entered into the religion of Allah in droves, arriving from all directions.

Source 10 from Abū Yūsuf, Kitāb al-Kharāj, *in John Alden Williams, ed.,* Themes of Islamic Civilization *(Berkeley: University of California Press, 1971), pp. 68–69, 72.*

10. From Abu Yusuf (d. A.H. 182/798 C.E.), *Book of Land-tax*

"I have heard," says Abū Yūsuf, "from Ismāʿīl ibn Abī Khālid, on the authority of Zubayd ibn al-Ḥārith, that when death was drawing near to Abū Bakr, he sent for ʿUmar to make him the Caliph, his successor, and people said 'Will you appoint as Caliph over us this hard, harsh man to be hard and harsh to us? What will you say to your Lord when you meet Him having appointed ʿUmar over us?' He said 'Would you frighten me with my Lord? I shall tell Him "God, I have appointed over them the best of Thy people!" ' Then he sent for ʿUmar and said 'I shall give you a piece of advice such that if you follow it, nothing will be dearer to you than your death when it comes, and if you do not follow it, nothing will be more hateful to you than the death you shall not escape. You have obligations to God at night that He will not accept from you by day, and obligations by day that He will not accept at night, and a work of supererogation is not accepted until after the performance of the obligatory works. The scales on Judgement Day will not weigh lighter for anyone than for those who sought light things, and they will not weigh heavier for anyone than for the man who sought justice in the world. . . . I have only appointed you my successor thinking of those whom I leave behind me. For I was a Companion of the Prophet, and saw one who preferred us to himself, and our people to his own family, so that we should give to them from the abundance of what is given to us. You have been my companion, and you have seen that I have only followed the path of him who was before me, and the first thing I counsel you against, ʿUmar, is your self, for every self has selfish desires, and if one gives in to one of them, it demands another. Beware also of those persons among the Companions of the Messenger of God who have filled their bellies and raised their eyes. Every man of them loves himself, and all of them will be in perplexity if one of them stumbles. Take care that that one is not you. They will never cease to fear you so long as you fear God, or cease to go straight with you so long as your way is straight. That is my counsel to you, and now I wish you farewell.' "

Chapter 5
International
Religious
Communities
(300 B.C.E.–
800 C.E.)

When 'Umar was dying, he left this advice: "I advise my successor to fear God, and to respect the rights and the merits of the first emigrants to Medina; and as to the Anṣār, who lived in Medina, and in the Faith, to accept their good deeds and to be indulgent to the bad among them. As to the people of the garrison towns, they are the help of Islam, the fury of the enemy, and the bringers of wealth, so he should take only their superfluity, and by their agreement. I advise him as to the beduins that they are the source of the Arabs, and the raw stuff of Islam, and he should take only a little of their possessions, to return to the poorest among them. As to the protected peoples, let him fulfill his agreement with them and fight their enemies and not burden them beyond their endurance. . . ."

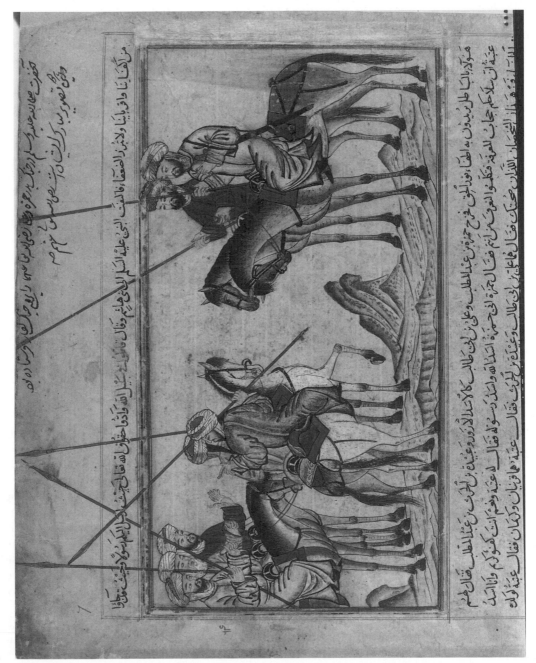

Source 11 from The Nasser D. Khalili Collection of Islamic Art. MSS 727, folio 66a.

11. Muhammad Addresses Ali and Other Leaders Before the Battle of Badr, from Rashid al-Din, *Jami'al-tawarikh*

Chapter 5
International
Religious
Communities
(300 B.C.E.–
800 C.E.)

QUESTIONS TO CONSIDER

Before you begin to make specific comparisons between the leaders and their methods of advancing their religious commitments, you should probably step back a minute and think about the different types of sources you have used. In some cases, there are quite comparable sources for two cases, but not for the third. For example, it is clear that both Ashoka and Constantine ordered the edicts included in the evidence to be inscribed or issued; we have nothing directly comparable for Muhammad. Our ability to compare the edicts of Ashoka and Constantine stops with the texts themselves, however, for though we have quite a bit of evidence about how Constantine and his successors enforced his edicts and proclamations, we have no way of knowing what impact Ashoka's edicts had on his actual reign. The language in which Ashoka's edicts were written ceased to be spoken shortly after his reign, so subsequent generations could not read them; in fact, the script in which they were written was deciphered for the first time only in 1837. Unlike the stories of Constantine told by Eusebius and others, the legends that grew up about Ashoka, including the one you read here, did so without reference to his actual edicts; people claimed the inscriptions referred to events in the legends, but they had no way of actually reading them the way Roman Christians could the laws and proclamations of Constantine.

For another example of similarity, the biographies of Eusebius and Ibn Ishaq are more like each other than the *Asokavadana*. All of these contain material that may be in the realm of legend, but we can check both Eusebius and Ibn Ishaq against other sources, something that is not possible for the *Asokavadana*. Eusebius in particular also notes his source when he is telling something his readers may have difficulty believing; in the section on Constantine's vision of the cross, for example, he stresses that Constantine himself told him about this, using "he said" rather than relating the story directly the way most of the biography is written. This same noting of sources appears even more prominently in the hadith (Source 8), where it serves to stress the authenticity of the words of Muhammad. Most of the hadith were actually written in the two centuries after Muhammad's life, when Islam had already split into Sunni and Shi'ite factions, and they are interpreted so as to argue one point of view or another. As you can see, for example, Source 8c gives a Sunni view of Muhammad's last words.

Keeping the limitations of our sources in mind, then, you can begin to compare the actions and ideas of the individuals and groups. Ashoka, Constantine, and Muhammad all had clear conversion experiences. How would you compare these and the actions that resulted directly from them? How do these experiences shape their attitudes toward military conquest as a means of expanding a religious community? What humanitarian aims develop after the conversions, and how do they seek to achieve these?

All of these leaders had to deal with dissenters—both people who followed other religious traditions and those within their own religion who disagreed with them. How did the leaders enforce their own views? What did they advise regarding the toleration of those who disagreed? How important was unity within their religious community to these leaders? Ashoka and Constantine each had to foster a relationship with a body of clergy that already existed, the Buddhist sangha and the Christian bishops. How would you characterize their relationship with these clerics? Where did ultimate authority lie in terms of making religious policy? (For some of these questions, the sources may give contradictory information, and you may wish to turn to your textbook for further information, or else simply note the contradiction.)

The sources for each of the three groups make explicit reference to the conflict between social status and religious status or authority. How do the leaders treat individuals of modest social status but high religious or moral status? What advice do they give to their followers in this regard?

The relationship between church and state is much discussed in the contemporary American political scene. What do these sources reveal about this relationship in these three religious traditions? In the minds of these leaders, should the religious community and the political community be unified, related, or separate?

Though all of these sources describe the actions of real individuals, they also convey what each tradition regarded as qualities of the ideal ruler. How would you compare the ideal ruler in these three traditions? What qualities would ideal religious communities exhibit under the leadership of such individuals? From your initial lists and comparisons, you are now ready to answer the central questions in this chapter: How did political leaders within Buddhism, Christianity, and Islam encourage the growth of their chosen religious community? What differences and similarities do you see in their actions and in what they viewed as most important in the lives of these communities?

EPILOGUE

The three religions we have explored in this chapter are three of the four largest religions found in the world today: Buddhism has around 376 million adherents, Christianity 2.1 billion, and Islam 1.5 billion.[17] (The fourth major world religion is Hinduism with 900 million adherents, though it is more concentrated in certain geographic areas than the other three.) All three of these continue to be missionary religions; that is, they seek new converts just as they did in the days of Ashoka, Constantine, and Muhammad. Some of the issues we have explored in this

17. These numbers represent 2001 statistics and come from www.adherents.com. There are, of course, many ways to count allegiance to religion, and the numbers change every day, so these are estimates; adherents.com has an excellent discussion of these issues.

Chapter 5

International

Religious

Communities

(300 B.C.E.–

800 C.E.)

chapter continue to be matters of concern or over the centuries have become even more complicated.

For example, each of these religions has splintered further since the periods we focused on in this chapter. Shortly after Ashoka's reign, Buddhism split into two main groups, Mahayana and Theravada (sometimes called Hinayana), and then continued to divide into a number of different sects. Christianity gradually divided into two main churches, Roman Catholicism and Eastern Orthodoxy, and the Roman Catholic Church was further split by the Protestant Reformation in the sixteenth century. New Christian denominations are created every year as groups choose to emphasize certain aspects of Christian teaching. The rift between Shi'ites and Sunnis was only the first of many within Islam, for Shi'ites themselves divided into two major groups, and other sects developed as well. Thus the unity sought by the leaders we have investigated has not been achieved, although there are movements within each of these three religions today to heal internal schisms or at least to downplay them in a desire for tolerance and understanding.

As these three religions have expanded, they have continued to confront the issue of the relationship between church and state, between the religious and political community. In some cases, the relationship is extremely intimate, in that all three are official state religions in some countries of the world. This role may have a widely differing impact, however. In some of the countries of the Middle East, for example, Islam

structures almost all aspects of life, whereas in some European countries that are officially Christian, few people attend church and the church has little impact on national policies. Even in those countries where the power of the state church is extremely strong, there are still disputes about overlapping or conflicting authority and the proper role of religious leaders: Should they be spiritual guides or heads of state?

On the other hand, many adherents of these religions live in countries where their religion is not the one sanctioned by the state, or where there is no official state religion, such as the United States. They, and their religious leaders, thus have to address the issues we have explored in this chapter in a different way. What should the relationship between the religious and political communities be in a country of religious pluralism? How should a person's allegiance to a country be weighed against allegiance to a religion? What are the limits of acceptable diversity within a religious community, and who has the power of exclusion? How do you handle someone who violates what is viewed as God's law in a religious tradition but has broken no state laws? Should there be a line between church and state, between the sacred and profane? Should political leaders follow the path of Ashoka, Constantine, and Muhammad and seek to expand their own religion, or should such crusades be left to those who do not hold public office?

None of these were issues when religion was closely tied to membership in a particular tribe or residence in a particular village, but as religions became international, as they came to be practiced by people over large geographic areas, the questions became pressing and problematic. Conflicts within and between religious communities are some of the most bitter, deadly, and long-lasting in the world today, and the words of Ashoka, carved in stone over two thousand years ago, still bear repeating: "The faiths of others all deserve to be honored for one reason or another. By honoring them, one exalts one's own faith and at the same time performs a service to the faith of others. By acting otherwise, one injures one's own faith and also does disservice to that of others."

CHAPTER SIX

VIKINGS AND POLYNESIANS:

EXPLORING NEW WORLDS

(300–1100)

THE PROBLEM

William Fitzhugh, the curator of a new exhibit on Vikings at the Smithsonian Institution, has recently warned that the historical record has badly distorted our view of early Scandinavians. "Only in the past 20 years or so," he points out, "have archeological and other studies begun to provide information that fleshes out and in some cases contradicts or even replaces the historical record. . . . This contrasts sharply with the early accounts, which were all from Europe, were inevitably based on victims' reports, and were extremely one-sided."[1]

The portrayal of Vikings represents a common historical problem: how

1. William Fitzhugh's remarks appeared in an interview on a *Nova* program on the Vikings, for which a partial transcript has been made available on *Nova*'s web site, **http://www.pbs. org/wgbh/nova/vikings/who.html.**

people who left few or no writings of their own appear in the historical record. The study of history has traditionally been based on evidence gleaned from written sources. But this approach has forced us to view the past almost exclusively from the vantage point of literate people, the ones who kept written records—often a small minority. The narrowness of their perspective, troubling enough with regard to their own societies, becomes highly problematic when they discuss neighbors who were nonliterate or who failed to keep historical records. For they often lacked a complete or dispassionate picture of those whose "history" they presumed to tell.

This chapter addresses the problem of how to deal with these voiceless people of history by looking at two outstanding examples that have begun to attract considerable attention of late, the Vikings and the Polynesians. Both were long relegated to the role of archetypal "barbarians," either as brutal despoilers in the case of the Vikings or as noble savages in the case of the Polynesians. Recently, however, some scholars have begun to argue that both of these seafaring peoples developed advanced maritime technologies that allowed them to carry out significant voyages of discovery, trade, and colonization long before the modern age of Western European exploration began and thus merit greater acknowledgment for their accomplishments.

Most of these findings come from nontraditional methods of historical study. Many depend upon the use of techniques that allow us to interpret the past through "material culture" or physical remains. With these methods, historians not only recover artifacts from the past but deduce from them information about how their makers lived and thought. New ways of studying oral traditions handed down by nonliterate people have also supplied historians with yet another set of tools. Together with recent scientific techniques, these approaches allow us to explore the world of formerly "voiceless" peoples as never before. In this chapter, you will have a chance to compare evidence relating to the Vikings and Polynesians that derives from some of these new approaches as well as from more traditional sources.

The mixed nature of these materials makes this chapter noticeably different from others, and you may be disconcerted at first by some of the sources presented in the Evidence section. Archaeological site plans and tables of scientific data are admittedly unlike traditional written documents. However, historians are turning more to such sources to recover the "material culture" of earlier people. A broad term, material culture refers not just to the physical objects left behind by a society, such as food, clothing, tools, structures, and other artifacts, but the cultural significance with which their creators invested them. When studying peoples like the Vikings and Polynesians who left few or no written records, we have to focus almost entirely upon their material culture to reconstruct their lives. But historians are finding non-literary objects to be equally revealing when dealing with societies that left written records. Learning to work with such materials, therefore, is increasingly important.

Your task in looking over this material is to decide how seriously these new findings need to be taken. That question is not a simple one to resolve, for it involves dealing with a number of other questions as well. First and foremost, of course, is there sufficient evidence to indicate that these peoples did carry out major voyages of discovery and colonization? Second, if they did, what was significant about these achievements from a historical point of view? That is to say, what impact or effect did they have on other peoples, past or present? This last issue raises a still broader question to think about, although the answer is not to be found in the evidence: What value is there in studying people whose experience and feats have long been lost or forgotten?

Chapter 6

Vikings and

Polynesians:

Exploring

New Worlds

(300–1100)

BACKGROUND

Reconsideration of the Vikings' reputation dates from the early 1960s, when the Norwegian Helge Ingstad and his archaeologist wife, Anne Stine Ingstad, discovered the remains of a Scandinavian settlement in North America at L'Anse aux Meadows on the Newfoundland coast of Canada. Although scholars had long known of Icelandic sagas or tales that spoke of Viking visits to a place called *Vinland*, or Wine Land, west of Greenland, they had dismissed them as fanciful. But evidence found at L'Anse aux Meadows revealed that some Vikings did make it to America around the year 1000, nearly five centuries before Columbus's celebrated voyage of 1492. In the years since 1960, further work has shown that the Viking discovery of America was only one part of a vast maritime expansion of Scandinavian people during the years from 750 to 1050, an era that has come to be called the Viking Age. To appreciate the scale of this expansion, which reached from the Caspian Sea to the shores of Labrador, look at the map on page 141.

Before their great expansion began, the Vikings dwelt in southern Scandinavia, where their forebears had settled in late Roman times. An offshoot of Germanic peoples, they were already differentiating into Danes, Norwegians, and Swedes, but they still shared a common language, called Norse, and continued to worship old Germanic gods like Odin, Thor, and Frey. Because of the harsh winters and short growing seasons in their homeland, they could not rely entirely on cereal crops for food

and engaged in herding, hunting, and trapping to survive. Given the territorial demands of this lifestyle, they usually lived dispersed on individual farms or in small hamlets. Political unification was difficult under these circumstances, and regional lords called *Jarls* ruled through local landed elites. Beneath these freemen, who could hold estates, command others, and speak out in a council known as a *thing*, was an enslaved class of *thralls* burdened with menial work.

Living around the North Sea, Scandinavians early came to rely on ships for communication and trade. Archaeological finds from Denmark reveal that people there devised the forerunner of the famous "longboat" well before the Viking Age. Fourth century ships unearthed in a Danish bog at Nydam Mose already show most of its characteristics: the tall, matching, upcurved bow and stern, the "clinkerbuilt" or overlapping oak side planks, and the open hull fitted with dozens of long oars. Only the addition of a mast and woolen sail, innovations that came in the seventh or eighth century, were required to complete the evolution of this unique craft. Shallow in draft to negotiate the fiords and coastal streams of Scandinavia yet flexibly built to withstand the forces of ocean storms, the Viking longboat was the basis of a maritime tradition that was unequaled in Europe until the Portuguese and Spanish developed an alternative one in the fifteenth century.

Such ships enabled Viking expansion, but they did not cause it. Christian churchmen, beginning with Alcuin, attributed it to God's doing, deeming Viking raids punishment

Viking Expansion

Source: Adapted from National Geographic, vol. 197, no. 5 (May 2000): 12–13. Map by Laszlo Kubinyi/NGS Image Collection.

Chapter 6

Vikings and

Polynesians:

Exploring

New Worlds

(300–1100)

for religious laxity. But an eleventh century Saxon cleric claimed that it resulted from overpopulation and poverty in the Viking homeland. His view accords with accounts in a thirteenth century Icelandic source called the *Landnámábok* or *Book of Settlement*. It portrays early Norse émigrés to the Atlantic islands as landless sons, social outcasts, and political refugees—all forced by adversity to leave their homes in search of opportunities elsewhere, much like later European immigrants to the New World.[2]

Whatever its causes, Viking emigration flowed in many directions. Danes spread south across modern Holland and France, then on to England or down through Spain into the Mediterranean. Swedes swept east across the Baltic Sea into Slavic lands to the fringes of the Byzantine and Islamic worlds. And Norwegians ventured west, hopping from one island to another across the North Atlantic. Settled neighbors seldom grasped the full scope of this exodus. Western Europeans were as unfamiliar with Viking voyages across the Atlantic or down the Volga River in Russia as Eastern peoples were of their western migrations. Slavs called them the *Rus* (a Baltic term later appropriated by Russians), while Byzantine Greeks, who prized their fighting ability and recruited them as mercenaries, called them Varangians. Such names meant nothing to Western Europeans, who dubbed them the Normanni or Normans, meaning men of the north. When meeting former members of the

Varangian Guard who were accompanying a Byzantine embassy, Frankish rulers were amazed to learn that they were akin to the Normans.

Most of these migrations began as small enterprises organized by a local chieftain to explore opportunities abroad. If successful, the chieftain would return to recruit additional chieftains and their war bands to accompany him on larger expeditions to establish beachheads from which they could march inland to pillage the countryside and collect *danegeld*, or tribute. If unopposed, they would proceed to seize land and impose their rule over the indigenous people, creating colonies that would attract further immigration from Scandinavia. By the late ninth century, Viking colonies spread across most of northern Europe and the North Atlantic. Swedes not only established important trade sites like Staraja Ladoga and Novgorod in Russia but founded the first known state there at Kiev. Meanwhile, Danes overran much of Britain after carving out enclaves throughout the coastal Netherlands and France, and Norwegians seized the Faroe, Orkney, and Shetland Islands before planting the first European settlements in Iceland and Greenland. Some of these lands, like the duchy of Normandy in France, they held as nominal fiefs under local rulers, but more often they ruled them independently, as they did in the British Isles, where they established separate kingdoms centered in York, Dublin, and the Isle of Man.

Contact between these enclaves and the Viking homeland nourished trade. Centers like Birka in Sweden and Heddeby in Denmark became

2. Adam of Bremen, *History of the Archbishops of Hamburg-Bremen*, trans. Francs J. Tscan (New York: Columbia University Press, 1959), p. 211.

Pacific Migrations

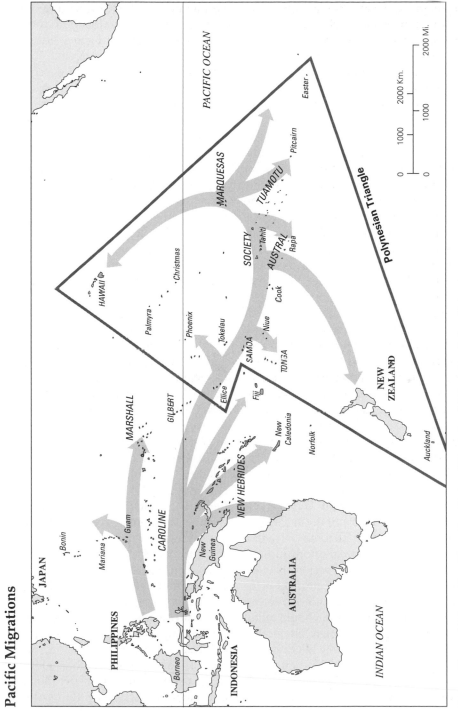

Source: Tommy Holmes, The Hawaiian Canoe *(Honolulu: Editions Limited, 1981), p. 4.*

Chapter 6

Vikings and

Polynesians:

Exploring

New Worlds

(300–1100)

rich and important cities as commerce flowed into them from regional markets as far off as Dublin and York in the west and Staraja Ladoga and Kiev in the east. For a while, a vast network of Viking-controlled trade linked the North Atlantic and Middle East into a single great market with Europe. Danish and Norwegian rulers made occasional efforts to unify this far-flung Viking world. Knut the Great of Denmark almost succeeded in the early eleventh century, bringing the Danes, Norwegians, English, Atlantic outliers, and some Swedes together in a brief-lived northern empire that lasted until his death in 1035. But his reign marked both the apogee of the Viking world and the start of its collapse. Over the ensuing two centuries, it broke apart as assimilation into local populations and conversion to Christianity deprived it of a common Scandinavian language and identity.

A similar expansion and fragmentation occurred among the Polynesian peoples of the Pacific, although they are much less well understood. Long ignored by scholars, Polynesia began to attract attention in 1947 when adventurers captained by a modern "Viking," the Norwegian Thor Heyerdahl, sailed a balsa raft from Peru to Raroia Atoll in the Tuaomotu Islands to prove that South American Indians could have peopled the region. Though Heyerdahl's subsequent effort to elaborate his theory of South American colonization in a popular book called *Kon-tiki*, published in 1952, generated many scholarly rebuttals, his dramatic voyage had much the same effect on Polynesian studies as the Ingstads' discovery of the L'Anse aux Meadows site

had on Viking studies, sparking a new era of research based upon innovative approaches. Until then, little was known of the Polynesian past, for the Polynesians (with but one exception) neither possessed writing themselves nor encountered literate people who could record their history until Europeans reached the Pacific in the sixteenth century. By then, most Polynesians had lost the ability to conduct distant voyages and, following long isolation on widely scattered islands, had only vague memories left of their origins.

Recent discoveries, however, suggest that their ancestors spread four thousand miles across the central Pacific to colonize the vast complex of islands known as Polynesia. As you can see from the map on page 143, most of Polynesia falls within a great triangle with its points at Hawaii in the north, New Zealand in the southwest, and Easter Island in the east, although a scattering of outlying islands stretches westward between Melanesia and Micronesia. Despite being dispersed over an area twice the size of the United States, Polynesians remain a relatively homogeneous population, speaking closely related languages of the Austronesian family that derive from a single ancestral form spoken back around 1500 B.C.E. Archaeological findings, though sparse for Polynesia as a whole, shed some light on that formative era. They show that from 1500 to 500 B.C.E., a Lapita culture with a distinctive pottery tradition flourished along an island chain running from New Guinea through Fiji to Tonga and Samoa. Not yet true farmers, the Lapita people were horticulturists who set plants out in temporary clearings created by slash and burn methods. But they already grew taro, yams, and breadfruit, the staples of later Polynesian life, and kept the region's only domesticated animals: pigs, chickens, and dogs. They must have already been good sailors, too, for they spread over closely spaced islands as far as Tonga and Samoa. Unlike the low atolls and rocky islands of the western Pacific, these islands are high and volcanic, with features more akin to those further east in the central Pacific. Here, where clay and stone materials were sparse and plant and animal life restricted, Lapita colonists had to adapt to a more typically Polynesian environment, fashioning baskets in place of clay pots, making implements out of shells and pumice rather than hard rock, and turning from the land to the sea for food. Tonga and Samoa thus seem most likely to be the places where Polynesians first emerged as a distinct people.

Before they could voyage into the central and eastern Pacific, where distances between islands were much greater, however, they had to perfect better craft than the outrigger canoes that ostensibly brought their Lapita ancestors to Tonga and Samoa from islands further west. The outrigger canoe, probably devised in Southeast Asia long before the Lapita people emerged, was a simple vessel made by hollowing out a single log and lashing a separate float to one side to improve its balance. Limited in size and low in the water, it was suitable only for offshore fishing and short trips between near islands on a calm sea, not voyages of a month or more over thousands of miles of stormy seas with large groups of people who had to be fed. For such voyages, early Polynesians developed a different craft, a twin-hulled vessel similar to a modern catamaran. Although called canoes, these were true ships and could be as much as ninety to a hundred feet in length. Their twin hulls were built up of separate planks, tied edge to edge in carvel fashion (as opposed to the clinker or overlapped construction of Viking ships). Beams lashed across the hulls bound them into a single assembly and supported wide decks and even raised platforms that could hold considerable cargo or passengers. Although such vessels could be rowed by oarsmen, they were equipped with masts and triangular sails to take advantage of the wind whenever possible. Using ships of this sort, Polynesians leapfrogged from island to island across four thousand miles of open ocean, probably using the position of stars on the horizon and an intimate knowledge of winds, currents, and bird flights to chart their way.

As Polynesians dispersed over the Pacific, differences evolved that distinguished one island people from another. Those who dwelled on resource-poor atolls and islands, which could not sustain large populations, lived in small-scale, usually egalitarian communities. But on bigger islands and archipelagoes like Tonga, Samoa, and the Society, Hawaiian, and Easter Islands, as on New Zealand, populous societies with a high degree of stratification developed. By the time Europeans reached the area, hereditary chieftains ruled many of these areas. Often distinguishing themselves as a caste apart, they used their elevated

[145]

Chapter 6

Vikings and

Polynesians:

Exploring

New Worlds

(300–1100)

status to exercise life-and-death power over kinsmen. Aided by centralized governments, many were capable of organizing a sufficient number of workers to build large burial mounds and monumental stone structures, terrace hillsides for taro beds, and construct fleets of oceangoing canoes. But because of the great distances between island groups, the local chiefdom remained the usual polity throughout Polynesia. Trade, too, was largely local, although archaeological findings indicate that long-distance exchanges did take place, if only through successive stages of barter between adjacent archipelagos. Isolation also affected religious practice. Worship varied from one archipelago to another despite a common polytheism. Cults of the sea god Tangaroa prevailed in the west, while eastern Polynesians worshiped a more eclectic pantheon featuring the war god Tu along with Rongo and Tane, gods of horticulture and procreation. Most eastern Polynesians nonetheless retained legends of a sacred homeland in the west called Hawaiki, of which the names Hawaii and Savai'i, an island in the Samoan chain, are variants. Perhaps Savai'i, which contains the ruins of an impressive ceremonial site built on a great stone mound, had a special cult role that inspired such legends. Similar *marae* or temple

complexes became even more elaborate in eastern Polynesia, where they were raised on stepped pyramids or stone terraces adorned with effigies of spirits such as the *Moai* of Easter Island.

That island, the easternmost that Polynesians settled, became a focus of controversy when Thor Heyerdahl led an archaeological expedition there in 1955 to seek traces of Native American movements into the Pacific. Only 2,500 miles off the coast of Chile, to which it now belongs, Easter Island lies within plausible sailing distance of Latin America, but no proof of Native American colonization has been found there. Less certain is whether Easter Islanders had contact with mainland America in pre-Columbian times. Striking resemblances between the stonework and art found on the island and that in the Andes as well as the existence on Easter Island of the only known system of writing in Polynesia, the ideographic *rongorongo* script, hint at possible connections with literate Amerindian peoples. Unfortunately, like the Viking communities in Greenland, this Polynesian outpost underwent a sharp demographic and cultural decline in late traditional times. After Peruvian slavers decimated its population in 1862, no elders survived who could read the island's unique script or keep alive memories of its past.

THE METHOD

In the Evidence section that follows, you will encounter material used by scholars to reconstruct the lost worlds

of the Vikings and Polynesians. You may notice a considerable difference in the nature of the sources presented for each people. In part this is because physical remains survive far better in the northern bogs and tundra of the Vikings' homelands than they do in tropical islands, and so we have far richer materials through which to study the Vikings than we have for the Polynesians. Also, the Vikings have attracted much more present-day study than the Polynesians, often from European descendants who are culturally akin to them. We are thus usually able to "read" Viking materials better and to get more out of them. Keep these factors in mind as you look over the evidence and consider how this situation affects our picture of the two peoples' respective activities.

As you might expect, the evidence is presented in two parts, one focused on the Vikings and the other on the Polynesians. Each opens with documents that reflect early efforts by outsiders to portray the people in question, followed by sources drawn from recent scholarship that try to illuminate them through their own artifacts and traditions. Compare the information presented through each. An important issue to be addressed here is the degree to which more recent material "fleshes out and in some cases contradicts or even replaces the historical record," as Fitzhugh put it. So consider how newer evidence adds to or changes our picture of the Vikings and Polynesians.

The section on the Vikings begins with a chronicle by a Saxon or German cleric known only as Adam of Bremen. In the 1060s he set out to record the history of the Catholic archbishops of Hamburg-Bremen but added digressions on the Scandinavians, whom they were then seeking to convert to Christianity. Though favorable to Scandinavians overall, he held a low opinion of the Viking adventurers who raided into Saxony. Source 2, an illustration from a manuscript on the life of St. Aubin dating from the same century, gives a similar view, portraying Vikings as they may have looked to clerics whose churches and monasteries they looted along the French coast.

Source 3 presents a very different image. Erected near a warrior's grave, this ninth-century stone from Gotland, Sweden, depicts a crew's journey to Valhalla, the legendary resting place of heroes. It shows the warrior god Odin riding his eight-legged horse Sleipnir, while one of his *valkyries*, or battle maidens, welcomes the crew to his realm. The ship is remarkably similar to the remnants of actual Viking vessels uncovered by archaeologists, like the one shown in Source 4, a photograph of the Oseberg *drakkar* or long ship discovered in a grave mound in Norway. The next items suggest where Vikings went in such ships and what they did. Source 5 consists of runic inscriptions on stones raised over the graves of Scandinavian notables to memorialize their feats at home and abroad. Source 6, a hoard or treasure trove of the sort often buried throughout Viking lands for religious or security reasons, yields more clues to Scandinavian activities abroad. Coins found in such hoards bear dates and mint marks that tell when and where they were obtained, and distinctive items of jewelry can be identified with their lands of origin.

That Scandinavians made it even farther afield can be deduced from the next items. Source 7, an excerpt from the *Greenlanders' Saga,* a prose tale produced during the thirteenth century flowering of Icelandic literature,

Chapter 6

Vikings and

Polynesians:

Exploring

New Worlds

(300–1100)

portrays Norwegian efforts to explore and settle the Atlantic isles. Though fictional, its version of Greenland's colonization and the exploration of Vinland parallels other Icelandic accounts and may preserve lore left by early settlers who knew firsthand about such affairs.[3] As Source 8, an archaeological plan of the L'Anse aux Meadows site, shows, the foundations of the long, narrow houses found there exactly conform in outline to the distinctive sod farmhouses that Scandinavians built in timber-poor Iceland. Along with a typical Viking bronze pin and stone lamp found at the site, these foundations establish a Viking presence in North America.

Source 9, which begins the Polynesian section, comes from the *Polynesian Researches* of William Ellis, an early American missionary in the Pacific. Published in 1833, it was one of the first efforts by a sympathetic Westerner to describe Polynesians in detail. Still, Ellis missed no opportunity to point out their uncivilized ways and what he termed their "licentiousness and moral degradation." The open sexuality and tolerance for premarital and homosexual activity that drew his contempt fascinated other early Western visitors to Polynesia. William Hodges's 1776 painting *Tahiti Revisited*, a detail of which appears as Source 10, reveals this reaction, portraying Polynesians as "noble savages" at home with nature and

with their bodies. An official artist on explorer James Cook's expedition to the Pacific in the 1770s, Hodges helped to foster this view in paintings on his return to London. By the nineteenth century, it had become a cliché in European art and literature, often used as a foil to Victorian stuffiness and prudery.

Efforts to dispel such stereotypes began only in the twentieth century as a few Western scholars became interested in the history of the Pacific peoples and tried to overcome the lack of early written records by looking for other kinds of evidence on the Polynesian past. One of the earliest approaches was to study maritime technology throughout the Pacific for clues about the way people moved into the region and settled where they did. But, because wood and fiber rot quickly in the tropics, no actual examples of the ancient vessels made of these materials survived for them to find. Petroglyphs or stone pictures such as those from Hawaii shown in Source 11 give a rough approximation of what ancient Polynesian double-hulled canoes may have looked like. Using such hints along with details gleaned from boat builders still active elsewhere in the Pacific, modern researchers have attempted reconstructions like the *Hokule'a*, depicted in Source 12. On voyages like the one charted on the map, they have also shown that such craft could sail closely enough into the wind to contend with the westerly trade winds and accurately find their way from one archipelago to another relying on traditional methods of navigation.

3. L'Anse aux Meadows was only a temporary camp, and the exact location of Vinland remains unclear. The issue of its location has been complicated by a so-called Vinland map that emerged in the 1960s, only to be soon discredited.

Memories of such voyages and links to other islands survived among Polynesians in popular traditions long after many had lost the ability to continue long-range travel, as Source 13 attests. Excerpted from an early-nineteenth century work called *Hawaiian Antiquities*, this material represents an attempt by its author, a traditional Hawaiian poet and storyteller named David Malo, to preserve oral accounts in writing before they were lost. Having learned to read and write Hawaiian at a missionary school, Malo was clearly influenced by Western ideas of historical narrative. Source 14, stories collected directly from elders on the islands of Rennel and Bellona by Western ethnographers in the 1950s, more directly reproduces the way oral traditions deal with historical events. Both, however, indicate that Polynesians did retain some memory of their own origins and the connections between distant island groups.

To trace these origins in more detail, modern historians have turned to linguists for help. By studying similarities and dissimilarities in related languages, they have worked out the chart shown here as Source 15 to indicate the likely steps by which Polynesians colonized different island groups. It is based on the assumption that as colonists who struck out to settle new islands lost regular contact with their former homelands, their speech evolved differently, eventually forming a new dialect or even a new language. The pattern of linguistic evolution may thus roughly chart the stages and paths of Polynesian movement across the Pacific. Historians have also sought the aid of ethnobotanists, who study how different cultures identify and use plants. Source 16 presents some of their findings on the origin and distribution of plants introduced into Polynesia by humans. Not surprisingly, the places from which most of these plants must have been obtained hint at a basic movement eastward out of Asia into Polynesia through the western Pacific. But the presence of several South American plants spread widely throughout Polynesia also hints at contacts with the New World and movement back westward.

Similarities between Polynesian and Andean art and architecture provide another suggestion of contact. Source 17 illustrates how, in the eyes of some, the *Moai* ancestral figures of Easter Island mark an intermediate step in the development of Polynesian *tiki* or sacred effigies out of Latin American models like the stella from Tiahuanaco, Peru. Advocates of this view also argue that the close-laid stone terraces on which these Easter Island figures were erected, as well as similar terraces in Hawaii and the stepped pyramids of ancient Tahiti, derive from Andean prototypes. But without direct archaeological proof of contact between Polynesians and Native Americans, such claims remain conjectural.

Chapter 6

Vikings and

Polynesians:

Exploring

New Worlds

(300–1100)

Source 1 from Adam of Bremen, History of the Archbishoprics of Hamburg-Bremen, *trans. Francis J. Tschan (New York: Columbia University Press, 1959), pp. 75–76, 190–191. Copyright © 1959 Columbia University Press. Reprinted by permission of the publisher.*

1. From Adam of Bremen, *History of the Archbishoprics of Hamburg-Bremen,* 11th century

BOOK TWO, XXXI.

At that time a fleet [994] of pirates whom our people call Ascomanni landed in Saxony and devastated all the coastland of Frisia and Hadeln.[4] And as they went up the mouth of the Elbe River, they fell upon the province. Then the chief men of the Saxons met, and although their forces were small, engaged the Barbarians, who had left their ships at Stade, which is a convenient port and stronghold on the Elbe. Mighty and memorable, but exceedingly unhappy, was the battle in which, though it was manfully contested on both sides, our men finally proved too few. The victorious Swedes and Danes completely destroyed the whole Saxon troop. Captured there were the margrave Siegfried, Count Dietrich and other distinguished men whom the barbarians dragged to the ships with their hands tied behind their backs, and their feet shackled with chains. After that the barbarians ravaged the whole province with impunity. But since one of the captives, the margrave Siegfried, stealthily slipped away by night with the aid of a certain fisherman and escaped, the pirates forthwith fell into a rage and, mocking all the nobles whom they had in chains, severed their hands and feet and cut off their noses. Thus maimed and half dead, they cast them upon the land. . . .

BOOK FOUR, VI.

There is very much gold in Zealand,[5] accumulated by the plundering of pirates. These pirates, called Vikings by the people of Zealand, by our people, Ascommani, pay tribute to the Danish king for leave to plunder the barbarians who live about this sea in great numbers. Hence it also happens that the license granted them with respect to enemies is frequently misused against their own

---

4. **Ascomanni:** literally "shipmen," but conveying the sense of pirates or sea raiders. Frisia and Hadeln roughly corresponded with the modern Netherlands and the North Sea coastal portion of Germany. Saxony, the northwestern part of modern Germany, was then a province in the Carolingian empire.

5. **Zealand:** a Danish island in the North Sea between the Jutland Peninsula and modern Sweden.

people. So it is true they have no faith in one another, and as soon as one of them catches another, he mercilessly sells him into slavery, either to one of his fellows or to a barbarian. In many other respects, indeed, both in their laws and their customs, do the Danes run contrary to what is fair and good. None of these points appears to me to be worth discussing, unless it be that they immediately sell women who have been violated and that men who have been caught betraying his royal majesty or in some other crime would rather be beheaded than flogged. No kind of punishment exists among them other than the ax and servitude, and then it is glorious for a man who is convicted to take his punishment joyfully. Tears and plaints and other forms of compunction, by us regarded as wholesome, are by the Danes so much abominated that one may weep neither over his sins nor over his beloved dead. . . .

Chapter 6

Vikings and

Polynesians:

Exploring

New Worlds

(300–1100)

Source 2: Bibliothèque nationale de France. Manuscript 01 NAL 1390 Fol 7.

2. Illuminated French Manuscript on Life of St. Aubin, St. Aubin Abbey, ca. 1100

3. Memorial Stone, Gotland, Sweden, 8th to 9th century

Chapter 6
Vikings and
Polynesians:
Exploring
New Worlds
(300–1100)

Source 4: University Museum of Cultural Heritage/University of Oslo.

4. Oseberg Viking Ship, Norway, 9th to 10th century

Source 5 from R. I. Paige, Runes *(Berkeley and Los Angeles: University of California Press, 1987), pp. 46–51.*

5. Runic Memorial Inscriptions, Germany, Norway, and Sweden

1. Haddeby Stone, Schleswig, Germany: "[This stone was raised by Thórófr, Svein's retainer for his comrade Eiríkr] who met his death when *drengiar* . . . besieged Haddeby. He was master of a ship, and a very good *drengr.*"[6]

2. Uppland Stone, Uppland, Sweden: "Áli had this stone put up in his own honour. He took Knútr's *danegeld* in England. May God help his soul!"[7]

3. Veda Stone, Uppland, Sweden: "[Irenmuder set up this stone.] He bought this estate and made his money in the east, in Gardar."[8]

4. Fjuckby Stone, Uppland, Sweden: "[Liótr set up this stone in memory of his son, Áki.] He was master of a freighter, docking in the harbors of Greece. He died at home."

5. Gripsholm Stone, Södermanland, Sweden: "Tola set up this stone in memory of her son Haraldr, Ingvarr's brother. Like men they went far to seek gold, and in the east they fed the eagle. Died south, in Serkland."[9]

6. Dynna Pillar, Opland, Norway: "Gunnvor, Thrýdrik's daughter, made a bridge in memory of her daughter, Ástrídr. She was the most skilful girl in Hadeland."

---

6. *drengr:* a young warrior; *drengiar* is its plural form.
7. *danegeld:* "Danish gold," the money Danish invaders exacted from the Anglo-Saxons in England.
8. **Gardar:** the name Scandinavians used for eastern Russia.
9. **Serkland:** Norse for "Saracen land," the usual European term for Muslim territories.

Chapter 6

Vikings and

Polynesians:

Exploring

New Worlds

(300–1100)

Source 6 from Vikings: The North Atlantic Saga, *ed. William W. Fitzhugh and Elizabeth I. Ward (Washington and London: Smithsonian Institution Press, 2000), p. 120. Photo: University Museum of Cultural Heritage, Oslo, Norway.*

6. Buried Viking Hoard, Hon, Norway

Trefoil Frankish broach

Russian neck rings

Greek-inscribed ring

Danish or Swedish pendant

Coins (Arabic, Byzantine, Anglo-Saxon)

Source 7 from Gwyn Jones, The Norse Atlantic Saga *(London: Oxford University Press, 1964), pp. 142–152. By permission of Oxford University Press.*

7. From *Greenlanders' Saga,* 13th century

I

Learned men tell us that this same summer Eirik the Red went off to colonize Greenland, thirty-five [some versions say twenty-five] ships set sail from Breidafjord and Borgarfjord, but only fourteen of them succeeded in getting there. Some were forced back and some perished. . . .

II

[Bjarni Herjolfsson, an Icelander, away in Norway when his father accompanied the settlers to Greenland, decided to follow him in his own ship, but was blown off course.] . . . Then their following wind died down, and north winds and fogs overtook them, so that they had no idea which way they were going. This continued over many days, but eventually they saw the sun and could then get their bearings [or determine the quarters of the heavens]. They now hoisted sail, and sailed that day before sighting land, and debated among themselves what land this could be. To his way of thinking, said Bjarni, it could not be Greenland . . . [for] the land was not mountainous and was covered with forest, with low hills there, so they left the land to port of them and let their sheet turn towards the land.

III

[After more landfalls, none of which he was willing to explore, Bjarni reached Greenland itself.] . . . There was now much talk about voyages of discovery. Leif, son of Eirik the Red of Brattahlid, went to see Bjarni Herjolfsson, bought his ship from him, and found her a crew, so that they were thirty-five all told. . . .

. . . They now prepared their ship and sailed out to sea once they were ready, and they lighted on that land first which Bjarni his people had lighted on last. They sailed to land there, anchor and put off a boat, then went ashore, and could see no grass there. The background was all great glaciers, and right up to the glaciers from the sea as it were a single slab of rock. The land impressed them as barren and useless. "At least," said Leif, "it has not happened to us as to Bjarni over this land, that we failed to get ourselves ashore. I shall now give the land a name, and call it Helluland, Flatstone Land." After which they returned to the ship.

After that they sailed out to sea and lighted on another land. This time too they sailed to land, cast anchor, then put off a boat and went ashore. The country

Chapter 6

Vikings and

Polynesians:

Exploring

New Worlds

(300–1100)

was flat and covered with forest, with extensive white sands wherever they went, and shelving gently to the sea. "This land," said Leif, "shall be given a name in accordance with its nature, and be called Markland, Wood Land." After which they got back down to the ship as fast as they could.

From there they now sailed out to sea with a north-east wind and were at sea two days before catching sight of land. They sailed to land, reaching an island which lay north of it. . . . After which they returned to their ship and sailed into the sound which lay between the island and the cape projecting north from the land itself. . . . Later they decided to winter there and built a big house.

There was no lack of salmon there in river or lake, and salmon bigger than they had ever seen before. The nature of the land was so choice, it seemed to them that none of the cattle would require fodder for the winter. No frost came during the winter, and the grass was hardly withered. Day and night were of a more equal length there than in Greenland or Iceland. On the shortest day of winter the sun was visible in the middle of the afternoon as well as at breakfast time.

One evening it turned out that a man of their company was missing. This was Tyrkir the German. Leif was greatly put out by this, for Tyrkir had lived a long while with him and his father, and had shown great affection for Leif as a child. He gave his shipmates the rough edge of his tongue, then turned out to go and look for him, taking a dozen men with him. But when they had got only a short way from the hall there was Tyrkir coming to meet them. . . .

"Why are you so late, foster-father," Leif asked him, "and parted this way from your companions."

By way of a start Tyrkir held forth a long while in German, rolling his eyes all ways, and pulling faces. They had no notion what he was talking about. Then after a while he spoke in Norse. "I went no great way further than you, yet I have a real novelty to report. I have found vines and grapes."

. . . They slept overnight, then in the morning Leif made this announcement to his crew. "We now have two jobs to get on with, and on alternate days must gather grapes or cut vines and fell timber, so as to provide a cargo of such things for my ship. . . ."

. . . Leif gave the land a name in accordance with the good things they found in it, calling it Vinland, Wineland; after which they sailed out to sea and had a good wind till they sighted Greenland and the mountains under the glaciers.

IV

There was now much discussion of Leif's expedition to Vinland. His brother Thorvald considered that the land had been explored in too restricted a fashion. So Leif said to Thorvald, "If you want to, go you to Vinland, brother, in my ship. . . ."

. . . Next summer Thorvald set off eastwards with the merchantship and further north along the land . . . and into the mouth of the next fjord they came to, and to a headland jutting out there which was entirely covered with forest.

They brought the ship to where they could moor her, thrust out a gangway to the shore, and Thorvald walked ashore with his full ship's company. "This is a lovely place," he said, "and here I should like to make my home." Then they made for the ship, and saw three mounds on the sands up inside the headland. They walked up to them and could see three skin-boats there, and three men under each. So they divided forces and laid hands on them all, except for one who got away in his canoe. The other eight they killed, and afterwards walked back to the headland, where they had a good look round and could see various mounds on up the fjord which they judged to be human habitations. Then after this so great a drowsiness overtook them that they could not keep awake, and all fell asleep. Then a cry carried to them, so that they were all roused up, and the words of the cry were these: "Rouse ye, Thorvald, and all your company, if you would stay alive. Back to your ship with all your men, and leave this land as fast as you can!" With that there came from inside the fjord a countless fleet of skin-boats and attacked them. . . . The Skrælings kept shooting at them for a while, but then fled away, each one as fast as he could [leaving the party intact, save for Thorvald, who was mortally wounded].

. . . Then they stayed there that winter and gathered grapes and vines for the ship. The following spring they prepared to leave for Greenland, and brought their ship into Eiriksfjord, and the news they had to tell Leif was great news, indeed.

Chapter 6

Vikings and

Polynesians:

Exploring

New Worlds

(300–1100)

Source 8 site plan from Anne S. Ingstad, The Discovery of a Norse Settlement in America *(Oslo: Norwegian University Press, 1977); reconstructed Stöng Farmhouse from James Graham-Cambell,* The Viking World *(New Haven and New York: Ticknor & Fields, 1980), p. 81.*

8. Site Plan, L'Anse aux Meadows, Newfoundland, Canada and House, Stöng, Iceland

SKETCH MAP BASED ON TOPOGRAPHIC SURVEY MAP
PREPARED BY NATIONAL PARKS BRANCH, OTTAWA
ENGINEERING SERVICES DIVISION

ÉPAVES BAY

N
MAGNETIC

BLACK DUCK BROOK

A - J   HOUSE-SITES.
I - II   COOKING PIT I AND II.
1 - 8   FEATURES.
12 =   HEARTHS.
13 =   CHARCOAL KILN.
14-17   BOAT-SHEDS.
—5—   CONTOUR INTERVAL 5 FOOT
~~   CONTOUR LINE.
☐   EXCAVATED AREA.
- - -   TRAIL.
    TURF WALLS OF HOUSES.
    OUTLINES OF BOAT-SHEDS

0   10   20   30 M

living room
hearth
benches

hall

vats

entrance

dairy

hearth
platforms
lavatory

Source 9 from William Ellis, Polynesian Researches, *vol. I (New York: J. & J. Harper, 1833), pp. 72, 86–87, 95, 97, 106.*

9. From William Ellis,
Polynesian Researches,
19th century

. . . The greater part of Polynesia appears to be inhabited by those who present in their physical character many points of resemblance to the Malay and South Americans, but yet differ materially from either, and seem to form an intermediate race.

Next to their hospitality, their cheerfulness and good nature strike a stranger. They are seldom melancholy or reserved, always willing to enter into conversation, and ready to be pleased, and to attempt to please their associates. They are generally careful not to give offense to each other: but though, since the introduction of Christianity, families dwell together, and find an increasing interest in social intercourse, yet they do not realize that high satisfaction experienced by members of families more advanced in civilization. . . .

Their humour and jests were, however, but rarely what might be termed innocent sallies of wit; they were in general low and immoral to a disgusting degree. . . . Awfully Dark, indeed, was their moral character, and notwithstanding the apparent mildness of their disposition, and the cheerful vivacity of their conversation, no portion of the human race was ever perhaps sunk lower in brutal licentiousness and moral degradation than this isolated people.

To a missionary, the business of whose life is with the people among whom he is stationed, everything relating to their history is, at least, interesting; and the origin of the islanders has often engaged our attention, and formed the subject of our inquiries. The early history of a people destitute of all records, and remote from nations in whose annals contemporaneous events would be preserved, is necessarily involved in obscurity. The greater part of the traditions of this people are adapted to perplex rather than facilitate the investigation.

The origin of the inhabitants of the Pacific is involved in great mystery, and the evidences are certainly strongest in favor of their derivation from Malayan tribes inhabiting the Asiatic islands; but allowing this to be their source, the means by which they have arrived at the remote and isolated stations they now occupy are inexplicable. If they were peopled from the Malayan islands, they must have possessed better vehicles and more accurate knowledge of navigation than they now exhibit, to have made their way against the constant tradewinds prevailing within the tropics, and blowing regularly, with but transient and uncertain interruptions, from east to west. . . .

. . . The monuments or vestiges of former population found in these islands are all exceedingly rude, and therefore warrant the inference that the people to whom they belong were rude and uncivilized, and must have emigrated from a

Chapter 6

Vikings and

Polynesians:

Exploring

New Worlds

(300–1100)

nation but little removed from a state of barbarism—a nation less civilized than those must have been who could have constructed vessels, and traversed this ocean six or seven thousand miles against the prevailing winds, which must have been the fact, if we conclude they were peopled only by the Malays.

On the other hand, it is easy to imagine how they could have proceeded from the east. The winds would favour their passage, and the incipient stages of civilization in which they were found would resemble the condition of the aborigines of America far more than that of the Asiatics. . . .

10. Detail from William Hodges, *Tahiti Revisited*, 1776

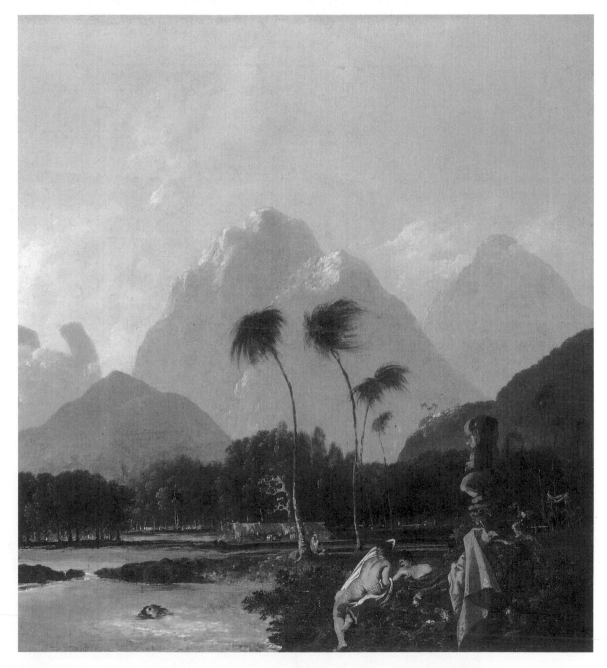

Chapter 6

Vikings and

Polynesians:

Exploring

New Worlds

(300–1100)

Source 11 from Tommy Holmes, The Hawaiian Canoe *(Honolulu: Editions Limited, 1981), pp. 154–155. Both photos: Ray Mains/Pacific Stock.*

11. Petroglyphs of Hawaiian Canoes

Source 12 photo from Tommy Holmes, The Hawaiian Canoe *(Honolulu: Editions Limited, 1993), p. 7. Photo: Ed George/National Geographic/NGS Collection, 1976/10514-5; map reprinted by permission from Ben F. Finney, "Voyaging Canoes and the Settlement of Polynesia," SCIENCE (1977), 196: 1277–1285. Copyright 2001 American Association for the Advancement of Science.*

12. Reconstructed Double-Hulled Hawaiian Canoe *Hokule'a* and Route of Its Voyages

Chapter 6

Vikings and

Polynesians:

Exploring

New Worlds

(300–1100)

Source 13 from David Malo, Hawaiian Antiquities (Moolelo Hawaii), *trans. Nathaniel Emerson (Honolulu, Bishop Museum, 1951), pp. 4–7.*

13. From David Malo, *Hawaiian Antiquities*, early 19th century

CHAPTER 4

4. It is thought that this people came from lands near Tahiti and from Tahiti itself, because the ancient Hawaiians at an early date mentioned the name of Tahiti in their *mele,* prayers, and legends.[10]

7. Perhaps because of their affection for Tahiti and Hawaii they applied the name Kahiki-nui to a district of Maui, and named this group . . . Hawaii. . . .[11]

8. The following is one way by which knowledge regarding Tahiti actually did reach these shores: we are informed (by historical tradition) that two men named Paao and Makua-kaumana, with a company of others, voyaged hither, observing the stars as a compass; and that Paao remained in Kohala, while Makua-kaumana returned to Tahiti.

10. Paao continued to live in Kohala until the kings of Hawaii became degraded and corrupted (*hewa*); then he sailed away to Tahiti to fetch a king from thence. Pili (Kaaiea) was that king and he became one of Hawaii's line of kings (*papa alii*).

13. There is also a tradition of a man named Moikeha, who came to this country from Tahiti in the reign of Kala, king of Hawaii.

15. When Kila [Moikeha's son] was grown up he in turn sailed on an expedition to Tahiti, taking his departure, it is said, from the western point of Kahoolawe, for which reason that cape to this day called Ke-ala-I-kahiki (the route to Tahiti).

16. Kila arrived in safety at Tahiti and on his return to these shores brought back with him Laa-mai-Kahiki [his son, whose name meant Tahiti-born Laa]. On the arrival of Laa was introduced the use of the *kaekeeke* drum. An impetus was given at the same time to the use of sinnet in canoe lashing (*aha hoa waa*),

---

10. **mele:** a traditional song or chant. Malo cites several traditional *mele* and prayers (*hainaki*) that make reference to Kahiki, generally assumed to be the Hawaiian pronunciation of Tahiti. One, a prayer to the god Lono, claims "The stem of Lono links our dynasties with Kahiki," (p. 146).

11. Many eastern Polynesian peoples had legends and songs recalling an ancient homeland called Hawaii or Hawaiki, a term that may have referred to western Polynesian as a whole or perhaps just a similar-sounding island like Savai'i in Samoa.

together with improvements in the plaited ornamental knots or lashings, called *lana-lana*. . . .

17. The Hawaiian are thought to be of one race with the people of Tahiti and the islands adjacent to it. The reason for this belief is that the people closely resemble each other in their physical features, language, genealogies, traditions (and legends) as well as in (the names of) their deities. It is thought that very likely they came to Hawaii in small detachments.

19. It seems probable that this was the case from the fact that in Tahiti they have large canoes called *pahi;* and it seems likely that its possession enabled them to make their long voyages to Hawaii. The ancients are said to have been skilled also in observing the stars, which served them as a mariner's compass directing their course.

Source 14 from Samuel H. Elbert and Torben Monberg, From the Two Canoes. Oral Traditions of Rennell and Bellona *(Honolulu and Copenhagen: University of Hawaii Press, 1965), pp. 82, 174–176, 188, 257, and 301. Copyright © 1965. Reprinted by permission of the University of Hawaii Press.*

14. Excerpts from the Oral Traditions of Rennell and Bellona

Text 124 *Story of the Voyage of the Ancients, told by Basiana, April 13, 1958*

1. The coming of the voyage of the ancients, that reached Rennell and Bellona here. They made no settlement, but first just traveled about on Bellona here and on Rennell and looked about. Afterwards they made their settlements, and made their two temples brought from 'Ubea.[12] The name of the great temple that Tongo brought was Teuse and Manga-ma'ubea. They dug up the earth and made the settlement of the gods there, and erected the house there. The house was very sacred.—

12. **Ubea:** the name the Polynesians of Bellona and Rennel used for their homeland.
   Bellona and **Rennell:** "outliers" or western extensions of Polynesia in the Solomon Islands about 200 miles south of Guadalcanal. 'Ubea was probably Uvea Island, located about midway between Samoa and Fiji, over 1,200 miles to the east.

Chapter 6

Vikings and

Polynesians:

Exploring

New Worlds

(300–1100)

Text 153 The Story of the Seven
Originals, told by Tupe'uhi,
March 19, 1958

1. The seven originals were brought here from 'Ubea and had different gods, and Kaitu'u had two. The Taupongi clan, Ekeitehua; and the Sau clan, theirs was Baabenga. 2. The Tanga clan's were Guatupu'a and Tepoutu'igangi. . . . Sikigimoemoe was the god of the Nikatemono clan. 3. The Puka clan and the Togo clan had their gods, but their names are not known. . . .[13]

Text 66 From the story of Kaitu'u
and Taupongi, told by Taupongi,
December 12, 1958

1. Taupongi and Tanga and Ngoha and Nikatemono and Puka and Sau and To'a and Suki and Pua made the search for land. These are the things which they brought from 'Ubeangango (West-'Ubea): two black stones and the temple named Mangama'ubea and the life-of-the-land [staff]. 2. [They] came and arrived at the eastern 'Ubea, where a person was strolling. . . . 3. And Tanga and Pua said as follows: "What is your name?" And [he] said: "I am Kaitu'u. . . ." 6. . . . And they took [him] to Tongo, his classificatory uncle, and they cast off away from eastern 'Ubea and came this way.

Text 67 Kaitu'u, told by Tetamogi,
January 6, 1958

[*Kaitu'u, whom the original migrants met on eastern 'Ubea, joined the group with his own kinsmen because he dreamed that two gods wanted him to carry them to a new location.*]

10. After his dream [Kaitu'u] awoke at daylight and made preparations and boarded the double canoe of Tahasi and To'a and Suke, the two chiefs and owners of the canoe. Kaitu'u's wife is not known. 11. The mother was taken aboard, her name being Nautaga. Togo made preparations. These people were uncle and nephew, Togo and Kaitu'u. 12. Togo boarded the canoe with his two gods, two stones named Tepoutapu (the-sacred-post), a male god, and Guatupu'a and Gau'eteaki (two names), a goddess. 13. [They all] boarded the canoe and got settled there; Kaitu'u and his mother and his two gods, and Togo and his two gods sat in the lesser hull. 14. And Tahasi and To'a and Suki sat in the main

---

13. The original Polynesian migrants who set out from western 'Ubea represented seven clans, but only two chiefs, Kaitu'u and Taupongi, made it safely to Rennell and Bellona with their followers intact.

hull. 15. Casting off from 'Ubea, coming this way, going and landing at many islands. 16. Coming this way, landing at a land, not knowing the name of the land, To'a and Suki were killed by the people of this land. 17. Casting off the canoe, coming this way, landing at another land. So Tahasi was also killed. The two people who had been chiefs and owners of the canoe were no more. 18. Kaitu'u and Togo were left, and [they] got into the main canoe and left the other hull.

Text 66 *From the story of Kaitu'u and Taupongi, told by Taupongi, December 12, 1958*

9. And Tongo and Kaitu'u boarded the main hull [of the double] canoe, and came and reached Henuatai (Marine-land). And the sea was rough, and the black stone sank [into the sea], and the people of the canoe came ashore at Henuatai, where [they] hammered and broke a stalactite and replaced the black stone with it, and slept in the neighborhood.

14. ... And all the people then took the canoes through the reef out to the sea and said: "Tengenga is my woman." 15. ... There were one hundred [people]; all were out to sea. Only the double canoe was left on the shore, and only Tongo and Kaitu'u stayed upon it. ...

18. When Tongo and Kaitu'u came out, the whole fleet of canoes had sunk. Only the one belonging to Taupongi was left. And Tongo took on board a man and his wife of another clan.

19. And in this way Tongo went on picking up all the clans. And the woman of the Tanga clan said: "Every clan now survives, each through one couple [baa-ghabu], but my clan will die out." 20. And Tongo picked up the Tanga clan in the double canoe, and [they] were now seven. And then the two canoes came this way, the double canoe in front and behind the one belonging to Taupongi. When [they] met rough seas, the double canoe fell astern, and so the one belonging to Taupongi was ahead.

22. [They] came and reached Ahanga at the lake and came to the north side of Rennell. Came on and came out from the point at Kangiata, and Bellona here appeared. 28. ... And the two canoes came ashore, [people] went up and walked about in Ahanga and danced their sauhongi.

Text 5 *Story of Ekeitehua, told by Taupongi, January 2, 1959*

4. The canoe belonging to Kaitu'u, the double canoe, came from 'Ubea, but the canoe belonging to Taupongi came here first. It was a small canoe, its name was *hua*. And the canoe came and arrived here at Bellona, and installed its district

Chapter 6

Vikings and

Polynesians:

Exploring

New Worlds

(300–1100)

god here and named [him] Ekeitehua. [They] called his district god that name because he arrived before the double canoe.[14]

Text 67 *Kaitu'u, told by Tetamogi,*
January 6, 1958

[*Conflict subsequently broke out with an indigenous people called the* hiti *already living on the island when they killed Togo in a dispute over the spoils of a hunt.*]

49. Then Kaitu'u stayed with the *hiti* and then thought he would revenge his uncle Togo, so Kaitu'u stood and fought the *hiti*, and Kaitu'u killed the *hiti*, and in revenge for Togo, killed and ate [the *hiti*].

14. Kaitu'u made the voyage in a great double canoe, whereas Taupongi had only a lesser small canoe or outrigger. But because the latter arrived first, his descendants called their clan god Ekeite-hua: "rest-on-the-small-canoe."

Source 15 based on charts in Patrick V. Kirch, The Evolution of the Polynesian Chiefdoms *(Cambridge and London: Cambridge University Press, 1984), pp. 27, 43.*

15. Development Sequence of Polynesian Languages

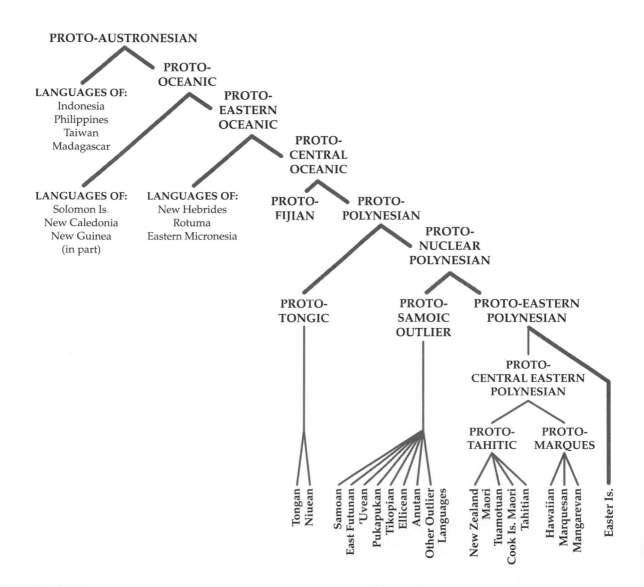

Chapter 6

Vikings and

Polynesians:

Exploring

New Worlds

(300–1100)

Source 16 charts created from data in W. Arthur Whistler, "Polynesian Plant Introduction," from Islands, Plants, and Polynesians: An Introduction to Polynesian Ethnobotany, *ed. Paul Allen Cox and Sandra Anne Banack (Portland, Ore.: Dioscorides Press, 1991), pp. 41–66.*

16. Plant Species Introduced into Polynesia Before European Contact

(a) *Origin of 72 known plant species introduced into Polynesia*

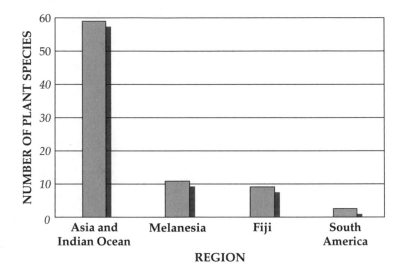

(b) *Distribution in Polynesia of three plant species of South American origin*

	Islands					
Species	*Tonga*	*Samoa*	*Cook*	*Society*	*Marquesas*	*Hawaii*
Ipomea batatas sweet potato	P	P	P	P	P	P
Lagenaria siceraria bottle gourd	—	—	P	P	P	P
Solanum repandum fruit-bearing shrub	P	P	P	P	P	Modern?

Note: P indicates the presence of a plant. *Solanum repandum* is found in Hawaii, but it was probably a modern plant introduction.

Source 17: Photo (a): Holton Collection/Superstock; Photo (b): Tony Morrison/South American Pictures, #BBA0211D; Photo (c): Jo Anne Van Tilburg, Easter Island (London: British Museum Press, 1994), p. 119. Drawing by Cristian Arevalo Pakarati, © Jo Anne Van Tilburg/EISP; Photo (d): Bernice Pauahi Bishop Museum.

17. Monolithic Statues

(a) *Ahu Akivi Platform, Easter Island*

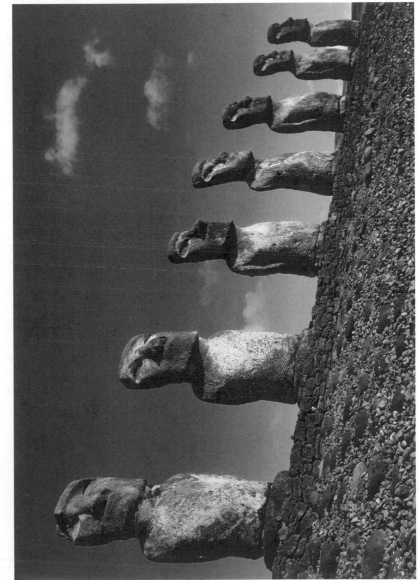

Chapter 6
Vikings and
Polynesians:
Exploring
New Worlds
(300–1100)

(d) Marquesan Tiki

(c) Easter Island Moai

(b) Tiahuanaco Stella

QUESTIONS TO CONSIDER

Begin your review of the evidence on the Vikings by asking how early historical documents like Sources 1 and 2 portrayed them. One way to approach this task with regard to Source 1 is to list the descriptive terms that Adam of Bremen uses to describe the Vikings. Taken together, what image do these terms evoke? Adam, like many chroniclers, employs stories and anecdotes to dramatize his account and provide representative examples of behavior. Do these present a consistent picture of Vikings? In particular, how does the story of Margrave Siegfried reflect on the Vikings' image as warriors? Compare this view with the one that emerges in the discussion of Danish morals and character. Does Adam accord any positive traits to the Danes or the Swedes? Now turn to Source 2 and ask yourself what specific aspect of Viking life this picture illustrates, and in what perspective. Does it challenge or reinforce the image provided by Adam's account? Does either suggest a heroic people or a people with significant historical accomplishments?

By contrast, look at how Source 3, the memorial stone, presents the subject of a party of Viking warriors. In what context are they shown here, and how does this affect the perspective? Do these seem to be treacherous, greedy, or disloyal men? Compare the ship depicted here with the one illustrated in Source 2. Which shows details of such things as hull outline, rigging, and sails, which would affect the seaworthiness of a craft? By implication, which shows a craft that might be

capable of an extended journey? Now compare the ship on the memorial stone with the one found at Oseberg. How well do they agree in details? Does the Oseberg vessel seem like a crude and clumsy craft? Replicas of such ships, which were up to ninety feet in length and sixteen feet in breadth, have been made and sailed across the Atlantic since the 1890s, leaving little doubt about their seaworthiness. How do such ships compare with those of later European explorers?

In going over the inscriptions in Source 5, note where Vikings went and how far they traveled. Note, too, what they did. Were they just pirates? What other activities did they pursue? Most inscriptions record the feats of men, but women did not go unrecognized, as you can see from the sixth inscription. How does this inscription in particular contrast with Adam's claim that Danes lacked compunction over the dead? Relying on what you have learned from these inscriptions, how do you think the Viking owner of the Hon hoard obtained the items displayed in Source 6? Note the places where these objects were made. How do you think they were obtained? Items from Western Europe may have come from pillaging, but Vikings did not raid the Muslim city of Bagdhad or the Bzyantine capital, Constantinople.

Source 7, the *Greenlander's Saga*, reveals still other Viking activities. Why did men like Erik the Red sail to Greenland? Assuming crews of the size Leif recruited for his ship, how many people accompanied his father to Greenland? How does this venture compare with later European attempts to start colonies in North America?

Chapter 6
Vikings and
Polynesians:
Exploring
New Worlds
(300–1100)

The voyages to Vinland later made by Leif and his brother Thorvald may have been for more than exploration, to judge from the cargoes they elected to bring back. Why might timber and grapes be of value to colonists in Greenland and Iceland? As you might guess from looking at the Icelandic farmhouse shown in Source 8, these are cold, northern lands with sparse forest cover that demanded extreme adaptation if settlers were to survive. The Vikings had to learn how to use the sparse materials at hand in these new places, and then developed a distinctive kind of sod building. Compare the outline of the house foundations (marked A–J) on the archaeological site plan of L'Anse aux Meadows with that of the reconstructed Icelandic farmhouse shown at the bottom of the page. Do you see the resemblance? Conditions further south on the North America coast were more favorable. Does the saga suggest why Vikings did not settle there?

As you turn to the material on the Polynesians, note how differently their "barbarism" is portrayed in Source 9, Ellis's account. What are the words Ellis uses to characterize them and what do the qualities these words evoke suggest—savage warriors, dignified chieftains, or degraded children? Compare the image you get of them here with the one conveyed in Hodges's painting, Source 10. By focusing on nude women bathing in a lush tropical setting, Hodges provided a very selective view of Polynesian life. Does it contrast sharply with Ellis's view or other views of South Sea islanders that you have encountered? What does such a view imply about these people? Would

you expect such people to plan and carry out arduous projects or have expert knowledge about navigation? Consider in this context Ellis's doubt that Polynesian ancestors came from Asia.

Like Ellis, many early Western observers felt that "a nation but little removed from a state of barbarism" could not "have constructed vessels, and traversed this ocean six or seven thousand miles against prevailing winds." But Source 11, the Hawaiian petroglyphs, indicates otherwise. Compare the canoes scratched on these rocks—particularly the outline of their hulls and sails—with Source 12, the photo of a replica of a traditional ocean-going canoe. Successful voyages over thousands of miles by replicas such as *Hokule'a* show that such vessels could cross vast stretches of open ocean. And as the map of *Hokule'a*'s voyages proves, their triangular rig would allow them to sail close enough into the wind to avoid being blown off course to the west.

As Sources 13 and 14 verify, memories of such voyages were kept alive in oral traditions. Note the number of trips between Tahiti and Hawaii listed in Source 13. Were any two-way? Why were such voyages undertaken, and what consequences did they have? Clearly settlement was one motive, but on what scale did it take place? How did such migrants find their way on such voyages? Stories from Rennell and Bellona in Source 14 give more detail on Polynesian colonization. What led the Seven Originals to leave 'Ubea? How many people set out, and how many arrived? What prized possessions did they bring with them? Like the Vikings in Vinland, these newcomers encountered prior occupants. Were their relations more amicable? What do you make of their treatment of the *hiti*? Rennell and Bellona lie far west of Uvea, the likely 'Ubea from which the Seven Originals came, suggesting two-way traffic across the Pacific.

The linguistic evidence presented in Source 15, however, shows that the main direction of Polynesian movement was from west to east. New branches in the line of language development probably occurred as groups broke away from older populations to settle a new home. What locations would then mark key stages in the migration of peoples into Polynesia? Find these on the map and note the course of migration that they indicate. Notice that this route runs counter to the direction of the trade winds. What does this fact imply about navigation into the Pacific from Asia—or South America. Source 16 provides data on the diffusion of South American plants into the Pacific. What does this suggest about human movements into the area? The interpretation of Source 17, the stone figures, is more problematic, because all representations of the human form look somewhat alike. But note that all are free-standing figures carved in similar crouching positions with arms clasped around their midriffs and large, staring eyes. Note, too, the similar headdress on both the Easter Island *Moai* and the South American stella. If we could prove that the Polynesians reached America from the west, would that feat give them new significance in history?

EPILOGUE

Both the Vikings and the Polynesians suffered from declines that cost them their seagoing prowess. Without the means of continuing long-range voyages, their scattered settlements lost touch with one another and sank into isolation and obscurity. Eventually most Viking states outside of Scandinavia foundered, as migrant communities died out or were assimilated into indigenous populations. Vinland was abandoned early, and by the fourteenth century the Greenland colonies had vanished, too. Settlements elsewhere fared little better, being incorporated into new states created and governed by other peoples. Only the duchy of Normandy in France, whose Duke William went on to conquer England in 1066, and Iceland endured to preserve some of their legacy. But in these lands, as in Scandinavia proper, conversion to Christianity and adoption of Western European ways brought a break with tradition and a loss of old identity. We know less about the course of events in Polynesia. However, when Europeans arrived in the Pacific, most eastern Polynesian peoples had lost their ability to build and sail the double canoes of the past. Trade and communication between major island groups had ceased, and little remained to indicate that Polynesians had once crossed the

Chapter 6

Vikings and

Polynesians:

Exploring

New Worlds

(300–1100)

ocean on voyages of discovery and colonization.

Only recently have we begun to see how great a break occurred and how worthwhile it may be to rediscover the lost worlds of people like the Vikings and the Polynesians. The picture that is emerging from modern studies of these two peoples, though certainly more detailed for the Vikings than for the Polynesians, shows in both cases not savages, but sophisticated peoples with a surprising degree of material and cultural development. Their transoceanic exploration, trade, and colonization certainly narrowed the great ocean barriers of the Atlantic and Pacific. And long before Columbus launched Western Europe's celebrated age of discovery with his expedition of 1492, they may have closed the final gap between the Old World and the New.

CHAPTER SEVEN

TWO FACES OF "HOLY WAR":[1]

CHRISTIANS AND MUSLIMS

(1095–1270s)

THE PROBLEM

According to the Book of Matthew in the Christian New Testament, after his resurrection from the dead, Jesus appeared before his eleven remaining disciples in Galilee, where he commanded them, "Go ye, therefore, and teach all nations, baptizing them in the name of the Father, and of the Son, and of the Holy Ghost, [t]eaching them to observe all things whatsoever I have commanded you."[2] Similarly, in the Qur'an (Koran), the book containing the revelations to Islam's founder, Muhammad ibn Abdullah, the Prophet commanded his followers to "Invite [all] to the way of your Lord . . . For your Lord knows best who has strayed from His Path,

and who receives guidance."[3] Thus Christianity and Islam, both of which saw themselves as the keepers of God's ultimate revelation of Himself to humanity, from their respective beginnings had built within their doctrines the commandment to proselytize and spread to include all peoples.

At their beginnings, neither Christianity nor Islam preached the expansion of the faiths by use of the sword. Muhammad counseled his followers to make converts "with wisdom and beautiful preaching; and argue with them in ways that are best and most gracious,"[4] while earlier the apostle Paul, himself a convert to Christianity, wrote to his fellow Christians in Rome to "follow after the things that make for peace, and things therewith one may edify another," so that "through your mercy they also may obtain mercy."[5]

---

1. The term *holy war* is of European origin, first coined by Friedrich Schwally in his book *Der Heilege Kreig im alten Israel [Holy War in Ancient Israel]* (Leipzig, 1901).

2. King James Version (KJV) 28:19–20. See also Acts 1:8.

3. Qur'an, Sūra 16:125.

4. Ibid.

5. Romans 14:19, 11:31, KJV.

Chapter 7

Two Faces of

"Holy War":

Christians and

Muslims

(1095–1270s)

Yet ultimately both Christians and Muslims were willing to spread their respective faiths by force. As Christians swelled in numbers, they increasingly embraced violence both to punish unbelievers and heretics and to expand the faith. For justification, they often reached back into the Old Testament, in which Israelites had been told to "utterly destroy them [unbelievers], as the Lord thy God hath commanded thee."[6] For their part, after the *hijra*[7] of Muhammad and his followers to Medina, the Prophet began to report revelations of *jihads al-sayf* (jihads of the sword). Originally the term *jihad* was shorthand for *jihad fi sabil Allah* (struggle in the path of God) and had no relation to warfare at all. Most often the term referred to an *internal* struggle of a Muslim against temptations, or a particular internal struggle against Muslim heretics or impious leaders. But, as noted above, within a few years of the *hijra*, Muhammad was saying such things as "Whoever fights in the path of God, whether he be killed or be victorious, on him We shall bestow a great reward," and "those who strive and fight has He distinguished above those who sit [at home] by a great reward."[8]

For centuries the proponents of these two religions maintained comparatively good relations with one another. In lands conquered by Muslims, Christians and Jews (known to Muslims as "People of the Book") were able to practice their respective faiths so long as they paid tribute and taxes to Muslim political authorities. Christians and Jews also were able to make pilgrimages to Jerusalem. And in Italy and Spain, Muslims lived in close proximity to Christians for hundreds of years without major altercations. Yet while their respective intellectual elites shared knowledge with one another, the two kept a careful—and enforced—distance. The papacy labeled Christians who dealt with Muslims as traitors and warned that such treason meant loss of all their property. For their part, most Muslims thought Western Christians were primitive and had little to teach them (Usamah ibn-Munqidh called Christians "animals").

Sometime after 1071 C.E., however, that brittle peace was broken. Seljuk Turks, new converts to Islam who interpreted the term *jihad* in its most warlike way, seized control of Jerusalem from the more tolerant Abbasid Muslims. On November 27, 1095, in a field of Clermont, France, Pope Urban II called on Western Christians to undertake a *peregrinatio* (pilgrimage) to capture Jerusalem from the Muslims.[9] By the time the first Christian army arrived in Palestine in 1098, written accounts by one side about the other had been circulated and read (or listened to). Appearing when they did

6. Deuteronomy 20:17, KJV.

7. **hijra:** the flight or emigration of Muhammad from Mecca to Medina, in 622 C.E.

8. Qur'an, Sūra 4:74, 95. Muhammad's revelations in the Qur'an are in order of length, with the longest sūra first. For one interpretation of the *chronology* of the revelations, see Reuven Firestone, *Jihad: The Origins of Holy War in Islam* (New York: Oxford University Press, 1999), pp. 67–91, 115–125.

9. Those Christians who went on these expeditions referred to themselves as "pilgrims." The term *crusade* (from the French word *croix*, "cross" in English) was not used for some time.

during the period Europeans refer to as the Crusades, there is little doubt that these accounts created perceptions and stereotypes in the minds of Christians who had never met Muslims, and vice versa. Moreover, it is clear that these accounts helped to formulate ideas in each camp of how the other should be treated.

Your task in this chapter is twofold. First, by examining the accounts written by Christians and by Muslims, determine the impressions that each side created of the other. Second, reach some conclusions about how those perceptions and stereotypes (whether accurate or inaccurate) might have influenced the ways in which Christians and Muslims chose to deal with one another.

Before you begin, we must issue a note of caution. From the evidence provided by Christians, you will *not* be able to determine what Muslims were *really* like, but only what Christians perceived (or wanted their readers to perceive) Muslims were like. This is equally true of the Muslim accounts. Indeed, it is quite possible that some of the writers had never even met the people about whom they were writing. Even so, what you *do* learn will prove extremely important, for perceptions, impressions, and stereotypes are often just as powerful as facts in prompting individuals to action. To paraphrase historian Claude Van Tyne, what people *think* is true may be more important to them than what is *really* true.

BACKGROUND

The 500s and early 600s was a period of great change in the Arab world. Increased trade had brought a new level of prosperity, but that prosperity in turn had produced tribal and class divisions. Old values of tribal unity and sharing wealth were giving way to new values of individual and family accumulation. At the same time, Arabs began to feel a strong sense of religious inferiority. Neighboring Jews and Christians (with whom Arab merchants traded) boasted that their respective faiths were superior to other religions because they were built on divine revelations, something Arabs had not received. Hence one could say that the Arabian peninsula was in economic, social, political, and intellectual crisis.

The appearance of Muhammad ibn Abdullah (ca. 570–632) ultimately solved each of these crises. Orphaned at an early age and raised by an uncle, Muhammad became a merchant, traveling in mercantile caravans as far as Palestine, where he surely became familiar with both Judaism and Christianity. Marriage to a wealthy widow freed him from the need to work long hours to make a living, and the extremely pious merchant spent a good deal of time in meditation and prayer.

Around the year 610, Muhammad began to experience what he said were divine revelations from God (*Allah* in Arabic) and God's messengers (he claimed that his first vision was of the angel Gabriel). Gathering around him

[181]

Chapter 7

Two Faces of

"Holy War":

Christians and

Muslims

(1095–1270s)

a small group of followers, he began to preach what he insisted was not a new religious faith but a reform of Arabs' traditional faith. Initially, Muhammad's message was a simple one: There was but one God (Allah), the same God, he said, who was worshiped by Jews and Christians; humans must prepare themselves for a last judgment; it was the duty of each believer to care for the poor and oppressed and to work to create a just society based on God's will and divine revelations. One can see how Muhammad and his teachings filled several needs in Arabic society. He advocated Arab unity over class and tribal divisions, care for the poor in a region of growing prosperity but unequal distribution of wealth, and Islam's parity with other religions because of the revelations Muhammad experienced.[10]

By the time of Muhammad's death in 632, most people living in the Arabian peninsula had become Muslims. Muhammad's successor Abu Bakr (called a *caliph,* or "successor to the Prophet") ordered that all of Muhammad's revelations be collected and printed in one book, the Qur'an (Koran), which was published in 651. Muslims accepted the teachings of both Jews and Christians (the most significant exception being the Christian assertion of Jesus' deity) and claimed that Muhammad was the last and ultimate prophet in a long line that included Abraham, Moses, and Jesus.

The death of Abu Bakr in 634 brought Umar to the caliphate. Under Umar, Arabs launched a series of wars to expand their power to North Africa, the Middle East, India, China, and Europe. In addition to the religious imperative, there also were economic reasons for these wars of expansion, especially the extension of trade routes under Arab control and the reaping of tribute paid by vanquished peoples. Jews and Christians living in conquered lands were allowed to practice their faiths, but economically and politically they were definitely second-class citizens. Christians were allowed to make pilgrimages to Jerusalem, a holy city that they now shared with Jews and Muslims.[11]

Beneath the surface, Islam was never as unified as Muslims claimed. In 656 the third caliph, Uthman, was murdered, and a division arose among Muslims as to who would succeed him. The two resulting groups, the Sunnis and the Shi'ites, also differed over whether caliphs, like the Prophet, were divinely inspired.[12] In time, the split became permanent, and even today it is the source of much internal strife within Islam, seen most recently in Iraq. Thus, by the time Christians from Western Europe began their own "holy war" in 1097 (later called by Europeans the First Crusade), the Muslim world was badly fragmented and vulnerable to outside intrusions.

11. Muslims believed that Muhammad ascended to heaven from the Dome of the Rock, located in Jerusalem on the very site of the Temple where Jesus taught, which was destroyed by Roman armies in the first century. In 691, Caliph Abd al-Malik built a pavilion on the rock. Both Christians and Muslims believed that the rock possessed curative powers, and pilgrims chipped off fragments to take them home.

12. The name *Sunni* was derived from the Arabic word *Sunna,* a collection of the Prophet's sayings and instructions for conduct in certain situations. *Shi'ite* is Arabic for "supporter" or "partisan."

10. *Islam,* in Arabic, means "submission (to God)," and a *Muslim* is "one who submits."

Chapter 7

Two Faces of

"Holy War":

Christians and

Muslims

(1095–1270s)

At the same time that the Muslim world was becoming increasingly divided, Western Europe was showing signs of increased energy. After centuries of comparatively modest population increases, suddenly population grew more rapidly, creating a surplus agricultural population and a resulting desire for more land. For example, it has been estimated that between about 950 and 1347 (the year the Black Death first appeared in Europe), the population of Europe increased threefold—in some areas, like Saxony, it increased tenfold. At the same time, trade with the eastern Mediterranean grew significantly, which fed the desires, especially in the commercial cities of Italy, for more trade connections with the Middle East. Finally, the social order produced a class of knightly warriors who were anxious to extend their power through combat.

Politically, however, Europe was even more fragmented than the Muslim world. Kings, for the most part weak, were unable to enforce peace within their domains. In an effort to keep the lords of Europe away from each other's throats as well as to enhance the power of the papacy, popes in the eleventh century attempted to promote the Peace of God movement among Christians. European nobles, the movement proclaimed, would not engage in warfare against one another.

The Peace of God movement shows that the power of the popes was increasing and that religious enthusiasm was on the rise in Europe. Itinerant preachers whipped up crowds into fevers of religious excitement in which visions and miracles of healing were reported. In about the year 1000, an old Christian myth was revived and spread throughout much of Europe. Before the second coming of Christ and the resulting end of the world, the story went, an emperor from the West would be crowned in Jerusalem and would battle the Antichrist in that holy city. The circulation of this myth was especially rampant during the widespread famine of 1033.

Hence a number of factors were pushing Christian Europe toward its own version of a "holy war." Population growth spurred a hunger for land, and, in turn, a drive for new lands to be brought under Europeans' control gained momentum. The knightly warriors could maintain the Peace of God among Christians while at the same time uniting to battle "pagans" elsewhere. Crusades could also increase the power of the papacy and would direct the religious enthusiasm toward a productive end. Therefore, when Pope Urban II in 1095 issued his call for a crusade, many Christians took up the cry "God wills it!" "You should be especially aroused," Urban challenged his listeners at Clermont, "by the knowledge that . . . the holy places are shamelessly misused and sacrilegiously defiled with their filth." The first armies set off in August 1097[13]; they captured Jerusalem on July 15, 1099.

Earlier Muslim incursions into North Africa, the eastern Mediterranean, Sicily, Italy, Spain, and southern France

13. A ragtag army of peasants led by the itinerant holy man Peter the Hermit began its march earlier, slaughtered Jews on its way across Europe, and was wiped out before reaching Palestine. It has been estimated that one-fourth of all "crusaders" (more often they referred to themselves as pilgrims) died on their way to the Holy Land.

did not mean that they had learned a great deal about Christian Europe, or that European Christians had learned a great deal about them. Instead, what is striking is the apparent utter lack of curiosity that each side displayed toward the other. Beginning about the time of the First Crusade, however, the number of written accounts by both Christians and Muslims increased dramatically. Your tasks are to determine what the perceptions presented were *and* how they helped to shape opinion on how the other side was to be treated.

THE METHOD

The Evidence section of this chapter contains three Muslim accounts of European crusaders and six shorter European Christian accounts of Muslims. Usamah ibn-Munqidh (1095–1188) was born in Syria and educated by private tutors; he was a merchant and government administrator, and knew Europeans quite well. Source 1 is his account of the "curious" crusaders. For his part, Ibn al-Athir (1160–1233) was one of three brothers, all of whom became noted Arabic scholars. He traveled extensively to collect material for his historical writing, and in Source 2, he glories in the 1187 retaking of Jerusalem. Imad ad-Din (1125–1201) was a scholar who was best known as a secretary to the sultan Saladin. Source 3 is an excerpt from his *History of the Fall of Jerusalem*.

As to the Christian sources, *History of the Jerusalem Journey* (Source 4) is by Peter Tudebode, a priest who accompanied the warriors on the First Crusade. One or possibly two of his brothers were killed in battle during the siege of Antioch. Some controversy continues to surround Peter Tudebode's account because many scholars believe that some of it was plagiarized from earlier writers. Since you are concerned with the perceptions that readers or listeners might have gleaned from the account, whether Tudebode actually saw some of what he chronicled or not is less important than those perceptions.

Fulcher of Chartres (1058?–1127?) was a chaplain on the First Crusade, first to Stephen of Blois and then to Baldwin of Boulogne. When Jerusalem fell (on July 15, 1099), Baldwin's older brother Godfrey was offered the kingship of Jerusalem but declined that title, preferring to be called the Defender of the Holy Sepulcher. When he died the next year, Baldwin was named his successor and thus became King Baldwin I of Jerusalem. Fulcher, therefore, was in a position to witness most of the events he described. Since only four Western eyewitness narratives of the First Crusade survive (one other being that of Peter Tudebode), Fulcher's history (Source 5) was much read by Fulcher's contemporaries and is of great value to historians. Because Fulcher's narrative simply stops in 1127, as he was recounting a plague of rats in Jerusalem, some historians believe he died in that year.

A History of Deeds Done Beyond the Sea by William of Tyre (Source 6), is almost certainly the most widely read account by a Christian of the Crusades.

Chapter 7

Two Faces of

"Holy War":

Christians and

Muslims

(1095–1270s)

William was born around 1130 in or near Jerusalem to European parents. He was extremely well educated both in Palestine and in Europe and had command of six languages, including Arabic and Persian. He was ordained a Roman Catholic priest, returned to what Christians referred to as the Holy Land, and was made Archbishop of Tyre, a position he held from 1175 to approximately 1185. By the time Saladin conquered Jerusalem in 1187, William had disappeared from view and probably had died.

Both Geoffrey de Vinsauf and Ambrose (Sources 7 and 8) wrote accounts of the Third Crusade (1189–1192). Geoffrey was a well-educated English monk and poet, whereas Ambrose was a *jongleur* (minstrel and storyteller) in the service of Richard I of England. Finally, Jean de Joinville (Source 9) was a French nobleman (1224–1317) who accompanied Louis IX of France on the Seventh Crusade (1249–1254) and who played an important role in convincing the papacy to canonize Louis in 1297 (27 years after Louis's death).

At first glance, all of these sources present some potential problems. To begin with, we cannot be certain that any of the authors (exceptions being Peter Tudebode, Fulcher of Chartres, and Jean de Joinville) were eyewitnesses to the events they describe. For example, some events that William of Tyre wrote about took place before he was born. To be sure, as secretary to Saladin, Imad ad-Din was in an excellent position to witness the events that he recounted. But that is not proof that he actually *did* see them, and we cannot be sure how much he embellished what he saw or heard.

And yet, in this chapter, these are not the obstacles that they might be elsewhere. This is because, as noted above, we are seeking the *perceptions* that each side had of the other and the images and stereotypes that were deliberately created for a myriad of purposes (the author of one of the sources, Fulcher of Chartres, described people "so tall that they can mount elephants as easily as horses").[14] Each author is attempting to create an impression in the minds of readers. To that end, he may accurately report events, or he may liberally exaggerate, interpret, or simply invent. That these writers were helping to create or perpetuate what ultimately would become very unhealthy stereotypes that in some cases continue to exist today does not appear to have bothered them in the least. Indeed, for some of these men, such stereotypes were good things that people should believe when facing their enemies.

As you finish each selection, think of some adjectives that readers of the account might have used to describe "the enemy." Keep a running list of these adjectives as you proceed through the evidence. Be willing also to read between the lines. Sometimes a particular author, in genuinely trying to describe or explain a specific incident, may have nevertheless created a perception in the minds of his readers, intentionally or unintentionally. Be alert for such instances.

Keep the central questions of the chapter in mind: In the written accounts by Muslims and Christians,

14. See Fulcher of Chartres, *A History of the Expedition to Jerusalem, 1095–1127*, trans. Frances Rita Ryan and ed. Harold S. Fink (Knoxville: University of Tennessee Press, 1969), p. 287.

what impressions did each side create of the other? How might those perceptions or stereotypes have influenced the way each side chose to deal with and treat each other, both during and after the period Europeans refer to as the Crusades?

MUSLIMS ON CHRISTIANS

Source 1 from Usamah ibn-Munqidh, An Arab-Syrian Gentleman and Warrior in the Period of the Crusades, *trans. Philip K. Hitti (New York: Columbia University Press, 1929; reprint, Princeton: Princeton University Press, 1987), pp. 161–169. © 1987 by Princeton University Press. Reprinted by permission of Princeton University Press.*

1. Usamah ibn-Munqidh Describes the Franks

Their lack of sense.—Mysterious are the works of the Creator, the author of all things! When one comes to recount cases regarding the Franks,[15] he cannot but glorify Allah (exalted is he!) and sanctify him, for he sees them as animals possessing the virtues of courage and fighting, but nothing else; just as animals have only the virtues of strength and carrying loads. I shall now give some instances of their doings and their curious mentality.

In the army of King Fulk, son of Fulk, was a Frankish reverend knight who had just arrived from their land in order to make the holy pilgrimage and then return home. He was of my intimate fellowship and kept such constant company with me that he began to call me "my brother." Between us were mutual bonds of amity and friendship. When he resolved to return by sea to his homeland, he said to me:

> My brother, I am leaving for my country and I want thee to send with me thy son (my son, who was then fourteen years old, was at that time in my company) to our country, where he can see the knights and learn wisdom and chivalry. When he returns, he will be like a wise man.

Thus there fell upon my ears words which would never come out of the head of a sensible man; for even if my son were to be taken captive, his captivity could not bring him a worse misfortune than carrying him into the lands of the Franks. However, I said to the man:

> By thy life, this has exactly been my idea. But the only thing that prevented me from carrying it out was the fact that his grandmother, my mother, is so fond of

15. Most Muslims called all the crusaders "Franks" even though they knew full well that they were not all French.

Chapter 7

Two Faces of

"Holy War":

Christians and

Muslims

(1095–1270s)

him and did not this time let him come out with me until she exacted an oath from me to the effect that I would return him to her.

Thereupon he asked, "Is thy mother still alive?" "Yes," I replied. "Well," said he, "disobey her not." . . .

Their curious medication.—A case illustrating their curious medicine is the following:

The lord of al-Munaytirah wrote to my uncle asking him to dispatch a physician to treat certain sick persons among his people. My uncle sent him a [Arab] Christian physician named Thābit. Thābit was absent but ten days when he returned. So we said to him, "How quickly hast thou healed thy patients!" He said:

They brought before me a knight in whose leg an abscess had grown; and a woman afflicted with imbecility. To the knight I applied a small poultice until the abscess opened and became well; and the woman I put on diet and made her humor wet. Then a Frankish physician came to them and said, "This man knows nothing about treating them." He then said to the knight, "Which wouldst thou prefer, living with one leg or dying with two?" The latter replied, "Living with one leg." The physician said, "Bring me a strong knight and a sharp ax." A knight came with the ax. And I was standing by. Then the physician laid the leg of the patient on a block of wood and bade the knight strike his leg with the ax and chop it off at one blow. Accordingly he struck it—while I was looking on—one blow, but the leg was not severed. He dealt another blow, upon which the marrow of the leg flowed out and the patient died on the spot. He then examined the woman and said, "This is a woman in whose head there is a devil which has possessed her. Shave off her hair." Accordingly they shaved it off and the woman began once more to eat their ordinary diet—garlic and mustard. Her imbecility took a turn for the worse. The physician then said, "The devil has penetrated through her head." He therefore took a razor, made a deep cruciform incision on it, peeled off the skin at the middle of the incision until the bone of the skull was exposed and rubbed it with salt. The woman also expired instantly. Thereupon I asked them whether my services were needed any longer, and when they replied in the negative I returned home, having learned of their medicine what I knew not before. . . .

Another wants to show to a Moslem God as a child.—I saw one of the Franks come to al-Amīr Mu'īn-al-Dīn (may Allah's mercy rest upon his soul!) when he was in the Dome of the Rock and say to him, "Dost thou want to see God as a child?" Mu'īn-al-Dīn said, "Yes." The Frank walked ahead of us until he showed us the picture of Mary with Christ (may peace be upon him!) as an infant in her lap. He then said, "This is God as a child." But Allah is exalted far above what the infidels say about him! . . .

Source 2 from Francesco Gabrieli, Arab Historians of the Crusades *(Berkeley: University of California Press, 1969), pp. 141–142, 144. Copyright 1969 by University of California Press–Books. Reproduced with permission of University of California Press–Books in the format Textbook via Copyright Clearance Center.*

2. Ibn al-Athir, The Capture of Jerusalem, 1187

When the Franks saw how violently the Muslims were attacking, how continuous and effective was the fire from the ballistas and how busily the sappers were breaching the walls, meeting no resistance, they grew desperate, and their leaders assembled to take counsel. They decided to ask for safe-conduct out of the city and to hand Jerusalem over to Saladin.[16] They sent a deputation of their lords and nobles to ask for terms, but when they spoke of it to Saladin he refused to grant their request. "We shall deal with you," he said, "just as you dealt with the population of Jerusalem when you took it in 492/1099, with murder and enslavement and other such savageries!" The messengers returned empty-handed. Then Balian ibn Barzan asked for safe-conduct for himself so that he might appear before Saladin to discuss developments. Consent was given, and he presented himself and once again began asking for a general amnesty in return for surrender. The Sultan still refused his requests and entreaties to show mercy. Finally, despairing of this approach, Balian said: "Know, O Sultan, that there are very many of us in this city, God alone knows how many. At the moment we are fighting half-heartedly in the hope of saving our lives, hoping to be spared by you as you have spared others; this is because of our horror of death and our love of life. But if we see that death is inevitable, then by God we shall kill our children and our wives, burn our possessions, so as not to leave you with a *dinar* or a *drachma* or a single man or woman to enslave. When this is done, we shall pull down the Sanctuary of the Rock and the Masjid al-Aqsa and the other sacred places, slaughtering the Muslim prisoners we hold—5,000 of them—and killing every horse and animal we possess. Then we shall come out to fight you like men fighting for their lives, when each man, before he falls dead, kills his equals; we shall die with honour, or win a noble victory!" Then Saladin took counsel with his advisers, all of whom were in favour of his granting the assurances requested by the Franks, without forcing them to take extreme measures whose outcome could not be foreseen. "Let us consider them as being already our prisoners," they said, "and allow them to ransom themselves on terms agreed between us." The Sultan agreed to give the Franks assurances of safety on the understanding that each man, rich and poor alike, should pay ten *dinar*, children of both sexes two *dinar* and women five *dinar*. All who paid this sum within forty days should go free, and those who had not paid at the end of the time should be enslaved. Balian ibn Barzan [Balian of Ibelin] offered 30,000 *dinar* as ransom

---

16. **Saladin:** Muslim sultan Salah ad-Din, whose real name was Yusuf ibn-Ayyub. *Salah-ad-Din* means "Rectifier of the Faith," a name Yusuf took up when he began his jihad against Christians.

Chapter 7

Two Faces of

"Holy War":

Christians and

Muslims

(1095–1270s)

for the poor, which was accepted, and the city surrendered on Friday 27 rajab/2 October 1187, a memorable day on which the Muslim flags were hoisted over the walls of Jerusalem. . . .

At the top of the cupola of the Dome of the Rock there was a great gilded cross. When the Muslims entered the city on the Friday, some of them climbed to the top of the cupola to take down the cross. When they reached the top a great cry went up from the city and from outside the walls, the Muslims crying the *Allāh akbar* in their joy, the Franks groaning in consternation and grief. So loud and piercing was the cry that the earth shook. . . .

Source 3 from Francesco Gabrieli, Arab Historians of the Crusades *(Berkeley: University of California Press, 1969), pp. 136–137, 148–149, 163, 170–171, 204, 207. Copyright © 1969 by University of California Press—Books. Reproduced with permission of University of California Press—Books in the format Textbook via Copyright Clearance Center.*

3. From Imad ad-Din, *History of the Fall of Jerusalem*

At the same time as the King was taken the "True Cross"[17] was also captured, and the idolaters who were trying to defend it were routed. It was this cross, brought into position and raised on high, to which all Christians prostrated themselves and bowed their heads. Indeed, they maintain that it is made of the wood of the cross on which, they say, he whom they adore was hung, and so they venerate it and prostrate themselves before it. They had housed it in a casing of gold, adorned with pearls and gems, and kept it ready for the festival of the Passion, for the observance of their yearly ceremony. When the priests exposed it to view and the heads (of the bearers) bore it along all would run and cast themselves down around it, and no one was allowed to lag behind or hang back without forfeiting his liberty. Its capture was for them more important than the loss of the King and was the gravest blow that they sustained in that battle. The cross was a prize without equal, for it was the supreme object of their faith. To venerate it was their prescribed duty, for it was their God, before whom they would bow their foreheads to the ground, and to which their mouths sang hymns. They fainted at its appearance, they raised their eyes to contemplate it, they were consumed with passion when it was exhibited and boasted of nothing else when they had seen it. They went into ecstasies at its reappearance, they offered up their lives for it and sought comfort from it, so much so that they had copies made of it which they worshipped, before which they prostrated themselves in their houses and on which they called when they gave evidence. So when the Great Cross was taken great was the calamity that befell them, and

17. The religious excitement in Europe led to the "discovery" of numerous relics both before and during the Crusades. Some of these relics were portions of the "True Cross" of Christ's crucifixion (see above), the Holy Lance (that pierced Jesus's side), and the Crown of Thorns. Thus, the loss of what was believed to have been the cross to Saladin was a devastating blow to the crusaders.

the strength drained from their loins. Great was the number of the defeated, exalted the feelings of the victorious army. It seemed as if, once they knew of the capture of the Cross, none of them would survive that day of ill-omen. They perished in death or imprisonment, and were overcome by force and violence.

They continued to attach errors like this to the object of their cult, wandering with false beliefs far from the true forms of faith, and said: "We shall die in defence of our Lord's sepulchre, and we shall die in fear of its slipping from our hands; we shall fight and struggle for it: how could we not fight, not contend and join battle, how could we leave this for them to take, and permit them to take from us what we took from them?" They made far-reaching and elaborate preparations, stretching out endlessly to infinity. They mounted deadly weapons on the walls, and veiled the face of light with the sombre curtain of walls. They sent out their demons, their wolves ran hither and thither, their impetuous tyrants raged; their swords were unsheathed, the fabric of their downfall displayed, their blazing firebrands lit. . . .

There arrived by ship three hundred lovely Frankish women, full of youth and beauty, assembled from beyond the sea and offering themselves for sin. They were expatriates come to help expatriates, ready to cheer the fallen and sustained in turn to give support and assistance, and they glowed with ardour for carnal intercourse. They were all licentious harlots, proud and scornful, who took and gave, foul-fleshed and sinful, singers and coquettes, appearing proudly in public, ardent and inflamed, tinted and painted, desirable and appetizing, exquisite and graceful, who ripped open and patched up, lacerated and mended, erred and ogled, urged and seduced, consoled and solicited, seductive and languid, desired and desiring, amused and amusing, versatile and cunning, like tipsy adolescents, making love and selling themselves for gold, bold and ardent, loving and passionate, pink-faced and unblushing, black-eyed and bullying, callipygian[18] and graceful, with nasal voices and fleshy thighs, blue-eyed and grey-eyed, broken-down little fools. . . .

Among the Franks there were indeed women who rode into battle with cuirasses [armor breastplates] and helmets, dressed in men's clothes; who rode out into the thick of the fray and acted like brave men although they were but tender women, maintaining that all this was an act of piety, thinking to gain heavenly rewards by it, and making it their way of life. Praise be to him who led them into such error and out of the paths of wisdom! On the day of battle more than one woman rode out with them like a knight and showed (masculine) endurance in spite of the weakness (of her sex); clothed only in a coat of mail they were not recognized as women until they had been stripped of their arms. Some of them were discovered and sold as slaves; and everywhere was full of old women. These were sometimes a support and sometimes a source of weakness. They exhorted and incited men to summon their pride, saying that the Cross imposed on them the obligation to resist to the bitter end, and that the combatants would

18. **callipygian:** having shapely buttocks.

[191]

Chapter 7

Two Faces of

"Holy War":

Christians and

Muslims

(1095–1270s)

win eternal life only by sacrificing their lives, and that their God's sepulchre was in enemy hands. Observe how men and women led them into error; the latter in their religious zeal tired of feminine delicacy, and to save themselves from the terror of dismay (on the day of Judgment) became the close companions of perplexity, and having succumbed to the lust for vengeance, became hardened, and stupid and foolish because of the harm they had suffered. . . .

EUROPEANS ON MUSLIMS

Source 4 from Memoirs of the American Philosophical Society, volume 101. *Peter Tudebode,* Historia de Hierosolymitano Itinere (History of the Jerusalem Journey), *trans. with Introduction and Notes by John Hugh Hill and Laurita L. Hill.* Memoirs of the American Philosophical Society, vol. 101 *(Philadelphia, 1974), pp. 54–55, 58–59, 115.*

4. From Peter Tudebode, *History of the Jerusalem Journey*

On another day the Turks led to the top of an Antiochian wall a noble knight, Rainald Porchet, whom they had imprisoned in a foul dungeon. They then told him that he should inquire from the Christian pilgrims how much they would pay for his ransom before he lost his head. From the heights of the wall Rainald addressed the leaders: "My lords, it matters not if I die, and I pray you, my brothers, that you pay no ransom for me. But be certain in the faith of Christ and the Holy Sepulchre that God is with you and shall be forever. You have slain all the leaders and the bravest men of Antioch; namely, twelve emirs and fifteen thousand noblemen, and no one remains to give battle with you or to defend the city."

The Turks asked what Rainald had said. The interpreter replied: "Nothing good concerning you was said."

The emir, Yaghi Siyan, immediately ordered him to descend from the wall and spoke to him through an interpreter: "Rainald, do you wish to enjoy life honorably with us?"

Rainald replied: "How can I live honorably with you without sinning?"

The emir answered: "Deny your God, whom you worship and believe, and accept Mohammed and our other gods. If you do so we shall give to you all that you desire such as gold, horses, mules, and many other worldly goods which you wish, as well as wives and inheritances; and we shall enrich you with great lands."

Rainald replied to the emir: "Give me time for consideration;" and the emir gladly agreed. Rainald with clasped hands knelt in prayer to the east; humbly he asked God that He come to his aid and transport with dignity his soul to the bosom of Abraham.

When the emir saw Rainald in prayer, he called his interpreter and said to him: "What was Rainald's answer?"

The interpreter then said: "He completely denies your god. He also refuses your worldly goods and your gods."

After hearing this report, the emir was extremely irritated and ordered the immediate beheading of Rainald, and so the Turks with great pleasure chopped off his head. Swiftly the angels, joyfully singing the Psalms of David, bore his soul and lifted it before the sight of God for Whose love he had undergone martyrdom.

Then the emir, in a towering rage because he could not make Rainald turn apostate, at once ordered all the pilgrims in Antioch to be brought before him with their hands bound behind their backs. When they had come before him, he ordered them stripped stark naked, and as they stood in the nude he commanded that they be bound with ropes in a circle. He then had chaff, firewood, and hay piled around them, and finally as enemies of God he ordered them put to the torch.

The Christians, those knights of Christ, shrieked and screamed so that their voices resounded in heaven to God for whose love their flesh and bones were cremated; and so they all entered martyrdom on this day wearing in heaven their white stoles before the Lord, for Whom they had so loyally suffered in the reign of our Lord Jesus Christ, to Whom is the honor and glory now and throughout eternity. Amen. . . .

Source 5 from Fulcher of Chartres, A History of the Expedition to Jerusalem, 1095–1127, *trans. Frances Rita Ryan and ed. Harold S. Fink (Knoxville: University of Tennessee Press, 1969), pp. 121–123. Copyright © 1969. Reprinted by permission of the University of Tennessee.*

5. From Fulcher of Chartres, *A History of the Expedition to Jerusalem, 1095–1127*

Soon therefore the Franks gloriously entered the city at noon on the day known as Dies Veneris, the day in which Christ redeemed the whole world on the Cross.[19] Amid the sound of trumpets and with everything in an uproar they attacked boldly, shouting "God help us!" At once they raised a banner on the top of the wall. The pagans were completely terrified, for they all exchanged their former boldness for headlong flight through the narrow streets of the city. The more swiftly they fled the more swiftly they were pursued.

Count Raymond and his men, who were strongly pressing the offensive in another part of the city, did not notice this until they saw the Saracens jumping off from the top of the wall. When they noticed it they ran with the greatest exultation as fast as they could into the city and joined their companions in pursuing and slaying their wicked enemies without cessation.

Some of the latter, Arabs as well as Ethiopians, fled into the Tower of David, and others shut themselves up in the Temples of the Lord and of Solomon. In the courts of these buildings a fierce attack was pressed upon the Saracens. There was no place where they could escape our swordsmen.

19. Friday, July 15, 1099.

Chapter 7

Two Faces of

"Holy War":

Christians and

Muslims

(1095–1270s)

Many of the Saracens who had climbed to the top of the Temple of Solomon in their flight were shot to death with arrows and fell headlong from the roof. Nearly ten thousand were beheaded in this Temple. If you had been there your feet would have been stained to the ankles in the blood of the slain. What shall I say? None of them were left alive. Neither women nor children were spared.

The Spoils Taken by
the Christians

How astonishing it would have seemed to you to see our squires and footmen, after they had discovered the trickery of the Saracens, split open the bellies of those they had just slain in order to extract from the intestines the bezants[20] which the Saracens had gulped down their loathsome throats while alive! For the same reason a few days later our men made a great heap of corpses and burned them to ashes in order to find more easily the above-mentioned gold.

And also Tancred rushed into the Temple of the Lord and seized much gold and silver and many precious stones. But he restored these things, putting them or their equivalent back into the holy place. This was in spite of the fact that no divine services were conducted there at that time. The Saracens had practiced their rule of idolatry there with superstitious rite and moreover had not allowed any Christian to enter.

With drawn swords our men ran through the city
Not sparing anyone, even those begging for mercy.
The crowd fell just as rotten apples fall
From shaken branches and acorns from swaying oaks.

Source 6 from William of Tyre, A History of Deeds Done Beyond the Sea, *2 vols., trans. Emily Atwater Babcock and A. C. Krey (New York: Columbia University Press, 1943), vol. 1, pp. 60, 68–69, 306–307; vol. 2, p. 323. Copyright © 1943 Columbia University Press. Reprinted with permission of the publisher.*

6. From William of Tyre,
A History of Deeds Done
Beyond the Sea

In the time of the Roman Emperor Heraclius, according to ancient histories and Oriental tradition, the pernicious doctrines of Muhammad had gained a firm foothold in the Orient. This first-born son of Satan falsely declared that he was a prophet sent from God and thereby led astray the lands of the East, especially Arabia. The poisonous seed which he sowed so permeated the provinces that his successors employed sword and violence, instead of preaching and exhortation,

20. **bezant:** a gold coin minted in Byzantium.

[194]

to compel the people, however reluctant, to embrace the erroneous tenets of the prophet. . . .

There was a certain infidel living in the city, a treacherous and wicked man, who persecuted our people with insatiable hatred. This man was determined to devise some scheme that would bring about their destruction. One day, he stealthily threw the carcass of a dog into the temple court, a place which the custodians—and indeed the whole city as well—were most careful to keep scrupulously clean. Worshippers who came to the temple to pray the next morning found the mouldering body of the unclean animal. Almost frantic, they at once roused the whole city with their cries. The populace quickly ran to the temple, and all agreed that without question the Christians were responsible for the act. Need more be said? Death was decreed for all Christians, since it was judged that by death alone could they atone for such an act of sacrilege. The faithful, in full assurance of their innocence, prepared to suffer death for Christ's sake. As the executioners, with swords unsheathed, were about to carry out their orders, however, a young man, filled with the spirit, came forward and offered himself as the sacrifice. "It would be most disastrous, O brethren," he said, "that the entire church should die in this way. Far better were it that one man should give his life for the people, that the whole Christian race may not perish. Promise me that annually you will reverently honor my memory and that the respect and honor due to my family shall be maintained forever. On these terms, at the command of God, I will deliver you from this massacre." The Christians heard his words with great joy and readily granted what he asked. They promised that, on the day of palm branches, in perpetual memory of him, those of his lineage should bear into the city, in solemn procession, the olive which signifies our Lord Jesus Christ.

The young man then gave himself up to the chief men of Jerusalem and declared that he was the criminal. In this way he established the innocence of the other Christians, for, when the judges heard his story, they absolved the rest and put him to the sword. Thus he laid down his life for the brethren and, with pious resignation, met death, that most blessed sleep, confident that he had acquired grace in the sight of the Lord. . . .

The reason for the title caliph is as follows: Muhammad, their prophet, or rather their destroyer, who was the first to draw the peoples of the East to this kind of superstition, had as his immediate successor one of his disciples named Abu-Bakr. The latter was succeeded in the kingdom by Omar, son of Khattab, who was likewise followed by Uthman, and he by Ali, son of Abu-Talib. All these prophets were called caliphs, as were also all who followed them later, because they succeeded their famous master and were his heirs. But the fifth in the succession from Muhammad, namely Ali, was more warlike than his predecessors and had far greater experience in military matters than his contemporaries. He was, moreover, a cousin of Muhammad himself. He considered it unfitting that he should be called the successor of his cousin and not rather a great prophet himself, much greater, in fact, than Muhammad. The fact that in his own estimation and that of many others he

Chapter 7

Two Faces of

"Holy War":

Christians and

Muslims

(1095–1270s)

was greater did not satisfy him; he desired that this be generally acknowledged. Accordingly, he reviled Muhammad and spread among the people a story to the effect that the Angel Gabriel, the propounder of the law, had actually been sent to him from on high but by mistake had conferred the supreme honor on Muhammad. For this fault, he said, the angel had been severely blamed by the Lord. Although these claims seemed false to many from whose traditions they differed greatly, yet others believed them, and so a schism developed among that people which has lasted even to the present. Some maintain that Muhammad is the greater and, in fact, the greatest of all prophets, and these are called in their own tongue, Sunnites; others declare that Ali alone is the prophet of God, and they are called Shiites.

Source 7 from Geoffrey de Vinsauf, Chronicle of the Crusade, Being Contemporary Narratives of The Crusade of Richard Coeur de Lion *(London: Henry G. Bohn, 1848), pp. 84–85.*

7. Geoffrey de Vinsauf, *How Saladin, Extolling the Law of Mahomet, is Reproved by a Jester*

Saladin by these means had got possession of nearly all the kingdom, and every thing succeeded to his wishes. Elevated with his proud triumphs, he talked in magnificent terms of the law of Mahomet, and pointed to the result of his en-terprise as a proof that it was superior to the law of Christ.

These insolent vaunts he often threw out in the presence of the Christians, one of whom, well known to him for his loquacity,[21] on a certain occasion, inspired by the Almighty, turned him into ridicule by the following reply: "God, who is the father of the faithful, judging the Christians worthy of reproof and correction for their crimes, has chosen thee, O prince, as his agent in this matter: thus sometimes a worldly father in anger seizes a dirty stick out of the mire, wherewith when he has chastised his erring sons, he throws it back among the filth where he found it."

Source 8 from Ambrose, The History of the Holy War, Being an Account of the Third Crusade, *Composed in Verse by Ambrose,* A Jongleur in the Service of Richard Lion-Heart, About the Year 1196, *in Edward Noble Stone, ed.,* Three Old French Chronicles of the Crusades *(Seattle: University of Washington Press, 1939), p. 76. Copyright © 1939. Reprinted by permission of The University of Washington Press.*

8. Ambrose, *How the Infidels Had Desecrated the Churches of Acre*

The day when Acre was surrendered, as I have understood the matter, it was four years (this know I of a certainty) since the Saracens had taken it; and I have

21. **loquacity:** the habit of being talkative.

clearly in memory that it was surrendered on the day after the feast of Saint Benedict, in despite of that accursed folk whom may God curse with His mouth I cannot refrain myself from saying this. For then ought ye to have seen the churches that were left in Acre—how the Turks had broken and defaced the images, overthrown the altars, and beaten crosses and crucifixes, for to do despite to our belief and to satisfy their own misbelieve—and had made of them their own mameries.[22] But they paid dear for this thereafter. . . .

Source 9 from John Lord de Joinville, Memoirs of Louis IX. King of France. The Crusade of St. Louis, in Chronicles of the Crusades (London: Henry G. Bohn, 1848), pp. 420–421.

9. de Joinville, *Something Concerning These Bedouins*

As my subject requires it, I shall say something concerning these Bedouins, and what sort of people they be. The Bedouins reside in deserts and mountains, and have no great faith in Mahomet, like the Turks, but believe in the religion of Aly,[23] who, they say, was uncle to Mahomet. They are persuaded that when any one of them dies for the service of his lord, or when attempting any good design, his soul enters a superior body, and is much more comfortable than it was before; this makes them ready to die at the command of their superiors or elders. These Bedouins do not reside in town or city, but always lie in the fields and deserted places, where, whenever the weather is bad, they, their wives and children, make themselves an habitation, by sticking into the ground poles connected by hoops, like to what women use in drying their washed clothes; and over these hoops they throw skins of their large sheep, which they call skins of Somas,[24] tanned with alum.[25] The Bedouins have large pelisses[26] of coarse hair, which cover their whole bodies, and when evening comes, or when it is cold or wet, they wrap themselves up in them, and retire to rest. Those who follow war have their horses feeding near them during the night, and have only to take off their bridles, and let them eat. In the morning they spread their pelisses to the sun, and, when dry, rub them, so that they do not appear as if they had been wetted. They never are armed for combat, for they say, and believe, that no one can die but at his appointed hour: they have likewise a mode of cursing, alluding to their faith, when they swear at their children, saying, "Be thou accursed [like a Frank], who puts on armor for fear of death!" In battle they use only a

22. **mameries:** mosques
23. See the last paragraph of the excerpt by William of Tyre.
24. **Somas:** Damascus.
25. **alum:** potassium or sodium, often mixed with metals.
26. **pelisses:** long cloaks, usually made of fur.

Chapter 7

Two Faces of

"Holy War":

Christians and

Muslims

(1095–1270s)

sword, made after the Turkish manner, and are clothed in linen robes like to surplices.[27] They are an ugly race, and hideous to look at; for their hair and beards are long and black. They live on the superabundance of milk from their herds; and their numbers are not to be counted; for they dwell in the kingdoms of Jerusalem, Egypt, and throughout all the lands of the Saracens and infidels, to whom they are tributary. . . .[28]

27. **surplices:** loose-fitting white robe or gown.

28. Another translation reads, "to whom they pay, every year, a great tribute." See Sir Frank T. Marzials, trans., *Memoirs of the Crusades* (New York: E.P. Dutton & Co., 1958), p. 198.

QUESTIONS TO CONSIDER

Begin with the three Muslim accounts of Christians. Usamah's account (Source 1) is extremely valuable not only because he was well acquainted with Christians but also because he offers his readers numerous examples to support his main view of his European Christian foes. Examine and analyze each of Usamah's illustrations. What point is he trying to make by relating the story of the Frank who wanted to take Usamah's son back to Europe to make him a "wise man"? How does this story shed light on Usamah's perception of the Franks? Similarly, Usamah describes in some detail two medical "case studies," comparing the European remedies to the Muslim treatment. What does he intend his readers to think after reading about those two patients? What are those impressions likely to have been? In his "God as a child" story, Usamah is remarkably restrained (see later accounts by Muslims and Christians of each other's faith). What point is communicated?

Ibn al-Athir's account (Source 2) is primarily concerned with Saladin's conquest of Jerusalem in 1187, and his portraits of European crusaders seem extremely vague. From reading the two accounts (the first of Franks suing for surrender terms and the second of Franks leaving the city), what impressions would readers get of the European crusaders? What adjectives best describe their behavior?

It matters little that Imad ad-Din's view (Source 3) of Christianity contains a number of errors and misperceptions—each side was remarkably ignorant of the other's faith. What is important is the perception of Christian beliefs that he attempts to convey. What impressions would Imad's readers have gathered from his story of the devotion of the European crusaders to the "True Cross"? What stereotypes of European crusaders would that likely have put in the minds of Imad's readers? Finally, Imad portrays two groups of Frankish women. What do the descriptions tell readers about European women—and men?

Finally, reexamine each of the Muslim accounts. Do you notice any threads that are common to all three sources?

Like their Muslim counterparts, Western writers also recounted the immediate transportation of fallen warriors' souls to heaven (see, for example, the immensely popular *Song of Roland,* written by an anonymous author around 1100 about the Battle of Roncesvalles in 778).[29] Roman Catholic priest Peter Tudebode also wrote of Christian souls transported immediately to heaven (the martyrdom of Rainald Porchet) and the "everlasting death" of the Turks. According to Peter Tudebode, how does the Turkish emir react to the faithfulness of Rainald? What perceptions was Peter Tudebode trying to communicate to his readers in that account? in his account of Muslims' mockery of crosses?

William of Tyre was the Christian chronicler most familiar with Palestine and its Muslim population. Yet the first paragraph makes it clear that, to William, Muḥammad is the "first-born son of Satan," a false prophet whose successors were converted to Islam by force. The "dog carcass" story offers a vivid stereotype of Muslims. What is that stereotype?

On the surface Fulcher of Chartres barely mentions the Muslims in his account of the First Crusade. Even so, a stereotype of Muslims does emerge, in part in contrast to the Christian crusaders.[30] How does Fulcher accomplish this? You will have to "read between the lines" of his narrative.

Like the account by the Fulcher of Chartres, several European chronicles, in their efforts to blacken the

reputations of the Muslims, often unintentionally offer some rather unexpected—and unwelcomed— impressions of the Crusaders themselves. In the excerpt "The Spoils Taken by the Christians," how does Fulcher of Chartes characterize the Saracens? What impression do you get of the Crusaders from that same account?

By the time of the Third Crusade (1189–1192), the Muslim leader Salah-al-Din Yusuf ibn-Ayyub (Saladin, 1137–1193) had recaptured Jerusalem and was considered by both sides to be a military genius. What, then, was the aim of Geoffrey's anecdote? How was Saladin characterized by Geoffrey de Vinsauf?

As noted earlier, Ambrose was a *jongleur* in the service of Richard I (Lion-Heart), King of England. After the capture of Acre on the Mediterranean coast, Richard massacred every man, woman, and child he could lay his hands on. In the light of that event, what is the purpose of Ambrose's excerpt?

Jean de Joinville's extensive and interesting account is one of the best primary sources of the Crusades (in the case of his account, the Seventh Crusade, 1249–1254). How did he portray the Bedouins?

Now repeat for the Christian writers the process that you followed for the Muslim writers; that is, look for any common themes or stereotypes that all the accounts share.

As you examined and analyzed the Muslim and the European accounts, you doubtless noticed that some of the perceptions held by Muslims and European Christians about each other were remarkably similar. What similarities did you identify? How do you account for them?

---

29. *The Song of Roland* is based on a battle in which the rear guard of Charlemagne's army was overwhelmed and slaughtered by Basques. Writing during the First Crusade, however, the author substituted Muslims for Basques in the epic.

30. See note 9.

Chapter 7

Two Faces of

"Holy War":

Christians and

Muslims

(1095–1270s)

Finally, without being too explicit, all of the accounts advocate ways in which the other side should be treated. How do the perceptions (and misperceptions) lead directly to those conclusions? What attitudes and behaviors do you think might have been recommended? To answer these questions, you will have to exercise some historical imagination. Put yourself in the position of an intelligent but uninformed person who is reading these accounts soon after they were written. How do the implicit stereotypes affect your view of how the targeted group should be treated? Explain.

EPILOGUE

The perceptions that Muslims and European Christians had of one another made it almost inevitable that the wars later known in the West as the Crusades would be carried on with extreme ferocity. As some of the evidence above suggests, civilians and combatants often were slaughtered indiscriminately, as Christians were exhorted to "slay for God's love," and both Muslim and Christian warriors were promised immediate admission to heaven if they died while fighting in a holy war (jihad).[31] Although no accurate estimates of losses are available (some historians insist the Crusades cost the West between 4 and 5 *million* people out of a total population of around 50 million, a figure most historians believe is too high), it can be said that fewer than one-half of the pilgrims who set out on a crusade ever returned. Muslim losses, although not that high, were also frightful.

Gradually the crusading spirit declined in the West, partly because of the meager results they achieved and partly because Europe had turned to other concerns. The Black Death struck Europe in 1347, killing over five times the number felled in the Crusades. England lost between a quarter and a half of its total population to the plague, and the number of deaths were just as appalling in other parts of Europe and Asia (the plague had struck China in 1331, and a more serious outbreak occurred in 1353). In addition, the Hundred Years War (1337–1453) kept Europe in an almost perpetual state of upheaval, diverting its attention from any future crusades. In the Muslim world, political disunity and the Mongol threat turned Muslim attention away from Europeans. Too, the so-called crusader states (four European-ruled principalities on the eastern shores of the Mediterranean) all had succumbed again to Muslim control.

One would expect that the long period of contact between the Muslim and Christian worlds would have produced a great deal of cross-fertilization of culture, ideas, goods,

31. St. Bernard wrote that "a Christian glories in the death of a pagan because Christ is glorified; the liberality of the King [God] is revealed in the death of the Christian, because he is led out to his reward." Quoted in Norman Daniel, *Islam and the West: The Making of an Image,* rev. ed. (Oxford: Oneworld Publishing, 1993), p. 136.

[200]

and knowledge. Indeed, this was the case, although more of these kinds of exchanges took place in Spain and Italy than in the Middle East. From the Arabs, the West acquired a great deal of knowledge of medicine, astronomy, chemistry, physics, and mathematics. Paper, invented in China, was adopted by the Arabs and transmitted to Europe.[32] Arabs had preserved a great deal of Greek philosophy (much of which had been lost in the West), and it was by way of the Arabs that Europe "rediscovered" Aristotle. Arabic courtly literature (*adab*) was translated and became the bases of some European literature (including Shakespeare's *Taming of the Shrew*). Trade between the two worlds was intensified.

Not surprisingly, Muslims borrowed almost nothing from the West. The Islamic world simply didn't think it had much to learn from the West. Muslims did adopt some European clothing and liked some European food, but these were minor compared to what Muslims exported to Europeans.

Yet, although the spirit of holy warfare declined in both the Muslim and Christian worlds, the perceptions and misperceptions that each side created of the other remained strong for centuries, and one can find their unhealthy residues even today in the struggles between the West and Iran and (later) Iraq, in the Arab-Israeli conflicts, and in the reemergence of Islamic fundamentalism. Behind the struggles over oil and geopolitics lie images, perceptions, and stereotypes that are centuries old and durable even today.

Writing at the time of the Crusades, Friar Felix Fabari wrote of Muslims, "The easterners are men of a different kind to us, they have other passions, other ways of thinking, other ideas . . . they are influenced by other stars. . . ." Even as Westerners have come to learn a great deal more about Islamic religion, society, politics, and the arts, the notions of Fabari and others remain.

---

32. In medicine, the Arab *al-Qanun* (The Canon) became *the* medical textbook in the West. In physics the Arabs gave the West the pendulum; in astronomy a more accurate method of predicting an eclipse; in mathematics the field of algebra (practically an Arab creation), the zero, and the decimal point. Before Europeans borrowed paper from the Arabs, they wrote on papyrus or parchment.

CHAPTER EIGHT

FICTION AND THE EMOTIONS

IN JAPANESE, ARABIAN, AND IRISH

CULTURE (1000–1400 C.E.)

In every culture of the world, people have created larger-than-life heroes and heroines, and more ordinary figures, whose desires and emotions led them to great heights and depths of feeling and motivated them to action. Initially, stories about these characters were shared orally, and listeners expanded on them, telling familiar stories in new ways, adding characters, and making up new situations. Then, in many places, they were written down, collected, reworked, and further expanded, and in a few places, authors invented new characters out of their own imaginations. Those who could read told or read written stories to those who could not, so that written stories came to shape the oral tradition as well as the other way around. Certain stories became especially popular, and were told, copied, and enhanced over centuries, forming

the foundation of what we have since come to call "literature."

Such works are studied, of course, in departments of literature, but historians use literary sources as well. The characters in oral traditions and the literature based on them are often described as having lived at some point in the past, and in using literature, earlier historians sometimes focused on whether the characters were "real" or not—that is, whether they were actual historical figures. This was not an important issue to most of the people who listened to or read these stories over the many centuries since they were first told, however. Instead, they avidly followed the characters because of their adventures, their personalities, and their reactions to the situations in which they found themselves. The stories did have to be "real" in another sense, however, for even mythical heroes needed to have emotions that would be understandable to those who heard about them.

[202]

Their reactions might be extreme, and their actions superhuman, but their inner feelings and passions needed to be believable. Thus, more recent historians often use literature to explore what earlier cultures found interesting in the private lives of men and women, and how they understood love, anger, passion, fear, sadness, and other emotions that shaped human action. They have discovered that the way emotions are expressed, and to some degree the way they are felt, differs from culture to culture, so that emotions themselves have a history. In addition to providing evidence about private life and the emotions, many of the tales directly or indirectly provide evidence for the role of storytelling itself, suggesting ways in which people viewed the importance of literature and the imagination.

This chapter includes small segments of three very long stories or story-groups that are part of the foundational literary heritage of three different parts of the world: *The Tale of Genji*, written by Murasaki Shikibu in tenth-century Japan; *The Arabian Nights*, a group of stories apparently first written down in Persian and then in Arabic in the late ninth century; and the Ulster Cycle, a group of Irish myths and stories that began to be written down in the seventh century. For this chapter, you have two tasks: the first is to analyze similarities and differences in the personal qualities and emotional responses of the men and women created in these stories. What makes an interesting character in these fictional stories, and how do these characters feel and act? The second is to think more broadly about fiction. What role does telling, hearing, and reading stories play in the cultures in which these stories originated? What opportunities does fiction provide for us as historians, and what special problems arise in using fiction as a historical source?

BACKGROUND

The three stories in this chapter come from cultures that were widely separated geographically, and yet they shared certain characteristics at the time in which the stories were first written down. All three were aristocratic cultures, in which one's social level and family of birth largely determined one's opportunities in life, but in which there was some social mobility. Marriage among the upper classes was regarded as an opportunity to increase family wealth and prestige, so that one's family had a great deal to say about whom one married. Women could inherit and own property, but only rarely held official positions of power. Thus women appeared infrequently in what was understood as "history," although they are important figures in all of these stories.

The Tale of Genji was, in fact, written by a woman, the daughter of an ambitious government official in Heian Japan who gained an education in classical Chinese literature and history by sitting in on the lessons her father provided for her brother in the late tenth century. Her real name is

Chapter 8

Fiction and

the Emotions

in Japanese,

Arabian, and

Irish Culture

(1000–1400 C.E.)

unknown, as women in Heian Japan were usually simply referred to by their fathers' or brothers' titles, but she is usually called Murasaki (the name of one of the female characters in *Genji*) Shikibu (a title once held by her father). At about age twenty, she married a much older man, who died soon afterward, leaving Murasaki Shikibu with a daughter. For a while she lived in seclusion and probably began work on *The Tale of Genji* during this time. In about 1005, her father secured her a position as a lady-in-waiting to the empress, and Murasaki was welcomed into the imperial court. During this time, she worked on a diary as well as *Genji* and was joined in her literary pursuits by a number of other women. The most famous of these was Sei Shonagon, the author of *The Pillow Book*, a long collection of stories and descriptions of upper-class life; Murasaki's daughter also became a well-known author.

The Tale of Genji is extremely long and complex, over twice as long as *War and Peace* and containing over 430 characters. It tells the story of Genji, the son of the emperor and his favorite concubine, who grows up at court and marries a princess slightly older than himself. He becomes good friends with his wife's brother, To-no-Chujo, and they both have many love affairs. Genji later takes To-no-Chujo's daughter from one of these affairs, Tamakazura, into his household, and also takes in the abandoned daughter of another prince, Lady Murasaki, who becomes his second wife after his first wife dies. Murasaki is often thought of as the romantic heroine of the story, as she becomes Genji's favorite.

Murasaki Shikibu did not set her story in the distant past, but in the near past in a milieu familiar to her readers. Although she was not explicit in providing historical details, she does refer to past emperors and events, and most commentators believe her story to have been set sometime between 900 and 925, or just about 100 years before she wrote *Genji*. Though Genji and the other characters in the book are not actual historical people, they correspond loosely to real figures, and when the emperor ruling during her lifetime heard *Genji* being read aloud he commented: "She [Murasaki Shikibu] must have read the *Chronicles of Japan*. . . she seems very learned."

Virtually every facet of *Genji* has provoked great arguments since it was written. We do not know exactly what order Murasaki wrote it in, because to some degree each chapter stands alone and they often circulated independently. *Genji* appeared long before the invention of the printing press, so that those who wished to have a copy for themselves had to copy it or pay someone to do so. It quickly became a classic, and one modern commentator has estimated that there have been more than 10,000 books about *Genji* since the original was written. Its reputation and complexity led later Japanese critics to doubt whether it could really have been written by a woman, although Murasaki's authorship is not questioned at all today. (This often happened with great literary works written by women throughout the world, and Japan is unusual in that almost all its literary classics were written by women. This was the result of the fact that men regarded Chinese as the appropriate language for their writings, a feeling so strong that when men did write in Japanese, they pretended that their works were written by women. The opposite pattern is found throughout most of the rest of the world: women used male pen names to make it more likely that their works would be taken seriously.)

The Arabian Nights did not have a single author, but the most important character is a woman, Shahrazad, the daughter of king's vizier, or highest official. The earliest stories that became part of *The Arabian Nights* were of Persian or Indian origin, and were first written down sometime before the late ninth century in Arabic and perhaps in Persian as well. This includes what is known as the "framing story" of King Shahrayar and Shahrazad, which sets the scene in which all the other stories are told. In the tenth century, an Arabic historian and an Arabic bookseller both mentioned—disparagingly—collections of stories that people were reading, referring to them by a name they have often had since, the *Thousand and One Nights*. Most of the early written versions of the stories have been lost; the oldest surviving manuscript, produced in Syria, dates from the fourteenth century. The stories continued to be told and retold orally as well as in writing, modified over the centuries to suit the teller and the audience. Gradually, more stories were added to the collection as various copyists decided that there really needed to be a thousand and one nights of tales. Along with the very old Persian tales, another group originated in Baghdad in the tenth to twelfth centuries, at a time when Baghdad was the capital of the Abbasid Caliphate and thus the cultural and economic center of the Muslim world. Unsurprisingly, many of these stories involve wise caliphs and their officials, although others relate the voyages of Sindbad, an ordinary (though courageous and lucky) sailor. A third group originated in Cairo in the twelfth to the fourteenth centuries, many of which center on genies, demons, and tricksters, characters that had long been part of the oral folktales and fables of Egypt. Various stories from these three groups were put together and written down in different mixtures over the centuries, blending together Indian, Persian, Arabic, Turkish, Egyptian, and other elements.

The stories also spread beyond the Muslim world. They were known to writers of the Italian Renaissance and to Shakespeare, who used elements from them as plot devices. European interest in these stories intensified in the early eighteenth century when Antoine Galland, who had lived for many years in the eastern Mediterranean working as a diplomat and a buyer of artifacts for collectors, began to translate manuscripts of stories he had obtained from Arabic into French. He translated stories of the voyages of Sindbad the sailor, and then the fourteenth-century Syrian manuscript that contained the oldest Persian tales, which he had brought back to Paris. (This manuscript is now in the French National Library in Paris.) These were so popular that his publisher urged him to do more, and he began translating and publishing stories told to him orally by

Chapter 8

Fiction and

the Emotions

in Japanese,

Arabian, and

Irish Culture

(1000–1400 C.E.)

a Syrian visitor to France. These stories included tales that were probably not part of *The Arabian Nights* in its Arabic versions at all, such as those of Aladdin and his magic lamp, and Ali Baba and the forty thieves.

In the nineteenth century, Arabic scholars in India, Germany, and Egypt published what they regarded as "complete" editions in Arabic, changing the language to make it more literary and including Egyptian and Turkish stories that had been added over the centuries. In the late twentieth century, the eminent scholar of medieval Arabic Muhsin Mahdi decided to go back to the fourteenth-century Syrian manuscript and publish an accurate edition in Arabic of the original stories; this has now served as the basis for translations into other languages, including the one in this chapter, and gives us a version much closer to the one people would have heard or read centuries ago.

Like the stories in *The Arabian Nights,* the stories in the Ulster Cycle first circulated orally. Some were written down, in Old Irish, by Irish Christian monks in the seventh or perhaps as early as the sixth century. Almost all of these manuscripts were destroyed by the Vikings when they attacked Irish monasteries in the ninth and tenth centuries, and none of them have survived until today. When the invasions stopped in the eleventh century and things became more peaceful, monks began to write again, picking up stories from fragments that survived, from copies of the earlier manuscripts that were in the libraries of monasteries on the continent, and from oral traditions. The oldest surviving manuscripts date

from the eleventh century, and in the late nineteenth and twentieth centuries, scholars and writers interested in Irish literature translated them into English, often basing their translations on several manuscript versions at the same time to tell a fuller story.

The Ulster Cycle tells the story of Conchobar, king of the Ulaid people who lived in northern Ireland, and his nephew, the warrior Cuchulaind (or Cú Chulainn). The Ulaid were a real people—their name is the origin of "Ulster," a modern term for northern Ireland—and some earlier scholars assumed that Conchobar and Cuchulaind were also real, and that they lived perhaps in the first century c.e., about four hundred years before Christianity was introduced into Ireland and written sources begin. Most historians and literary scholars today do not regard them as historical individuals, but as mythical heroes; Cuchulaind, in fact, is half-divine in the stories, as he is the son of Conchobar's sister and the god Lugh. In the stories, King Conchobar and Cuchulaind are the center of a group of warriors called the Knights of the Red Branch, similar to King Arthur and the Knights of the Round Table, whose stories originated at about the same time. We do not know exactly when stories about the Knights of the Red Branch began to be told, and it is difficult to separate their many layers—the original oral version, later oral versions, seventh-century written versions, eleventh-century written versions, and so on. The story that is told predates the coming of Christianity and the characters are not Christian, but the written versions were made by Irish Christian monks, whose values no doubt influenced the way they told the story. The very fact that the stories kept being retold, and written down century after century, however, indicates that people in Ireland over a long period found them compelling.

THE METHOD

The first task in this chapter is to compare the personal qualities and emotional responses of the male and female characters created in the three stories. To do this, the method is quite simple: read carefully, draw conclusions and inferences from your reading, and make comparisons based on these conclusions. As you read, first identify the major characters, and begin to jot down your impressions of their qualities, actions, and emotions. Begin with those that are explicit in the texts: How are the characters described in terms of external and internal qualities? What emotions do the stories attribute to them? How do they respond to these feelings? Then think about qualities that are implicit: Given the way certain characters respond, what qualities would you use to describe them, even if the story does not mention these explicitly? How would you characterize the feelings behind their actions? Are their emotions and actions presented in a positive way—that is, as praiseworthy—or does the narrator seem to disapprove of them? Once you have done this for all three texts, you will be able to trace similarities and differences among them.

The second task in this chapter is to consider the role of fiction, and again there is direct and indirect evidence. First, note places in which the narrator of the story or the characters say something about telling, hearing, and reading stories. Then, think about the ways in which telling or hearing stories influences the plot. What does this suggest about the role of fiction?

Source 1 presents four scenes from *The Tale of Genji*. The first describes Genji as he is growing up. What qualities does he exhibit to the emperor, the ladies and court, and the visiting Korean physiognomist? In the second scene, the grown-up Genji, his friend and brother-in-law To-no-Chujo, and several courtiers discuss women. What does To-no-Chujo's attitude about the letters from women that Genji has lying about reveal about the qualities he expects in men? (Remember that Genji is the husband of his sister, and that he himself is married.) In women? What does his discussion about women reveal about his own emotions? About those he expects in women? The third scene occurs later in the same chapter, when Genji spends the night at the household of the governor of Kii after spending the day with his wife. What emotions are ascribed to Genji as this scene unfolds? To the woman involved? What do they do in response to their feelings? Buddhism, which was becoming more widely accepted in Japan in Murasaki's time, taught that

Chapter 8

Fiction and

the Emotions

in Japanese,

Arabian, and

Irish Culture

(1000–1400 C.E.)

one should regard worldly things as transitory, and strive to control one's passions to eliminate desire. The most proper attitude was one of *aware*, a gentle melancholy and sadness at the world's passing things. Because of the quickness with which they faded, flowers captured the essence of these ideas, and both men and women used flowers and perfume to express their thoughts. How is *aware* expressed in this scene?

The final scene in Source 1 occurs much later in the book, when Genji comes upon To-no-Chujo's daughter Tamakazura and others reading romantic stories; through this scene we can learn about the role that stories were understood to play in Japanese culture, as well as observe more of Genji's emotional responses. Who does Genji expect will read fictional stories? What purpose do they serve, in his opinion? How does this fit with the type of storytelling he and his friends engage in, as we have just seen? How does Tamakazura differ in her opinions about these issues? As you can tell from reading the scene, Genji is attracted to Tamakazura, the daughter of his best friend. How does this shape his view of the relation between stories and real life? At the end of this scene, he talks to Murasaki, his wife, about the stories that he views as appropriate reading for their daughter. Why does he want her to read certain types of stories and not others? How would you describe his feelings toward his daughter?

Source 2 starts with the very beginning of *The Arabian Nights*. How is King Shahrayar described? What emotions does he show at the beginning? How does his brother react to his wife's infidelity, and how do his emotions change in response to this? How does King Shahrayar react to his own wife's infidelity, and how do his subjects react to this? Does this fit with the way he was described at the beginning of the story? Turning to Shahrazad: How is she described? What does she plan in response to the king's actions, and what does this suggest about her? What emotions does her father show in reaction to this? How does her plan work? What emotions do the characters in the very brief excerpts from stories she tells exhibit? What do these stories, and the way the plot unfolds, suggest about the role of storytelling in Arabian culture?

Source 3 is an excerpt from one of the stories about Cuchulaind, usually titled "The Wooing of Emer." What qualities are attributed to Cuchulaind at the beginning of the story? What emotions does Cuchulaind provoke in the men of Ulster? What qualities are attributed to Emer? Why is Cuchulaind attracted to her? How does he describe himself to her, and how does she describe herself to him? What does Cuchulaind do after Emer's father Vorgall sends him away? How does the story portray Cuchulaind's feelings during all this? "The Wooing of Emer" does not contain direct comments about the role of stories as does *The Tale of Genji*, nor is the plot driven by storytelling the way *The Arabian Nights* is, so you will have to infer information about stories in Irish culture. Do any of the "gifts" that Cuchulaind or Emer is said to possess suggest that telling stories was important? When the two first meet, what do they do? How does Cuchulaind's ability to speak, as well as fight, shape the plot?

Once you have taken notes and thought about the characters and the role of stories in each of the three sources for this chapter, you can compare them. What personal qualities do the central male characters share across these stories, and in what ways are they different? What about the female characters? What emotions do the characters show openly, either in descriptions or through their behavior, and how is this influenced by gender in the three stories? All of the stories involve a father who is trying to keep his daughter from something: Genji is trying to keep his daughter from reading love stories (while encouraging the daughter of his good friend to do so), the vizier is trying to keep Shahrazad from marrying the king, and Forgall is trying to keep Emer from marrying Cuchulaind. How do the stories portray the fathers' emotions? Why do you think this might have been a common theme in stories told at this period of history? All three of the stories also involve people having sex with individuals to whom they are not married. We probably do not need to ask why this was a common theme, but how are the stories similar, and how are they different, in the way they portray the emotions involved in these encounters? Does this suggest that the emotions themselves differ in the three cultures? In Source 1, Genji and Tamakazura talk at length about romantic stories and their relation to truth. Based on their comments there, how do you think they might regard Shahrazad's plan?

As you read, you also need to keep the final question in mind: What opportunities does fiction provide for us as historians, and what special problems arise in using fiction as a historical source? So far you have discovered some answers to the first part of the question, but you may have also found yourself questioning your assumptions. Fictional characters are often interesting because they are extraordinary, or at least have extraordinary things happen to them. Are they thus models for normal behavior, or counter-models whose experiences are meant to contrast with the normal? In other words, were hearers or readers supposed to be like them, or pleased they were not? Might we be safer in using fiction as a source for historical details—such as the way houses were laid out in Japan or the use of weapons in Ireland—than as a source for ideas about the range of human emotions and acceptable human behavior?

Chapter 8

Fiction and

the Emotions

in Japanese,

Arabian, and

Irish Culture

(1000–1400 C.E.)

THE EVIDENCE

Source 1 from Lady Murasaki Shikibu, The Tale of Genji, *vol. I and vol. II, trans. Edward Seidensticker (New York: Alfred Knopf, 1976), pp. 16, 18, 32–33, 40–46, 436–439. Translation copyright © 1976, copyright renewed 2004 by Edward G. Seidensticker. Used by permission of Alfred A. Knopf, a division of Random House, Inc.*

1. From *The Tale of Genji*

He had grown into a lad of such beauty that he hardly seemed meant for this world—and indeed one almost feared that he might only briefly be a part of it . . .

He now lived at court. When he was seven he went through the ceremonial reading of the Chinese classics, and never before had there been so fine a performance . . . .

The lesser ladies crowded about, not in the least ashamed to show their faces, all eager to amuse him, though aware that he set them off to disadvantage. I need not speak of his accomplishments in the compulsory subjects, the classics and the like. When it came to music his flute and koto made the heavens echo—but to recount all his virtues would, I fear, give rise to a suspicion that I distort the truth. . . .

An embassy came from Korea. Hearing that among the emissaries was a skilled physiognomist,[1] the emperor would have liked to summon him for consultation. He decided, however, that he must defer to the emperor Uda's injunction against receiving foreigners, and instead sent this favored son to the Kōro mansion, where the party was lodged. The boy was disguised as the son of the grand moderator, his guardian at the court. The wise Korean cocked his head in astonishment.

"It is the face of one who should ascend to the highest place and be father to the nation," he said quietly, as if to himself . . .

The sobriquet[2] "the shining Genji," one hears, was bestowed upon him by the Korean.

It had been raining all day. There were fewer courtiers than usual in the royal presence. Back in his own palace quarters, also unusually quiet, Genji pulled a lamp near and sought to while away the time with his books. He had Tō no Chūjō with him. Numerous pieces of colored paper, obviously letters, lay on a shelf. Tō no Chūjō made no attempt to hide his curiosity.

"Well," said Genji, "there are some I might let you see. But there are some I think it better not to."

"You miss the point. The ones I want to see are precisely the ones you want to hide. The ordinary ones—I'm not much of a hand at the game, you know, but

1. A person who studies someone's face for clues to that person's character.
2. Nickname.

even I am up to the ordinary give and take. But the ones from ladies who think you are not doing right by them, who sit alone through an evening and wait for you to come—those are the ones I want to see."

It was not likely that really delicate letters would be left scattered on a shelf, and it may be assumed that the papers treated so carelessly were the less important ones.

"You do have a variety of them," said Tō no Chūjō, reading the correspondence through piece by piece. This will be from her, and this will be from *her*, he would say. Sometimes he guessed correctly and sometimes he was far afield, to Genji's great amusement. Genji was brief with his replies and let out no secrets.

"It is I who should be asking to see *your* collection. No doubt it is huge. When I have seen it I shall be happy to throw my files open to you."

"I fear there is nothing that would interest you." Tō no Chūjō was in a contemplative mood. "It is with women as it is with everything else: the flawless ones are very few indeed. This a sad fact which I have learned over the years. All manner of women seem presentable enough at first. Little notes, replies to this and that, they all suggest sensibility and cultivation. But when you begin sorting out the really superior ones you find that there are not many who have to be on your list. Each has her little tricks and she makes the most of them, getting in her slights at rivals, so broad sometimes that you almost have to blush. Hidden away by loving parents who build brilliant futures for them, they let word get out of this little talent and that little accomplishment and you are all in a stir. They are young and pretty and amiable and carefree, and in their boredom they begin to pick up a little from their elders, and in the natural course of things they begin to concentrate on one particular hobby and make something of it. A woman tells you all about it and hides the weak points and brings out the strong ones as if they were everything, and you can't very well call her a liar. So you begin keeping company, and it is always the same. The fact is not up to the advance notices."

Tō no Chūjō sighed, a sigh clearly based on experience. Some of what he had said, though not all, accorded with Genji's own experience . . .

They talked on, of the varieties of women. . . .

At this point two young courtiers, a guards officer and a functionary in the ministry of rites, appeared on the scene, to attend the emperor in his retreat. Both were devotees of the way of love and both were good talkers. . . .

[Genji goes to visit his wife at her house but spends the night at the household of the governor of Kii.]

Having heard that his host's stepmother, who would be in residence, was a high-spirited lady, he listened for signs of her presence. There were signs of someone's presence immediately to the west. He heard a swishing of silk and young voices that were not at all displeasing. Young ladies seemed to be

[211]

Chapter 8

Fiction and

the Emotions

in Japanese,

Arabian, and

Irish Culture

(1000–1400 C.E.)

giggling self-consciously and trying to contain themselves. The shutters were raised, it seemed, but upon a word from the governor they were lowered. There was a faint light over the sliding doors. Genji went for a look, but could find no opening large enough to see through. Listening for a time, he concluded that the women had gathered in the main room, next to his. . . .

Genji lay wide awake, not pleased at the prospect of sleeping alone. He sensed that there was someone in the room to the north. It would be the lady of whom they had spoken. Holding his breath, he went to the door and listened.

"Where are you?" The pleasantly husky voice was that of the boy who had caught his eye [the brother of the stepmother].

"Over here." It would be the sister. The two voices, very sleepy, resembled each other. "And where is our guest? I had thought he might be somewhere near, but he seems to have gone away."

"He's in the east room." The boy's voice was low. "I saw him. He is every bit as handsome as everyone says."

"If it were daylight I might have a look at him myself." The sister yawned, and seemed to draw the bedclothes over her face.

Genji was a little annoyed. She might have questioned her brother more energetically.

"I'll sleep out toward the veranda. But we should have more light." The boy turned up the lamp. The lady apparently lay at a diagonal remove from Genji. "And where is Chūjō?[3] I don't like being left alone."

"She went to have a bath. She said she'd be right back." He spoke from out near the veranda.

All was quiet again. Genji slipped the latch open and tried the doors. They had not been bolted. A curtain had been set up just inside, and in the dim light he could make out Chinese chests and other furniture scattered in some disorder. He made his way through to her side. She lay by herself, a slight little figure. Though vaguely annoyed at being disturbed, she evidently took him for the woman Chūjō until he pulled back the covers.

"I heard you summoning a captain, " he said, "and I thought my prayers over the months had been answered."[4]

She gave a little gasp. It was muffled by the bedclothes and no one else heard.

"You are perfectly correct if you think me unable to control myself. But I wish you to know that I have been thinking of you for a very long time. And the fact that I have finally found my opportunity and am taking advantage of it should show that my feelings are by no means shallow."

His manner was so gently persuasive that devils and demons could not have gainsaid him. The lady would have liked to announce to the world that a strange man had invaded her boudoir.

---

3. **Chūjō:** one of her ladies-in-waiting.

4. Chujo means "captain," the rank that Genji holds.

"I think you have mistaken me for someone else," she said, outraged, though the remark was under her breath

The little figure, pathetically fragile and as if on the point of expiring from the shock, seemed to him very beautiful.

"I am driven by thoughts so powerful that a mistake is completely out of the question. It is cruel of you to pretend otherwise. I promise you that I will do nothing unseemly. I must ask you to listen to a little of what is on my mind."

She was so small that he lifted her easily. As he passed through the doors to his own room, he came upon the Chūjō who had been summoned earlier. He called out in surprise. Surprised in turn, Chūjō peered into the darkness. The perfume that came from his robes like a cloud of smoke told her who he was. She stood in confusion, unable to speak. Had he been a more ordinary intruder she might have ripped her mistress away by main force. But she would not have wished to raise an alarm all through the house.

She followed after, but Genji was quite unmoved by her pleas.

"Come for her in the morning," he said, sliding the doors closed.

The lady was bathed in perspiration and quite beside herself at the thought of what Chūjō, and the others too, would be thinking. Genji had to feel sorry for her. Yet the sweet words poured forth, the whole gamut of pretty devices for making a woman surrender. . . . .

. . . She was weeping. He had his hands full but would not for the world have missed the experience.

"Why must you so dislike me?" he asked with a sigh, unable to stop the weeping. "Don't you know that the unexpected encounters are the ones we were fated for? Really, my dear, you do seem to know altogether too little of the world."

"If I had met you before I came to this,"[5] she replied, and he had to admit the truth of it, "then I might have consoled myself with the thought—it might have been no more than self-deception, of course—that you would someday come to think fondly of me. But this is hopeless, worse than I can tell you. Well, it has happened. Say no to those who ask if you have seen me."

One may imagine that he found many kind promises with which to comfort her.

The first cock was crowing and Genji's men were awake.

"Did you sleep well? I certainly did."

"Let's get the carriage ready."

Some of the women were heard asking whether people who were avoiding taboos were expected to leave again in the middle of the night.

Genji was very unhappy. He feared he could not find an excuse for another meeting. He did not see how he could visit her, and he did not see how they could write. Chūjō came out, also very unhappy. He let the lady go and then took her back again.

5. That is, before she was married.

[213]

Chapter 8

Fiction and

the Emotions

in Japanese,

Arabian, and

Irish Culture

(1000–1400 C.E.)

"How shall I write to you? Your feelings and my own—they are not shallow, and we may expect deep memories. Has anything ever been so strange?" He was in tears, which made him yet handsomer. The cocks were now crowing insistently. He was feeling somewhat harried as he composed his farewell verse:

"Why must they startle with their dawn alarums
When hours are yet required to thaw the ice?"

The lady was ashamed of herself that she had caught the eye of a man so far above her. His kind words had little effect. She was thinking of her husband, whom for the most part she considered a clown and a dolt. She trembled to think that a dream might have told him of the night's happenings.

This was the verse with which she replied:

"Day has broken without an end to my tears.
To my cries of sorrow are added the calls of the roosters" . . .

[Much later in the novel, Tō no Chūjo's
daughter Tamakazura and Genji's second
wife Murasaki spend their time at Genji's
house at Rokujo.]

The rains of early summer continued without a break, even gloomier than in most years. The ladies at Rokujo amused themselves with illustrated romances . . .

Tamakazura was the most avid reader of all. She quite lost herself in pictures and stories and would spend whole days with them. Several of her young women were well informed in literary matters. She came upon all sorts of interesting and shocking incidents (she could not be sure whether they were true or not), but she found little that resembled her own unfortunate career. There was *The Tale of Sumiyoshi*, popular in its day, of course, and still well thought of. She compared the plight of the heroine, within a hairbreadth of being taken by the chief accountant, with her own escape from the Higo person.[6]

Genji could not help noticing the clutter of pictures and manuscripts. "What a nuisance this all is," he said one day. "Women seem to have been born to be cheerfully deceived. They know perfectly well that in all these old stories there is scarcely a shred of truth, and yet they are captured and made sport of by the whole range of trivialities and go on scribbling them down, quite unaware that in these warm rains their hair is all dank and knotted."

He smiled. "What would we do if there were not these old romances to relieve our boredom? But amid all the fabrication I must admit that I do find real emotions and plausible chains of events. We can be quite aware of the frivolity and

6. **Higo:** an obnoxious rural suitor of Tamakazura.

the idleness and still be moved. We have to feel a little sorry for a charming princess in the depths of gloom. Sometimes a series of absurd and grotesque incidents which we know to be quite improbable holds our interest, and afterwards we must blush that it was so. Yet even then we can see what it was that held us. Sometimes I stand and listen to the stories they read to my daughter, and I think to myself that there certainly are good talkers in the world. I think that these yarns must come from people much practiced in lying. But perhaps that is not the whole of the story?"

She pushed away her inkstone. "I can see that that would be the view of someone much given to lying himself. For my part, I am convinced of their truthfulness."

He laughed. "I have been rude and unfair to your romances, haven't I. They have set down and preserved happenings from the age of the gods to our own. *The Chronicles of Japan* and the rest are a mere fragment of the whole truth. It is your romances that fill in the details.

"We are not told of things that happened to specific people exactly as they happened; but the beginning is when there are good things and bad things, things that happen in this life which one never tires of seeing and hearing about, things which one cannot bear not to tell of and must pass on for all generations. If the storyteller wishes to speak well, then he chooses the good things; and if he wishes to hold the reader's attention he chooses bad things, extraordinarily bad things. Good things and bad things alike, they are things of this world and no other.

"Writers in other countries approach the matter differently. Old stories in our own are different from new. There are differences in the degree of seriousness. But to dismiss them as lies is itself to depart from the truth. Even in the writ which the Buddha drew from his noble heart are parables, devices for pointing obliquely at the truth. To the ignorant they may seem to operate at cross purposes. The Greater Vehicle[7] is full of them, but the general burden is always the same. The difference between enlightenment and confusion is of about the same order as the difference between the good and the bad in a romance. If one takes the generous view, then nothing is empty and useless."

He now seemed bent on establishing the uses of fiction.

"But tell me: is there in any of your old stories a proper, upright fool like myself?" He came closer. "I doubt that even among the most unworldly of your heroines there is one who manages to be as distant and unnoticing as you are. Suppose the two of us set down our story and give the world a really interesting one."

"I think it very likely that the world will take notice of our curious story even if we do not go to the trouble." She hid her face in her sleeves.

"Our curious story? Yes, incomparably curious, I should think." Smiling and playful, he pressed nearer.

---

7. **Greater Vehicle:** Mahayana Buddhism, the type of Buddhism that had spread to Heian Japan.

Chapter 8

Fiction and

the Emotions

in Japanese,

Arabian, and

Irish Culture

(1000–1400 C.E.)

"Beside myself, I search through all the books,
And come upon no daughter so unfilial."

"You are breaking one of the commandments."
He stroked her hair as he spoke, but she refused to look up. Presently, however, she managed a reply:

"So too it is with me. I too have searched,
And found no cases quite so unparental."

Somewhat chastened, he pursued the matter no further. Yet one worried. What was to become of her?

Murasaki too had become addicted to romances. Her excuse was that Genji's little daughter insisted on being read to.

"Just see what a fine one this is," she said, showing Genji an illustration for *The Tale of Kumano*. The young girl in tranquil and confident slumber made her think of her own younger self. "How precocious even very little children seem to have been. I suppose I might have set myself up as a specimen of the slow, plodding variety. I would have won that competition easily."

Genji might have been the hero of some rather more eccentric stories.

"You must not read love stories to her. I doubt that clandestine affairs would arouse her unduly, but we would not want her to think them commonplace."

What would Tamakazura have made of the difference between his remarks to her and these remarks to Murasaki?

"I would not of course offer the wanton ones as a model," replied Murasaki, "but I would have doubts too about the other sort. Lady Atemiya in *The Tale of the Hollow Tree*, for instance. She is always very brisk and efficient and in control of things, and she never makes mistakes; but there is something unwomanly about her cool manner and clipped speech."

[Genji replied:] "I should imagine that it is in real life as in fiction. We are all human and we all have our ways. It is not easy to be unerringly right. Proper, well-educated parents go to great trouble over a daughter's education and tell themselves that they have done well if something quiet and demure emerges. It seems a pity when defects come to light one after another and people start asking what her good parents can possibly have been up to. Yet the rewards are very great when a girl's manner and behavior seem just right for her station. Even then empty praise is not satisfying. One knows that the girl is not perfect and looks at her more critically than before. I would not wish my own daughter to be praised by people who have no standards."

He was genuinely concerned that she acquit herself well in the tests that lay before her.

2. From *The Arabian Nights*

It is related—but God knows and sees best what lies hidden in the old accounts of bygone people and times—that long ago, during the time of the Sasanid dynasty, in the peninsulas of India and Indochina, there lived two kings who were brothers. The older brother was named Shahrayar, the younger Shahzaman. The older, Shahrayar, was a towering knight and a daring champion, invincible, energetic, and implacable. His power reached the remotest corners of the land and its people, so that the country was loyal to him, and his subjects obeyed him. Shahrayar himself lived and ruled in India and Indochina, while to his brother he gave the land of Samarkand to rule as king.

Ten years went by, when one day Shahrayar: felt a longing for his brother the king, summoned his vizier[8] (who had two daughters, one called Shahrazad, the other Dinarzad) and bade him go to his brother. Having made preparations, the vizier journeyed day and night until he reached Samarkand. When Shahzaman heard of the vizier's arrival, he went out with his retainers to meet him. He dismounted, embraced him, and asked him for news from his older brother, Shahrayar. The vizier replied that he was well, and that he had sent him to request his brother to visit him. Shahzaman complied with his brother's request and proceeded to make preparations for the journey. In the meantime, he had the vizier camp on the outskirts of the city, and took care of his needs. He sent him what he required of food and fodder, slaughtered many sheep in his honor, and provided him with money and supplies, as well as many horses and camels.

For ten full days he prepared himself for the journey; then he appointed a chamberlain in his place, and left the city to spend the night in his tent, near the vizier. At midnight he returned to his palace in the city, to bid his wife good-bye. But when he entered the palace, he found his wife lying in the arms of one the kitchen boys. When he saw them, the world turned dark before his eyes and, shaking his head, he said to himself, "I am still here, and this is what she has done when I was barely outside the city. How will it be and what will happen behind my back when I go to visit my brother in India? No. Women are not to be trusted." He got exceedingly angry, adding, "By God, I am king and sovereign in Samarkand, yet my wife has betrayed me and has inflicted this on me."

---

8. **Vizier:** The highest state official or administrator under a caliph or a king (literally, "one who bears burdens").

Chapter 8

Fiction and

the Emotions

in Japanese,

Arabian, and

Irish Culture

(1000–1400 C.E.)

As his anger boiled, he drew his sword and struck both his wife and the cook. Then he dragged them by the heels and threw them from the top of the palace to the trench below. He then left the city and, going to the vizier, ordered that they depart that very hour. The drum was struck, and they set out on their journey, while Shahzaman's heart was on fire because of what his wife had done to him and how she had betrayed him with some cook, some kitchen boy. They journeyed hurriedly, day and night, through deserts and wilds, until they reached the land of King Shahrayar, who had gone out to receive them.

When Shahrayar met them, he embraced his brother, showed him favors, and treated him generously. He offered him quarters in a palace adjoining his own, for King Shahrayar had built two beautiful towering palaces in his garden, one for the guests, the other for the women and members of his household. He gave the guest house to his brother, Shahzaman, after the attendants had gone to scrub it, dry it, furnish it, and open its windows, which overlooked the garden. Thereafter, Shahzaman would spend the whole day at his brother's, return at night to sleep at the palace, then go back to his brother the next morning. But whenever he found himself alone and thought of his ordeal with his wife, he would sigh deeply, then stifle his grief, and say, "Alas, that this great misfortune should have happened to one in my position!" Then he would fret with anxiety, his spirit would sag, and he would say, "None has seen what I have seen." In his depression, he ate less and less, grew pale, and his health deteriorated. He neglected everything, wasted away, and looked ill. . . .

[Shahzaman sees his brother's wife and ten
of her female slaves having sex with males
slaves, and arranges for Shahrayar to see
this as well.]

When King Shahrayar saw the spectacle of his wife and the slave girls, he went out of his mind, and when he and his brother came down from upstairs, he said, "No one is safe in this world. Such doings are going on in my kingdom, and in my very palace. Perish the world and perish life! This is a great calamity, indeed." . . .

He went to his own palace and ordered his chief vizier, the father of the two girls Shahrazad and Dinarzad, who will be mentioned below, and said to him, "Take that wife of mine and put her to death." Then Shahrayar went to her himself, bound her, and handed her over to the vizier, who took her out and put her to death. Then King Shahrayar grabbed his sword, brandished it, and, entering the place chambers, killed every one of his slave-girls and replaced them with others. He then swore to marry for one night only and kill the woman the next morning, in order to save himself from the wickedness and cunning of women, saying, "There is not a single chaste woman anywhere on the entire face of the earth." Shortly thereafter he provided his brother Shahzaman with supplies for his journey and sent him back to his own country with gifts, rarities, and money. The brother bade him good-bye and set out for home.

Shahrayar sat on his throne and ordered his vizier, the father of the two girls, to find him a wife from among the princes' daughters. The vizier found him one, and he slept with her and was done with her, and the next morning he ordered the vizier to put her to death. That very night he took one of his army officers' daughters, slept with her, and the next morning ordered the vizier to put her to death. The vizier, who could not disobey him, put her to death. The third night he took one of the merchants' daughters, slept with her till the morning, then ordered his vizier to put her to death, and the vizier did so. It became King Shahrayar's custom to take every night the daughter of a merchant or a commoner, spend the night with her, then have her put to death the next morning. He continued to do this until all the girls perished, their mothers mourned, and there arose a clamor among the fathers and mothers, who called the plague upon his head, complained to the Creator of the heavens; and called for help on Him who hears and answers prayers.

Now, as mentioned earlier, the vizier, who put the girls to death, had an older daughter called Shahrazad and a younger one called Dinarzad. The older daughter, Shahrazad, had read the books of literature, philosophy, and medicine. She knew poetry by heart, had studied historical reports, and was acquainted with the sayings of men and the maxims of sages and kings. She was intelligent, knowledgeable, wise, and refined. She had read and learned. One day she said to her father, "Father, I will tell you what is in my mind." He asked, "What is it?" She answered, "I would like you to marry me to King Shahrayar, so that I may either succeed in saving the people or perish and die like the rest." When the vizier heard what his daughter Shahrazad said, he got angry and said to her, "Foolish one, don't you know that King Shahrayar has sworn to spend but one night with a girl and have her put to death the next morning? If I give you to him, he will sleep with you for one night and will ask me to put you to death the next morning, and I shall have to do it, since I cannot disobey him." She said, "'Father, you must give me to him, even if he kills me." He asked, "What has possessed you that you wish to imperil yourself?" She replied, "Father, you must give me to him. This is absolute and final. . . .

"If you don't take me to King Shahrayar, I shall go to him by myself behind your back and tell him that you have refused to give me to one like him and that you have begrudged your master one like me." The vizier asked, "Must you really do this?" She replied, "Yes, I must."

Tired and exhausted, the vizier went to King Shahrayar and, kissing the ground before him, told him about his daughter, adding that he would give her to him that very night. The king was astonished and said to him, "Vizier, how is it that you have found it possible to give me your daughter, knowing that I will, by God, the Creator of heaven, ask you to put her to death the next morning and

Chapter 8

Fiction and

the Emotions

in Japanese,

Arabian, and

Irish Culture

(1000–1400 C.E.)

that if you refuse, I will have you put to death too?" He replied, "My King and Lord, I have told her everything and explained all this to her, but she refuses and insists on being with you tonight." The king was delighted and said, "Go to her, prepare her and bring her to me early in the evening."

The vizier went down, repeated the king's message to his daughter, and said, "May God not deprive me of you." She was very happy and, after preparing herself and packing what she needed, went to her younger sister, Dinarzad, and said, "Sister, listen well to what I am telling you. When I go to the king, I will send for you, and when you come and see that the king has finished with me, say, `Sister, if you are not sleepy, tell us a story.' Then I will begin to tell a story, and it will cause the king to stop his practice, save myself, and deliver the people." Dinarzad replied, "'Very well."

At nightfall the vizier took Shahrazad and went with her to the great King Shahrayar. But when Shahrayar took her to bed and began to fondle her, she wept, and when he asked her, "Why are you crying?" she replied, "I have a sister, and I wish to bid her good-bye before daybreak." Then the king sent for the sister, who came and went to sleep under the bed. When the night wore on, she woke up and waited until the king had satisfied himself with her sister Shahrazad and they were by now all fully awake. Then Dinarzad cleared her throat and said, "Sister, if you are not sleepy, tell us one of your lovely little tales to while away the night, before I bid you good-bye at daybreak, for I don't know what will happen to you tomorrow." Shahrazad turned to King Shahrayar and said, "May I have your permission to tell a story?" He replied, "'Yes,"' and Shahrazad was very happy and said, "Listen":

The Story of the Merchant and the Demon

It is said, O wise and happy King, that once there was a prosperous merchant who had abundant wealth and investments and commitments in every country. He had many women and children and kept many servants and slaves. One day, having resolved to visit another country, he took provisions, filling his saddlebag with loaves of bread and with dates, mounted his horse, and set out on his journey. . . .

[The merchant accidentally kills the son of
the demon with a date pit and the demon
threatens to kill him.]

Then he seized him and, throwing him to the ground, raised the sword to strike him. The merchant began to weep and mourn his family and his wife and children . . ..

When the merchant finished and stopped weeping, the demon said, "By God, I must kill you, as you killed my son, even if you weep blood." The merchant asked, "Must you?" The demon replied, "I must," and raised his sword to strike.

[220]

But morning overtook Shahrazad, and she lapsed into silence, leaving King Shahrayar burning with curiosity to hear the rest of the story. Then Dinarzad said to her sister Shahrazad, "What a strange and lovely story!" Shahrazad replied, "What is this compared with what I shall tell you tomorrow night if the king spares me and lets me live? It will be even better and more entertaining." The king thought to himself, "I will spare her until I hear the rest of the story; then I will have her put to death the next day."

When morning broke, the day dawned, and the sun rose; the king left to attend to the affairs of the kingdom, and vizier, Shahrazad's father, was amazed and delighted. Then Dinarzad said to her sister Shahrazad, "Please sister if you are not sleepy, tell us one of your lovely little tales to while away the night." The king added, let it be the conclusion of the story of the demon and the merchant, for I would like to hear it." Shahrazad replied, "With the greatest pleasure, dear, happy King":

It is related, O wise and happy King, that when the demon raised his sword, the merchant asked the demon again, "Must you kill me?" and the demon replied, "Yes." Then the merchant said, "Please give me time to say good-bye to my family and my wife and children, divide my property among them, and appoint guardians. Then I shall come back, so that you may kill me." The demon replied, "I am afraid that if I release you and grant you time, you will go and do what you wish, but will not come back." The merchant said, "I swear to keep my pledge to come back, as the God of Heaven and earth is my witness." The demon asked, "How much time do you need?" The merchant replied, "One year, so that I may see enough of my children, bid my wife good-bye, discharge my obligations to people, and come back on New Year's Day." The demon asked, "Do you swear to God that if I let you go, you will come back on New Year's Day?" The merchant replied, "'Yes, I swear to God." . . .

[The merchant says good-bye to his family and returns to face the demon. Three old men approach and hear his story, and when the demon comes to kill the merchant, each old man gets the demon to agree to release the merchant from one-third of his obligations if he tells a story the demon finds "strange and amazing." The first two old men do, and their stories take six nights to tell.]

Then the third old man said, "Demon, don't disappoint me. If I told you a story that is stranger and more amazing than the first two, would you grant me one-third of your claim on him for his crime?" The demon replied, "I will." Then the old man said, "Demon, listen":

[221]

Chapter 8

Fiction and

the Emotions

in Japanese,

Arabian, and

Irish Culture

(1000–1400 C.E.)

But morning overtook Shahrazad, and she lapsed into silence. Then her sister said, "What an amazing story!" Shahrazad replied, "The rest is even more amazing." The king said to himself, "I will not have her put to death until I hear what happened to the old man and the demon; then I will have her put to death, as is my custom with the others."

The following night Dinarzad said to her sister Shahrazad, "For God's sake, sister, if you are not sleepy, tell us one of your lovely little tales to while away the night." Shahrazad replied, "With the greatest pleasure":

I heard, O happy King, that the third old man told the demon a story that was even stranger and more amazing than the first two. The demon was very much amazed and, swaying with delight, said, "I grant you one-third of my claim on him for his crime." Then the demon released the merchant and departed. The merchant turned to the three old men and thanked them, and they congratulated him on his deliverance and bade him good-bye. Then they separated, and each of them went on his way. The merchant himself went back home to his family, his wife, and his children, and he lived with them until the day he died. But this story is not as so strange or as amazing as the story of the fisherman.

Dinarzad asked, "Please, sister, what is the story of the fisherman?" Shahrazad said:

[*She tells another series of interrelated
stories that take 20 nights, and so on. After
271 nights, the translator adds the
following:*]

Tradition has it that in the course of time Shahrazad bore Shahrayar three children and that, having learned to trust and love her he spared her life and kept her as his queen.

Source 3 from Kuno Meyer, ed. "The Wooing of Emer," in Archaeological Review *1(1888), pp. 70–71, 72, 73–75, 150, 151, 301, 305–306.*

3. From "The Wooing of Emer"

Cuchulaind surpassed all of them at those feats for quickness and deftness. The women of Ulster loved Cuchulaind greatly for his quickness at the feats, for the nimbleness of his leap, for the excellency of his wisdom; for the sweetness of his speech, for the beauty of his face, for the loveliness of his look. Many were his gifts. First, his gift of prudence until his warrior's flame appeared, the gift of feats, the gift of game-playing, the gift of calculating, the gift of sooth-saying, the gift of sense, the gift of beauty. But three faults had Cuchulaind—that he was too young (for his moustache had not grown, and all the more would unknown youths deride him), that he was too daring, that he was too beautiful.

The men of Ulster took counsel about Cuchulaind, for their women and maidens loved him greatly. For there was no wife with Cuchulaind at that time. This was the counsel, that they would seek a woman whom Cuchulaind might choose to woo. For they were sure that a man who had a wife to attend to him would less ravish their maidens and accept the love of their women. And, besides, they were troubled and afraid that Cuchulaind would perish early, so that for that reason they wished to give him a wife that he might leave an heir; for they knew that his re-birth would be of himself.

Then Conchobor sent out nine men into each province of Erinn to seek a wife for Cuchulaind, to see if they would find in any dun or in any chief place in Erinn the daughter of a king, or of a chief, or of a lord of land, whom Cuchulaind might be pleased to choose and woo. All the messengers returned that day a year gone, and had not found a maiden whom Cuchulaind chose to woo.

Thereupon Cuchulaind himself went to woo a maiden that he knew in Luglochta Loga—viz., Emer, the daughter of Forgall the Wily. Then Cuchulaind himself and his charioteer Loeg, son of Riangabar, went in his chariot. That was the one chariot which the host of the horses of the chariots of Ulster could not follow, on account of the swiftness and speed of the chariot and of who sat in it. Then Cuchulaind found the maiden on her playing field, with her foster-sister around her. These were daughters of the lords of land that lived around the dun of Forgall. They were learning needle-work and fine handiwork from Emer. She was the one maiden whom he deigned to address and woo of the maidens of Erinn. For she had the six gifts—viz., the the gift of beauty, the gift of voice, the gift of sweet speech, the gift of needle-work, the gift of wisdom, the gift of chastity. Cuchulaind said that no maiden should go with him but she who was his equal in age and shape and race, and skill and deftness, who was the best handworker of the maidens of Erinn, and that none was a fitting wife for him unless such were she. And as she was the one maiden that fulfilled all those conditions, Cuchulaind went to woo her above all . . .

Emer lifted up her lovely fair face and recognised Cuchulaind. And then she said: "May God make smooth the path before you!" "May you be safe from every harm!" said he. "Whence hast thou come?" she asked. "From Intide Emna," he replied. "Where did you sleep?" said she. "We slept," he said, "in the house of the man who tends the cattle of the plain of Tethra." "What was your food there?" she asked. "The ruin of a chariot was cooked for us there," he replied. "Which way didst thou come?" said she. "Between the Two Mountains of the Wood," said he . . . .

"Truly I swear, oh maiden," said Cuchulaind, "that I shall make my deeds recounted among the glories of the strength of heroes." "What then is thy strength?" said Emer. "Not hard to tell, truly," said he. "When I am weak in fight, I defend twenty. Sufficient for thirty is a third of my strength. I alone make combat against forty. My protection guards a hundred. Fords and battlefields

Chapter 8

Fiction and

the Emotions

in Japanese,

Arabian, and

Irish Culture

(1000–1400 C.E.)

are avoided for fear and dread of me. Hosts and multitudes and many armed men flee with the terror of my face. . . .

"I am a skilful student of the arts of the god of druidism, so that I am learned in the excellencies of knowledge. All the men of Ulster have equally brought me up, both charioteers and chariot-chiefs, both kings and chief-poets so that I am the darling of the host and multitude, so that I fight for the honour of them all alike.

"And thou, oh maiden," said Cuchulaind, "how hast thou been reared in Luglochta Loga?"

"Not hard to tell, truly," answered the maiden. "I was brought up," said she, "in ancient virtues, in lawful behaviour in keeping chastity, in equal queen, in stately form,so that to me is attributed every noble stately form among the hosts of women.""Good are those virtues, truly," said Cuchulaind. "Why then," said he, "should it not befitting for us both to become one? For I have not hitherto found a maiden capable of holding converse with me at a meeting in this wise."

While they were thus conversing, Cuchulaind saw the breasts of the maiden over the bosom of her smock. Then he said, "Fair is this plain, the plain of the noble yoke." Then the maiden spoke these words: "No one comes to this plain," said Emer, "who does not slay as many as a hundred on each ford from the Ford of Scennmenn at Ollbine, to Banchuing Arcait where swift Brea breads the brow of Fedelm."

"Fair is this plain, the plain of the noble yoke," said Cuchulaind.

"No one comes to this plain," said she, "who has not achieved the feat of slaying three times nine men with one blow" . . .

After those noble words, Cuchulaind went from them, and they did not hold any further converse on that day. When Cuchulaind was driving across Bray, Loeg, his charioteer, asked him: "Now," said he, "the words which thou and the maiden Emer spoke [about the "fair plan of the noble yoke"], what did you mean by them?" "Dost thou not know," answered Cuchulaind, "that I am wooing Emer? And it is for this reason that we disguised our words lest the girls should understand that I am wooing her, for if Forgall knew it, we should not meet with his consent."

[Despite Cuchulaind's attempt to hide his intentions with coded language, Emer's father Forgall learns that Cuchulaind is courting Emer, which he opposes. He suggests to Cuchulaind that he train with the warrior-women Scathach "to learn soldierly feats," hoping he will be killed in the process.]

Scathach was at that time carrying on war against other tribes over which the Princess Aife was ruling. Then the two hosts assembled to fight. Cuchulaind was put in bonds by Scathach, and a sleeping potion had been given him before, that he might not go to the battle lest anything should happen to him there. As a precaution she did this. Then forthwith out of his sleep started Cuchulaind after an hour. While anybody else would have slept twenty-four hours with this sleeping potion, it was only one hour for him. He then went with the two sons of Scathach against the three sons of Ilsuanach, viz. Cuar and Cett and Cruife, three warriors of Aife's. Alone he met them all three, and they fell by him. There was a meeting in battle on the next morning, and both hosts went until the two arrays were face to face. Then went the three sons of Esse Enchinde, viz. Cire and Bire and Blaicne, three other warriors of Aife, and began combat against the two sons of Scathach. They went on the path of feats. Scathach uttered a sigh at this, for she knew not what would come of it, first, as there was no third man with her three sons against those three and then she was afraid of Aife, because she was the hardest woman-warrior in the world. Then Cuchulaind went up to her two sons, and sprang on the path, and met them all three, and they fell by him.

Aife challenged Scathach to combat, Cuchulaind went up before Aife, and asked what it was she loved most. Scathach said: "What she loves most," said she, "is her two horses and her chariot and her charioteer." Cuchulaind and Aife went on the path of feats and began combat there. Then Aife shattered Cuchulaind's weapon so that his sword was no longer than his fist. "Ah," cried he, "the charioteer of Aife and her two horses and her chariot have fallen down in the glen, and have all perished!" At that Aife [was distracted and] looked up. Then Cuchulaind approached her, seized her at her two breasts, took her on his back like a shoulder-load, and carried her with him to his own host. Then he threw her from him to the ground, and placed his bare sword over him. And Aife said: "Life for life, oh Cuchulaind!" "My three wishes to me!" said he, "Thou shalt have them, as they come with thy breath," said she. "These are my three wishes," said he, "thou to give hostage to Scathach, without ever afterwards opposing her, thou to be with me this night before thy dun, and to bear me a son." "I promise it all thus," said she. It was done in that wise. Cuchulaind then went with Aife and slept with her that night.

Then Aife said she was with child, and that she would bear a boy.

[After his training with Scathach,
Cuchainland returns and kills many of the
warriors Forgall sends against him.]

Forgall then made a leap on to the rampart of the rath without, in fleeing from Cuchulaind, and he fell and was without life. Cuchulaind took Emer with him and her foster-sister, with their two loads of gold and silver, and took a leap back again across the third rampart with the two maidens and went forth.

Cries were raised around them from every direction.

Now Cuchulaind killed one hundred on each ford from Ath Scennmend at Ollbine to the Boyne of Bray, and he fulfilled all the deeds that he had vowed

[225]

Chapter 8

Fiction and

the Emotions

in Japanese,

Arabian, and

Irish Culture

(1000–1400 C.E.)

to the maiden, and he came safely out of it, and reached Emain Macha towards the darkness of that night. Emer was brought into the Red Branch to Conchobor and to the men of Ulster, and they bade her welcome . . . .

Conchobor paid Emer's wedding gift on the morrow, and Cuchulaind's honour price was paid, and he slept then with his wife, and they did not separate after that until they both died.

QUESTIONS TO CONSIDER

All types of sources from the past must be used very carefully, for even those that appear simply to relate historical facts, such as events during the reign of a monarch or the births and deaths of family members, were written for a specific purpose and with a specific audience in mind. This is even more the case when we use fiction, for their tellers or authors were not attempting to tell a true story but one that would interest hearers or readers and support a certain theme.

Literary conventions also shape fictional works. All storytellers and authors, even the most innovative, work within certain literary forms. For instance, even if they are repeating a well-known tale, they decide whether their story will be first-person narrative or third-person, whether they as an author will speak in the narrative or not. They adjust their style and vocabulary to suit the audience. They decide whether they will claim that their characters are real individuals or based on real individuals, and decide whether to use actual historical events as the setting for the plot. They may weave in elements drawn from other things they have

heard or read, incorporating familiar themes and motifs. Other storytellers and authors intentionally break with tradition, adding unexpected plot twists and unconventional characters, but their stories are effective precisely because both they as authors and we as hearers or readers realize they are doing this. Thus, even stories that break with traditional plot lines or characterization expect readers to be familiar with certain conventions. (You can see this most easily in satire. A dialogue, for example, between the Lone Ranger and Tonto in which the Lone Ranger begins with "How! Me Lone Ranger, him Tonto" is recognizable as satire only if you know that normally Tonto's lines are written in this way.)

Stories also create conventions, of course. They reflect their own culture, but they also help to shape it, as readers often learn what is expected of a woman or man faced with a certain problem by reading how fictional characters responded. Fiction does not teach directly like sermons or collections of the sayings of wise men, but it often gives a clear idea of what is desirable and undesirable behavior, what are proper and improper ways of expressing one's emotions.

You probably feel you know little about Japanese, Arabic, or Irish literary conventions from a thousand years ago, but the stories in this chapter all influenced later literature, and certain aspects of them became common features of many works of fiction. In *Genji,* for example, the convention of writing poems to one's lover might at first seem odd, but can you think of an equivalent in contemporary fiction? Have you read dialogue in recent novels (or heard it in movies or television programs) similar to To-no-Chujo's comments that all women seem wonderful at first, until you learn more about them? Have you read scenes of seduction similar to that of Genji and his host's stepmother, in which "sweet words poured forth" designed to "make a woman surrender"? Similarly, the setting of *The Arabian Nights* might at first seem very exotic and King Shahrayar's reaction to his wife's infidelity extreme. When you read or watch scenes involving a wife's affair in a contemporary setting, however, how do you expect the husband to act, even before he appears? Will "his anger boil" and will he "go out of his mind"? Have conventions about what a husband will do changed much? (You may wish to argue that these are not conventions, but represent the "natural" reaction to marital infidelity. From what you have read in *Genji,* however, does it seem that Genji would react in this way?) The structure of *The Arabian Nights,* in which night after night Shahrazad gets up to a point in a story and then stops, might seem artificial to you, but can you think of contemporary examples of this technique? How does modern fiction, in books and on screen, use "framing stories"? (Consider, for example, the first two minutes of any television crime drama, such as *Law and Order* or *CSI.*)

"The Wooing of Emer" tells a story that has been repeated so often that it, too, might seem "natural": gorgeous guy charms beautiful woman, but her family (or someone else) wants to keep them apart, so he performs valiant deeds in order to win her, and at the end, they get married and live happily ever after. This plot line is not as universal as its ubiquity in contemporary novels and movies might make it seem, however. Heterosexual passion is not an important factor in the epics, myths, and other stories of many cultures, and when it is, it leads to disaster, not marriage. Very few of the stories in *The Arabian Nights,* in fact, revolve around a man doing something in order to win a woman, although the power of this convention is so strong today that contemporary retellings of the stories—such as the 1992 Disney movie *Aladdin*—have to add this. Psychologists and family counselors have found that the idea that "love conquers all," repeated so often in fiction, shapes people's expectations of real life. Can you identify other contemporary conventions about the ways in which emotions shape (or should shape) behavior? Can you think of works of fiction, including fiction told through movies and songs, that have helped create these conventions?

Chapter 8

Fiction and

the Emotions

in Japanese,

Arabian, and

Irish Culture

(1000–1400 C.E.)

EPILOGUE

Each of the stories or story-cycles in this chapter has had a very long life. By two centuries after *The Tale of Genji* was written, scholars in Japan were trying to produce an authoritative and complete version from the many manuscripts and partial copies that existed, and considered the work required reading for anyone who wanted to be considered learned. Thus, *Genji* became a classic, in the same way that Homer's *Iliad* and Virgil's *Aeneid* did in Europe. Like these works, *Genji* was looked to not only as great literature, but as a historical source, a description of the way things had actually been in Genji's time. Like many classics, it was also viewed as a comment on the way things were supposed to be, and was used by scholars as a way to criticize what they perceived as a cultural decline in their own day. Even people who had not read it became familiar with many scenes and characters because these were discussed in other literary works or depicted in art, in the same way that people who have not read the *Iliad* know about the Trojan War it describes. In fact, some scholars would say that *Genji* served one of the functions of the Bible in the West—not, of course, as a source of religious teaching and inspiration, but as a common point of cultural reference, with Japanese people referring to it all the time and assuming everyone was familiar with the stories it contained. In the twentieth century, *Genji* was adapted into an opera and several films, and within the past several decades it has been retold in manga form and as an anime television series.

Genji's influence was primarily in Japan, but *The Arabian Nights* has become familiar around the world. Galland's French volumes were translated into English almost as soon as they were published. People noted that Galland's translations sometimes deviate significantly from the Arabic original—and the various English editions deviate even more—but they are the version that has been most influential. The stories that Galland added are the ones most often retold, and it is hard to think about *The Arabian Nights* without them. French, English, and American authors began to write more stories based on Galland's set in exotic "Oriental" locations, sanitized and moralized versions were published as children's literature, and composers used them as inspiration for symphonies and operas. For Western audiences, *The Arabian Nights* helped to create an image of an exotic East of violent monarchs, harems full of beautiful women, and sly tricksters who used devious means to get what they wanted. This image—what recent historians have termed "Orientalism"—shaped the ways nineteenth- and twentieth-century Westerners responded to actual events in the Near East, and continues to do so today.

The stories of the Ulster Cycle did not circulate as widely as those of *The Arabian Nights,* but they may also have had a political impact. In the late nineteenth century, the Ulster Cycle was rediscovered by people who were agitating for Irish independence from British rule, including the poet W. B. Yeats. They collected myths, stories, and folklore, and used characters in them as symbols of an independent Ireland in patriotic poetry and plays. Later, Yeats wondered whether these writings played a part in the 1916 Easter Rebellion in Dublin, whose leaders were subsequently executed by the British but whose goals were ultimately achieved when Ireland became independent. Thus, "old stories in which there is scarcely a shred of truth," as Genji put it, have continued to exert their power.

CHAPTER NINE

THE MONGOL CONQUEST:

SCOURGE OR STIMULUS?

(1206–1360)

The traditional image of the Mongols has generally been a negative one. Even in an age in which warfare was generally brutal in nature and accompanied by frequent atrocities, they acquired a reputation for unusual cruelty. This view of the Mongols first arose during the years of the conquest at the start of the thirteenth century, as reports and rumors spread before their advance. News of Mongol reprisals in captured cities from Kaifeng to Samarkand exacerbated fears elsewhere. By the time they reached the Middle East and Europe, their enemies attributed them with superhuman ferocity. In the Christian West, where they came to be seen as a form of divine punishment loosed on a sinful world, they were even called "the Scourge of God."

As chroniclers in conquered and threatened lands began to look back and assess the history of the conquest, many perpetuated these views. The mid-thirteenth-century Persian writer Ata al-Mulk Juvaini, for example, frequently stressed in his *History of the World Conqueror* how Chinggis Khan and his generals willingly butchered defenseless prisoners and civilians in their sweep across Muslim lands. A contemporary British cleric, Matthew Paris, went even further in writing his *History of the Tartars*, accusing them of fiendishness for their delight in mass murder and cannibalism: "And thus they use their captives like beasts of burden. The men are inhuman and bestial, they can be said to be monsters rather than men, they thirst for blood and drink it. . ."[1] So portrayed in historical accounts as well as popular myths, the Mongols were to be

---

1. Translated by Daniel Baraz in *Medieval Cruelty: Changing Perceptions, Late Antiquity to the Early Modern Period* (Ithaca, NY: Cornell University Press, 2003), p. 98.

remembered in later eras for their rapacity rather than glory.

Mongol leaders, especially at the beginning of their imperial expansion, did deliberately use mass slaughter to terrorize enemies and cow them into submission. There can be no doubt, therefore, that they resorted to atrocities when it served their interests. Such ruthlessness has been seen as a contributing factor in their defeat of far more powerful enemies and swift creation of the world's largest empire up to that time, an empire that at its height stretched across Eurasia from the Pacific to the Danube. It has also been seen as a factor in their equally sudden decline, because of the legacy of hatred it left among most of their subjects.

But a new generation of scholars has begun to challenge the view that Mongol armies were particularly more vicious than others and to assert that there were many positive aspects of their rule. Noting that most contemporary forces were equally brutal, they suggest that accounts of the Mongols' cruelty may have been exaggerated or even made up by those whom they defeated to discredit them. Not only do they question the scale of alleged slaughter, they tend to refute claims of mass rape and cannibalism as pure fabrications. They also shift attention away from discussions of battles and conquests, the traditional focus of interest in the Mongols, looking instead at the progressive ways in which the Mongols ruled their empire, encouraging trade, artisanship, and religious toleration. Above all, they argue, in building a transcontinental empire, the Mongols brought diverse peoples together as never before, hastening an unprecedented exchange of goods and ideas. This exchange, some even claim, may have been a key first step toward global integration. Rather than destroyers of what others had built, this approach suggests, the Mongols may have been a positive force that helped to launch the modern, integrated world:

> The Mongols' receptiveness to foreigners was a critical factor in promoting cultural exchange and a truly "global" history. Their attitude of relative openness toward foreigners and foreign influence led to an extraordinary interchange of products, peoples, technology, and science throughout the Mongol domains. . . . And if we remember that Christopher Columbus was actually looking for a new route to Asia when he landed in America—and that one of the few books he had with him was Marco Polo's account of his travels in Asia—we could even say that global history begins with the Mongols and the bridge they built between the East and the West.[2]

Your task in this chapter, using primary materials that date from the thirteenth and fourteenth centuries, is to decide which of these views is more creditable—that is to say, were the Mongols a scourge or stimulus? Do the allegations of Mongol narrow-mindedness and brutality seem justifiable? And if so, should we then regard the Mongol conquest as no more than an example of historical cruelty—a cautionary tale, perhaps, of

2. The Mongols in World History, 2004. Part of the *Asia for Educators* online series of Columbia University. http://afe.easia.columbia.edu/mongols/history/history2.htm

Chapter 9
The Mongol
Conquest:
Scourge or
Stimulus?
(1206–1360)

what happens when people abandon themselves to license and cruelty? Or should we instead look upon the event more favorably, paying attention to the ways in which the Mongols proved receptive to the goods, skills, ideas, and even beliefs of others and fostered their spread across the breadth of Eurasia as never before? Is there, in short, evidence to suggest that the Mongol conquest may have set in motion a level of cultural interaction leading to the start of a new era of global history?

BACKGROUND

Chinggis Khan[3] (1167?–1227), the founder of the Mongol empire, probably did not think about the broad impact of his acts. A man of the steppe or grassland, he set out just to unite the nomads of Mongolia. He began by gaining control over his own tribe of Mongols and then leading them to force other Mongol and Turcic tribes into an expanded confederation. Master of all eastern Mongolia north of the Gobi desert by 1206, he called a great council or *kuriltai* of all "the dwellers of the tents," at which he took the title Khagan, or Khan of Khans, and laid the basis of a cohesive *ulus* or steppe polity.

To overcome old tribal and ethnic loyalties and strengthen this state, known as a khanate after the title of its ruler, Chinggis Khan reorganized its people into hereditary military bands. As members' households and herds were attached to these bands, they also doubled as basic units of government and taxation. In search of further unity, Chinggis Khan had the Uighurs, a literate Turcic people, create a Mongolian script based upon Middle Eastern rather than Chinese models. Set down in this medium, his collected decrees formed a sacred body of rules, called the *yasa*, which all followers had to swear to uphold, making it, rather than tribes or leaders, the focus of Mongol unity. Once able to mobilize the scarce resources of the steppe through these reforms, Chinggis Khan felt confident to challenge much larger and better-endowed neighbors, whose rivalries with each other would allow him to confront them one by one.

Starting in 1210, Chinggis struck at the weakest, the Tangut empire on his southwestern flank. No sooner was it reduced to vassalage than he attacked the far more powerful Jürched empire based in north China and forced it to into submission by 1215. Next, he turned westward against Karakhitai, a state recently forged in eastern Central Asia by Khitan[4] refugees, whom the Jürched had driven out of north China.

3. Mongol names and titles appear in many variant forms because of transmission through different languages and transcriptions. This title, for example, is often written as Jenghiz or Genghis Khan. Khan or *Qa'an* is the Mongolian word for a lord or ruler, to which the term *Chinggis* (probably meaning "oceanic" or all-encompassing) was added as an epithet. His personal name, Temüjin, also appears in other forms.

4. The Khitans, another branch of Mongol people, had ruled north China for nearly two centuries. During that era, the area they ruled came to be called Khitai or Kitay, giving rise to the English variant, Cathay. Muslim and Christians long continued to call north China by this name—and the north Chinese Kitayans.

Chapter 9

The Mongol

Conquest:

Scourge or

Stimulus?

(1206–1360)

Their collapse led him, in 1219, to attack the even more formidable Kwarezm empire, which dominated the western steppes of Central Asia. But Kwarezm, based on the Iranian plateau, proved a more difficult foe, and by 1223–1224, Mongol armies were attacking in a great arc from the Indus to the Dneiper rivers in an effort to outflank it. With success in the west finally likely, Chinggis Khan returned east to crush a Tangut revolt. His death in 1227 kept him from enjoying ultimate victory, but by then, he had already taken more territory and people than any other ruler in history. And to this, his successors would add yet more.

That Chinggis Khan allowed both the Tangut and Jürched rulers limited autonomy as vassals suggests that he was reluctant to absorb agrarian territories into his steppe state. No such qualms checked his successors. Beginning with Ögödei, who was installed as khan at a *kuriltai* in 1229, they sought to annex outright all defeated states. Ögödei first absorbed the Tangut lands and then seized most of Afghanistan and Iran following Kwarezm's fall in 1231. Meanwhile, he reopened war with the Jürched and appropriated the whole of north China when they collapsed in 1234. These victories enormously increased Mongol resources, inspiring a further push westward. Thus, in 1241, General Batu took Kiev, drove into Poland, and went on to occupy Hungary. Only the death of Ögödei in December of 1241 slowed the pace of conquest. During the brief reign of his son Güyük in the 1240s, internal quarrels preoccupied Mongol leaders.

Batu's installment of Möngke, another of Chinggis Khan's grandsons, as the fourth khan ended these quarrels and allowed expansion to resume. During Möngke's reign from 1251 to 1259, the western armies took the offensive again, defeating the Islamic Caliphate and occupying Baghdad and much of Mesopotamia in 1258. Meanwhile, in the East, Möngke attacked the Song in southern China. Though he died before the defeat of the Song, his brother and successor, Qubilai Khan, resolutely prosecuted the war with Song China for twenty years. When in 1279 his forces finally defeated the Song and annexed south China, Qubilai Khan was nominal master of an unparalleled empire reaching from Baghdad to the Pacific.

But by the time Qubilai became khagan in 1260, the bonds of empire were fraying. Möngke left no clear successor, and his death occasioned a quarrel over who should succeed him. Though Qubilai's followers proclaimed him Khagan at a *kuriltai* convened in north China, where he was directing the war against the Song, a rival faction of steppe leaders in the Altai region refused to acknowledge him and rebelled. Their defection isolated western Mongol lands, allowing commanders there to act with increasing autonomy. What had been a single khanate now split along the lines of the four Hordes (Mongol *Orda*), through which the empire had been administered: the Il-Khanate based in Iran, the Golden Horde of southwestern Russia, Chagatai centered around Samarkand in Central Asia, and Qubilai's domain in eastern Asia.

Qubilai's response was to shift his base to north China. Abandoning Karakorum, he built Khanbaligh, the city Chinese would later rename Beijing, as a new capital. There he turned to Khitan and Chinese aides to rule through a Song-style bureaucracy and relied increasingly on his agrarian lands. By 1271, he so identified with this new seat of power that he proclaimed himself the founding emperor of a Chinese-style Yuan dynasty. As part of this policy, he intensified his attacks on Song China, finally defeating and annexing it in 1279. But even this victory did not satisfy him, and he set out to conquer an even greater East Asian realm. He succeeded in imposing indirect rule over Tibet and forced most of Indochina into vassalage. But his efforts to conquer Japan and parts of Indonesia with captured Song fleets proved a failure, though they did mark the world's first projection of sea power on a massive scale. So in the end, his East Asian realm remained a much smaller and more regional empire than the vast, steppe-based *ulus* created by his grandfather, Chinggis Khan. Thus, the period of a united Mongol empire stretching across the breadth of Eurasia was really very brief, lasting only from the 1220s into the 1260s.

THE METHOD

The usual way to resolve historical problems is to turn to the earliest available documents for possible answers. But we face a problem in doing so with regard to the Mongol conquest, for the Mongols proved surprisingly unconcerned with recording their achievements for later ages. Having become a literate people only at the beginning of their imperial expansion, they lacked a tradition of historical or other writings, so we have very few documents produced by the Mongols themselves. Moreover, they left almost no lasting material remains. Originally a nomadic people unaccustomed to permanent residences, they did not build imposing monuments to awe future ages. Karakorum, their first capital, was built entirely of perishable materials and quickly fell into ruin once abandoned in 1259. As a result, we are unusually dependent upon the accounts made by others, often their victims and conquered subjects. Keep this fact in mind as you work through the evidence section, giving special attention to who produced what—and for what likely purpose.

Source 1 consists of a selection of passages translated from *The Secret History of the Mongols*. This work, probably produced by an anonymous court scribe in about 1240, seems to be the only extensive historical piece actually written down by Mongols. But as its readership was restricted to only a small court elite, copies of the Mongolian text disappeared soon after the fall of the empire. All that survives are Chinese transcriptions and translations. Aside from the question of how faithful such transmissions may be, they are hard to understand on

[235]

Chapter 9
The Mongol
Conquest:
Scourge or
Stimulus?
(1206–1360)

stylistic grounds, being terse chronicles that use many colloquial terms and assume knowledge of contemporary names and events unfamiliar to a current reader. Nonetheless, this is the single best account we have of the Mongols' own view of the conquest at the height of their power.

The next two sources, though not from Mongol authors, were written by men who served closely with them in the administration of conquered lands. The first, Source 2, is taken from *A Journey to the West*, a travel journal written in Chinese by Yelü Chucai, a sinified Khitan who served Chinggis as a top administrator in North China. It probably dates from 1228 and reflects his experiences accompanying Chinggis in the field on his Central Asian wars. The other, Source 3, is excerpted from a history of the world called the *Ta'rīkh-i Gāzānī*, written by Rashīd al-Dīn Tabib, a Persian who served as a minister to the Il-Khanate that came to rule Iran and Mesopotamia. Completed in 1307, it offers the most detailed account of the Mongols produced by any early writer. Disseminated widely in both Persian and Arabic, it became a standard work throughout the Muslim world. The selections here, drawn from the third volume, *The Successors of Genghis Khan*, concern the election of Chinggis Khan's immediate heir, Ögödei, as khan and his efforts to give the empire a more formal institutional structure.

Source 4, selections from the *Ta'rī kh-i-Jahan-Gusha*, or *The History of The World Conqueror*, comes from another Persian writer, Ata al-Mulk Juvaini, who also collaborated with the Mongol conquerors of his homeland. Focused mainly on Chinggis's career and the early years of the conquest, it is narrower in scope than Rashīd's work. Juvaini apparently owed his position to his father, who shifted allegiance from Kwarezm to the Mongols at an early point in the conquest. And it was apparently while accompanying his father on a visit to the imperial capital of Karakorum in 1252 that Juvaini became sufficiently impressed with the Mongol's achievements that he resolved to set them down in a history. Eventually rising to serve as an advisor to Möngke Khan's brother, Hülegü, the founder of the Il-Khan line, he had access to high Mongol leaders and official documents not available to others. For that reason, his work is often considered the second most important source on the conquest after *The Secret History*. The part given here deals with the election of the fourth Khan Möngke due to the backing of General Batu. Histories of this sort were often illustrated in the Persian manner with small paintings like Source 5. This one, which graced a fourteenth-century copy of Juvaini's work, shows the Mongols besieging a walled city during the conquest of Kwarezm. The scene depicts a rather conventional battle, focusing mostly on weaponry and military details rather than bold or dramatic action.

Source 6, *The Tale of the Destruction of Riazan*, stands in high contrast to these initial documents. An epic poem, probably composed by Russian clergymen during the first half of the fourteenth century, *The Tale* reflects the viewpoint of those whom the Mongols attacked. Focused upon Batu's invasion of Russia, it recounts the heroic defense—and fall—of a small Russian principality called Riazin in 1237. Its unflattering portrait of the "godless" Batu leaves no doubt about the authors' view of the Mongols. Source 7, taken from *The Account of John de Plano Carpini*, presents another Christian cleric's view of the Mongols. Its author was sent out in 1245 by Pope Innocent IV to secure Batu's help in arranging a meeting with Ögödei Khan and to assess the nature of the Mongol threat. As the report he brought back was one of the earliest first-hand accounts of the Mongols available to Europe, it played an important role in establishing how they were seen there. Despite an effort at impartiality, John ultimately did not find the Mongols to his liking and complained of their insolence, treachery, and nonchalant slaughter of others.

Once the immediate threat of a Mongol invasion of Europe passed, however, Western travelers who ventured into their territory no longer seemed to stress Mongol violence, as the next two documents demonstrate. The first, Source 8, selections from *The Travel Account of William of Rubruck*, recounts the experiences of another cleric turned envoy, in this case one sent out by Louis IX of France in 1253 to explore the possibility of securing Mongol aid for a crusade. Though clearly unimpressed by the Mongol capital, Karakorum, William seems not to have been much troubled by Mongol behavior. Neither was the author of the final selection, Source 9, drawn from Francis Balducci Pegolotti's *Book of Description of Countries*. Pegolotti, a Florentine merchant working in the firm of Bardi, wrote the book sometime in the early 1300s to encourage fellow Western merchants to expand their activities further afield. Though not as famous as Marco Polo's work, which comes from about the same time, Pegolotti's supplies more practical information for merchants about travel conditions and trade across the Mongol empire. The picture he paints is certainly not one of turmoil and oppression but of secure trade routes and prosperous cities where foreigners and locals can mix freely.

In going through this diverse material, your first task is obviously to determine what information each source provides about the Mongol impact upon the people and conditions of their time, especially as it relates to the question of their being a scourge or stimulus. Pay particular attention to remarks about Mongol destructiveness, on one hand, and more positive comments about the benefits of their actions, on the other. What light does each piece shed on allegations of Mongol narrow-mindedness, cruelty, or their delight in rape and slaughter? Conversely, do you find evidence that Mongol interest in others—or what they had to offer—promoted an expanding exchange of goods, skills, or ideas? What concrete information does each provide about the conquest's effect on migration, travel, or trade? Are there, in fact, clear suggestions that Mongol activities were intensifying either the scope or pace of cultural interaction?

Keeping track of all this information may not be easy. You may find it worthwhile to lay out a simple chart

Chapter 9

The Mongol

Conquest:

Scourge or

Stimulus?

(1206–1360)

in which to note what you find in each source to facilitate comparison between them. Make it four columns wide horizontally, and divide each column into nine vertical spaces. Title the first column "Sources" and, under that heading, list the sources one by one, spacing them out equally to fill the nine vertical spaces. Leave the other columns blank, but label the second one "Scourge" and the third "Stimulus." Finally, title the fourth column "Conclusions." As you review each source, briefly note whatever

information it offers in support of the interpretations designated in columns two and three (one or both), and then indicate in column four which interpretation it seems to support best. Be aware, of course, that the evidence may support more than a simple choice between the two interpretations, so be prepared to note that as well. After you have filled in the appropriate spaces for all the documents, go over your various conclusions and decide what the overall weight of evidence best supports.

THE EVIDENCE

1. From *The Secret History of the Mongols*

And so

Making straight
The people having skirts of felt [which cover their tents as outward walls]

and, in the year of the tiger [1206], assembling themselves at the head of the Onan [River], having made [one] to set up a white standard having nine feet, then they gave unto Cinggis Qahan the title *qan*. Then also he gave unto Muqali the title *gui ong*.[5] Making Jebe to pursue Güčülüg Qan of the Naiman, then also he made him to go a warfare. When he had made an end of setting in order the Mongγoljin people, when Činggis Qahan made a decree, he made a decree, saying, "For [those] who are gone with [me], together setting up a nation, I shall, making bands of thousands and appointing captains of the thousands, speak words of favour. . . ."

5. **gui ong:** a Chinese title *guo wang*, meaning "king of a state," which Khitan rulers had been giving to allied chieftains.

. . . He made a decree, saying, "At the moment when [I am] being protected by Everlasting Heaven and am rectifying the entire people, becoming

[Mine] eyes for seeing,
[Mine] ears for hearing,

the entire people part thou and give [as] parts unto [Our] Mother, unto Us, unto [Our] younger brethren, and unto [Our] sons, according to the names of the people,

Dividing
Those who have skirts of felt [which cover their tents as outward walls],
Making to separate themselves
Those who have doors of boards [on their tents].

Let not anyone violate thy word." Again saying that Šigi Qutuqu, of the entire people,

Making thieves to beware,
Making lies to be vain,

should make to die [those] for whom holdeth the custom, that they should be made to die and should make to punish [those] for whom holdeth the custom that they should be made to be punished, he committed [unto him] the judgments of over all [the people]. Again he made a decree, saying, "Let him, writing write in the blue register, make into registers the fact that, of the entire people,

He shall have parted parts
and the fact that
He shall have judged judgments

and unto the seed of the seed, let one not alter the blue writing which Šigi Qutuqu, [after] taking counsel with me, shall, [after] deciding [it], have made into registers on white paper. . . ."

    Činggis Qahan, at that fact of having set forth, in making the Altan Qa'an of the Kitad people to submit himself, took many satins; making Burqan of the Qašin people to submit himself, he took many camels; Činggis Qahan, at that fact of having set forth, in the year of the sheep [1211], making the Altan Qan of the Kitad people, named Aqutai, to submit himself and making Iluqu Burqan of the Tang'ud people to submit himself, returning, pitched [on] the Sa'ari Steppe.[6]

    . . . Again, after that, his many ambassadors having Ĵubqan at their head, [ambassadors] which he had sent to make peace with Ĵau Gon, being hindered by the Altan Qa'an, [named] Aqutai, of the Kitad people, Činggis Qahan in the year of the dog [1214] again set forth against the Kitad people. . . . When [Činggis Qahan] arrived at the Tonggon Pass, the soldiers of the Kitad, saying, "[Let us defend our] soil," came to stay [his] passage. Činggis Qahan, joining battle with Ile, Qada,

---

6. The Altan or Golden Khan was the emperor of the Jürched Jin or Golden Dynasty ruling north China, which the Mongols called Kitad after the Khitan who ruled it earlier. The Tang'ud were the Tanguts of the Xi-xia empire.

Chapter 9

The Mongol

Conquest:

Scourge or

Stimulus?

(1206–1360)

Höbögetür—[all] three—, made Ile and Qada to remove. Both Tolui and Čügü Gürigen, rushing upon [them] from athwart, making the Hula'an Degelen to withdraw themselves, arriving, making Ile and Qada to remove, overcoming [them], slew the Kitad till they stood [as] rotten trees. Altan Qan, knowing that his Kitad troops had suffered [their] slaying and making an end of [them], going out from Ĵungdu, fleeing, entered the city of Namging. When their soldiers which remained grew lean and died, among themselves they together ate the flesh of men. . . .

Spoiling the Tang'ud people, making Iluqu Burqan be Šiduryu, accomplishing him, causing the mothers and the fathers of the Tang'ud people, unto the seed of the seed, to vanish . . . he made a decree, saying, "While [I] eat food, saying, [They are] vanished . . . be [ye], saying [this]." Because the Tang'ud people, [after] speaking a word, kept not to the word, Činggis Qahan going a warfare a second time against the Tang'ud people, destroying the Tang'ud people, coming [back], in the year of the pig [1227] Činggis Qahan is ascended to Heaven. . . .

In the year of the rat the princes of the right hand having at their head Ča'adai and Batu, the princes of the left hand having at their head Odčigin, Noyan, Yegü, and Yesünge, the princes of the middle having at their head Tolui, the daughters, the sons in law, the captains of ten thousand and [those] of a thousand, being a multitude, wholly assembling at Köde'ü Aral of the Kelüren [River], according to the same decree by which Činggis Qahan had named [him], raised up Ögödei Qahan as qan. . . .

Ögödei Qahan suffering himself to be raised up as *qan*, after suffering [one] to cause the ten thousand guards which walk within and the people of the middle to be for himself, first [of all] taking counsel with Elder Brother Ča'adai, made to go a warfare both Oqotur and Münggetü, succourers of Čormaqan Qorči which was gone a warfare against the Qalibai Soltan of the Baɣtad people of the peoples which his father Cinggis Qahan had left undone . . . such was the manner in which he made to go a warfare the princes having at their head Batu, Büri, Güyüg, and Möngge.[7]

Source 2 from Inscribed Landscapes: Travel Writings from Imperial China, trans. *Richard E. Strassberg (Berkeley: University of California Press, 1994), pp. 229–232. Copyright © 1994 by University of California Press—Books. Reproduced with permission of California Press— Books in the format Textbook via Copyright Clearance Center.*

2. Selections from "A Journey to the West" by Yelü Chucai

In the spring of the year wu-yin, the day after the moon reached its height in the third month [April 12, 1218], I, the Lay Scholar of Profound Clarity, was commanded to be in attendance on a journey to the West. . . .

7. The Qalibai Soltai of Baɣtad people means the Caliph Sultan of Baghdad, who was the caliph or secular head of the Arab caliphate; the leaders Ögödei sent out against him were his sons and nephews, two of whom would succeed him as khagan.

In less than a hundred days, I reached the Traveling Court. Mountains and rivers crisscrossed; how lush was the verdant land! The covered wagons were like clouds; the army, like rain drops. Horses and oxen covered the plains; foot soldiers and troops in armor emblazoned the sky. Fires and smoke viewed each other from afar; fortified camps stretched for thousands of miles. Never has there been such magnificence throughout all history!

In the following year [1219], the Imperial Army commenced its Western Campaign, the route passing through the Golden Mountains.[8] It was just at the height of summer, yet snow flew about on the mountain peaks and the accumulated ice was more than a thousand feet high. His Majesty commanded that the ice be cut through to create a road for the army. . . . West of the Golden Mountains, the rivers all flow westward into the Western Ocean. Thus has Heaven defined the boundary between East and West!

. . . After traveling about three hundred fifty miles beyond the Desert Ocean Army Region, there is the city of Bolat, which controls several other towns nearby. South of Bolat are the Dark Mountains, which stretch for some three hundred fifty miles east to west and seventy miles north to south. . . . After coming out of the Dark Mountains, there is the city of Almalik.[9] When men of the Western Region saw these apple groves they called it 'Almalik,' for the entire surrounding area contains apple farms, and it is from these that it derived its name. It controls eight or nine cities where many grapes and pears can be found. They also raise the five kinds of grain, just like in the Central Plains of China.

. . . Farther west more than a hundred miles is the city of Talas. Farther southwest more than a hundred forty miles are the cities of Khojend, Pap, Kasan, and Pa-lan. Khojend has many pomegranate trees; the fruits are as large as two hands clasped together, and are sweet with a tinge of sourness. Three to five pieces yield about one large cup of juice, excellent for quenching thirst. Beside the city of Pa-lan are pa-lan groves, hence the name. The flowers of the *pa-lan* are like those of the common apricot tree, but somewhat lighter in shade; the leaves are like those of the peach tree, but smaller. Every winter they blossom; by the height of summer, the fruit ripens. It is shaped like the flat peach, but the flesh is not fit to eat, only the pits are consumed. The large watermelons of Pa-p'u weigh as much as sixty-five pounds; a mule can carry only two at a time. Their flavor is sweet, cool, and delicious.

About one hundred seventy-five miles farther northwest of Khojend is the city of Otrar, which controls more than ten neighboring cities. The leader of this city murdered our dynasty's ambassador and a number of his entourage as well as more than a hundred merchants, plundering their goods. This was the initial reason for this Western Campaign.

---

8. The Golden Mountains are the Altai range—*altai* or *altan* being the Mongol word for "golden."

9. The Desert Ocean refers to the Gobi. Today the Dark or Yin Mountains beyond are called the Tianshan.

Chapter 9

The Mongol

Conquest:

Scourge or

Stimulus?

(1206–1360)

More than three hundred fifty miles west of Otrar is a great city, named "Samarkand."[10] "Samarkand" means "fertile" among the men of the Western Region, and this place was so named because of its fertile soil. The Western Liao named this city "the Superior Prefecture of Hochung" because of its proximity to the river. Samarkand is extremely rich. They use gold and copper coins without holes or raised edges; all merchandise is weighed out by scales. There are gardens everywhere in the surrounding outskirts, stretching for several tens of miles. Every house must have a garden, and these gardens are always fascinating in design. They all employ canals and fountains, square ponds, and round pools; cypresses grow next to willows, and peach trees intertwine with plum, creating one of the most impressive scenes today. Large melons are the size of a horse's head and long enough to contain a fox. Of the eight kinds of grain, they lack millet, glutinous rice, and soybeans, but they have all the others. At the height of summer there is no rain, so they transport water by means of canals. Every third acre of land is irrigated with over two hundred gallons of water. They ferment grapes, the flavor resembling the 'Nine Fermentations Wine' of Chung-shan. Though there are plenty of mulberry trees, few people know how to raise silkworms, so silk is extremely rare and they all wear cotton. The local people consider white an auspicious color, while black clothing is worn at funerals, so everyone wears white.

Between two hundred and two hundred fifty miles west of Samarkand is the city of Bokhara. The produce here is even more plentiful, and the cities and towns quite numerous. Samarkand was the capital of the Shah of the Moslems. Bokhara, Khojend, and Otrar were subject to it.

West of Bokhara is a great river named the Amu Darya, slightly inferior to the Yellow River, which flows west into the Great Sea. . . . Farther west along this great river is Bactria, which is quite prosperous. Farther west is the city of T'uan, which is also magnificent. In the city can be found many items made of lacquer that bear the mark of Ch'ang-an.

I proceeded directly west of here, arriving at the city of Black India. The people of this kingdom also have a written language, but it differs in alphabet and sound from that used in the Buddhist kingdoms. There are many Buddhist statues throughout this kingdom. The people do not butcher cows or goats but do drink their milk. According to their custom, when the husbands die first, their wives are cremated together with them. I inquired about the location of the Buddhist kingdoms, and they indicated that they lay to the southeast. After investigation, I concluded that this kingdom is not northern India proper; the inhabitants are a border people on the north of India. . . . South of this kingdom is a great river as broad as the Yellow River, as cold as ice and snow, whose swirling current is swift and dangerous. It comes from slightly west of here and bows directly south and slightly east. I would reason that it must enter

10. Samarkand was the greatest city and trade emporium of Central Asia as well as the seat of the Kwarezm empire.

into the Southern Ocean. Furthermore, the land produces much sugarcane on fields as wide as those which grow millet. The local people squeeze out its juice, fermenting it into wine and boiling it to make sugar.

Northwest of Black India is the kingdom of Kipchak.[11] For a thousand miles there are calm rivers everywhere without any hills. Ah, it is a strange place indeed! There are no cities, and the people mostly raise goats and horses. They make wine from honey, but the flavor is not too different from the wine of the Central Plains of China. . . . Samarkand is almost seven thousand miles from the Central Plains of China, India is the same distance from Samarkand, and Kipchak is the same distance from India. Even though the road is circuitous and winding, I would not consider these places nearby, for they are I don't know how many tens of thousands of *li* away.

When the year fell on chun-t'an [1224], the Imperial Army set forth on a campaign. The Hsi-Hsia had betrayed our trust and violated treaties, so, in the second month of spring of the year ping-hsu [March 1226], the entire Six Armies attacked in successive waves and in one blow conquered it. Their leader was executed, but the common people were allowed to dwell in peace.

Source 3 from Rashīd al-Dīn Tabib, The Successors of Genghis Khan, *trans. John Andrew Boyle (New York: Columbia University Press, 1971), pp. 29–33, 61–62. Copyright © 1971 Columbia University Press. Reprinted with permission of the publisher.*

3. Selections from Rashīd al-Dīn Tabib's *The Successors of Genghiz Khan*

In the *qaqa yil*, that is, the Year of the Pig, falling within the months of the year 624 / 1226–1227, Chingiz-Khan, by reason of that condition which no mortal can escape, passed away in the region of Tangqut, having set out for the country of the Nangiyas and having reached the frontier [of that country].[12] As has been described in his history, his coffin was borne to Kelüren, which is their original *yurt*, and the mourning ceremonies were performed. All the princes and emirs then consulted together regarding the kingdom and departed each to his own place of residence, where, as had been agreed, they took their rest. For nearly 2 years throne and kingdom were deprived of a king. [Then] they reflected that [if] something happened and no leader or king had been appointed, falsehood and confusion would find their way into the foundations of the kingdom. It was therefore advisable to make haste in the matter of the accession to the Khanate. And on this delicate business they dispatched

11. Kipchak was the steppe area of southern Russia, stretching eastward from the Black Sea.
12. **Nangiyas:** a Mongol term for the southern Chinese Song state.

Chapter 9

The Mongol

Conquest:

Scourge or

Stimulus?

(1206–1360)

ambassadors to one another from every side and busied themselves with preparing a *quriltai*. When the violence of the cold had abated and the first days of spring had come round, all the princes and emirs set out from every side and direction for the ancient *yurt* and great *ordo*. From Qipchaq [came] the sons of Jochi: Orda, Batu, Shiban, Tangqut, Berke, Berkecher, and Toqa-Temür; from Qayaliq [came] Chaghatai Khan with all his sons and grandsons; from the Emil and the Qobaq, Ögetei Qa'an with his sons and descendants; from the East, their uncles Otchigin and Bilgütei Noyan and their cousin Elchidei Noyan, the son of Qachi'un; and from all sides [came] the emirs and great men of the army. All of these now presented themselves at Kelüren. Tolui Khan, whose title is Yeke-Noyan or Ulugh-Noyan, the lord of his father's house and original yurt, was already there. The aforesaid company for 3 days and nights concerned themselves with pleasure, conviviality, and merrymaking, after which they spoke about the affairs of the empire and the kingship, and in accordance with the will of Chingiz-Khan they settled the Khanate upon Ögetei Qa'an. First all the sons and princes in one voice said to Ögetei Qa'an: "By the command of Chingiz-Khan it behooves thee with divine assistance to set thy [foot] upon the land of kingship in order that the haughty leaders may gird the loins of their lives with the girdle of servitude and that far and near, whether Turk or Tāzīk, [they] may be obedient and submissive to thy command. . . ."

. . . And when he had done with feasting and making presents he ordered that in accordance with the ancient *yasaq* and their usage and custom they should provide victuals for the soul of Chingiz-Khan, and should choose forty beautiful girls of the race and seed of the emirs that had been in attendance on him and having decked them out in precious garments embroidered with gold and jewels, dispatch them along with choice horses to join his spirit. . . .

. . . When Qa'an had been established on the throne of the kingdom, he first of all made a *yasa* that all the ordinances that had previously been issued by Chingiz-Khan should be upheld and preserved and protected from change and alteration. [He also commanded:] "Any crime or offense that has been committed by anyone up to the day of our accession, we have forgiven them all. If after today any person behaves with impudence and proceeds to an act that contravenes the old and new *yasas*, there shall befall him such chastisement and requital as are fitting to his crime. . . ."

. . . Thereafter he dispatched armies to all the borders and sides of the empire to protect the frontiers and the provinces. In the direction of Persia, unrest and insurrection had not yet abated, and Sultan Jalāl al-Din was still active there.[13] He dispatched Chormaghun Noyan and a group of emirs with thirty thousand horsemen to deal with him. He dispatched Köketei and Sübedei Bahadur with a like army against the Qipchaq, Saqsin, and Bulghar;

13. Sultan Jalāl al-Din was the Muslim ruler of Kwarezm.

toward Khitai, Tibet, Solanga, Jürche, and that general region he sent on in advance a party of great *noyans* with an army, whilst he himself with his younger brother, Möngke Qa'an, set out in the wake of that army toward Khitai, which had not yet submitted and where the Emperor of Khitai was still in possession. . . .

. . . And in no way did he neglect the finest points in whatever related to laying the foundations of world sovereignty and raising the edifices of prosperity. Having brought with him from Khitai masters of every craft and trade, he commanded them to build in the *yurt* of Qara-Qorum, where he for the most part had his auspicious residence, a palace exceedingly tall in structure and with lofty pillars, such as was in keeping with the high resolve of such a king. The length of every wing of it was the distance of a bowshot, and in the middle they raised up an exceedingly tall pavilion. These buildings were finished off in the best possible fashion and painted with all kinds of designs and pictures. They called it Qarshi: he made it his residence and orders were given that each of his brothers and sons and the rest of the princes that were in attendance should build tall houses in that neighborhood. They all obeyed the command, and when those buildings were completed and joined one to another they covered a great area. . . .

He asked: "Which is the fairest city in the whole world?" They answered: "Baghdad." He ordered a great city to be built on the banks of the Orkhon and given the name of Qara-Qorum. Between the countries of Khitai and that town other *yams* were established in addition to the *tayan yams*. At every stage a *tümen* was posted for the protection of the *yams*.[14] And he had issued a *yasa* to the effect that every day five hundred wagons fully loaded with food and drink should arrive thither from the provinces to be placed in stores and then dispensed therefrom. For [corn] and [wine] there were provided great wagons drawn by six oxen each. . . .

Source 4 from 'Ala ad-Din 'Ata-Malik Juvaini, The History of the World Conqueror, *translated by John Andrew Boyle (Cambridge, Mass.: Harvard University Press, 1958), pp. 549–550, 552–553, 559–560, 562, 568, 607–610. Collection of Representatives Works: Persian Series, 1958. Copyright © UNESCO 1958. Used by permission of UNESCO.*

4. Selections from Juvaini's *The History of the World Conqueror*

By the *yasa* and custom of the Mongols the father's place passes to the youngest son by the chief wife. Such was Ulugh-Noyan, but it was Chingiz-Khan's *yasa* that Ögetei should be Khan and in obedience to his father's command Ulugh-Noyan went to great pains in order to set Qa'an upon the throne of the Khanate

---

14. **yams:** uniform post and caravan stations established by Ögödei along a system of arterial roads built to connect the various parts of the empire; the *tümen* were military units attached to them as garrisons.

Chapter 9

The Mongol

Conquest:

Scourge or

Stimulus?

(1206–1360)

and was most assiduous in his exertions to establish him firmly upon the seat of kingship. For between the brothers, and especially between Qa'an and himself, there was affection beyond the degree of brotherhood. . . .

After Ulugh-Noyan's death Qa'an commanded that as long as he lived affairs of state should be administered in accordance with the counsel of his wife Sorqotani Beki, the niece of Ong-Khan, by whom he had his eldest sons, Mengü Qa'an, Qubilai, Hülegü and Arigh Böke, and that the above-mentioned sons, the army and the people, great and small, should be under the control of her command and prohibition, her loosening and binding, and should not turn their heads from her commandment.[15] Now in the management and education of all her sons, in the administration of affairs of state, in the maintenance of dignity and prestige and in the execution of business, Beki, by the nicety of her judgement and discrimination, constructed such a basis and for the strengthening of these edifices laid such a foundation that no turban-wearer (*kulah-dar*) would have been capable of the like or could have dealt with these matters with the like brilliance. In any business which Qa'an undertook, whether with regard to the weal of the Empire or the disposal of the army, he used first to consult and confer with her and would suffer no change or alteration of whatever she recommended. The ambassadors and *elchis* too held her in great honour and respect. . . .

Furthermore, in the management of her household and in the ceremonial of her court she laid for kinsmen and stranger such a foundation as the khans of the world had not been capable of. And so she continued until the time when God Almighty through the mediation of her experience laid the bride of kingship in the bosom of Mengü Qa'an's distinction. And her hand was ever open in munificence and benefaction, and although she was a follower and devotee of the religion of Jesus she would bestow alms and presents upon *imams* and *shaikhs* and strove also to revive the sacred observances of the faith of Mohammed (may God bless him and give him peace!). And the token and proof of this statement is that she gave 1000 silver *balish* that a college (*madrasa*) might be built in Bokhara, of which pious foundation the *shaikh-al-Islam* Saif-ad-Din of Bakharz should be administrator and superintendent; and she commanded that villages should be bought, and endowment made and teachers and students accommodated [in the college]. And always she would send alms to all parts to be distributed among the poor and needy of the Moslems. . . .

The princes [on Güyük's death] now presented themselves from every side. Of the sons of Qa'an there came Qadaghan Oghul and of the sons and grandsons of Chaghatai, Qara-Hülegü and Mochi. [There came also] Mengü Qa'an with his brothers Möge and Arigh Böke and of the emirs Uhatai and Yesü-Buqa;

15. Sorqotani Beki was originally the wife of Chinggis Khan's youngest brother, Ulugh-Noyan or Tolui, but, following Mongol custom, on his death she married his brother, Ögödei. Möngke was her son by Tolui, not Ögödei. She had to overcome considerable opposition from the latter's descendants in pressing for Möngke's election.

and from other directions came the emirs and *noyans* and the other princes and nephews of Batu. They held a great assembly and after feasting for some days deliberated together about the entrusting of the Khanate to a person who was fitted thereto and had experienced the good and ill, the weal and woe of action, and tasted the sweet and bitter of life, and led armies far and near, and won renown in banquets and victory in battles. . . .

. . . Batu took up the speeches of that day and none having anything to add thereto he continued as follows: "The administration of so great a realm and the advancement of so delicate a matter can be effected by such a person . . . as has known and experienced the *yasa* of Chingiz Khan and the customs of Qa'an [Ögödei] . . . and has in person supervised important affairs and been in charge of weighty matters, and in the overcoming of difficulties and the crushing of rebels has provided unanswerable proofs. Now of the lineage (*urugh*) of Chingiz-Khan is Mengü Qa'an, who is famous for his shrewdness and bravery and celebrated for his sagacity and valour. The affairs of the Khanate should be ordered and regulated by the excellence of his world-adorning counsel and the welfare of the land and people assured by the good fortune of his knot-loosening resolution and forethought. . . .

. . . I shall place the reins of this affair in the hands of his proficiency and put the signet of the Empire upon the finger of his resolve and experience, for that unbroken horse, the world, will be tamed beneath the thighs of his severity and valour and the sword that protects the commonweal and guards the frontiers will be unsheathed from the scabbard of his resolve and intrepidity."

. . . As for those who spoke evasively and postponed [a decision] on this matter, fabricating tales and inventing stories, on the pretext that the Khanate ought to remain in the family (urugh) of Qa'an or Güyük Khan, they forgot the subtlety of *"Thou givest power to whom thou wilt"* and therefore dispatched messenger after messenger in all directions and also sent messages to Batu to say that they dissented from that agreement and did not acquiesce in that covenant.[16]

[But] . . . those present—the princes . . . and the emirs, *noyans* and great officials of the *ordu* of Chingiz-Khan as well as such other leaders as were in that neighbourhood, together with troops beyond number or computation—[of all these] the princes took off their hats inside the *ordu*, slung their belts over their shoulders and raising up Mengü set him upon the throne of sovereignty and kingship. . . .

. . . Accordingly in the great quriltai, after he had been firmly seated on the throne of the Khanate and his attention was no longer concerned with the case of the self-seeking and the envious, he turned his mind towards the subjugation of the farthest East and West of the world. And first he dispatched Qubilai

---

16. Often, as here, Juvaini quotes from the Qur'an. The line in question comes from the Qur'an, 3:25.

Chapter 9

The Mongol

Conquest:

Scourge or

Stimulus?

(1206–1360)

to the Eastern parts consisting of Khitai and then in the year 650/1252–3 proceeded to arrange and organize the affairs of his other brother Hülegü and charged him with the conquest of the Western parts. . . . And he sent to Khitai to fetch mangonel experts and naphtha throwers; and they brought from Khitai 1,000 households (*khana*) of Khitayan mangonel-men, who with a stone missile would convert the eye of a needle into a passage for a camel. . . . [17]

And *elchis* were sent on in advance to reserve all pasturage and meadowland wherever the World-King's troops might be expected to pass, from the Qanghai mountains between Qara-Qorum and Besh-Baligh; and all animals were forbidden to graze there lest the pastures might be harmed or the meadows injured. And all the garden-like mountains and plains were banned and prohibited and the teeth of cattle were prevented from browsing thereon. And in all countries from Turkestan to Khorasan and uttermost Rum and Georgia grass fell into the category. . . .

As for the provisioning of the troops orders were given that all the lands should provide one *taghar*, i.e., 100 *maunds*, of flour and 50 *maunds*, i.e., one skin, of wine for each man. And the emirs and local rulers, whoever they were, began to prepare provisions (*ulafa*) and get together *tuzghu* or offerings of food; and they set down their offerings at every stage [of the army's advance]. At the same time the Mongol and Moslem emirs brought herds of mares and each in turn manufactured *qumiz* until the troops passed on to another emir.[18] And the route along which it was calculated that the World-King would pass was cleared, parasang by parasang, of thorns and boulders; and bridges were built over the rivers and streams and boats held in readiness at the ferries.[19]

---

17. A mangonel was a small catapult.

18. **Qumiz** or *koumiss* is an alcoholic beverage made from mare's milk.

19. A parasang was a Persian land measure equal to about four miles.

Source 5 from an illuminated manuscript of Rashīd al-Dīn Tabib's al-Tawarikh, *written in about 1307. Edinburgh University Library. © The University of Edinburgh.*

5. Persian miniature illustrating a Mongol attack on a city

Chapter 9

The Mongol

Conquest:

Scourge or

Stimulus?

(1206–1360)

Source 6 from Medieval Russia's Epics, Chronicles, and Tales *translated by Serge A. Venkovsky (New York: Meridian Books, 1996), pp. 199–203.*

6. Tale of the Destruction of Riazan

Within twelve years after bringing the miraculous icon of St. Nicholas from Kherson, the godless Emperor Batu invaded the Russian land with a great multitude of his Tatar warriors and set up camp on the river Voronezh in the vicinity of the principality of Riazan. And he sent his infidel envoys to the city of Riazan, to Great Prince Yury Ingvarevich, demanding tithes from everyone—from the princes and from all ranks of people. And the Great Prince decided to send his son, Fedor Yurevich, to Batu with many gifts and supplications that he not invade the land of Riazan. . .

Prince Fedor came to the Emperor Batu. . . And Batu began to entertain the Riazan Princes, and after this entertainment asked that they send their sisters and daughters to be his concubines. And one envious Riazan courtier told Batu that the wife of Prince Fedor belonged to the Byzantine imperial family and that she had a most beautiful body. Emperor Batu, who was false and merciless, became excited, and told Prince Fedor: "Prince, give me your wife so that I may enjoy her beauty." And Prince Fedor said, "It is not our Christian custom to bring to you, the godless emperor, our wives so that your lust may be satisfied. If you conquer us then you will be the ruler of our wives."

The godless Batu felt offended, and became angry. He ordered the immediate death of Prince Fedor, and commanded that his body be thrown in a field where it would be devoured by beasts and birds. And the retinue and the warriors of Prince Fedor were also put to death.

. . . The accursed Batu began the conquest of the land of Riazan and soon approached the city of Riazan itself. They encircled the city and fought without surcease for five days. Batu changed his regiments frequently, replacing them with fresh troops, while the citizens of Riazan fought without relief. And many citizens were killed and others wounded. Still others were exhausted by their great efforts and their wounds. On the dawn of the sixth day the pagan warriors began to storm the city, some with firebrands, some with battering rams, and others with countless scaling ladders for ascending the walls of the city. And they took the city of Riazan on the 21st day of December.

And they killed without exception all monks and priests. And they burned this holy city with all its beauty and wealth. . . And churches of God were destroyed, and much blood was spilled on the holy altars. And not one man remained alive in the city. All had drunk the same bitter cup to the dregs. And there was not even anyone to mourn the dead. Neither father nor mother could mourn their dear children, nor the children their fathers or mothers. Nor could a brother mourn the death of his brother, or a relative, his relative. All were dead. And this happened for our sins.

Seeing this terrible letting of Christian blood, the heart of godless Batu became even more hardened, and he marched against the cities of Suzdal and Vladimir, intending to conquer all Russian lands. . . At that time a Riazan lord, Eupaty Kolovrat, in Chernigov at the time of the destruction of the city of Riazan, heard of Batu's invasion. He left Chernigov with a force and hurried to Riazan. When he came to the land of Riazan he saw it devastated and the cities destroyed, the rulers killed, and the people dead. . .

And Eupaty wept . . . [and] became angry. He gathered a small force of seventeen hundred men who had been preserved by God outside the city. And they hurriedly pursued the godless Batu. And with difficulty they caught up with him in the principality of Suzdal, and suddenly fell upon his camp. And there began a battle without mercy, and confusion reigned.

And the Tatars lost their heads from fear as Eupaty fought so fiercely that his sword became dull, and, taking a sword from a fallen Tatar, he would cut them down with their own swords. The Tatars thought that the Russians had risen from the dead, and Eupaty was riding through the ranks of the Tatar regiments so bravely that Batu himself became frightened. With great effort the Tatars managed to capture five men from Eupaty's regiments, and then only because they were exhausted from their wounds. They were brought before the Tatar emperor, and he asked them: "Why do you cause me such evil?" The warriors answered: "We are of the Christian faith, knights of the Great Prince Yury of Riazan, and from the regiment of Eupaty Kolovrat. We were sent by Prince Ingvar Ingvarevich to you, the powerful emperor, to honor you, to chase you away with honors, and to render unto you all honors. Do not wonder, Emperor, that we have not had time to serve up the bitter cup to your entire army." And Batu sent his brother-in-law, Hostovrul, against Eupaty, and with Hostovrul went strong regiments. Hostovrul bragged the emperor, and promised to bring back Eupaty alive. Eupaty was encircled by Tatar troops. And Hostovrul rode out against Eupaty, but Eupaty cleft with one blow to the saddle. . .

And once more he began to cut down the Tatar troops, and he killed many of Batu's best knights. Some were cut down, while others were cleft to their waist, and still others were to their saddles. . . The Tatars brought up catapults and began showering rocks upon him. And they finally killed Eupaty Kolovrat.

Chapter 9

The Mongol

Conquest:

Scourge or

Stimulus?

(1206–1360)

Source 7 from The Travels of Sir John Mandeville, the version of the Cotton Manuscript in modern spelling with three narrative in illustration of it, from Hakluyt's Navigations, Voyages, and Discoveries. (London: MacMillan & Co., 1923), pp. 215–216, 217–218, 232.

7. The Account of John de Plano Carpini

The Mongals, or Tartars, in outward shape, are unlike to all other people. For they are broader between the eyes, and the balls of their cheeks, than men of other nations be. They have flat and small noses, little eyes, and eyelids standing straight upright, they are shaven on the crowns like priests.

. . . Their manners are partly praiseworthy, and partly detestable; for they are more obedient unto their lords and masters, than any other either clergy or lay-people in the whole world. For they do highly reverence them, and will deceive them neither in words nor deeds. They seldom or never fall out amongst themselves, and, as for fightings or brawlings, wounds or manslaughters, they never happen among them. There are neither thieves nor robbers of great riches to be found, and therefore the tabernacles and carts of them that have any treasures are not strengthened with locks or bars. If any beast go astray, the finder thereof either lets it go, or driveth it to them that are put in office for the same purpose, at whose hands the owner of the said beast demandeth it, and without any difficulty receiveth it again. One of them honoureth another exceedingly, and bestoweth banquets very familiarly and liberally, notwithstanding that good victuals are dainty and scarce among them. They are also very hardy, and when they have fasted a day or two without any manner of sustenance, they sing and are merry as if they had eaten their bellies full. In riding, they endure much cold and extreme heat. There be, in a manner, no contentions among them, and though they use commonly to be drunken, yet do they not quarrel in their drunkenness, and no one among them despiseths another, but helpeth and furthereth him, as much as conveniently he can. Their women are chaste, neither is there so much as a word uttered concerning their dishonesty. Some of them will notwithstanding speak filthy and immodest words. But towards other people, the said Tartars be most insolent, and they scorn and set naught by all other noble and ignoble persons whatsoever. . . . Moreover they are angry and of a disdainful nature unto other people, and beyond all measure deceitful, and treacherous towards them. They speak fair in the beginning, but in conclusion they sting like scorpions. For crafty they are, and full of falsehood, circumventing all men whom they are able, by their sleights. Whatsoever mischief they intend to practice against a man, they keep it wonderfully secret, so that he may by no means provide for himself, nor find a remedy against their conspiracies. They are unmannerly also and uncleanly in taking their meat and their drink, and in other actions. Drunkenness is honourable among them, and when any of them hath taken more drink than his stomach can well bear, he calleth it up and falls to drinking again. They are most intolerable exactors, most covetous possessors, and most niggardly givers. The slaughter of other people is accounted a matter of nothing with them.

. . . [T]hey set forth against Russia, and made foul havoc there, destroying cities and cattles and murdering the people. They laid siege a long while unto Kiow, the chief city of Russia, and at length they took it and slew the citizens. Whereupon, travelling through that country, we found an innumerable multitude of dead men's skulls and bones lying upon the earth. For it was a very large and populous city, but it is now in a manner brought to nothing: for there do scarce remain 200 houses, the inhabitants whereof are kept in extreme bondage.

Source 8 from Mission to Asia: Narratives and Letters of the Franciscan Missionaries in Mongolia and China in the Thirteenth and Fourteenth Centuries, *ed. Christopher Dawson (New York: Harper and Row, 1966), pp. 91, 117, 119–121, 126–127, 128, 149, 183–184, 187–188, 201–202. Copyright © 1966. Reprinted by permission of Continuum International Publishing Group.*

8. Selections from the Travel Account of William of Rubruck

And so we reached Soldaia[20] on May 21st. Certain merchants from Constantinople had arrived before us and had announced that envoys were coming thither from the Holy Land who wished to visit Sartach. Now I had preached publicly on Palm Sunday in St. Sophia's that I was not an envoy either of you or anybody else, but that I was going among these unbelievers in accordance with our Rule. Then when we landed the said merchants warned me to mind my words, for they had given out that I was an envoy, and if I were to deny that I was such, then I would not be allowed to proceed.

. . . So we found Sartach three days' journey from the Etilia, and his orda seemed very large to us, for he has six wives, and his firstborn son, who was with him, has two or three, and each wife has a large house and perhaps two hundred carts. Our guide went to a certain Nestorian, Coiac by name, who is one of the chief men of his court. The latter made us go a very long way to the house of the *Yam*. *Yam* is what they call the man whose duty it is to receive envoys.[21] In the evening the said Coiac ordered us to come to Sartach.

. . . In the evening Coiac called us and said, "The Lord King has written fair words to my master, but they contain certain difficult matters about which he dare not do anything without the advice of his father; you must therefore journey to his father. . . ."

20. **Soldaia:** a port on the Black Sea through which caravan trade with the East funneled.

21. The Etilia or Volga River marked the border of Batu's territory. The *Yam* was the Mongol post station, which also served as a state-run hostel and local garrison.

Chapter 9
The Mongol
Conquest:
Scourge or
Stimulus?
(1206–1360)

. . . And so travelling due east in the direction of Baatu, on the third day we reached the Etilia and when I saw the river I wondered from what part of the north so much water flowed. Before we took our leave of Sartach, the aforesaid Coiac together with many other scribes of the court said to us, "Do not say that our master is a Christian, for he is not a Christian but a Mongol." This is because the word Christianity appears to them to be the name of a race, and they are proud to such a degree that although perhaps they believe something of Christ, nevertheless they are unwilling to be called Christians, wanting their own name, that is, Mongol, to be exalted above every other name. . . .

When I saw Baatu's orda I was overcome with fear, for his own houses seemed like a great city stretching out a long way and crowded round on every side by people to a distance of three or four leagues. . . . In their tongue the court is called "orda," which means the middle, because it is always in the middle of his people, with the exception that no one places him self due south, for the doors of the court open in that direction. . . .

And so first we were taken to a Saracen who did not provide us with any food. The following day we were taken to the court. Baatu had had a large pavilion set up, as his house could not hold as many men and women as had assembled. The man who was conducting us told us that we were to say nothing until bidden by Baatu, and then we were to speak briefly. He also asked whether you had ever sent envoys to them. I told him how you had sent to Keu Chan, and I said you would have sent neither envoys to him nor a letter to Sartach, if you had not believed that they were Christians, for it was not from any fear but in order to congratulate them because you had heard that they were Christians that you sent. Then he led us in front of the pavilion and warned us not to touch the ropes of the tent, which they consider take the place of the threshold of a house. We stood there in our habits, bare-footed and heads uncovered, and we were a great gazing stock for their eyes. Friar John of Policarp had been there but he had changed out of his habit in order not to be despised, for he was an envoy of our Lord the Pope.

. . . Then we went out, and after a little the man who was conducting us came and, taking us to the lodging, he said to me, "The Lord King asks that you be retained in this country, and Baatu cannot do this without the knowledge of Mangu, so you and your interpreter are to go to Mangu. Your companion, however, and the other man will return to Sartach's orda and wait there. . . ." It was also on this part of the Journey that I was told by the scribe for whom we had waited at Cailac that in the letter which Baatu was sending to Mangu Chan it said that you were asking for an army and help against the Saracens from Sartach. At that I began to wonder greatly and also to be worried for I knew the gist of your letter and knew that there was no mention of this in it, save that you admonished him to be the friend of all Christians, to exalt the Cross, and to be the enemy of all enemies of the Cross. I was also afraid that, since the interpreters were Armenians from Greater Armenia with a deep hatred of the

Saracens, they had, out of loathing for them and to do them harm, interpreted your letter more strongly in accordance with their own desires. . . .

AND so we came on the aforementioned day to the orda. Our guide was assigned a large dwelling; we three were given a tiny hut in which we could only just put our baggage and make our beds and a little fire. Many came to visit our guide and he was brought rice wine in long-shaped flagons with narrow necks. I could not tell the difference between it and the best Auxerre wine, except that it had not the bouquet of wine.

We were summoned and closely questioned as to the business on which we had come. I replied: "We heard that Sartach was a Christian; we went to him, the French King sent him a private letter by us; Sartach sent us to his father, his father sent us here. He must have written the reason why. . . ."

As for the city of Caracorum I can tell you that, not counting the Chan's palace, it is not as large as the village of Saint Denis, and the monastery of Saint Denis is worth ten times more than the palace. There are two districts there: the Saracens' quarter where the markets are, and many merchants flock thither on account of the court which is always near it and on account of the number of envoys. The other district is that of the Cathayans who are all craftsmen. Apart from these districts there are the large palaces of the court scribes. There are twelve pagan temples belonging to the different nations, two mosques in which the law of Mahomet is proclaimed, and one church for the Christian at the far end of the town. The town is surrounded by a mud wall and has four gates. At the east gate are sold millet and other grain, which is however seldom brought there; at the west sheep and goats are sold; at the south oxen and carts; at the north horses.

. . . I had enquiry made of Mangu Chan what he wished to do with us, saying that we would gladly stay there forever if it so pleased him; if, however, we were to go back it would be easier for us to make the return journey in the summer than in the winter. He immediately sent a message to me telling me not to go far away for he wished to speak with me the next day. . . .

The one who spoke with me was a Saracen and had been ambassador to Vastacius.[22] Blinded by gifts, he had advised Vastacius to send envoys to Mangu Chan and thus play for time, for Vastacius believed that they were on the point of invading his territory. He sent the envoys and after he got to know the Mongols he took little heed of them; neither has he made peace with them, nor have they up to the present invaded his country. . . . The man then began to ask me many questions about the Pope and the King of the French and of routes leading to them. . . .

AFTER the feast of Pentecost they began to compose the letter which the Chan was to send to you. In the meantime he returned to Caracorum and held his great reception just on the octave of Pentecost, and he wanted all the envoys to be present on the last day. . . . He then began to address them, saying: "I have parted with my brothers and have sent them into danger against foreign

22. **Vestacius:** Vastasius (1222–1255) was the Byzantine emperor who was also sending embassies to Karakorum.

Chapter 9

The Mongol

Conquest:

Scourge or

Stimulus?

(1206–1360)

nations. Now we shall see what you will do when I wish to send you to extend our empire. . . ."

At that time I saw the envoy of the Caliph of Baghdad there; he had himself conveyed to the court in a litter between two mule, which led some to say that the Chan had made peace with them, the condition being that they should provide him with an army of ten thousand horsemen. Others were saying that Mangu had declared he would not make peace with them unless they destroyed all their fortifications, and the envoy had replied: "When you take all the hooves off your horses, we will destroy all our fortifications."

I also saw there the envoys of a Sultan of India who had brought eight leopards and ten greyhounds trained to sit on the back of a horse like leopards. When I asked about India, in what direction it was from that spot, they pointed towards the west, and the envoys accompanied me on our return journey for about three weeks, travelling all the time westwards. I saw, too, envoys of the Sultan of Turkey, who brought costly presents for the Chan; he replied, so I heard, that he had need of neither gold nor silver but of men; by this he meant he wanted them to provide him with an army.

Source 9 from Henry Yule, Cathay and the Way Thither, *vol. 3 (London: The Hakluyt Society, 1914), pp. 143–155.*

9. From Francis Balducci Pegolotti, *Book of Description of Countries*

THINGS NEEDFUL FOR MERCHANTS WHO DESIRE TO MAKE THE JOURNEY TO CATHAY ABOVE DESCRIBED.

In the first place, you must let your beard grow long and not shave. And at Tana you should furnish yourself with a dragoman [interpreter]. And you must not try to save money in the matter of dragomen by taking a bad one instead of a good one. For the additional wages of the good one will not cost you so much as you will save by having him. And besides the dragoman it will be well to take at least two good men servants, who are acquainted with the Cumanian tongue [language of the Kipchak Turks]. And if the merchant likes to take a woman with him from Tana, he can do so; if he does not like to take one there is no obligation, only if he does take one he will be kept much more comfortably than if he does not take one. Howbeit, if he do take one, it will be well that she be acquainted with the Cumanian tongue as well as the men.

[256]

And from Tana travelling to Gintarchan you should take with you twenty-five days' provisions, that is to say, flour and salt fish, for as to meat you will find enough of it at all the places along the road. And so also at all the chief stations noted in going from one country to another in the route, according to the number of days set down above, you should furnish yourself with flour and salt fish; other things you will find in sufficiency, and especially meat.

The road you travel from Tana to Cathay is perfectly safe, whether by day or by night, according to what the merchants say who have used it. Only if the merchant, in going or coming, should die upon the road, everything belonging to him will become the perquisite of the lord of the country in which he dies, and the officers of the lord will take possession of all. And in like manner if he die in Cathay. But if his brother be with him, or an intimate friend and comrade calling himself his brother, then to such a one they will surrender the property of the deceased, and so it will be rescued.

And there is another danger: this is when the lord of the country dies, and before the new lord who is to have the lordship is proclaimed; during such intervals there have sometimes been irregularities practiced on the Franks, and other foreigners. (They call *Franks* all the Christians of these parts from Romania westward.) And neither will the roads be safe to travel until the other lord be proclaimed who is to reign in room of him who is deceased.

Cathay is a province which contained a multitude of cities and towns. Among others there is one in particular, that is to say the capital city, to which is great resort of merchants, and in which there is a vast amount of trade; and this city is called Cambalec. And the said city hath a circuit of one hundred miles, and is all full of people and houses and of dwellers in the said city.

You may calculate that a merchant with a dragoman, and with two men servants, and with goods to the value of twenty-five thousand golden florins, should spend on his way to Cathay from sixty to eighty *sommi* of silver, and not more if he manage well; and for all the road back again from Cathay to Tana, including the expenses of living and the pay of servants, and all other charges, the cost will be about five *sommi* per head of pack animals, or something less. And you may reckon the *sommo* to be worth five golden florins. You may reckon also that each ox-waggon will require one ox, and will carry ten cantars Genoese weight; and the camel-waggon will require three camels, and will carry thirty cantars Genoese weight; and the horse-waggon will require one horse, and will commonly carry six and half cantars of silk, at 250 Genoese pounds to the cantar. And a bale of silk may be reckoned at between 110 and 115 Genoese pounds.

You may reckon also that from Tana to Sara the road is less safe than on any other part of the journey; and yet even when this part of the road is at its worst, if you are some sixty men in the company you will go as safely as if you were in your own house.

Anyone from Genoa or from Venice, wishing to go to the places above-named, and to make the journey to Cathay, should carry linens with him, and

[257]

Chapter 9

The Mongol

Conquest:

Scourge or

Stimulus?

(1206–1360)

if he visit Organci he will dispose of these well. In Organci he should purchase *sommi* of silver, and with these he should proceed without making any further investment, unless it be some bales of the very finest stuffs which go in small bulk, and cost no more for carriage than coarser stuffs would do.

Merchants who travel this road can ride on horseback or on asses, or mounted in any way that they list to be mounted.

Whatever silver the merchants may carry with them as far as Cathay the lord of Cathay will take from them and put into his treasury. And to merchants who thus bring silver they give that paper money of theirs in exchange. This is of yellow paper, stamped with the seal of the lord aforesaid. And this money is called balishi; and with this money you can readily buy silk and all other merchandize that you have a desire to buy. And all the people of the country are bound to receive it. And yet you shall not pay a higher price for your goods because your money is of paper. And of the said paper money there are three kinds, one being worth more than another, according to the value which has been established for each by that lord.

QUESTIONS TO CONSIDER

Given the variety of materials presented here, you will undoubtedly find discrepancies in what they reveal about the Mongols. Unique points of view are certainly worth noting, but you need to be on the lookout for the bigger picture. This approach, of course, requires you not only to go over each source individually but to compare one to another. The most consistent and reliable information will probably be whatever appears in more than one. In searching through the different sources for common features, however, you may run into difficulty due to the variant spellings of names, places, and terms, which can complicate comparisons. Usually you can overcome this problem by sounding out words and looking for phonetic similarity. Terms like *Khan, Qa'an,* and *Qan* look different in print, but their correspondence should become apparent when you sound them out. Still, it might even be a good idea to make a list of such terms to help you in identifying them.

As you work your way through the Evidence section, looking for agreement, remember that not all of the sources may be equally credible. In addition to seeking information from each document, ask yourself how reliable it may be with regard to the question at hand. Consider whether or not the author was well placed enough to offer accurate comments. Was the account based on first-hand observation or access to reliable reports from others as opposed to conjecture or rumors? Consider, too, how the author's relationship with the Mongols may have shaped the perspective of an account. Was the author a supporter of the Mongol regime, an outsider seeking something from the Mongols, or a victim or someone threatened by them? Try to imagine, for example, how each of these relationships would have affected an observer's point of view with regard to the question of cruelty or openness to others. If you follow the advice given earlier about creating a chart, you can add comments about the relative credibility of each document in the Conclusions column and then refer back to them when weighing the overall evidence to decide how best to regard the Mongol conquest.

That the authors of Source 1, *The Secret History of the Mongols*, purported to reveal a "secret" account implies that they felt themselves privileged to special information. Does it, in fact, seem to offer the viewpoint of "insiders"? How does it compare stylistically with other pieces— and what does this suggest? Consider, too, how it portrays Chinggis Khan and his son Ögödei. Which of their activities does it highlight? And what does it tell us of their interests or motives? Were matters of trade or cultural interchange significant to them? Note the stress on "nation" building through the division of the people into "thousands" and the commitment of "judgments" into a new writing system. These are references to Chinggis Khan's reorganization of his followers and his use of the *yasa* to achieve a new unity transcending tribal or ethnic divisions. But notice also how he "slew the Kitad till they stood [as] rotten trees" and his "spoiling" of enemies like the Tanguts down to the "seed of the seed." Does such treatment suggest a long-range interest in building

a vast new empire or a warrior's immediate, perhaps parochial, interest in revenge?

Compare the perspective of this first piece with that of Yelü Chucai in Source 2. As a Khitan, he came from another, more distant branch of Mongols. Yet he calls himself a "Scholar of Profound Clarity" and seemed to regard China, not the Mongol steppes, as his home. Compare his view on the treatment of the Tangut state with that in *The Secret History*. He, too, justified its conquest as payment for betrayal, yet he also stressed that only its leader was killed, not the common people. Does he appear to be a warrior who glories in slaughter? For that matter, was the issue of steppe unity of much importance to him? He did seem to be impressed with the size of Chinggis' army and gives us some impression of how its march westward spread and displaced people on a vast scale. But most of his attention appears to have been fixed on the conquered territories rather than the conquerors. What do you make of his many remarks about the cities he saw in the West and his careful attention to their local products? Do his comments suggest a widening exchange of goods and technology? What may have prompted his observation that "Samarkand is extremely rich" or that in Bokhara "produce . . . is even more plentiful"? Was he interested in trade or the economic development of the empire? Notice his many references to the "Central Plains of China" and his use of that area as a point of reference. What does his discussion of distances imply about his sense of expanding horizons?

[259]

Chapter 9
The Mongol
Conquest:
Scourge or
Stimulus?
(1206–1360)

Like Yelü Chucai, the author of Source 3, Rashīd al-Dīn Tabib, also served in the Mongol administration, although his masters were the Il-Khans who ruled Iran and the Middle East rather than Chinggis or any of his successors as Khagan. A Persian and Muslim, he was even at a further remove ethnically and culturally from the Mongols. Yet, as his account makes clear, his position was far from unique: Turks, Tāzīks (Iranians), and Khitans (a term encompassing northern Chinese as well as the original Khitan Mongols) made up a significant part of the Mongol establishment by his day. How did he seem to view the relationship between them and the Mongols proper? Do you detect any sign of tension or embarrassment? Does he even mention negative aspects of the conquest such as destruction and slaughter? China, of course, was not his point of reference. As a Muslim, he rather looked westward. Note, in this regard, what he reported was said to be "the fairest city in the whole world" and a model to be imitated in constructing Karakorum. But observe whom Ögödei drafted to build and furnish his capital. Imperial horizons were clearly expanding to both ends of Eurasia. In this context, pay heed to Rashīd's remarks about the far-flung system of postal and garrison points called *yams* that Ögödei set up. What was the likely impact of this system on communication, travel, and trade across Eurasia?

Juvaini, the author of Source 4, *The History of the World Conqueror*, was also a Persian who held office in the administration of the Mongol empire. Did he seem to regard them as cruel or overbearing conquerors? He does quote Batu to the effect that the newly installed Khagan, Möngke, would tame "the unbroken horse" of the world "between the thighs of his severity." But does he speak of atrocities or even cruel behavior toward the conquered? And how does he portray top Mongol leaders like Batu? Pay particular attention in this respect to his assessment of the dowager, Sorqotani Beki. Though she was especially astute in managing her son's rise to power, she was no anomaly: the mothers of both Chinggis and Güyük also played important political roles. Does such behavior match conventional views of the Mongols? What does this account—and particularly Batu's speech in nomination of Möngke to the position of supreme Khan—suggest about the qualities Mongols valued in their leaders? Juvaini's discussion of Sorqotani Beki's religious activities also deserves notice.[23] What does it tell us about Mongol attitudes toward foreign religions and the impact their rule was having on them? For all his focus here on the more benign aspects of Mongol rule, Juvaini still takes care to point out that the Mongols intensified their military efforts under Möngke. Indeed, as he indicates, they mobilized vast numbers of men and goods to be sent off on new campaigns across the whole of the Old World. In the process, they dispatched hundreds of thousands of soldiers, officials, and craftsmen far from their homelands. What do you suppose was the likely result of relocating men like the Khitan mangonel experts

23. Refer back to footnote 15 for particulars.

and naphtha throwers mentioned here halfway across Inner Asia? Think of the effect such actions had on the level of intercontinental cultural and technological exchanges. The Persian painting of a city under a siege by the Mongols, Source 5, offers a good illustration. It shows the Mongols using a mangonel, which was a large catapult, against a walled city somewhere in Iran. In their homeland on the steppes, where there were no walled cities or citadels, the Mongols knew nothing of such heavy war engines. They soon found them necessary, however, once their invasion of the Tangut and Khitan empires brought them face to face with massive fortifications. As the previous source notes, they then turned to captured experts for help in acquiring what they needed. Does this seem to be a unique case of borrowing? Are there other examples of Mongol interest in or receptivity to the higher technology of others?

Unlike the painting, which presents an almost serene picture of battle in which no one is hurt, Source 6, *The Tale of the Destruction of Riazan*, dramatizes the bloodletting. Can there be any doubt of Mongol rapacity here? Notice the stress on Batu's initial treachery and his lust for the wives of the nobles. What effect is achieved by having Prince Feodor say his demands run counter to "Christian custom"? Does the *Tale* draw upon a religious undercurrent to discredit the Mongols? Could that be why the epic stresses the fact that "all the monks and priests" were slaughtered and "much blood was spilled on the holy altars" during the massacre of the population—or why it concludes "this happened for our sins"? Does that mean we cannot trust anything it says? The Russian churchmen who composed the *Tale* were far from unique in portraying the Mongols unsympathetically: no less a figure than the Pope's own official emissary to the Khagan, John de Plano Carpini, who wrote Source 7, shared their distain. He claimed to regard them as both praiseworthy in some ways and detestable in others. But do you find his list of their good and bad points equal in weight? What negative traits did he single out? How do they compare with those shown or implied in *The Tale of the Destruction of Riazan*? The image of rowdy, unclean, drunken, and unmannerly behavior bears a close resemblance to earlier Western ideas of generic barbarian behavior. Could cultural stereotyping have played a part in shaping John's perception of the Mongols? Cultural differences certainly seem to have confounded him. He clearly realized that they treated outsiders very differently from each other, but he never reflects on why that may have been the case. A tribal mentality, for example, might explain their insolence and cruelty to those who stood apart from them. John did not himself witness any Mongol battles or massacres, yet he concluded that "slaughter of other people is accounted a matter of nothing with them." On what did he base this view? Does he provide any credible evidence to support the claim?

Not all Western clerics who met Mongols held them in such disapproval. William of Rubruck, a priest who ventured to Karakorum as an emissary of Louis IV of France, regarded them

Chapter 9

The Mongol

Conquest:

Scourge or

Stimulus?

(1206–1360)

almost favorably, as you can see from his report, parts of which make up Source 8. Of course, though a churchman, William traveled as the envoy of a political rather than a religious leader, a fact that, as he indicates, may have accorded him better treatment. Still, for all that he noted a Mongol discomfort in being labeled Christian and in dealing with Christian priests, he never noted any mistreatment of them—or any other foreigners. Did he, too, see the Mongols as drunken, insolent, and unmannerly? True, he didn't find Karakorum very impressive. But to what did he compare it? Whom besides the Mongols did he find living there? And what other envoys did he see at Möngke's court? What do his observations suggest about the movement of peoples, skills, and ideas through the empire?

Source 9, Pegolotti's manual, provides insight into another kind of movement across the continent, those of goods and merchants engaged in private trade. Writing as an Italian merchant to encourage others to enter the booming Eurasian trade, he may have played down the rigors of intercontinental travel. How difficult or dangerous does it seem from what he reported? He did remark on certain "irregularities" suffered by foreign merchants, but did he warn of

Mongol violence or treachery? As a trader, his interest was on the cities of Cathay, and Khanbaligh in particular, not Karakorum. Why?

In the post-Mongol period, the impact of Europe's seaborne trade on the formation of a global economy and an interdependent world has long been appreciated. But some scholars now suggest that this trend may have started with an upsurge of trans-regional trade in the Mongol era. That Pegolotti wrote his work to encourage Europeans to enter the lucrative Eurasian trade suggests that they were not yet accustomed to it but perhaps were showing new interest in it. His focus, of course, was on reaching Qubilai's capital Khanbaligh and other cities of Cathay. Why there? How safe a trip did he think it would be? Like Marco Polo in his more famous account, Pegolotti was careful to enumerate the cost of key trade goods in the East and the likely profits to be made bringing them back to Europe. What did he say merchants should buy—and using what? Note his fascination with *balishi*, the paper money that the Mongols adopted from the Song Chinese. From his information about goods and prices, do you think Europeans had a better or less developed economy at this time?

EPILOGUE

Attempts to rebuild the transcontinental *ulus* of the early Mongol khans failed. Qubilai's immediate heir in

Khanbaligh, Temür, affected a pretense of universal rule, but the other khans ignored him. As each Horde began to function separately, Mongol leaders identified more and more with local people and came to be separated

[262]

by different religious and cultural traditions. Those in the West converted to Islam and culturally assimilated with their Russian, Turcic, and Persian subjects, while those in the East adopted Lamaist Buddhism and identified with China's Confucian tradition. In their isolation, they were easily overthrown one by one and replaced by indigenous challengers in the fourteenth century. Thus the Il-Khanate, weakened by wars with the Golden Horde and the Black Plague in the early 1300s, collapsed in a round of civil wars by 1359. Qubilai's regime soon followed. Destabilized by a great flood of the Yellow River in the 1350s, it was engulfed by Chinese revolts, and when rebels took Khanbaligh in 1368 to proclaim the native Ming dynasty, its last khan abandoned China and fled to Mongolia.

In the end, the Khanate of Chagatai fared little better, although it mounted a brief effort at rebuilding the old empire. Following the partition of its territories by quarreling factions in the mid-fourteenth century, a Mongol upstart, Timur the Lame, wrested control from Chinggis Khan's descendants. Determined to rebuild the old empire, he invaded and annexed the Golden Horde and then conquered most of western Asia from the Indus to the Black Sea. But he failed to build a lasting administration and was better known for slaughtering vanquished enemies and leaving behind pyramids of their skulls. At his death in 1405, his empire too disintegrated, ending the last serious threat of a Mongol revival. The small, surviving Mongol regimes from the Russian steppes to Mongolia had all they could do to defend themselves from new powers rising across Asia. Yet so great was the memory of the Pax Mongolica that many of these new powers incorporated aspects of Mongol rule, and one, the Mogul Empire founded in northern India, even associated itself with the Mongols by name. Thus, a Mongol mystique long outlived the Mongol Empire in Asia.

But that mystique did not survive into the Modern era. For as Westerners began to dominate the world, first lacing it together in new trade networks and then imposing imperial control over most of it, the achievements of others fell into the shadows. When remembered at all, the Mongol empire came to be associated mainly with what was termed Oriental Despotism and seen as a symbol of oppression and cruelty. That the Pax Mongolia had allowed an earlier expansion of communication and commerce across Eurasia, which may have catalyzed modern integration, was ignored or forgotten. It is only more recently, as the tide of Western empires too has waned, that some contemporary scholars are re-examining the role the Mongols may have played both in encouraging the first phase of global integration and, perhaps, even in inspiring Westerners to complete it. And yet, there remain the allegations of atrocities and claims of their readiness to resort to cruelty and slaughter in pursuit of empire. In the end, what conclusion have you reached? Were the Mongols a scourge—or a stimulus?

CHAPTER TEN

REGIONAL METROPOLISES:

CONSTANTINOPLE AND

TENOCHTITLÁN (1160–1521)

As noted in an earlier chapter, the words for civilization in most Western European languages derive from the Latin term for a city, *civitas*. The implied connection between high cultural attainment and "civic" or urban life reflects a measure of truth. First emerging in the third millennium B.C.E., in what has sometimes been termed the urban revolution, cities provided dynamic, new foci for human development. Within the next few millennia, they appeared not only across the entire breadth of Eurasia but in Africa and America as well. Originally small, largely self-contained city-states, urban communities began to change with the widening of political, religious, and economic networks during the centuries that immediately preceded the start of the common era. As imperial capitals, religious seats, or trade emporia, a few centers here and there began to evolve

into cities on a scale much larger and far more complex in nature. Over the next thousand years, some of these, like imperial Rome in the West and Changan in East Asia, grew into a new kind of city that served as the hub of a huge, far-flung region. To contemporaries they were not just the biggest urban areas in their respective spheres but regional "metropolises," world-class cities that outranked all peers. Typically seats of political and religious power as well as cultural and economic magnets, they attracted polyglot populations from all over a vast hinterland. Long before the advent of modern mass society, therefore, great international cities began to emerge as trans-regional, cosmopolitan centers.

Although imposing in their own ways, these pre-modern metropolises were quite different from the big cities of the twentieth century. Built before the Industrial Revolution and the emergence of modern utilities and mass transit, they had to solve basic urban problems of housing, supply, sanitation, and transportation with far fewer technological means. For that very reason, of course, economics and technology played a smaller role in shaping them. Both the modern industrial city, whose concentric rings of commercial, manufacturing, and residential zones centered around a "downtown" complex of railroad depots and office buildings, and the contemporary "edge city" with its malls, airports, and theme parks strung out along arterial highways typically evolved in haphazard response to the changing technologies and material needs of mass, democratic societies. Older cities, though certainly affected by physical considerations, tended to be shaped more by ideals than by material concerns. And the patterns and rhythms of life within them conveyed a very different urban experience from that of the modern West. To comprehend the nature of any premodern metropolis, therefore, we need to free ourselves from current conceptions of what constitutes a city.

Unfortunately, neither historians nor others who study cities have agreed on a simple, generic definition, and efforts to list a comprehensive set of urban characteristics have generally met with much criticism. For in addition to such commonly accepted features as the presence of a large population, a ruling elite or class, diversified manufacturing, and long-distance trade, regionally unique traits like the possession of writing or metallurgy complicate the issue. Lewis Mumford in his classic study *The City in History* thus cautions: "No single definition will apply to all its manifestations and no single

description will cover all its transformations."[1] In truth, a certain amount of consensus does exist. All scholars, for example, agree that urban life entails a high concentration of people living together in some sort of interdependent community. And most regard a population of about five thousand as the minimum necessary for a true city. Furthermore, experts generally concur that cities are primarily non-agricultural communities with formal institutions that provide diverse services to surrounding areas as well as to their own inhabitants. But beyond these few essentials, cities have varied widely in size, role, and character, making it difficult to generalize about their historical identity. For that reason, an understanding of any urban type has to be sought first and foremost through an analysis of actual examples.

This chapter accordingly asks you to consider two of the world's greatest cities in late traditional times, roughly speaking, from about the twelfth through the fifteenth centuries. The two presented here, Constantinople and Tenochtitlán, do not represent especially unique examples for this era, which coincides with the end of the Middle Ages in Europe. Other contemporary metropolises such as Baghdad or the Chinese city of Hangzhou would serve equally well as case studies. The choice of Constantinople and Tenochtitlán, however, highlights the global nature of the phenomena, contrasting as it does two cities, one in the Mediterranean and the other in

---

1. Lewis Mumford, *The City in History: Its Origins, Its Transformations, Its Prospects* (New York: Harcourt Brace Jovanovich, 1961), p. 3.

Chapter 10

Regional

Metropolises:

Constantinople

and Tenochtitlán

(1160–1521)

Mesoamerica, that were quite literally worlds apart. Moreover, because Western Europeans visited and recorded their impressions of both sites during this era, this choice invites implicit comparisons with their homelands where truly great urban centers had yet to develop.

Your task in this chapter is to determine what the characteristics of these two great cities were. Go over the materials presented in the Evidence section for each of the cities, looking for information on the dominant physical features. Then think about what these features represent in terms of urban life or activities. The prominence of railroad stations, factories,

office buildings, and department stores at the heart of most modern cities, for example, provides clear indications of their industrial and commercial nature. What physical elements stood out in Constantinople and Tenochtitlán, and how do these elements provide clues to these cities' identity and nature? Once you have arrived at some idea of what each city was like, compare them to see if they shared enough common features to represent a generic type. By considering what characterized them, you should not only discover what these metropolises were like in their heyday but gain some insight into the nature of big, pre-modern cities in general.

BACKGROUND

Although differing in many respects, Constantinople and Tenochtitlán both achieved regional preeminence primarily as imperial capitals. First and foremost seats of government, they represented conscious attempts by rulers to legitimize political authority. For this reason, both were built in imitation of older and more renowned centers of power whose grandeur and might their founders hoped to regain. Yet neither remained merely a political seat. Each in its own way became a major religious site and a hub of interregional trade as well as the dominant center of high culture in its sphere. Nonetheless, their fortunes remained closely tied to those of the empires that they represented, and when these

fell, both cities quickly lost their original grandeur.

Of the two, Constantinople was by far the older, but its rise to fame as a Roman capital came late in its history. The city dates back to 658 B.C.E., when Greek colonists from Megara first settled it. Named Byzantium in honor of their leader Byzas, it remained no more than a provincial port throughout most of antiquity. Its only noteworthy feature was its location: It stood at the tip of a promontory jutting out into the narrow strait, known as the Bosphorus, that separates Europe from Asia. This strait connects the Black Sea to the north with the Sea of Marmara to the south and through it—and the even narrower channel of the Hellespont— to the Aegean entrance of the Mediterranean. By imperial times, Roman expansion into Greece and Asia Minor

[266]

made this waterway the most important artery in the rich, eastern half of the empire. With the decline of Rome and its western provinces in the fourth century c.e., this eastern portion of the empire gained ever greater importance as a reservoir of wealth and manpower. And Byzantium, perched upon an easily defended headland dominating the most crucial waterway in the East, assumed new strategic value. It was apparently this strategic consideration that led Emperor Constantine to select the city as a replacement for Rome in 324 when he sought a better base from which to revive the empire.

Though Rome itself had ceased to be the actual imperial residence for some time before this change, it continued to hold great symbolic importance. In selecting Byzantium, therefore, Constantine apparently made much of its similarity with the older capital, particularly the fact that it, like Rome, stood among hills. To enhance the similarity, he refurbished the city in typical Roman style. But Constantinople, or "Constantine's city," as the site came to be called after its formal consecration in 330, was a seaport rather than an inland center. Built on a triangular peninsula, it faced water on two sides: the Sea of Marmara on the south and a deep inlet off the Bosphorus on the north. This inlet, called the Golden Horn because of its crescent-like shape, provided the city with a well-protected deep-water harbor that made it one of the best ports in the Mediterranean world. Taking full advantage of the maritime character of the site, its original Megaran founders had concentrated most of their public buildings in Greek fashion atop a tall

hill, named the Acropolis, that overlooked the water at the very tip of the peninsula. The sea and seafarers thus dominated the city.

Byzantium differed from Rome in another respect as well. Imperial Rome rose to fame without walls, adding them only in 268 when the growing threat of barbarian invasion from across the Alps led Emperor Aurelius to see to the city's defenses. But the unsettled conditions of his time led Constantine to wall off Byzantium's landward side immediately, giving the city a well defined western boundary. Later, Emperor Theodosius built an even more massive rampart farther to the west, considerably enlarging the city, and subsequent rulers raised sea walls along both the Golden Horn and the Marmaran shore. These defenses, which gave Constantinople a reputation for impregnability, attracted attention throughout the West and made the city a frequently copied prototype for the walled cities of medieval times.

Despite its extensive fortification, however, Constantinople ultimately covered four times the area of Rome. The heart of the city remained near the tip of the peninsula, where Constantine refurbished existing buildings and added what came to be called simply the Great Palace. As the first Christian emperor and one who actively patronized his faith, Constantine also built a number of churches throughout the city. Later emperors continued his interest in public construction. Emperor Theodosius not only built new land walls to the west of those erected under Constantine to enlarge the city but also added many internal

Chapter 10
Regional
Metropolises:
Constantinople
and Tenochtitlán
(1160–1521)

monuments and improvements. Even more lavish, however, was Emperor Justinian, who launched an extensive building program to renovate the city as part of his effort to revitalize the Roman state. Along with many secular works, he ordered the construction of St. Sophia, a colossal church designed to be the greatest and most impressive building in all Christendom. During Justinian's reign from 527 to 565, in fact, the city probably reached the peak of its development with a population somewhere around 500,000 to 600,000—far in excess of that of contemporary Rome, which had shrunk rapidly in size as well as in stature.

By the time of Justinian, the city assumed the basic layout that it was to retain for the better part of the next millennium. Public life centered around a complex of buildings that stood just southwest of the Acropolis, the original heart of the city, near the tip of the peninsula. These included not only the Great Palace and the church of St. Sophia, the chief seats, respectively, of imperial political and religious life, but a great stadium-like race course called the Hippodrome and the Baths of Zeuxippus, both of which offered important public entertainments. Between them passed the Mese, or "Midway," the city's principal street. This grand avenue ran westward from the foot of St. Sophia to the Forum of Theodosius, where it forked into branches that continued out to the two most important entry points in the landward walls—the Golden Gate and the Gate of Charisos—which opened to the main imperial highways linking the city to the rest of the empire. Along its approximately two-mile

course stood additional forums, colonnaded squares in which markets and other public affairs could be conducted with some shelter from the weather. The largest and most imposing of these, the Forum of Theodosius, also served as the terminus of the raised aqueduct, built by order of Emperor Valens, that kept the many fountains and cisterns of the city filled with an adequate supply of fresh water. Most private homes and shops lined the secondary streets that branched off the Mese to thread their way up and down the six hills across which the city spread.

The decline of imperial might and wealth following Justinian's reign curtailed further building, and subsequent rulers added little to the city other than an occasional small church or monument. Moreover, by the eighth century, dwindling imperial fortunes together with a series of earthquakes and plagues appear to have severely reduced the population to perhaps a third or less of its peak figure. Thus it was a much smaller city that survived to become the regional metropolis of the Western world during Europe's Middle Ages. It was also a more complex city, combining its original Roman heritage with strong Greek and Christian influences. In its layout and most prominent secular buildings, of course, Constantinople continued to reflect the urban ideals of ancient Rome. But because of the Hellenistic culture of its populace, who spoke mainly Greek, the city's distinctly eastern character soon overpowered its Latin legacy. This feature was especially marked in religious affairs, for the city served as the seat of the Orthodox Christian faith

[268]

whose churches conformed to the Greek or Eastern rites rather than those of Rome. Moreover, as an important trade as well as political and religious center throughout the Middle Ages, the city continued to attract people from all over the Mediterranean and Asia Minor. Its many foreign quarters, filled with Italians, Jews, Armenians, and Slavs, gave it a cosmopolitan flavor that was enriched by a constant influx of still more exotic traders and diplomats coming from as far away as Britain and Persia.

Relative to Constantinople, Tenochtitlán was a young city. Founded by a people known as the Aztecs in the fourteenth century, the city quickly grew from a small local center into the largest city in the Americas as they expanded their control over Mesoamerica. The Aztecs, a Nahuatl-speaking group who called themselves the Mexica or Tenocha, came late into this area from an original homeland located somewhere in the arid lands farther to the northwest. According to their legends, they had dwelt there in a city called Azatlán, the "Place of the Herons," built on a paradisiacal island located in the midst of a desert lake. At the beginning of the twelfth century, however, they and seven neighboring tribes left their homeland at the order of their chief god, Huitzilopochtli, on a long migration southward. By the century's end they reached the shores of a new lake, Lake Texcoco, high up in the Valley of Mexico, where for nearly a century, they served indigenous tribes as mercenaries. In 1325, however, the Aztecs retreated into the marshes of Lake Texcoco to found a new city of their own at a site where,

in fulfillment of a prophecy attributed to their god Huitzilopochtli, they found an eagle perched on a cactus growing out of a stone.

The city they erected in the marshes took its name, Tenochtitlán—the "Place of the Prickly Pear Cactus"—from this prophecy. And the image of an eagle on a cactus not only provided a glyph or written emblem for the city but, combined with a sheaf of spears, served as the imperial symbol of the Aztecs. Like the founders of Constantinople, the Aztec builders of Tenochtitlán developed their city in imitation of an older ideal. But two different models influenced its design. One was the legendary paradise, Azatlán, in imitation of which they founded their new city on an island off the southwestern shore of Lake Texcoco. But in actual layout, Tenochtitlán followed another more historic model, an impressive ruin lying less than fifty miles away in the northeastern part of the Valley of Mexico.

All that remained of a great city dating back to the middle of the first millennium of the common era, this deserted ruin exercised a tremendous influence over all the peoples of Mesoamerica. The Aztecs, who knew nothing of its builders' identity, called it simply Teotihuacán, or the "City of the Gods," on the assumption that only divine beings could have built so grand a place. Despite extensive archaeological work in recent decades, we know little more about its builders than the Aztecs did. This first great metropolis of the Americas, however, clearly attests to a long prior tradition of urban development in the area. At its height around the year 500 C.E., Teotihuacán

Chapter 10

Regional

Metropolises:

Constantinople

and Tenochtitlán

(1160–1521)

may have been home to as many as 200,000 people, making it one of the world's largest cities at the time. Even more impressive than its immense pyramids, its great residential quarters and workshops, or its vast market compound is its careful layout around an expansive avenue of monumental buildings leading to the city's titanic Pyramid of the Sun. In spite of the grandeur of their city, Teotihuacán's inhabitants began to drift away sometime after 750 for reasons still unknown to us, eventually leaving it an empty ruin. Even in abandonment, the old site continued to serve as an urban model for subsequent Central American people. None, however, succeeded as well as the Aztecs in recapturing its grandeur.

In order to duplicate the monumental scale of Teotihuacán, the Aztecs had to expand their original island site through extensive landfills and hydraulic projects, allowing them to enlarge its shoreline and connect it with an adjacent island that held a separate community named Tlaltelolco. As part of this endeavor, they also found a solution to the damaging alkalinity of the landlocked Lake Texcoco: They built a huge dike across the southwest corner to isolate streams bringing in fresh water from the brackish main body of the lake lying east and north of the city. Within this fresh water zone, they reclaimed many acres of marshland around the city's edge for agricultural use by building up *chinampas,* floating fields of heaped-up mud and vegetation anchored in place with stakes and willow trees. In addition, they built great causeways to the north, south, and west to link the island complex to

the mainland. These connected the city to trade routes that fanned out across the Valley of Mexico, making it the hub of a mammoth network of commerce that spread across the whole of Central America.

Because the northern community of Tlaltelolco developed independently until conquered and annexed by the expanding Aztecs in the 1470s, the island complex retained two distinct populations, each focused upon its own *teocalli,* or ceremonial center. That of Tenochtitlán proper occupied the geographic center, but the more northerly *teocalli* of Tlaltelolco outshone it in magnificence. Both featured enormous enclosures containing temples and priestly quarters around which clustered ancillary markets, administrative courts, and palaces. Beyond these great centers spread a maze of streets and canals along which stood many smaller markets, workshops, and residential sections. Made primarily of stucco-covered adobe, most of the buildings in these latter sections were low, one- or two-storied structures that adjoined open courtyards. Those in Tenochtitlán were organized into four wards dispersed around the central temple enclosure.

By its zenith at the end of the fifteenth century, this prodigious urban complex probably held 200,000 to 300,000 people, a population greater than that of any contemporary European city, including Constantinople. But this figure fails to include the population of the half dozen or so satellite communities that developed on the shore of the lake, particularly where the causeways began. The larger metropolitan area of Tenochtitlán, therefore, may well have contained a population twice or more in size, making it one of the world's greatest urban areas at the time. Many of these people were not Aztecs but older inhabitants of the region whose city-states had been subjected to Aztec rule. They and other ethnic groups who migrated into the metropolitan area from more distant vassal states or came as traveling merchants infused it with a very diverse population. A constant flow into the city of tribute missions and organized merchant groups from as far away as the deserts of the north and Yucatan to the south added even more to its cosmopolitanism. Many of these immigrant groups and visitors tended to settle in separate neighborhoods and markets where they perpetuated their own customs and languages, adding great cultural variety to the city's life.

THE METHOD

The physical remains of old cities, whether ancient or more recent, provide the best information about their main features. Ideally, then, we should turn to archaeology, the science that studies the material culture of the past, for evidence about the nature of these early metropolises. But because modern Mexico City and Istanbul overlie old Tenochtitlán and Constantinople, archaeologists have not been able to do the extensive work required to uncover them. Although occasionally new construction, particularly in Mexico City, has allowed them to excavate a few important sites, for the most part they have not been able to do much fieldwork. So historical archaeology, or the investigation of material sites built in historical times, provides only limited evidence for us to use in understanding these particular cities.

As a result, the bulk of our information must come from documents. You will find two sets in the Evidence section that follows, one for Constantinople and one for Tenochtitlán. Sources 1 and 2 present eyewitness accounts of Constantinople left behind by two medieval European travelers, Benjamin of Tudela, a Spanish rabbi who visited the city in the course of a long trip across the Mediterranean in the years 1160–1173, and Robert of Clari, a French soldier who took part in the sack of the city in 1203 by Western Europeans bound on the Fourth Crusade. Nicetas Choniates, a Byzantine writer and historian, who was present during the sack of the city by Robert and his companions, registers something of the impact it had among residents in Source 3, excerpted from his *Historia*. But his account of the sack also provides more details about the monuments that graced the city. You can identify many of the sites these writers describe in Source 4, a medieval illustrated map of Constantinople. Source 5 provides an illustration of the most celebrated of these, the great church of St. Sophia. Two Byzantine accounts complete this picture of medieval Constantinople: Source 6, an account from the *Historia* of the chronicler George Acropolites, describes an imperial procession through the city in celebration of its recovery from

Chapter 10

Regional

Metropolises:

Constantinople

and Tenochtitlán

(1160–1521)

invaders in 1261 by Emperor Michael VIII; and Source 7, an imperial Chryso-bull (or decree) of 1082, sheds light on economic matters in the city.

Similar materials reflect life in Tenochtitlán at its height. Source 8 comes from a letter written by the Spanish conqueror of the city, Hernan Cortés, to King Charles V of Spain, and Source 9 presents the recollections of one of his lieutenants, Bernal Díaz del Castillo, as recorded in his history *The Discovery and Conquest of Mexico*. A parallel visual record appears in Source 10, a Spanish map of the city made at the time of its conquest in the sixteenth century. Source 11 shows a line drawing of the excavated site of the Great Temple area, and Source 12, an Aztec drawing from the so-called Florentine Codex, depicts the Great Temple that formed the city's central feature. This Codex, an illustrated manuscript now in Madrid, preserves Aztec accounts of traditional life as transcribed into both Nahuatl and Spanish by Bernardino de Sahagún soon after the conquest.

Interpreting the sources for Tenoch-titlán presents special problems. Unlike the Byzantines, the Aztecs had no writing system of their own, and so the oldest written descriptions of their capital date from the time of its downfall and come from the hands of the Europeans who destroyed it. Despite their obvious appreciation of many aspects of Tenochtitlán, such observers hardly viewed the city with dispassionate eyes, and their remarks need to be considered cau-tiously. The inhabitants of Constanti-nople, of course, did write, and they left us considerable records of their

own. But here, too, we must be wary of problems. Many of the surviving accounts come from outsiders who either passed through the city them-selves or obtained their information second-hand from other visitors. And outsiders necessarily view places from an unusual perspective.

Before historians can use such testi-mony, then, they have to determine its degree of credibility. Obvious cultural and religious biases leading to overex-aggerations and false observations are often easy to spot. Those who openly glorify their own cultural or religious superiority, for example, may well play down the impressiveness of what they have seen elsewhere. Other fac-tors, however, may cause more subtle distortions. Invaders often inflate the size and splendor of conquered sites to enhance their reputation at home or to awe rivals. Be aware, too, that out-siders generally have interests and purposes quite different from those of the inhabitants, and they may frequent only certain quarters to the exclusion of others. For example, a religious pilgrim might remain unaware of the activities of a market or craft quarter, whereas a merchant hurrying to sell his wares could be completely obliv-ious to major religious sites. So as you analyze the materials that follow, try to discern not only who wrote each account but for whom and why. The answers to these questions should tell you which source may be more believ-able for a particular aspect of city life. By then crosschecking and integrating pieces from different accounts, you should be able to obtain a reasonably clear and accurate picture of what these cities were like.

Begin this attempt by trying to determine what physical features stood out most in each of these cities. Did certain districts or complexes catch the eye of visitors more than others? What constituted the most imposing public monuments and civic symbols? Were there special places for work, residence, and entertainment? How did people move about within the city, and where did the principal lines of access take them? Once you have a list of these features, locate each of them on the maps included and give some thought to the general pattern that emerges. Ask yourself how the parts inter-related and what elements seemed most to shape the overall layout of the city. Do any clear centers of city life seem to stand out from others? Can you tell what sorts of activities dominated city life?

Once you have gained a general sense of the layout and chief structures of each city, ask yourself what such features indicate about the course of events in Constantinople and Tenochtitlán. Try to determine from the physical elements those chief concerns or activities around which public life revolved. Did certain of them predominate? Were there, for example, defensive works? What would such features indicate about urban life and the relationship between the cities and their surrounding countryside? What, if anything, seemed to provide the locus for communal life? Were there large open spaces or public buildings where crowds could gather? What would they have done there? What provisions existed for mass movement and supply of resources like food? Similarly, try to determine what most defined civic identity through a consideration of the nature of public spaces and monuments. Did certain complexes command more notice than others? What did they house or commemorate? Who would have participated in or benefited from them?

On the basis of this analysis, ask yourself what such elements suggest about the function and nature of these early metropolises. Both were obviously imperial capitals, but were they merely political centers? To what extent did they also function as important focal points for economic, religious, or cultural life? It might help to compare them with more recent cities. Think for a moment how cities are laid out today and what features dominate contemporary urban landscapes. Note how airports, freeways, corporate headquarters, malls, and theme parks reflect the pattern and rhythm of the contemporary urban life with its emphasis on commercial activities and preoccupation with *mass* mobility, consumerism, and entertainment. What do the features of Constantinople and Tenochtitlán reveal about the nature of earlier urban life? Whose interests did they most seem to serve? How might you define or characterize such cities?

Chapter 10

Regional

Metropolises:

Constantinople

and Tenochtitlán

(1160–1521)

Source 1 from Manuel Komroff, ed., Contemporaries of Marco Polo *(New York: Liveright, 1928), pp. 264–267.*

1. From Benjamin of Tudela, *Travels of Rabbi Benjamin of Tudela, 1160–1173*

The circumference of the city of Constantinople is eighteen miles; one-half of the city being bounded by the continent, the other by the sea, two arms of which meet here; the one a branch or outlet of the Russian, the other of the Spanish sea. Great stir and bustle prevails at Constantinople in consequence of the conflux of many merchants, who resort thither, both by land and by sea, from all parts of the world for purposes of trade, including merchants from Babylon and from Mesopotamia, from Media and Persia, from Egypt and Palestine, as well as from Russia, Hungary, Patzinakia, Budia, Lombardy and Spain. In this respect the city is equalled only by Baghdad, the metropolis of the Mahometans [Muhammadans].

At Constantinople is the place of worship called St. Sophia, and the metropolitan seat of the Pope of the Greeks, who are at variance with the Pope of Rome. It contains as many altars as there are days of the year, and possesses innumerable riches, which are augmented every year by the contributions of the two islands and of the adjacent towns and villages. All the other places of worship in the whole world do not equal St. Sophia in riches. It is ornamented with pillars of gold and silver, and with innumerable lamps of the same precious materials.

The Hippodrome is a public place near the wall of the palace, set aside for the king's sports. Every year the birthday of Jesus the Nazarene is celebrated there with public rejoicings. On these occasions you may see there representations of all the nations who inhabit the different parts of the world, with surprising feats of jugglery. Lions, bears, leopards, and wild asses, as well as birds, which have been trained to fight each other, are also exhibited. All this sport, the equal of which is nowhere to be met with, is carried on in the presence of the king and the queen.

King Manuel has built a large palace for his residence on the sea-shore, near the palace built by his predecessors; and to this edifice is given the name of Blachernes [Blachernae]. The pillars and walls are covered with pure gold, and all the wars of the ancients, as well as his own wars, are represented in pictures. The throne in this palace is of gold, and ornamented with precious stones; a golden crown hangs over it, suspended on a chain of the same material, the length of which exactly admits the emperor to sit under it. This crown is ornamented with precious stones of inestimable value. Such is the lustre of these diamonds, that, even without any other light, they illumine the room in which they are kept. Other objects of curiosity are met with here which it would be impossible to describe adequately.

The tribute, which is brought to Constantinople every year from all parts of Greece, consisting of silks, and purple cloths, and gold, fills many towers. These riches and buildings are equalled nowhere in the world. They say that the tribute of the city alone amounts every day to twenty thousand florins, arising from rents of hostelries and bazaars, and from the duties paid by merchants who arrive by sea and by land. The Greeks who inhabit the country are extremely rich, and possess great wealth in gold and precious stones. They dress in garments of silk, ornamented with gold and other valuable materials. They ride upon horses, and in their appearance they are like princes. The country is rich, producing all sorts of delicacies, as well as abundance of bread, meat, and wine. They are well skilled in the Greek sciences, and live comfortably, "every man under his vine and his fig tree." The Greeks hire soldiers of all nations, whom they call barbarians, for the purpose of carrying on their wars with the sultan of the Thogarmim, who are called Turks. They have no martial spirit themselves, and, like women, are unfit for warlike enterprises. . . .

No Jews dwell in the city with them; they are obliged to reside beyond the one arm of the sea, where they are shut in by the channel of Sophia on one side, and they can reach the city by water only, when they want to visit it for purposes of trade. The number of Jews at Constantinople amounts to two thousand Rabbanites and five hundred Caraites, who live on one spot, but divided by a wall. The principals of the Rabbanites, who are learned in the law, are the rabbi Abtalion, Obadiah, Aaron Khuspo, Joseph Sargeno and Eliakim the elder. Many of them are manufacturers of silk cloth, many others are merchants, some being extremely rich; but no Jew is allowed to ride upon a horse, except Solomon Hamitsri, who is the king's physician, and by whose influence the Jews enjoy many advantages even in their state of oppression, which is very severely felt by them; and the hatred against them is increased by the practise of the tanners, who pour out their filthy water in the streets and even before the very doors of the Jews, who, being thus defiled, become objects of contempt to the Greeks.

Their yoke is severely felt by the Jews, both good and bad; for they are exposed to be beaten in the streets, and must submit to all sorts of bad treatment. Still the Jews are rich, good, benevolent, and religious men, who bear the misfortunes of their exile with humility. The quarter inhabited by the Jews is called Pera.

Chapter 10

Regional

Metropolises:

Constantinople

and Tenochtitlán

(1160–1521)

Source 2 from Robert of Clari, The Conquest of Constantinople, *trans. Edgar Holmes McNeal (New York: W. W. Norton, 1969), pp. 101, 102–103, 105, 107, 108–110, 111–112. Copyright © 1969 by Columbia University Press. Reprinted with permission of the publisher.*

2. From Robert of Clari, *Conquest of Constantinople,* 1203

Not since the world was made, was there ever seen or won so great a treasure or so noble or so rich, not in the time of Alexander nor in the time of Charlemagne nor before nor after. Nor do I think, myself, that in the forty richest cities of the world there had been so much wealth as was found in Constantinople. For the Greeks say that two thirds of the wealth of this world is in Constantinople and the other third scattered throughout the world. . . .

When the city was captured and the pilgrims were quartered, as I have told you, and the palaces were taken over, then they found in the palaces riches more than a great deal. And the palace of Boukoleon was very rich and was made in such a way as I shall tell you. Within this palace, which was held by the marquis, there were fully five hundred halls, all connected with one another and all made with gold mosaic. And in it there were fully thirty chapels, great and small, and there was one of them which was called the Holy Chapel, which was so rich and noble that there was not a hinge nor a band nor any other part such as is usually made of iron that was not all of silver, and there was no column that was not of jasper or porphyry or some other rich precious stone. . . .

[And there was another palace in the city, called the palace of Blachernae.] And there were fully twenty chapels there and at least two hundred chambers, or three hundred, all connected with one another and all made of gold mosaic. And this palace was so rich and so noble that no one could describe it to you or recount its great nobility and richness. In this palace of Blachernae there was found a very great treasure, for one found there the rich crowns which had belonged to former emperors and the rich ornaments of gold and the rich cloth of silk and gold and the rich imperial robes and the rich precious stones and so many other riches that no one could number the great treasure of gold and silver that was found in the palaces and in many other places in the city. . . .

Then the pilgrims regarded the great size of the city, and the palaces and fine abbeys and churches and the great wonders which were in the city, and they marveled at it greatly. And they marveled greatly at the church of Saint Sophia and at the riches which were in it.

Now I will tell you about the church of Saint Sophia, how it was made. Saint Sophia in Greek means Sainte Trinité ["Holy Trinity"] in French [*sic*].[2] The church of Saint Sophia was entirely round, and within the church there were domes, round all about, which were borne by great and very rich columns,

2. Robert of Clari apparently knew no Greek and so misunderstood the meaning of the church's name. *Saint Sophia* means "Holy Wisdom," not "Holy Trinity."

and there was no column which was not of jasper or porphyry or some other precious stone, nor was there one of these columns that did not work cures. . . .

Elsewhere in the city there is another gate which is called the Golden Gate. On this gate there were two elephants made of copper which were so large that it was a fair marvel. This gate was never opened except when an emperor was returning from battle after conquering territory. And when an emperor returned from battle after conquering territory, then the clergy of the city would come out in procession to meet him, and the gate would be opened, and they would bring out a chariot of gold, which was made like a cart with four wheels, such as we call a *curre*.

Now in another part of the city there was another marvel. There was an open place near the palace of Boukoleon which was called the Games of the Emperor. This place was a good bowshot and a half long and nearly a bowshot wide. Around this place there were fully thirty rows of seats or forty, on which the Greeks used to mount to watch the games, and above these rows there was a loge, very dainty and very noble, where the emperor and the empress sat when the games were held, and the other high men and ladies. And if there were two sides playing at the same time, the emperor and the empress would wager with each other that one side would play better than the other, and so would all the others who watched the games.

. . . Now about the rest of the Greeks, high and low, rich and poor, about the size of the city, about the palaces and the other marvels that are there, we shall leave off telling you. For no man on earth, however long he might have lived in the city, could number them or recount them to you. And if anyone should recount to you the hundredth part of the richness and the beauty and the nobility that was found in the abbeys and in the churches and in the palaces and in the city, it would seem like a lie and you would not believe it.

Source 3 from Byzantium: Church, Society, and Civilization Seen Through Contemporary Eyes, *ed. Deno John Geanakopolos (Chicago and London: University of Chicago Press, 1984), pp. 371–372. Copyright © 1984. Reprinted by permission of the publisher, The University of Chicago Press.*

3. Nicetas Choniates, *"Destruction of Ancient Art in the Latin Sack of Constantinople"*

From the very beginning they [the Latins] revealed their race to be lovers of gold; they conceived of a new method of plundering, which had completely escaped the notice of all who had [just] sacked the imperial city. Having opened the graves of those emperors which were in the burial ground situated in the area of the church of Christ's Holy Apostles, they stripped all of them during the

Chapter 10

Regional

Metropolises:

Constantinople

and Tenochtitlán

(1160–1521)

night and, if any golden ornament, pearl, or precious stone still lay inviolate in these [tombs], they sacrilegiously seized it. When they found the corpse of the Emperor Justinian, which had remained undisturbed for so many years, they marveled at it, but they did not refrain from [looting] the funerary adornments. We may say that these Westerners spared neither the living nor the dead. They manifested [toward all], beginning with God and his servants [i.e. the clergy], complete indifference and impiety: quickly enough they tore down the curtain in the Great Church [Hagia Sophia], the value of which was reckoned in millions of purest silver pieces, since it was entirely interwoven with gold.

Even now they were still desirous of money (for nothing can satiate the avarice of the barbarians). They eyed the bronze statues and threw them into the fire. And so the bronze statue of Hera, standing in the agora of Constantine, was broken into pieces and consigned to the flames. The head of this statue, which could hardly be drawn by four oxen yoked together, was brought to the great palace. The [statue of] Paris [also called] Alexander opposite it, was cast off its base. This statue was connected with that of the goddess Aphrodite to whom the apple of Eris [Discord] was depicted as being awarded by Paris. . . .

These barbarians—who do not appreciate beauty—did not neglect to overturn the statues standing in the Hippodrome or any other marvelous works. Rather, these too they turned into coinage [*nomisa*], exchanging great things [i.e. art] for small [i.e. money], thus acquiring petty coins at the expense of those things created at enormous cost. They then threw down the great Hercules Trihesperus, magnificently constructed on a base and girded with the skin of a lion, a terrifying thing to see even in bronze. . . . He was represented as standing, carrying in his hands neither quiver nor arrows nor club, but having his right foot and right hand extended and his left foot bent at the knee with the left hand raised at the elbow. . . . He [the statue of Hercules] was very broad in the chest and shoulders and had thick hair, plumb buttocks, and strong arms, and was of such huge size, I think, as Lysimachus [Lysippus?] considered the real Hercules to have been—Lysimachus who sculpted from bronze this first and last great masterpiece of his hands. The statue was so large that the rope around his thumb had the size of a man's belt and the lower portion of the leg, the height of a man. But those [i.e. the Latins] who separate manly vigor from other virtues and claim it for themselves (considering it the most important quality) did not leave this Hercules (although it was the epitome of this attribute) untouched.

4. Illustrated Map of Constantinople, 13th century

Chapter 10
Regional
Metropolises:
Constantinople
and Tenochtitlán
(1160–1521)

Source 5: Bildarchiv Foto Marburg/Art Resource, NY.

5. Interior, Saint Sophia

6. George Acropolites, "The Byzantine Recovery of Constantinople: Thanksgiving and Celebration," 1261

The emperor [Michael VIII Palaeologus] reached Constantinople on the fourteenth day of August, but he did not wish to enter the city the same day, so he pitched his tents in the monastery of Cosmidion. . . . And after spending the night there and arising, he made his entrance as follows: since the Patriarch Arsenios was not present . . . it was at once necessary that one of the prelates pronounce the prayers. George, metropolitan of Cyzicus . . . whom they call Kleidas, fulfilled this task. Getting up on one of the towers of the Golden Gate and having with him also the icon of the *Theotokos,* the image named after the monastery of the *Hodegetria,* he recited prayers for all to hear. Then the emperor, putting aside his mantle, fell to his knees on the ground, and with him all those behind fell to their knees. And after the first prayer was over, the deacon motioned them to rise, and all standing chanted *Kyrie eleison* [Lord have mercy] one hundred times.

When this was over, another prayer was recited by the prelate. And then the same thing happened as after the first. And this was done until the completion of all the prayers. When the religious part of the ceremony had been performed, the emperor entered the Golden Gate in a way which honored God more than the emperor, for he marched on foot with the icon of the Mother of God preceding him. And he went up to the monastery of Studius, and after leaving there the icon of the most immaculate Mother of God, he mounted his horse and went to the Church of the Wisdom of God [St. Sophia]. There he worshiped Our Lord Christ and rendered proper thanks to him. Then he arrived at the Great Palace and the Byzantine population was filled with great and immense joy and exultation. For there was no one who could not dance or exult with joy, being scarcely able to believe this event because of its unexpectedness and the enormous outpouring of jubilation. Since it was necessary that the patriarch also be in Constantinople, . . . after a few days the emperor entered the holy building, the temple of Great Wisdom, in order that he might hand over the *cathedra* [the patriarch's throne] to the prelate. And finally there assembled with the emperor all the notables of the archons and the entire multitude. Then the emperor, taking the arm of the patriarch, said, "Take your throne now, O lord, and enjoy it, that of which you were so long deprived."

Chapter 10

Regional

Metropolises:

Constantinople

and Tenochtitlán

(1160–1521)

Source 7 from G. Tafel and G. Thomas, eds., Urkunden zur Älteren Handelsund Staatsgeschichte der Republik Venedig, *in* Byzantium: Church, Society, and Civilization Seen Through Contemporary Eyes, *ed. Deno John Geanakopolos (Chicago: University of Chicago Press, 1984), pp. 286–287. Copyright © 1984. Reprinted by permission of the publisher, The University of Chicago Press.*

7. Chrysobull Detailing
Extraordinary Privileges for
the Venetians, 1082

No one is ignorant of those things which have been done by the faithful Venetians, how after they had gathered together different types of ships, they came to Epidamnus (which we call Dyrrachium) and how they provided for our assistance numerous seaborne fighting men, how their fleet conquered by force the wicked expedition [of the Normans], and how they lost some of their own men. We also know how even now they continue to be our allies, and about those things which have been done by their rowers [*thalattokopi*], men who work on the sea. Even if we should not mention this, everyone knows it perfectly well.

Wherefore, in recompense for their services of this kind, Our Majesty decrees through this present chrysobull, that the Venetians annually receive a gift of twenty pounds [of gold], so that they might distribute this among their own churches in whatever manner they see fit. . . . In addition, those workshops situated in the quarter of Perama [on the Golden Horn across from Pera], together with their upper chambers, which have an entrance and exit throughout, which extend from the Ebraica [gate] up to the Vigla [gate], both inhabited or uninhabited, and in which Venetians and Greeks stay—[all of] these we grant to them as factories, as well as three docks [*scalae*] which end in this aforementioned area. We also grant to St. Akyndinos the property, that is, a mill, lying alongside this church, which belongs to the house of Peter and which has an income of twenty bezants [Byzantine gold coins]. Similarly, we give the church of the Holy Apostle Andrew in Dyrrachium, together with all the imperial payments except the one which is set aside there to be given to the [harbor] barges.

It is also granted to the Venetians that they may conduct business in every type of merchandise in all parts of the empire, that is around great Laodicea, Antioch, Mamistra, Adana, Tarsus, Attalia, Strobilos, Chios, Ephesus, Phocea, Dyrrachium, Valona, Corfu, Bonditza, Methone, Coron, Nauplia, Corinth, Thebes, Athens, Negropont, Demetrias, Thessalonika, Chrysopolis, Perithorion, Abydos, Redestos, Adrianople, Apros, Heraclea, Selymbria, and the megalopolis itself [Constantinople], and indeed in all other places which are under the authority of our pious clemency, without their paying anything at all for any favor of commerce or for any other condition on behalf of their business—[payments] which are made to the fisc [*demosion*] such as the *xylokalamos, limenatikos, poriatikos, kaniskios, hexafolleos, archontikios* [i.e. charges for mooring ships, disembarking, and unloading cargo, and taxes on imports, exports, purchases, and sales], and

[282]

exemption from all other taxes which have to be paid to engage in commerce. For in all places of business Our Majesty has given them the permission that they be free of such exactions. And the Venetians are removed [from the authority of] the *eparchos parathalassitos* [sic] himself, the *heleoparochos*, the *genikos*, the *chartularii*, the *hypologoi*, and of all officials of this sort. Let no one who carries out imperial or other duties presume to be contemptuous of the provisions which have been specified here. For permission has been granted to the Venetians to deal in whatever types of goods and merchandise anyone may mention, and they have the ability to make any purchase and remain free from all exactions [*dationes*].

Source 8 from Hernan Cortés: Letters from Mexico, *ed. and trans. A. R. Pagden (New York: Grossman, 1971), pp. 83–84, 102–106, 107–108, 109.*

8. Letter of Hernan Cortés to Charles V, King of Spain

This great city of Temixtitan [Tenochtitlán] is built on the salt lake, and no matter by what road you travel there are two leagues from the main body of the city to the mainland. There are four artificial causeways leading to it, and each is as wide as two cavalry lances. The city itself is as big as Seville or Córdoba. The main streets are very wide and very straight; some of these are on the land, but the rest and all the smaller ones are half on land, half canals where they paddle their canoes. All the streets have openings in places so that the water may pass from one canal to another. Over all these openings, and some of them are very wide, there are bridges made of long and wide beams joined together very firmly and so well made that on some of them ten horsemen may ride abreast. . . .

This city has many squares where trading is done and markets are held continuously. There is also one square twice as big as that of Salamanca, with arcades all around, where more than sixty thousand people come each day to buy and sell, and where every kind of merchandise produced in these lands is found; provisions as well as ornaments of gold and silver, lead, brass, copper, tin, stones, shells, bones, and feathers. . . .

Finally, besides those things which I have already mentioned, they sell in the market everything else to be found in this land, but they are so many and so varied that because of their great number and because I cannot remember many of them nor do I know what they are called I shall not mention them. Each kind of merchandise is sold in its own street without any mixture whatever; they are very particular in this. Everything is sold by number and size, and until now I have seen nothing sold by weight. There is in this great square a very large building like a courthouse, where ten or twelve persons sit as judges. They preside over all that happens in the markets, and sentence criminals. There are in this square other persons who walk among the people to see what they are selling

Chapter 10

Regional

Metropolises:

Constantinople

and Tenochtitlán

(1160–1521)

and the measures they are using; and they have been seen to break some that were false. . . .

There are, in all districts of this great city, many temples or houses for their idols. . . .

Amongst these temples there is one, the principal one, whose great size and magnificence no human tongue could describe, for it is so large that within the precincts, which are surrounded by a very high wall, a town of some five hundred inhabitants could easily be built. All round inside this wall there are very elegant quarters with very large rooms and corridors where their priests live. There are as many as forty towers, all of which are so high that in the case of the largest there are fifty steps leading up to the main part of it; and the most important of these towers is higher than that of the cathedral of Seville. . . .

There are three rooms within this great temple for the principal idols, which are of remarkable size and stature and decorated with many designs and sculptures, both in stone and in wood. Within these rooms are other chapels, and the doors to them are very small. Inside there is no light whatsoever; there only some of the priests may enter, for inside are the sculptured figures of the idols, although, as I have said, there are also many outside.

There are in the city many large and beautiful houses, and the reason for this is that all the chiefs of the land, who are Mutezuma's [Montezuma's] vassals, have houses in the city and live there for part of the year; and in addition there are many rich citizens who likewise have very good houses. All these houses have very large and very good rooms and also very pleasant gardens of various sorts of flowers both on the upper and lower floors.

Along one of the causeways to this great city run two aqueducts made of mortar. Each one is two paces wide and some six feet deep, and along one of them a stream of very good fresh water, as wide as a man's body, flows into the heart of the city and from this they all drink. The other, which is empty, is used when they wish to clean the first channel. Where the aqueducts cross the bridges, the water passes along some channels which are as wide as an ox; and so they serve the whole city.

Canoes paddle through all the streets selling the water; they take it from the aqueduct by placing the canoes beneath the bridges where those channels are, and on top there are men who fill the canoes and are paid for their work. At all the gateways to the city and at the places where these canoes are unloaded, which is where the greater part of the provisions enter the city, there are guards in huts who receive a *certum quid* of all that enters. I have not yet discovered whether this goes to the chief or to the city, but I think to the chief, because in other markets in other parts I have seen this tax paid to the ruler of the place. Every day, in all the markets and public places there are many workmen and craftsmen of every sort, waiting to be employed by the day. The people of this city are dressed with more elegance and are more courtly in their bearing than those of the other cities and provinces, and because Mutezuma and all those

[284]

chieftains, his vassals, are always coming to the city, the people have more manners and politeness in all matters. Yet so as not to tire Your Highness with the description of the things of this city (although I would not complete it so briefly), I will say only that these people live almost like those in Spain, and in as much harmony and order as there, and considering that they are barbarous and so far from the knowledge of God and cut off from all civilized nations, it is truly remarkable to see what they have achieved in all things.

Source 9 from Bernal Díaz del Castillo, The Discovery and Conquest of Mexico, *trans. A. P. Maudsley (New York: Farras, Straus and Cudahy, 1956), pp. 191–192, 215–219.*

9. From Bernal Díaz del Castillo, *The Discovery and Conquest of Mexico*

Our Captain and all of those who had horses went to Tlaltelolco on horseback, and nearly all of us soldiers were fully equipped, and many Caciques whom Montezuma had sent for that purpose went in our company. When we arrived at the great market place, called Tlaltelolco, we were astounded at the number of people and the quantity of merchandise that it contained, and at the good order and control that was maintained, for we had never seen such a thing before. . . . In this way one could see every sort of merchandise that is to be found in the whole of New Spain. . . .

When we arrived near the Great Cue and before we had ascended a single step of it, the Great Montezuma sent down from above, where he was making his sacrifices, six priests and two chieftains to accompany our Captain.[3] On ascending the steps, which are one hundred and fourteen in number, they attempted to take him by the arms so as to help him to ascend (thinking that he would get tired) as they were accustomed to assist their lord Montezuma, but Cortés would not allow them to come near him. When we got to the top of the great Cue, on a small plaza which has been made on the top where there was a space like a platform with some large stones placed on it, on which they put the poor Indians for sacrifice, there was a bulky image like a dragon and other evil figures and much blood shed that very day.

So we stood looking about us, for that huge and cursed temple stood so high that from it one could see over everything very well, and we saw the three causeways which led into Mexico, that is the causeway of Iztapalapa by which

---

3. Díaz uses the term *Cue* to refer to the tall, flat-topped pyramid on which the Aztecs built their temples. Note his care in recounting its impressive height, some 114 steps above the surrounding plaza.

Chapter 10

Regional

Metropolises:

Constantinople

and Tenochtitlán

(1160–1521)

we had entered four days before, and that of Tacuba, and that of Tepeaquilla, and we saw the fresh water that comes from Chapultepec which supplies the city, and we saw the bridges on the three causeways which were built at certain distances apart through which the water of the lake flowed in and out from one side to the other, and we beheld on that great lake a great multitude of canoes, some coming with supplies of food and others returning loaded with cargoes of merchandise; and we saw that from every house of that great city and of all the other cities that were built in the water it was impossible to pass from house to house, except by drawbridges which were made of wood or in canoes; and we saw in those cities Cues and oratories like towers and fortresses and all gleaming white, and it was a wonderful thing to behold; then the houses with flat roofs, and on the causeways other small towers and oratories which were like fortresses.

After having examined and considered all that we had seen we turned to look at the great market place and the crowds of people that were in it, some buying and others selling, so that the murmur and hum of their voices and words that they used could be heard more than a league off. Some of the soldiers among us who had been in many parts of the world, in Constantinople, and all over Italy, and in Rome, said that so large a market place and so full of people, and so well regulated and arranged, they had never beheld before.

Then our Cortés said to Montezuma: "Your Highness is indeed a very great prince and worthy of even greater things. We are rejoiced to see your cities, and as we are here in your temple, what I now beg as a favour is that you will show us your gods and Teules." Montezuma replied that he must first speak with his high priests, and when he had spoken to them he said that we might enter into a small tower and apartment, a sort of hall, where there were two altars, with very richly carved boardings on the top of the roof. On each altar were two figures, like giants with very tall bodies and very fat, and the first which stood on the right hand they said was the figure of Huichilobos their god of War. . . . Then we saw on the other side of the left hand there stood the other great image the same height as Huichilobos, and it had a face like a bear and eyes that shone, made of their mirrors which they call *Tezcat,* and the body plastered with precious stones like that of Huichilobos, for they say that the two are brothers; and this Tezcatepuca was the god of Hell and had charge of the souls of the Mexicans, and his body was girt with figures like little devils with snakes' tails. The walls were so clotted with blood and the soil so bathed with it that in the slaughter houses of Spain there is not such another stench.

10. Spanish Illustrated Map of Tenochtitlán, Printed in Nuremberg, 1524

Chapter 10
Regional
Metropolises:
Constantinople
and Tenochtitlán
(1160–1521)

Source 11: Museo del Templo Mayor. Photographer: Saturnino Vallejo y German Zuniga.

11. The Excavated Site of the Great Temple Enclosure

Source 12 from Bernardino de Sahagún, Historia de las Cosas de Nueva España, *trans. Arthur J. O. Anderson and Charles E. Dibble (Santa Fe, N.M.: The School of American Research and the University of Utah, 1954). Photograph: Courtesy, Patrimonio Nacional, Biblioteca Real.*

12. The Great Temple Enclosure at Tenochtitlán, from the Florentine Codex

Chapter 10
Regional
Metropolises:
Constantinople
and Tenochtitlán
(1160–1521)

QUESTIONS TO CONSIDER

As you go over the sources in search of clues that will help you determine the nature of these early metropolises, look for features that reappear in more than one account. Benjamin of Tudela and Robert Clari, the authors of Sources 1 and 2, had different reasons for visiting Constantinople, and their personal interests may have affected what they saw and remembered of the city. Yet both call attention to three of the city's dominant structures: St. Sophia, the Boukoleon palace, and the Hippodrome. Symbolic of the city's mixed Christian, Roman, and Greek heritage, these buildings all stood near the base of the original Acropolis. They formed the Capitolium, a central complex where the great thoroughfare known as the Mese, the city's main artery, began its course out to the landward walls. Together with public baths and the nearby Forum of Constantine, they defined the heart of the city as well as the administrative center of the imperial government. From Nicetas Choniates' remarks in Source 3, it is clear that these sites, particularly the agora of Constantine and the Hippodrome, were adorned with many ancient Greek and Roman statues, which preserved an air of classical antiquity even in the medieval city. All three sites provided dramatic arenas for public spectacles. But note how, according to Sources 1 and 2, all three, including the stadium, housed religious as well as imperial functions. What explains the close connection between sports, religion, and politics in the life of this city? Would this same combination be likely in a twentieth-century city?

You can easily locate these and other major sites in Source 4, an illustrated medieval map of Constantinople. The map clearly shows one of the city's most often remarked features—its great encircling walls. What do such fortifications suggest about the city's relationship to the surrounding countryside and its regional position? Built by a series of early emperors, these walls were primarily intended to protect the administrative machinery of the empire. Most of the major government buildings, in fact, clustered together near the Capitolium. If you look at the apex of the triangular peninsula that juts out into the water on the map, you can see this area. Can you identify any of the buildings depicted?

The domed structure is the church of St. Sophia, or "Holy Wisdom." Why does it appear so large? St. Sophia was the biggest building then known in the Christian world, and, as Source 5 shows, it did enclose a vast space under its dome. But its size here is probably symbolic of its eminent role as the seat of the patriarch or head of the Greek Orthodox Church and the sacred light it was said to radiate throughout the Byzantine Empire. Like the entire complex of which it formed the hub, the church served an important civic function, too. It provided a staging area for great public processions that proceeded down the Mese to the Golden Gate, symbolically the most important entry into the city. Something of their appearance can be glimpsed in

Source 6, which describes the return of Emperor Michael VIII Palaeologus into the city following its recovery from the Crusaders. Note how St. Sophia plays a prominent role in the celebrations. Of course, as the drawing of the city shows, and Robert of Clari's account confirms, many smaller churches, abbeys, and imperial monuments dotted the rest of the cityscape. What do they tell about this metropolis?

Perhaps less obvious in the general accounts of Constantinople is its role as a major seaport and center of economic activity. The medieval map clearly reveals the city's maritime character showing many *porta*, or sea gates, giving direct access to the waterfront. Think for a moment how the encircling sea would have eased problems of sanitation, transportation, and supply in a premodern city of this size. Constantinople's proximity to important sea routes also promoted a great deal of trade and industry. Both Rabbi Benjamin and Robert of Clari hint at this aspect of the city's life. Notice how both dwell on the fabulous material wealth of the city, the one finding it comparable only to Baghdad, the center of the Muslim world, and the other rating it as without peer. Much of this wealth derived from what the rabbi called "the conflux of many merchants" who came "from all parts of the world," giving the city a very cosmopolitan and mercantile character. Whom does he specifically mention as inhabitants or visitors? By the eleventh century, Italians dominated most of the commerce in the eastern Mediterranean and Black Seas. What role did they play in the life of Constantinople?

Source 7, a Chrysobull, or imperial edict, authorizing Venetian trade rights, not only indicates the extent of their privileges but also affords a brief glimpse into the complex economic life of the city. Note its mention of specialized workshops, factories, mills, docks, and barges as well as its list of various taxes levied on different port activities and commercial transactions. Clearly commerce and manufacturing flourished in Constantinople during Europe's Middle Ages. Observe, too, the high concentration of Venetians in a section of the city along the fashionable port side of the Golden Horn called Perama—just opposite the separate walled community of Pera, which, according to Rabbi Benjamin, served as the Jewish quarter and a center of silk manufacturing. Apparently the splendid harbor of the Golden Horn had drawn most of the economic activity and commercial wealth of the city to its shores by this time. The map hints at this trend in its depiction of many multistoried houses in these quarters, presumably the residences of rich merchants. The allure of this essentially mercantile quarter seems to have attracted members of the political elite, too. Can you find the Blanchernae Palace overlooking the water of the Golden Horn near the end of the land wall? What might this indicate about the impact of the sea and commerce on the character of the city?

Water influenced the layout of Tenochtitlán even more than that of Constantinople, for it was an island city, surrounded on all sides by water. Its watery setting, of course, was an

Chapter 10

Regional

Metropolises:

Constantinople

and Tenochtitlán

(1160–1521)

inland lake, as the city stood on a high plateau far from the sea. The Spanish conquistadors Hernan Cortés and Bernal Díaz made much of this setting, as you can see from Sources 8 and 9. Note that both remark on the lake's contribution to the city's defense as well as to its transportation system. Because of Lake Texcoco— and the strength of Aztec forces—the city needed no walls. Instead of ramparts, therefore, the most impressive external features of the city were the great causeways that linked it with the lakeshore. As Cortés writes, two of these doubled as aqueducts, bringing an ample supply of fresh water into the city from landward sources. These causeways appear clearly in Source 10, an early Spanish map of the city. Notice their great extent as well as the many outlying communities that clustered around their junction with the shore. This drawing also shows the great wickerwork dike built east of the city to hold back brackish water and the many channels weaving in and out of the *chinampas* (floating fields) on its perimeter. What impression do you gain from these documents about the likely role waterways played in the city's life? Would they have facilitated trade over a vast region? Or would they merely have made a widely dispersed urban area possible in the premodern period?

Of the various causeways, the most impressive seems to have been the one that entered from the south, along which Cortés and his party first entered the city. As he relates, this causeway, which began in the satellite city of Ixtapalapa and spanned Lake Xochimilco before continuing across Lake Texcoco proper, led directly to the enclosure of the Great Temple that formed the center of Tenochtitlán. Within the walls of this temple, built high on a pyramid of stone, stood sanctuaries dedicated to the Aztecs' patron god Huitzilpochtli and the rain god Tlaloc. All around it, Cortés says, spread towers and courts inhabited by priests. A large plaza, which served as the main market, occupied the area in front of this enclosure, and various imperial and noble residences flanked it on either side. Like the Capitolium of Constantinople, this entire complex, known as the Great Teocalli, provided the main focus of public life. The drawing of the excavated site shown in Source 11 gives some idea of its original layout. It was named after the large temple, or *teocalli*, that loomed over it, but, as you can see, it contained many other components. How do these compare with those of the Capitolium in Constantinople?

The nature of the activities that occurred around the Great Temple complex can be inferred from Díaz's detailed description of the similar, though somewhat larger, *teocalli* of Tlatelolco, the neighboring city that became virtually one with the Aztec capital after its conquest. Note Díaz's open astonishment at the number of people and the amount of goods in the arcaded marketplace associated with this compound, as well as his keen interest in the wealth seen there. Like Constantinople, Tenochtitlán served as a regional economic center whose merchants, according to Díaz, traded in "every sort of merchandise that is to be found in the whole of New Spain," that is, all of Mesoamerica. His

description of the marketplace at Tla-
teloco matches Cortés's portrayal of a
great square in the city "twice as big as
that of Salamanca" where "more than
sixty thousand people come each day
to buy and sell." They both note the
orderliness of the trading as well as the
wide variety of produce on display. To
what do they attribute this order?

Díaz shows equal astonishment
over the vast court of the temple
itself and the Great Cue (pyramid)
that stood in its center. From the sum-
mit, the highest point in the city, he
could look out beyond the immediate
precincts of the capital to survey the
entire metropolitan area spread out
across the shores of the surrounding
lakes. His comparisons of Tenochtitlán's size with that of Europe's great
cities of the time, including Constantinople, merit special notice. One of
Cortés's letters to Charles V echoes
Díaz's praise of Tenochtitlán, claiming
that even "in Spain there is nothing
to compare" with the main palace
adjacent to the Tenochtitlán *teocalli*
in which the Aztec ruler Montezuma
lived. But both accounts evince dis-
gust over the ceremonies conducted
in its temple enclosures, for Europeans found the human sacrifice practiced by the Aztecs as part of their
religion upsetting. What does Díaz
reveal about his feelings on this issue?
Clearly he regards Europeans as culturally superior in this respect, though
they, too, engaged in mass killing
under other circumstances and did
not refrain from eventually slaughtering large numbers of Aztecs.

Source 12, an Aztec drawing of the
Great Temple enclosure at Tenochtitlán, illustrates the kind of sacrificial
ceremonies that so repulsed the Spaniards. At the top center appears the
Great Temple itself with sacrificial
blood streaming down the steps from
its two sanctuaries. Like many other
Mesoamerican peoples, the Aztecs
considered blood to be a source of
vitality that supported the cycle of
life. They thus sacrificed people in
order to replenish the vitality of the
gods, who they believed returned it
to humanity in full measure through
the fecundity of life. Although only
a few victims were killed in ordinary
rituals, as many as eighty thousand
prisoners were sacrificed here on the
altar stones in victory celebrations
following the conquest of rival states.
On these latter occasions, the Aztecs
invited vassal chieftains and allied
rulers to witness the gory spectacle,
suggesting that such rites had important political as well as religious functions. What might these have been?
How may such activities have shaped
the way in which neighboring peoples
understood the nature or significance
of the city?

As you can see from a comparison
with the excavated site, the drawing
of the Great Temple provides a faithful picture of this ceremonial heart
of the city where its people sought
daily renewal through sacrifice.
Note, in this context, Díaz's account
of the emperor personally assisting
the priests in such rites as part of a
state religion. In Tenochtitlán, like
Constantinople, palace and temple
stood together, creating an almost
inseparable focus for public life.
What does this fusion of sacred and
secular suggest about their nature as
cities?

Chapter 10

Regional

Metropolises:

Constantinople

and Tenochtitlán

(1160–1521)

EPILOGUE

Because of their grandeur and wealth in late traditional times, both Constantinople and Tenochtitlán attracted the attention of covetous outsiders who eventually brought them to grief. The Spanish conquest and sack of Tenochtitlán in 1521 are, of course, generally well known. For all of his earlier admiration of the city, after seizing control of it, Cortés set about its complete destruction. He had already torn down the great dike during his attack on the city, destroying its immediate agricultural environs; and after occupying it, he ordered all the principal buildings razed, the waterways filled in with the rubble, and most of its former inhabitants relocated, claiming the need to purge it of its barbaric religious cults. A Nahuatl lament for the dying city preserves some of the anguish this destruction wrought: "Let me not be angry that the grandeur of Mexico is to be destroyed./ The smoking stars gather together against it; the one who cares for flowers is about to be destroyed."[4] Using the labor of allied tribes whom he brought to the area, Cortés built a new, Spanish-style colonial settlement renamed Mexico City upon the ruins of the old Aztec capital. Ironically, the builders of the new city erected the Metropolitan Cathedral over part of the old *teocalli* enclosure on a site adjacent to their colonial headquarters (where the present National Palace stands), thus perpetuating in a new form the close conjunction of temple and palace.

Constantinople's plight was neither as dramatic nor as complete, but Constantine's city, too, suffered from invasion. The first of these came in 1203 when "Latin" participants of the Fourth Crusade, diverted from their original purpose by the lure of Constantinople's wealth and what they deemed its heretical Greek church, sacked and occupied the city. Remarking that "they revealed their race to be lovers of gold," a Byzantine chronicler complained that "these Westerners spared neither the living nor the dead" when they looted the city and showed "complete indifference and impiety" in stripping St. Sophia and other churches of all valuables.[5] Though dominated by Venetians, who coveted Constantinople's economic superiority, most of these so-called Latin conquerors were Franks, who, after thoroughly looting its moveable wealth, attempted to control the city for the next few decades. But a great fire that broke out during their occupation had devastated nearly half the city; and under their subsequent colonial rule, Constantinople not only failed to rebuild but slid into a rapid economic decline.

Thus, though restored to Greek control under Michael VIII Palaeologus in 1261, the city never regained its former wealth or stature. Its trade and territories passed gradually into the hands

---

4. This lament is translated by Daniel G. Brinton in his *Ancient Nahuatl Poetry* (New York: AMS Press, Inc., 1969), p. 123; this version is a reprint of an older edition printed in Philadelphia in 1890.

5. These remarks by Nicetas Chomates appear in an excerpt from his *Historia* translated in *Byzantium: Church, Society, and Civilization Seen Through Contemporary Eyes*, ed. Deno John Geanakopolos (Chicago: University of Chicago Press, 1984), p. 371. Copyright © 1984. Reprinted by permission of the publisher, The University of Chicago Press.

of others, and by the early fifteenth century it was reduced to a shadow of its original glory, with wide empty spaces within its walls given over to orchards and fields of grain or filled with crumbling ruins. As a result of their declining fortunes, the Byzantines could not stem the tide of Turkish-speaking Muslim people moving in from the east. In 1453 one of these, known as the Ottoman Turks, seized the city and ended Byzantine rule for good. Unlike the earlier Latin conquerors, however, they successfully rebuilt the city under the name Istanbul to serve as the capital of an expansionary, new Islamic empire that straddled the Bosphorus and spread westward into Europe as well as southeastward into Palestine and Africa. Symbolically, they transformed St. Sophia into a mosque and built a new imperial residence, known as the Topkapi Sarayi, nearby on the old Acropolis, reaffirming afresh the traditional importance of temple and palace in the city's identity.

The role that Western Europeans played in the decline of both of these metropolises merits some thought. Many of the sources imply that religious beliefs underlay their violent behavior. And their almost obsessive interest in gold and other material wealth is also well documented. As various of the above accounts demonstrate, Venetians, Franks, and later Spaniards, too, found these cities far richer than anything they knew. Their often naive amazement over the wealth and size of such metropolises points out the relative "underdevelopment" of urban centers in their homelands during this era. Because of this relative backwardness, Westerners later tended to equate the emergence of great urban centers with modern economic development. An appreciation of the scope of premodern metropolises like Constantinople, Tenochtitlán, Baghdad, Hangzhow, and Osaka, however, calls this view into question. Their impressive scale, in fact, suggests that efforts to understand world history using Western European patterns of development as a standard may be misleading.

CHAPTER ELEVEN

SACRED JOURNEYS:

PILGRIMAGES IN BUDDHISM

AND ISLAM (629–1324)

Early in 1964, a thirty-eight-year-old American boarded a plane for Germany, his ultimate destination the city of Mecca in Saudi Arabia. As a Muslim, his faith required that he visit the holy sites of Islam and perform the prescribed rituals of the *hajj*. As a black man coming from a society deeply divided by race, the strongest impression this pilgrimage left on him was the complete irrelevance of racial concerns amongst his hosts and fellow pilgrims. He wrote his wife:

> You may be shocked by these words coming from me. But on this pilgrimage, what I have seen, and experienced, has forced me to *re-arrange* much of my thought-patterns previously held, and to *toss aside* some of my previous conclusions. . . . During the past eleven days here in the Muslim world,

I have eaten from the same plate, drunk from the same glass, and slept in the same bed (or on the same rug)—while praying to the *same* God—with fellow Muslims whose eyes were the bluest of blue, whose hair was the blondest of blond, and whose skin was the whitest of white. . . . We were *truly* all the same (brothers)—because their belief in one God had removed the "white" from their *minds,* the "white" from their *behavior,* and the "white" from their *attitude.* . . . All praise is due to Allah, the Lord of the Worlds.[1]

A year after his realization that true brotherhood was possible across racial lines, the author was felled by an assassin.

The experiences of Malcolm X in Mecca were highly personal, but

1. *The Autobiography of Malcolm X,* as told to Alex Haley (New York: Ballantine, 1964), pp. 391–393.

they were also part of a larger fabric of history. His journey to Mecca, and the rites he performed while there, repeated the experiences of generations of Muslims over a thousand years. Like so many of these pilgrims, Malcolm brought his own concerns and the issues of his own society with him, only to have his preconceptions challenged by the international, cosmopolitan experience of the hajj.

It is logical to begin this chapter on sacred journeys with an account from the world of Islam. No other religious tradition has placed more emphasis on the sacred pilgrimage, requiring a very specific set of rites of *every* believer who has the resources to make at least one journey to the heartland of its prophets. But Islam is remarkable only for the intense centralization and codification of its sacred journey. The impulse to travel to holy sites appears to be a nearly universal component of human spirituality.

For most people in most places and times, the destinations of these journeys have probably been relatively local. Sacred spaces, often associated with nature or with the presence of living or departed spiritual leaders, might be relatively easy to visit. But with the rise of major world religions, such as Buddhism and Islam, sacred journeys came to involve long sojourns in which pilgrims, like Malcolm X, crossed significant cultural frontiers. In the process, pilgrims performed the same role that long-distance traders often played in disseminating culture. Pilgrimage routes became broad avenues on which people and ideas, cultures and languages, moved and mixed.

In each of these traditions there is a sense of the need for a return to places associated with the founding of that religion: to the parts of India most closely associated with Siddhartha Gautama, the Buddha; and to Mecca and Medina, where Islam states that Muhammad received God's final revelation and initiated the incredible expansion of the world's fastest-growing religion. Modern transportation has made such journeys relatively easy today, although political and economic circumstances can still create dangers and uncertainties. In the period covered in this chapter, from the seventh through the fourteenth centuries, the decision to set out on a long-distance pilgrimage was not one that could be taken lightly. As we will see, such an act of spiritual devotion could take years of the pilgrims' lives and expose them to extreme hazards.

In the sources that follow, you will consider the motivations and experiences of Buddhist and Muslim pilgrims. What role does pilgrimage seem to play in each particular religion in general terms and in the faith experiences of the individual pilgrims? Why did these pilgrims set out? What do their experiences along the way tell us about their own view of the world and that of the societies through which they pass? As outsiders, how are they viewed and how do they view others? What types of challenges did they have to overcome to reach their destination? Were they ultimately successful in their spiritual quest?

Chapter 11

Sacred Journeys:

Pilgrimages in

Buddhism

and Islam

(629–1324)

BACKGROUND

In comparing the religions to be considered in this chapter and their traditions of pilgrimage, it is important to note that Buddhism gained millions of followers outside its place of origin while becoming a minority religion in the land of its founder, Siddhartha Gautama (the Buddha). Islam, by contrast, has remained dominant in the areas where Muhammad lived and preached. As a result, patterns of pilgrimage in Buddhism have been less centralized than those in Islam, less focused on a particular route or a predictable pattern.

The early success of Buddhism in India following the death of Siddhartha Gautama (ca. 483 B.C.E.) reached its height in the reign of Emperor Ashoka (ca. 264–223 B.C.E.), who made Buddhism the state religion and patronized its art and architecture (see Chapter 5). The *stupas* and pillars erected under Ashoka still attract pilgrims. Most importantly for our story, Ashoka sponsored missionary activities outside of India. By the time caste-based Hinduism reasserted itself in South Asia, Buddhist monasteries had been founded across Central and Southeast Asia, as well as in China.

The pilgrimage impulse was strong in Buddhism from the beginning. It is said that when the Buddha died, his disciples cremated his remains and scattered the ashes among the most important of their communities. Before long, the Buddha's followers began visiting the sites of his life's most important activities: "To visit the scenes of the eight great events is to experience in a direct way the life of the Buddha as both a demonstration of his perfection and the perfection of all Buddhas."[2] The further across Asia the religion spread, however, the more difficult it was for Buddhists to visit these original sites, and as Buddhism waned in India, social and political circumstances made such journeys much more problematic.

That did not stop intrepid travelers from going to India to visit the holy sites. A number of Chinese Buddhist monks made such journeys in the fourth through sixth centuries. Their numbers were never great, but they were very important in the development of East Asian Buddhism. Buddhism had arrived in China via the Silk Road during the Han dynasty. Christian, Zoroastrian, and Manichean communities were also established in China at this time, but Buddhism became far and away the most prominent of these imported faiths, even while having to contend with competition from two well-established religious and ethical traditions: Confucianism and Daoism. In spite of occasional persecution, Buddhism flourished, and by the time of the T'ang dynasty (626–960), monasteries had been established throughout the land. From this time forward, Chinese Buddhism was relatively self-sufficient, and pilgrimages to India became more infrequent.

2. John Huntington, "Sowing the Seeds of the Lotus: A Journey to the Great Pilgrimage Sites of Buddhism," *Orientations*, November 1985, p. 48, cited in Sally Hovey Wriggins, *Xuanzang: A Buddhist Pilgrim on the Silk Road* (Boulder, Colo.: Westview, 1996), p. 82.

As well as personal spiritual fulfill-ment, Chinese pilgrims to India were concerned with gathering material that could be used to purify and rectify the Chinese practice of Buddhism. In returning to the source, they sought out original texts and learned to read them in their original languages, con-sulting with Buddhist sages in the monasteries they visited along the way. Buddhism had adapted itself to local customs as it spread from its original homeland. These monks saw the need to return to its place of ori-gin to purify their faith. Meanwhile, missionaries from China had reached Korea and Japan by the sixth century. As Buddhism once again flourished and adapted itself to local culture, Korean and Japanese monks were fired by the same impulses that had led Chinese monks to India. Now China itself became a destination for pilgrimage.

The resources that earlier pilgrims had previously sought in India—sacred texts, relics, learned authori-ties, and holy sites—became widely available in China. The Mahay-ana school, to which the Chinese belonged, appealed to a wider pop-ulation than the stricter and more ascetic Theravada school primar-ily because it offered an easier path to Enlightenment and emphasized the passage of the individual soul to a blessed realm rather than the complete extinction of the individual. The deification of Siddhartha Gau-tama under Mahayana gave an out-ward focus to spirituality, meaning that veneration of statues of Buddha became a focal point of worship. Par-ticularly impressive images of Buddha could become destinations of pilgrim-age wherever they might be found. Mahayana Buddhists also emphasized that common people could be helped toward Enlightenment through the aid of compassionate beings known as *bodhisattvas*. These were individu-als who were further along on the path to *nirvana* but who remained in the world as benefactors of humanity. As they achieved Buddhahood them-selves and passed from the earth, their places of residence could also become shrines to which pilgrims flocked. In other words, the multiplicity of bod-hisattvas and Buddhas in China itself meant that there was no special need to go to the land of Siddhartha Gau-tama, who could at any rate be prayed to at local shrines.

Just as Chinese monks had once looked to India, Japanese and Korean monks now saw China as a destina-tion for sacred journeys. By the sev-enth century, Buddhism was taken up by Japanese emperors. In the early days it was missionaries from China who brought doctrines, images, rel-ics, and sacred texts to Japan. Soon, however, Japanese monks made the journey in the opposite direction, to visit the holy sites and schol-ars of China. In 607 the Emperor Shotoku authorized an embassy to China to establish diplomatic rela-tions and sent hundreds of young men, Buddhist monks included, to study in China. The best known of the Japanese Buddhists who traveled to China was a monk named Ennin who kept a diary of his long and arduous trip (838–847 C.E.). You will encounter Ennin's story later in this chapter.

Chapter 11

Sacred Journeys:
Pilgrimages in
Buddhism
and Islam
(629–1324)

Of the five "pillars" of Islam—the statement of faith, the five daily prayers, the requirement of charity, the need to fast during the month of Ramadan, and the Qur'anic injunction to perform the hajj—none is more difficult to achieve than the pilgrimage to Mecca. For most Muslims in today's world, it has been an unachievable goal: Two million pilgrims from 125 countries come to Mecca for the hajj each year, but that accounts for only two in a thousand adult Muslims. For those who have the means and the opportunity, however, it is the journey of a lifetime.

In the second half of the first millennium, Islam expanded beyond its original Arabian heartland with amazing speed. It was not long before most believers neither spoke Arabic as their native language nor fully connected with the Arab culture in which Islamic belief and practice was so deeply rooted. Even in the immediate geographic environs of the Arab world, cultural diversity soon became the rule rather than the exception in the world of Islam. The Persians are close neighbors, but their language is Indo-European rather than Semitic, and their cultural and religious traditions are quite different from those of the Arabs. The Turks originated in the very different environment of the Central Asian steppes, and again both their language and their culture were and are nothing like those of the Arabs among whom Islam had originated. Needless to say, when Islam spread to West Africa, Europe and Southeast Asia, its cultural complexity increased dramatically. The possibility has always existed that interaction with local languages and cultures would dilute the purity of the faith. The hajj acts as a check on that process. Every year pilgrims arrive from across the world, representing diverse cultural backgrounds. But in the hajj all distinctions are removed: The pilgrims adopt the same dress, speak the same words, and precisely follow the same rituals. When the pilgrims circle the black building known as the *ka'ba* at the center of Mecca, they are at the physical and spiritual center of the Islamic world.

The ka'ba is a very ancient building that already stood where it does today when Muhammad was a child. At that time it was filled with images and objects sacred to many faiths, representing the religious pluralism that prevailed in seventh-century Arabia. After Muhammad received his first revelation and spread the word about the one true God, the polytheism of the ka'ba could only seem an abomination. When he returned from his exile in Medina, Muhammad ordered that the ka'ba be cleared of the objects and images it contained and be sanctified for God. The fact that religious travelers were already accustomed to visiting the ka'ba might have eased the adjustment of converts to the new religion. Muhammad himself established the precedent for all the main elements of the pilgrimage as still practiced today, and to the believer those directions came straight from God.

Only Muslims may enter Mecca, which is seen as *haram*, a sanctuary of their faith. As they enter, the pilgrims exchange their personal clothing for special white garments, which eliminate all distinctions of rank and status. Men and women wear different types of garments, but women who are in Mecca as pilgrims are not veiled, and men and women mix very freely. Ritual bathing prepares the pilgrims for the holy rites that are about to begin. No violent thoughts or actions and no sexual activity are allowed. Seven counterclockwise circuits of the ka'ba are performed at three key points during the hajj, though few pilgrims are lucky enough to achieve their goal of actually touching this edifice as thousands swirl about the ka'ba in unison. Five times each day every Muslim faces the ka'ba in order to pray; for believers to actually be there is to feel that they are at the center of human communication with God. After leaving Mecca, and after a night spent in desert tents, the pilgrims move on to Arafat to perform the ritual known as the Day of Standing Together Before God. After another night in the desert, the pilgrims participate in a ritual stoning of the devil before returning to Mecca and repeating their circuit of the ka'ba. Most will then go on to Medina to visit the Prophet's grave.

While the world has changed dramatically, the pilgrimage itself has changed little over the centuries. It therefore serves to connect Muslims not only with their contemporaries, but with past generations. Above all, it-is the ultimate expression of the personal religious devotion of the pilgrim:

Muslims are drawn to Mecca like filings to a magnet, attracted by the integrative power of a journey to the heartland. More than a city, Mecca is a principal part of speech in a sacred language and the direction Muslims pray in throughout their lives. Simply to set foot there may answer years of longing. . . . Over the centuries, in times of peace and war, Mecca has offered its visitors a dependable retreat, a sort of ritual greenhouse reserved for forcing the spirit into blossom no matter what may be going on beyond the Haram borders. As a reminder of how life ought to be lived, the journey has inspired peasants, princes, mystics and revolutionaries. For all these reasons, it represents a literal trip of a lifetime.[3]

Muslims have clearly invested much of their spiritual energy in the hajj.

Politics and historical chronology are not irrelevant to the story of the hajj: Whoever controls the holy sites has a position of great power and responsibility in the Islamic world, an authority exercised today by the royal house of Saudi Arabia. Certainly political and military circumstances in the world outside Mecca have greatly affected the ability of pilgrims to reach the holy city over time. Having said that, there is a timeless quality to the hajj that sets it apart from its Buddhist equivalent. While the stories of the Buddhist pilgrims that follow seem to come from a far different world, the essential experiences of Muslim pilgrims in the city of Mecca have never fundamentally changed.

3. Michael Wolfe, introduction to *One Thousand Roads to Mecca: Ten Centuries of Travelers Writing About the Muslim Pilgrimage* (New York: Grove, 1999), p. xxiv.

Chapter 11

Sacred Journeys:

Pilgrimages in

Buddhism

and Islam

(629–1324)

THE METHOD

The first thing to bear in mind when reading the pilgrimage accounts that follow is the variety of narrative styles. Some are first-person narratives, while others are impersonal chronicles. As always when reading historical documents, you should ask: Who wrote this, and why? How might these documents have affected the attitude of a reader at that time toward pilgrimages and holy sites?

Because the sources are so different in structure and intent, not every one will be relevant to each of the questions we pose. But as you read, keep separate lists for Buddhist and Islamic sources and make note of any information you run across that is relevant to the following questions:

- What were the primary religious factors that inspired the pilgrims to set out on their journey? What were their most powerful spiritual experiences? Did their religious beliefs or attitudes change in any way as a result of the pilgrimage?

- How was the pilgrimage organized— on an individual basis or in a large or small group? What might account for each form or organization?

- How were the pilgrims affected by the political systems they encountered? Did political leaders along the way do more to help or to hinder the pilgrims? What hazards did the pilgrims face, and how did they overcome them? How did the pilgrims sustain themselves economically?

- As the pilgrims observed peoples whose cultures and customs were different from their own, what did they especially notice, and how did they react? Alternatively, how did people from different backgrounds seem to view the pilgrims?

- Although the pilgrims represented here are all men, what do the sources tell us about women's participation in sacred journeys, and more generally about gender relations in the societies described?

With these questions as a starting point, you will return to make systematic comparisons among the documents. Meanwhile, the following paragraphs provide some additional background for each. You will want to refer back to this section as you consider the evidence.

Source 1 consists of a series of extracts from the diary kept by the Japanese monk Ennin during his nine-year pilgrimage to China. Ennin's journey of 838 to 847 took place during the period mentioned above when the Japanese emperors, who were interested in learning from Chinese examples in government, culture, and religion, sponsored "embassies" to achieve that end. As you will see in this reading, however, official sponsorship from Japan was not sufficient to guarantee the success of a pilgrimage. Apart from the sometimes grave difficulties Ennin encountered in traveling by both sea and land, Chinese officials both great and small placed impediments in his path. Showing remarkable fortitude, however, Ennin and his companions were successful in their sacred journey, learning from Buddhist monks in various monasteries and visiting holy sites. Ennin's experience in China was an international one, for while he was there he met and interacted not only with Chinese Buddhists but also with monks from Korea, India, and other lands. His diary demonstrates that pilgrimages of this type had cultural and linguistic as well as spiritual dynamics.

Source 2 is taken from one of the most popular books ever written, *Journey to the West,* or *The Monkey-King.* Though also set in T'ang-era China, it was written in the seventeenth century by Wu Ch'êng-ên, who appealed to popular tastes for tales of magic, monsters, and mystery. But the goal of the story's heroes, the Buddhist priest Tripitaka and his disciple Monkey, is a serious one. Paralleling Ennin's quest, they travel from China to India in search of sacred Buddhist texts.

A portrait of Xuanzang, the greatest of all Chinese pilgrims to India, is shown in Source 3. Xuanzang's journey of 629 to 645 resulted in a religious renaissance. The sacred texts and relics he brought back to China served as a foundation for the further development of Buddhism in the context of the powerful and centralized T'ang state. He also composed a record of his travels entitled *Record of the Western Regions* and was the subject of a well-known biography, *The Life of Xuanzang.* This work helped to establish the legend of Xuanzang as a man of great fortitude, wisdom, and compassion. The portrait reproduced here gives us some insight into how Chinese Buddhists conceptualized Xuanzang as the "ideal pilgrim" in terms of both his physical and spiritual attributes.

The rest of the documents take us to the world of Islam. Source 4 is the story of Naser-e Khosraw, a Persian pilgrim who performed his hajj in the 1060s when Jerusalem was ruled by Christian crusaders. Khosraw was an administrator in Persia (today's Iran) who seems to have had a midlife crisis: Disenchanted with the corruption of government and concerned about his own moral failings, he had a dream that led him on a new path, and he departed for Mecca. The full text of his story has much to say not only about the hajj itself but also about the whole Islamic world through which he passed.

While Naser-e Khorsaw traveled west to visit Mecca, the author of Source 5, Abu al-Husayn Muhammad ibn Ahmad ibn Jubayr (1145–1217), traveled east from Spain, then the far western edge of the Dar al-Islam ("Abode of Islam"). Ibn Jubayr, an Arab, was a native of Valencia in the Muslim-ruled Andalusian region of southern Spain. He moved to the capital city of Grenada to study law, later serving secretary to the emir (governor). The English translator of *The Travels of Ibn Jubayr* tells an intriguing story behind the book's origins. The emir had offered Ibn Jubaryr, his servant, a cup of wine to drink. Ibn Jubayr, keeping to the law of his faith, refused. Insulted, the emir forced him instead to drink seven cups. Then the emir's guilt led him to offer Ibn Jubayr seven cups of gold in recompense for his transgression. Now with the means provided by the emir's gift, Ibn Jubayr set off for Mecca in 1183.

[303]

Chapter 11

Sacred Journeys:

Pilgrimages in

Buddhism

and Islam

(629–1324)

The journey from Spain to Arabia required travel across the Mediterranean Sea, which in that crusader era was contested between Muslim and Christian forces; Ibn Jubayr traveled to Egypt on an Italian ship. Once in Egypt he had entered the lands of the greatest Muslim monarch of the age, Salah al-Din, known in the West as Saladin (c.1138–1193), on whom he lavished praise. On his return he described Baghdad and Damascus, important political, cultural. and economic centers, before traveling to the Syrian coast for passage by ship back to Spain. It was here on the Eastern Mediterranean coast, and on the island of Sicily en route home, that Ibn Jubayr's contacts with Christians were strongest. While a staunch defender of Islam, his critiques of the Christians he encounters are never simple stereotypes, but show an appreciation for the diversity of Christian (and Muslim) behavior. The story of his travels was widely distributed in its original Arabic.

The final readings in this chapter, Sources 6, 7, and 8, take our view of the Islamic world even further. These documents by three Arabs—al-Maqrizi, al-Umari, and Ibn Khaldun—concern a great West African king, Mansa Musa. This king of Mali was perhaps the best-known African of his period, and his story is still considered central to African history today. In the fourteenth century, the Islamic kingdom of Mali was the latest of the large-scale states that had appeared in the West African region known to Arab geographers as the Sahel. The wealth of Mali, and therefore of its king, had several sources. Trade in goods produced in different environmental zones within West Africa was one source of wealth and urbanization, as was trade across the desert with the Arabs and Berbers of North Africa. The most important foundation of Malian power, however, was control of gold, and it is as a man of gold that Mansa Musa is still remembered. His story is quite important to world economic history, since the supply of gold he commanded played a crucial role in the economic growth of the Mediterranean region in this period. In these sources, however, while Mansa Musa's wealth and power are not forgotten, we also see him as a Muslim who took his faith seriously enough to brave the difficult journey across the Sahara to complete the hajj. The authors collected stories of Mansa Musa and his kingdom as part of a larger effort to inform their cosmopolitan audience about the *Dar al-Islam* ("the Abode of Islam") in the world at large.

THE EVIDENCE

Source 1 from Ennin's Diary: The Record of a Pilgrimage to China in Search of the Law, *trans. Edwin O. Reischauer (New York: The Ronald Press Company, 1955), pp. 6–23 passim, 58–63 passim, 93, 148–153 passim, 302, 305, 347–376 passim. Copyright © 1955. Reproduced with permission of John Wiley & Sons, Inc.*

1. From the Diary of Ennin, 838–847

[*Ennin has arrived in China from Japan aboard an official "tributary" ship, and he visits the monastery of Yangchou.*]

. . . It is the festival of the winter solstice. Monks and laymen all offer congratulations. Those who are laymen pay their respects to the officials and congratulate them on the festival of the winter solstice. . . . Officials of high and low rank and the common people all offer one another congratulations when they meet. . . .

The congregation of monks said to us foreign monks, "Today is the festival of the winter solstice. May you have a myriad of blessings; may the propagation of the lamp [of the Law] be without end; and may you return soon to your own land and long be National Teachers." . . .

This festival is exactly the same as New Year's Day in Japan. Each lay and monastic establishment provides rare delicacies, and all sorts of dishes are assembled. All use congratulatory phrases on the season, conforming to the tastes of the men of former times. . . .

Today was a national anniversary day. . . . Early in the morning the monastic congregations gathered in this monastery and seated themselves in rows in the flanking buildings on the east, north, and west. At 8 A.M. the Minister of State and the General entered the monastery by the great gate. The Minister of State and the General walked in slowly side by side. Soldiers in ranks guarded them on all sides, and all the officials of the prefecture and of the regional commandery followed behind. . . .

After that, several tens of monks lined up in rows at both the east and west doors of the hall. Each one held artificial lotus flowers and green banners. A monk struck a stone triangle and chanted, "All be worshipful and reverence the three eternal treasures." After that the Minister of State and the General arose and took censers, and the prefectural officials all followed after them, taking incense cups. . . . After all the monks had burned incense, they returned toward the hall by this route, chanting Sanskrit hymns without cease. . . .

. . . The leader of the chants, standing alone and motionless, struck a stone triangle, and the Sanskrit [chanting] stopped. Then they again recited, "Honor the three eternal treasures." The Minister of State and the General sat down

Chapter 11

Sacred Journeys:

Pilgrimages in

Buddhism

and Islam

(629–1324)

together in their original seats. . . . A venerable monk, Yüan-ch'eng Ho-shang, read a prayer after which the leader of the chants intoned hymns in behalf of the eight classes of demi-gods. The purport of the wording was to glorify the spirit of the [late] Emperor. At the end of each verse he recited, "Honor the three eternal treasures." The Minister of State and the officials rose to their feet together and did reverence to the Buddha, chanting three or four times. Then all [were free] to do as they wished. . . .

[*The Chinese emperor has refused to grant Ennin and his fellow monks permission to travel. Ennin communicates with a Japanese ambassador.*]

I presented a letter to the Ambassador Consultant Counselor, [saying that] I should remain in China because I was having difficulties in accomplishing my search for the Law. . . . The Consultant Counselor notified me saying, "If you desire to remain, that is for the sake of Buddhism, and I dare not stand in the way of your determination. If you wish to stay, then do remain. The government of this land, however, is extremely severe, and, if the officials learn of this, it will [entail] the crime of disobeying an Imperial order, and you will probably have trouble. You should think it over." . . .

[*Ennin writes to the Chinese government minister in charge of monasteries.*]

We monks, having in mind merely our longing for the Buddhist teachings, have come from afar to this benevolent land with our hearts set on sacred places and our spirits rejoicing in the pilgrimage. It is said that Mt. [Wu]-t'ai and some other places are the source of the teaching and the places where the great saints have manifested themselves. Eminent monks from India have visited them, crossing their precipitous slopes, and famous patriarchs of China have there attained enlightenment. We monks have admired these glorious places, and having chanced to meet with this happy destiny, have by good fortune come to this holy land. Now we wish to go to these places to fulfill our long-cherished hopes, but we fear that on the road [others] will not honor our reasons for traveling. We have heard that the Learned Doctor Prajñā petitioned for official credentials on behalf of some mendicant monks, and that they [were allowed] by Imperial edict to practice [their mendicancy. Thus,] this started of old and has continued until recent times.

We humbly hope that this monastery, in accordance with the laws and precedents of the land, will address the prefecture and the subprefecture, asking for official credentials. If it does so, the . . . glorious fame of the Monastery Administrators will stir foreign lands afar, their encouraging magnanimity will make gloriously manifest the sun-like Buddha, and we shall be more than indebted to you.

[*Ennin visits a Korean monastery.*]

At 8 A.M. they struck the bell for the scripture lecturing, apprising the group, after which the congregation spent quite a little time entering the hall. At the moment the bell sounded for the congregation to settle down, the lecturer entered the hall and mounted to a high seat, while the congregation in unison called on the name of the Buddha. Their intonation was wholly Korean and did not resemble the Chinese sounds. After the lecturer had mounted to his seat, the invocation of the name of the Buddha stopped. A monk seated below him chanted in Sanskrit, entirely in the Chinese manner, the one-line hymn, "How through this scripture," etc. When he reached the phrase, "We desire the Buddha to open to us the subtle mystery," the crowd chanted together, "The fragrance of the rules, the fragrance of meditation, the fragrance of deliverance," etc. After the singing of the Sanskrit hymn had ended, the lecturer changed the headings of the scripture and dividing them into the three parts, explained the headings. . . . After that the debaters argued the principles, raising questions. While they were raising a question, the lecturer would hold up his chowry, and when a questioner had finished asking his question, he would lower it and then raise it again, thank [the questioner] for his question, and then answer it. They recorded both the questions and the answers. It was the same as in Japan, except that the rite of [pointing out doctrinal] difficulties was somewhat different. After lowering his hand at his side three times and before making any explanation, [a debater] would suddenly proclaim the difficulty, shouting with all his might like a man enraged, and the lecturer would accept the problem and would reply without raising problems in return. . . .

[After being further delayed by bureaucracy, Ennin finally sets out for Mt. Wu-t'ai, an area known as the home of the bodhisattva Monju, also referred to in this document as Monjushiri. Monju was a great spiritual leader who delayed his own achievement of nirvana in order to help his fellow men attain Enlightenment. Ennin's long stay at Mt. Wu-t'ai was the spiritual center of his pilgrimage.]

. . . When one enters this region of His Holiness [Monju], if one sees a very lowly man, one does not dare to feel contemptuous, and if one meets a donkey, one wonders if it might be a manifestation of Monju. Everything before one's eyes raises thoughts of the manifestations of Monju. The holy land makes one have a spontaneous feeling of respect for the region. . . .

. . . We opened the hall and worshiped an image of His Holiness the Bodhisattva Monju. Its appearance is solemn and majestic beyond compare. The figure riding on a lion fills the five-bay hall. The lion is supernatural. Its body is majestic, and it seems to be walking, and vapors come from its mouth. We looked at it for quite a while, and it looked just as if it were moving. . . .

. . . Regardless of rank or position, here all persons make one think of Monju. Long ago, the Ta-hua-yen-ssu held a great . . . feast, and commoners, both men and women, and beggars and the destitute all came to receive food, but the patron was displeased and said, "My intention in coming here far up the mountain slopes and holding a . . . feast was merely to provide for the monks of the

Chapter 11

Sacred Journeys:

Pilgrimages in

Buddhism

and Islam

(629–1324)

mountain, and it was not my intention that these worldly laymen and beggars should all come and receive my food. If such beggars are to be provided for, then . . . feasts can be arranged in their native places. Why should I come all the way to this mountain [to feed them]?" The monks persuaded him to have food given to all. Among the beggars was a pregnant woman, heavy with child, and, when at her seat she received her full portion, she demanded a portion for the child in her womb. The patron cursed her and would not give it to her. The pregnant woman said several times, "Although the child in my womb has not yet been born, he counts as a person, so why don't you give him his food?" The patron said, "You are a fool. Even though the child in your belly should count as one, he does not come out to ask for it. If he gets the food, to whom should we give it to eat?" The woman replied, "If the child in my belly does not get food, then I too should not eat," and, rising, she left the dining hall. Just as she went out of the door of the hall, she was transformed into Monjushiri, emitting light which filled the hall with dazzling brightness. With his bright jade-[like] countenance and seated on a lion with golden hair and surrounded by a myriad of Bodhisattvas, he soared up into the sky. The whole assembly of several thousand persons rushed out together and fell dumbfounded and insensible to the ground. They raised their voices in repentance and wept bitterly, raining down tears, and called out together, "His Holiness Monjushiri," until their voices gave way and their throats were dry, but he never deigned to turn around and grew indistinct and then disappeared. The whole assembly had no appetite for the food, and each one of them made vows. Thenceforth, when offerings were sent and . . . feasts arranged, all were provided for equally, regardless of whether they were clerics or laymen, men or women, great or small, noble or lowly, poor or rich. Accordingly, the custom of the mountain is to have a system of equality. There have been many other miracles of divine manifestation besides this one, of which the whole empire knows.

[*After years of study at the monastery in Mt. Wu-t'ai, Ennin's achievements in Buddhist knowledge are confirmed.*]

. . . My instruction in the Great Law of the *Kongōkai* was concluded, and I made offerings to the *Kongōkai Mandara* and received Baptism as a Transmitter of the Law. Five jars of water were poured on my head. At night I made offerings to the Twelve Heavens. Everything went auspiciously.

I finished copying the newly translated scriptures of the Hsing-shan-ssu and the *Methods of Reciting Religious Formulae* on the twenty-second day of the fourth moon. [Yüan-cheng] Ho-shang said to me, "I have told you all that I understand about the Great Law of the *Kongōkai*, and you have copies down all of these practices. If there is anything further that you lack, you should seek it elsewhere."

[*Just as Ennin achieves the main goals of his pilgrimage, the political situation becomes volatile. As Uighur armies attack from Central Asia, foreigners and foreign religions come under attack. The emperor begins to suppress Buddhism and promote Taoism.*]

In the wards within the city of Ch'ang-an there are more than three hundred Buddha halls. Their Buddhist images, scripture towers, and so forth are as magnificent as [those described] in the Law, and all are the work of famous artisans. A single Buddha hall or cloister rivals a great monastery in the provinces. But in accordance with the edict they are being destroyed. I do not know how many Buddha halls and cloisters of the land in the various provinces are being done away with. There [also] was an Imperial edict ordering the destruction of all the revered stone pillars and the grave monuments of monks. [Another] Imperial edict called upon the University for Sons of the State, the Scholars, those who had achieved the status of Accomplished Literati of the land, and those of learning, to take up Taoism, but so far not a single person has done so. . . .

[*The emperor declares that all Buddhist monks and nuns are to be returned to lay life, and that foreign monks are to be sent home.*]

. . . The Commissioners of Good Works, in accordance with the Imperial edict, included us in the return to lay life. They also notified the monasteries that, if a monk or nun does not submit to being returned to lay life, he is guilty of disobedience to an Imperial edict and will be condemned to death on the spot.

On hearing this I bound up my written materials, wrapping up all the scriptures I had copied, the teachings on devotion, and my *mandara*. . . . I do not regret my return to lay life. I merely regret that I shall not be able to take with me the holy teachings I have copied. Buddhism has been proscribed on Imperial order, and I fear that, [were I to take the writings with me], on my way the various prefectures and commanderies would examine me and, discovering the truth, would accuse me of disobedience to an Imperial edict. . . .

After fifteen *li* I turned around and saw the Chief Administrator Ilsin far to the west, coming after us on a horse. . . . We had tea with him in a wayside store and talked for a long time. When we parted he said, "Buddhism no longer exists in this land. But Buddhism flows toward the east. So has it been said since ancient times. I hope that you will do your best to reach your homeland and propagate Buddhism there. Your disciple has been very fortunate to have seen you many times. Today we part, and in this life we are not likely to meet again. When you have attained Buddhahood, I hope that you will not abandon your disciple."

. . . We reached Yang-chou and saw the monks and nuns of the city being sent back to their places of origin with their heads wrapped up. The monasteries are to be destroyed, and their money, estates, and bells are being confiscated by the government. . . .

[*Finally, Ennin gets the news that the anti-Buddhist emperor has died. The dark cloud of repression is lifted as the new emperor immediately takes steps to restore the monasteries to official favor. Ennin begins his homeward voyage.*]

Chapter 11

Sacred Journeys:

Pilgrimages in

Buddhism

and Islam

(629–1324)

. . . We boarded the ship and waited for a wind.

. . . The group on board cast away mirrors and the like in sacrifice to the spirits to obtain a wind. We monks burned incense and recited prayers on behalf of the spirits of the soil of this island and the spirits of the great and the lowly, praying that we might safely reach our homeland. Then at this place we read the *Diamond Sutra* in one hundred scrolls on behalf of the spirits of this soil and the spirits of the great and the lowly. In the fifth watch (4 A.M.), we started out even though there was no wind. Scarcely had we gotten out of the mouth of the inlet when a west wind suddenly blew up, so we hoisted sail and headed east. It seemed as though the spirits were aiding us. . . .

. . . At noon we saw ahead of us the mountains of Japan stretching out clearly from the east to the southwest. At nightfall we reached Shika Island in the northern part of Matsura District in the Province of Ilizen and tied up.

Source 2 excerpts from Wu Ch'êng-ên, Monkey: Folk Novel of China, *trans. Arthur Waley, copyright © 1943 by John Day Company, Inc., pp. 126–128, 202–209, 279–284, 288–289, 302–305. Copyright © renewed 1970 by Alison Waley. Used by permission of Grove/Atlantic, Inc. and Penguin Books Ltd.*

2. From *Journey to the West,* or *The Monkey-King,* 17th century

CHAPTER XIV

[The priest Tripitaka, accompanied by a hunter he has met on his long road to India, encounters his first disciple, Monkey.]

The hunter and Tripitaka were still wondering who had spoken, when again they heard the voice saying, "The Master has come." The hunter's servants said, "That is the voice of the old monkey who is shut up in the stone casket of the mountain side." "Why, to be sure it is!" said the hunter. "What old monkey is that?" asked Tripitaka. . . . "Years ago [said the hunter,] a very old man told me that at the time when Wang Mang overthrew the First Han Dynasty, Heaven dropped this mountain in order to imprison a magic monkey under it. He has local spirits as his gaolers, who, when he is hungry give him iron pills to eat, and when he is thirsty give him copper-juice to drink, so that despite cold and short commons he is still alive. That cry certainly comes from him. You need not be uneasy. We'll go down and have a look."

After going downhill for some way they came to the stone box, in which there was really a monkey. Only his head was visible, and one paw, which he waved violently through the opening, saying, "Welcome, Master! Welcome! Get me out of here, and I will protect you on your journey to the West." The hunter stepped boldly up, and removing the grasses from Monkey's hair and brushing away the grit from under his chin, "What have you got to say for yourself?" he asked. "To

[310]

you, nothing," said Monkey. "But I have something to ask of that priest. Tell him to come here." "What do you want to ask me?" said Tripitaka. "Were you sent by the Emperor of T'ang to look for Scriptures in India?" asked Monkey. "I was," said Tripitaka. "And what of that?" "I am the Great Sage Equal of Heaven," said Monkey. "Five hundred years ago I made trouble in the Halls of Heaven, and Buddha clamped me down in this place. Not long ago the Bodhisattva Kuan-yin, whom Buddha had ordered to look around for someone to fetch Scriptures from India, came here and promised me that if I would amend my ways and faithfully protect the pilgrim on his way, I was to be released, and afterwards would find salvation. Ever since then I have been waiting impatiently night and day for you to come and let me out. I will protect you while you are going to get Scriptures and follow you as your disciple."

Tripitaka was delighted. "The only trouble is," he said, "that I have no axe or chisel, so how am I to get you out?" "There is no need for axe or chisel," said Monkey. "You have only to want me to be out, and I shall be out." "How can that be?" asked Tripitaka. "On the top of the mountain," said Monkey, "is a seal stamped with golden letters by Buddha himself. Take it away, and I shall be out." Tripitaka . . . did indeed see innumerable beams of golden light streaming from a great square slab of rock, on which was imprinted in golden letters the inscription Om Mani Padme Hum.

Tripitaka knelt down and did reverence to the inscription, saying, "If this monkey is indeed worthy to be a disciple, may this imprint be removed and may the monkey be released and accompany me to the seat of Buddha. But if he is not fit to be a disciple, but an unruly monster who would discredit my undertaking, may the imprint of this seal remain where it is." At once there came a gust of fragrant wind that carried the six letters of the inscription up into the air, and a voice was heard saying, "I am the Great Sage's gaoler. Today the time of his penance is ended and I am going to ask Buddha to let him loose." Having bowed reverently in the direction from which the voice came, Tripitaka and the hunter went back to the stone casket and said to Monkey, "The inscription is removed. You can come out." "You must go to a little distance," said Monkey. "I don't want to frighten you." They withdrew a little way, but heard Monkey calling to them. "Further, further!" They did as they were bid, and presently heard a tremendous crushing and rending. They were all in great consternation, expecting the mountain to come hurtling on top of them, when suddenly the noise subsided, and Monkey appeared, kneeling in front of Tripitaka's horse, crying, "Master, I am out!" . . .

Tripitaka . . . said to him, "Disciple, we must give you a name in religion." "No need for that," said Monkey, "I have one already. My name in religion is 'Aware-of-Vacuity.'" "Excellent!" said Tripitaka. . . . "You shall be Monkey Aware-of-Vacuity." . . .

[*Tripitaka and his disciples meet the ghost of a king who was killed and his power usurped by a sorcerer. In this passage they unmask the "false king" and return power to the rightful ruler, who has been brought back to life and is posing as their servant.*]

Chapter 11

Sacred Journeys:

Pilgrimages in

Buddhism

and Islam

(629–1324)

. . . At last they reached the Hall of Golden Bells, where they saw the two rows of officials civil and military, and the four hundred Court officers, all of imposing stature and magnificently apparelled. Monkey led forward Tripitaka to the white jade steps, where they both stood motionless and erect. The officials were in consternation. "Are these priests so utterly bereft of decency and reason?" they exclaimed. "How comes it that, seeing our king, they do not bow down or greet him with any word of blessing? Not even a cry of salutation escaped their lips. Never have we seen such impudent lack of manners!" "Where do they come from?" interrupted the false king. "We were sent from the eastern land of T'ang in Southern Jambudvīpa," said Monkey haughtily, "by royal command, to go to India that is in the Western Region, and there to worship the Living Buddha in the Temple of the Great Thunder Clap, and obtain true scriptures. Having arrived here we dare not proceed without coming first to you to have our passports put in order." The false king was very angry. "What is this eastern land of yours?" he said. "Do I pay tribute to it, that you should appear before me in this rude fashion, without bowing down? I have never had any dealings with your country." "Our eastern land," said Monkey, "long ago set up a Heavenly Court and became a Great Power. Whereas yours is a Minor Power, a mere frontier land. There is an old saying, 'The king of a Great Country is father and lord; the king of a lesser country is vassal and son.' You admit that you have had no dealings with our country. How dare you contend that we ought to bow down?" . . .

"My Master," said Monkey haughtily, "is called Tripitaka, and is treated by the Emperor of China as his younger brother. The Emperor in a vision went to the Realms of Death, and on his return he ordered a great Mass for all souls in torment. On this occasion my Master recited so well and showed such compassionate piety that the Goddess Kuan-yin chose him to go on a mission to the West. My Master vowed that he would faithfully perform this task in return for this sovereign's bounties, and he was furnished by the Emperor with credentials for the journey. . . . After leaving China, he came first to the Land of the Two Frontiers, where he picked up me, and made me his chief disciple. In the hamlet of the Kao family, on the borders of the country of Wu-ssu, he picked up a second disciple, called Pigsy; and at the river of Flowing Sands he picked up a third, whom we call Sandy. Finally a few days ago, at the Temple of the Treasure Wood, he found another recruit—the servant who is carrying the luggage."

The false king . . . turned savagely upon Monkey and addressed to him a crafty question. "I can accept," he said, "that one priest set out from China, and picked up three priests on the way. But your story about the fourth member of your party I altogether disbelieve. This servant is certainly someone whom you have kidnapped. What is his name? Has he a passport, or has he none? Bring him before me to make his deposition!" . . .

Dear Monkey! He stepped boldly forward and cried to the magician in a loud, clear voice: "Your Majesty, this old man is dumb and rather hard of hearing. But it so happens that when he was young, he travelled in India, and knows the way there. I know all about his career and origins and with your Majesty's permission I will make a deposition on his behalf." "Make haste," said the false king, "and furnish a true deposition or you will get into trouble."

Monkey then recited as follows:

The subject of this deposition is far advanced in years; he is deaf and dumb, and has fallen upon evil days. His family for generations has lived in these parts; but five years ago disaster overtook his house. Heaven sent no rain; the people perished of drought, the lord king and all his subjects fasted and did penance. They burned incense, purified themselves and called upon the Lord of Heaven; but in all the sky not a wisp of cloud appeared. The hungry peasants dropped by the roadside, when suddenly there came a Taoist magician from the Chung-nan Mountains, a monster in human form. He called to the winds and summoned the rain, displaying godlike power; but soon after secretly destroyed this wretched man's life. In the flower-garden he pushed him down into the crystal well; then set himself on the Dragon Throne, none knowing it was he. Luckily I came and achieved a great success; I raised him from the dead and restored him to life without hurt or harm. He earnestly begged to be admitted to our faith, and act as carrier on the road, to join with us in our quest and journey to the Western Land. The false king who sits on the throne is that foul magician; he that now carries our load is Crow-cock's rightful king!

When the false king in the Palace of Golden Bells heard these words, he was so startled that his heart fluttered like the heart of a small deer. Then clouds of shame suffused his face, and leaping to his feet he was about to flee, when he remembered that he was unarmed. Looking round he saw a captain of the Guard with a dagger at his waist, standing there dumb and foolish as a result of Monkey's spell. The false king rushed at him and snatched the dagger; then leapt upon a cloud and disappeared into space. . . .

Dear Monkey! He instructed Pigsy and Sandy to take good care of the prince, king, ministers, queen and Tripitaka; . . . and was peering round on every side, looking for the wizard. Presently he saw that monster flying for his life towards the north-east. Monkey caught him up and shouted, "Monster, where are you off to? Monkey has come." The wizard turned swiftly, drew his dagger and cried, "Monkey, you scamp, what has it got to do with you whether I usurp someone else's throne? Why should you come calling me to account and letting out my secrets?" "Ho, ho," laughed Monkey. "You impudent rascal! Do you think I am going to allow you to play the emperor? Knowing who I am you would have done well to keep out of my way. Why did you bully my master, demanding depositions and what not? You must admit now that the deposition was not far from the truth. Stand your ground and take old Monkey's cudgel like a man!"

The wizard dodged and parried with a thrust of his dagger at Monkey's face. It was a fine fight! After several bouts the magician could no longer stand up

[313]

Chapter 11

Sacred Journeys:
Pilgrimages in
Buddhism
and Islam
(629–1324)

against Monkey, and suddenly turning he fled back the way he had come, leapt into the city and slipped in among the officers who were assembled before the steps of the throne. Then giving himself a shake, he changed into an absolute counterpart of Tripitaka and stood beside him in front of the steps. Monkey rushed up and was about to strike what he supposed to be the wizard, when this Tripitaka said, "Disciple, do not strike! It is I!" It was impossible to distinguish between them. "If I kill Tripitaka, who is a transformation of the wizard, then I shall have achieved a glorious success; but supposing, on the other hand, it turns out that I have killed the real Tripitaka, that would not be so good. . . ." There was nothing for it but to stay his hand. . . .

Much to Monkey's annoyance, Pigsy stood by, laughing at his discomfiture. "You've nothing to laugh at, you hulking brute," he said. "This means you've got two masters to order you about. It's not going to do you much good." "Brother," said Pigsy, "you call me a fool, but you're a worse fool than I. You can't recognize your own Master, and it's a waste of effort to go on trying. But you would at least recognize your own headache, and if you ask our Master to recite his spell, Sandy and I will stand by and listen. The one who doesn't know the spell will certainly be the wizard Then all will be easy." "Brother," said Monkey, "I am much obliged to you. There are only three people who know that spell. It sprouted from the heart of the Lord Buddha himself; it was handed down to the Bodhisattva Kuan-yin, and was then taught to our master by the Bodhisattva herself. No one else knows it. Good, then! Master, recite!"

The real Tripitaka at once began to recite the spell; while the wizard could do nothing but mumble senseless sounds. "That's the wizard," cried Pigsy. "He's only mumbling." And at the same time he raised his rake and was about to strike when the wizard sprang into the air and ran up along the clouds. Dear Pigsy! With a loud cry he set off in pursuit, and Sandy, leaving Tripitaka, hastened to the attack with his priest's staff. Tripitaka stopped reciting, and Monkey . . . seized his iron cudgel and sped through the air. . . . He sprang up into the empyrean, and was about to deliver a tremendous blow when, from a many-coloured cloud in the north-east, there came a voice which said, "Monkey, stay your hand!" Monkey looked round and saw it was the Bodhisattva Manjuśrī. He withdrew his cudgel, and coming forward did obeisance, saying "Bodhisattva, where are you going to?" "I came to take this monster off your hands," said Manjuśrī. "I am sorry you should have the trouble," said Monkey. The Bodhisattva then drew from his sleeve a magic mirror that showed demons in their true form. Monkey called to the other two to come and look, and in the mirror they saw the wizard in his true shape. He was Manjuśrī's lion! . . .

. . . Manjuśrī then recited a spell and said, "Creature, back to your true shape and look sharp about it!" The wizard at once changed into his real lion form, and Manjuśrī, putting down the lotus that he carried in his hand, harnessed the lion, mounted him and rode away over the clouds. . . .

[314]

CHAPTER XXVIII

[After many more adventures, the travelers reach the Holy Mountain and meet Buddha himself.]

They travelled westward for many months, and at last began to be aware that the country through which they were now passing was different from any that they had seen. Everywhere they came across gem-like flowers and magical grasses, with many ancient cypresses and hoary pines. In the villages through which they passed every family seemed to devote itself to the entertainment of priests and other pious works. On every hill were hermits practising austerities, in every wood pilgrims chanting holy writ. Finding hospitality each night and starting again at dawn, they journeyed for many days, till they came at last within sudden sight of a cluster of high eaves and towers. "Monkey, that's a fine place," said Tripitaka, pointing to it with his whip. "Considering," said Monkey, "how often you have insisted upon prostrating yourself at the sight of false magicians' palaces and arch impostors' lairs, it is strange that when at last you see before you Buddha's true citadel, you should not even dismount from your horse." At this Tripitaka in great excitement sprang from his saddle, and walking beside the horse was soon at the gates of the high building. A young Taoist came out to meet them. "Aren't you the people who have come from the east to fetch scriptures?" he asked. Tripitaka hastily tidied his clothes and looking up saw that the boy was clad in gorgeous brocades and carried a bowl of jade dust in his hand. Monkey knew him at once. "This," he said to Tripitaka, "is the Golden Crested Great Immortal of the Jade Truth Temple at the foot of the Holy Mountain." Tripitaka at once advanced bowing. . . .

. . . Monkey led them up the hill at a leisurely pace. They had not gone more than five or six leagues when they came to a great water about eight leagues wide. It was exceedingly swift and rough. No one was to be seen in any direction. "I don't think this can be the right way," said Tripitaka. "Do you think the Immortal can possibly have been mistaken. This water is so wide and so rough that we cannot possibly get across." "This is the way all right," said Monkey. "Look! Just over there is a bridge. That's the right way to Salvation." Presently Tripitaka came to a notice-board on which was written Cloud Reach Bridge. But it proved, when they came up to it, that the bridge consisted simply of slim tree trunks laid end on end, and was hardly wider than the palm of a man's hand. "Monkey," protested Tripitaka in great alarm, "it's not humanly possible to balance on such a bridge as that. We must find some other way to get across." "This is the right way," said Monkey, grinning. "It may be the right way," said Pigsy, "but it's so narrow and slippery that no one would ever dare set foot on it. And think how far there is to go, and what it's like underneath." "All wait where you are, and watch while I show you how," cried Monkey. Dear Monkey! He strode up to the bridge, leapt lightly on to it and had soon slipped across. "I'm over!" he shouted, waving from the other side. Tripitaka showed no sign of following

Chapter 11

Sacred Journeys:

Pilgrimages in

Buddhism

and Islam

(629–1324)

him, and Pigsy and Sandy bit their fingers murmuring, "Can't be done! Can't be done!" Monkey sprang back again and pulled at Pigsy, saying, "Fool, follow me across." But Pigsy lay on the ground and would not budge. "It's much too slippery," he said. "Let me off. Why can't I have a wind to carry me?" "What would be the good of that?"said Monkey. "Unless you go by the bridge you won't turn into a Buddha." "Buddha or no Buddha," said Pigsy, "I'm not going on to that bridge." The quarrel was at its height, when Sandy ran between them and at last succeeded in making peace. Suddenly Tripitaka saw someone punting a boat towards the shore and crying, "Ferry, ferry!" "Stop your quarrelling, disciples," said Tripitaka. "A boat is coming." They all gazed with one accord at the spot to which he pointed. A boat was coming indeed; but when it was a little nearer they saw to their consternation that it had no bottom. Monkey with his sharp eyes had already recognized the ferryman as the Conductor of Souls, also called Light of the Banner. But he did not tell the others, merely crying "Ahoy, ferry, ahoy!" When the boat was along shore, the ferryman again cried "Ferry, ferry!" "Your boat is broken and bottomless," said Tripitaka, much perturbed. "How can you take people across?" "You may well think," said the ferryman, "that in a bottomless boat such a river as this could never be crossed. But since the beginning of time I have carried countless souls to their Salvation." "Get on board, Master," said Monkey. "You will find that this boat, although it has no bottom, is remarkably steady, however rough the waters may be." Seeing Tripitaka still hesitate, Monkey took him by the scruff of the neck and pushed him on board. There was nothing for Tripitaka's feet to rest on, and he went straight into the water. The ferryman caught at him and dragged him up to the side of the boat. Sitting miserably here, he wrung out his clothes, shook out his shoes, and grumbled at Monkey for having got him into this scrape. But Monkey, taking no notice, put Pigsy and Sandy, horse and baggage, all on board, ensconcing them as best he could in the gunwale. The ferryman punted them dexterously out from shore. Suddenly they saw a body in the water, drifting rapidly down stream. Tripitaka stared at it in consternation. Monkey laughed. "Don't be frightened, Master," he said. "That's you." And Pigsy said, "It's you, it's you." Sandy clapped his hands. "It's you, it's you," he cried. The ferryman too joined in the chorus. "There *you* go!" he cried. "My best congratulations." He went on punting, and in a very short while they were all safe and sound at the other side. Tripitaka stepped lightly ashore. He had discarded his earthly body; he was cleansed from the corruption of the senses, from the fleshly inheritance of those bygone years. His was now the transcendent wisdom that leads to the Further Shore, the mastery that knows no bounds.

When they were at the top of the bank, they turned round and found to their astonishment that boat and ferryman had both vanished. Only then did Monkey tell them who the ferryman was. Tripitaka began thanking his disciples for all they had done for him. "Every one of us," said Monkey, "is equally indebted to the other. If the Master had not received our vows and accepted us as his disciples we should not have had the chance to do good works and win salvation. If we had not protected the Master and mounted guard over him, he would never have got rid of his mortal body. Look, Master, at this realm of flowers and happy creatures—of phoenixes, cranes and deer. Is it not a better place indeed than the haunted deserts through which you and I have passed?" Tripitaka still murmured his thanks, and with a strange feeling of lightness and exhilaration they all set off up the Holy Mountain and were soon in sight of the Temple of the Thunder Clap, with its mighty towers brushing the firmament, its giant foundations rooted in the seams of the Hill of Life. . . .

. . . Twitching with excitement Tripitaka followed Monkey to the gates of the Temple. . . .

. . . Father Buddha was delighted. He ordered the Bodhisattva, Vajrapanis, Arhats, Protectors, Planets and Temple Guardians to form up in two lines. Then he gave orders that the priest of T'ang was to be shown in. Again the word was passed along from gate to gate: "The priest of T'ang is to be shown in." Tripitaka, Monkey, Pigsy and Sandy, carefully following the rules of etiquette prescribed to them, all went forward, horse and baggage following. When they reached the Great Hall they first prostrated themselves before the [Buddha] and then bowed to right and left. This they repeated three times, and then knelt before the Buddha and presented their passports. He looked through them one by one and handed them back to Tripitaka, who bent his head in acknowledgment, saying, "The disciple Hsüan Tsang has come by order of the Emperor of the great land of T'ang, all the way to this Holy Mountain, to fetch the true scriptures which are to be the salvation of all mankind. May the Lord Buddha accord this favour and grant me a quick return to my native land."

Hereupon the [Buddha] opened the mouth of compassion and gave vent to the mercy of his heart: "In all the vast and populous bounds of your Eastern Land, greed, slaughter, lust and lying have long prevailed. There is no respect for Buddha's teaching, no striving towards good works. So full and abundant is the measure of the people's sins that they go down forever into the darkness of Hell, where some are pounded in mortars, some take on animal form, furry and horned. In which guise they are done by as they did on earth, their flesh becoming men's food. Confucius stood by their side teaching them all the virtues, king after king in vain corrected them with fresh penalties and pains. No law could curb their reckless debauches, no ray of wisdom penetrate their blindness.

"But I have three Baskets of Scripture that can save mankind from its torments and afflictions. One contains the Law, which tells of Heaven, one contains the Discourses, which speak of Earth, one contains the Scriptures, which save the dead. They are divided into thirty-five sections and are written upon fifteen thousand one hundred and forty-four scrolls. They are the path to Perfection, the gate that leads to True Good. In them may be learnt all the motions of the stars and divisions of earth, all that appertains to man, bird, beast, flower, tree and implement of use; in short, all that concerns mankind is found therein. In consideration of the fact that you have come so far, I would give you them all to take . . . back to the East, to be a boon there forever." . . .

Chapter 11

Sacred Journeys:
Pilgrimages in
Buddhism
and Islam
(629–1324)

After dismissing the pilgrims, Buddha broke up the assembly. Presently the Bodhisattva Kuan-yin appeared before the throne, saying, "Long ago I was instructed by you to find someone in China who would come here to fetch scriptures. He has now achieved this task, which has taken him five thousand and forty days. The number of the scrolls delivered to him is five thousand and forty-eight. I suggest that it would be appropriate if he were given eight days in which to complete his mission, so that the two figures may concord." "A very good idea," said Buddha. "You may have that put into effect." He then sent for the eight Vajrapanis and said to them, "You are to exert your magic powers and carry back Tripitaka to the East. When he has deposited the scriptures, you are to bring him back here. All this must be done in eight days, that the number of days taken by the journey may concord with the number of scrolls allotted to him." The Vajrapanis at once went after Tripitaka, caught him up and said to him, "Scripture-taker, follow us." A sudden lightness and agility possessed the pilgrims and they were borne aloft upon a magic cloud. . . .

[*After bringing the sacred scriptures to the T'ang emperor, the companions return to the Holy Mountain.*]

Meanwhile the four pilgrims and the white horse were carried back to Paradise by the eight Vajrapanis, and counting up the time taken by their going and coming, it proved that the whole journey had barely taken the eight stipulated days. It happened that when they arrived, all the deities of the Holy Mountain were assembled before Buddha, to receive his instructions. "We beg to state that the pilgrims have been to Ch'ang-an, as commanded, have handed over the scriptures and have now returned to report," said the Vajrapanis. They then motioned to Tripitaka and the rest to come forward and receive their heavenly rank.

"Holy priest," said the [Buddha] "you in a previous existence were my second disciple and were called Golden Cicada. But because you paid no heed to my teaching and scoffed at my doctrine, I caused you to be reborn in the East. But now by the true devotion you have shown in the fetching of my holy scriptures, you have won great merit and I herewith appoint you to be a Buddha, with the title "Buddha of Precocious Merit."

"Monkey, because you made trouble in Heaven, it was found necessary to imprison you under the Mountain of the Five Elements. But fortunately, when the time of your retribution was ended, you turned your heart to the Great Faith and your endeavour to the scourging of evil and the promotion of good. Upon your recent journey you distinguished yourself by the subjugation of monsters and demons, and have done, first and last, so well that I hereby promote you to be the Buddha Victorious in Strife.

"Pigsy, you were once a marshal of the watery hosts of Heaven. But at a peach banquet you drank too much and made free with a fairy maiden. For this you were condemned to be born into the common world, with a shape near to animal.

"However, when you were haunting the cave of the Cloud Ladder, you were converted to the Higher Religion, eventually became a priest and gave your protection to Tripitaka on his journey. Greed and lust are not yet utterly extinct in you; but remembering that you carried the luggage all the way, I now promote you to be Cleanser of the Altar." "Hey! What's this? I don't understand," said Pigsy. "You've just made the other two into Buddhas. Why aren't I a Buddha too?" "Because," said Buddha, "your conversation and appearance still lack refinement, and your appetite is still too large. But the number of my worshippers in all the four continents of the Universe is very large, and it will be your job to clean up the altar everywhere and whenever there is a Buddhist ceremony and offerings are made. So you'll get plenty of pickings. I don't see what you've got to complain of.

"Sandy, you were a great Captain of Spirits; but one day at the Peach Banquet you broke a crystal dish and were banished to the common world, where you settled in the River of Flowing Sands and lived by devouring human flesh. Fortunately you were converted, zealously and faithfully carried out your vows and protected Tripitaka. In recognition of the way you got his horse over the mountain passes, I now promote you to the rank of an Arhat, with the title 'Golden Bodied Arhat'."

Then he turned to the white horse. "You," he said, "were a child of the Dragon King of the Western Ocean, but you disobeyed your father and were found guilty of unfilial conduct. Fortunately you were converted to the Faith and became attached to our Order. Because you carried Tripitaka to the West and on the return journey transported the scriptures, your services too must be rewarded, and I hereby promote you to be one of the eight senior Heavenly Dragons."

The four pilgrims all kowtowed their thanks, and the white horse also made sign of its gratitude. . . .

The promotion of the five saints took place in the presence of all the spirits of Heaven—Buddhas, Bodhisattvas, Arhats, monkey local deities and Guardian Spirits. While the newcomers took their appointed places in the great assembly, multitudinous voices rose in prayer: "Praise to the Buddha of the Past, Praise to Bhaishajya, Praise to Sākyamuni . . ." and so on through all the Buddhas, till finally for the first time they chanted "Praise to the Buddha of Precocious Merit, Praise to the Buddha Victorious in Strife." Next they invoked the names of all the Bodhisattvas, Kuan-yin, Mahāsthāmprāpta, Manjuśrī, Samantabhadra and the rest, ending with "Praise to the Cleanser of the Altar, praise to the Golden Bodied Arhat, praise to the Heavenly Dragon."

I dedicate this work to the glory of Buddha's Pure Land. May it repay the kindness of patron and preceptor, may it mitigate the sufferings of the lost and damned. May all that read it or hear it read find their hearts turned towards Truth, in the end be born again in the Realms of Utter Bliss, and by their common intercession requite me for the ardours of my task.

Chapter 11
Sacred Journeys:
Pilgrimages in
Buddhism
and Islam
(629–1324)

3. Modern Portrait of Xuanzang

Source 4 from Naser-e Khosraw (Safarnama), *trans. Wheeler Thackston (CUNY Press, 1985), the Persian Heritage Series No. 36.*

4. From Naser-e Khosraw,
Book of Travels

I was a clerk by profession and one of those in charge of the sultan's revenue service. In my administrative position I had applied myself for a period of time and acquired no small reputation among my peers. . . .

In the month of Rabi II in the year 437 [October 1045], when the prince of Khurasan was Abu Solayman Chaghri Beg Daud son of Mika'il son of Seljuk, I set out from Marv on official business to the district of Panjdeh and Marv Rud, where I stopped off . . .

From there I went to Juzjanan, where I stayed nearly a month and was constantly drunk on wine. (The Prophet says, "Tell the truth, even if on your own selves.") One night in a dream I saw someone saying to me, "How long will you continue to drink of this wine, which destroys man's intellect? If you were to stay sober, it would be better for you."

In reply I said, "The wise have not been able to come up with anything other than this to lessen the sorrow of this world."

"To be without one's senses is no repose," he answered me. "He cannot be called wise who leads men to senselessness. Rather, one should seek out that which increases reason and wisdom."

"Where can I find such a thing?" I asked.

"Seek and ye shall find," he said, and then he pointed toward the *qibla* and said nothing more. When I awoke, I remembered everything, which had truly made a great impression on me. "You have waked from last night's sleep," I said to myself. "When are you going to wake from that of forty years?" And I reflected that until I changed all my ways I would never find happiness.

On Thursday . . . [19 December 1045] . . . , I cleansed myself from head to foot, went to the mosque, and prayed to God for help both in accomplishing what I had to do and in abstaining from what he had forbidden.

Afterwards I went to Shoburghan and spent the night in a village in Faryab. From there I went via Samangan and Talaqan to Marv Rud and thence to Marv. Taking leave from my job, I announced that I was setting out for the Pilgrimage to Mecca, I settled what debts I owed and renounced everything worldly, except for a few necessities.

. . . After Jerusalem I decided to voyage to Egypt by sea and thence again to Mecca. . . .

. . . Whoever wants to go to Mecca from Egypt must go east. From Qolzom there are two ways, one by land and one by sea. The land route can be traversed in fifteen days, but it is all desert and three hundred parasangs long. Most of

Chapter 11

Sacred Journeys:

Pilgrimages in

Buddhism

and Islam

(629–1324)

the caravans from Egypt take that way. By sea it takes twenty days to reach Jar, a small town in the Hijaz on the sea. From Jar to Medina it takes three days. From Medina to Mecca is one hundred parasangs. Following the coastline from Jar, you will come to the Yemen and the coast of Aden; continuing in that direction, you will eventually wind up in India and China. Continuing southward from Aden and slightly westward, you will come to Zanzibar and Ethiopia. . . . Going south from Egypt through Nubia, you come to the province of the Masmudis, which is a land of broad pasturelands, many animals, and heavyset, strong-limbed, squat, black-skinned men; there are many soldiers of this sort in Egypt . . .

A DESCRIPTION OF THE CITY OF MECCA

The city of Mecca is situated low in the midst of mountains such that from whatever direction you approach, the city cannot be seen until you are there. The tallest mountain near Mecca is Abu Qubays, which is round like a dome, so that if you shoot an arrow from the foot of the mountain it reaches its top. Abu Qubays is to the east of the city, so that if you should be in the Haram Mosque in the month of Capricorn you see the sun rise from behind the top of the mountain. On top of the mountain is a stone stele said to have been erected by Abraham. The city lies on a plain between the mountains and measures only two arrow shots square. The Haram Mosque is in the middle of the plain, and the city lanes and bazaars are built all around it. Wherever there is an opening in the mountain a rampart wall has been made with a gate. The only trees in the city are at the western gate to the Haram Mosque, called Abraham's Gate, where there are several tall trees around a well. On the eastern side of the Haram Mosque a large bazaar extends from south to north. At the south end is Abu Qubays. At the foot of Abu Qubays is Mount Safa, which is like a staircase, as rocks have been set in such a fashion that people can go up to pray, which is what is meant by [the expression] "to do Safa and Marwa." At the other, the north end of the bazaar, is Mount Marwa, which is less tall and has many edifices built on it, as it lies in the midst of the city. In running between Safa and Marwa the people run inside this bazaar.

For people who have come from faraway places to perform the Minor Pilgrimage, there are milestones and mosques set up half a parasang away from Mecca, where they bind their *ihram*. To bind the *ihram* means to take off all sewn garments and to wrap a seamless garment about the waist and another about the body. Then, in loud voice, you say, "*Labayk Allahumma, labayk,*"[4] and approach Mecca. When anyone already inside Mecca wants to perform the Minor Pilgrimage, he goes out to one of the markets, binds his *ihram*, says the Labayk, and comes back into Mecca with an intention to perform the Minor Pilgrimage. Having come into the city, you enter the Haram Mosque, approach the Ka'ba, and circumambulate . . . always keeping the Ka'ba to your left

---

4. The words of the *labayk* mean approximately "[Thy servant] has answered thy call, O God."

[shoulder]. Then you go to the corner containing the Black Stone, kiss it, and pass on. When the Stone is kissed once again in the same manner, one *tawaf*, or circumambulation, has been completed. This continues for seven *tawafs*, three times quickly and four slowly. When the circumambulation is finished, you go to the Station of Abraham opposite the Ka'ba and stand behind the Station. There you perform two *rakats* called the Circumambulation Prayer. Afterwards you go [to] the Well of Zamzam, drink some water or rub some on the face, and leave the Haram Mosque by the Safa Gate. Just outside this gate are the steps up Mount Safa, and here you face the Ka'ba and say the prescribed prayer, which is well-known. When the prayer has been said, you come down from Safa and go from south to north through the bazaar to Marwa. Passing through the bazaar, you go past the gates to the Haram Mosque, where the Prophet ran and commanded others to run also. The length is about fifty paces, and on either side are two minarets. When the people coming from Safa reach the first two minarets, they break into a run until they pass the other two at the other end of the bazaar. Then they proceed slowly to Marwa. Upon reaching the end they go up Marwa and recite the prescribed prayer. Then they return through the bazaar and repeat the run until they have gone four times from Safa to Marwa and three times from Marwa to Safa, making seven runs the length of the bazaar. Coming down from Marwa the last time, you find a bazaar with about twenty barbershops facing each other. You have your head shaved and, with the Minor Pilgrimage completed, come out of the Sanctuary. The large bazaar on the east side is called Souk al-Attarin [Druggists' Market]. It has nice buildings, and all the shopkeepers are druggists. In Mecca there are two [public] baths each paved with a green stone from which flints are made.

I reckoned that there were not more than two thousand citizens of Mecca, the rest, about five hundred, being foreigners and *mojawirs*.[5] Just at this time there was a famine, with sixteen maunds of wheat costing one dinar, for which reason a number of people had left.

Inside the city of Mecca are hospices for the natives of every region—Khurasan, Transoxiana, the Iraq, and so on. Most of them, however, had fallen into ruination. The Baghdad caliphs had built many beautiful structures, but when we arrived some had fallen to ruin and others had been expropriated. All the well water in Mecca is too brackish and bitter to drink, but there are many large pools and reservoirs, costing up to ten thousand dinars each, that catch the rainwater from the hills. When we were there, however, they were empty. A certain prince of Aden, known as Pesar-e Shaddel, had brought water underground to Mecca at great personal expense. This water was used to irrigate crops at Arafat and was limited to there, although conduits had been constructed and a little water reached Mecca, but not inside the city; therefore, a pool had been made to collect the water, and water carriers drew the water

5. *mojawir:* a sojourner, one who resides for an unusually long period near a holy place on sacred shrine to receive the blessings attendant upon it.

Chapter 11

Sacred Journeys:

Pilgrimages in

Buddhism

and Islam

(629–1324)

and brought it to the city to sell. Half a parasang out on the Borqa Road is a well called Bir al-Zahed [the Ascetic's Well]. A nice mosque is located there, and the water is good. The water carriers also bring water from that place for sale.

The climate of Mecca is extremely hot. I saw fresh cucumbers and eggplants at the end of the month of Aquarius. This was the fourth time I had been to Mecca.

From . . . [19 November 1050] until . . . [5 May 1051] I was a *mojawer* in Mecca. On the fifteenth of Aries the grapes were ripe and were brought to town from the villages to be sold in the market. On the first of Taurus melons were plentiful. All kinds of fruit are available in winter, and [the markets] are never empty.

THE HAJJ

On the ninth of Dhu al-Hijja 442 [24 April 1051], with God's help, I completed my fourth pilgrimage. After the sun had set and the pilgrims and preacher had left Arafat, everyone traveled one parasang to Mash'ar al-Haram [Sacred Shrine], which is called Muzdalifa. Here a nice structure like a *maqsura* has been built for people to pray in. The stones that are cast in Mina are gathered up here. It is customary to spend the holiday eve in this spot and then to proceed to Mina early the next morning after the dawn prayer for making the sacrifice. A large mosque called Khayif is there, although it is not customary to deliver the sermon or to perform the holiday prayer at Mina, as the Prophet did not establish a precedent.

The tenth day is spent at Mina, and stones are cast, which practice is explained as a supererogatory act connected with the Pilgrimage.

On the twelfth, everyone who intends to leave departs directly from Mina, and those who intend to remain awhile in Mecca go there. Hiring a camel from an Arab for the thirteen-day journey to Lahsa, I bade farewell to God's House.

A DESCRIPTION OF BASRA

The city has a large wall, except for the portion that faces the water, where there is no wall. The water here is all marsh, the Tigris and Euphrates coming together at the beginning of the Basra district, and when the water of the Hawiza joins the confluence, it is called Shatt-al-Arab. . . . To the southwest of Basra is open plain that supports neither settlement nor agriculture. . . .

When we arrived we were as naked and destitute as madmen, for it had been three months since we had unloosed our hair. I wanted to enter a bath in order to get warm, the weather being chilly and our clothing scant. My brother and I were clad only in old *lungis* with a piece of coarse fabric on our backs to keep out the cold. "In this state who would let us into a bath?" I asked. Therefore, I sold a small satchel in which I kept my books and wrapped the few rusty dirhems I had received in a piece of paper to give the bath attendant, thinking that he might give us a little while longer in the bath in order for us to remove the grime from our bodies. When I handed him the change, he looked at us as though we were madmen and said, "Get away from here! People are coming out of the bath." As he would not allow us in, we came away humiliated and in haste. Even the children who were playing at the bathhouse door thought we were madmen and, throwing stones and yelling, chased after us. We retired into a corner and reflected in amazement on the state of the world.

Now, as we were in debt to the camel driver for thirty dinars, we had no recourse save the Vizier of the King of Ahwaz, Abu al-Fath Ali son of Ahmad, a worthy man, learned in poetry and belles lettres, and very generous, who had come to Basra with his sons and retinue and taken up residence but who, at present, had no administrative position. Therefore, I got in touch with a Persian, also a man of learning, with whom I had some acquaintance and who had entrée to the Vizier but who was also in straightened circumstances and totally without means to be of assistance to me. He mentioned my situation to the Vizier, who, as soon as he heard, sent a man with a horse for me to come to him just as I was. Too ashamed of my destitution and nakedness, I hardly thought it fitting to appear before him, so I wrote a note of regret, saying that I would come to him later. I had two reasons for doing this: one was my poverty, and the other was, as I said to myself, that he now imagines that I have some claim to being learned, but when he sees my note he will figure out just what my worth is, so that when I go before him I need not be ashamed.

Immediately he sent me thirty dinars to have a suit of clothing made. With that amount I bought two fine suits and on the third day appeared at the Vizier's assembly. I found him to be a worthy, polite, and scholarly man of pleasant appearance, humble, religious, and well-spoken. He had four sons, the eldest of whom was an eloquent, polite, and reasonable youth called Ra'is Abu Abd Allah Ahmad son of Ali son of Ahmad. Not only a poet and administrator, he was wise and devout beyond his youthful age. We were taken in and stayed there from the first of Shaban until the middle of Ramadan. The thirty dinars due the Arab for our camel were paid by the Vizier, and I was relieved of that burden. (May God thus deliver all his servants from the torment of debt!)

When I desired to depart he sent me off by sea with gifts and bounteous good things so that I reached Fars in ease and comfort, thanks to the generosity of that noble man. (May God delight in such noble men!) . . .

After our worldly condition had taken a turn for the better and we each had on decent clothing, we went back one day to the bathhouse we had not been allowed to enter. As soon as we came through the door the attendant and everyone there stood up respectfully. We went inside, and the scrubber and servant came to attend to us. When we emerged from the bath all who were in the dressing room rose and remained standing until we had put on our clothes and departed. During that time the attendant had said to a friend of his, "These are those very young men whom we refused admission one day." They imagined that we did not know their language, but I said in Arabic, "You are perfectly correct. We are the very ones who had old sacks tied to our backs." The man was ashamed and

Chapter 11

Sacred Journeys:

Pilgrimages in

Buddhism

and Islam

(629–1324)

most apologetic. Now these two events transpired within twenty days, and I have included the story so that men may know not to lament adversity brought on by fate and not to despair of the Creator's mercy, for he is merciful indeed.

Source 5 from The Travels of Ibn Jubayr, being the chronicle of a medieval Spanish Moor concerning his journey to the Egypt of Saladin, the holy cities of Arabia, Baghdad and the city of the caliphs, the Latin Kingdom of Jerusalem, and the Norman Kingdom of Sicily, *translated from the original Arabic by R. J. C. Broadhurst, (London: J.Cape, 1952), pp. 26–28; 30–34; 36–38; 45–48; 60; 63–66; 75; 78; 80; 107; 110–111; 116–117; 137–138; 188–189; 226–227; 291; 297–301; 314–315; 316–322; 336–338; 349–350; 361–362. Reprinted by permission of The Random House Group Ltd.*

5. The Travels of Ibn Jubayr

We traveled to Ceuta [on the North African coast] where we found a [Christian] Genoese ship about to sail to al-Iskandariyah [Alexandria] . . . and we set sail with the power and help of God Most High. There is no God but He . . .

Early on the night of Wednesday the wind blew with violence upon us, throwing the sea into turmoil and bringing rain and driving it with such force that it was like a shower of arrows. The affair became serious and our distress increased. Waves like mountains came upon us from every side. Thus we passed the night, filled with despair, but hoping yet for relief in the morning . . . But day came . . . with increasing dread and anguish. The sea raged more, the horizon blackened, and the wind and rain rose to a tumult so that the sails of the ship could not withstand it . . . Despair then overcame our spirits and the hands of the Muslims were raised in supplication to Great and Glorious God . . . We spent that night . . . hovering between hope and despair, but with the break of day, God spread His mercy so that clouds dispersed, the wind abated, the sun shone and the sea was calmed. Men rejoiced, conviviality returned, and despair departed. Praise be to God who showed us the greatness of His power and restored us with His gracious mercy and bounteous compassions. . . . Christian sea-captains who were present, and Muslims who had gone through journeys and storms at sea, all agreed that they had never in their lives seen such a tempest . . .

The first day of the month was a Sunday and the day after our arrival in Alexandria. The day of our landing, one of the first things we saw was the coming on board of the agents of the Sultan to record all that had been brought in the ship. All the Muslims in it were brought forward one by one, and their names and descriptions, together with the names of their countries, recorded . . . Most of them were on their way to discharge a religious duty and had nothing but bare provisions for the journey. But they were compelled to pay the *zakat* [tax] without being questioned as to what had been possessed by them for the complete year and what had not . . . The Muslims were then ordered to take their belongings, and what remained of their provisions, to the shore, where

[326]

there were attendants responsible for them and for carrying to the Customs all that they had brought ashore . . . The Customs was packed to choking. All their goods, great and small, were searched and confusedly thrown together, while hands were thrust into their waistbands in search of what might be within . . . During all this, because of the confusion of hands and the excessive throng, many possessions disappeared. After this scene of abasement and shame, for which we pray God to recompense us amply, the pilgrims were allowed to go. There is no doubt that this is one of the matters concealed from the great Sultan known as Salah al-Din [Saladin]. If he heard of it, from what is related of his justice and leanings toward pity, he would end it . . . In the lands of Saladin we found nothing bad that merits mention save this affair, which was provoked by the officials of the Customs . . .

Amongst the glories of Alexandria, and owing in truth to the Sultan, are the colleges and hostels erected there for students and pious men from other lands. There each may find lodging where he may retreat, and a tutor to teach him the branch of learning he desires, and an allowance to cover all his needs. The care of the Sultan for these strangers from afar extends to the assigning of baths in which they may cleanse themselves when they need, to the setting up of a hospital for the treatment of those of them that are sick, and to the appointment of doctors to attend to them . . . One of the Sultan's most generous acts was the allotting of two loaves daily for each of the Moorish [Spanish] "sons of the road" whatever their number . . .

[Of Cairo] we shall begin by mentioning the monuments and blessed shrines, which for their beneficence are preserved by Great and Glorious God. Of such in the great tomb in Cairo in which is kept the head of Husayn, the son of 'Ali ibn Abi Talib, may God hold them in favor. It is in a silver casket and over it has been built a mausoleum so superb as to be beyond description and beyond the power of the mind to comprehend . . . We observed men kissing the blessed tomb, surrounding it, throwing themselves upon it, smoothing with their hands the covering that was over it, moving around it in a surging throng, calling out invocations, weeping and entreating Glorious God to bless the hallowed dust, and offering up humble supplications such as would melt the heart and split the hardest flint . . . I do not believe that in all existence there is a more . . . exquisite and wonderful building. May God in His grace and favor sanctify the noble bones that are within it. The night of that day we passed in the cemetery known as al-Qarafah. This is also one of the wonders of the world for the tombs it contains of prophets–God's benedictions upon them–of the kindred of Muhammad–May God hold them in His favor–of [Muhammad's] Companions, of the followers of the Companions, of learned men and ascetics, and of saintly men renowned for their miracles . . .

Another of the Sultan's benefactions, and a monument of enduring usefulness to Muslims, are the bridges he has begun to construct . . . Near to these new bridges are the ancient pyramids, of miraculous construction and wonderful to look upon . . . If men sought to tear them down they must fail. There is

[327]

Chapter 11

Sacred Journeys:

Pilgrimages in

Buddhism

and Islam

(629–1324)

dispute concerning them, some saying that they are the tombs of Adam and his sons; others have different views. To be short, none but Great and Glorious God can know their story . . .

Another of the generous deeds of Sultan Salah al-Din close to God Most High . . . was his annulling of the customs duty imposed as a tax on pilgrims during the Fatimid dynasty. The pilgrims had suffered distress from its harsh exactment and were much wasted by it, and felt wronged by this humbling and crushing device. At times there came some who had with them no more than the bare cost of the journey, or had not even this provision, but they were compelled to pay the fixed tax . . . Those who could not suffered the most painful punishment . . . Among the various inflictions devised was hanging by the testicles, or such foul acts. May God protect use from the abuse of his decrees . . . [Salah al-Din] abolished this cursed impost . . . Thus did he make a most happy reform, lightening the way of the pilgrim, who had been abandoned, with no one to whom he could turn. God, at the hands of this just Sultan, was sufficient to deliver the Muslims from a grievous case and a most painful state . . .

[After leaving Cairo] across this desert no one will journey save on camel, by reason of their endurance of thirst. The best and most comfortable camel litters used upon them are . . . made in Yemen for they are covered with leather and are roomy. Two of them are bound together by stout ropes and are put across the camel. They have supports at each corner, and on these rests a canopy. The traveler and his companion in counterpoise will thus be veiled from the blaze of the midday heat and may sit reclining and at ease beneath its covering. With his companion he may partake of what he needs of food and the like, or read, when he wishes, the Koran or a book; and whoso deems it lawful to play chess may, if he wish, play his companion, for diversion and to relieve his spirit. To be short, it eases the hardship of travel. Most travelers [however] rode their camels on top of their baggage and so painfully endure the rigors of the burning heat . . .

On the evening of Saturday, we entered 'Aydhab, a city of the shores of the Jiddah [Red] Sea. It has no walls and most of its houses are built of reeds . . . It is one of the most frequented ports in the world because of the ships of India and Yemen that sail to and from it, as well as the pilgrim ships that come and go. It is in the desert with no vegetation and nothing to eat save what is brought to it. Yet its people, by reason of the pilgrims, enjoy many benefits, especially at the time of their passing through, for of each load of victuals that the pilgrims bring, they receive a fixed food tax, light in comparison with the former customs duties . . . A further advantage they gain from the pilgrims is in the hiring of their *jihab:* ships which bring them much profit in conveying the pilgrims to Jiddah and returning them when dispersing after the discharge of their pious duty . . . The journey from Jiddah to 'Aydhab is most calamitous for pilgrims, save those few whom Great and Glorious God preserves, for the wind takes most of them to anchorages on the desert far south of 'Aydhab. There the Bujat, a type of Sudanese living in the mountains, come down to them and hire them their camels, and lead them through a waterless track. Often the greater number of them perish from thirst, and the Bujat seize the money and other things that they have left behind. Not seldom pilgrims will stray on foot through the wayless desert and, being lost, die of thirst . . . This race from the Sudan is more astray from the right path, and have less reason, than the animals. They have no religion save the formal words professing the unity of God, which they utter to display that they are Muslims. But behind that are corrupt beliefs and practices that cannot be condoned and are unlawful. Their men and women go naked abroad, wearing nothing but the rag which covers their genitals, and most not even this. In a word, they are a breed of no regard and it is no sin to pour maledictions upon them. . . .

We passed on our way that night until we arrived at al-Qurayn, with the rising of the sun. This place is a staging post for pilgrims and a place of their encampment. There they put on the *ihram* [simple white cloth worn by pilgrims to Mecca] and there they rest throughout the day of their arrival . . . We entered Mecca–God protect it–by the 'Umrah Gate. As we marched that night, the full moon had thrown its rays upon the earth, the night had lifted its veil, voices struck the ears with the *Talbiyat* ['Here I am, O God, here I am'] from all sides, and tongues were loud in invocation, humbling beseeching God to grant them their requests, sometimes redoubling their *Talbiyat*, and sometimes imploring with prayers. Oh night most happy, the bride of all nights of life, the virgin of the maidens of time . . .

The new moon of this month was the most auspicious our eyes had seen in all that had passed in our life. It rose after we had already entered the seat of the venerable enclosure, the sacred Haram [precinct] of God, the dome in which is the *maqam* [enclosure] of Abraham, the place from which the Prophet's mission went forth, and the alighting place of the faithful spirit Gabriel with inspiration and revelation . . . The venerable House has four corners and is almost square . . . The principal corner is the one containing the Black Stone [the *Kaaba*]. There the circumambulation begins, the circumambulator drawing back a little from it so that all of his body might pass by it, the blessed House being on the left . . . The outside of the *Kaaba*, on all its four sides, is clothed in coverings of green silk . . . and on their upper part is a band of red silk on which is written the verse, 'Verily the first house founded for mankind was that at Mecca' [Koran III, 96] . . .

We gazed upon [Abraham's stone] and were blessed by touching and kissing it. The water of Zamzam was poured for us into the imprints of the two blessed feet [of Abraham who stood on this stone when he built the *Kaaba*], and we drank it–may God profit us by it. The traces of both feet are visible, as are the traces of the honored and blessed big toes. Glory to God who softened the stone beneath the tread so that it left its trace . . . The contemplation of this place and the venerable House is an awesome sight which distracts the senses in amazement, and ravishes the heart and mind. You will see only revenant gazes, flowing tears, eyes dissolved in weeping, and tongues in humble entreaty to Great and Glorious God . . .

Chapter 11

Sacred Journeys:

Pilgrimages in

Buddhism

and Islam

(629–1324)

In the 'Abbassid Dome is a store containing a large chest that the Koran of one of the four Caliphs who were Companions of the Messenger of God–may God bless and preserve him. It is written in the hand of Zayd ibn Thabit–may God hold him in his favor–and was copied in the eighteenth year after the death of the Messenger of God . . . the custodian of this dome, whose task it was to show it to us, told us that when the people of Mecca are smitten with a drought, or suffer a rising of prices, they take out this Koran and, opening the door of the venerated House, place it on the blessed threshold with the venerated maqam, the maqam of the friend of God Abraham–may God bless both the Prophet and him. With bared heads they gather round, humbly beseeching and entreating God by the venerated Koran and the sublime maqam, and leaving not their place until the mercy of God, Great and Glorious is He, has overtaken them . . .

As you leave [Mecca] at the distance of a mile, you will find a mosque beside which is a stone placed on the road like a bench, and overtopping it and leaning against it is another stone with an inscription have become effaced. It is reported that this is the place where the Prophet–may God bless and preserve him–sat and rested . . . Men win blessings by kissing it and smoothing their cheeks against it, as indeed they should in duty, and they lean against it that their bodies might receive blessings by contact. After this place, at the distance of a bow-shot, you will find. . . two tombs piled high with heaps of large stones. It is said that they are the tombs of Abu Lahab and his wife [leaders of a prominent family which rejected the prophecy of Muhammad]. God's curses on them. From old times on, men have not ceased the custom of stoning them, until now they are covered by two large mountains . . .

Mecca–may God exalt it–is all a noble shrine . . . it is the Haram [sacred precinct] of God, and His place of security. Enough that it is the place of origin of the Prophet–may God bless and preserve him–whom God distinguished with honor and liberality, sending with him the verses of the Koran and wise invocations. It is the source of inspiration and revelation, and the first place where the spirit of the faithful, Gabriel, descended . . . this blessed town and its peoples have from ancient times profited from the prayers of the friend of God, Abraham [and] the hearts of men yearn towards it from far countries and distant regions. The road to it is a place of encounter for those, coming and going, to whom the blessed claims of Islam have reached. From all parts produce is brought to it, and it is the most prosperous of countries in its fruits, useful requisites, commodities, and commerce. And although there is no commerce save in the pilgrim period, nevertheless, since people gather in it from east and west, there will be sold in one day, apart from those that follow, precious objects such as pearls, sapphires, and other stones, various kinds of perfume such as musk, camphor, amber and aloes, Indian drugs and other articles brought from India and Ethiopia, the products of the industries of Iraq and Yemen, as well as the merchandise of Khurasan [in Central Asia], the goods of the Maghrib [in North Africa] and other wares such as it is impossible to enumerate or correctly assess . . .

On the 29th of the month the [Sacred] House was reserved for women exclusively, and they congregated from all parts. They had assembled for it some days before . . . and there was no woman in Mecca but that day went to the Sacred Mosque. When the [hereditary guardians] arrived to open the venerated House, they made haste that they might depart to leave it free to the women, and likewise the men left clear to them the place of circumambulation and the *Hijr* [corner of the *Kaaba*], so that not a man remained around the blessed House. The women rushed to ascend the steps, and the [guardians] could hardly get through them as they made their descent from the venerated House. They formed a chain, the one holding the other, and fell into such a state of confusion that they collapsed. Some shrieked, some wailed, and some cried, 'God is Great,' and others, 'There is no God but God'. . . It was their grandest and most splendid and most solemn day. May God give them advantage from it, and make it noble before His noble countenance. Yet on the whole, in comparison with the men, they are wretched and cheated. They see the venerated House and may not enter it, they gaze upon the blessed Stone but cannot touch it, and their lot is wholly one of staring and feeling the sadness that moves and holds them . . . May God, by His grace and favor, advantage them for their sincere intentions and their faith . . .

Our stay in Mecca . . . amounted to two hundred and forty-five felicitous and blessed days . . .

Baghdad is an ancient city, and although it has never ceased to be the capital of the Abbasid Caliphate . . . most of its traces have gone, leaving only a famous name. In comparison with its former state, before misfortune struck it and the eyes of adversity turned towards it, it is like an effaced ruin, a remain washed out, or the statue of a ghost. It has no beauty that attracts the eye, or calls him who is restless to depart to neglect his business and to gaze . . . And the beauty of its women, wrought between its waters and its airs, is talked of and celebrated throughout the lands, so that if God does not give protection, there are the dangers of love's seductions. As to its people, you scarce can find among them any who do not affect humility, but who yet are vain and proud. Strangers they despise, and they show scorn and disdain to their inferiors, while the stories and news of other men they belittle. Each conceives, in belief and thought, that the whole world is but trivial in comparison with his land, and over the face of the world they find no noble place of living save their own. It is as if they are persuaded that God has no lands or people save theirs . . . The stranger with them is without fellowship, his expenses are doubled, and he will find amongst them none who do not practice hypocrisy with him or make merry with him only for some profit or benefit . . . The ill conduct of the people of this town is stronger than the character of its air and water, and detracts from the probity of its traditions and its reports . . .

In these [Iraqi] lands the Shi'ites have strange manifestations. They are more numerous than the Sunnis, and have filled the land with their doctrines. They have diverse sects . . . who are infidels for they attribute divinity to

Chapter 11

Sacred Journeys:

Pilgrimages in

Buddhism

and Islam

(629–1324)

[Muhammed's son-in-law] 'Ali–may God hold him in His favor. God is above what they say . . . God has allowed them to go astray, and with them many of His creatures . . .

As for the convents which they call *khawaniq*, they are many and are used by the [mystic] Sufis. They are elaborately decorated palaces, with water flowing to all their parts forming the most agreeable sight one could see . . . They follow a noble path, and their social conduct is admirable. The style of their ritual in worship is remarkable, and excellent is their custom of assembling to listen to impassioned dance music. In these ecstacied and abstracted states the world forsakes them, such is their rapture and transport. In a word, all their affairs are wonderful, and they hope for a future life of bliss and felicity . . .

[In Damascus] the conveniences for strangers are beyond computation, more especially for those who commit to memory the Book of Great and Glorious God and those devoted to study, to whom the attitude of this town is most extraordinary. All these Eastern cities are of this fashion, but this city is more populous and wealthy. Whoever of the young men of [Islamic Spain and North Africa] seeks prosperity let him move to these lands and leave country in the pursuit of knowledge and he will find many forms of help. The first of these is the release of the mind from the consideration of livelihood, and this is the greatest and most important . . . Well then the door of this East is open, so enter it in peace industrious youth and seize the chance of undistracted study and seclusion before a wife and children cling to you and you gnash your teeth in regret at the time you have lost . . .

If in all these Eastern lands there was nothing but the readiness of its people to show bounty to strangers and generosity to the poor, especially in the case of the inhabitants of the countryside, it would be enough. For you will find admirable their eagerness to show kindness to guests, which is enough to bring them honor . . . One of their admirable traits is their respect for the pilgrim, despite the shortness of the distance to Mecca and the ease with which they could make the journey. When the pilgrims return, they stroke them with their hands and press upon them to secure their benedictions . . . Any stranger in these parts whom God has rendered fit for solitude may, if he wishes, attach himself to a farm and live there the pleasantest life with the most contented mind. Bread in plenty will be given to him by the people of the farm, and he may engage himself in the duties of an imam [religious leader] or in teaching, or what he will, and when he is wearied of the place he may remove to another farm, or climb Mount Lebanon . . . and find the saintly hermits who nothing seek but to please Great and Glorious God and remain with them so long as he wishes, and then go where he wills. It is strange how the Christians around Mount Lebanon, when they see any Muslim hermits, bring them food and treat them kindly, saying that these men are dedicated to Great and Glorious God and that they should therefore share with them . . . And if the Christians treat the opponents of their religion in this fashion, what think you of the treatment that Muslims give each other?

One of the astonishing things that is talked of is that though the fires of discord burn between the two parties, Muslim and Christian, two armies of them may meet and dispose themselves in battle array, and yet Muslim and Christian travelers will come and go between them without interference . . . The Muslims continuously journeyed from Damascus to Acre (though Christian territory), and likewise not one of the Christian merchants was stopped or hindered (in Muslim territories). The Christians impose a tax on the Muslims in their land which gives them full security; and likewise the Christian merchants pay a tax upon their goods in Muslim lands. Agreement exists between them, and there is equal treatment in all cases. The soldiers engage themselves in their war, while the people are at peace and the world goes to him who conquers . . . The state of these countries in this regard is truly more astonishing than our story can fully convey. May God by His favor exalt the world of Islam . . .

We passed the night of Friday in Darayah, a village belonging to Damascus . . . Halfway on the road, we came upon an oak tree of great proportions and with wide-spreading branches. We learnt that it is called the 'Tree of Measure,' and when we enquired concerning it, we were told that it was the boundary on this road between security and danger, by reason of some Frankish [Christian] brigands who prowl and rob thereon. He whom they seize on the Muslim side, be it by the length of the arms or a span, they capture; but he whom they seize on the Frankish side at a like distance, they release. This is a pact they faithfully observe and is one of the most pleasing and singular conventions of the Franks . . .

Our way lay through continuous farms and ordered settlements, whose inhabitants were all Muslims, living comfortably with the [Christians]. God protect us from such temptation. They surrender half their crops to the Franks at harvest time . . . other than that they are not interfered with save for a light tax on the fruits of trees. Their houses and all their effects are left to their full possession . . . But their hearts have been seduced, for they observe how unlike them in ease and comfort are their brethren in the Muslim regions . . . This is one of the misfortunes afflicting the Muslims. The Muslim community bewails the injustice of a landlord of its own faith, and applauds the conduct of its opponent and enemy, the Christian landlord, and is accustomed to justice from him. He who laments this state must turn to God . . .

Acre is the capital of the Frankish cities in Syria . . . and a port of call for all ships. In its greatness it resembles Constantinople. It is the focus of ships and caravans, and the meeting-place of Muslim and Christian merchants from all regions. Its roads and streets are choked by the press of men, so that it is hard to put foot to ground. Unbelief and unpiousness there burn fiercely and pigs and crosses abound. It stinks and is filthy, being full of refuse and excrement. The Franks ravished it from Muslims hands . . . and the eyes of Islam were swollen with weeping for it . . . Mosques became churches and minarets bell towers, but God kept undefiled one part of the principal mosque . . .

Tyre has become proverbial for its impregnability, and he who seeks to conquer it will meet with no surrender or humility. The Franks prepared it as a

[333]

Chapter 11

Sacred Journeys:

Pilgrimages in

Buddhism

and Islam

(629–1324)

refuge in case of unforeseen emergency, making it a strong point for their safety. Its roads and streets are cleaner that those of Acre. Its people are by disposition less stubborn in their unbelief, and by nature and habit they are kinder to the Muslim stranger. Their manners, in other words, are gentler. Their dwellings are larger and more spacious. The state of Muslims in the city is easier and more peaceful . . .

An alluring worldly spectacle deserving of record was a wedding procession which we witnessed one day in the port of Tyre. All the Christians, men and women, had assembled, and were formed in two lines at the bride's door. Trumpets, flutes, and all musical instruments were played until she proudly emerged between two men who held her right and left as though they were her kindred. She was most elegantly garbed in a beautiful dress from which she trailed, according to their traditional style, a long train of golden silk. On her head she wore a golden diadem covered by a net of woven gold, and on her breast was a like arrangement. Proud she was in her ornament and dress, walking with little steps of half a span, like a dove, or in the manner of a wisp of cloud . . . The Muslims and other Christian onlookers formed two ranks along the route, and gazed on them without reproof . . . We thus were given the chance of seeing this alluring sight, from the seducement of which God preserve us . . .

There can be no excuse in the eyes of God for a Muslim to stay in any infidel country, save when passing through it, while the way lies clear in Muslim lands. They will face pains and terrors . . . more especially, amongst their base and lower orders, the hearing of what will distress the hearts in the reviling of him [Muhammad] whose memory God has sanctified, and whose rank He has exalted; there is also the absence of cleanliness, the mixing with the pigs, and all other prohibited matters . . . Beware, beware of entering their lands . . .

[W]ith the favor of God toward the Muslims, we embarked on a large ship, taking water and provisions. The Muslims secured places apart from the Franks. Some Christian pilgrims came aboard. They had been on the pilgrimage to Jerusalem and were too numerous to count, but were more than two thousand . . . So, under the will of Great and Glorious God, we awaited a favoring wind and the completion of the ship's stowing . . .

When . . . we were overlooking the city of Messina [on the island of Sicily] the sudden cries of the sailors gave us the grievous knowledge that the ship had been driven by the force of the wind towards one of the shore lines and had struck it . . . Dreadful cries were raised on the ship, and the Last Judgment had come; the break that has no mending and the great calamity which allows us no fortitude. The Christians gave themselves over to grief, and the Muslims submitted themselves to the decree of their Lord . . . holding fast to the rope of hopefulness in the life to come. In turn the wind and the waves buffeted the ship until one of its rudders broke. The captain then threw out one of the anchors, hoping to take hold with it, but to no purpose. . . The sun then rose and small boats came out to us. Our cries had fallen on the city, and the King of Sicily, William himself, came out with some of his retinue to survey the affair. We made speed to go down to the boats, but the violence of the waves would not allow them to reach the ship. We at last descended into them at the end of the terrible storm. . . The strangest thing that we were told was that the Christian King, when he perceived some needy Muslims staring from the ship, having not the means to pay for their landing because of the owners of the boats were asking so high a price for their rescue, enquired, this King, concerning them and, learning their story, ordered that they be given one hundred ruba'i of his coinage in order that they might alight. All the Muslims were thus saved and cried, 'Praise be to God, Lord of the Universe'. . .

The Muslims of [Palermo, the capital of Sicily] preserve the remaining evidence of their faith [after being conquered by the Christians.] They keep in repair the great number of their mosques, and come to prayers at the call of the muezzin. In their own suburbs they live apart from the Christians. The markets are full of them, and they are the merchants of the place. They do not congregate for the Friday service, since [that] is forbidden. . . They have a *qadi* (judge) to whom they refer their law-suits, and a cathedral mosque where, in this holy month [of Ramadan] they assemble under its lamps. The ordinary mosques are countless, and most of them are used as schools for Koran teachers. But in general these Muslims do not mix with their brethren under infidel patronage, and enjoy no security for their goods, their women, or their children. May God, by His favor, amend their lot with His beneficence . . .

The Christian women [of Palermo] follow the fashion of Muslim women, are fluent of speech, wrap their cloaks about them, and are veiled. They go forth on this Feast Day dressed in robes of gold-embroidered silk, wrapped in elegant cloaks, concealed by colorful veils, and shod with gilt slippers. Thus they parade to their churches . . . bearing all the adornments of Muslim women, including jewelry, henna on the fingers, and perfumes . . .

We passed the night ready for traveling–God grant that our journey be expeditious–and on the morning of the Feast of Sacrifice we were on the deck of the ship . . . We sailed, by the blessings of God Most High, in three Christian ships which had agreed to keep course together, the foremost keeping contact with the last . . . By [God's] goodness the wind continued and spread so that we came to Cartagena [in Spain] and landed . . . On Thursday . . . we came to hour home in Grenada. . . Praise be to God for His beneficent works, and for the easement and relief. His blessings upon. . . Muhammad, His noble Messenger and Chosen One, and upon his family, and his Companions who followed the true course by his guidance . . . The span of our journey, from the time of our leaving Grenada, to that of our return, was full two years and three months and a half. Praise be to God, Lord of the Universe.

Chapter 11
Sacred Journeys:
Pilgrimages in
Buddhism
and Islam
(629–1324)

Source 6 from Corpus of Early Arabic Sources for West African History, *trans. J. F. P. Hopkins, ed., N. Levtzion and J. F. P. Hopkins (Cambridge: Cambridge University Press, 1981), Bibliothèque Nationale, Paris, MS. 4657. Copyright © 1981 by University of Ghana, International Academic Union, Cambridge University Press, 1981. Reprinted with the permission of Cambridge University Press.*

6. From al-Maqrizi's Account of Mansa Musa

Mansā Mūsā arrived in Egypt in 724/1324 with magnificent gifts and much gold. The sultan al-Malik al-Nāsir Muhammad b. Qalāwūn sent the *mihmandār* to receive him and Mūsā rode to the Citadel on the day of his official reception. . . . He refused to kiss the ground and said to the interpreter: "I am a man of the Malikite school and do not prostrate myself before any but God." So the sultan excused him and drew him near to him and did him honour. The sultan asked him the reason for his coming and he replied: "I wish to make the Pilgrimage." So the sultan ordered the *wazīr* to equip him with everything he might need.

It is said that he brought with him 14,000 slave girls for his personal service. The members of his entourage proceeded to buy Turkish and Ethiopian slave girls, singing girls, and garments, so that the rate of the gold dinar fell by six dirhams. Having presented his gift he set off with the caravan. The sultan had committed him to the care of the emir Sayf al-Dīn Itmish, commander of the caravan (*amīr al-rakb*), and he [and his companions] travelled as a self-contained company in the rear of the pilgrim caravan. When he had completed his Pilgrimage he remained behind for several days at Mecca after the ceremonies. Then he turned back but many of his followers and camels perished from cold so that only about a third of them arrived with him. Consequently he needed to borrow much money from the merchants. He bought several books on Malikite jurisprudence. The sultan presented him with horses and camels and he set off for his own country, having given away much wealth as alms in the two holy cities. Whenever his companions addressed him on any subject they bared their heads while speaking to him according to a custom of theirs.

Source 7 from Corpus of Early Arabic Sources for West African History, *trans. J. F. P. Hopkins, ed. N. Levtzion and J. F. P. Hopkins (Cambridge: Cambridge University Press, 1981), Bibliothèque Nationale, Paris, MS. 5868. Copyright © 1981 by University of Ghana, International Academic Union, Cambridge University Press, 1981. Reprinted with the permission of Cambridge University Press.*

7. From al-Umari's Account of Mansa Musa

The king of this realm sits in his palace on a big dais . . . , on a big seat . . . made of ebony like a throne. . . . Over the dais, on all sides, are elephant tusks one beside the other. He has with him his arms, which are all of gold—sword, javelin . . . , quiver, bow, and arrows. . . . About 30 slaves, . . . stand behind him, Turks and others who are bought for him in Egypt. One of them carries in his hand a parasol . . . of silk surmounted by a dome and a bird of gold in the shape of a falcon. This is borne on the king's left. His emirs sit around and below him in two ranks to right and left. Further away are seated the chief horsemen of his army. In front of him there stands a man to attend him, who is his . . . swordbearer . . . , and another, called *shā'ir* "poet" who is his intermediary . . . between him and the people. Around all these are people with drums in their hands, which they beat. Before the kings are people dancing and he is pleased with them and laughs at them. Behind him two flags are unfurled, and before him two horses are tied ready for him to ride whenever he wishes. . . .

They wear turbans with ends tied under the chin like the Arabs. Their cloth is white and made of cotton which they cultivate and weave in the most excellent fashion. . . . Their brave cavaliers wear golden bracelets. Those whose knightly valour is greater wear gold necklets also. If it is greater still they add gold anklets. Whenever a hero . . . adds to the list of his exploits the king gives him a pair of wide trousers, and the greater the number of a knight's exploits the bigger the size of his trousers. These trousers are characterized by narrowness in the leg and ampleness in the seat. The king is distinguished in his costume by the fact that he lets a turban-end dangle down in front of him. His trousers are of twenty pieces and nobody dares to wear the same. . . .

The king of this country imports Arab horses and pays high prices for them. His army numbers about 100,000, of whom about 10,000 are cavalry mounted on horses and the remainder infantry without horses or other mounts. They have camels but do not know how to ride them with saddles.

The emir Abū 'l-Ḥasan 'Alī b. Amīr Ḥājib told me that he was often in the company of sultan Mūsā the king of this country when he came to Egypt on the Pilgrimage. He was staying in [the] Qarāfa [district of Cairo] and Ibn Amīr Ḥājib was governor of Old Cairo and Qarāfa at that time. A friendship grew up between them and this sultan Mūsā told him a great deal about himself and his country and the people of the Sūdān who were his neighbors. One of the things which he told him was that his country was very extensive and contiguous with the Ocean. By his sword and his armies he had conquered 24 cities each with its surrounding district with villages and estates. It is a country rich in livestock— cattle, sheep, goats, horses, mules—and different kinds of poultry—geese, doves, chickens. The inhabitants of his country are numerous, a vast concourse. . . . He has a truce with the gold-plant people, who pay him tribute.

Ibn Amīr Ḥājib said that he asked him about the gold-plant, and he said: "It is found in two forms. One is found in the spring and blossoms after the rains in open country (*ṣaḥrā'*). It has leaves like the *najīl* grass and its roots are gold (*tibr*). The other kind is found all the year round at known sites on the banks of the Nīl and is dug up. There are holes there and roots of gold are found like stones or gravel and gathered up. Both kinds are known as *tibr* but the first is of superior fineness (*afḍal fī'l-'iyār*) and worth more." Sultan Mūsā told Ibn Amīr

Chapter 11

Sacred Journeys:

Pilgrimages in

Buddhism

and Islam

(629–1324)

Ḥājib that gold was his prerogative and he collected the crop as a tribute except for what the people of that country took by theft.

. . . A custom of this sultan is that he does not eat in the presence of anybody, be he who he may, but eats always alone. And it is a custom of his people that if one of them should have reared a beautiful daughter he offers her to the king as a concubine . . . and he possesses her, without a marriage ceremony as slaves are possessed, and this in spite of the fact that Islam has triumphed among them and that they follow the Malikite school and that this sultan Mūsā was pious and assiduous in prayer, Koran reading, and mentioning God. . . .

"I said to him (said Ibn Amīr Ḥājib) that this was not permissible for a Muslim, whether in law . . . or reason . . . , and he said: 'Not even for kings?' and I replied: 'No! not even for kings! Ask the scholars!' He said: 'By God, I did not know that. I hereby leave it and abandon it utterly!'

"I saw that this sultan Mūsā loved virtue and people of virtue. He left his kingdom and appointed as his deputy there his son Muḥammad and emigrated to God and His Messenger. He accomplished the obligations of the Pilgrimage, visited [the tomb of] the Prophet [at Medina] (God's blessing and peace be upon him!) and returned to his country with the intention of handing over his sovereignty to his son and abandoning it entirely to him and returning to Mecca the Venerated to remain there as a dweller near the sanctuary . . . , but death overtook him, may God (who is great) have mercy upon him.

"This sultan Mūsā, during his stay in Egypt both before and after his journey to the Noble Ḥijāz, maintained a uniform attitude of worship and turning towards God. It was as though he were standing before Him because of His continual presence in his mind. He and all those with him behaved in the same manner and were well-dressed, grave, and dignified. He was noble and generous and performed many acts of charity and kindness. He had left his country with 100 loads of gold which he spent during his Pilgrimage on the tribes who lay along his route from his country to Egypt, while he was in Egypt, and again from Egypt to the Noble Ḥijāz and back. As a consequence he needed to borrow money in Egypt and pledged his credit with the merchants at a very high rate of gain so that they made 700 dinars profit on 300. Later he paid them back amply. . . . He sent to me 500 mithqals of gold by way of honorarium. . . .

From the beginning of my coming to stay in Egypt I heard talk of the arrival of this sultan Mūsā on his Pilgrimage and found the Cairenes eager to recount what they had seen of the Africans' prodigal spending. I asked the emir Abū 'l-'Abbās Aḥmad b. al-Ḥāk . . . and he told me of the opulence, manly virtues, and piety of this sultan. "When I went out to meet him (he said), that is, on behalf of the mighty sultan al-Malik al-Nāṣir, he did me extreme honour and treated me with the greatest courtesy. He addressed me, however, only through an interpreter despite his perfect ability to speak in the Arabic tongue. Then he forwarded to the royal treasury many loads of unworked native gold and other valuables. I tried to persuade him to go up to the Citadel to meet the sultan, but he refused persistently, saying: 'I came for the Pilgrimage and nothing else.

[338]

I do not wish to mix anything else with my Pilgrimage.' He had begun to use this argument but I realized that the audience was repugnant to him because he would be obliged to kiss the ground and the sultan's hand. I continued to cajole him and he continued to make excuses but the sultan's protocol demanded that I should bring him into the royal presence, so I kept on at him till he agreed.

"When we came in the sultan's presence we said to him: 'Kiss the ground!' but he refused outright saying: 'How may this be?' Then an intelligent man who was with him whispered to him something we could not understand and he said: 'I make obeisance to God who created me!' then he prostrated himself and went forward to the sultan. The sultan half rose to greet him and sat him by his side. They conversed together for a long time, then sultan Mūsā went out. The sultan sent to him several complete suits of honour for himself, his courtiers, and all those who had come with him, and saddled and bridled horses for himself and his chief courtiers. His robe of honour consisted of an Alexandrian open-fronted cloak . . . embellished with . . . cloth containing much gold thread and miniver fur, bordered with beaver fur and embroidered with metallic thread, along with golden fastenings, a silken skull-cap with caliphal emblems, a gold-inlaid belt, a damascened sword, a kerchief [embroidered] with pure gold, standards, and two horses saddled and bridled and equipped with decorated . . . saddles. He also furnished him with accommodation and abundant supplies during his stay.

"When the time to leave for the Pilgrimage came round the sultan sent to him a large sum of money with ordinary and thoroughbred camels complete with saddles and equipment to serve as mounts for him, and purchased abundant supplies for his entourage and others who had come with him. He arranged for deposits of fodder to be placed along the road and ordered the caravan commanders to treat him with honour and respect.

"On his return I received him and supervised his accommodation. The sultan continued to supply him with provisions and lodgings and he sent gifts from the Noble Ḥijāz to the sultan as a blessing. The sultan accepted them and sent in exchange complete suits of honour for him and his courtiers together with other gifts, various kinds of Alexandrian cloth, and other precious objects. Then he returned to his country.

"This man flooded Cairo with his benefactions. He left no court emir . . . nor holder of a royal office without the gift of a load of gold. The Cairenes made incalculable profits out of him and his suite in buying and selling and giving and taking. They exchanged gold until they depressed its value in Egypt and caused its price to fall." . . .

Merchants of . . . Cairo have told me of the profits which they made from the Africans, saying that one of them might buy a shirt or cloak . . . or robe . . . or other garment for five dinars when it was not worth one. Such was their simplicity and trustfulness that it was possible to practice any deception on them. They greeted anything that was said to them with credulous acceptance. But later they formed the very poorest opinion of the Egyptians because of the

Chapter 11

Sacred Journeys:

Pilgrimages in

Buddhism

and Islam

(629–1324)

obvious falseness of everything they said to them and their outrageous behaviour in fixing the prices of the provisions and other goods which were sold to them, so much so that were they to encounter today the most learned doctor of religious science and he were to say that he was Egyptian they would be rude to him and view him with disfavour because of the ill treatment which they had experienced at their hands.

Muhanna' b. 'Abd al-Bāqī al-'Ujrumī the guide informed me that he accompanied sultan Mūsā when he made the Pilgrimage and that the sultan was very open-handed towards the pilgrims and the inhabitants of the Holy Places. He and his companions maintained great pomp and dressed magnificently during the journey. He gave away much wealth in alms. "About 200 mithqals of gold fell to me" said Muhanna' "and he gave other sums to my companions." Muhanna' waxed eloquent in describing the sultan's generosity, magnanimity, and opulence.

Gold was at a high price in Egypt until they came in that year. The mithqal did not go below 25 *dirhams* and was generally above, but from that time its value fell and it cheapened in price and has remained cheap till now. The mithqal does not exceed 22 *dirhams* or less. This has been the state of affairs for about twelve years until this day by reason of the large amount of gold which they brought into Egypt and spent there. . . .

Al-Zawāwī also said: . . .

"The king of this country wages a permanently Holy War on the pagans of the Sūdān who are his neighbours. They are more numerous than could ever be counted."

Source 8 from Corpus of Early Arabic Sources for West African History, *trans. J. F. P. Hopkins, ed. N. Levtzion and J. F. P. Hopkins (Cambridge: Cambridge University Press, 1981). Copyright © 1981 by University of Ghana, International Academic Union, Cambridge University Press, 1981. Reprinted with the permission of Cambridge University Press.*

8. From Ibn Khaldun's Account of Mansa Musa

According to *al-ḥājj* Yūnus, the interpreter for this nation at Cairo, this man Mansā Mūsā came from his country with 80 loads of gold dust . . . , each load weighing three *qinṭārs*. In their own country they use only slave women and men for transport but for distant journeys such as the Pilgrimage they have mounts.

Ibn Khadīja continues: "We returned with him to the capital of his kingdom. He wished to acquire a house as the seat of his authority, solidly constructed and clothed with plaster on account of its unfamiliarity in their land, so Abū Isḥāq al-Ṭuwayjin made something novel for him by erecting a square building with a dome. He had a good knowledge of handicrafts and lavished all his skill on it. He plastered it over and covered it with coloured patterns so that it turned out to be the most elegant of buildings. It caused the sultan great astonishment because of the ignorance of the art of building in their land and he rewarded Abū Isḥāq for it with 12,000 mithqals of gold dust . . . apart from the preference, favour . . . and splendid gifts which he enjoyed."

There were diplomatic relations and exchanges of gifts between this sultan Mansā Mūsā and the contemporary Merinid king of the Maghrib, sultan Abū 'l-Ḥasan. High-ranking statesmen of the two kingdoms were exchanged as ambassadors. The ruler of the Maghrib chose with care such products and novelties of his kingdom as people spoke of for long after . . . and sent them by the hand of 'Alī b. Ghānim, the emir of the Ma'qil, and other dignitaries of his state.

QUESTIONS TO CONSIDER

The questions relating to "sacred journeys" that might be of greatest interest to us as modern readers, those having to do with the inner spiritual lives of the pilgrims, can be very difficult to answer given the nature of the sources available to us. Individual, personal narratives are often not available. Nevertheless, several documents here give us some insight. In reading the sources, how would you compare the *intentions* of the pilgrims? Did the Buddhist and Muslim pilgrims you have read about seem to have similar goals in undertaking their journeys, or were their intentions specific to their particular religion? You will have to speculate to answer the next questions, but do you think the experience of pilgrimage had any permanent effects on these travelers after they returned home? What new perspectives might Ennin, for example, have brought back to the Buddhist monasteries of Japan? How might Mansa Musa's experiences have affected political and religious practices in Mali? What other evidence of changed attitudes or practices do you see in these sources?

Scale of organization was one factor that clearly had a major effect on the experiences of pilgrims. As a general rule, the smaller the group you travel with, the more you need to rely on the help of strangers and the more culturally accommodating you have to be, learning other people's languages and adapting yourself to their customs. Does that statement seem to hold true in these texts? How different were the experiences of pilgrims who traveled alone or with a few people (Naser-e Khosraw or Ennin) from those who traveled as part of much larger groups?

A related issue is the life of the pilgrims on the road and the reception they met from the people among whom they traveled. In what ways did the government and bureaucracy of China, for example, aid or hinder Ennin in achieving his goals? Considering other dangers the pilgrims

Chapter 11

Sacred Journeys:

Pilgrimages in

Buddhism

and Islam

(629–1324)

faced on the road, were they better off traveling in an area of strong or weak government? Some pilgrims, like Mansa Musa, brought considerable wealth with them when they journeyed and were able to pay their own way. If like Ibn Jubayr they were not as rich as the king of Mali, how did they sustain themselves while living in foreign lands?

A central question in today's world is the dynamic of cross-cultural exchange in a rapidly globalizing human society. While the pace of such interactions has certainly quickened dramatically, world historians have stressed that we should not assume that people in earlier times lived in utter isolation within separate "civilizations."[6] Pilgrimage routes could act as pathways of cultural borrowing in areas such as language, music, architecture, technology, taste in foodstuffs, and many

6. Jerry Bentley, *Old World Encounters* (New York: Oxford University Press, 1993).

other areas of life. For world historians, travelers' tales such as these in this chapter can provide valuable information regarding cross-cultural exchanges in pre-modern times. So how *did* the pilgrims relate culturally to the people they encountered on their travels, and how were they viewed by their hosts? What might these pilgrims have brought back from their journeys that would have had an influence back home? How did the Arabs who returned to Mali with Mansa Musa, for example, leave their mark on his capital?

Finally, you may want to compare these sources in terms of their relevance or lack of it to today's world. Does Ennin's story have anything to tell us about the relationship between nationalism and religion that might be applied to our own times? Do the attitudes and actions of the Muslim pilgrims have any continuing relevance to the situation in the Middle East today? Are there other questions raised by these sources that seem to have continuing relevance?

EPILOGUE

The final questions above lead us to consider the issue of sacred journeys in today's world. In some ways, it seems that little has changed. While improvements in transportation and the creation of modern facilities have certainly had an effect, Muslims still perform the same hajj rituals as Naser-e Khosraw and Ibn Jubayr.

Buddhism is still an international religion with significant movement of believers across national and cultural boundaries (and the Communist government of China seems to be just as interested as its T'ang-era predecessors in the regulation of religion). On the other hand, our world sometimes seems so urbanized, commercialized, and focused on recreation and entertainment that the whole concept of "sacred spaces" seems to be on the wane. Does it seem that we are less likely than our ancestors to aspire to sacred journeys? Or do our journeys take us to places regarded as "sacred" in a non-religious sense, such as the Lincoln Memorial or the national Baseball Hall of Fame?

Whatever the answer, there can be no doubt about the importance of religiously inspired pilgrimages over the long course of world history.

CHAPTER TWELVE

THE WELL-EDUCATED MAN:

STUDENTS AND SCHOLARS IN CHINA,

PARIS, AND TIMBUKTU (1180–1600)

THE PROBLEM

Most of you using this book are attending a college or university in which it has been assigned as a course textbook, or perhaps are enrolled in a high school course taught at the college level. The course is led by an instructor, who probably stands in front of you at least part of the time lecturing while you take notes. The course will end with an examination, on which you will compete with your fellow classmates to show your mastery of the material. You may also demonstrate what you have learned by writing papers, giving a speech, or debating with your fellow students. To succeed in the course, you will need to have developed certain patterns of behavior, such as coming to class and studying. If you are successful, you might go on to more advanced courses, in which you are taught more complex material and

can work on your own, doing research and extensive reading. This course is most likely part of a specified group of courses, such as general education requirements or requirements for a history major. These requirements are designed to give you knowledge and skills, and also to transform you into a well-educated person, someone who has read books judged worthy and understood ideas judged important. They thus reflect cultural values about what it means to be well-educated, as well as practical needs. At the end of this group of courses, you may go through a ceremony in which you and your instructors wear garments that indicate the level of your studies, and you may receive a certificate written in a language you do not normally speak indicating that you have successfully completed your studies. Even those of you who never see the inside of a classroom, but are using this book for a course delivered completely online,

[344]

might go through such a ceremony and receive such a certificate, often on paper designed to look antique.

The paper on which your diploma is printed is not the only thing about colleges and universities that is rooted in the distant past. Every aspect of courses, programs of study, requirements, ceremonies, and expectations noted in the first paragraph was shared by students eight hundred years ago. During the twelfth and thirteenth centuries, institutions of higher learning developed or expanded in many parts of the world, in which young men came together to study written texts judged authoritative and important. These institutions, which went by various titles usually translated into university, college, or academy in English, were designed to transmit a body of knowledge and cultural values from one generation to the next, provide students with skills that were judged politically and economically useful, and transform the best of those students into well-educated men. (Institutions of higher learning throughout the world were limited to male students until the nineteenth or twentieth century.) Individual scholars gained prominence through their teaching in these schools, where learning was based on memorization and interpretation of basic texts along with debate and argumentation. Student life was closely regulated, with rules designed to develop patterns of behavior that would contribute to students' success.

Your task in this chapter will be to analyze similarities and differences in the education offered at institutions of higher learning in the post-Classical era in three places widely separated geographically: southern China, Timbuktu in western Africa, and Paris in western Europe. What courses of study did they prescribe for students, and why? What was expected of a well-educated man, and what cultural values do these expectations reveal?

BACKGROUND

The first large institution in the world specifically devoted to the advanced education of young men—what would later come to be called a university—was in China. In 124 B.C.E., Emperor Han Wudi (140–87, the "Martial Emperor") established an imperial university at the capital at Xian designed to prepare talented young men to become officials and bureaucrats who could centralize and run the enormous empire. The university took the philosophy of Confucius (551–479 B.C.E.) as the basis for its curriculum. Confucius had lived during a turbulent period in Chinese history, and he decided that the best way to keep a society peaceful and prosperous was to make sure that all positions of power were held by wise and honest men. (Confucianism is sometimes called a religion, but it does not teach the worship of a god or gods and is more accurately called a philosophy or way of life.) Wisdom and honesty were to be found naturally in some individuals, but they could be further enhanced through education.

Chapter 12

The Well-
Educated Man:
Students and
Scholars in
China, Paris,
and Timbuktu
(1180–1600)

Thus the purpose of education was to produce a small and select group of highly qualified leaders dedicated to a life of service, and these leaders would provide advice and guidance to rulers and society at large. Under the leadership of this elite group of scholar-bureaucrats (sometimes also called "scholar-officials" or "literati" or, in Chinese, *shi* or *shidafu*) society would be a well-ordered hierarchy in which everyone was arranged in ranks and knew his or her place.

Confucius failed in his attempts to become just such an advisor, and his ideas were largely unknown when he died. The writings in which they were recorded, known as the *Analects* ("sayings") were not lost, however, and later Chinese thinkers, including those Han Wudi relied on to set up the university, recovered and built on Confucius's ideas. Education began with learning—often to the point of memorizing—the Confucian classics, which included learning how to write the thousands of characters in which they were written.

The imperial university had fifty students when it first opened, but the financial support for study that it offered and the possibility of a high-ranking government job for its graduates quickly drew talented students. By the end of the Han dynasty in 220 C.E. the number of government-supported students had reached 30,000. The fall of the Han dynasty brought disruption in the educational system that lasted for centuries, but the founders of the Song dynasty (960–1279) made a deliberate effort to revive and strengthen Confucian-style education and support Confucian teachings. They developed a three-tier system of civil service

examinations that tested knowledge in philosophy, law, and literature. Success in a local examination allowed a man to progress to the regional level, and success there could lead to a scholarship at the imperial university and the chance to take the national examination. These exams could be grueling, with candidates watched closely by guards to prevent cheating as they composed eight-part answers called "eight-legged essays" to literary and philosophical questions posed by the examiners.

Many of the successful scholar-bureaucrats came from wealthy noble families who could afford the best schools, but a few were bright commoners who rose in prominence on the basis of their ability, for affluent parents in expanding Song cities were willing to support their sons through this long process. Smaller universities and private academies (*shu-yuan*) were set up in many parts of China to train young men for these examinations, which were often staffed by teachers who had made it through the first two tiers but had failed to go on and secure a top degree and government employment. The development of woodblock-printed books dramatically lowered the cost of books and broadened access to texts at all educational levels.

The Mongols who ruled China during the thirteenth and fourteenth centuries replaced the Confucian scholar-bureaucrats with foreign administrators, but the Hongwu emperor (r. 1368–1398), who defeated the Mongols and founded the Ming dynasty, reestablished the imperial civil service examinations. Ming emperors also restored state support for students at the imperial university and many regional academies. From the fourteenth century through the early twentieth, boys (or their families) hoping to gain the government salary, official position, and special title that success in the national examinations could bring studied in academies and universities all over China. They studied classical works to provide content for their examination essays, and they also practiced calligraphy, poetry, and composition so that the form of their essay would catch the eye of examiners and allow it to rise above those of the tens of thousands of other students competing for the same opportunities.

Islam also promoted education based on a group of core texts, beginning with the Qur'an, which was revealed to Muhammad in Arabic, so that study of that language was central to all Muslim learning. Schools focusing on study of the Qur'an were established in many places where Islam spread, and institutions of advanced learning, called *madrasas,* were opened in larger cities and capitals throughout the Islamic world. *Madrasas* were usually funded by private endowments, for which their donors received spiritual benefits. By the twelfth century Islamic learning had spread to Timbuktu on the Niger River in West Africa, which was a center of trade for salt, textiles, gold, slaves, and metal goods. Teachers opened small schools in their own homes teaching basic reading in Arabic and recitation of the Qur'an, and scholars (*ulama*) began providing advanced philosophical, theological, and legal training at schools attached to several mosques.

The scholars of Timbuktu were supported by powerful rulers. In the 1320s, the emperor Mansa Musa (r. 1312–1337) made Timbuktu part of the Mali Empire, ordered the construction of a larger and more impressive mosque, and brought in scholars from Cairo and Baghdad, the oldest centers of Islamic learning. The Muslim scholar Ibn Battuta visited Timbuktu in the 1350s on one of his legendary journeys, though he was not particularly impressed with the city. During the next century, however, Timbuktu became an even more important center of Islamic scholarship and book production; manuscript books joined salt and gold as Timbuktu's most important commodities. In 1468, the city was conquered by Sunni Ali Ber (r. 1464–1493), the founder of the Songhay Empire along the Niger River. Though Sunni Ali Ber was officially a Muslim, he thought that the scholars of Timbuktu, many of whom were Arabs from North Africa and the Middle East, did not pay enough respect to the African religions people had followed before Islam came to West Africa. Sunni Ali threatened to arrest the Timbuktu scholars, and many of them fled the city, taking their manuscripts with them. The scholars returned when one of Sunni Ali's generals, Askia Muhammad Turé (r. 1493–1538), took over the throne in 1493. Later known as "Askia the Great," he thought that Islam would be more helpful in making the Songhay Empire strong and united than traditional religions, so he used Islamic scholars as advisors on legal and political matters, supported the building of mosques, and encouraged the writing of books on Muslim history and law.

Centers of learning in Timbuktu, of which the largest was that attached to

Chapter 12

The Well-

Educated Man:

Students and

Scholars in

China, Paris,

and Timbuktu

(1180–1600)

Sankore mosque in the north part of the city, are sometimes called universities, but they had no central administration, official curriculum, or buildings. They were organized around specific scholar-professors, who taught texts of their choosing in the courtyards and rooms of the mosque complexes or in their own homes. These scholars and their students produced and bought huge numbers of manuscripts during the thirteenth through the sixteenth centuries, of which about 700,000 survive in and around Timbuktu today. In his multivolume *Description of Africa* first published in 1550, Leo Africanus, a Spanish Muslim later baptized as a Christian and employed by the pope, wrote of Timbuktu: "Here are great store of doctors, judges, priests, and other learned men, that are bountifully maintained at the king's cost and charges. Hither are brought diverse manuscripts or written books, which are sold for more money than any other merchandise."[1] The city attracted scholars from North Africa and from towns further up the Niger River such as Jenne and Daikha, and it educated thousands of students. By the sixteenth century there may have been as many as 150 Qur'anic schools, with several hundred advanced students and scholars regarded as part of the *ulama*, the highly respected body of scholars.

Students began by studying Arabic and memorizing the Qur'an, and they then advanced to a second level studying other texts. They also studied practical courses in carpentry, business,

navigation, tailoring, or other subjects designed to give them skills with which they could support themselves. Students hoped they would eventually become officials supported by a government salary, but the number of graduates was always greater than the number of positions. As men learned in Islamic law (*imams*), they might still be called on to give legal opinions, and it was thought that their opinions would be fairer and more just if they did not depend on the patronage of the wealthy but earned their own living.

Especially able students moved on to a third level, in which they usually studied under one particular teacher and developed expertise in specific areas of Islamic law, philosophy, or theology. Students researched topics in the thousands of books that were held in various libraries in Timbuktu and then presented their ideas in public debates, where professors and other students queried and disputed them. Once a teacher decided a student had progressed far enough, he issued him an individual license to teach a particular text. Those who reached this higher stage were awarded special turbans, with various knots and circles with symbolic meaning.

Universities in Timbuktu flourished especially during the reign of Askia the Great, with Muslim rulers from throughout northern and western Africa seeking opinions from their scholars on legal and political matters. Timbuktu's reputation was captured in a West African proverb: "Salt comes from the north, gold from the south, and silver from the country of the white men. But the word of God and the treasure of wisdom are only to be

1. Leo Africanus, *The History and Description of Africa*, Vol. 3, trans. John Pory, Hakluyt Society, vol. 94 (New York: Burt Franklin, 1896), p. 825.

found in Timbuktu." The city's prominence ended when it was conquered and sacked by the Moroccan army in the 1590s, and many of its leading scholars were deported to Marrakesh, the capital of Morocco.

In Europe during the Classical Period education was handled by private tutors and small schools, and during the early Middle Ages most education was carried out by monasteries and convents, which gave children basic training in Latin and provided more advanced education for a few individuals who would become leaders in the Church or administrators for secular rulers. Education centered on the Bible and the works of Christian authors, though the writings of a few pagan authors, most prominently Aristotle, were also studied and copied. Beginning in the early eleventh century, bishops in the growing cities of France and Italy opened schools attached to their cathedrals that offered more advanced subjects. These cathedral schools took in boys and young men who had learned their Latin in monasteries or private schools, and they developed a curriculum based on the works of Christian and classical authors.

Like Timbuktu, the city of Paris was a center of trade and production by the twelfth century. It was the capital of the expanding kingdom of France and home to a powerful bishop, well-endowed monasteries, and many schools teaching basic Latin. In 1163, Bishop Maurice de Sully began building a new cathedral dedicated to the Virgin Mary ("Our Lady," or Notre Dame in French) on an island in the Seine River in the middle of the city. His cathedral school soon outgrew

other centers of learning in the city, and in 1200 it received a royal charter from the king of France. Popes as well as kings took an interest in the school, and they or their representatives issued statutes about the proper content of courses and methods of instruction. Students were drawn by excellent teachers and by the fact that only an official of the bishop, called the *scholasticus* or chancellor, had the authority to issue licenses to teach, which would allow them to offer classes once they had finished their studies.

The number of students spilled out from the island to the left bank of the Seine, which came to be known as the "Latin Quarter" after the official academic language. Special residence halls for students, called *colleges*, were opened, though, as in Timbuktu, the university itself had no classrooms and teachers simply taught in rented rooms. Students paid teachers directly for their classes, which were advertised by signs noting their location, cost, and special features. As the number of students in Paris increased, the teachers joined together into a "universal society of teachers," or *university* for short. Believing that the chancellor often either granted the right to teach to unqualified parties or simply sold licenses outright, they began to require that prospective teachers pass an examination set by the university besides getting the chancellor's approval. This certificate to teach, which was the earliest form of academic degree, granted the holder one of the titles, *master* or *doctor*, that we still use today. (Bachelor's degrees were to come later.) Men with doctoral degrees were allowed to wear garments trimmed in velvet, a cloth usually reserved for the

Chapter 12

The Well-

Educated Man:

Students and

Scholars in

China, Paris,

and Timbuktu

(1180–1600)

nobility. Most of the students studied theology, and Paris became the model for later universities such as Oxford and Cambridge in England and Heidelberg in Germany.

In Paris, as in China and Timbuktu, learning centered on hard, close drill of the works of standard authorities. Professors lectured on these texts, and students copied the text itself and the professors' comments. During the thirteenth century, professors at Paris developed the "scholastic method" of argument, which applied logic to theological and philosophical questions. Students were attracted by the logical and rhetorical skills of certain teachers, who used the scholastic method to address seeming contradictions between the ideas of various authorities on basic issues like the relationship between reason and faith or the omnipotence of God. More advanced students used this method to develop elaborate arguments, and they presented these at oral disputations, which were eagerly attended by other students as a welcome break from formal lectures.

THE METHOD

To answer the central questions in this chapter, you will be using different types of sources that discuss courses of study and set out expectations for students and for the well-educated man. Some of these are philosophical statements that directly discuss the purposes of education. Others are regulations for students and teachers that describe how and what they should study and how they should behave while studying or teaching. These rules, which were all drawn up by those in charge of educational institutions, reveal their ideas of the qualities they were trying to instill in their students as they attempted to transform them into model scholars. Others are biographies of individuals held up as models of the perfect scholar that discuss their course of study and personal characteristics. These biographies do not directly say, "Students should do this or this" or "Education should accomplish this" or "Education should accomplish this or this" the way that regulations do, but they give a clear indication of the ideal educated man. Thus even though they are *descriptive* sources, tracing the life of a particular individual, they are also obliquely *prescriptive,* setting out an exemplary standard of behavior for others to follow.

This chapter asks you to analyze similarities and differences in higher education in three different geographic areas on two different questions. Thus it might be helpful before you begin reading to make a simple six-cell chart, with the three areas—China, Timbuktu, and Paris—as vertical columns and the two questions—courses of study and cultural values—as horizontal rows. Each of the sources contains information on both questions, so as you read, jot information in the appropriate place on the chart. Organizing your findings in this way will make your final comparisons easier. Information on courses of study is stated quite directly in the sources; information on cultural values and expectations emerges somewhat indirectly, so you will need to evaluate the sources more carefully to fill in this row on your chart.

Sources 1 to 3 come from China. Sources 1 and 2 were written by Zhu Xi (1130–1200), the most influential neo-Confucian scholar of the Song dynasty, whose ideas became an essential part of all discussions of education in China for centuries. Zhu Xi wrote, compiled, or edited nearly one hundred books, established or reestablished academies in several places, served as an official, and had a huge group of disciples, who recorded thousands of conversations with him on many subjects. He wrote on practical and ethical matters such as the proper way to celebrate family rituals, and also on abstract philosophical issues, such as the relation between mind and heart and the ultimate nature of things. In 1180, he helped revive the White Deer Grotto Academy near the city of Nanchang in Jiangxi province in southern China, which had fallen into ruins. He raised money to build new buildings and buy books, and he reorganized the academy based on his own teachings.

Source 1 is a set of guidelines written by Zhu Xi posted on the wall of the academy when it reopened; the first part consists of quotations from the works of Confucius and other classics, and the second of Zhu's own ideas about the goals of learning. What does he see as the most important values that students should learn? What are the best ways to learn these? What qualities would a well-educated man exhibit, in Zhu's opinion?

Source 2 is from Zhu Xi's proposals for the reform of education at academies and universities throughout China, written in 1195. What was good about education in the past, and wrong about education now? What subjects and texts should be studied, and why? What should students avoid doing? Why does he think it was important that students all study the views of earlier scholars and follow one particular school of interpretation?

In 1315, the educational reformer Cheng Duanli (1271–1345) attached several of Zhu Xi's writings (including the *Articles of the White Deer Grotto Academy*) to his extensive *Schedule for Learning*, which became a model for students. Source 3 includes the preface to this work and also another work that Cheng Duanli included in his first chapter, the "School Regulations Established by Masters Cheng and Dong," drawn up by two of Zhu Xi's followers to set out the procedures in their school. Like Zhu Xi, Cheng Duanli also thinks that education in his own day had serious problems. In the preface, what does he see as wrong? How could improvements be made, and what would be the result? The "School Regulations Established by Masters Cheng and Dong" gives quite detailed rules for student conduct. How would you describe the ideal student based on these rules? How does this fit with the ideals set out by Zhu Xi in the rules for the White Deer Grotto Academy?

Rules for students similar to those in China are not available for Timbuktu, but information about courses of study, cultural values, and ideals for behavior can be found in many biographies of revered scholars. Sources 4 and 5 are just such biographies. They are both included in the *Tar'rikh al-sudan*, a history of Timbuktu and the surrounding

Chapter 12

The Well-

Educated Man:

Students and

Scholars in

China, Paris,

and Timbuktu

(1180–1600)

area written around 1655 by Abd al-Rahman b. Abd Allah b. Imran al-Sadi (1594–1656?) a scholar, imam at a major mosque, and official in the Timbuktu government. Al-Sadi's history chronicles the rise and decline of the Songhay Empire and its eventual overthrow by the Moroccans. He also includes—with proper citation of his sources—several sections from the works of earlier scholars. The longest of these is a group of biographies of Timbuktu scholars taken from the biographical dictionary called *al-Dhayl* or *Kifāyat al-muhtāj*, written by the prominent scholar and jurist Ahmad Baba (1556–1627). Ahmad Baba was the son, grandson, nephew, and great-grandson of scholars. He studied and then taught in Timbuktu until he was exiled to Morocco in 1593, and he wrote more than fifty books over the course of his long career, some of which are still used by Islamic scholars. His library of 1,600 volumes was seized when he was arrested, though he was allowed to continue writing in Morocco, and eventually to return to Timbuktu.

In Source 4, Ahmad Baba describes his grandfather. What scholarly activities does he praise? What character traits? In Source 5, Ahmad Baba goes into great detail about his teacher Muhammad Baghayogho (1523–1594) and his course of study. What subjects did Baghayogho study and then teach, and how did the teaching day go? What personal characteristics did Ahmad Baba especially praise? What activities as a teacher? What cultural values would teachers like Baghayogho model and try to instill in their students?

Sources 6 through 8 come from Paris. Source 6 consists of the statutes issued

for the University of Paris by Cardinal Robert Courçon in 1215. Courçon, a representative of Pope Innocent III, took a special interest in the university and approved rules governing academic life. Innocent had been a student at Paris himself and wanted to ensure that the university's traditions continued. What does Courçon prescribe as the books to be read? Not to be read? How were students and teachers supposed to behave at promotions and meetings? How were the rules for teachers in the arts different from those for teachers in theology? Why do you think there was this difference, and what does it reveal about the values of those who ran the university?

Source 7 contains rules for licensing a student to teach issued by the Faculty of the Arts (which included Latin language and literature, philosophy, and natural history) and the Faculty of Medicine at the University of Paris. What procedures were established to make sure that the licensing was fair? Why do you think these were needed? What books were students in these two areas expected to have learned? What personal characteristics were they expected to demonstrate if they wanted to teach?

Source 8 is a series of rules governing life in one of the residential colleges at Paris, not the university as a whole. They were issued by Robert de Sorbon, the chaplain of King Louis IX, who established the college in the thirteenth century as a residence hall for students of theology. (By the sixteenth century, the word *Sorbonne* was used to describe the faculty of theology; since the nineteenth century the entire University of Paris has been called the

Sorbonne.) What aspects of student life did he regulate? What qualities did he attempt to encourage in the students living at his college? If students suc- cessfully internalized these qualities, what sort of well-educated men would emerge from Sorbon's college?

Sources 1 and 2 from William Theodore de Bary and Irene Bloom, eds., Sources of Chinese Tradition, *2d ed., vol. 1 (New York: Columbia University Press, 1999), pp. 743–744, 737–742. Copyright © 1999 Columbia University Press. Reprinted with permission of the publisher.*

1. Zhu Xi, *Articles of the White Deer Grotto Academy*, 1180

[*Zhu Xi lays out precepts from Confucius and others.*]

Affection between parent and child;
Rightness between ruler and minister;
Differentiation between husband and wife;
Precedence between elder and younger;
Trust between friends. [*Mencius* 3A:4][2]

The above are the items of the Five Teachings. . . . For those who engage in learning, these are all they need to learn. As to the proper procedure for study, there are also five items, as follows:

Study extensively, inquire carefully, ponder thoroughly, sift clearly, and practice earnestly. [*Mean* 20]

The above is the proper sequence for the pursuit of learning. Study, inquiry, pondering, and sifting are for fathoming principle to the utmost. As to earnest practice, there are also essential elements at each stage from personal cultivation to the handling of affairs and dealing with others, as listed separately below:

Be faithful and true to your words and firm and sincere in conduct. [*Analects* 15:5]

Curb your anger and restrain your lust; turn to the good and correct your errors. [*Yijing*, hexagrams 41, 42]

2. The items in brackets refer to the classical text Zhu is quoting: Mencius (390?–305?) is a Confucian philosopher; *Mean* is a Confucian text about moral human conduct; *Analects* are the main writings of Confucius; *Yijing* (also spelled *I Ching*) is the *Classic of Changes,* a very old text that provided advice for interpreting the future by consulting six-line symbolic diagrams called hexagrams.

Chapter 12

The Well-

Educated Man:

Students and

Scholars in

China, Paris,

and Timbuktu

(1180–1600)

The foregoing are the essentials of personal cultivation.

Be true to moral principles and do not scheme for profit; illuminate [exemplify] the Way and do not calculate the advantages [for oneself].

The foregoing are the essentials for handling affairs.

Do not do to others what you would not want them to do to you. [*Analects* 12:2; 15:24]
When in your conduct you are unable to succeed, reflect and look [for the cause] within yourself. [*Mencius* 4A:4]

The foregoing are the essentials for dealing with others.

[*Zhu Xi explains important points.*]

I [Zhu] have observed that the sages and worthies of antiquity taught people to pursue learning with one intention only, which is to make students understand the meaning of moral principle through discussion, so that they can cultivate their own persons and then extend it to others. The sages and worthies did not wish them merely to engage in memorizing texts or in composing poetry and essays as a means of gaining fame or seeking office. Students today obviously act contrary [to what the sages and worthies intended]. The methods that the sages and worthies employed in teaching people are all found in the classics. Dedicated scholars should by all means read them frequently, ponder them deeply, and then inquire into them and sift them.

If one understands the necessity for principles and accepts the need to take responsibility oneself for seeing that they are so, then what need will there be for someone else to set up such contrivances as rules and prohibitions for one to follow? In recent times regulations have been instituted in schools, and students have been treated in a shallow manner. This method of making regulations does not at all conform with the intention of the ancients. Therefore I shall not now try to put them into effect in this lecture hall. Rather, I have specifically selected all the essential principles that the sages and the worthies have used in teaching people how to pursue learning; I have listed them, as above, one by one, and posted them on the crossbar over the gate. You, sirs, discuss them with one another, follow them, and take personal responsibility for their observance. Then in whatever a man should be cautious or careful about in thought, word, or deed, he will certainly be more demanding of himself than he would be the other way [of complying with regulations]. If you do otherwise or even reject what I have said, then the "regulations" others talk about will have to take over and in no way can they be dispensed with. You, sirs, please think this over.

2. Zhu Xi, *Proposals for Schools and Official Recruitment*, 1195

In antiquity the method of selecting officials from the schools began with [schools] in the villages and communities and reached up to [the Imperial College] at the capital. Students were taught moral conduct and the [six] arts (*daoyi*), and those who were worthy and capable were promoted [to become officials]. There was just one place where students were educated, just one means by which they were made officials, and just one method by which they were selected. Therefore, scholars (*shi*) had a fixed purpose and suffered no distractions. They made diligent efforts from morning until night and were only concerned about failing in moral cultivation rather than possible failure in attaining office or emoluments.[3] This is what is meant by Confucius's saying "to have few errors in words and few regrets in conduct, one can find emolument [enough] in that" and by Mencius's saying that "[men of antiquity] cultivated heavenly rank [true nobility] and human rank followed after it." With respect to education in the Three Dynasties [Xia, Shang, Zhou], the applied arts were considered the least important. Nevertheless, they were practical and indispensable. As a systematic process this could help people to cultivate their minds and nourish their life force. Consequently people were able to make progress toward the goal of virtuous conduct. It was for this reason that the ancient system could develop human talents, enrich culture, regulate society's affairs, and bring about great peace. This is not so, however, of the present system. . . .

It has been my view that if one wants to take advantage of the present opportunity to reform the current system so as gradually to restore the ancient order of the Three Kings and improve today's customs, one must . . . establish moral conduct as a category in the examinations so as to give students a firm foundation; . . . abolish the composition of [*shi*] poetry in the examinations and instead . . . test on the classics, masters, histories, and current affairs in separate years so as to make students' learning complete. Moreover, students should be made to base themselves on a definite school of exegesis[4] (*jiafa*) in dealing with the classics, and examiners should see that they follow the correct punctuation of the text, that in their replies students show a thorough understanding of the text, and that they expound the various commentaries one by one before concluding with their own personal views. Moreover, in schools persons of authentic moral character should be chosen diligently to teach and guide students and to attract scholars who are committed to solid learning.

Then, having changed the system, you will have genuine commitment and not a spirit of opportunism, real practical conduct and not just empty words, solid learning and unfailingly useful talent. The foregoing is just an outline; the details follow. . . .

3. **emolument:** payment for work.
4. **exegesis:** interpretation.

Chapter 12

The Well-

Educated Man:

Students and

Scholars in

China, Paris,

and Timbuktu

(1180–1600)

2. The reason it is necessary to establish moral conduct as an examination category is that virtuous conduct has great importance for humankind. In fact, morality is inherent in human nature and is what is proper to the human Way. It is called virtue [*de*] because it is inherent [*de*] in the mind-and-heart. It is called conduct [*xing*] because it is carried out [*xing*] by the individual person. [Moral conduct] certainly is not an ornament one puts on in order to please others' eyes and ears. If scholars truly make an effort in this, they can not only cultivate their own persons but also extend it to governing others, the state, and all-under-Heaven. Therefore there was no educator in antiquity who did not consider moral conduct as the first priority. . . .

[4.] The learning of the masters originates from the same source as that of the sages. Each master has his strengths and shortcomings. One has to learn from their strengths and evaluate their shortcomings. The histories reflect changes in rise and decline, order and disorder, gain and loss from ancient times to the present. Matters of great importance, such as rituals and music, systems and institutions, astronomy, geography, military strategy, and penal codes, are indispensable in contemporary society and cannot be neglected. Students cannot afford not to study them. But it is impossible to require students to master all of these thoroughly in a short period of time, and it will not do to impose such a demand on them. However, if the books that students must study are divided and tested in different years, then it will not be too difficult to have all scholars master one third or one quarter of the requirements in three years. Therefore, I propose that the [*Classic of*] *Changes,* the [*Classic of*] *Documents,* and the [*Classic of*] *Odes* be considered one subject and be tested in the first and seventh year of the twelve-year cycle.[5] The *Rites of Zhou,* the *Ceremonial Rites* (*Yili*), and the *Rites of the Two Dai* are to be considered one subject and be tested in the fourth year.[6] The *Spring and Autumn Annals* and its three commentaries are to be one subject and be tested in the tenth year.[7] (The years of examinations should be the same as for provincial examinations, and there should be two questions about the meaning of each subject.) All examinations on the classics should include the *Great Learning,*[8] the *Analects,* the *Mean,* and the *Mencius.* (There should be one question about the meaning of each). Essay questions should consist of four subjects on the masters, which would be tested in different years. . . . [(]It should also be

---

5. *Classic of Documents*: a collection of speeches and pronouncements understood to have been made by the earliest Chinese rulers and their ministers, and edited by Confucius. The *Classic of Odes* is an anthology of poetry from the early Zhou dynasty (1100–256 B.C.E.).

6. *Rites:* collections of various texts, most dating from the Zhou dynasty.

7. *Spring and Autumn Annals:* a chronicle of events from 722 to 481 B.C.E.

8. *Great Learning:* a highly influential work written about 400 B.C.E. by a disciple of Confucius that links higher education in the individual with harmony and order in the family, the state, and the world.

permitted that two essay questions be asked in each year that the examinations deal with the histories and the annals.)

The policy questions should include histories and current affairs and be conducted in a similar manner. . . . In consequence of this, there would be no classic that a scholar had not mastered and no history that scholars had not studied. They will all be useful to present-day society.

5. The reason for dealing with the classics according to a particular school's method of exegesis is that while the principles of all-under-Heaven are not external to one's mind, the words of the sages and worthies, which contain profound meanings and require textual analysis, cannot be understood through mere conjecture. Moreover, the ancient institutions and ways of conducting affairs are not something we can now observe. Therefore those who study the classics must first have recourse to what earlier scholars have arrived at and then go on from there. Some might say that these [earlier] views are not without error, but still, one should examine the reasons why they may be correct or incorrect so that one can reflect on them in one's mind and correct any of their errors. . . .

In recent years the habits of scholars have become imprudent and reckless, and students have no focus or goal [in their studies]. Those who purport to deal with the classics no longer bother to read the original texts themselves or the commentaries of earlier scholars. They merely read and imitate essays that have been successful in the examinations in recent years. Then they compose practice essays on a theme selected from the classics and deliberately bend the original meaning of the text to suit their erroneous views. Although they know they distort the meaning of the classics, they care only about the flow of their prose, not the meaning of the texts. . . . Now the way to rectify the problem is, after considering various interpretations of the classics, to base oneself on a particular school's method (*jiafa*) for interpreting commentaries on the classics. . . .

The Imperial College in antiquity was created primarily for educating people, and the role it played in selecting scholars for office was secondary. For this reason, scholars who came to the Imperial College were motivated by rightness, not profit. . . . Since the Xining reign, [however,] the Imperial College has become a place where people strive for fame and profit. As for the instructors, they have been selected solely because of their skill in writing examination essays and winning some fame in the examination halls. . . . If one wishes to get rid of these evils . . . [o]ne should select scholars who have moral character and are qualified as teachers and appoint them to be school officials. They should be given long tenure and entrusted with expounding moral teachings to the students. . . .

If these proposals are adopted, one can expect that, with the teachings of the sages illuminated above and customs beautified among the people below, the way of the ancient kings will be restored to its [former] brilliance in the present age, and its beneficial legacy will reach on down to posterity.

Chapter 12

The Well-

Educated Man:

Students and

Scholars in

China, Paris,

and Timbuktu

(1180–1600)

3. Cheng Duanli, *A Schedule for Learning*, 1315

PREFACE

Nowadays, fathers and older brothers who wish to benefit their youngsters give them an education, and yet hardly two or three out of every ten of our youths actually achieve anything academically. This is not solely the fault of the youngsters and their teachers; the elders, for their lack of foresight, should also share the blame. Before the youngsters have studied and understood the nature of things, they are forced by their elders to compose essays. The teachers, though aware of the danger of such a practice, nevertheless wish to display their own talents; they are therefore willing to comply with such requests. In this way, the sequence of the learning process is confused. Instead of attaining their goals by a shortcut, the youngsters end up not getting anywhere at all. Not only are their writings worthless, but they usually do not even know one book thoroughly. Months and years go by; when they finally realize their mistakes and begin to regret them, they have become too old. Furthermore, when incorrect methods are used in the beginning, various wrong ideas are likely to stick because of the importance of first impressions. This in turn causes the students to wander on the periphery of true learning all their lives, ignorant of their own mistakes.

The sequence of teaching practiced by Confucius was as follows: first he made the students concentrate their minds on the Way; then he taught them virtues; then he made them act in accordance with the principle of humanity. Only after these principles had been incorporated in their daily lives did the students begin to study. In the *Rituals of the Zhou* the grand educator listed the six arts after the six virtues and six model behaviors, which clearly indicates the order of significance. Our present system of selecting government officials still regards personal virtue as the first criterion; next comes knowledge of the classics and the ability to govern, with writing ability as the last consideration. This is a very reasonable system. The examinations on the classics, furthermore, are based on the teachings of Master Zhu Xi, combining study of philosophy with advancement in officialdom, much to the benefit of those who devote themselves to the Way. This is what the civil service examinations of the Han, Tang, and Song dynasties lacked, and therefore scholars are now offered a rare opportunity. Unfortunately, our students fail to take advantage of this system.

Our students try to follow the teachings of Master Zhu in their study of the classics, yet they are ignorant of his method of study. Because they have no method, they tend to use flowery language to promote themselves. During the period when the teachings of Master Cheng flourished, Hu Wending lamented the wordiness of most people's writing. I fear that the same trend is returning in our time. To correct the situation, I have compiled a "Schedule for Learning," which I would like to share with my friends. This work is based on the selection of Master Zhu's method of study compiled by Fu Hanqing. I have also included other helpful theories by scholars in earlier eras.

In my humble opinion, if we wish to study the classics, to understand the nature of things, to be familiar with all political theories, to investigate our institutions, to be well versed in everything ancient and modern, to wield language at will, and finally, to popularize our discoveries and contributions throughout the entire nation, we should follow this schedule for learning. For it is the purpose of this work to differentiate between the essential and the trivial and to retain a proper order of progress. In this manner we will not forget what we have learned thoroughly, and we will review and reflect daily on what has not yet been fully digested until it becomes a part of ourselves. Eventually, mind and reason will become one, and a profound tranquillity will be achieved amidst constant changes and movements. There will be a convergence of the self and the Way, and virtues will be reflected naturally in our discourse and writings, which will become models for our contemporaries as well as for posterity. Our method is thus not to be compared with the ordinary methods of studying one narrow subject.

Written by Cheng Duanli, in the eighth month, 1315, at the Academy for Establishing Virtue in Chizhou.

SCHOOL REGULATIONS
ESTABLISHED BY MASTERS
CHENG AND DONG

All students of this school must observe closely the following regulations.

1. *Ceremonies held on the 1st and 15th of every month.* At daybreak, the student on duty for that day will sound his clappers. At the first round of the clappers, you should rise, wash your face, comb your hair, and put on proper clothing. By the second round of the clappers, you should be dressed either in ceremonial robes or in summer robes and gather in the main hall. The teachers will then lead you to the image of Confucius, to which you will bow twice. After the incense has been lit, you will make two more bows.

Afterwards, the teachers walk over to the southwestern corner, and you line up in order of your ages in the northeast. Then you pay respect to the teachers by making two bows to them, while the teachers accept the salutation, standing erect. An older student then comes forward and delivers a short greeting; this is followed by two more bows to the teachers. Afterwards, the teachers retire into a room, and you form a circle and bow to each other twice. When this is done, you go to your seats.

2. *Daily salutations held in the morning and in the evening.* On ordinary days, the student on duty sounds the clappers as described above. At the second

Chapter 12

The Well-

Educated Man:

Students and

Scholars in

China, Paris,

and Timbuktu

(1180–1600)

round of the clappers you will enter the hall and line up to wait for the teachers to come out. Then the teachers and you bow to each other with hands folded in front. Next, you divide into two groups and bow to each other, after which you begin your daily studies.

At night, before bedtime, the clappers are sounded again. You must all gather to repeat the same ceremony as in the morning.

Whenever there is an assembly of students, such as at a group lecture, a dinner, or a tea, the salutations are the same as just described. For a lecture, you should wear ceremonial robes or summer robes. For all other occasions you may dress less formally.

3. *Daily behavior.* You should have a defined living area. When in a group you will be seated according to your ages. When sitting, you must straighten your backs and sit squarely in the chair. You should not squat, lean to one side, cross your legs, or dangle your feet. At night, you should always wait for the elders to go to bed first. After they are in bed, you should keep quiet. Also, you should not sleep during the day.

4. *Gait and posture.* You should walk slowly. When standing, keep your hands folded in front. Never walk or stand in front of an elder. Never turn your back on those who are your superiors in age or status. Do not step on doorsills. Do not limp. Do not lean on anything.

5. *Looking and listening.* Do not gape. Do not eavesdrop.

6. *Discourse.* Statements should always be verifiable. Keep your promises. Your manners should be serious. Do not be boisterous or playful. Do not gossip about your neighbors. Do not engage in conversations about vulgar matters.

7. *Appearance.* Be dignified and serious. Do not be insolent. Do not be rough or rude. Do not be vicious or proud. Do not reveal your joy or anger.

8. *Attire.* Do not wear unusual or extravagant clothing. Yet do not go to the other extreme and appear in clothes that are ragged, dirty, or in bad taste. Even in your private quarters you should never expose your body or take off your cap. Even in the hottest days of summer you should not take off your socks or shoes at will.

9. *Eating.* Do not fill yourself. Do not seek fancy foods. Eat at regular hours. Do not be discontent with coarse fare. Never drink unless on a holiday or unless you are ordered to do so by your elders. Never drink more than three cups or get drunk.

10. *Travel.* Unless you are called upon by your elders, ordered to run errands by your teachers, or faced by a personal emergency, you are not allowed to leave the school grounds at will. Before your departure and after your return you should report to your teacher. You must not change your reported destination, and you must return by the set time.

11. *Reading.* You should concentrate on your book and keep a dignified appearance. You should count the number of times you read an assigned piece.

If, upon completion of the assigned number, you still have not memorized the piece, you should continue until you are able to recite it. On the other hand, if you have memorized the piece quickly, you should still go on to complete the assigned number of readings.

Only after a book has been thoroughly learned should you go on to another. Do not read too many things on a superficial level. Do not attempt to memorize a piece without understanding it. Read only those books which expound virtues. Do not look into useless writings.

12. *Writing.* Do not scribble. Do not write slanted or sloppy characters.

13. *Keep your desk tidy.* The assigned seats should be kept in order. Your study area should be simple but tidy. All book chests and clothing trunks should be locked up carefully.

14. *Keep the lecture halls and private rooms clean.* Each day one student is on duty. After sounding the second round of the clappers, he should sprinkle water on the floor of the lecture hall. Then, after an appropriate wait, he should sweep the floor and wipe the desks. The other cleaning jobs should be assigned to the pages. Whenever there is cleaning to be done, they should be ordered to do it, regardless of the time of the day.

15. *Terms of address.* You should address those who are twice your age as "elder," those who are ten years older than you as "older brothers," and those who are about your age by their polite names. Never address one another as "you." The same rules should be followed in letter writing.

16. *Visits.* The following rules should be observed when a guest requests to visit the school. After the teacher is seated and the student on duty has sounded the clappers, all students, properly dressed, enter the lecture hall. After the morning salutation, the students remain standing; only when the teacher orders them to retire may they leave. If the guest should wish to speak to a student privately, he should, after seeing the teacher, approach the student at his seat. If the student finds the visitor incompatible, he is not obliged to be congenial.

17. *Recreational.* There are rules for the playing of musical instruments, for archery, as well as for other games. You should seek recreation only at the right time. Gambling and chess games are lowly pastimes and should be avoided by our students.

18. *Servants.* Select those who are prudent, honest, and hardworking. Treat them with dignity and forbearance. When they make mistakes, scold them or report to the teacher. If they do not improve after being punished, report to the teacher to have them discharged. A student should not expel his page at will.

If you can follow the above regulations closely, you are approaching the true realm of virtue.

Chapter 12

The Well-

Educated Man:

Students and

Scholars in

China, Paris,

and Timbuktu

(1180–1600)

Sources 4 and 5 from John O. Hunwick, Timbuktu and the Songhay Empire: Al-Sa'di's Ta'rikh al-sudan Down to 1613. *Copyright Leiden: Brill, 2003, pp. 52–53, 62–68. Reprinted by permission of Koninklijke Brill NV.*

4. Description of Ahmad al-Tinbuktī, from Ahmad Baba, *al-Dhayl*, ca. 1600

Aḥmad b. ʿUmar b. Muḥammad Aqīt b. ʿUmar b. ʿAlī b. Yaḥyā b. Guddāla al-Ṣanhājī al-Tinbuktī, my grandfather, the father of my father, know as *al-hājj* Ahmad.[9] He was the eldest of three brothers celebrated in their region for learning and religion, a man of goodness, virtue and religious faith, upholding the Sunna,[10] practising manly virtues and chaste behaviour, scrupulous [in his conduct], a man who loved the Prophet—may God bless him and grant him peace—and continuously devoted himself to reciting poems in his praise. . . . He was a jurist, a lexicologist, a grammarian, a prosodist, and a man who avidly sought after knowledge his whole life, being the owner of many books which he had copied in his own hand and annotated. He left some seven hundred volumes.

He studied under his maternal grandfather, the jurist Anda Ag-Muḥammad, and his maternal uncle, the jurist al-Mukhtār al-Naḥwī, and others. In the year 890/1485 he travelled to the east and performed the pilgrimage, coming into contact with [Egyptian scholars]. He returned during the time of upheaval . . . caused by the tyrant . . . Sunni ʿAlī, and went to Kano and other cities of the land of Sūdān. Many people benefitted from his teaching of the Islamic sciences, the most illustrious of them being the jurist Maḥmūd b. ʿUmar, who read the *Mudawwana* with him.[11] He exerted himself to gain knowledge of the Islamic sciences and to teach them right down to his death, which occurred on a Friday night in Rabīʿ II 943 [1536],[12] at about the age of eighty. He was invited to be imam of the mosque but he declined the post, and others as well.

One of his most celebrated manifestations of divine grace occurred when he visited the Noble Tomb [of the Prophet] and asked to be allowed to go inside. When the guardian refused him, he sat down outside the tomb praising the Prophet—may God bless him and grant him peace—and the door opened of itself, without any agent, and people rushed to kiss his hand. This is how I heard the account from a group of people.

9. *al-hājj:* honorary title given to those who have fulfilled the religious duty of a pilgrimage to Mecca.

10. **Sunna:** code of behavior for Sunni Muslims.

11. *Mudawwana:* a collection of legal problems and solutions.

12. Dates are given according to the Muslim and Christian calendars.

5. Description of Muhammad Baghayogho, from Ahmad Baba, *al-Dhayl*, ca. 1600

Muḥammad b. Maḥmūd b. Abī Bakr al-Wangarī al-Tinbuktī, known as Baghayogho. . . . Our shaykh and our [source of] blessing, the jurist, and accomplished scholar, a pious and ascetic man of God, who was among the finest of God's righteous servants and practising scholars. He was a man given by nature to goodness and benign intent, guileless, and naturally disposed to goodness, believing in people to such an extent that all men were virtually equal in his sight, so well did he think of them and absolve them of wrongdoing. Moreover, he was constantly attending to people's needs, even at cost to himself, becoming distressed at their misfortunes, mediating their disputes, and giving counsel.

Add to this his love of learning, and his devotion to teaching—in which pursuit he spent his days—his close association . . . with men of learning, and his own utter humility, his lending of his most rare and precious books in all fields without asking for them back again, no matter what discipline they were in. Thus it was that he lost a [large] portion of his books—may God shower his beneficence upon him for that! Sometimes a student would come to his door asking for a book, and he would give it to him without even knowing who the student was. In this matter he was truly astonishing, doing this for the sake of God Most High, despite his love for books and [his zeal in] acquiring them, whether by purchase or copying. One day I came to him asking for books on grammar, and he hunted through his library and brought me everything he could find on the subject.

He also had enormous patience in teaching throughout the entire day, and was able to get his matter across to even the dull-witted, never feeling bored or tired, so that others attending his class would grow fed-up, whilst he would remain so unruffled that I once heard one of our colleagues say, "I think this jurist must have drunk Zamzam water so that he would not get fed-up during teaching," so greatly did his patience surprise him.[13]

With all this he was constant in his devotions, shunning immorality, thinking well of all mankind, even oppressors, minding his own business, and eschewing curiosity over what was not his concern. He wore the finest cloak of decency and humbleness, and bore in his hand the firmest banner of integrity. These qualities were matched by his tranquillity, dignity, shyness and good moral qualities, which made all dealings with him easy. All men's hearts were possessed by love for him, and they lauded him with one accord. You could find no one who did not love him, giving him sincere praise and showing admiration for his good qualities.

---

13. **Zamzam:** the well inside the Sacred Mosque in Mecca. Its water is reputed to have miraculous properties. Pilgrims often return home with a small bottle of it.

Chapter 12

The Well-

Educated Man:

Students and

Scholars in

China, Paris,

and Timbuktu

(1180–1600)

Muḥammad Baghayogho was long-suffering as a teacher, disdaining neither the beginner nor the dull-witted. Indeed, he devoted his whole life to teaching, even while faithfully attending to the needs of the common man, and to judicial matters, since they found no one to emulate him or replace him. The sultan invited him to accept appointment as *qāḍī* [judge] of his capital [Gao], but he scorned the offer, holding himself aloof from it. He asked someone to intervene on his behalf, and God Most High spared him from it.

He devoted himself to teaching. . . . When I first came in contact with him he was teaching various classes at the beginning of his day from the hour of the early morning worship until mid-morning. Then he would go to his house and perform the mid-morning worship . . . , remaining a while, and after that sometimes going to the *qāḍī* to plead for people, or to effect a reconciliation. During the noon hour, he would teach in his house, lead people in the midday worship, and then give instruction again until the mid-afternoon worship. After this, he would go out to teach in some other place until dusk or thereabouts. After the sunset worship he would teach in the mosque until the evening worship, then return home. I heard that he always used to spend the last part of the night in devotions.

He was a [scholar] of sound and precise knowledge, and rapid comprehension, intelligent and astute, who delved into the finer points, and had a ready response and a swift understanding. A man of illuminated inner vision, he was taciturn and grave. Sometimes he would open himself up to people, while on others he would be harsh with them. His excellent understanding and swift comprehension were legendary. He studied jurisprudence with his father and his maternal uncle, two righteous jurists. Then he and his brother, the righteous jurist Aḥmad, settled in Timbuktu, where they followed Aḥmad b [Muḥammad b.] Saʿīd's teaching of the *Mukhtaṣar* of Khalīl.[14] Together they then travelled to perform the pilgrimage with their maternal uncle, and met with [many legal scholars]. . . .

After their pilgrimage and the death of their maternal uncle, they returned and took up residence in Timbuktu. Under [Aḥmad b. Muḥammad] b. Saʿīd they studied jurisprudence and *ḥadīth*, reading with him the *Muwaṭṭa*,[15] . . . the *Mukhtaṣar*, and other works, following his teaching devotedly. Under my respected father they studied the principles [of jurisprudence], rhetoric and logic. . . .

Besides all this he devoted himself to teaching until finally he became the unparalleled shaykh of his age in the various branches of learning. I remained attached to him for more than ten years, and completed with him the *Mukhtaṣar* of Khalīl in my own reading and that of others some eight times. I completed with him the *Muwaṭṭa,* reading it for comprehension, as well as the *Tas'hīl* of Ibn Mālik,[16] spending three years on it, in an exhaustive analytical study. . . .

14. ***Mukhtasar of Khalīl:*** compendium of law in the Maliki tradition of legal thought, dominant in northern and western Africa.

15. ***Muwatta:*** primary legal text of the founder of the Maliki tradition, Ibn Mālik b. Anas (d. 179/796).

16. ***Tas'hīl:*** another of Ibn Mālik's works.

. . . I undertook exegesis of the Mighty Qurʾān with him to part way through [the seventh chapter]. . . .

In sum, he is my shaykh and teacher; from no one else did I derive so much benefit as I did from him and from his books—may God Most High have mercy on him and recompense him with Paradise. He gave me a licence in his own hand for everything for which he had a licence and for those works for which he gave his own. I drew his attention to one of my writings, and he was pleased with it, and wrote praise of it in his own hand; indeed, he wrote down portions of my scholarly research, and I heard him quoting some of it in his classes, for he was fair-minded and humble, and ready to accept the truth from wherever it came.

He was with us on the day of the tribulation,[17] and that was the last time I saw him. I heard later that he had died on Friday [19th] Shawwāl, 1002/8 July 1594. He had been born in 930/1523–4.

Source 6 from Dana Carleton Munro, ed. and trans., Translations and Reprints from the Original Sources of European History, *vol. 2, no. 3 (Philadelphia: University of Pennsylvania Press, no date), pp. 12–15.*

6. Statutes for the University of Paris Issued by Robert Courçon, 1215

R., servant of the cross of Christ, by the divine mercy cardinal priest of the title of St. Stephen in Monte Celio and legate of the apostolic seat, to all the masters and scholars at Paris—eternal safety in the Lord.

Let all know, that having been especially commanded by the lord pope to devote our energy effectively to the betterment of the condition of the students at Paris, and wishing by the advice of good men to provide for the tranquillity of the students in the future, we have ordered and prescribed the following rules: No one is to lecture at Paris in arts before he is twenty-one years old. He is to listen in arts at least six years, before he begins to lecture. He is to promise that he will lecture for at least two years, unless he is prevented by some good reason, which he ought to prove either in public or before the examiners. He must not be smirched by any infamy. When he is ready to lecture, each one is to be examined according to the form contained in the letter of lord P. bishop of Paris (in which is contained the peace established between the chancellor and the students by the judges appointed by the lord pope, approved and confirmed namely by the bishop and deacon of Troyes and by P., the bishop, and J., the chancellor of Paris).

The treatises of Aristotle on logic, both the old and the new, are to be read in the schools in the regular and not in the extraordinary courses. The two

17. **tribulation:** when Ahmad Baba and other scholars were arrested by the Moroccans.

Chapter 12

The Well-

Educated Man:

Students and

Scholars in

China, Paris,

and Timbuktu

(1180–1600)

Priscians,[18] or at least the second, are also to be read in the schools in the regular courses. On the feast-days nothing is to be read except philosophy, rhetoric, *quadrivialia*,[19] the Barbarism, the Ethics, if they like, and the fourth book of the Topics. The books of Aristotle on Metaphysics or Natural Philosophy, or the abridgements of these works, are not to be read, nor the writings of Master David of Dinant, the heretic Amauri, or the Spaniard Mauricius.[20]

In the promotions and meetings of the masters and in the confutations or arguments of the boys or youths there [shall be no drinking]. But they may call in some friends or associates, but only a few. We also advise that donations of garments and other things be made, as is customary or even to a greater extent, and especially to the poor. No master lecturing in arts is to wear anything except a cope,[21] round and black and reaching to the heels—at least, when it is new. But he may well wear a pallium.[22] He is not to wear under the round cope embroidered shoes and never any with long bands. . . .

Each master is to have jurisdiction over his scholars. No one is to receive either schools or a house without the consent of the occupant, if he is able to obtain it. No one is to receive a license from the chancellor or any one else through a gift of money, or furnishing a pledge or making an agreement. Also, the masters and students can make among themselves or with others agreements and regulations, confirmed by a pledge, penalty or oath, about the following matters: namely, if a student is killed, mutilated or receives some outrageous injury—if justice is not done; for fixing the prices of lodgings; concerning the dress, burial, lectures, and disputations; in such a manner, however, that the university is not scattered or destroyed on this account.

We decide concerning the theologians, that no one shall lecture at Paris before he is thirty-five years old, and not unless he has studied at least eight years, and has heard the books faithfully and in the schools. He is to listen in theology for five years, before he reads his own lectures in public. No one of them is to lecture before the third hour on the days when the masters lecture. No one is to be received at Paris for the important lectures or sermons unless he is of approved character and learning. There is to be no student at Paris who does not have a regular master.

18. **Priscian:** a Roman grammarian whose two works, *Priscian minor* and *Priscian major*, presented models of correct letters and legal documents.

19. *quadrivialia:* the four more advanced fields of study within the seven liberal arts: arithmetic, geometry, astronomy, and music.

20. Aristotle's treaties on metaphysics and natural philosophy were forbidden by the pope because they stated that the world was eternal (rather than created by God) and that the human soul was not immortal. The last three authors the Church regarded as heretics.

21. **cope:** a long cloak or cape.

22. **pallium:** a white stole usually worn by popes and archbishops as a symbol of their authority. In this case, a master teacher was allowed to wear one as an indication of his level of academic achievement and its corresponding institutional authority; the pallium thus served a function similar to the master's or doctoral hood.

Sources 7 and 8 from Lynn Thorndike, ed. and trans., University Records and Life in the Middle Ages *(New York: Columbia University Press, 1944), pp. 52–55, 81–82, 92–98. Copyright © 1944 Columbia University Press. Reprinted by permission of the publisher.*

7. Rules for Licensing a Student to Teach at the University of Paris

[In the Faculty of Art, 1252]

In the year since the Incarnation, 1251, the masters of the English nation,[23] teaching in arts at Paris and for the good of the university and of learning taking multifold measures, and by God's grace continuing in the future without diminution, decreed by their common counsel and that of good men the form noted below for bachelors in arts determining in Lent,[24] as is the custom. In the first place the proctor, touching the Bible, shall select two persons whom he believes qualified to choose examiners of those determining, who, touching the Bible, shall swear that without hate or love of any person or any part of their nation, they will choose three masters, whom they know to be strict and qualified in examining faithfully, more intent on the promotion and advantage of the university, less susceptible to prayer or bribe. These three when chosen shall similarly swear on the Bible that they will faithfully examine and proceed with rigor of examination, licentiating the worthy and conducting themselves without hate of any person or group of their nation, also without envy or any rancor of mind or other sinister perturbation. Moreover, those who have insufficient standing in the examination and are unworthy to pass they shall fail, sparing no one, moved neither by prayer nor bribe nor fear nor love or any other occasion or indirect favor of persons.

The masters presenting candidates, moreover, and the bachelors themselves shall give personal security that they will make no entreaties on behalf of bachelors nor seek favor from the examiners or from the nation or from the university, either by themselves or through others, but will accept the simple statement of the examiners. By the same token, if it happens that bachelors are failed, that they will not bring . . . complaints or threats or other evils against the examiners, either by themselves or through others, because they ought to suppose that the examiners have acted according to their consciences and good faith for the honor of the university and the nation.

Moreover, a bachelor coming up for the licentiate in arts at Paris should be twenty years old or at least in his twentieth year, and of honorable life and laudable conversation. He should not have a cope without a hood of the same cloth,

23. **English nation:** one of the four divisions of the school of the arts at the University of Paris, loosely related to the origin of its teachers and students. The others were French, Norman, and Picard.

24. Determinations were long public debates in which bachelors (lower-level students) seeking a license to teach showed off their abilities. They were held during Lent, the forty days preceding Easter.

Chapter 12

The Well-

Educated Man:

Students and

Scholars in

China, Paris,

and Timbuktu

(1180–1600)

nor a hood with knots. He should not wear a mitre on his head in the classrooms while he is determining. . . . [He shall swear] that he has attended lectures in arts for five years or four at least at Paris continuously or elsewhere in a university of arts. Further, that he has heard the books of Aristotle on the Old Logic, namely, the *Praedicamenta* and *Periarmeniae* at least twice in ordinary lectures and once cursorily,[25] the *Six Principles*[26] at least once in ordinary lectures and once cursorily, the three first books of the *Topics* and the *Divisions* once in ordinary lectures or at least cursorily, the *Topics* of Aristotle and *Elenci* twice in ordinary lectures and once at least cursorily or if not cursorily at least thrice in ordinary, the *Prior Analytics* once in ordinary lectures and once cursorily, or, if he is now attending, so that he has heard at least half before Lent and is to continue, the *Posterior Analytics* once in ordinary lectures completely.[27] Also that he shall have heard *Priscian minor* (books 17–18) and the *Barbarismus*[28] twice in ordinary lectures and at least once cursorily, *Priscian major* (books 1–16) once cursorily. Also he shall have heard *De anima*[29] once or be hearing it as aforesaid. Also he shall give satisfaction that he has diligently attended the disputations of masters in a recognized university for two years and for the same length of time has answered as required. . . . in class. Also he shall promise that he will respond to questions for a full year from the beginning of one Lent to the beginning of the next. . . .

Also, it shall be enjoined on him that all through Lent, and thereafter so long as he shall belong to the faculty of arts as student or teacher, he shall obey the mandate of rector and proctor in lawful and honorable matters. Also he shall not give drinks except on the first day he begins to determine and the last, unless this is done by the permission of the rector or the proctor of his nation, who can give him a dispensation in this regard. . . .

Also, in addition to the aforesaid, after the candidates shall have been licensed, let them be present every Friday at the Vespers of the blessed Virgin and at mass the Saturday following, until Palm Sunday, under the penalty by which masters are bound.

[*In the Faculty of Medicine, 1270*]

Let it be known that bachelors in the faculty of medicine wishing to open a course for the first time are held on oath to all the following requirements. They shall give security that they will observe the ordinances, statutes, honors and customs of the faculty which shall be indicated to them by the dean or someone acting in the dean's place or by the whole faculty. Also they shall assure the dean . . . or before the whole faculty that they have attended lectures in medicine

25. Ordinary lectures were given by older and more respected professors and discussed a text in detail. Cursory lectures were shorter and more superficial, often given by younger professors with only a master's degree.

26. The *Book of Six Principles* was a study of logic by an unknown author.

27. Most of the books in this sentence are works by Aristotle on logic.

28. *Barbarismus:* a section on grammar and rhetoric from Donatus's *Ars Major*.

29. *De anima:* Aristotle's work in natural history.

for three years and are in their fourth year of which they have attended for five months. . . . Also, they shall swear that they responded twice concerning a question in the classes of two masters. . . . Also, they shall pledge that on each Sabbath day they will attend mass, just as masters do, so long as they are lecturing, this in penalty of twopence.

This is the form of licenciating bachelors in medicine. First the master in charge of the bachelor should testify to the chancellor in the presence of masters summoned for this purpose as to the fitness of the bachelor to be licensed. The duration of his attendance he ought to prove by two witnesses at least. . . . The form as to texts heard is that he should have heard twice in ordinary lectures the *Art of Medicine*[30] . . . ; the *Viaticum*[31] twice in ordinary lectures, the other books of Isaac[32] once in ordinary, twice cursorily. . . . Also he should have read one book of theory and another of practice. And to this he should swear; if, moreover, anyone is convicted of perjury or lying, he can be refused the licentiate.

8. Robert de Sorbon's Regulations for His College, Before 1274

I wish that the custom which was instituted from the beginning in this house by the counsel of good men may be kept, and if anyone ever has transgressed it, that henceforth he shall not presume to do so.

No one therefore shall eat meat in the house on Advent, nor on Monday or Tuesday of Lent, nor from Ascension Day to Pentecost.

Also, I will that the community be not charged for meals taken in rooms. If there cannot be equality, it is better that the fellow eating in his room be charged than the entire community.

Also, no one shall eat in his room except for cause. If anyone has a guest, he shall eat in hall. If, morever, it shall not seem expedient to the fellow to bring that guest to hall, let him eat in his room and he shall have the usual portion for himself, not for the guest. If, moreover, he wants more for himself or his guest, he should pay for it himself. . . .

Also, the fellows should be warned by the bearer of the roll that those eating in private rooms conduct themselves quietly and abstain from too much noise, lest those passing through the court and street be scandalized and lest the fellows in rooms adjoining be hindered in their studies. . . .

Also, the rule does not apply to the sick. If anyone eats in a private room because of sickness, he may have a fellow with him, if he wishes, to entertain and wait on him, who also shall have his due portion. What shall be the portion of a

---

30. **Art of Medicine:** perhaps the Greek physician Galen's major work, *Tegni.*

31. *Viaticum:* a Latin translation of a comprehensive medical textbook by the Muslim physician Ibn al-Jazzar.

32. Isaac Judaeus was a Jewish physician whose works had been translated into Latin.

Chapter 12

The Well-

Educated Man:

Students and

Scholars in

China, Paris,

and Timbuktu

(1180–1600)

fellow shall be left to the discretion of the dispenser. If a fellow shall come late to lunch, if he comes from classes or a sermon or business of the community, he shall have his full portion, but it from his own affairs, he shall have bread only. . . .

Also, all shall wear closed outer garments, nor shall they have trimmings of vair or grise[33] or of red or green silk on the outer garment or hood.

Also, no one shall have loud shoes or clothing by which scandal might be generated in any way.

Also, no one shall be received in the house unless he shall be willing to leave off such and to observe the aforesaid rules.

Also, no one shall be received in the house unless he pledges faith that, if he happens to receive books from the common store, he will treat them carefully as if his own and on no condition remove or lend them out of the house, and return them in good condition whenever required or whenever he leaves town.

Also, let every fellow have his own mark on his clothes and one only and different from the others. And let all the marks be written on a schedule and over each mark the name of whose it is. And let that schedule be given to the servant so that he may learn to recognize the mark of each one. And the servant shall not receive clothes from any fellow unless he sees the mark. And then the servant can return his clothes to each fellow. . . .

Also, for peace and utility we propound that no secular person living in town—scribe, corrector, or anyone else—unless for great cause eat, sleep in a room, or remain with the fellows when they eat, or have frequent conversations in the gardens or hall or other parts of the house, lest the secrets of the house and the remarks of the fellows be spread abroad.

Also, no outsider shall come to accountings or the special meetings of the fellows, and he whose guest he is shall see to this.

Also, no fellow shall bring in outsiders frequently to drink at commons, and if he does, he shall pay according to the estimate of the dispenser.

Also, no fellow shall have a key to the kitchen.

Also, no fellow shall presume to sleep outside the house in town, and if he did so for reason, he shall take pains to submit his excuse to the bearer of the roll. . . .

Also, no women of any sort shall eat in the private rooms. If anyone violates this rule, he shall pay the assessed penalty, namely, sixpence.[34] . . .

Also, if anyone has spoken opprobrious[35] words or shameful to a fellow, provided it is established by two fellows of the house, he shall pay a purse which ought to belong to the society.

Also, if one of the fellows shall have insulted, jostled or severely beaten one of the servants, he shall pay a sextarium of wine to the fellows, and this wine ought to be *vin superieur*[36] to boot. . . .

33. **vair:** squirrel fur. **grise:** any type of gray fur.

34. This was a substantial amount of money for most students.

35. **opprobrious:** scornful.

Also, at the deliberations of the fellows each shall peacefully remain silent until he has been called upon by the prior, and after he has had his say, he shall listen to the others calmly. . . .

Also, no one shall form the habit of talking too loudly at table. Whoever after he has been warned about this by the prior shall have offended by speaking too loudly, provided this is established afterwards by testimony of several fellows to the prior, shall be held to the usual house penalty, namely two quarts of wine.

The penalty for transgression of statutes which do not fall under an oath is twopence, if the offenders are not reported by someone, or if they were, the penalty becomes sixpence in the case of fines. I understand "not reported" to mean that, if before the matter has come to the attention of the prior, the offender accuses himself to the prior or has told the clerk to write down twopence against him for such an offence, for it is not enough to say to the fellows, "I accuse myself."

36. *vin superieur:* high-quality wine.

QUESTIONS TO CONSIDER

The questions for this chapter ask you to make comparisons, which involves finding both differences and similarities. Looking at your notes or the chart you have made, turn first to the question on the courses of study. Sources 2, 5, 6, and 7 all refer to specific books that students in China, Timbuktu, and Paris were to read; these are different books, but do you see certain similarities among them? What cultural values were expressed through the recommendation of these books? How do teachers present these texts to students? How does the normal day proceed? How would you compare the length of time students spent in advanced education in these three areas?

Sources 2 and 6 offer another point of comparison. In Source 2, Zhu Xi comments that students should all have masters and follow one particular school of interpretation, and in Source 6, Robert Courçon concludes with "there is to be no student at Paris who does not have a regular master." Why do you think they both regarded the link between student and teacher as so important? What evidence do you find in Source 5 of teacher-student links in Timbuktu?

Sources 5 and 7 discuss the ways in which students became teachers themselves. How would you compare these ways? What do you think are the reasons for the differences you find?

Sources 3 and 8 present regulations for many aspects of student conduct. What issues are similar in France and

Chapter 12

The Well-
Educated Man:
Students and
Scholars in
China, Paris,
and Timbuktu
(1180–1600)

China? Why do you think there is such concern about elaborate clothing, fancy foods, visitors, and boisterous behavior? What does the discussion of servants in each set of rules indicate about students? Now look for differences, or things that are mentioned in only one set of rules. What might these indicate?

There are often different ideas about the best way to facilitate student learning within any culture, and sometimes within the writings of one thinker. For example, at the end of Source 1, Zhu Xi comments that it is better if a student "accepts the need to take responsibility" for himself than if schools set up "such contrivances as rules and prohibitions." Yet in Source 2, he sets up quite specific rules, and by the time of Source 3—150 years later—Cheng Duanli uses "the teachings of Master Zhu Xi" as the source for his own rules. Why do you think Zhu's earlier words had been forgotten, by himself and his followers?

As you have worked through the sources relating to courses, books, and studying, you have learned many things about the ideals set for the perfect student. Many of these translated into ideals for the perfect scholar and well-educated man. Begin with similarities. What qualities do Zhu Xi, Cheng Duanli, Ahmad Baba, Robert Courçon, and the faculty of the University of Paris all prize in students and teachers? If Muhammad Baghayogho was really the person that Ahmad Baba described, what qualities would Zhu Xi find admirable in him? What might not be as noteworthy in a Chinese (or French) context?

Then move to differences, some of which may involve different understandings of the same word. How would, for example, *moral* or *virtuous* be understood differently in these three cultures? How did (or could) scholars demonstrate their virtue? Ahmad Baba finds humility and patience as important qualities in a scholar. Do these seem to have been as important in China or France? What does the pattern of similarities and differences reveal about the role of higher education, and about cultural values in these three areas?

In all three areas, organized higher education was limited to men, and schools were a place where boys were socialized into a certain ideal of masculinity. (The word *bachelor*, meaning "unmarried man," and *bachelor's degree* both come from the designation for the lowest level of knight or monk; at Paris and other European universities, students were prohibited from marrying, so they were bachelors in both senses of the word.) In Source 4, Ahmad Baba specifically describes his grandfather as "practicing manly virtues." What do these virtues appear to be in that source? What other indications do you find in the sources that these rules and statements were directed at men? A well-educated man was one who was different from women, of course, but also from other types of men. What do the sources portray as stereotypically masculine behavior that students or scholars should avoid or limit? What role did universities and academies play in establishing and enforcing gender norms, that is, ideas about the proper roles of men and women?

You are now ready to answer the questions for this chapter: What courses of study did they prescribe for students, and why? What was expected of a well-educated man, and what cultural values do these expectations reveal? In answering these questions, you have no doubt discovered differences among the three areas, as you might have expected given how widely they were separated, but also more similarities than you might initially have imagined there would be. What do those similarities suggest?

EPILOGUE

The patterns of learning and behavior that the institutions discussed in this chapter have had very long lives. The imperial examinations promising access to high official positions were held in China until the early twentieth century, and they serve as the basis for similar systems in the Republic of China (Taiwan) today. The centers of learning at Timbuktu largely disintegrated with the Moroccan invasions, but some scholars continued teaching, and since 2000 the Timbuktu Educational Foundation has been working to repair the buildings and reopen the university. It is also working to restore and preserve the hundreds of thousands of manuscripts that remain— many of them in the Ahmad Baba library—and to publish and translate the most significant of them. Scholars in western Africa are still understood to be part of the *ulama,* and they maintain *isnads,* lists somewhat like family genealogies that link them into chains of teachers and students back to the sixteenth century or even earlier. The University of Paris remains the most important university in France, and the "Latin Quarter" is still home to many students, though not many of them speak Latin. New disciplines have been added to its offerings, though not fast enough for many students; modernization of the curriculum was one of the demands of the 1968 student revolt in Paris. The robes specified in thirteenth-century Parisian ordinances can still be found on people with doctoral degrees around the world, complete with three bands of velvet on the sleeves.

Of course, the courses of study prescribed in the thirteenth century are not the only ones available for college and university students today, but they remain one option among many. You can certainly study the works of Confucius or Aristotle, and to reach an advanced level in these subjects you will need to learn classical Chinese or Greek. Islamic education around the world begins with the Qur'an, for which you will need to learn Arabic. Skills required of students have also remained strikingly similar. Though you might not compose "eight-legged essays," you have probably learned certain patterns for writing effective test answers or papers, such as an introduction, body, and conclusion.

What we might term extracurricular aspects of student life have not changed dramatically, either. The earliest prohibition of hazing freshmen dates from 1340 in Paris, which also orders anyone who "knows any person or persons to have afflicted bodily violence, threats

Chapter 12

The Well-

Educated Man:

Students and

Scholars in

China, Paris,

and Timbuktu

(1180–1600)

and any injury upon Freshmen because of their class" to report it and not be concerned about the disapproval of their fellow students if they did.[37] Nearly seven hundred years later, university administrators are still attempting to stop hazing, and also to limit excessive drinking, just as Robert de

37. Lynn Thorndike, *University Records and Life in the Middle Ages* (New York: Columbia University Press, 1944), p. 193. Copyright © 1944 Columbia University Press. Reprinted by permission of the publisher.

Sorbon and Masters Cheng and Dong did. Hazing, drinking, and many other things that are mentioned in the rules for students in this chapter are still considered expected behavior in young men, though today they are part of college life for many young women as well. Zhu Xi or Robert Courçon would no doubt be shocked by the presence of women as students and as teachers, but they might be comforted in knowing that so many other aspects of advanced learning have changed so little.

CHAPTER THIRTEEN

FACING THE BLACK DEATH

(1300–1400)

THE PROBLEM

Traditional accounts have often emphasized human decision making as the driving force of history. More recently, however, world historians have looked more closely at factors that lie outside direct control by individuals and societies, most notably the disease environments in which our ancestors lived. Outbreaks of epidemic disease have had a profound effect on human history since ancient times.

One of the best-known and best-studied examples is the terror of the Black Death, the epidemic of bubonic plague that struck Europe in the middle of the fourteenth century and killed somewhere between a quarter and a third of its people. Those who exhibited the telltale buboes usually had less than three days to live. Those who contracted the pneumatic form of the illness, spread by respiration from person to person, would be perfectly healthy one day and dead the next. "Ring around the rosies" shows how ancient memories of dramatic events can be retained in the popular imagination.

When the plague epidemic hit Europe in 1347–1348, people faced the crisis with little useful knowledge about how the plague was spread or how it could be treated. One thing they did know: The disease had come from the east. While most historical attention has been focused on the Black Death in Europe, historians have followed through on that single bit of knowledge and now understand that the fourteenth-century outbreak of the plague was a *pandemic*, that is, a widespread epidemic that struck most of Eurasia and North Africa almost simultaneously. The tragedy of the Black Death was not limited to a single corner of the world, and it has therefore become a major topic among world historians.

Where did the plague come from? Why did it arise so suddenly and spread so rapidly? What could be done about it? Societies across Eurasia and North Africa were faced with these questions in the fourteenth century. Your task in this chapter will be to examine a number of contemporary accounts of the Black Death drawn from both Christian and Islamic sources. How did these authors answer the questions posed above? What were some of the medical, religious, political, and economic reactions to the Black Death? Do you see any similarities between Christian and Muslim reactions? Or are there some fundamental differences in how people from the two religious traditions dealt with the plague?

BACKGROUND

The answers to some of these questions are not absolutely clear even today, but we certainly know a great deal more about bubonic plague than did the Asian, European, and African victims of the fourteenth-century pestilence. Much of our scientific knowledge about bubonic plague comes from studies conducted in the late nineteenth and early twentieth centuries. In the 1890s a devastating new outbreak of plague afflicted Asia; millions died in India and China. Stirred to action, bacteriologists identified the bacterium that causes bubonic plague and the cycle of infection that produces epidemics of the disease. Fleas drink the blood of infected rats, after which the bacteria multiply in the flea's gut. When the flea bites another rat, the bacteria are regurgitated into the open wound. Usually this cycle of infection is limited to fleas and their rodent hosts. Under special circumstances, however, the fleas jump from their rodent hosts and bite people instead.

Thus the spread of the bubonic plague in the 1890s, as in earlier epidemics, resulted from increasing human contact with infected fleas and rats. This knowledge, however, still does not explain why it is that in certain times and places bubonic plague spreads with such speed and ferocity. Plague-infested rodent populations have lived in close proximity to humans from time immemorial. In such areas plague is endemic, that is, always present. But its effects among humans are usually minimized and localized by the small size of the affected population, their lack of contact with the wider world, and popular knowledge of the local environment, which often permits the development of folk strategies that lessen human contact with infected rodents.

Plague becomes *epidemic*, spreading to previously unaffected areas, when these balances are upset. A sudden growth in the rat population, environmental changes that drive rats carrying infected fleas into closer contact with humans, economic or cultural changes that challenge the folk wisdom that had kept the plague at bay—all have been implicated in the spread of plague epidemics. Finally, in order for a pandemic to occur—for the plague bacillus to infect huge numbers of humans very suddenly across vast distances—even more substantial changes must have taken place in the interactions between humans and the environment and among different societies.

Such was indeed the case in the fourteenth century. One factor may have been environmental changes in Inner Asia. A period of drought may have forced infected rat populations into closer contact with human societies in search of food and water. But human actors were certainly involved as well, as we see in William McNeill's imaginative reconstruction.[1] In his view, it was the great Mongol warriors who unwittingly created the conditions for the Black Death. It was the Mongols' conquests and the vast expansion of trade that accompanied their empire building that facilitated the spread of plague from a localized outbreak in China in 1331, through the Central Asian steppes in the 1330s, to the ports of the Black Sea and the Mediterranean in the 1340s, and finally to the most densely populated areas of Europe, Western Asia, and North Africa in 1347–1348.

The Mongol era saw an unprecedented unification of Eurasia, not only militarily and politically, but commercially and even environmentally as well. This was the thirteenth- and fourteenth-century world in which famous travelers such as the Italian Marco Polo (1254–1324) and the North African Ibn Battuta (1304–1368) crossed from one end of Eurasia to the other with unprecedented ease. Little did the merchants and other intercontinental travelers realize that in their saddlebags and on their carts and ships, plague-infested fleas had stowed away, ready to spread the disease to rodents and humans at the other end of their journey. By 1339 the plague was found in Samarkand, a famous Central Asian stopping point on the Silk Road. By 1345 it had reached the Volga River and the Caucasus Mountains. By 1347 it had reached the ports of the Black Sea, Constantinople, and Alexandria, and within a year it had spread to Mecca, Damascus, Tunis, Venice, and Paris. Far-away London was hit in 1349. In all of these areas the plague led to a devastating loss of population: By some estimates, the population of Egypt did not return to its pre-1347 level until the nineteenth century. The effects of the Black Death in Europe were so fundamental that the pandemic is often cited as one of the main causes of the decline of feudalism and the rise of the new ideas and institutions that would usher in the modern age.

Very little of this was known to the victims of the Black Death. Yet they could not have been expected to accept this scourge without attempts to find an explanation and a remedy. What caused the plague, and what could be done about it? There was, of course, no single answer to these questions. A great deal depended on religious beliefs: The responses of Latin Christians, Orthodox Christians, Muslims, Jews, Zoroastrians, Buddhists, and followers of other faiths were at least partially determined by the specific traditions of their religions.

1. William H. McNeill, *Plagues and Peoples* (New York: Anchor, 1977).

In Western Europe, the Black Death struck at societies that had experienced several centuries of economic growth, population increase, and relative political stability. The "high middle ages" were a period of spiritual optimism, as demonstrated by the magnificent cathedrals erected in the twelfth through early fourteenth centuries. With the growth of cities came an expansion of long-distance trade; Europeans came into greater contact with the rest of the Eurasian world. They had no way of knowing that increased contact with the wider world would bring the danger of a plague epidemic.

The *Dar-al-Islam* ("Abode of Islam") was at the epicenter of political and military events in Eurasia, and was both more stimulated and more destabilized than Western Europe by Asian-centered events such as the rise of the Mongols and the coming of the Turks. When the Mongols overran Baghdad in 1258, they not only brought the Abbasid caliphate to an end but also severed a link of authority between the Prophet and the caliphs ("successors") that has never to this day been reestablished. Muslims in Western Asia had therefore experienced cataclysmic political change less than a century before the arrival of the Black Death. By the early fourteenth century, Muslims often felt a sense of faded glory, of the best times having already passed, whether one looked at the fairly recent fall of the Abbasid

caliphate or at the glorious time when the Prophet Muhammad ruled the *umma* (community) with a perfect mixture of spiritual and political authority. Though the demographic effects of the Black Death were quite similar in Europe and the Middle East, these differences of experience and outlook conditioned the responses of various societies to this crisis.

Generalizations are just that; we should not let them obscure the very real differences that occur within given societies and between particular individuals. Even within a single tradition, people reacted to the trauma of the Black Death quite differently, and popular responses were frequently quite different from the policies adopted by secular and religious authorities. In Western Europe, for example, groups known as *flagellants,* convinced that the plague was sent by God as a punishment for their sins, beat themselves bloody as a form of penance. Others sought solace and deliverance through quiet contemplation. In Islamic lands, some regarded the Black Death as a blessing, guaranteeing a place in heaven to those who suffered it in dignity as an unfathomable expression of God's will. But in these same societies there were also those who resorted to magic, trying to find some secret combination of words or numbers that would protect them. It is variations on these themes that you will explore in the readings that follow.

THE METHOD

As you consider the texts and images that follow, keep three side-by-side lists:

- On the first list, note every idea that you encounter that has to do with the *cause* of the pestilence. You may want to differentiate *ultimate* causes (e.g., divine intervention) from *immediate* causes (e.g., environmental factors and human activities).

- On the second list, write down every idea you find that has to do with the *consequences* of the plague for the societies and individuals concerned. You may want to differentiate the demographic, social and political, economic, religious, and psychological consequences of the Black Death as reported in the sources.

- On the third list, keep track of all the actions that are described or recommended for *curing* or in some other way *coping* with the Black Death. As you add items to this list, you may want to consider the question of how effective these measures might have been.

When you encounter the same idea in more than one document, make a note of how many times it occurs and whether it is found only in Christian documents, only in Muslim ones, or in both. When these lists are completed, you should have the material you need to make comparisons between the documents and to generalize about the main questions at issue: How did people interpret the causes of the plague, what were its effects, and how did people respond to this calamity?

The paragraphs below provide some historical context to help you make sense of each of the readings. You will want to refer back to this section as you consider the evidence.

The first document is taken from a book that many consider to be the greatest work of history written by a Muslim of this period, Ibn Khaldun's *Introduction to History* (Source 1). Ibn Khaldun, a well-known Arab philosopher, historian, and statesman, was centrally concerned with describing and analyzing various types of civilization; he anticipated the work of later world historians by placing a great emphasis on environmental conditions in explaining how different civilizations arise and develop.

The next three documents, by contrast, give us a much more immediate and intimate portrait of the plague as it affected three very different cities: Florence, Damascus, and Constantinople. Giovanni Boccaccio was a literary scholar as well as one of the great writers of his day. His *Decameron* (Source 2) is renowned for its glorious tales of late medieval Florentine life, for bringing us much closer to the real world of kitchens, bedrooms, shop fronts, and back alleys than any previous work in European literature. The *Decameron* is a work of fiction, but these opening pages, where Florentine reactions to the plague are described, have the ring of truth.

The passage from Ibn Battuta is similar to Boccaccio in its close description of civic reactions to the plague. The greatest of medieval Arab geographers, Ibn Battuta was one of the most widely traveled men of his age, and his *Travels in Asia and Africa* (Source 3) is an important source of information about the world of Islam in the fourteenth century. In this passage he describes a procession in the city of Damascus. Though he does not dwell on the fact, we know that Ibn Battuta was deeply affected by the Black Death: His own mother was carried away by the plague. Family tragedy also infuses the reading from Ioannes Cautacuzenos (Source 4), better known as the Byzantine Emperor John VI. Adronikos, the young man whose death is mentioned in this passage, was John VI's own son. In 1355, eight years after this tragic event, John VI abdicated his throne and retired to a monastery. This passage is taken from the history of the Byzantine Empire he wrote while in retirement. While the other documents in this chapter come from either the Latin Christian or the Islamic tradition, this one represents an Orthodox Christian viewpoint.

Among the major elements of the account of Jean de Venette, a Carmelite friar (Source 5), are the great importance that Christians placed on dying a "good death" and the challenges that the huge mortality of 1348 posed to their doing so. Sudden death and the possibility of burial in unconsecrated ground were particularly horrible for people who believed that an eternity in hell awaited any soul that was not adequately prepared. Jean de Venette also comments, like Boccaccio, on the effects of the epidemic on standards of social conduct and morality. It is also important to note that this account indicates that some believed that the

Black Death was caused by the evil actions of particular groups of people. The attacks on Germany's Jewish population that he describes are a chilling anticipation of the genocide that would take place six hundred years later; 1349 was neither the first nor the last time that one response to harsh times has been to find a scapegoat.

The next source is a visual one, a reproduction of a painting that is included because it gets at both human and cosmological dimensions of the Black Death as it was experienced in Europe (Source 6). In interpreting this painting, it might be helpful to think in terms of several sets of contrasts. First, compare the left and right sides of the lower part of the painting, with the corpse in the foreground as a bridge between the two. Second, compare the lower and upper portions of the painting. St. Sebastian, who is seen near the top of the painting in a position of prayer, was one of several saints who became identified as offering help to plague victims. Sebastian was a soldier in the Roman army who was put to death for his adherence to Christianity. St. Sebastian was always represented with arrows piercing his flesh, a torture equivalent to being pierced by the hidden arrows of the plague. (Muslims also made a connection between being shot with arrows and being infected by bubonic plague: There were those who thought that the disease entered the human body by being shot with invisible arrows by evil *jinn*, or spirits.) The prayer to St. Sebastian (Source 7) exemplifies the concept of the "intercession of the saints." If God himself seemed too distant to be appealed to directly, you could pray to a saint to intercede on your behalf.

The following four documents all relate to the Black Death in the Islamic world. The quotation from theologian and legal scholar Muhammad ibn Isma'il (Source 8), while very brief, is of the greatest importance. There is a strong tendency in Islam to judge current behavior and practice in relation not only to a sacred text but also to historical precedent. In addition to the Qur'an, the accounts of the life and times of Muhammad as given in the *hadith*, the stories of the Prophet's life collected and codified in later generations, give believers the guidance they need for correct behavior, individual as well as social and political, in almost every situation. While the Qur'an itself has little to say about the plague, the three statements from the hadith proposed by Ibn Isma'il helped establish an understanding of the plague that was shared by most Muslim theologians. They are therefore powerfully authoritative. Those in the Islamic world who thought differently had to justify their positions in relation to this orthodoxy. In contrast, Ibn al-Khatib's perspective (Source 9) is a medical one, and his conclusions do not necessarily conform to the orthodoxy. His perspective is that of a physician, interested in concrete causes and cures, rather than that of a lawyer or theologian interested in the interpretation of texts for their own sake.

In addition to the medical perspective, there were other Islamic responses to the Black Death. Mysticism and magic have long had a role in the Islamic world, and the catastrophe of the Black Death seems to have reinforced these trends. Muslims do not have saints to pray to, but in the Sufi brotherhoods they do have spiritual leaders whose blessings can continue even after death. Visiting the graves of departed holy men, while not sanctioned by some Islamic thinkers, became a much more common practice in this period. While Sufi mystics usually accept the basic theological premises of the Islamic legal traditions, they try to go beyond them by finding a direct connection with the Divine. Often this involves achieving a meditative state through constant repetition of one or more of the many names they attribute to God. It is possible that the surge of interest in Islamic mysticism in the late medieval period may be at least partly attributable to the spiritual quest of Muslims seeking solace from the harsh world of the plague.

The images reproduced in Source 10 point to another response to the plague: the use of cryptograms—combinations of numbers, letters, or words—to stave off the epidemic. Often these strategies relied on the use of specific Qur'anic verses or names for God. The use of devices such as amulets was not, of course, limited to the Islamic world. However, because Muslims are not allowed to find relief and help from the types of portraits and statues that were familiar to medieval Christians, they were more likely to use the type of figurative devices shown in this source. The idea that salvation could come from writing a holy verse on a slip of paper, dissolving the ink in water, and then drinking it may have been opposed by orthodox thinkers like Ibn al-Isma'il, but it gave people a sense that there was something they could do other than simply accept their deaths as a martyrdom. The use of numbers to interpret the world, like the similar use of the stars by astrologers, could give people a sense of an underlying order of things when they were faced with the apparent randomness with which the plague chose its victims.[2] For Muslims, meditation on mathematical symbols or sacred words, like the Christian contemplation of statues or other sacred images, could help believers focus on the divine.[3]

2. Historian Michael Dols writes, "Obviously, the cryptograms show a great variety, being composed of words, letters, numbers, symbols, or any combination of these. . . . Their symbolism is often not readily apparent. In some instances, there is a perfect square in which the sum is always the same whether the numbers are added horizontally, vertically or diagonally, or when any group of four contiguous numbers are added together. . . . The instructions state that when the quadrants were completed by the inclusion of the numbers outside the diagram the square would avert the plague. . . . These magic quadrants may have been used in numerous ways, but it is certain that they were often inscribed on metal amulets." (From Michael Dols, *The Black Death in the Middle East* [Princeton: Princeton University Press, 1977], pp. 138–139)

3. Michael Dols elaborates, "Ibn Haydur relates that his teacher informed him that one night in the year 764/1362–63 he had gone to bed and thought about the epidemic of plague that was rampant in this year. He slept badly because of the distress caused by the epidemic. In his sleep, he saw a man take a small book from his own library and bring it to him. The man laid his hand on the last line on the right side of the page of the book and said: 'These names will intercede for you during the epidemic, and read them in this manner—'Oh Living One, Oh Patient One, Oh Loving One, Oh Wise One.' . . . When it was morning he told his friends about the dream. Among them was [one] who, when he heard the recitation of the names of God in this manner, said that these names were engraved on rings. . . . The stone engraved in this way would guard a person against the burning fever that accompanied plague, if he drank water in which the ring had been submerged." (Dols, *The Black Death*, pp. 133–135)

Ibn al-Wardi was an eyewitness to the spread of the plague in Aleppo (Syria), who died of the disease in 1349. The selection from his account of the plague (Source 11) seems less consistent than the accounts of some other authors, and in fact some of his arguments may even seem contradictory: If the plague for Muslims is really "a martyrdom and a reward," why would one seek to escape it? In spite of, or perhaps even because of, such inconsistencies, Ibn al-Wardi has a great deal to say about popular beliefs related to our core questions: Where did the plague come from, what were its consequences, and what could people do about it?

The following three selections give us varying European accounts of the causes of and remedies for the plague. The Fifteenth-Century Treatise on the Pestilence, reproduced as Source 12, gives the conventional Christian interpretation of that time. Thus, just as Ibn al-Khatib had to struggle with Islamic religious orthodoxy in his assertion of medical causes and cures for the plague, so the Paris Medical Faculty (Source 13) had to justify their effort to go beyond this type of strictly religious explanation. The Paris doctors distinguished their mode of inquiry from that of religious authorities by grounding their analysis in the works of the classical tradition of medicine, with reference to such figures as Hippocrates and Galen. (Though they do not acknowledge it in this passage, these doctors were deeply indebted to the Iranian Muslim physician Ibn Sina, whose very influential medical text synthesizing classical and Islamic medical knowledge had been translated into Latin in the twelfth century.) While the references to astrology and the "four humors" may not seem very scientific to us, this document represents the most sophisticated medical thinking of its day. The selection entitled "A Wholesome Medicine Against the Plague" (Source 14) reminds us that while reaction to the plague in Europe could take such violent forms as self-flagellation and attacks on Jews, there were many other Christians who were more moderate and balanced in their response.

These readings on the Black Death have taken us across many intellectual and cultural frontiers. The final reading, in which the great Humanist philosopher Petrarch (Source 15) describes the death of his friends, brings us back down to the most basic, human level. As we read Petrarch's letter, can we really imagine what it would have been like to be living in such circumstances?

THE EVIDENCE

Source 1 from Michael Dols, The Black Death in the Middle East *(Princeton: Princeton University Press), 1977, p. 270; Ibn Khaldun,* The Muqaddimah; *trans. Franz Rosenthal (Princeton: Princeton University Press, 1967), pp. 136–137. Copyright © 1977 Princeton University Press, 2005, renewed PUP. Reprinted by permission of Princeton University Press.*

1. From Ibn Khaldun, *The Muqaddimah: An Introduction to History*

Civilization in the East and West was visited by a destructive plague which devastated nations and caused populations to vanish. It swallowed up many of the good things of civilization and wiped them out. It overtook the dynasties at the time of their senility, when they had reached the limit of their duration. . . .

In the later (years) of dynasties, famines and pestilences become numerous. . . .
. . . There is much unrest and bloodshed, and plagues occur. The principal reason for the latter is the corruption of the air (climate) through (too) large a civilization (population). It results from the putrefaction and the many evil moistures with which (the air) has contact (in a dense civilization). Now, air nourishes the animal spirit and is constantly with it. When it is corrupted, corruption affects the temper of (the spirit). If the corruption is strong, the lung is afflicted with disease. This results in epidemics, which affect the lung in particular. (Even) if the corruption is not strong or great, putrefaction grows and multiplies under (its influence), resulting in many fevers that affect the tempers, and the bodies become sick and perish. The reason for the growth of putrefaction and evil moistures is invariably a dense and abundant civilization

such as exists in the later (years) of a dynasty. . . . This is obvious. Therefore, it has been clarified by science in the proper place that it is necessary to have empty spaces and waste regions interspersed between civilized areas. This makes circulation of the air possible. . . .

God determines whatever He wishes.

Source 2 from Giovanni Boccaccio, The Decameron, *trans. Mark Musa and Peter Bondanella (New York: W. W. Norton, 1982), pp. 6–12. Copyright © 1982 by Mark Musa and Peter Bondanella. Used by permission of W.W. Norton & Company, Inc.*

2. From Giovanni Boccaccio, *The Decameron*

Let me say, then, that thirteen hundred and forty-eight years[4] had already passed after the fruitful Incarnation of the Son of God when into the distinguished city of Florence, more noble than any other Italian city, there came a deadly pestilence. Either because of the influence of heavenly bodies or because of God's just wrath as a punishment to mortals for our wicked deeds, the pestilence, originating some years earlier in the East, killed an infinite number of people as it spread relentlessly from one place to another until finally it had stretched its miserable length all over the West. And against this pestilence no human wisdom or foresight was of any avail; quantities of filth were removed from the city by officials charged with the task; the entry of any sick person into the city was prohibited; and many directives were issued concerning the maintenance of good health. Nor were the humble supplications rendered not once but many times by the pious to God, through public processions or by other means, in any way efficacious; for almost at the beginning of springtime of the year in question the plague began to show its sorrowful effects in an extraordinary manner. . . . Neither a doctor's advice nor the strength of medicine could do anything to cure this illness; on the contrary, either the nature of the illness was such that it afforded no cure, or else the doctors were so ignorant that they did not recognize its cause and, as a result, could not prescribe the proper remedy (in fact, the number of doctors, other than the well-trained, was increased by a large number of men and women who had never had any medical training); at any rate, few of the sick were ever cured, and almost all died after the third day of the appearance of the previously described symptoms (some sooner, others later), and most of them died without fever or any other side effects.

This pestilence was so powerful that it was transmitted to the healthy by contact with the sick, the way a fire close to dry or oily things will set them

4. In Boccaccio's day, Florentines began the first of each year not with the first of January, as is done today, but rather with the traditional date of the Annunciation (March 25).

aflame. And the evil of the plague went even further: not only did talking to or being around the sick bring infection and a common death, but also touching the clothes of the sick or anything touched or used by them seemed to communicate this very disease to the person involved. . . . The plague described here was of such virulence in spreading from one person to another that not only did it pass from one man to the next, but, what's more, it was often transmitted from the garments of a sick or dead man to animals that not only became contaminated by the disease but also died within a brief period of time. My own eyes, as I said earlier, were witness to such a thing one day: when the rags of a poor man who died of this disease were thrown into the public street, two pigs came upon them, and, as they are wont to do, first with their snouts and then with their teeth they took the rags and shook them around; and within a short time, after a number of convulsions, both pigs fell dead upon the ill-fated rags, as if they had been poisoned. From these and many similar or worse occurrences there came about such fear and such fantastic notions among those who remained alive that almost all of them took a very cruel attitude in the matter; that is, they completely avoided the sick and their possessions, and in so doing, each one believed that he was protecting his own good health.

There were some people who thought that living moderately and avoiding any excess might help a great deal in resisting this disease, and so they gathered in small groups and lived entirely apart from everyone else. They shut themselves up in those houses where there were no sick people and where one could live well by eating the most delicate of foods and drinking the finest of wines (doing so always in moderation), allowing no one to speak about or listen to anything said about the sick and the dead outside; these people lived, entertaining themselves with music and other pleasures that they could arrange. Others thought the opposite: they believed that drinking excessively, enjoying life, going about singing and celebrating, satisfying in every way the appetites as best one could, laughing, and making light of everything that happened was the best medicine for such a disease; so they practiced to the fullest what they believed by going from one tavern to another all day and night, drinking to excess; and they would often make merry in private homes, doing everything that pleased or amused them the most. This they were able to do easily, for everyone felt he was doomed to die and, as a result, abandoned his property, so that most of the houses had become common property, and any stranger who came upon them used them as if he were their rightful owner. In addition to this bestial behavior, they always managed to avoid the sick as best they could. And in this great affliction and misery of our city the revered authority of the laws, both divine and human, had fallen and almost completely disappeared, for, like other men, the ministers and executors of the laws were either dead or sick or so short of help that it was impossible for them to fulfill their duties; as a result, everybody was free to do as he pleased.

Many others adopted a middle course between the two attitudes just described: neither did they restrict their food or drink so much as the first group nor did they fall into such dissoluteness and drunkenness as the second; rather, they satisfied their appetites to a moderate degree. They did not shut themselves up, but went around carrying in their hands flowers, or sweet-smelling herbs, or various kinds of spices; and they would often put these things to their noses, believing that such smells were a wonderful means of purifying the brain, for all the air seemed infected with the stench of dead bodies, sickness, and medicines.

Others were of a crueler opinion (though it was, perhaps, a safer one): they maintained that there was no better medicine against the plague than to flee from it; convinced of this reasoning and caring only about themselves, men and women in great numbers abandoned their city, their houses, their farms, their relatives, and their possessions and sought other places, going at least as far away as the Florentine countryside—as if the wrath of God could not pursue them with this pestilence wherever they went but would only strike those it found within the walls of the city! Or perhaps they thought that Florence's last hour had come and that no one in the city would remain alive.

And not all those who adopted these diverse opinions died, nor did they all escape with their lives; on the contrary, many of those who thought this way were falling sick everywhere, and since they had given, when they were healthy, the bad example of avoiding the sick, they in turn were abandoned and left to languish away without any care. The fact was that one citizen avoided another, that almost no one cared for his neighbor, and that relatives rarely or hardly ever visited each other—they stayed far apart. This disaster had struck such fear into the hearts of men and women that brother abandoned brother, uncle abandoned nephew, sister left brother, and very often wife abandoned husband, and—even worse, almost unbelievable—fathers and mothers neglected to tend and care for their children as if they were not their own.

Thus, for the countless multitude of men and women who fell sick, there remained no support except the charity of their friends (and these were few) or the greed of servants, who worked for inflated salaries without regard to the service they performed and who, in spite of this, were few and far between; and those few were men or women of little wit (most of them not trained for such service) who did little else but hand different things to the sick when requested to do so or watch over them while they died, and in this service, they very often lost their own lives and their profits. . . . Between the lack of competent attendants that the sick were unable to obtain and the violence of the pestilence itself, so many, many people died in the city both day and night that it was incredible just to hear this described, not to mention seeing it! Therefore, out of sheer necessity, there arose among those who remained alive customs which were contrary to the established practices of the time.

It was the custom, as it is again today, for the women relatives and neighbors to gather together in the house of a dead person and there to mourn with the women who had been dearest to him; on the other hand, in front of the deceased's home, his male relatives would gather together with his male neighbors and other citizens, and the clergy also came, many of them or sometimes just a few, depending upon the social class of the dead man. Then, upon the shoulders of his equals, he was carried to the church chosen by him before death with the funeral pomp of candles and chants. With the fury of the pestilence increasing, this custom, for the most part, died out and other practices took its place. And so not only did people die without having a number of women around them, but there were many who passed away without having even a single witness present, and very few were granted the piteous laments and bitter tears of their relatives; on the contrary, most relatives were somewhere else, laughing, joking, and amusing themselves; even the women learned this practice too well, having put aside, for the most part, their womanly compassion for their own safety. . . .

The plight of the lower class and, perhaps, a large part of the middle class was even more pathetic: most of them stayed in their homes or neighborhoods either because of their poverty or because of their hopes for remaining safe, and every day they fell sick by the thousands; and not having servants or attendants of any kind, they almost always died. Many ended their lives in the public streets, during the day or at night, while many others who died in their homes were discovered dead by their neighbors only by the smell of their decomposing bodies. The city was full of corpses. The dead were usually given the same treatment by their neighbors, who were moved more by the fear that the decomposing corpses would contaminate them than by any charity they might have felt toward the deceased: either by themselves or with the assistance of porters (when they were available), they would drag the corpse out of the home and place it in front of the doorstep, where, usually in the morning, quantities of dead bodies could be seen by any passerby; then they were laid out on biers, or for lack of biers, on a plank. . . . Moreover, the dead were honored with no tears or candles or funeral mourners; in fact, things had reached such a point that the people who died were cared for as we care for goats today. Thus it became quite obvious that the very thing which in normal times wise men had not been able to resign themselves to, even though then it struck seldom and less harshly, became as a result of this colossal misfortune a matter of indifference to even the most simpleminded people.

So many corpses would arrive in front of a church every day and at every hour that the amount of holy ground for burials was certainly insufficient for the ancient custom of giving each body its individual place; when all the graves were full, huge trenches were dug in all of the cemeteries of the churches and into them the new arrivals were dumped by the hundreds; and they were packed in there with dirt, one on top of another, like a ship's cargo, until the trench was filled. . . .

Oh, how many great palaces, beautiful homes, and noble dwellings, once filled with families, gentlemen, and ladies, were now emptied, down to the last servant! How many notable families, vast domains, and famous fortunes remained without legitimate heir! How many valiant men, beautiful women, and charming young boys, who might have been pronounced very healthy by Galen, Hippocrates, and Aesculapius (not to mention lesser physicians), ate breakfast in the morning with their relatives, companions, and friends and then in the evening dined with their ancestors in the other world!

Source 3 from Ibn Battuta: Travels in Asia and Africa, 1325–1354, *trans. and selected by H. A. R. Gibbs (New York: August M. Kelley, 1969), pp. 305, 68–69.*

3. From *Ibn Battuta, Travels in Asia and Africa, 1325–1354*

Early in June we heard at Aleppo that the plague had broken out at Gaza, and that the number of deaths there reached over a thousand a day. On travelling to Hims I found that the plague had broken out there: about three hundred persons died of it on the day that I arrived. So I went on to Damascus, and arrived there on a Thursday. . . .

One of the celebrated sanctuaries at Damascus is the Mosque of the Footprints (al-Aqdám), which lies two miles south of the city, alongside the main-highway which leads to the Hijáz, Jerusalem, and Egypt. It is a large mosque, very blessed, richly endowed, and very highly venerated by the Damascenes. . . . I saw a remarkable instance of the veneration in which the Damascenes hold this mosque during the great pestilence, on my return journey through Damascus in the latter part of July 1348. The viceroy Arghún Sháh ordered a crier to proclaim through Damascus that all the people should fast for three days and that no one should cook anything eatable in the market during the daytime. For most of the people there eat no food but what has been prepared in the market. So the people fasted for three successive days, the last of which was a Thursday, then they assembled in the Great Mosque, amírs, sharífs, qádís, theologians, and all the other classes of the people, until the place was filled to overflowing, and there they spent the Thursday night in prayers and litanies. After the dawn prayer next morning they all went out together on foot, holding Korans in their hands, and the amírs barefooted. The procession was joined by the entire population of the town, men and women, small and large; the Jews came with their Book of the Law and the Christians with their Gospel, all of them with their women and children. The whole concourse, weeping and supplicating and seeking the favour of God through His Books and His Prophets, made their way to the Mosque of the Footprints, and there they remained in supplication and invocation until near midday. They then returned to the city and held the Friday service, and God lightened their affliction; for the number of deaths in a single day at Damascus did not attain two thousand, while in Cairo and Old Cairo it reached the figure of twenty-four thousand a day.

Source 4 from Christos S. Bartsocas, "Two Fourteenth Century Descriptions of the 'Black Death,'" Journal of the History of Medicine, *October 1966, pp. 395–397.*

4. From Ioannes Cautacuzenos (John VI of Byzantium), *Historarum*

Upon arrival in Byzantium she [the empress] found Andronikos, the youngest born, dead from the invading plague, which starting first from the Hyperborean Scythians, attacked almost all the sea coasts of the world and killed most of their people. For it swept not only through Pontus, Thrace and Macedonia, but even Greece, Italy and all the islands, Egypt, Libya, Judaea and Syria, and spread throughout almost the entire world.

So incurable was the evil, that neither any regularity of life, nor any bodily strength could resist it. Strong and weak bodies were all similarly carried away, and those best cared for died in the same manner as the poor. No other [major] disease of any kind presented itself that year. If someone had a previous illness he always succumbed to this disease and no physician's art was sufficient; neither did the disease take the same course in all persons but the others, unable to resist, died the same day, a few even within the hour. Those who could resist for two or three days had a very violent fever at first, the disease in such cases attacking the head; they suffered from speechlessness and insensibility to all happenings and then appeared as if sunken into a deep sleep. . . .

Great abscesses were formed on the legs or the arms, from which, when cut, a large quantity of foul-smelling pus flowed and the disease was differentiated as that which discharged much annoying matter. Even many who were seized by all the symptoms unexpectedly recovered. There was no help from anywhere; if someone brought to another a remedy useful to himself, this became poison to the other patient. Some, by treating others, became infected with the disease. It caused great destruction and many homes were deserted by their inhabitants. Domestic animals died together with their masters. Most terrible was the discouragement. Whenever people felt sick there was no hope left for recovery, but by turning to despair, adding to their prostration and severely aggravating their sickness, they died at once. No words could express the nature of the disease. All that can be pointed out is that it had nothing in common with the everyday evils to which the nature of man is subject, but was something else sent by God to restore chastity. Many of the sick turned to better things in their minds, by being chastened, not only those who died, but also those who overcame the disease. They abstained from all vice during that time and they lived virtuously; many divided their property among the poor, even before they were attacked by the disease. If he ever felt himself seized, no one was so ruthless as not to show repentance of his faults and to appear before the judgment seat of God with the best chance of salvation, not believing that the soul was incurable

[389]

or unhealed. Many died in Byzantium then, and the king's son, Andronikos, was attacked and died the third day.

Source 5 from Rosemary Horrox, trans. and ed., The Black Death *(Manchester: Manchester University Press, 1994), pp. 55–57.*

5. From the Chronicle of Jean de Venette

In 1348 the people of France, and of virtually the whole world, were assailed by something more than war. For just as famine had befallen them, as described in the beginning of this account, and then war, as described in the course of the account, so now pestilences broke out in various parts of the world. In the August of that year a very large and bright star was seen in the west over Paris, after vespers, when the sun was still shining but beginning to set. It was not as high in the heavens as the rest of the stars; on the contrary, it seemed rather near. And as the sun set and night approached the star seemed to stay in one place, as I and many of my brethren observed. Once night had fallen, as we watched and greatly marvelled, the great star sent out many separate beams of light, and after shooting out rays eastwards over Paris it vanished totally: there one minute, gone the next. Whether it was a comet or something else—perhaps something condensed from some sort of exhalations which then returned to vapour—I leave to the judgment of astronomers. But it seems possible that it presaged the incredible pestilence which soon followed in Paris and throughout the whole of France, as I shall describe.

As a result of that pestilence a great many men and women died that year and the next in Paris and throughout the kingdom of France, as they also did in other parts of the world. . . .

. . . During the epidemic the Lord, of his goodness, deigned to confer such grace on those dying that, however suddenly they died, almost all of them faced death as joyfully as if they had been well prepared for it. Nor did any-one die without making confession and receiving the last sacrament. So that more of those dying would make a good end, Pope Clement mercifully gave the confessors in numerous cities and villages the power to absolve the sins of the dying, so that as a result they died the more happily, leaving much of their land and goods to churches or religious orders since their right heirs had predeceased them.

Men ascribed the pestilence to infected air or water, because there was no famine or lack of food at that time but, on the contrary, a great abundance. One result of this interpretation was that the infection, and the sudden death which it brought, were blamed on the Jews, who were said to have poisoned wells and rivers and corrupted the air. Accordingly the whole world brutally rose against

[390]

them, and in Germany and in other countries which had Jewish communities many thousands were indiscriminately butchered, slaughtered and burnt alive by the Christians.[5] The insane constancy shown by them and their wives was amazing. When Jews were being burnt mothers would throw their own children into the flames rather than risk them being baptised, and would then hurl themselves into the fire after them, to burn with their husbands and children.

It was claimed that many wicked Christians were discovered poisoning wells in a similar fashion. But in truth, such poisonings, even if they really happened, could not have been solely responsible for so great a plague or killed so many people. There must have been some other cause such as, for instance, the will of God, or corrupt humours and the badness of air and earth; although perhaps such poisonings, where they did occur, were a contributory factor. The mortality continued in France for most of 1348 and 1349 and then stopped, leaving many villages and many town houses virtually empty, stripped of their inhabitants. Then many houses fell quickly into ruin, including numerous houses in Paris, although the damage there was less than in many places.

When the epidemic was over the men and women still alive married each other. Everywhere women conceived more readily than usual. None proved barren, on the contrary, there were pregnant women wherever you looked. Several gave birth to twins, and some to living triplets. But what is particularly surprising is that when the children born after the plague started cutting their teeth they commonly turned out to have only 20 or 22, instead of the 32 usual before the plague. I am unsure what this means, unless it is, as some men say, a sign that the death of infinite numbers of people, and their replacement by those who survived, has somehow renewed the world and initiated a new age. But if so, the world, alas, has not been made any better by its renewal. For after the plague men became more miserly and grasping, although many owned more than they had before. They were also more greedy and quarrelsome, involving themselves in brawls, disputes and lawsuits. Nor did the dreadful plague inflicted by God bring about peace between kings and lords. On the contrary, the enemies of the king of France and of the Church were stronger and more evil than before and stirred up wars by land and sea. Evil spread like wildfire.

What was also amazing was that, in spite of there being plenty of everything, it was all twice as expensive: household equipment and foodstuffs, as well as merchandise, hired labour, farm workers and servants. The only exception was property and houses, of which there is a glut to this day. Also from that time charity began to grow cold, and wrongdoing flourished, along with sinfulness and ignorance—for few men could be found in houses, towns or castles who were able or willing to instruct boys in the rudiments of Latin.

---

5. The Jews had been expelled from France by Philip the Fair in 1322.

Source 6: Walters Art Museum, Baltimore.

6. Lieferinxe, *St. Sebastian Interceding for the Plague-Stricken*

Source 7 from Rosemary Horrox, trans. and ed., The Black Death *(Manchester: Manchester University Press, 1994), pp. 125–126.*

7. A Prayer to St. Sebastian

O St Sebastian, guard and defend me, morning and evening, every minute of every hour, while I am still of sound mind; and, Martyr, diminish the strength of that vile illness called an epidemic which is threatening me. Protect and keep me and all my friends from this plague. We put our trust in God and St Mary, and in you, O holy Martyr. . . . Be with us always, and by your merits keep us safe and sound and protected from plague. Commend us to the Trinity and to the Virgin Mary, so that when we die we may have our reward: to behold God in the company of martyrs.

Source 8 from William H. McNeill, Plagues and Peoples *(New York: Anchor, 1977), p. 198.*

8. Citations from the Hadith

When you learn that epidemic disease exists in a county, do not go there; but if it breaks out in the county where you are, do not leave.

He who dies of epidemic disease is a martyr.

It is a punishment that God inflicts on whom he wills, but He has granted a modicum of clemency with respect to Believers.

Source 9 from Manfred Ullman, Islamic Medicine *(Edinburgh: Edinburgh University Press, 1978), pp. 94–95. Copyright © 1978. Reprinted with permission of Edinburgh University Press, www.euppublishing.com.*

9. An Arab Doctor's Medical Perspective on the Black Death

If one asks, 'How can you admit the assertion, there is infection, when the revealed word (*ash-shar'*) denies this?' we answer: that infection exists, is confirmed by experience, research, insight and observation and through constantly recurring accounts. These are the elements of proof. For him who has treated or recognized this case, it cannot remain concealed that mostly the man who has had contact with a patient infected with this disease must die, and that, on the other hand, the man who has had no contact remains healthy. So it is with the appearance of the illness in a house or quarter because of a garment or a vessel;

[393]

even an earring can destroy him who puts it in his ear, and all the inhabitants of the house. The illness can first appear in a town in a single house; then, from there, it can break out among individual contacts, then among their neighbours, relatives, and especially their visitors, until the breach becomes even greater. The illness can appear in coastal towns that enjoyed good health until there lands in them a man with plague, come from across the sea, from another coast where the plague already exists, as reports tell. The date of the appearance of the illness in the town tallies with the date of debarcation of this man. Many remained healthy who kept themselves strictly cut off from the outside world, like the pious Ibn-Abī-Madyan in Salé. He belonged to those who believed in contagion. He had stored up provisions for a long period and bricked up his door behind him and his large family. The town succumbed but during that period, he was not deprived of a single soul. One had repeatedly heard that places which lie remote from highways and traffic remained untouched. But there is nothing more wonderful at this time than the prison camp of the Muslims—may God free them!—in the Arsenal of Seville: there were thousands but the plague did not touch them although it practically destroyed the town itself. The report is also correct that the itinerant nomads living in tents in North Africa and elsewhere remained healthy because there the air is not shut in and the corruption proceeding from it could only gain a slight hold. . . .

But it belongs to principles which one may not ignore that a proof taken from tradition (Hadīth), if observation and inspection are contrary, must be interpreted allegorically. In this matter it is essential that it should be interpreted in accordance with the views of those who hold the theory of contagion. There are numerous compassionate passages in revealed scripture, for example, the utterance of the Prophet: 'an owner of sick animals should not drive these to the owner of healthy animals.'

Source 10 from Michael Dols, The Black Death in the Middle East *(Princeton: Princeton University Press, 1977), pp. 139, 135. Copyright © 1977 Princeton University Press, 2005 renewed PUP. Reprinted by permission of Princeton University Press.*

10. Cryptograms

406	409	412	398
411	399	405	410
400		407	404
408	403	401	413

414

Source 11 from "Ibn al-Wardi's Risalah al naba' 'an al-Waba,' *A Translation of a Major Source for the History of the Black Death in the Middle East," in* Near Eastern Numismatics, Iconography, Epigraphy and History: Studies in Honor of George C. Miles, *ed. Dickran K. Kouymjian (Beirut: American University, 1974), pp. 447–450, 452–455. Copyright © 1974. Reprinted by permission of the American University of Beirut.*

11. From Ibn al-Wardi, "An Essay on the Report of the Pestilence"

God is my security in every adversity. My sufficiency is in God alone. Is not God sufficient protection for His servant? Oh God, pray for our master, Muhammad, and give him peace. Save us for his sake from the attacks of the plague and give us shelter.

The plague frightened and killed. It began in the land of darkness. Oh, what a visitor! It has been current for fifteen years. China was not preserved from it nor could the strongest fortress hinder it. The plague afflicted the Indians in India. It weighed upon the Sind. It seized with its hand and ensnared even the lands of the Uzbeks. . . . The plague increased and spread further. It attacked the Persians, . . . and gnawed away at the Crimea. . . . The plague destroyed mankind in Cairo. . . . It stilled all movement in Alexandria. . . .

Oh Alexandria, this plague is like a lion which extends its arm to you.
Have patience with the fate of the plague, which leaves of seventy men only
   seven.

Then, the plague turned to Upper Egypt. It, also, sent forth its storm to Barqah.
The plague attacked Gaza, and it shook 'Asqalān severely. The plague oppressed
Acre. The scourge came to Jerusalem and paid the *zakāt* [with the souls of men].
It overtook those people who fled to the al-'Aqsā Mosque, which stands beside
the Dome of the Rock. If the door of mercy had not been opened, the end of
the world would have occurred in a moment. It, then, hastened its pace and
attacked the entire maritime plain. The plague trapped Sidon and descended
unexpectedly upon Beirut, cunningly. Next, it directed the shooting of its arrows
to Damascus. There the plague sat like a king on a throne and swayed with
power, killing daily one thousand or more and decimating the population. It
destroyed mankind with its pustules. May God the Most High spare Damascus
to pursue its own path and extinguish the plague's fires so that they do not
come close to her fragrant orchards.

Oh God, restore Damascus and protect her from insult.
Its morale has been so lowered that people in the city sell themselves for grain.
   . . .

Oh God, it is acting by Your command. Lift this from us. It happens where
You wish; keep the plague from us. Who will defend us against this horror
other than You the Almighty? . . .
   How many places has the plague entered. It swore not to leave the houses
without its inhabitants. It searched them out with a lamp. The pestilence caused
the people of Aleppo the same disturbance. . . .
   Oh, if you could see the nobles of Aleppo studying their inscrutable books of
medicine. They multiply its remedies by eating dried and sour foods. The buboes
which disturb men's healthy lives are smeared with Armenian clay. Each man
treated his humours and made life more comfortable. They perfumed their
homes with ambergris and camphor, cyperus and sandal. They wore ruby rings
and put onions, vinegar, and sardines together with the daily meal. They ate
less broth and fruit but ate the citron and similar things.
   If you see many biers and their carriers and hear in every quarter of Aleppo
the announcements of death and cries, you run from them and refuse to stay
with them. In Aleppo the profits of the undertakers have greatly increased. Oh
God, do not profit them. Those who sweat from carrying the coffins enjoy this
plague-time. Oh God, do not let them sweat and enjoy this. . . .
   We ask God's forgiveness for our souls' bad inclination; the plague is surely
part of His punishment. We take refuge from His wrath in His pleasure and
from His chastisement in His restoring.

[396]

They said: the air's corruption kills. I said: the love of corruption kills.
How many sins and how many offenses does the crier call our attention to. . . .

This plague is for the Muslims a martyrdom and a reward, and for the disbe-
lievers a punishment and a rebuke. When the Muslim endures misfortune, then
patience is his worship. It has been established by our Prophet, God bless him
and give him peace, that the plague-stricken are martyrs. This noble tradition
is true and assures martyrdom. And this secret should be pleasing to the true
believer. If someone says it causes infection and destruction, say: God creates
and recreates. If the liar, disputes the matter of infection and tries to find an
explanation, I say that the Prophet, on him be peace, said: who infected the
first? If we acknowledge the plague's devastation of the people, it is the will of
the Chosen Doer. So it happened again and again.

I take refuge in God from the yoke of the plague. Its high explosion has burst
into all countries and was an examiner of astonishing things. Its sudden attacks
perplex the people. The plague chases the screaming without pity and does not
accept a treasure for ransom. Its engine is far-reaching. The plague enters into the
house and swears it will not leave except with all of its inhabitants. "I have an
order from the *qādī* to arrest all those in the house." Among the benefits of this
order is the removal of one's hopes and the improvement of his earthly works. It
awakens men from their indifference for the provisioning of their final journey.

One man begs another to take care of his children, and one says goodbye to his
    neighbors.
A third perfects his works, and another prepares his shroud.
A fifth is reconciled with his enemies, and another treats his friends with kindness.
One is very generous; another makes friends with those who have betrayed
    him.
Another man puts aside his property; one frees his servants.
One man changes his character while another mends his ways.
For this plague has captured all people and is about to send its ultimate
    destruction.
There is no protection today from it other than His mercy, praise to be God.

Nothing prevented us from running away from the plague except our devotion to the noble tradition. Come then, seek the aid of God Almighty for raising
the plague, for He is the best helper. Oh God, we call You better than anyone did
before. We call You to raise from us the pestilence and plague. We do not take
refuge in its removal other than with You. We do not depend on our good health
against the plague but on You. We seek Your protection, Oh Lord of creation,
from the blows of this stick. We ask for Your mercy which is wider than our sins
even as they are the number of the sands and pebbles. We plead with You, by the
most honored of the advocates, Muhammad, the Prophet of mercy, that You take

away from us this distress. Protect us from the evil and the torture and preserve us. For You are our sole support; what a perfect trustee!

Source 12 from Rosemary Horrox, trans. and ed., The Black Death *(Manchester: Manchester University Press, 1994), pp. 193–194.*

12. A Fifteenth-Century Treatise on the Pestilence

It should be known to all Christians that pestilence, and every other manifestation of God's vengeance, arises because of sin. . . . Pestilence arises from a multitude of sins, but most especially from swearing worthless, deceitful and meaningless oaths.

If I am asked what is the cause of pestilence, what is its physical cause and by what means can someone save himself from it, I answer to the first question that sin is the cause, as set forth above. To the second question I say that it arises from the sea, as the evangelist says: 'There shall be signs in the sun and in the moon and in the stars; and upon the earth distress of nations, by reason of the confusion of the roaring of the sea and of the waves'.[6] For the devil, by the power committed to him, when the seas rise up high, is voiding his poison, sending it forth to be added to the poison in the air, and that air spreads gradually from place to place and enters men through the ears, eyes, nose, mouth, pores and the other orifices. Then if the man has a strong constitution, nature can expel the poison through ulcers, and if the ulcers putrify, are strangled and fully run their course the patient will be saved, as can be clearly seen. But if the poison should be stronger than his nature, so that his constitution cannot prevail against it, then the poison instantly lays siege to the heart, and the patient dies within a short time, without the relief which comes from the formation of ulcers.

To the third question I say that during the pestilence everyone over seven should be made to vomit daily from an empty stomach, and twice a week, or more often if necessary, he should lie well wrapped up in a warm bed and drink warm ale with ginger so that he sweats copiously, and he should never touch the sheets after that until they have been cleansed of the sweat, for if the person sweating had been in contact with the pestilence a healthy man could catch the plague from the sheets unless they have been well washed. And as soon as he feels an itch or prickling in his flesh he must use a goblet or cupping horn to let blood and draw down the blood from the heart, and this should be done two or three times at intervals of one or two days at most. And if he should feel himself oppressed deep within the body, then he should let blood in the nearest veins,

---

6. Luke 21.25. This occurs in a list of the signs which will precede Christ's second coming and the end of the world.

either in the arms or in the main veins of the feet. Likewise something which is extremely poisonous in itself may be of service in excluding the plague. And if a healthy adult does as I have described, they can save themselves whenever a great pestilence occurs.

Source 13 from Rosemary Horrox, trans. and ed., The Black Death *(Manchester: Manchester University Press, 1994), pp. 158–163.*

13. From Report of the Paris Medical Faculty, October 1348

Seeing things which cannot be explained, even by the most gifted intellects, initially stirs the human mind to amazement; but after marvelling, the prudent soul next yields to its desire for understanding and, anxious for its own perfection, strives with all its might to discover the causes of the amazing events. For there is within the human mind an innate desire to seize on goodness and truth. As the Philosopher makes plain, all things seek for the good and want to understand.[7] To attain this end we have listened to the opinions of many modern experts on astrology and medicine about the causes of the epidemic which has prevailed since 1345. However, because their conclusions still leave room for considerable uncertainty, we, the masters of the faculty of medicine at Paris, inspired by the command of the most illustrious prince, our most serene lord, Philip, King of France, and by our desire to achieve something of public benefit, have decided to compile, with God's help, a brief compendium of the distant and immediate causes of the present universal epidemic (as far as these can be understood by the human intellect) and of wholesome remedies; drawing on the opinions of the most brilliant ancient philosophers and modern experts, astronomers as well as doctors of medicine. And if we cannot explain everything as we would wish, for a sure explanation and perfect understanding of these matters is not always to be had (as Pliny says in book II, chapter 39: 'some accidental causes of storms are still uncertain, or cannot be explained'), it is open to any diligent reader to make good the deficiency.

We shall divide the work into two parts, in the first of which we shall investigate the causes of this pestilence and whence they come, for without knowledge of the causes no one can prescribe cures. In the second part we shall include methods of prevention and cure. There will be three chapters in the first part, for this epidemic arises from a double cause. One cause is distant and from above, and pertains to the heavens; the other is near and from below and pertains to the earth, and is dependent, causally and effectively, on the first cause.

7. "The Philosopher" is Aristotle.

Therefore the first chapter will deal with the first cause, the second with the second cause, and the third with the prognostications and signs associated with both of them. There will be two treatises in the second part. The first will deal with medical means of prevention and cure and will be divided into four chapters: the first on the disposition of the air and its rectification; the second on exercise and baths; the third on food and drink; the fourth on sleeping and waking, emptiness and fullness of the stomach and on the emotions. The second treatise will have three chapters: the first on universal remedies; the second on specific remedies appropriate to different patients; the third on antidotes.

CHAPTER 1 OF THE FIRST PART: CONCERNING THE UNIVERSAL AND DISTANT CAUSE

We say that the distant and first cause of this pestilence was and is the configuration of the heavens. In 1345, at one hour after noon on 20 March, there was a major conjunction of three planets in Aquarius. This conjunction, along with other earlier conjunctions and eclipses, by causing a deadly corruption of the air around us, signifies mortality and famine—and also other things about which we will not speak here because they are not relevant. Aristotle testifies that this is the case in his book *Concerning the causes of the properties of the elements*, in which he says that mortality of races and the depopulation of kingdoms occur at the conjunction of Saturn and Jupiter, for great events then arise, their nature depending on the trigon in which the conjunction occurs. And this is found in ancient philosophers, and Albertus Magnus in his book, *Concerning the causes of the properties of the elements* (treatise 2, chapter 1) says that the conjunction of Mars and Jupiter causes a great pestilence in the air, especially when they come together in a hot, wet sign, as was the case in 1345. For Jupiter, being wet and hot, draws up evil vapours from the earth and Mars, because it is immoderately hot and dry, then ignites the vapours, and as a result there were lightnings, sparks, noxious vapours and fires throughout the air.

These effects were intensified because Mars—a malevolent planet, breeding anger and wars—was in the sign of Leo from 6 October 1347 until the end of May this year, along with the head of the dragon, and because all these things are hot they attracted many vapours; which is why the winter was not as cold as it should have been. And Mars was also retrograde and therefore attracted many vapours from the earth and the sea which, when mixed with the air, corrupted its substance. Mars was also looking upon Jupiter with a hostile aspect, that is to say quartile, and that caused an evil disposition or quality in the air, harmful and hateful to our nature. This state of affairs generated strong winds (for according to Albertus in the first book of his *Meteora*, Jupiter has the property of raising powerful winds, particularly from the south) which gave rise to excess heat and moisture on the earth; although in fact it was the dampness which was most marked in our part of the world. And this is enough about the distant or universal cause for the moment.

CHAPTER 2 OF THE FIRST PART: CONCERNING THE PARTICULAR AND NEAR CAUSE

Although major pestilential illnesses can be caused by the corruption of water or food, as happens at times of famine and infertility, yet we still regard illnesses proceeding from the corruption of the air as much more dangerous. This is because bad air is more noxious than food or drink in that it can penetrate quickly to the heart and lungs to do its damage. We believe that the present epidemic or plague has arisen from air corrupt in its substance, and not changed in its attributes. By which we wish it be understood that air, being pure and clear by nature, can only become putrid or corrupt by being mixed with something else, that is to say, with evil vapours. What happened was that the many vapours which had been corrupted at the time of the conjunction were drawn up from the earth and water, and were then mixed with the air and spread abroad by frequent gusts of wind in the wild southerly gales, and because of these alien vapours which they carried the winds corrupted the air in its substance, and are still doing so. And this corrupted air, when breathed in, necessarily penetrates to the heart and corrupts the substance of the spirit there and rots the surrounding moisture, and the heat thus caused destroys the life force, and this is the immediate cause of the present epidemic.

And moreover these winds, which have become so common here, have carried among us (and may perhaps continue to do so in future) bad, rotten and poisonous vapours from elsewhere: from swamps, lakes and chasms, for instance, and also (which is even more dangerous) from unburied or unburnt corpses—which might well have been a cause of the epidemic. Another possible cause of corruption, which needs to be borne in mind, is the escape of the rottenness trapped in the centre of the earth as a result of earthquakes—something which has indeed recently occurred. But the conjunctions could have been the universal and distant cause of all these harmful things, by which air and water have been corrupted.

CHAPTER 3: CONCERNING PROGNOSTICATION AND SIGNS

Unseasonable weather is a particular cause of illness. For the ancients, notably Hippocrates, are agreed that if the four seasons run awry, and do not keep their proper course, then plagues and mortal passions are engendered that year. Experience tells us that for some time the seasons have not succeeded each other in the proper way. Last winter was not as cold as it should have been, with a great deal of rain; the spring windy and latterly wet. Summer was late, not as hot as it should have been, and extremely wet—the weather very changeable from day to day, and hour to hour; the air often troubled, and then still again, looking as if it was going to rain but then not doing so. Autumn too was very rainy and misty. It is because the whole year here—or most of it—was warm and wet that the air is pestilential. For it is a sign of pestilence for the air to be warm and wet at unseasonable times.

Wherefore we may fear a future pestilence here, which is particularly from the root beneath, because it is subject to the evil impress of the heavens, especially since that conjunction was in a western sign. Therefore if next winter is very rainy and less cold than it ought to be, we should expect an epidemic round about late winter and spring—and if it occurs it will be long and dangerous, for usually unseasonable weather is of only brief duration, but when it lasts over many seasons, as has obviously been the case here, it stands to reason that its effects will be longer-lasting and more dangerous, unless ensuing seasons change their nature in the opposite way. Thus if the winter in the north turns out to be cold and dry, the plagues might be arrested.

We have not said that the future pestilence will be exceptionally dangerous, for we do not wish to give the impression that it will be as dangerous here as in southern or eastern regions. For the conjunctions and the other causes discussed above had a more immediate impact on those regions than on ours. However, in the judgement of astrologers (who follow Ptolemy on this) plagues are likely, although not inevitable, because so many exhalations and inflammations have been observed, such as a comet and shooting stars. Also the sky has looked yellow and the air reddish because of the burnt vapours. There has also been much lightning and flashes and frequent thunder, and winds of such violence and strength that they have carried dust storms from the south. These things, and in particular the powerful earthquakes, have done universal harm and left a trail of corruption. There have been masses of dead fish, animals and other things along the sea shore, and in many places trees covered in dust, and some people claim to have seen a multitude of frogs and reptiles generated from the corrupt matter; and all these things seem to have come from the great corruption of the air and earth. All these things have been noted before as signs of plague by numerous wise men who are still remembered with respect and who experienced them themselves.

No wonder, therefore, that we fear that we are in for an epidemic. But it should be noted that in saying this we do not intend to exclude the possibility of illnesses arising from the character of the present year—for as the aphorism of Hippocrates has it: a year of many fogs and damps is a year of many illnesses. On the other hand, the susceptibility of the body of the patient is the most immediate cause in the breeding of illnesses, and therefore no cause is likely to have an effect unless the patient is susceptible to its effects. We must therefore emphasise that although, because everyone has to breathe, everyone will be at risk from the corrupted air, not everyone will be made ill by it but only those, who will no doubt be numerous, who have a susceptibility to it; and very few indeed of those who do succumb will escape.

The bodies most likely to take the stamp of this pestilence are those which are hot and moist, for they are the most susceptible to putrefaction. The following are also more at risk: bodies bunged up with evil humours, because the unconsumed waste matter is not being expelled as it should; those following a bad life style, with too much exercise, sex and bathing; the thin and weak, and persistent worriers; babies, women and young people; and corpulent people with a ruddy complexion. However those with dry bodies, purged of waste matter, who adopt a sensible and suitable regimen, will succumb to the pestilence more slowly.

[402]

We must not overlook the fact that any pestilence proceeds from the divine will, and our advice can therefore only be to return humbly to God. But this does not mean forsaking doctors. For the Most High created earthly medicine, and although God alone cures the sick, he does so through the medicine which in his generosity he provided. Blessed be the glorious and high God, who does not refuse his help, but has clearly set out a way of being cured for those who fear him. And this is enough of the third chapter, and of the whole first part.

Source 14 from Rosemary Horrox, trans. and ed., The Black Death *(Manchester: Manchester University Press, 1994), p. 149.*

14. A Wholesome Medicine
Against All Infirmities

The advice of the reverend father Dom Theophilus of Milan, of the order of St Benedict, against the plague; also a most wholesome medicine against all infirmities. Note it well.

Whenever anyone is struck down by the plague they should immediately provide themselves with a medicine like this. Let him first gather as much as he can of bitter loathing towards the sins committed by him, and the same quantity of true contrition of heart, and mix the two into an ointment with the water of tears. Then let him make a vomit of frank and honest confession, by which he shall be purged of the pestilential poison of sin, and the boil of his vices shall be totally liquified and melt away. Then the spirit, formerly weighed down by the plague of sin, will be left all light and full of blessed joy. Afterwards let him take the most delightful and precious medicine: the body of our lord and saviour Jesus Christ. And finally let him have himself anointed on the seat of his bodily senses with holy oil. And in a little while he will pass from transient life to the incorruptible country of eternal life, safe from plague and all other infirmities.

Compared with this all other remedies of doctors are futile and profit little against the plague, which God keeps for the chastisement of sin and which is without remedy save through him and his power.

Source 15 from Rosemary Horrox, The Black Death *(Manchester: Manchester University Press, 1994), pp. 248–249.*

15. From Petrarch, "Letters on
Familiar Matters"

a. What are we to do now, brother? Now that we have lost almost everything and found no rest. When can we expect it? Where shall we look for it? Time, as they say, has slipped through our fingers. Our former hopes are buried with our friends. The year 1348 left us lonely and bereft, for it took from us wealth which could not be restored by the Indian, Caspian or Carpathian Sea. Last losses are beyond recovery, and death's wound beyond cure. There is just one comfort: that we shall follow those who went before. I do not know how long we shall have to wait, but I know that it cannot be very long—although however short the time it will feel too long. . . .

b. There remained to me at least something salvaged from the wreck of last year: a most brilliant man, and (you must take my word for it) one great in action and counsel, Paganino da Milano, who after numerous proofs of his virtue became very dear to me, and seemed worthy of your friendship as well as mine. He was on the way to becoming another Socrates, displaying almost the same loyalty and good fellowship, and that friendship which lies in sharing good and bad fortune and in baring the hidden places of the heart in a trusting exchange of secrets.

How much he loved you, how much he longed to see you—you whom he could see only with the eyes of imagination. How much he worried about your safety during this shipwreck of the world. I was amazed that a man unknown to him could be so much loved. He never saw me graver than usual without becoming anxious himself and asking, 'Is something wrong? How is our friend?' But when he heard that you were in good health he would cast aside his fears with wonderful alacrity.

And this man (I speak it with many tears, and would speak it with more but my eyes are drained by previous misfortunes and I should save some tears for whatever may befall in the future), this man, I say, was suddenly seized by the pestilence which is now ravaging the world. This was at dusk, after dinner with his friends, and the evening hours that remained he spent talking with us, reminiscing about our friendship and shared concerns. He passed the night in extreme pain, which he endured with an undaunted spirit, and then died suddenly the next morning. None of the now-familiar horrors were abated, and within three days all his children and household followed him.

Go, mortals, sweat, pant, toil, range the lands and seas to pile up riches you cannot keep; glory that will not last. The life we lead is a sleep; whatever we do, dreams. Only death breaks the sleep and wakes us from dreaming. I wish I could have woken before this.

QUESTIONS TO CONSIDER

Now that you have looked at the evidence and made a list of the causes and consequences of the Black Death and the reactions to it, we can draw out some more detail and make some more systematic comparisons.

What, ultimately, caused the Black Death? Astrological causation is mentioned by the doctors of Paris, and several other authors refer to the alignment of the heavens or the actions of heavenly bodies. But was this really the ultimate cause? For most Christians and Muslims, the ultimate cause almost certainly had to be God. The documents you have examined make this clear, but a question still remains: *Why* would God bring such a pestilence to humanity? Taking the documents from Christian writers first, what seems to have been the most common answer to that question? The "Fifteenth-Century Treatise on the Pestilence" is characteristic in this regard, and also gives us an idea of the larger historical framework within which medieval Christians might understand the cause of the Black Death.

If we then compare the Islamic documents, a contrast becomes apparent: Meditations on God's intentions seem to be much less prominent in these sources. As Ibn Khaldun says, "God determines whatever He wishes." In general, Muslims are more reluctant than Christians to make authoritative pronouncements about God's intentions. The most rigid position articulated in these texts, Ibn Isma'il al Bukhari's relation of the *hadith*, implies that the plague is sent directly by God to the victim, as a punishment to the infidel and as a martyrdom (and therefore a blessing) to the Believer. No other explanation is necessary: God's will is unknowable. Nevertheless, you may be able to identify at least one passage from a Muslim writer who, like his Christian counterparts, ascribes a specific motivation for God's activities.

We find a greater range of possibilities when we turn from the ultimate causes in heaven to the immediate causes on earth. The first reading, from Ibn Khaldun, introduces us to the general area of environmental and demographic causation. While Ibn Khaldun locates the Black Death in a great scheme of the rise and fall of civilizations, other authors look more closely at particular environmental factors. As you look through the list of possible causes that you have identified in the documents, select those that have to do with environmental conditions or the size and distribution of population. From what you know of the "real" causes of the plague, how astute were these observations?

Many of our texts also refer to the means by which the plague is *transmitted* from one place to another and from one person to another. Again, issues of environment and demography are involved. How would you characterize the various theories of transmission, and which do you find to have been closest to the mark? Again, some variation between Christian and Islamic sources may be noted. The "orthodox" Islamic position, represented here by Muhammad ibn Isma' il, relies on an interpretation of the *hadith* that claims that since the disease is sent directly by God, there can be no belief in transmission through infection or contagion. How do the other Islamic authors react to this position?

Apart from theories of causation and transmission that refer to divine, heavenly, or environmental causes, there are also some texts that refer to the conscious activities of evil human beings who spread the disease on purpose. How were they said to have done so, and why? What groups were most likely to be singled out for such accusations, and what fate did they suffer as a consequence?

If we move from the question of causation to the question of the consequences of the Black Death, the most likely thing to notice first are the reports of mortality. How many people are said to have died? What percentage of the population is said to have been affected? How accurate do you think these reports might be?

Apart from the sheer number of people who died, many of the texts comment on the social, political, and economic effects of the Black Death. How did people's responses to the calamity affect social relationships within communities, between neighbors, between different social groups, and within families? According to the various authors, did the plague bring people closer together or push them apart? Were previously established forms of authority strengthened or weakened? How might some people benefit economically from the devastation of the plague? Does it seem that the changes in these societies brought about by the plague were temporary or permanent? Do the social, political, and economic effects of the plague seem to have been more concern to Christian or to Islamic commentators?

Many of these questions are posed in our sources in terms of public and private morality. As you compare entries in your list of consequences of the Black Death, also be aware of the contrast between those authors who saw standards of morality declining in the wake of the plague, and those who reported that at least some people were becoming more virtuous. What were some of the most striking examples of the breakdown of social conventions and the decline in morality? Under what circumstances might some people actually improve their behavior, and how might that positive response be shown?

What of the psychological effects of the plague? Several of the documents give us a close and immediate sense of the despair felt by survivors of the plague who had seen their friends and family carried away: Ioannes Cantacuzenos and Petrarch come to mind. Apart from those human emotions with which we can no doubt relate, however, there is another set of psychological concerns with which we may not immediately empathize. For medieval Christians in particular, it was of the greatest importance to die a "good death." This meant that one was properly prepared to leave this world for the next. One needed to be spiritually prepared, having received confession and the last rites of the Church. It was best if one had an opportunity to take leave of friends and family. After death, an elaborate wake and funeral ceremony would help the soul of the departed into heaven, as would the continued prayers of those left behind. Burial in consecrated ground was absolutely essential. From your reading of the documents in which such questions are raised, what might have been the psychological and emotional effects of the Black Death on medieval Christians? How might the reactions of Muslims have differed if they interpreted the *hadith* to mean that for Believers the plague was a martyrdom that guaranteed them a place in Heaven?

The ultimate logic of despair is to do nothing. If the plague really was sent by God and the doctors could do nothing about it, then why do anything other than simply wait to die? Perhaps you can find evidence of such attitudes in some of the documents, but clearly most people were on the lookout for things they could do to protect themselves and their communities. The Christian painting and Islamic cryptograms demonstrate how people might use visual images both to externalize their fears and to invoke divine aid as a protection from the plague.

In fact, many of the responses intended to remedy the situation were religious in nature. What seem to have been the most common religious activities that groups and individuals could pursue to protect themselves from the plague, or at least alleviate their suffering? Which ones seem to have been most approved of by religious leaders, or organized by them on behalf of the community? Were there other remedies that, while religious in inspiration, might have been disapproved of by the Catholic Church or by the most orthodox Islamic thinkers?

Other remedies that people might take involved changes in their living situations: People might change either where they lived, with whom they lived, or both. What different types of examples of this pattern did you find in the documents? How much of a change

did they represent from previous social practices? Did the commentators seem to approve or disapprove of these strategies? Were they effective?

There were also attempts at medical solutions to the problem, involving both diagnosis and remedy. The prescriptions could involve changes of diet, alteration of lifestyle, and the use of specific medications and cures, as well as "civic" solutions involving urban authorities. Which sources do you think are the most "medical" in their approach? Did you find any diagnoses or remedies that you thought were more sensible than others?

Now that you have drawn some comparisons and reached some conclusions, you may want to step back and consider more generally the people who lived through the Black Death as depicted in these documents. It is difficult for us, perhaps, to suspend our judgment when looking at the thoughts and beliefs of people who lived long ago in very different cultural, religious, and technological circumstances. But if we make the effort, we will be better able to engage the people of the past on their own terms. What, then, have you learned about the inner worlds of medieval Christians and Muslims through your work in this chapter?

EPILOGUE

The world afflicted by the Black Death more than seven centuries ago may seem quite remote from our own. Advances in medical science now shield us from such devastation. Or

do they? Is the lesson to be drawn from an examination of epidemic disease in world history really all that comforting? Two of the essential preconditions for the plague pandemic of the fourteenth century, increasing population density and a growth in intercontinental trade, should sound familiar to us today. In fact, Ibn Khaldun saw it as a general rule of history that civilizations create the conditions of their own collapse. The growth of population in general, and of cities in particular, and the growth of trade and overall prosperity seem to Ibn Khaldun to lead almost inevitably to a catastrophic decline marked by famine and pestilence.

We do not need to be as fatalistic as Ibn Khaldun to recognize that the connection between plagues and peoples is not merely a matter of history. Yet the tremendous strides of medical science have tended to blind us to this fact. Over the past century, sustained efforts to bring cleaner food, water, and living conditions to growing populations made significant headway, at least in the world's more prosperous regions. At the same time, medical science grew ever more sophisticated at identifying and attacking epidemic diseases—witness the development of the polio vaccine, the eradication of smallpox, the creation of more and more powerful antibiotics, and a huge reduction in the rates of tuberculosis and syphilis. It seemed that the age-old problem of epidemic disease was well on its way to solution.

This complacency was shattered by the AIDS outbreak of the 1980s. Differences of opinion are still to be found concerning the origin of AIDS. Since it is often the case that viruses develop in wild or domesticated animals and then somehow make the leap to human beings, it is possible that one or more of the HIV-related viruses endemic amongst certain species of monkeys in Africa made such a transition, perhaps

when a hunter was infected by the blood of his kill. In the past, such a virus would probably have had only a local impact. In today's world, however, that infected hunter is likely to travel to a city, spreading the virus outside its original confined environment. That city is likely to be connected to an international airport. A disease that might once have been confined to a small group or region now stands a much better chance of becoming a global epidemic. Whatever the origin of HIV-AIDS, there is no doubt that the conditions of modernity have contributed to the spread of the disease.

HIV-AIDS is only the most notorious of the new diseases that have appeared in the past two decades. We could add Ebola virus, Lyme disease, Legionnaire's disease, Lassa fever, and many others to the list. At the same time, there has been a resurgence of old scourges that we once thought were on their way out, and the rise of more deadly forms of diseases such as malaria and encephalitis. As Arno Karlen points out, we are constantly and unwittingly creating the conditions that make this possible:

We provide new ecological niches for microbes by tilling fields and domesticating animals, and by bringing into existence gardens and second-growth forests, villages and cities, homes and factories. We give them new homes in discarded truck tires and water tanks, air conditioners and hospital equipment. We transport them by automobile, ship and airplane. We alter their opportunities and affect their evolution when we change our abodes, our sex behavior, our diets, our clothing. The faster we change ourselves and our surroundings, the faster new infections reach us. In the past century we have changed the biosphere as much as any glacial change or meteor impact ever has. So we and microbes are dancing faster than ever in order to survive each other. As we do so, the burdens on our environment and our immune defenses increase.[8]

Far from having conquered epidemic disease, we seem to have speeded up the process in a way that threatens to get out of hand. As in the period reviewed in this chapter, population growth and expanded intercontinental trade bring both opportunity and danger.

Karlen advises us to be concerned, but not to despair. Our immune systems are very powerful and highly adaptable. Perhaps even more important, history shows that the human race has been through this before and has always survived. Then as now our responses are conditioned by our cultural presuppositions. As we think back on the tragic story of the Black Death, perhaps our attitude should be one of understanding and appreciation for the way our forebears dealt with problems that we still face today.

8. Arlo Karlen, "The New Epidemic," in *The Black Death,* ed. Dan Nardo (San Diego: Greenhaven, 1999), p. 126.

CHAPTER FOURTEEN

CROSS-CULTURAL ENCOUNTERS:

TRAVEL, RELIGION, CONQUESTS,

AND TRADE (1400–1700)

THE PROBLEM

For the vast majority of humans alive in 1400, the world was an exceedingly small place. Most people never traveled more than a few miles from their birthplaces, living lives that were hard, restrictive, and for the most part short, as they died of hunger, in childbirth, of countless ailments, or from mysterious diseases that killed them by the thousands. Their perspectives were almost entirely confined to a small village of a few dozen families and to a nearby regional marketplace. Work, justice, medicine, marriage, entertainment, and social life were almost entirely local. Over 50 percent of their caloric intake was made up of one of the world's five major crops: wheat, corn, rice, barley, and sorghum. When those crops failed, sickness and death were very near.

Hardly any of these folk realized the profound changes that were taking place in their world, in not a few cases not far away. Travelers, missionaries, pilgrims, explorers/conquerors, and countless merchants, seamen, and caravan leaders all were participating in the process of gradually knitting together diverse peoples and already established regional trade networks into a nearly global web of information and commerce. Travelers widened perspectives and acted as cross-cultural carriers of knowledge and inventions. Religious proselytizers and pilgrims helped the folk to see beyond their local temple or church or mosque toward a multicultural religious community. Explorers and conquerors swept people into the expanding web, albeit often against their wills. Merchants were crucial in this process of proto-globalization, even though some cultures looked down on them, relegated them to lower stations, or restricted their activities. As the global web expanded, however, their wealth, power, and status rose enormously. This process of commercial globalization would not be completed for centuries, probably not until the middle to late nineteenth century. But the foundations were laid here, in the so-called pre-modern era of roughly 1400 to 1700.

The Evidence in this chapter includes accounts by travelers, missionaries, pilgrims, explorers, conquerors, and merchants as well as some helpful statistics and factual information. Using this evidence, the Background section of this chapter, your textbook, and your historical imagination, explain the cultural/

economic/political readiness of each major region to participate in the emerging global commercial network and how this network affected each region, both positively and negatively.

The major regions dealt with in this chapter are (1) East Asia (China and Japan), (2) Southern Asia (India and Southeast Asia), (3) North Africa and Middle East, (4) sub-Saharan West and East Africa, and (5) Western Europe. The two major commercial regions in the Americas (Aztec and Inca empires) will be touched on when addressing European expansion.

BACKGROUND

By the 15th century C.E., much of the world was recovering from a series of natural disasters that were followed soon thereafter by the horrific pandemic known as the Black Death.[1] Abnormally heavy rainfalls caused crop failures from China through Europe, whereas severe droughts from India through sub-Saharan Africa had the same effect. Then, beginning in 1320 in Southeast Asia, the terrible plague swept across China, Mongolia, the steppes of Central Asia to the Middle East, Egypt, North Africa and the Arabian peninsula, the Mediterranean, Western Europe, and finally to

1. See Chapter 13. The Black Death got its name from the black splotches on the skins of its victims.

Scandinavia and Ireland. Whole villages were devastated and in some areas the populations did not return to their pre-plague levels for 500 years.

Although mass starvation and the Black Death undoubtedly decreased the number of travelers, missionaries, and traders, it did not stop these interregional contacts altogether, and in fact this may well have been one way that the plague spread. Almost all of these people passed through lands touched by the plague, and it has been said that the Moroccan pilgrim Ibn Battuta "barely outran the Black Death" during his thirty-year journey of some 75,000 miles. Merchant caravans, some of which numbered hundreds or even thousands of camels, traversed the Great Silk Road from East Asia to the Mediterranean, carrying silk, tea, spices, porcelains, Buddhism, and, doubtless, the Black

Chapter 14

Cross-Cultural

Encounters:

Travel, Religion,

Conquests and

Trade (1400–1700)

Death[2]. Whether by land or water, trade routes connected cities (Venice, Genoa, Amsterdam, Istanbul, Calicut, Malacca, Maco, Jedda, London, etc.) where good locations, capital for investments, merchant combinations into companies, seafaring expertise, and boldness of leadership made these urban ports the capitals of early inter-regional commerce. And although the majority of trade in the 1400s through the 1600s was local, bartering food for often crudely made handicrafts or goods that could not be made at home, an increasing number of travelers, missionaries, and merchants were journeying farther afield, across regional cultural, economic, and political lines.[3]

Without a doubt the wealthiest and most advanced region, and therefore the region one would assume was best prepared to participate in the emerging global commercial network, was

East Asia, dominated by China. The Ming dynasty had come to power in 1368, and once a brief intra-family struggle for power (1398–1402) had been settled, the new emperor Yongle broke the Mongol power in China, brought political stability to the region, began to consolidate the authority of the emperor (called "the Son of Heaven"), and moved the capital to Beijing, which by 1500 boasted 672,000 inhabitants and was one of the ten largest cities in the world. To be sure, the famines and the Black Death had killed approximately one-third of China's people, but by 1500 the population had rebounded to exceed pre-plague levels, representing roughly 23 percent of the world's people.[4]

Pre-Ming China was the technological and economic powerhouse of the world. With the world's largest internal market system, Chinese tradesmen also sent silk, porcelain ware, and jade along the Great Silk Road, while Buddhist monks brought Chinese manufactures (especially much-coveted ironware) to Korea and Japan. Inventions such as gunpowder, fireworks, paper, the printing press, the magnetic compass, the sternpost rudder, and ships' hulls divided into watertight compartments often were more appreciated elsewhere than in China itself.

Although pre-Ming China carried on a significant amount of inter-regional trade, the first Ming emperor

2. Camels were used on the Great Silk Road and in the North African and sub-Saharan trade. As opposed to common folklore, camels do not store water in their humps but instead distribute it throughout their bodies. See William J. Bernstein, *A Splendid Exchange: How Trade Shaped the World* (New York: Atlantic Monthly Press, 2008), p. 55. On religious pilgrimages, Buddhism, Christianity, and Islam all strongly encouraged travel by the laity to holy places. The Christian crusaders of the 11th through 13th centuries referred to themselves as "pilgrims." See Chapter 7. For Ibn Battuta see Roxanne L. Euben, *Journeys to the Other Shore: Muslim and Western Travelers in Search of Knowledge* (Princeton: Princeton University Press, 2006), p. 38.

3. For cities see Fernand Braudel, *The Perspective of the World*, vol. 3 of *Civilization and Capitalism, 15th–18th Century*, trans. Sian Reynolds (New York: Harper and Row, 1984), pp. 27, 34. For an interesting survey of the spice trade see Michael Krondl, *The Taste of Conquest: The Rise and Fall of the Three Great Cities of Spice* (New York: Ballantine Books, 2007). For a map showing the Great Silk Road see ibid., pp. 18–19.

4. For China's population see Angus Maddison, *The World Economy: A Millennial Perspective* (Development Centre of the Organisation for Economic Co-Operation and Development, 2001), p. 40; Andre Gunder Frank, *ReORIENT: Global Economy in the Asian Age* (Berkeley: University of California Press, 1998), p. 170.

(Hongwu) prohibited Chinese merchants from engaging in foreign trade, possibly because he feared an influx of foreigners and their ideas. Hongwu's edict was strengthened by the collapse of the Mongol Empire, which made travel on the Great Silk Road extremely dangerous. Several merchants avoided the edict by moving their operations to Macao, a small island in the South China Sea.

The third Ming emperor, Yongle, was determined to demonstrate his power throughout East Asia, Southern Asia, and the Middle East by constructing an enormous fleet that would visit other regions and exact tribute from their rulers. To build and command the fleet Yongle chose Zheng He, who had proved his loyalty and talents in years of service to the emperor. Captured as a young man in a Ming war against his homeland, Zheng He was castrated and awarded to Yongle as a eunuch servant. Proving his loyalty during Yongle's successful *coup d'état*, Zheng He constructed a navy that at its height had over 250 vessels and 27,000 men, most of them warriors. From 1405 to 1433 this impressive fleet made seven voyages, returning with enormous amounts of tribute for the emperor. And wherever Zheng He's fleet went, Chinese merchants were soon to follow. Indeed, from all appearances, it would seem most likely that East Asia and especially China would be the region most likely to benefit from the emergence of an early commercial globalization.[5]

Another region that appeared to be in a good position to gain from the new global commercial patterns was that of the Middle East and Southern Asia, made up of the three Muslim empires of the Ottomans, the Safavids, and the Mughuls. The Ottoman Empire originated in the 1300s in what we now know as western Turkey. Expanding its political, religious, and economic power through conquests, by the 1400s it extended across North Africa, through present-day Turkey, Iraq, Israel, Syria, Saudi Arabia, Eastern Europe, and southern Spain. In 1453 Sultan Mehmed II captured Constantinople, thus giving him control of the vast majority of the trade passing eastward into Europe. Western merchants were permitted to do business in the Ottoman Empire, although they were required to pay fees for the privilege.[6] Throughout this vast empire, the Ottomans built magnificent architecture and impressive libraries (which included many "rescued" ancient European texts) and wrote interesting and elaborate poetry, music, and literature. A multi-ethnic empire, subjects were allowed to retain their own cultures and religions by paying modest tributes to regional government officials (Jews often said they were more tolerated by Ottoman Muslims than they were by anti-Semitic European Christians). Hence, in large part due to its advantageous geographic location, the Ottoman Empire, like early Ming China, was in a good position to benefit from proto-globalization.

---

5. The best recent account is Edward L. Dreyer, *Zheng He: China and the Oceans in the Early Ming Dynasty*, 1405–1433 (New York: Pearson/ Longman, 2007).

6. For Christian merchants in the Ottoman Empire see Braudel, *The Perspective of the World*, p. 22.

Chapter 14
Cross-Cultural
Encounters:
Travel, Religion,
Conquests and
Trade (1400–1700)

The Safavid Empire was founded by a mystical Islamic religious order's military campaign to reunite the old Persian Empire. An impressive trading and cultural center, the empire ultimately included present-day Iran and much of Afghanistan.

The wealthiest of the three so-called gunpowder empires (because of the role those weapons played in the three empires' establishing their power) was the Mughul Empire of northern India.[7] With its huge trade caravans and its near-domination of the Indian Ocean and South China Sea trade lanes, the Mughul merchants were the primary sources of carpets, fine cloth, pepper, and sugar. Indeed, before European development of its sugar colonies in Brazil and the West Indies, the Mughul traders were one of the principal sources of sugar in the world.

In spite of its impressive resources, the region of West Africa was not in an advantageous position to benefit from proto-globalization, in large part because of increased regional instability. Earlier, however, North African Berber and Arab traders pushing across the Sahara had found organized kingdoms in West Africa and had carried on a brisk commerce in gold, silk and cotton cloth, dates, ivory, salt, and slaves.[8] By the year 1100 camel caravans regularly crossed the Sahara to reach the bustling trade centers of Timbuktu and Gao, bringing trade goods from East Asia as well as the Islamic religion. Politically, the Kingdom of Ghana, a highly centralized military state, had been the dominant force in the region, but by 1200 it had declined, giving way to the Kingdom of Mali, an area so rich that when emperor Musa of Mali (a convert to Islam by Arab merchants from North Africa) arrived in Mecca in 1324 after a 3,500-mile pilgrimage, everyone's eyes were caught by Musa's hundreds of retainers leading a huge caravan of camels, one hundred of which were loaded with gold bars and gold dust.

And yet, by the 1400s the region had grown progressively unstable. North of Mali, the state of Songhai (also spelled Songhay and Songhi) had broken off from Mali, taking with it the opulent trade centers of Timbuktu and Gao. In turn, population increases as well as invasions from Senegambia and Guinea left all of West Africa politically and economically weakened and increasingly vulnerable to outside intrusion. By the 1500s, inter-ethnic rivalries had increased the number of slaves captured in battle, slaves that Muslim and European traders were only too willing to purchase.

As noted earlier, by the end of the Black Death around 1400,[9] Europe was the least prosperous and most provincial of all the global regions, a

---

7. For the "gunpowder empires" see Clive Ponting, *Gunpowder* (London: Chatto & Windus, 2005), pp. 79–99.

8. The Arabs called West Africa *Bilad al-Sudan*, or "Land of the Blacks."

9. Actually the plague reappeared sporadically throughout the entire 1400s and some of the 1500s, but by then much of the population had developed immunity.

virtual backwater of squalid villages, periodic hunger, near-constant intra-regional warfare, and peasant and urban uprisings that were crushed with incredible ferocity. Trade with other regions was not strong, since virtually no one wanted the crude goods that European merchants offered for sale or barter. To many travelers from other regions, Europe's situation appeared bleak indeed.[10]

And yet, by 1700 Western Europe no longer was the poor stepchild of the world's commercial regions. In nearly every aspect of Western European life, it appears that a significant awakening was taking place that over time would overthrow lethargy and backwardness and would make Western Europe the world's dominant commercial region.

Descendants of Western Europeans (including many Americans) take this commercial revolution for granted, assuming it was the inevitable bounty paid to a superior people. Closer examination, however, reveals that leaders were not always enlightened, merchants were not always bold or innovative, important technological improvements were more often borrowed from other cultures, and

as much responsible for Western Europe's resurgence as anything was incredibly good luck. Yet that resurgence did happen and, moreover, it lifted much of the population and not just the most prosperous and perfumed. By 1700 the *per capita gross domestic product*[11] in Western Europe was 166% that of China, 181% that of India, and 236% that of Africa. To be sure, Western peasants were still poor, often hungry, and periodically sick, but they were not nearly so bad off as those in other world regions. Therefore, although it did not appear so at the time, Western Europe was indeed in a very favorable position to benefit enormously from the emerging global trade networks and to use a combination of beneficial factors, aggressive attitudes, and good fortune to dominate many of those networks by 1600.

What strengths and weakness did each of the world's major commercial regions possess in the 1400s that prepared (or did not prepare) it to enter the emerging global marketplace? How did that emerging network affect each region, positively and negatively? How would you explain the rise of Western Europe?

---

10. Perhaps the only exceptions were the bustling commercial centers of Venice, Genoa, Milan, Florence, and Naples, whose brisk Mediterranean trade with Muslim traders made these prosperous cities. In 1500 the most populous three cities in Europe were Naples, Venice, and Milan. By 1700, however, they were London, Paris, and Lisbon.

11. The per capita gross domestic product is the total of all goods produced in an area (including food) divided by the area's population. See Angus Maddison, *Contours of the World Economy, 1–2030 AD:* Essays in *Macro-Economic History* (Oxford, UK: Oxford University Press, 2007), p. 382.

Chapter 14

Cross-Cultural

Encounters:

Travel, Religion,

Conquests and

Trade (1400–1700)

THE METHOD

In this chapter you will be working with three types of evidence: (1) primary source accounts by travelers, explorers, missionaries, and merchants, (2) some helpful statistics that will allow you to measure with some precision the populations, wealth, commerce, and living standards of the major cultural/economic regions, and (3) some factual information that will help you to answer the chapter's central questions.

By now you are no stranger to primary source accounts. You have already learned to elicit the main points and/or arguments of a source, to read between the lines to determine the source's bias/prejudice, to draw conclusions as to what is *not* being said, and to speculate about what conclusions the readers of the source at the time were expected to draw. In this chapter, you will have to go one step farther, for not one primary source in the chapter ever directly attempts to answer the chapter's central questions. But by reading each primary source carefully *and* by using your historical imagination, you may be able to tell how the source's author would have answered those questions. It

would be helpful if you made a chart for each source, summarizing the points made and noting your opinions about the author's statements, biases, and so forth.

Some of the primary sources include descriptions of people from a culture (or cultures) different from that of the source's author. How does the author depict those people (adjectives are important here)? What does that tell you about the author's opinion of inter-regional contacts? Unleash your historical imagination here.

Although some students are uncomfortable when working with statistics, in this chapter the statistical sets are few and very uncomplicated. Some of the sets will help you to compare different cultures over time (population gain/loss, standards of living, etc.) while other sets will simply show you increases or decreases in one thing (imports of tobacco, gold shipments, etc.). By themselves these statistics will not answer the chapter's central questions, but combined with primary sources and factual information, they will prove to be very helpful.

Similarly, the list of facts is to be used along with primary sources and statistics. For additional factual information, if you believe you need it, consult your text or your instructor.

PRIMARY SOURCES

A. CHINA

Source 1 from Edward L. Dreyer, Zheng He: China and the Oceans in the Early Ming Dynasty, 1405–1433 *(Library of the World Biography Series), 1st, © 2007, pp. 192–195. Printed and electronically reproduced by permission of Pearson Education, Inc., Upper Saddle River, New Jersey.*[12]

1. Zheng He's Inscriptions in Stone, 1431

[We have] traversed over hundred li of vast ocean waves, rising as high as the sky and swelling endlessly. Whether in dense fog and drizzling rain or in wind-driven waves rising like mountains, no matter what the sudden changes in sea conditions, we spread our cloudlike sails aloft and sailed by the stars day and night. [Had we] not trusted her divine merit, how could we have done this in peace and safety? When we met with danger, once we invoked the divine name, her answer to our prayer was like an echo; suddenly there was a divine lamp which illuminated the masts and sails, and once this miraculous light appeared, then apprehension turned to calm. The personnel of the fleet were then at rest, and all trusted they had nothing to fear. This is the general outline of the goddess' merit.

When we arrived at the foreign countries, barbarian kings who resisted transformation [by Chinese civilization] and were not respectful we captured alive, and bandit soldiers who looted and plundered recklessly we exterminated. Because of this the sea routes became pure and peaceful and the foreign peoples could rely upon them and pursue their occupations in safety. All of this was due to the aid of the goddess . . .

[I] In the third year of Yongle (1405) we went in command of the fleet to Calicut (*Guli*) and other countries. At that time pirate Chen Zuyi and his gang had gathered together at Palembang, where they plundered the foreign merchants. We captured their chieftains alive and returned in the fifth year (1407).

[II] In the fifth year of Yongle (1407) we went in command of the fleet to Java, Calicut, Cochin Thailand and other countries, whose kings each. . . presented tributes of local products, precious birds, and [rare] animals. In the seventh year (1409) we returned.

12. Zheng He (1371–1433) was born in Yunnan, which was under the control of the Mongols. In 1381 he was captured in a battle with Ming forces, castrated, and given as a servant to future Ming emperor Yongle. He was chosen by Yongle to build and command the huge Ming fleet, which made seven expeditions.

Chapter 14

Cross-Cultural

Encounters:

Travel, Religion,

Conquests and

Trade (1400–1700)

[III] In the seventh year of Yongle (1409) we went in command of the fleet to the afore[mentioned] countries, passing by the island of Ceylon on our way. The king of that country, Alagakkonra, trusted to his own strength and plotted to do harm to the fleet. Trusting to a divine manifestation of the spirit of the goddess, we perceived and understood this, and in consequence captured that king alive and presented him [to the emperor] on our return in the ninth year (1411). Afterward he received the favor of a pardon and was returned again to [his own] country. . . . The Imperial Ming [Dynasty] has unified [the lands within the four] seas [and under the] canopy [of Heaven], excelling the Three Dynasties and surpassing the Han and Tang. From the edge of the sky to the ends of the earth there are none who have not become subjects and slaves. To the most western of the Western Regions and to the most northern of the northern extremities, the length of a journey may be calculated, and thus the barbarians from beyond the seas, even those who are truly distant, [so that their languages require] double translation (*into another language that can then be translated into Chinese*), all have come to court bearing precious objects and presents.

2. Zhang Han's Essay on Merchants[13]

Money and profit are of great importance to men. They seek profit, then suffer by it, yet they cannot forget it. They exhaust their bodies and spirits run day and night, yet they still regard what they have gained as insufficient.

Those who become merchants eat fine food and wear elegant clothes. They ride on beautifully caparisoned, double-harnessed horses, dust flying as they race through the streets and the horses' precious sweat falling like rain. Opportunistic persons attracted by their wealth offer to serve them. Pretty girls in beautiful long-sleeved dresses and delicate slippers play stringed and wind instruments for them and compete to please them.

Merchants boast that their wisdom and ability are such as to give them a free hand in affairs. They believe that they know all the possible transformations in the universe and therefore can calculate all the changes in the human world, and that the rise and fall of prices are under their command. They are confident that they will not make one mistake in a hundred in their calculations. These merchants do not know how insignificant their wisdom and ability really are.

13. Zhang Han (1511–1593) was a Chinese government official whose family had grown rich in the textile trade. His family also may have been engaged in the animal breeding business and claimed to own 10,000 sheep.

As Zhuangzi says, "Great understanding is broad and unhurried; little understanding is cramped and busy.". . .

The profits from the tea and salt trades are especially great, but only large-scale merchants can undertake these businesses. Furthermore, there are government regulations on their distribution...

Profits from selling tea and officials' income from tea tax are usually ten to twenty percent of the original investment. By contrast, merchants' profits from selling salt and official income from the salt tax can reach seventy to eighty percent of the original invested capital. In either case, the more the invested capital, the greater the profit; the less the invested capital, the less the profit. The profits from selling tea and salt enrich the nation as well as the merchants. Skillful merchants can make great profits for themselves while the inept ones suffer losses. This is the present state of the tea and salt business. . . .

As to the foreign trade on the northwestern frontier and the foreign sea trade in the southeast, if we compare their advantages and disadvantages with respect to our nation's wealth and the people's well-being, we will discover that they are as different as black and white. But those who are in charge of state economic matters know only the benefits of the Northwest trade, ignoring the benefits of the sea trade. How can they be so blind? . . .

Foreigners are recalcitrant and their greed knows no bounds. At the present time our nation spends over one million cash yearly from our treasury on these foreigners; still we cannot rid ourselves of their demands. What is more, the greedy heart is unpredictable. If one day these foreigners break the treaties and invade our frontiers, who will be able to defend us against them? I do not think our present trade with them will ensure us a century of peace . . . . . .

Turning to the taxes levied on Chinese merchants, though these taxes are needed to fill the national treasury, excessive exploitation should be prohibited. . . .

3. The Biography of Zhu Jiefu[14]

After the funeral, Jiefu was short of funds. Since for generations his family had been in commerce, he decided not to suffer just to preserve his Scholar's cap. Therefore he handed in his resignation to the academic officials and devoted himself to the salt business. He thoroughly studied the laws on salt merchandising and was always able to talk about the strength and weakness of the law. When the envoy from the salt manufacturing division asked for his suggestions, Jiefu would respond promptly. As a result, all the other salt merchants respected him as their leader.

---

14. Zhu Jiefu was a Confucian scholar whose father was a salt merchant. His father's death forced him to abandon his studies to take over his father's business. In 1568 he was falsely accused of violating government regulations of the salt trade, was found guilty, and was sentenced to banishment to the frontier. He died at age 65.

Chapter 14

Cross-Cultural

Encounters:

Travel, Religion,

Conquests and

Trade (1400–1700)

During the Jiajing period [1522–1567] salt affairs were handled by the central law officer, who increased the taxes suddenly, causing great inconvenience for the merchants. They gathered in Jiefu's house and asked him to serve as their negotiator. Jiefu entered the office and stated the advantages and disadvantages of the new law eloquently in thousands of words. Leaning against his couch, the central law officer listened to Jiefu's argument and finally adopted his suggestions.

At that time, the merchants suffered greatly from two scoundrels who often took them to court in the hopes of getting bribes from them. During tense moments at trials, the merchants usually turned to Jiefu as their spokesman. Being lofty and righteous, he always disclosed the scoundrels' crimes and incriminated them. The merchants thus esteemed Jiefu for his virtue and wanted to give him a hundred taels of gold as a birthday present. But he protested, "Even if my acts have not been at the lofty level of a knight-errant, I did not do them for the sake of money." Thus, the merchants respected him even more and no longer talked about giving him money. . . .

The populace in Tunxi city where Jiefu lived was militant and litigious. When he returned home for his father's funeral, slanderous rumors were spread about him but Jiefu humbled himself and never tried to get back at the instigators. Later, when he rapidly grew rich, people became even more critical. Jiefu merely behaved with even greater deference.

He gained a reputation for his hospitality, and even when common people visited him, he always treated them very well. Some people came to rely upon Jiefu as much as if he were a relative. If he did not offer them enough, they would complain, "You stupid little rich merchant, why are you so stingy with me?"

Source 4 from Basil Davidson, The African Past: Chronicles from Antiquity to Modern Times *(Boston: Atlantic Monthly Press, 1964), p. 115. Copyright © 1964 by Basil Davidson. Reprinted by permission of Curtis Brown, Ltd.; and Joseph Needham, Wang Ling, and Lu Gwei Djen,* Science and Civilisation in China *(Cambridge: Cambridge University Press, 1971), vol. 4, pp. 533–534. Copyright © 1971 by Cambridge University Press.*

4. Chang Hsieh's Advice to Traders (1618)

The time has come to draw all these threads together. Sofala, by the sea-routes, was just about half-way between Lisbon and Nanking. Might it not perhaps have changed the course of history if the first Portuguese vessels coming past Sofala to Malindi had met much greater fleets of bigger ships with company more numerous than their own—and people, too, with very different ideas about the proper relations between civilized men and barbarians? "Coming into contact with barbarian peoples," wrote Chang Hsieh in 1618 in a passage we shall shortly read, "you have nothing more to fear than touching the left horn of a snail. The only things one should really be anxious about are the means of mastery of the waves of the seas—and, worst of all dangers, the minds of those avid for profit and greedy of gain." And indeed it was in accordance with this enlightened conception of inter-cultural contact that the Chinese set up no factories, demanded no forts, made no slave-raids, accomplished no conquests. Their total lack of any proselytising religion precluded friction from that source. The governmental character of their enterprises helped to restrain individual avarice and the crimes to which it could give rise. On the other hand, it is clear enough that the Portuguese behaviour originated as a development of the Crusader mentality. They were at war. But if the naval struggle against the Muslim mercantile States on the shores of the Indian Ocean was a continuation of the "Holy War" for the holy places, it turned insensibly into something quite different, an insatiable thirst for gold, not only Muslim gold, and an obsessive desire for power over all African and Asian peoples, whether or not they had anything to do with Islam. And now too there began to come into play that decisive superiority of armaments which the scientific Renaissance was to give to Europeans, enabling them to dominate the Old World and the New for three centuries. . . .

B. EUROPE

Source 5 from Christopher Columbus, Journal of the First Voyage to America (New York: Albert Boni & Charles Boni, 1924), pp. 24–29.[15]

5. Christopher Columbus
Journal, 1530s

As I saw that they were very friendly to us, and perceived that they could be much more easily converted to our holy faith by gentle means than by force, I presented them with some red caps, and strings of beads to wear upon the neck, and many other trifles of small value, wherewith they were much delighted, and became wonderfully attached to us. Afterwards they came swimming to the boats, bringing parrots, balls of cotton thread, javelins and many other things which they exchanged for articles we gave them, such as glass beads, and hawk's bells; which trade was carried on with the utmost good will. But they seemed on the whole to me, to be a very poor people. They all go completely naked, even the women, though I saw but one girl. All whom I saw were young, not above thirty years of age, well made, with fine shapes and faces; their hair short, and coarse like that of a horse's tail, combed toward the forehead, except a small portion which they suffer to hang down behind, and never cut. Some paint themselves with black, which makes them appear like

---

15. Christopher Columbus (1451–1506) was a Genoese seaman, navigator, and explorer. Although not the first European to reach the Western Hemisphere, his initial voyage of 1492 was the first to make educated Europeans aware of the so-called New World and its possibilities for exploitation.

Chapter 14

Cross-Cultural

Encounters:

Travel, Religion,

Conquests and

Trade (1400–1700)

those of the Canaries, neither black nor white; others with white, others with red, and others with such colours as they can find. Some paint the face, and some the whole body; others only the eyes, and others the nose. Weapons they have none, nor are acquainted with them, for I showed them swords which they grasped by the blades, and cut themselves through ignorance. They have no iron, their javelins being without it, and nothing more than sticks, though some have fish-bones or other things at the ends. They are all of a good size and stature, and handsomely formed. I saw some with scars of wounds upon their bodies, and demanded by signs the cause of them; they answered me in the same way, that there came people from other islands in the neighbourhood who endeavoured to make prisoners of them, and they defended themselves. I thought then, and still believe, that these were from the continent. It appears to me, that the people are ingenious, and would be good servants; and I am of opinion that they would very readily become Christians, as they appear to have no religion. They very quickly learn such words as are spoken to them. If it please our Lord, I intend at my return to carry home six of them to your Highnesses [Spain's monarchs, Ferdinand and Isabella] that they may learn our language . . .

At daybreak great multitudes of men came to the shore, all young and of fine shapes, very handsome; their hair not curled but straight and coarse like horse hair, and all with foreheads and heads much broader than any people I had hitherto seen; their eyes were large and very beautiful . . .

They were straight-limbed without exception, and not with prominent bellies but handsomely shaped. They came to the ship in canoes, made of a single trunk of a tree, wrought in a wonderful manner considering the country; some of them large enough to contain forty or forty-five men, other of different sizes down to those fitted to hold but a single person. They rowed with an oar like a baker's peel, and wonderfully swift . . .

Seeing some of them with little bits of this metal hanging at their noses, I gathered from them by signs that by going southward or steering round the island in that direction, there would be found a king who possessed large vessels of gold, and in great quantities. I endeavoured to procure them to lead the way thither, but found they were unacquainted with the route . . .

The natives are an inoffensive people, and so desirous to possess any thing they saw with us, that they kept swimming off to the ships with whatever they could find, and readily bartered for any article we saw fit to give them in return, even such as broken platters and fragments of glass . . .

I do not . . . see the necessity of fortifying the place, as the people here are simple in war-like matters, as your Highnesses will see by those seven which I have ordered to be taken and carried to Spain in order to learn our language and return, unless your Highnesses should choose to have them all transported to Castile, or held captive in the island. I could conquer the whole of them with fifty men, and govern them as I pleased. . . .

Source 6 from Bartolomé de Las Casas: A Selection of His Writings, *trans. & ed. George Sanderlin (New York: Alfred A. Knopf, 1971), pp. 158–161. Translation copyright © 1971 by Alfred A. Knopf, a division of Random House, Inc. Used by permission of Alfred A. Knopf, a division of Random House, Inc.*[16]

6. Las Casas, Teaching the True Religion (1530s)

The one and only method of teaching men the true religion was established by Divine Providence for the whole world, and for all times: that is, by persuadmg the understanding through reasons, and by gently attracting or exhorting the will. This method should be common to all men throughout the world, without any distinction made for sects, errors, or corrupt customs.

This conclusion will be proved in many ways: by arguments drawn from reason; by examples of the ancient Fathers; by the rule and manner of preaching which Christ instituted for all times; by the practices of the Apostles; by quotations from holy teachers; by the most ancient tradition of the Church and by her numerous ecclesiastical decrees . . .

And first, this conclusion will be proved by arguments drawn from reason, among which let this be the first. There is only one method peculiar to Divine Wisdom by which it disposes and moves created beings gently to actions and to their natural ends. But among created beings, rational creatures are higher and more excellent than all others which were not made in the Image of God. . . . Therefore, Divine Wisdom moves rational creatures, that is, men, to their actions or operations gently . . . Therefore, the method of teaching men the true religion ought to be gentle, enticing, and pleasant. This method is by persuading the understanding and by attracting the will. . . .

A method contrary to the one we have been defending would be the following: that. . . the pagans should first be subjected, whether they wished to be or not, to the rule of the Christian people, and that once they were subjected, organized preaching would follow... [But a] rational creature has a natural capacity for being moved, directed and drawn to any good gently . . . because of his freedom of choice. But if pagans find themselves first injured, oppressed, saddened, and afflicted by the misfortunes of wars, through the loss of their children, their goods, and their own liberty . . . how can they be moved voluntarily to listen to what is proposed to them about faith, religion, justice and truth? Or how will they be able to adhere to what has been preached? Likewise, if a soft word multiplies friends and, on the contrary, "An ill-tempered man stirs up strife" (Prov. 15, 18), how many enemies will not such bitter words and works make? . . .

16. Bartolomé de Las Casas (1484–1566) was born in Spain, the son of a merchant. At age 18, he went to the "New World" as part of an expedition to conquer Santo Domingo, and also participated in the conquests of Cuba and Mexico. In a change of heart, he became a Dominican priest and wrote numerous treatises urging humane treatment for the Native Americans. In 1537, Pope Paul III issued a papal bull declaring that "the Indians are truly men [and] ... by no means [should they] be deprived of their liberty." The bull was generally ignored by Spanish and Portuguese conquerors and slave masters.

Chapter 14

Cross-Cultural

Encounters:

Travel, Religion,

Conquests and

Trade (1400–1700)

Source 7 from Richard Hakluyt (the Younger), Discourse of Western Planting *(1584), in David B. Quinn, ed.,* English Plans for North America, *vol. 3 of* New American World: A Documentary History of North America to 1612 *(New York: Arno Press, 1979), vol. 3, pp. 71–72, 82.*[17]

7. Richard Hakluyt (the Younger), Discourse of Western Planting (1584)

1. That this westerne discoverie will be greately for thinlargement of the gospell of Christe whereunto the Princes of the refourmed relligion are chefely bounde amongest whome her mattie ys principall.

2. That all other englishe Trades are growen beggerly or daungerous, especially in all the kinge of Spayne his Domynions, where our men are dryven to flinge their Bibles and prayer Bokes into the sea, and to forsweare and renownce their relligion and conscience and consequently theyr obedience to her Majestie.

3. That this westerne voyadge will yelde unto us all the commodities of Europe, Affrica, and Asia, as far as wee were wonte to travell, and supply the wantes of all our decayed trades. . . .

That this enterprise will be for the manifolde imploymente of nombers of idle men, and for bredinge of many sufficient, and for utterance of the greate quantitie of the commodities of our Realme. . . .

[W]e are growen more populous than ever. . . that they can hardly lyve one by another. . . and often fall to pilferinge and thevinge and other lewdness, whereby all the prisons of the lande are daily . . . stuffed full of them, where either they pitifully pyne awaye, or els at lengthe are miserably hanged. . . .

13. That hereby the Revenewes and customes of her Majestie bothe outwards and inwardes shall mightely be inlarged by the toll, excises, and other dueties which withoute oppression may be raised.

14. That this action will be greately for thincrease, mayneteynaunce and safetie of our Navye, and especially of greate shippinge which is the strengthe of our Realme, and for the supportation of all those occupations that depende upon the same.

15. That spedie plantinge in divers fitt places is moste necessarie upon these luckye westerne discoveries for feare of the daunger of being prevented by other nations which have the like intentions, with the order thereof and other reasons therwithall alleaged. . . .

17. Richard Hakluyt the Younger (1552–1616) was an English clergyman and author and, with his cousin Richard Hakluyt the Elder, was an articulate and insistent advocate of English colonization.

17. That by these Colonies the Northwest passage to Cathaio and China may easely quickly and perfectly be searched oute aswell by river and overlande, as by sea, for proofe whereof here are quoted and alleaged divers rare Testymonies oute of the three volumes of voyadges gathered by Ramusius and other grave authors

18. That the Queene of Englande title to all the west Indies, or at the leaste to as moche as is from Florida to the Circle articke, is more lawfull and righte then the Spaniardes or any other Christian Princes. . . .

Source 8 from Sir John Chardin, Travels in Persia, 1673–1677 *(New York: Dover Publications, 1988), pp. 282–283. Copyright © 1988. Reprinted by permission of Dover Publications.*[18]

8. Sir John Chardin, Travels in Persia

Trading is a very honourable Profession in the *East*, as being the best of those that have any Stability, and are not so liable to change. 'Tis not to be wonder'd at, for it cannot be otherwise in Kingdoms, where on the one hand there is no Title of Nobility, and therefore little Authority annexed to the Birth; and where on the other Hand, the form of Government being altogether Despotick and Arbitrary, the Authority annexed to Places and Employments cannot last longer than the Employments themselves, which are likewise precarious; for which Reason Trading is much set by in that part of the World, as a lasting and independent Station. Another Reason why it is valu'd is, because the Noblemen profess it, and the Kings also; they have their Deputies as the Merchants have, and under the same Denomination: They have most of them their Trading Ships, and their Store-Houses. The King of *Persia*, for Instance, sells and sends to the Neighbouring Kingdoms, Silk, Brocades, and other rich Goods, Carpets and Precious Stones. The Name of Merchant, is a Name much respected in the East, and is not allowed to Shop-keepers or Dealers in trifling Goods; nor to those who Trade not in foreign Countries: 'Tis allow'd only to such as employ Deputies or Factors in the remotest Countries: And those Men are sometimes rais'd to the highest Ranks, and are usually employed in Embassies. There are Merchants in *Persia* who have Deputies in all parts of the world: And when those Deputies are returned Home, they wait on their Master, under no better Denomination than that of a Servant, standing up always before them, and waiting at Table, tho' some of those Deputies are

---

18. Sir John Chardin (1643–1713) was a wealthy jeweler and jewelry merchant who sold his merchandise throughout the Safavid Empire. He served as the court jeweler to King Charles II of England and was knighted for those endeavors.

Chapter 14

Cross-Cultural

Encounters:

Travel, Religion,

Conquests and

Trade (1400–1700)

worth above threescore thousand Crowns. In the Indies the Laws are still more favourable to Traders, for tho' they are much more numerous than in Persia, they are nevertheless more set by. The Reason of this additional Respect, is, because in the East, Traders are Sacred Person, who are never molested even in time of War; and are allowed a free Passage, they and their Effects, through the middle of Armies: 'Tis upon their account especially that the Roads are so safe all over Asia, and especially in *Persia*. The *Persians* call a Trader *Saudaguer*, i.e. Gain-Monger.

The Eastern Merchants affect Grandure in Trading, notwithstanding they send their Deputies into all Parts, and stay at Home themselves, as in the Center of their grand Concern; they make no Bargains themselves directly, there is no publick place of Exchange in their Towns; the Trade is carried on by Stock-jobbers, who are the subtilest, the cunningest, the slyest, the complaisantest, the patientest, and the most intriguing Men of the whole Society, having a valuable and insinuating Tongue beyond Expression: They are called *Delal*, which answers to Great Talkers, that Word being of a contrary Signification to Lal, i.e. Dumb. The *Mabometans* have a Proverb alluding to the Name of those Men, viz. That at the last Day, Delal Lal, the Stock-jobbers, or Talkers, will be Dumb; intimating that they will have nothing to say for themselves. 'Tis very curious to see them make Bargains: After they have Argued and Discoursed a while before the Seller, and commonly at his own House, they agree with their Fingers about the Price: They take hold of one another's right Hand under a Cloak or Handkerchief, and entertain one another in that manner; the strait Finger stands for Ten, the bent Finger for Five; the Finger end for One; the whole Hand for a Hundred; and the Fist for a Thousand. Thus they denote Pounds, Pence, and Farthings, with a Motion of their Fingers: While they bargain they put on such a grave and steady Countenance, that 'tis impossible to know in the least either what they think or say.

However, the *Mahometans* are not the greatest Traders in Asia, tho' they be dispers'd almost in every Part of it; and tho' their Religion bears sway in the larger part of it. Some of them are too Effeminate, and some too severe to apply themselves to Trade, especially foreign Trading. Wherefore in *Turky*, the *Christians* and *Jews* carry on the main foreign Trade: And in *Persia* the *Christians* and *Indian Gentiles*. As to the Persians they Trade with their own Countrymen, one Province with another, and most of them Trade with the *Indians*. . . .

Source 9 from Thomas Mun, England's Treasure by Forraign Trade, or the Balance of our Forraign Trade is The Rule of Our Treasure *(London: J.G. for Thomas Clark, 1664), pp. 5–6, 25.*[19]

9. Thomas Mun, England's Treasure (1664)

Although a Kingdom may be enriched by gifts received, or by purchase taken from some other Nations, Yet these are things uncertain and of small consideration when they happen. The ordinary means therefore to encrease our wealth and treasure is by *Forraign Trade,* wherein wee must ever observe this rule; to sell more to strangers yearly than wee consume of theirs in value. For suppose that when this Kingdom is plentifully served with the Cloth, Lead, Tinn, Iron, Fish and other native commodities, we doe yearly export the overplus to forraign Countries to the value of twenty two hundred thousand pounds; by which means we are enabled beyond the Seas to buy and bring in forraign wares for our use and Consumptions, to the value of twenty hundred thousand pounds; By this order duly kept in our trading, we may rest assured that the Kingdom shall be enriched yearly two hundred thousand pounds, which must be brought to us in so much Treasure; because that part of our stock which is not returned to us in wares must necessarily be brought home in treasure.

For in this case it cometh to pass in the stock of a Kingdom, as in the estate of a private man; who is supposed to have one thousand pounds yearly revenue and two thousand pounds of ready money in his Chest: If such a man through excess shall spend one thousand five hundred pounds *per annum,* all his ready mony will be gone in four years; and in the like time his said money will be doubled if he take a Frugal course to spend but five hundred pounds *per annum;* which rule never faileth likewise in the Commonwealth, but in some cases (of no great moment) which I will hereafter declare, when I shall shew by whom and in what manner this balance of the Kingdoms account ought to be drawn up yearly, or so often as it shall please that State to discover how much we gain or lose by trade with forraign Nations. But first I will say something concerning those ways and means which will encrease our exportation and diminish our importation of wares; which being done, I will then set down some other arguments both affirmative and negative to strengthen that which is here declared, and thereby to shew that all the other means which are commonly supposed to enrich the Kingdom with Treasure are altogether insufficient and meer fallacies. . . .

In the course of forraign trade there are three sorts of gain, the first is that of the Commonwealth, which may be done when the Merchant (who is the principal Agent therein) shall lose. The second is the gain of the Merchant, which he doth sometimes justly and worthily effect, although the Commonwealth be

19. Thomas Mun (1571–1641) was a London merchant and a member of the East India Company.

Chapter 14

Cross-Cultural

Encounters:

Travel, Religion,

Conquests and

Trade (1400–1700)

a loser. The third is the gain of the King, whereof he is ever certain, even when the Commonwealth and the Merchant shall be both losers. . . .

C. MUSLIM REGIONS

Source 10 from Travels of Ibn Battuta, *trans. & ed. Samuel Lee (New York: Burt Franklin, n.d.),* pp. 169–170, 172–173.[20]

10. Travels of Ibn Battuta,
c. 1353

The first town we entered in the country of Malabar was that of Abi Sardar which is small, and is situated on a large estuary of the sea. We next came to the city of Kakanwar, which is large, and also upon an estuary of the sea. It abounds in the sugar-cane. The Sultan is an infidel. He sent his son as a pledge to our vessel, and we landed accordingly, and were honourably received. He also sent presents to the ship, as marks of respect to the Emperor of India. It is a custom with them, that every vessel which passes by one of their ports shall enter it, and give a present to its Sultan; in this case they let it pass, but otherwise they make war upon it with their vessels, they then board it out of contempt, and impose a double fine upon the cargo, just in proportion to the advantage they usually gain from merchants entering their country.

We next arrived at the city of Manjarun, which is situated upon a large estuary of the sea, called the *"estuary of the wolf,"* and which is the greatest estuary in the country of Malabar. In this place are some of the greatest merchants of Persia and Yemen. Ginger and black pepper are here in great abundance. The king of this place is the greatest of the kings of Malabar, and in it are about four thousand Mohammedan merchants. The king made us land, and sent us a present.

We next came to the town of Hīlī, which is large and situated upon an estuary of the sea. As far as this place come the ships of China, but they do not go beyond it; nor do they enter any harbour, except that of this place, of Kālikūt, and of Kawlam.

The city of Hīlī is much revered both by Mohammedans and infidels, on account of a mosque, the source of light and of blessings, which is found in it. To this seafaring persons make and pay their vows, whence its treasury is derived, which is placed under the control of the principal Moslem. The mosque

---

20. Ibn Battuta (1304–1368 or 1369) was a Moroccan scholar and traveler. A Muslim, after his hajj (pilgrimage to Mecca), he vowed to travel to everywhere that had embraced Islam, a journey that covered roughly 75,000 miles and took thirty years.

maintains a preacher, and has within it several students, as well as readers of the Korān, and persons who teach writing.

We next came to Kālikūt, one of the great ports of the district of Malabar, and in which merchants from all parts are found. The king of this place is an infidel who shaves his chin just as the Haidari Fakeers of Room do. When we approached this place, the people came out to meet us, and with a large concourse brought us into the port. The greatest part of the Mohammedan merchants of this place are so wealthy, that one of them can purchase the whole freightage of such vessels as put in here; and fit out others like them. Here we waited three months for the season to set sail for China: for there is only one season in the year in which the sea of China is navigable. Nor then is the voyage undertaken, except in vessels of the three descriptions following: the greatest is called a junk, the middlingsized a zaw, the least a kakam. The sails of these vessels are made of cane-reeds, woven together like a mat; which, when they into port, they leave standing in the wind. In some of these vessels there will be employed a thousand men, six hundred of these sailors, and four hundred soldiers. Each of the larger ships is followed by three others, a middle sized, a third, and a fourth sized. These vessels are nowhere made except in the city of El ZaitŪn [Chuanzhou] in China, or in Sīn Kīlān, which is Sin El Sin. They row in these ships with large oars, which may be compared to great masts, over some of which five and twenty men will be stationed, who work standing. The commander of each vessel is a great Emir. In the large ships too they sow garden herbs and ginger, which they cultivate in cisterns (made for that purpose), and placed on the sides of them. In these also are houses constructed of wood, in which the higher officers reside with their wives; but these they do not hire out to the merchants. Every vessel, therefore, is like an independent city. Of such ships as these, Chinese individuals will sometimes have large numbers: and, generally, the Chinese are the richest people in the world.

Source 11 from Evliyá Efendí, Narrative of Travels in Europe, Asia, and Africa in the Seventeenth Century, *trans. Joseph von Hammer, in* The Muslim World, 1100–1700 *(Oxford, UK: Routledge, 2007), pp. 323–324, 333–335. Copyright © 2007. Permission of the Royal Asiatic Society, Great Britain and Ireland.*[21]

11. Evliyá Efendí, Narrative of Travels

If I should minutely describe all the pleasure-places, gardens, yallis, and Koshks, it would be a long work; therefore according to my narrow intellect I have given only the most famous of all the buildings, foundations, pilgrimages, and walks. It now remains to speak of the shops and guilds which adorn the well-guarded

21. Evilyá Efendí (1611–c.1683) was the son of a prosperous Istanbul goldsmith. In 1630 he had a vision in which the Prophet Muhammad ordered him to travel throughout the whole world.

Chapter 14
Cross-Cultural
Encounters:
Travel, Religion,
Conquests and
Trade (1400–1700)

city of Constantinople, we are therefore about to enumerate, if it please God, all the handicraftsmen according to the constitutional laws of Sultán Suleiman, mentioning their patrons, and where they are buried, the number of shops, and men they employ.

God having created man in paradise, from whence he was seduced by the insinuation of Satan; Adam was taught by the mediation of Gabriel to sow the earth with corn during his life-time, and all the prophets similar arts necessary for sustaining life.

[Here the author lists all of the major prophets recognized by Islam and their occupations, some of which were Noah the joiner, Abraham the dairyman and mason, Joseph the watchmaker and then king, Moses the shepherd, Solomon the basketmaker, Daniel a fortuneteller, Jonas a fisherman, Jesus a traveler, "and six hundred years after him, Mohammed, the last of the prophets, a merchant, and soldier in God's ways. . . . All these prophets having been taught their above-mentioned arts by Gabriel, communicated them to mankind, and became the Sheikhs and protectors of those arts." Clearly the idea is that each occupation is divinely ordained and thereby equal to all others.]

The foundation of all science are the letters of the alphabet, wherein God, the Almighty, has manifested his eternal power in a way to confound all the powers of intellect. God has sent to his Prophets an hundred and four books. The four holy writs, the Pentateuch, the Psalter, the Gospel, and the Korán, and the hundred sent to other prophets are all composed by the combinations of the twenty-nine letters. It is said that there are seventy-two different languages in the world, but God knows there may be a thousand and seventy-two nations on the surface of the earth, each of whom has its particular language. I myself have, in the course of my travels of forty-one years, met with an hundred and forty-seven languages of different nations, whom I have heard to speak; and all these languages are combined of the twenty-nine elements of the alphabet. If there were to come into the world some hundred thousand more Aristotles they would never be able to add a letter more, nor to change the fundamental forms of language. In the Persian, it is true there are the letters *p, j* and *g* which are not found in the Arabic alphabet; they are, however, expressed by the same signs. In the Circassian language there are some rude sounds like those of a woodpecker, which cannot be written, and which are uttered and understood only by the Circassians themselves. The science of the alphabet is one of the most necessary to get on with in the secret and mystic sciences . . .

*The Description of Constantinople, made in the Year 1048 (1638),
by order the Sultán Murad IV, containing the summary
of Buildings of every kind.*

Sultán Murád IV, the conqueror of Baghdad, son of Ahmed I, (God's mercy upon him and all his ancestors) delighted in conversing with learned men, particularly with those skilled in chronology. One day at one of these assemblies of learned divines and historians, mention was made of the description of the old town of Constantinople. Sultán Murád said: "Though so many countries and residences have been minutely described by geographers and historians, yet this my residence of Constantinople remains undescribed." The Mufti, Yahyá Efendi, the son of Zekeria Efendi, who was present, answered: "My Emperor, in the Korán this noble town of Constantinople is mentioned by the verse: 'Have the Greeks not been vanquished in the lowest ground?' The builder of this spot marked out in the Korán was first Suleiman (Solomon), then Alexander Zulkarnin, who lived 882 years before the Prophet: it was then repaired by thy great ancestor Mohammed II, and then at your own order, my Emperor, by Lala Beirám Páshá, when you undertook the expedition of Eriván. It is in order to glorify this town and its inhabitants that the Prophet delivered these words. 'They shall conquer Constantinople, how good a Prince its Prince, what good troops its troops.' Travellers call this great capital, the splendour, the power, the magnificence of Greece, the pride of Macedonia, the star of Rum: the town, the excellent town, of which the Koran says: "Have the Greeks not been vanquished?"

The Mufti, having quoted these verses (of one of the town-revolts) in order to give a description of Constantinople, our master, Evliya Efendi declaimed the famous Arabic verse:

> I've seen the towns of all the world
> But nowhere saw I one like this.

Others who were of the assembly said: "My Emperor, we have read many curious books, we have travelled seventy or eighty years, we were present at the conquests of the greatest towns, but nowhere saw one like Constantinople; we saw travellers of an hundred and twenty to an hundred and fifty years old, who had spent their lives on the road, who also said that they had never seen a town, which as to situation, clime, and beauty, could be compared to Constantinople." The Sultán said: "Dear companions, and you, Mufti Yahyá Efendi, if it please God we will wrest Baghdad from the hands of the Persians. . . . May God preserve [Constantinople] from her decay and fall!"

Chapter 14
Cross-Cultural
Encounters:
Travel, Religion,
Conquests and
Trade (1400–1700)

D. AFRICA

Sources 12 and 13 from Basil Davidson, trans., The African Past *(London: Curtis Brown, 1964), pp. 191–194, 120–121.*

12. Nzinga Mbemba, King of Kongo, to the King of Portugal, 1526[22]

Sir, Your Highness [King of Portugal] should know how our Kingdom is being lost in so many ways that it is convenient to provide for the necessary remedy, since this is caused by the excessive freedom given by your agents and officials to the men and merchants who are allowed to come to this Kingdom to set up shops with goods and many things which have been prohibited by us, and which they spread throughout our kingdoms and Domains in such an abundance that many of our vassals, whom we had in obedience, do not comply because they have the things in greater abundance than we ourselves; and it was with these things that we had them content and subjected under our vassalage and jurisdiction, so it is doing a great harm not only to the service of God, but the security and peace of our Kingdoms and State as well.

And we cannot reckon how great the damage is, since the mentioned merchants are taking every day our natives, sons of the land and the sons of our noblemen and vassals and our relatives, because the thieves and men of bad conscience grab them wishing to have the things and wares of this Kingdom which they are ambitious of; they grab them and get them to be sold; and so great, Sir, is the corruption and licentiousness that our country is being completely depopulated, and Your Highness should not agree with this nor accept it as in your service. And to avoid it we need from those [your] Kingdoms no more than some priests and a few people to teach in schools, and no other goods except wine and flour for the holy sacrament. That is why we beg of Your Highness to help and assist us in this matter, commanding your factors that they should not send here either merchants or wares, because it is *our will that in these Kingdoms there should not be any trade of slaves nor outlet for them.* Concerning what is referred [to] above, again we beg of Your Highness to agree with it, since otherwise we cannot remedy such an obvious damage. Pray Our Lord in His mercy to have Your Highness under His guard and let you do forever the things of His service. . . .

Moreover, Sir, in our Kingdoms there is another great inconvenience which is of little service to God, and this is that many of our people, keenly desirous as they

22. Nzinga Mbemba (c. 1456–1542 or 1543) was King of Kongo from 1509 until his death. After the arrival of the Portuguese (who referred to him as King Afonso I), he was allowed to rule over Kongo's northern province of Nsundi. He became a devout Christian under tutelage by Portuguese priests.

[432]

are of the wares and things of your kingdoms, which are brought here by your people, and in order to satisfy their voracious appetite, seize many of our people, freed and exempt men, and very often it happens that they kidnap even noblemen and the sons of noblemen, and our relatives, and take them to be sold to the white men who are in our Kingdoms; and for this purpose they have concealed them; and others are brought during the night so that they might not be recognized.

And as soon as they are taken by the white men they are immediately ironed and branded with fire, and when they are carried to be embarked, if they are caught by our guards' men the whites allege that they have bought them but they cannot say from whom, so that it is our duty to do justice and to restore to the freemen their freedom, but it cannot be done if your subjects feel offended; as they claim to be.

And to avoid such a great evil we passed a law so that any white man living in our Kingdoms and wanting to purchase goods in any way should first inform three of our noblemen and officials of our court whom we rely upon in this matter, and these are Dom Pedro Manipanza and Dom Manuel Manissaba, our chief usher, and Gonçalo Pires our chief freighter, who should investigate if the mentioned goods are captives or free men, and if cleared by them there will be no further doubt nor embargo for them to be taken and embarked. But if the white men do not comply with it they will lose the aforementioned goods. And if we do them this favor and concession it is for the part Your Highness has in it, since we know that it is in your service too that these goods are taken from our Kingdom, otherwise we should not consent to this. . . .

13. Pate Chronicle[23]

Now in those days Arab and Indian vessels used to come to Pate harbor.

Sultan Omar had a nephew who was very fond of traveling. On his first journey he set out for India, but was completely lost and his ship sank, and he himself, after meeting with great hardships and difficulties and losing everything, returned home. He remained at home for a year, but the next year he wished to travel abroad again . . . [His parents now vainly attempted to dissuade him.] As they were unable to stop him they made up a fleet of seven ships for him and he voyaged away and wrecked all his ships. He returned alone, and he had nothing and no one with him . . . [But still he persisted in his wish to travel the seas, and again prevailed upon his parents and friends.] When his parents found that they were unable to prevent him, they gave him a fleet according to his wishes.

So he set out and arrived in India where he traded and made much profit. During the return they were lost at sea for many days till from the vessel on board of which he was they saw an island near them.

---

23. Pate Island is in the Indian Ocean off the coast of East Africa near present-day Kenya. It had been under Arab rule since the 14th century, until it was conquered by the Portuguese in 1597. The date of the Pate Chronicle is unknown.

Chapter 14

Cross-Cultural

Encounters:

Travel, Religion,

Conquests and

Trade (1400–1700)

So they disembarked as they were in need of water, and that youth wished to rest from the discomforts he had suffered. He lay under a tree and told his servants to cook his food and bring it to him here.

They sat down to cook, and when the fire blazed up they saw the sand of that place melt and run away. When it had gone a little from the fire it cooled in separate little pieces . . . [This the enterprising young man immediately recognized to be silver. He persuaded his crew to jettison most of the cargo they had bought and to load instead with this silver-bearing sand.]

So they took his advice and unloaded all their goods and filled up with sand for three days till the ship could carry no more . . . [They lost some in a storm but] afterwards they got a safe and favorable wind and arrived home [where he was joyfully received] . . .

He rested for three days and then at dead of night he brought some of the sand and put it in a store in his house. Then he called skilled workmen and showed them a little, and when they had made an ornament out of it they found that it was very pure silver.

Now it was at this time that the Portuguese arrived in Pate, and first they came in friendship. Afterwards he showed the ore to the Portuguese and they asked him where he got it. He told them the story from first to last because of his joy when he knew that it was real ore.

Those Portuguese wanted him to show them the spot, and they went together with the captain and searched for six months and returned again without finding it . . .

STATISTICS

Sources 14 through 21, 23, and 26 from Angus Maddison, Contours of the World Economy, 1–2030 AD: Essays in Macro-Economic History *(Oxford, UK: Oxford University Press, 2007), pp. 43, 112, 113, 123, 214, 223, 377–378, 382. By permission of Oxford University Press.*

14. Rates of Population Growth, 1000–1820 (ave. annual compound growth rates)

Region	1000–1500	1500–1820	% of world total 1700
Western Europe	0.16	0.26	13.5%
China	0.11	0.41	22.9%
India	0.08	0.20	27.4%
Africa	0.07	0.15	10.1%

15. Per Capita Gross Domestic Product (in 1990 international dollars), 1000–1700

Region	1000	1500	1600	1700
Western Europe	$427	$771	$889	$997
China	$450	$600	$600	$600
India	$450	$550	$550	$550
Africa	$425	$414	$422	$421

16. Population and Gross Domestic Product Growth, 1500–1700

Region	Population Growth 1500–1700	GDP Growth 1500–1700
Asia	+28%	0.0%
Africa	+72%	0.02%
Latin America	–29%	NA
Western Europe	+42%	+76.0%

17. Urbanization Ratios in China and Western Europe, 1000–1700 (population in cities 10,000 and over as percentage of total population)

Region	1000	1500	1600	1700
China	3.0%	3.8%	4.0%	NA
Western Europe	NA	5.8%	7.9%	9.5%

18. Slave Exports from Africa, by Destination (000s), 650–1800

Destination	650–1500	1500–1800	% of total 1500–1800
Trans-Sahara	4270	1950	18.20%
Asia	2200	1000	9.33%
Americas	81	7766	72.47%
Total	6551	10,716	100.00%

Chapter 14

Cross-Cultural

Encounters:

Travel, Religion,

Conquests and

Trade (1400–1700)

19. World Gold Output by Region, 1493–1700 (in million fine oz.)

Region	1493–1600	1601–1700
Africa	8153	6430
Americas	8976	19043
Europe	4758	3215

20. Gold and Silver Shipments from the Americas to Europe, 1500–1700 (metric tons)

Dates	Gold	Silver
1500–1600	150	7500
1601–1700	158	26,168

21. Exports of Gold and Silver from Europe, 1600–1700 (metric tons of silver equivalent)

Dates	To West Asia	Dutch to Asia	British to Asia	Total to Asia
1601–1650	2500	425	250	3175
1651–1700	2500	775	1050	4325

Source 22 from Social Science Research Council, Statistical History of the United States *(Stanford, CT: Fairfield Publishers, 1965), pp. 765–766. Copyright © 1965. Reprinted by permission of Social Science Research Council. Slightly different numbers can be found in Elizabeth Boody Schumpeter,* English Overseas Trade Statistics, 1697–1808 *(Oxford, UK: Clarendon Press, 1960), pp. 52–55.*

22. Tobacco Imported to England from Virginia and Maryland Colonies, 1620–1700

Dates	Total (in thousands of pounds)
1620	119.0
1640	1257.0
1663	7371.1
1672	17,559.0
1682	21,399.0
1700	37,166.0

23. Number of Ships Sailing to Asia, by Country, 1500–1700

Country	1500–1599	1600–1700
Portugal	705	371
Netherlands	65	1770
England	--	811
France	--	155

Source 24 from Russell R. Menard, Sweet Negotiations: Sugar, Slavery, and Plantation Agriculture in Early Barbados *(Charlottesville: University of Virginia Press, 2006), p. 18. © 2006 by the Rector and Visitors of the University of Virginia. Reproduced by permission of University of Virginia Press.*

24. Sugar Exports from Barbados to London, 1651–1700

Dates	Sugar Exported (tons)
1651	3750
1669	9525
1696	7613
1700	12,170

Source 25 from Joseph Smith, with Francisco Vinhosa, History of Brazil, 1500–2000 *(London: Pearson/Longman, 2002), p. 22. Copyright © 2002. Reprinted with permission of Pearson Education Ltd.*

25. Sugar Production in Brazil, 1600–1625 (in metric tons)

Dates	Sugar Production
1600	8000
1625	14,000

26. Wealth Distribution in Mughul Empire, c. 1600

Category	% of Labor Force	% of National Income
Emperor, royalty, court	1%	15%
Merchants, bankers, artisans	17%	37%
Village cultivators	72%	45%
Tribal groups	10%	3%

Chapter 14
Cross-Cultural
Encounters:
Travel, Religion,
Conquests and
Trade (1400–1700)

HELPFUL FACTUAL INFORMATION

A. CHINA

1. In 1421 emperor Yongle temporarily suspended further voyages by the Ming fleet. In 1433, after a seventh voyage was permitted, emperor Xuande said, "We do not have any desire for goods from distant regions." Finally, in 1436 emperor Zhu Qizhen ordered the fleet and all shipbuilding plans destroyed.

2. Japanese and Chinese pirates harassed coastal towns and actually controlled parts of the Ming Empire. Rather than build another navy to police its offshore waters, the Ming regime decided to close its ports, fortify the coastline, and withdraw into semi-isolation to discourage pirate attacks.

3. Nearly constant warfare on China's northeastern frontier drained both the military and the treasury. By the early 17th century the emperor was in virtual seclusion, the bureaucracy had broken down, and there was infighting at court. Support of the emperor's family and the building of more palaces also hurt the government's financial situation.

4. From 1629 to roughly 1647 a series of peasant rebellions broke out in northern Shensi province and spread throughout northern China. Some contemporaries estimated the death toll of the rebels to be over 200,000, although the most recent scholar of the revolts believes these estimates may be exaggerated.

5. The Ming Government did not support Chinese merchants engaged in foreign trade. The government did not protect them against the pirates.

6. In 1635 the Japanese emperor Tokugawa Iemitsu forbade Japanese ships to leave for foreign countries. Japanese could not travel or live abroad and would be executed if they returned to Japan.

7. Between 1400 and 1600 China's population more than doubled, from roughly 72 million in 1400 to 160 million in 1600. The vast majority of the population was very poor and could not purchase the wares of Chinese traders.

B. MUSLIM EMPIRES

8. By 1700 the Ottoman, Safavid, and Mughul empires all were facing difficult times. The Ottomans were drained by warfare. Moreover, the Ottomans did not control the rich commerce that passed through the empire, preferring to grow wealthy and complacent by charging fees to the foreign merchants. By the 1600s commerce was in the hands of foreigners.

[438]

9. The Safavid Empire's treasury was in serious difficulty due to the support of a very large army that was almost constantly crushing regional uprisings. By 1700 the army was unraveling and the regional revolts left the empire in near-anarchy.

10. The Mughul Empire overtaxed the peasantry to the point of revolt. Clashes with Hindus were a regular feature of Mughul life. Finally, the Mughuls had built no navy and therefore had no power to resist the armed European traders or the fortified European trade outposts.

C. AMERICAS

11. Prior to European discovery and intrusion, the Americas had two major trade networks: the Aztec in what is now Central America and the Inca along the west coast of South America.

12. Recent research has uncovered the fact that the Native Americans' health had been deteriorating for a long time prior to 1492, the major culprits being tuberculosis, joint disease, anemia, and arrested tissue development. Infant mortality (children who died before reaching the age of one) may have run as high as 40 percent.

13. Europeans brought with them diseases against which Native Americans had no immunity. It has been estimated that the total population had declined 63 percent by 1600, 78 percent by 1650, and up to 90 percent in all. This explains how Francisco Pizarro's army of 167 Spanish conquistadors was able to defeat an Inca army of 200,000.

14. Before European intrusion into the Americas, European merchants had almost no wares to allow them to participate in the emerging global commerce. In the Americas, however, Europeans found gold, silver, and lumber products and raised the profitable commercial crops of tobacco and sugar. See statistics on gold, silver, tobacco, and sugar trade.

D. AFRICA

15. As noted earlier, the rising political instability in sub-Saharan Africa kept the region in a state of periodic warfare. Muslim merchants took advantage of this by purchasing slaves, often taken in battle, and transporting them to North Africa, the Middle East, and the Mughul Empire.

16. When Europeans began growing sugarcane in Central America, the West Indies, and Brazil and tobacco in Virginia and Maryland, they began buying slaves from African businessmen, many of whom grew wealthy in the business of human commerce. Statistics are merely educated estimates, but the total of 10 million brought to the Western Hemisphere in the so-called Middle Passage has been accepted by most scholars.

Chapter 14

Cross-Cultural

Encounters:

Travel, Religion,

Conquests and

Trade (1400–1700)

17. The slave trade permitted Dutch, Portuguese, and English merchants to purchase slaves in Africa, transport them to the Americas, exchange them for sugar, and then either return to Europe, where the sugar would be sold, or carry it to England's New England colonies, where it would be converted to molasses or rum.

E. WESTERN EUROPE

18. The Age of Discovery in Europe also was the Age of Renaissance Humanism. Christopher Columbus, Amerigo Vespucci, Leonardo da Vinci, Michelangelo, Erasmus, and William Shakespeare were roughly contemporaries. This intellectual awakening brought forth new ideas, inventions, and broader horizons.

19. Among the features important in travel and commerce were the magnetic compass, the stern rudder, hulls of watertight compartments (borrowed from the Chinese via Muslims), the astrolabe (used to establish latitude) and the triangular ship's sail (from the Arabs), and cannons on ships (gunpowder was a Chinese invention).

20. Western Europe gradually embraced the notion of private property ownership. Prior to this, lands were owned by monarchs or feudal lords, who rented them to peasants. The concept of private property created a sense of security and stability.

21. In the 1400s and 1500s Europeans generally had more to eat, due to new crops (some of which came from the Columbian Exchange from the Americas), better equipment (including metal plowshares), and better techniques (planting clover to regenerate the soil). By the 1600s, 140,000 tons of surplus grain was being sent via rivers or overland to the growing cities.

22. Cities were important in the specialization of occupations, the bringing together of merchants (who often combined into companies) and artisans.

23. European birth rates, although high by today's standards, were "well below the biological maximum,"[24] allowing each person to enjoy a better standard of living and to afford some manufactured products.

24. Wealthy artisans and landowners began to invest their profits in commerce—hence the emergence of the "enterpriser," or the "entrepreneur," who made money by investing money.

---

24. See David S. Landes, *The Unbound Prometheus: Technological Change and Industrial Development in Western Europe from 1750 to the Present* (Cambridge: Cambridge University Press, 1969), p. 22.

25. The political institution of the nation-state was beginning to emerge, at first in Portugal and Spain and later in France, the Low Countries, and England. Monarchs often made alliances with wealthy commoners (merchants, bankers, entrepreneurs), exchanging money for status and power.

26. Nation-states often sponsored explorations and even colonization as money-making enterprises. Also, new laws (such as the English Navigation Acts of 1651 and later) attempted to bring order (and profit for the monarch) and self-sufficiency into their slowly emerging empires.

27. With Italian traders dominant in the Mediterranean and the Ottoman Turks' capture of Constantinople, trade with East Asia and the Muslim empires became costly and difficult. Therefore, Portugal's Prince Henry the Navigator began sending Portuguese ships down the western coast of Africa in attempts to find a new sea route to India and the East. In 1487 Bartolomeu Dias rounded the southern tip of Africa[25] and in May 1498 Vasco da Gama, with the help of an Indian navigator, at last reached India. The Portuguese ships carried cannon and the seamen constructed fortified trading posts.

28. In its effort to find an alternate route to the East, the Spanish crown sponsored the voyages of Columbus, who convinced the Spanish monarchs that he could reach the riches of the East by sailing due west into the uncharted Atlantic. Governments in France, the Netherlands, and England, although slow starters, also sponsored voyages.

25. Cape Agulhas, not the Cape of Good Hope, is actually the southernmost point of Africa. Dias originally called the Cape of Good Hope the Cape of Storms, but the name was changed by King John II of Portugal.

QUESTIONS TO CONSIDER

By now you have come to appreciate the fact that historians, like all other problem solvers, almost never work with just one type of source. From Chapter 1, which used both visual and written evidence, to Chapter 13, which relied on travel accounts, a prayer, a work of art, a medical perspective, and cryptograms, you have been expected to use all the sources at your disposal to answer each chapter's central question.

In this chapter, the Evidence comprises 13 written accounts, 13 sets of statistics, and 28 pieces of factual information. Remember that your two central questions are:

1. How prepared (culturally, economically, politically) was each major region to participate in the emerging global commercial network?

2. How did this emerging network affect each region, both positively and negatively?

Chapter 14

Cross-Cultural

Encounters:

Travel, Religion,

Conquests and

Trade (1400–1700)

The written accounts prove especially valuable in assessing the opinions of individuals in various regions regarding commerce, inter-regional trade, merchants themselves, people in other regions, the cultural climate regarding trade, and so forth. Begin by framing some direct questions for each source:

Example: What did Zhang Han (Source 2) think of merchants? Of the climate regarding trade? Of foreign traders?

Example: What reasons did Richard Hakluyt (Source 7) give for English colonization? Remember to whom his piece was addressed.

Example: What place (status) did merchants occupy in Constantinople, according to Evilyá Efendí (Source 11)?

Example: Is proto-globalization a positive or negative force for the Kingdom of Kongo (Source 12)?

Often the authors of the 13 written accounts do not answer those questions directly, and you will have to read between the lines. For example, in Zheng He's inscription (Source 1),

you will need to put some interpretive pressure on the account to infer his answers to your questions.

The 13 sets of statistics also will help to answer the chapter's central questions, albeit not directly. Sources 14 through 17 deal with population and per capita gross domestic product (the total production within a country or region divided by the number of people in that country or region). Historical statistics measure *change over time* (population gain/ loss, standard of living, etc.) and are particularly valuable in demonstrating what is *actually* taking place— whereas written accounts often tell what individuals *think* is taking place. Examine closely all the statistics for a particular region. Then read the written sources written by individuals from that region (Columbus is writing about Native Americans, but his account should be seen as a European perspective).

Finally there are 28 pieces of factual information that will help you connect the written and statistical information. Work carefully, examining and analyzing one major region at a time. Take careful notes as you go along.

EPILOGUE

By 1400 people throughout the world were in the process of recovering from the famines and Black Death of the 1300s. As political leaders sought to stabilize their positions and pilgrims of all the world's major religious faiths set out on their journeys to their

respective holy places, merchants were reviving old trade patterns while at the same time charting new ones.

The general recovery, while touching every major region either lightly or profoundly, at the same time altered the economic and political relationships between those regions. China, once the wealthiest, most innovative, and cultured region, by the

1400s was losing ground, a victim of its own provincialism, ethnocentrism, and astoundingly poor decisions. To the south and east, the Muslim empires (Ottoman, Safavid, and Mughul) maintained shaky authority in their multi-ethnic domains, potential victims to outside intruders. The Americas were decimated by European-borne diseases and the Western-imposed economic and political systems. Africa agonized over international warfare and the loss of millions of its youngest and strongest men and women through slavery.

As we know, the chief beneficiary of this fluid situation was Western Europe. Profiting enormously from the unexpected "discovery" of the "New World," Western Europe emerged on the international stage rich in gold, silver, trade goods, and a sense of superiority and destiny. In his introduction to an anthology of European accounts of Japan written between 1543 and 1640, historian Michael Cooper observed, "The Europeans had generally adopted the role of representative of a superior race," whereas almost 500 years before that Christopher Columbus noted, "I could conquer the whole of them with fifty men, and govern them as I pleased."[26]

Even today, many people of the West believe that their forebears were destined to dominate the world's economy, cultural life, and politics and that this domination was inevitable. As we have seen in this chapter, however, the West *did* emerge as the dominant region, but this was due to a complex interrelationship of factors and through incredibly good luck. At the conclusion of this volume, this chapter speaks to the present even as it informs us about the past.

A future chapter, albeit not in a history book, might say that the West has been the favored world region for approximately 500 years. But is this position a permanent one? Obviously, historians cannot answer that question—and should not. But historians can provide the crucial context and background information that will help others do so.

26. Michael Cooper, ed., *They Came to Japan* (Berkeley: University of California Press, 1965), pp. xi–xii.